MW00787661

The NEW TESTAMENT

Vitale Jan Tinker

The NEW TESTAMENT

A VERSION BY
JON MADSEN

First published by Floris Books in 1994
Reprinted with minor corrections 2000
Fourth printing 2017

British Library CIP Data available
ISBN 978-086315-184-2
Printed and bound by Gutenberg Press Limited, Malta

Contents

Foreword

In recent years, a wealth of New Testament translations has appeared. Some versions are strictly scholarly and literal in their approach; others have the intention of making the text more accessible to the general reader by using contemporary language and idioms. Either way, it is clear that there is a need to come to a fresh understanding of this fundamental book of Christianity.

The limitation of a more literal translation is that it can feel 'dry' to the general reader and make it hard to experience the living quality of the Gospel. Simply updating the language, on the other hand, involves the risk of trivializing the text; it can become 'lively' but lose some of its depth.

This present version is an attempt to find a middle way. Let me say at once that without the famous Nestle text and the literal translation into English by Marshall, my own efforts would have been severely hampered. One can only have the greatest respect and admiration for such expertise.

And yet there are problems; they are particularly apparent in the Pauline Epistles, and these were, in fact, the starting point of this version. Often, for example, one is disconcerted by the seeming contradiction in Paul between his frequent references to *love* and, on the other hand, his severity, his austere moralizing attitude and the dry and intellectual tone of much of what he writes.

In the translation into German by Emil Bock,* a liberating, wide-ranging style is used which opens doors to a fresh appreciation of Paul and the gospels. Bock had a deep feeling for the spirituality of the early Christians. To them, the Spirit was a decisive factor in their daily lives, and was a power at work in the writers of the texts which we now know as the New Testament.

Bock (1895–1959), co-founder and later leader of The Christian Community, attempted to formulate the texts of the Greek New Testament in such a way that something of the Spirit working in the

* Emil Bock, *Das Neue Testament,* Urachhaus, Stuttgart.

early Church could also become part of our modern experience. To achieve this, he often had to use more words than in the original texts, since many of the 'overtones' of the ancient languages are otherwise lost.

His is a courageous, even daring, attempt to approach the New Testament with the conviction that it contains eternal wisdom and that this living wisdom needs uncovering. This may mean creating unusual and perhaps initially awkward-seeming formulations of language, but the unsuspected depths which come to light are a great gain. That became part of my conviction and the basis for this present version too. I have made full use of the pioneer work of Bock.

But there is a third component which should be mentioned here. My work as a priest in The Christian Community deeply influenced my approach to this version, whenever I found the sacramental sphere in which I work coming to meet me, as it were, out of the text itself. The following three examples (of many which could be quoted) may be found helpful as illustrations of this.

In Colossians (1:27) we read (in the Revised Standard Version): 'To them God chose to make known how great among the Gentiles are the riches of the glory of this mystery, which is Christ in you, the hope of glory.' The present version runs thus: 'Now it is the will of God that they should become aware what immeasurable fullness of revealing light for all the peoples lies in this mystery: it is "Christ in you," the certain hope of all future revelation.' The phrase picked out by quotation marks is a fundamental and recurring one in the liturgy of the Communion Service of The Christian Community.

The second example also comes from Colossians: 'Continue steadfastly in prayer, being watchful in it with thanksgiving' (4:2, RSV). In this version: 'Cultivate your life of prayer with perseverance. Practise it in wakefulness of spirit and in that mood of thankfulness which grows out of the Eucharist.' Here it seemed not only interesting but actually essential to highlight the liturgical overtones of *eucharistia,* the actual word used by Paul.

My third example also touches on the liturgical realm. RSV: 'Do not neglect the gift you have, which was given you by prophetic utterances when the elders laid their hands upon you' (1Tim.4:14). That a ritual of some kind (Ordination?) is referred to is discernible, but I hope to have highlighted it by the following version: 'Do not neglect the spiritual gift which has come alive in your soul through the words, pointing to the future, and the laying on of hands of those who lead as priests.'

An attempt has been made to distinguish typographically between the three 'persons' of the Trinity. Thus 'HE' refers to the Father, 'he' to the Son. The Spirit with a capital S refers to the Holy Spirit, with the lower case to the individual spirit in human beings. Inevitably, in some instances, where the meaning is ambiguous, a choice had to be made – it seems quite in accordance with the mystery of the Trinity that it refuses to be so rigidly fixed!

My sincere wish is that the reader will derive joy and pleasure from working with this new version. It is intended as a help for the reader to make his or her own discoveries, for the width and depth of the Gospel are infinite.

I should like to express my grateful thanks to Margaret Rapson for her untiring and meticulous work in preparing and checking the manuscript, and for far more instances of help and inspiration in finding felicitous English phrases than I could possibly enumerate here.

Thanks are also due to several colleagues of mine for their comments and suggestions, and to Ken Robins for his care in proofreading.

J.M.

Synopsis

Matthew

1:1	*Genealogy of Jesus*
1:18	*The birth of Jesus*
2:1	*The priest-kings from the East*
2:13	*The flight into Egypt*
3:1	*John the Baptist*
3:13	*The Baptism of Jesus*
4:1	*The Temptation*
4:18	*The first disciples*
5:1	*The Sermon on the Mount*
8:1	*Healing a leper*
8:5	*The Roman officer from Capernaum*
8:14	*Peter's mother-in-law*
8:18	*Two enquiries*
8:23	*Calming the storm*
8:28	*Healing two demon-possessed Gadarenes*
9:1	*Healing a paralysed man*
9:9	*The call to Matthew*
9:14	*About fasting*
9:18	*The woman with a haemorrhage and raising Jairus' daughter*
9:27	*Healing two blind men*
9:32	*Healing a dumb man*
10:1	*The calling and mission of the twelve disciples*
11:2	*The Baptist's question*
12:1	*Disputes about the Sabbath and the Son of Man*
12:46	*New human relationships*
13:1	*Seven parables about the kingdom of heaven*
13:53	*Rejection in Nazareth*
14:1	*The death of John the Baptist*
14:13	*Feeding the five thousand*
14:22	*Walking on the sea*
15:1	*True purity*
15:21	*Healing a Canaanite woman*
15:29	*Healings*
15:32	*Feeding the four thousand*
16:1	*Signs of the times*

Mark

10:17 The rich young man
10:32 The third foretelling of death and resurrection
10:35 James' and John's request
10:46 Healing the blind man of Jericho
11:1 The entry into Jerusalem
11:12 The fig tree
11:15 Cleansing the Temple
11:27 The question about authority
12:1 The parable of the vine-growers
12:13 Paying taxes
12:18 The dispute with the Sadducees
12:28 The most important commandment
12:35 About the scribes, and the widow's offering
13:1 Apocalyptic words on the Mount of Olives
14:1 The anointing in Bethany and betrayal by Judas
14:12 The Last Supper
14:26 The prayer in Gethsemane and arrest
14:53 Accusation before the High Priest
14:66 Peter's denial
15:1 Interrogation before Pilate
15:16 Crowning with thorns
15:22 The Crucifixion
15:33 The hour of death
15:42 The burial
16:1 The Resurrection
16:9 The appearance of the Risen One

Luke

1:1 Introduction
1:5 Annunciation to Zechariah
1:26 Annunciation to Mary
1:39 Meeting of Mary and Elizabeth
1:57 The birth of John
1:67 Zechariah's song of praise
2:1 The birth of Jesus
2:21 Presentation in the Temple
2:25 Simeon and Anna
2:41 The twelve-year-old Jesus in the Temple
3:1 John the Baptist
3:21 Baptism and genealogy of Jesus
4:1 The Temptation
4:14 Teaching in the synagogues and rejection in Nazareth
4:31 First healing: Healing a man possessed by a demon

13:22 The question about attaining to the Kingdom of God
13:31 Enmity of Herod
14:1 Meal with a Pharisee and healing a man with dropsy
14:16 Parable of the great banquet
14:25 Conditions of discipleship
15:1 Three parables: The lost sheep, lost coin, lost son
16:1 Parable of the unjust steward
16:14 The Pharisees and the Law
16:19 The rich man and Lazarus
17:1 Obligations of inner growth: Parable of the servant's duty
17:11 Healing ten lepers and the grateful Samaritan
17:20 The coming of the Kingdom and foretelling the suffering
18:1 Parable of the widow who asked
18:9 Parable of the Pharisee and the tax-collector
18:15 Blessing the children
18:18 The rich leader of the people
18:31 Foretelling death and resurrection
18:35 Healing the blind man of Jericho
19:1 Meal with the chief tax-collector Zacchaeus
19:11 Parable of the silver pounds
19:28 The entry into Jerusalem
19:45 Cleansing the Temple
20:1 The question about authority
20:9 Parable of the wine growers
20:19 Paying taxes
20:27 Dispute with the Sadducees
20:45 Beware of scribes
21:1 The widow's offering
21:5 Apocalyptic words
22:1 Betrayal by Judas
22:7 The Last Supper
22:24 Conversation with the disciples
22:39 The Prayer in Gethsemane and arrest
22:54 Peter's denial
22:63 Accusation before the Sanhedrin
23:1 Interrogation before Pilate and Herod
23:26 Bearing the cross
23:32 The Crucifixion
23:44 The hour of death
23:50 The burial
24:1 The Resurrection
24:13 The walk to Emmaus
24:33 The appearance of the Risen One in Jerusalem

John

1:1	*Prologue*
1:19	*John the Baptist*
1:35	*The first disciples*
2:1	*The first sign: The marriage at Cana*
2:12	*The first Passover: Cleansing the Temple*
2:23	*Conversation with Nicodemus by night*
3:22	*The last witnessing by the Baptist*
4:1	*Conversation with the Samaritan woman*
4:43	*The second sign: Healing the son of a courtier*
5:1	*The third sign: Healing a paralysed man*
5:17	*The working of the Father and of the Son*
5:31	*Witnessing for the Son*
6:1	*The fourth sign: Feeding the five thousand*
6:16	*The fifth sign: Walking on the sea*
6:22	*I AM the bread of life*
6:60	*Division in the circle of the disciples*
6:67	*Peter's confession*
7:1	*Journey to Jerusalem*
7:14	*His working at the festival*
7:31	*Chief priests and Pharisees plan his arrest*
7:45	*Division of the Sanhedrin*
8:1	*The adulteress*
8:12	*I AM the light of the world*
8:21	*Descent from above and from below*
8:30	*Abraham and Christ*
9:1	*The sixth sign: Healing a man born blind*
10:1	*I AM the door*
10:11	*I AM the good shepherd*
10:22	*Further attacks by the Jews*
11:1	*Lazarus*
11:25	*I AM the resurrection and the life*
11:33	*The seventh sign: The raising of Lazarus*
11:45	*The Sanhedrin decides to kill him*
11:54	*The last Passover*
12:1	*Anointing in Bethany*
12:12	*The entry into Jerusalem*
12:20	*Meeting with Greeks*
12:36	*The unbelief of the Jews*
13:1	*Washing the feet of the disciples*
13:21	*Indicating the traitor*
13:31	*Foretelling Peter's denial*
14:1	*I AM the way and the truth and the life*

14:15 The promise of the Holy Spirit
15:1 I AM the true vine
15:18 The world's hatred
15:26 The working of the Holy Spirit
16:1 Reunion with the disciples
16:25 Speaking openly about the Father
17:1 The High Priestly prayer
18:1 The arrest
18:15 Peter's denial and Jesus before the High Priest
18:28 Interrogation before Pilate
19:1 Crowning with thorns
19:8 The judgment
19:17 The Crucifixion
19:28 The death
19:38 The burial
20:1 The Resurrection
20:11 Appearance before Mary of Magdala
20:19 Appearance before the disciples
20:26 Appearance before Thomas
21:1T he early meal by the sea
21:15 The tasks of Peter and the beloved disciple

Acts
1:1 Prologue
1:4 Ascension
1:13 Choosing Matthias
2:1 The Pentecost event
2:14 Peter's Pentecost address
2:37 The first congregation
2:42 Life in the congregation
3:1 Healing a paralysed man
4:1 The apostles are arrested
4:23 Return to the congregation
4:32 Property held in common in the Jerusalem congregation
5:1 Ananias and Sapphira
5:12 Healings in the Temple portico
5:17 The apostles are arrested for the second time
6:1 Choosing the seven deacons
6:8 The work of Stephen and his address
7:54 Death of Stephen and persecution of the congregation
8:4 Philip in Samaria
8:9 Simon the magician
8:26 Philip and the Ethiopian

Synopsis

9:1	*Saul before Damascus*
9:26	*Saul in Jerusalem and his return to Tarsus*
9:32	*Peter's work near the Mediterranean Sea*
10:1	*Peter and the Roman centurion*
11:1	*Justification before the apostles in Jerusalem*
11:19	*Antioch, where the term 'Christians' was first used*
12:1	*Persecution in Jerusalem and death of James*
12:5	*Peter's arrest and escape*
13:1	*Mission through the Holy Spirit*
13:4	*Paul's first journey: in Cyprus*
13:13	*In Pamphylia and Pisidia*
14:1	*Mistaken for gods in Lycaonia*
14:21	*Return journey*
15:1	*Paul and Barnabas in Jerusalem*
15:6	*Peter's and James' address at the council in Jerusalem*
15:22	*The council's decision and conveying it to Antioch*
15:36	*Paul's second journey: separating from Barnabas*
16:1	*Paul in Galatia*
16:10	*Paul in Macedonia: entering Europe*
17:1	*Paul in Thessalonica*
17:10	*Paul in Beroea*
17:16	*Paul in Athens*
18:1	*Paul in Corinth*
18:18	*Return journey*
18:23	*The third journey. Apollos in Ephesus*
19:1	*Paul in Ephesus*
19:23	*The riot in Ephesus*
20:1	*Journeying through Greece and Macedonia*
20:7	*In Troas*
20:13	*Continuing to Miletus and farewell to Asia*
21:1	*From Miletus to Tyre, Ptolemais and Caesarea*
21:15	*Paul before the apostles in Jerusalem*
21:27	*Paul's arrest*
21:37	*Address to the Jews*
22:22	*The effect of his address*
22:30	*Paul before the Sanhedrin*
23:11	*Murder plot against Paul*
23:31	*Paul protected by the Romans and moved to Caesarea*
24:1	*Interrogation before the governor Felix*
25:1	*Paul before the new governor Festus*
25:8	*Paul's appeal to Caesar*
25:23	*Paul before King Agrippa*
27:1	*The way to Rome: journey from Caesarea to Crete*

27:9 Paul gives warning
27:14 Shipwreck
28:1 Stay on Melite
28:11 Continuing the journey via Sicily
28:15 Arrival in Rome

Romans

Introduction
1:1 Greeting to the congregation
1:8 Thanks, and his intention to visit
The fall of humanity and the way of salvation
1:18 God's anger over the non-Jews
2:1 God's anger over the Jews
3:21 Redemption through faith
4:1 Abraham the father of faith
5:1 The Fall of Adam and Christ's deed of grace
The new life
6:1 Sin and holiness
7:1 Living under the Law
8:1 Living in the spirit
8:18 The future hope for creation
God's way with Israel
9:1 The divine will in Israel
9:30 Israel has not reached the goal of its Law
11:1 Through grace, a remnant of Israel may become worthy
11:11 The heathen peoples are the spur for Israel
Advice to the congregation
12:1 Make your personal life holy
13:1 Subordination to the God-given order
14:1 Weakness of the individual and strength of community
Conclusion
15:14 Looking back, and announcing a visit to Rome
16:1 Greetings to individual members
16:17 Beware of fraudulent teachers
16:21 Greetings from the fellow workers, and concluding adulation

1 Corinthians

Introduction
1:1 Greeting to the congregation
1:4 Words of thanks
Shortcomings in the congregation
1:10 Partisanship
1:18 Proclamation works either as foolishness or as wisdom
3:1 Partisanship renders the proclamation ineffectual

4:9 *Personal experiences*
5:1 *Moral strayings in the congregation*
6:1 *The effect of our bearing on the world, the angels, the future*

Answers to a letter from the Corinthians

7:1 *Being single or married*
8:1 *About eating meat from sacrifices to idols*
9:1 *The apostle's freedom*
10:1 *The dangers of taking part in ritual meals of sacrifice*
11:2 *The conduct of men and women at worship*
11:17 *Worthy celebration of the Christ-meal*

About the gifts of grace

12:1 *The organism of the congregation*
12:31 *The Hymn to Love*
14:1 *Speaking in tongues and speaking prophecy*
15:1 *About the resurrection of the dead*

Conclusion

16:1 *Appeal for a collection*
16:5 *The travel plans of Paul and his fellow workers*
16:13 *Final advice and greetings*

2 Corinthians

Suffering with Christ

1:1 *Introduction*
1:3 *Words of thanks*
1:8 *Rescue from the danger of death*
1:12 *Defence against being reproached for untruthfulness*
2:12 *Experience in Troas*

Service in the Old Covenant and in the New Covenant

3:1 *The immediacy of the new revelation*
4:5 *Overcoming the forces of decline*
5:1 *The earthly and the heavenly dwelling*
5:20 *The task of the apostle in troubled times*
6:11 *Keeping apart from those without faith*
7:5 *Joy over the change of heart of the Corinthians*
8:1 *Report of the collecting of gifts in Macedonia*
9:1 *Encouragement to generosity*

Paul justifies his way of working

10:1 *Justification against reproaches by Jewish Christians*
11:1 *Justification on the basis of the Gospel*
11:16 *Justification on the basis of his being persecuted*
12:1 *Justification on the basis of his visions*
12:7 *The thorn in the body*

Conclusion
12:14 *Announcing another visit*
13:11 *Greeting and words of blessing*

Galatians

1:1 *Prologue*
1:6 *Reason for writing: the true Gospel is under threat*
1:13 *The stages of becoming an apostle to the foreigners*
2:1 *Meeting with the first apostles in Jerusalem and Antioch*
2:19 *Christ in me*
3:1 *Only faith, not the Law, leads to righteousness*
3:19 *The Law is our teacher towards Christ*
4:1 *Free from the Law through the Son*
5:1 *Call to freedom*
5:16 *Living out of the spirit*
6:1 *Life in the congregation*
6:11 *Concluding words*

Ephesians

1:1 *Introduction*
1:3 *Song of praise*
1:15 *Prayer of thanksgiving for the community*
2:1 *New life as an endowment from God*
2:11 *The new community*
3:1 *The share of the heathens in the Christ mystery*
3:14 *Prayer for the community*
4:1 *Exhortation to peaceful co-operation in the community*
4:17 *A call to live out of the strength of renewal*
5:1 *Life in the light*
5:21 *Order in the home*
6:10 *The armour of God*
6:21 *Conclusion*

Philippians

1:1 *Introduction*
1:3 *Prayer of thanks for the congregation*
1:12 *News of the work in Rome*
1:27 *Call to order the life of the congregation worthily*
2:5 *Christ emptied himself and offered up his divine form*
2:19 *News of Timothy and Epaphroditus*
3:1 *Faith in Christ and the Law*
3:12 *The apostle's example*
4:1 *Rejoice!*

4:10	*Thanks for the gift that was sent*
4:19	*Concluding words*

Colossians

1:1	*Introduction*
1:3	*Prayer of thanks*
1:9	*Prayer for the congregation*
1:15	*The cosmic dimension of Christ*
1:24	*The mystery revealed: Christ in you*
2:4	*Warning against teachings which lead astray*
3:1	*The old and the new human being*
3:13	*Life in the congregations*
3:18	*Ordering the house-community*
4:2	*Call to prayer*
4:5	*Attitude towards outsiders*
4:7	*News about Tychicus and Onesimus*
4:10	*Greetings*

1 Thessalonians

1:1	*Introduction and words of thanks*
1:4	*The special position of the congregation in Thessalonica*
2:1	*Remembering the apostle's work in Macedonia*
2:13	*How the Gospel was received in the congregation*
2:17	*The apostle's visit thwarted*
3:1	*The sending out of Timothy*
4:1	*Encouragement to strive on the right way*
4:13	*Those who have died, and the coming of Christ*
5:12	*Conduct within the congregation*
5:23	*Words of blessing and greeting*

2 Thessalonians

1:1	*Introduction and words of thanks*
1:7	*The renewed coming of Christ*
2:1	*The coming of Christ and the approach of the Adversary*
3:1	*Request for the prayer of the congregation*
3:6	*Keeping one's distance from dissolute people*
3:16	*Words of blessing and greeting*

1 Timothy

1:1	*Introduction*
1:3	*Defending the teaching against distortions*
1:12	*Words of thanks and the summons to fight in the spirit*
2:1	*Summons to earnest prayer*

10:19 *Free access to the Holy of Holies*
11:1 *The path of faith in the Old Covenant*
12:1 *The path of faith in the New Covenant*
13:1 *Advice on various matters*
13:20 *Words of blessing, greetings*

James

1:1 *Introduction*
1:2 *Standing firm in temptation*
1:13 *The origin of temptation*
1:19 *Right hearing and right doing*
2:1 *Before God all human beings are equal*
2:14 *Faith without works is fruitless*
3:1 *The power of the tongue*
3:13 *Wisdom from above*
4:1 *The origin of conflicts*
4:11 *Warning against disparaging judgments and self-praise*
5:1 *The judgment upon the rich*
5:7 *Reminder to be patient*
5:13 *Anointing the sick and the healing power of prayer*
5:19 *Responsibility for those who have strayed*

1 Peter

1:1 *Introduction*
1:3 *Words of thanks for hope fulfilled*
1:13 *Summons to a holy life*
2:1 *The living edifice of those born anew*
2:11 *The good example*
2:18 *Admonition to slaves*
3:1 *Admonitions to women and men*
3:8 *Admonitions to the congregation*
4:1 *About the meaning of suffering*
5:1 *Admonition to the elders and to the young*
5:12 *Conclusion: greetings and words of blessing*

2 Peter

1:1 *Introduction*
1:3 *The importance of the Promise*
1:15 *The Transfiguration: the fundamental experience*
2:1 *Judgment upon false teachers*
3:1 *The apparent delay in the reappearing of Christ*
3:14 *Concluding admonition and reference to Paul*

1 John

1:1	*The message concerning the divine Word*
1:5	*Life in the Light*
2:7	*Brotherly love*
2:18	*The signs of Antichrist*
3:1	*Distinguishing features of the children of God*
4:1	*The Spirit of God and the spirit of Antichrist*
4:7	*The love of God and brotherly love*
5:1	*The power of faith*
5:5	*The threefold testimony to Christ*
5:13	*Certainty that prayer is heard*
5:18	*Shelter in Christ*

2 John

1	*Greeting*
4	*Love for the brothers*
7	*Warning against being led astray*
12	*Concluding words and greeting*

3 John

1	*Greetings and words of blessing*
5	*Conduct towards foreign brothers*
9	*Diotrephes and Demetrius*
13	*Concluding words and greeting*

Judas (Jude)

1	*Greetings and words of blessing*
3	*Fight for the faith*
11	*The error of Balaam and Korah's rebellion*
20	*Stand firm in love*
24	*Words of praise*

Revelation

1:1	*The origin of the revelation*
1:4	*Greetings to the seven congregations*
2:1	*To Ephesus*
2:8	*To Smyrna*
2:12	*To Pergamum*
2:18	*To Thyatira*
3:1	*To Sardis*
3:7	*To Philadelphia*
3:14	*To Laodicea*
4:1	*The throne in the heavens*

Synopsis

The Gospel of Matthew

1 *Genealogy of Jesus*

This is the book of how Jesus Christ became Man, a son of David who is a son of Abraham.

[2]Abraham awakened to life Isaac,
Isaac Jacob,
Jacob Judah and his brothers,
[3]Judah Perez and Zerah from the womb of Tamar,
Perez Hezron,
Hezron Ram,
[4]Ram Amminadab,
Amminadab Nahshon,
Nahshon Salmon,
[5]Salmon Boaz from the womb of Rahab,
Boaz Obed from the womb of Ruth,
Obed Jesse,
[6]Jesse David the king.
David awakened to life Solomon from the womb of the wife of Uriah,
[7]Solomon Rehoboam,
Rehoboam Abijah,
Abijah Asa,
[8]Asa Jehoshaphat
Jehoshaphat Joram,
Joram Uzziah,
[9]Uzziah Jotham,
Jotham Ahaz,
Ahaz Hezekiah,
[10]Hezekiah Manasseh,

Manasseh Amon,
Amon Josiah,
[11]Josiah Jechoniah and his brothers when the people was deported into captivity in Babylon.
[12]After the banishment to Babylon:
Jechoniah awakened to life Shealtiel,
Shealtiel Zerubbabel,
[13]Zerubbabel Abiud,
Abiud Eliakim,
Eliakim Azor,
[14]Azor Zadok,
Zadok Achim,
Achim Eliud,
[15]Eliud Eleazar,
Eleazar Matthan,
Matthan Jacob,
[16]Jacob Joseph, the husband of Mary.
From her womb was born Jesus who is called the Christ.

[17]This is the number of all the generations:

From Abraham to David fourteen generations, from David to the deportation to Babylon fourteen generations, from the deportation to Babylon to the Christ fourteen generations.

The birth of Jesus

[18]And the birth of Jesus Christ took place in this way: Mary, his
mother, was betrothed to Joseph; but before they were aware of
having come together, she was found to have conceived a child
through the power of the Holy Spirit. [19]Her husband Joseph,
who was an upright man, did not wish to speak ill of her, and
he considered whether he should set her free without causing
any stir. [20]While he was still pondering this, see, the angel of
the Lord appeared to him in a dream and said to him, 'Joseph,
Son of David, do not let yourself be swayed from taking Mary
to yourself as your wife. What is stirring in her womb has been
conceived through the power of the Holy Spirit. [21]She will bear a

son. You shall give him the name Jesus, for he will heal his own of their sins.'

22All this took place, so that the word of the Lord, spoken by the mouth of the prophet, might be fulfilled:

23See, the maiden will conceive;
she will bear a son,
he shall be called Emmanuel.

Translated, that means: God is in our midst.

24When Joseph rose from sleep, he followed the directions of the angel and took Mary to himself as his wife. 25He was not aware of any coming together with her until she bore her son. And he gave him the name Jesus.

2 *The priest-kings from the East*

Now when Jesus had been born in Bethlehem in Judea in the reign of King Herod, see: Priest-kings from the realms of the East came
to Jerusalem and said, 2'Where is the newborn child who is destined to be king of the Jews? We saw his star in the realms of the East and have come to bow down to him.'

3When King Herod heard the question he was alarmed, and
the whole of Jerusalem with him. 4He called together all the chief priests and scribes of the people and enquired of them: 'Where is
the Christ to be born?' 5And they answered, 'In Bethlehem in Judea; for thus it is written by the prophet:

Bethlehem in the land of Judah,
6you are not the least among
the leading places in Judah;
for from you shall come the ruler,
the shepherd of my people Israel.'

7Then Herod invited the priest-kings to come, and in confidential conversation he learnt from them the precise time when the star
had appeared. 8And he directed them to Bethlehem and said, 'Go and see what you can find out about the child. And when you have found him, bring me word; then I, too, will go to bow down before him.'

9After these words from the king they went on their way; and
see, the star which they had seen in the realms of the East showed
them the way, until it stood over the house where the child was.
10And when they saw the star they were filled with exceedingly
great joy. 11They entered the house and beheld the child and Mary
his mother, and they fell down and worshipped him and opened
their treasures and offered him gifts: Gold, frankincense and myrrh.
12And a dreamvision directed them not to return to Herod, so they
departed to their own country by another way.

The flight into Egypt

13When they had gone, see, the angel of the Lord appeared to Joseph
in a dream and said, 'Get up, take the child and his mother and flee
to Egypt. Remain there until I speak to you again. For Herod will
hunt for the child to destroy him.'

14And he got up, took the child and his mother and set off in the
night for Egypt. 15There he remained until the death of Herod. The
word of the Lord, spoken by the prophet, had to be fulfilled:

> Out of Egypt I called my son.

16When Herod realized that it was futile to expect the priest-
kings to return to him, his rage flared up. And he ordered that all
the boys who had been born in the last two years in Bethlehem and
all the surrounding region be killed. That corresponded to the time
which he had discovered from the priest-kings.

17Thus was fulfilled the word of the prophet Jeremiah:

> 18A voice is heard in Ramah,
> wailing and great lamentation;
> Rachel weeps for her children,
> and she refuses all consolation,
> because they are no more.

19When Herod had died, see, the angel of the Lord appeared in a
dream to Joseph in Egypt and said, 20'Get up, take the child and his
mother and journey to the land of Israel; for now those who hunted
for the child's life and soul are dead.'

21And he got up, took the child and his mother and travelled to the land of Israel. [22]But when he heard that Archelaus reigned in Judea in place of his father Herod, he was afraid to go there. Following a revelation which he received in a dream he went to Galilee [23]and settled in the town called Nazareth.

The word of the prophet was to be fulfilled:

He is predestined to be a Nazarene.

3 *John the Baptist*

In those days John the Baptist came. He proclaimed his message in the isolation of the Judean desert. He said, [2]'Change your hearts and minds. The realm of the heavens has come close.'

[3]He it is of whom the prophet Isaiah speaks:

A voice is heard, calling in the loneliness:
'Prepare the way for the highest leader,
make his path straight and good!'

[4]John wore a garment of camel's hair and a leather girdle around his waist. Hard fruits and wild honey was his food.

[5]At that time people came out to him from Jerusalem and the whole of Judea and from the region around the Jordan, [6]and they were baptized by him in the flowing waters of the Jordan and confessed their sins.

[7]When he saw that many Pharisees and Sadducees also came for baptism, he said to them, 'You sons of the serpent, who has told you how to escape from the coming World-Fire? [8]Now therefore strive after the right fruits of the change of heart and mind. [9]Do not think that you are safe by saying: We have Abraham as our father. I say to you: The heavenly Father is just as able to raise Abraham-sons from these dead stones. [10]Already the axe is laid to the root of the trees, and every tree that does not bear good fruit is felled and thrown into the fire. [11]I baptize you with water to lead you to a change of consciousness. He who comes after me is mightier than I; unworthy am I even to carry his shoes. He will baptize you with the Holy Spirit and with fire. [12]The winnowing fork is in his hand, and he will cleanse his grain of the chaff. He will gather the wheat into the barn, but the chaff he will burn in an unquenchable fire.'

The Baptism of Jesus

13Then Jesus came from Galilee to the Jordan to John, to be baptized by him. 14But John refused and said, 'It is I who need to be
baptized by you – and you come to me?' 15Jesus answered him,
'Let it be so now. It is good thus, so that we fulfil properly all that
destiny requires.' Then he consented. 16When Jesus had received
the baptism and was already coming out of the water again, see,
the heavens opened and he saw the Spirit of God descending in the
form of a dove and hovering over him. 17And see, a voice spoke out
of the heavens:

> 'This is my Son whom I love,
> in him will I reveal myself.'

4 *The Temptation*

After this Jesus was driven by the Spirit into the loneliness of the desert to be tested by the Adversary.

2After forty days and forty nights subjected to fasting, he felt
hunger; 3and all at once the Adversary stood before him and said,
'If you are the Son of God, let these stones change into bread
through the power of your word.' 4But he replied, 'Scripture
says:

> Man does not live by bread alone.
> He lives by every word that comes from the mouth of God.'

5Then the Adversary carried him away to the holy city and set
him on the parapet of the Temple 6and said, 'If you are the Son of
God, throw yourself down. For scripture says:

> He has given you into the charge of HIS angels,
> and they will bear you up on their hands,
> so that you shall not strike your foot against a stone.'

7Jesus said, 'But it also says:

> You shall not make the divine power who guides you serve your caprice.'

8Again the Adversary carried him away. He took him to a very
high mountain and showed him all the realms of the world and the

gleaming interplay of their forces, 9and he said, 'All this I will give
into your power if you will fall down and acknowledge me as your
Lord.' 10Then Jesus said to him, 'Vanish, Satan! Scripture says:

> You shall bow before the divine power who guides
> you, and only serve HIM.'

11Then the Adversary left him, and see, angels came to him and
served him.

12When Jesus became aware that John had fallen into the hands
of his enemies, he went to Galilee. 13He went from Nazareth and
chose for his dwelling-place Capernaum, a town by the sea in the
territory of the tribes Zebulun and Naphtali. 14The word of the
prophet Isaiah was to be fulfilled:

> 15Land of Zebulun, land of Naphtali,
> toward the sea, across the Jordan,
> Galilee, land of the peoples:
> 16The people who dwell in darkness see a great light.
> And for those who dwell in the realm of death and shadows
> the sun rises.

17From that time on Jesus began his proclamation: 'Change your
hearts and minds. The realms of the heavens have come close.'

The first disciples

18As he walked by the Sea of Galilee, he saw two brothers, Simon
who later was called Peter, and Andrew, his brother. They were
casting a net into the sea, for they were fishermen. 19And he said to
them, 'Follow me! I will make you fishers of men.' 20And at once
they left their nets and followed him.

21As he walked on he saw two other brothers, James the son of
Zebedee and John, his brother. They were sitting in the boat with
Zebedee their father, mending their nets. He called them to him,
22and at once they left the boat and their father and followed him.

23And he wandered through all Galilee and taught in the synagogues there and proclaimed the message of salvation from the
heavenly world and healed all the illnesses and infirmities from

which the people suffered. 24Soon he was spoken about in the whole
of Syria and they brought to him all who were ill with many kinds
of disease, those who were suffering, those possessed, somnambu-
lists and those who were paralysed, and he healed them all.
25And great crowds followed him from Galilee and the Decapolis,
from Jerusalem and Judea and from the land beyond the Jordan.

5 *The Sermon on the Mount*

When he saw the crowd of people, he went up on the mountain.
Then he sat down, and his disciples came to him. 2And he opened
his mouth and began to teach them:
3'Blessed are the beggars for spirit, for within themselves they
find the realm of the heavens.
4'Blessed are those who endure earthly suffering, for within
themselves they find the comfort of the spirit.
5'Blessed are those who achieve harmony of soul, for in their
innermost self they will grasp the meaning of the earth.
6'Blessed are those who hunger and thirst for the Good, for their
own doing will satisfy their hunger.
7'Blessed are the merciful, for they, in their turn, will receive
mercy.
8'Blessed are those whose hearts are pure, for within them they
shall behold God.
9'Blessed are those who bring peace into the world, for they will
be called sons of God.
10'Blessed are those who are persecuted because they serve the
higher life; the realm of the heavens is within them.
11'Blessed are you when you are reviled and persecuted, when
lying and hate-filled words are hurled at you because my Being
lives in you. 12Rejoice and be glad; in the heavens the full compensation of destiny has been prepared for you. Were not the prophets
before you reviled and persecuted just as much?
13'You are the salt of the earth. If the salt loses its power to
crystallize, how can it be restored? It becomes useless; it has to be
thrown away and it is trodden underfoot by men.

14‘You are the light of the world. A city on a mountain cannot remain hidden, 15and a light is not lit to be put under a corn-measure. It is put on a stand so that it shines for all who are in the house. 16Your light should shine for men like that, so that they see how your Being radiates and give praise to your Father in the heavens.

17‘You must not think that I have come to abolish the Law or the prophets. My task is not to abolish but to fulfil. 18Yes, I say to you: Until heaven and earth pass away, not a letter, not a dot of the Law will lose its validity. Everything must be fulfilled first. 19Whoever relaxes one of the commandments of the Law even in the slightest and teaches others accordingly will have a name of little value in the realms of the heavens. But he who does justice to these commandments in his actions and in his teaching will have a great name in the realms of the heavens. 20I say this to you: If your share of the Good is not greater than that of the scribes and Pharisees, you will not find the way to the realms of the heavens.

21‘You have heard the word that was spoken to mankind in the past:

> You shall not kill.

And:

> Whoever kills brings crisis to his destiny.

22But out of my own power I say to you: Even he who allows impulses of anger to burn against his fellow men brings crisis to his destiny. And whoever turns against his fellow men with arrogant disdain, sins against the spiritual guidance of his people. And as for him who curses his fellow men out of hate and enmity, he causes his soul to become prey to the cosmic flames.

23‘So, if, as you are making your offering, you become conscious of having done someone an injustice, 24let your gift lie before the altar, and first go and be reconciled to your fellow man, and then offer your gift.

25‘Be quick to show your good will to him who accuses you, as long as you still can find a way with him. Otherwise your accuser will hand you over to the judge, and the judge to the gaoler who

throws you into prison. 26Yes, I say to you, you will not be released
from there until you have paid the last penny of your debt. 27You
have heard the word that was spoken to mankind in the past:

> You shall not dishonour marriage.

28But out of my own power I say to you: Everyone who looks at a
woman with a lustful eye has committed adultery with her in his
heart. 29If your physical eye causes you to become alienated from
your higher being, then rather tear it out and throw it from you. It
is better for you to lose one of your members than that your whole
bodily nature should fall into the abyss. 30And if your active hand
separates you from your higher being, then cut it off and throw it
from you. It is better for you to lose one of your members than that
your whole bodily nature should fall into the abyss.

31'It was said:

> Whoever divorces his wife must give her a letter
> which sets her free.

32But out of my own power I say to you: Every one who divorces his
wife, except on the ground of unchastity, makes her an adulteress;
and every one who marries a woman who has been set free by her
husband becomes an adulterer.

33'You have also heard the word that was spoken to mankind in
the past:

> Do not swear beyond your powers, for you owe the
> Lord fulfilment of what you have sworn.

34But out of my own power I say to you: Do not swear by spiritual
powers at all, neither those of heaven – for it is the throne of God
– 35nor those of the earth – for it is HIS footstool – nor those of
Jerusalem – for it is the city of the great King. 36Nor must you swear
by your head, for you cannot make a single hair white or black.
37Let your words be Yes or No. Everything which goes beyond that
comes from evil.

38'You have heard that it was said:

> An eye for an eye, a tooth for a tooth.

39But out of my own power I say to you: Do not resist evil. If
someone strikes you on the right cheek, turn the left cheek to him

also. [40]If someone wants to fight with you and take your coat, let
him have your cloak also. [41]And if someone forces you to go with
him one mile, go with him two miles. [42]Give to him who asks
you, and do not turn away from him who wants to borrow from
you.

[43]'You have heard that it was said:

Love your neighbour and hate your enemy.

[44]But out of my own power I say to you: Love your enemies, pray
for your persecutors. [45]Then you will be sons of your Father in the
heavens. HE makes HIS sun rise on evil and good, and sends rain on
the friends and the enemies of the true being. [46]Does it bring you
forward if you only love those who love you? Do not the tax-collectors also do that? [47]If you only bid your brothers welcome, what
is so great about that? Do not the pagan peoples do that? [48]You are
to come close to the holy aims, as your Father in the heavens is the
epitome of all holy aims.

6 'Take care that you do not make your spiritual striving into a
display for other people, for then you will not achieve any results
which will endure before the countenance of your Father in the
heavens.

[2]'When you do deeds of love, make no great performance of it
as do the hypocrites in the synagogues and in the streets who only
wish to be applauded by men. Yes, I say to you, they themselves
forfeit any gain.

[3]'When you do deeds of love, let your left hand not know what
your right hand is doing. [4]Then your deeds of love become reality
in the realm which is hidden from the senses; and the Father, the
Ground of the World, before whose gaze the invisible is apparent,
will reward you in the course of destiny.

[5]'Also when you pray, do not be like the hypocrites. They love
to stand in the synagogues and on the street corners when they say
their prayers, because they want to be noticed by people. Yes, I say
to you, they themselves forfeit any gain. [6]But you, when you pray,
go into your innermost room and close the door. Then send your
prayer up to the Father, the Ground of the World, into the realm

which is hidden from the senses. And the Father, before whose gaze the invisible is apparent, will reward you.

7‘In your prayers do not mutter empty words as the pagan peoples do. They think that they will be heard because of the great number of their words. 8Do not follow their example; for your Father knows what you need before you ask HIM. 9Let your prayer be like this:

Our Father in the heavens,
Your name be hallowed,
10Your kingdom come,
Your will be done, as in heaven so also on earth.
11Our daily bread give us today,
12And forgive us our debts, as we forgive our debtors;
13And lead us not into temptation,
But deliver us from the evil.

14‘If you forgive your fellow men their shortcomings, then your heavenly Father will also forgive your shortcomings. 15And if you do not forgive your fellow men, then your Father will not forgive you your shortcomings, either.

16‘When you are practising self-discipline, do not put on a gloomy face like the hypocrites. They distort their faces, so that all shall see that they are practising asceticism. Yes, I say to you: They themselves render their doing fruitless. 17But you, when you practise self discipline, anoint your head and wash your face, 18so that your asceticism is not visible to men, but to the Father, the Ground of the World, in the realm which is hidden from the senses. And the Father, the Ground of the World, before whose gaze the invisible is apparent, will reward you.

19‘Do not collect earthly treasures, for they are eaten up by moths and rust, and thieves rummage through them and steal them. 20Rather, gather treasures in the spiritual world. They cannot be eaten by moths and rust, nor can thieves rummage through them and steal them. 21Where you have gathered a treasure, thither your heart forces will bear you.

22‘The eye is the lamp of your body; now if your eye is clear

throughout, your whole body will be filled with light. [23]But if your
eye is dull, your whole body will be full of darkness; and if the light
in you turns into darkness, how dark that darkness will be!

[24]'No one can serve two masters. Either he hates the one and
loves the other, or he will follow the one and despise the other.
You cannot serve the world of God and at the same time the world
of hardened materialism. [25]Therefore I say to you: Do not let your
soul be anxious about what you shall eat and drink, nor about
the clothing you shall put on. Is not the soul more than food and
the body more than clothing? [26]Look up to the birds of the sky.
They do not sow, they do not reap, nor do they gather into barns;
and yet your Father in the heavens feeds them. Are you not much
more than they? [27]Which of you can add even a moment to the
years of his life by taking extra care? [28]And why do you worry
about clothing? Learn from the lilies of the field. See how they
grow without any effort and without weaving their garment. [29]I
tell you: Solomon in his greatest glory was not arrayed like one of
them. [30]If God clothes even the grass of the field like this, which
grows today and is burnt tomorrow, will HE not much more clothe
you? How weak is your faith! [31]So turn away from anxiety; do
not say: What shall we eat, and what shall we drink, and what
shall we wear? [32]All these things are the desires and concerns of
the heathen peoples. Your Father in the heavens knows all your
needs. [33]Above all strive for the divine kingdom and its harmonious order. Then all these other things will be yours as well. [34]Do
not be anxious about tomorrow; let tomorrow take care of itself. It
is enough that each day has its own problems.

7 'Do not judge, or the judgment will fall upon yourselves; for
with every slighting judgment that you make you actually judge
yourselves. [2]With the measure that you use, you too will be measured. [3]Why do you see the splinter in your brother's eye and are
not aware of the beam in your own eye? [4]And how can you say
to your brother, "Come here. I will take the splinter out of your
eye," whilst you yourself have a beam in your own eye? [5]You
hypocrite, first remove the beam from your own eye and then you

may concern yourself with taking the splinter out of your brother's
eye.

6‘Do not give what is holy to dogs. And do not throw pearls
before swine; they only trample on them and turn on you to tear
you apart.

> 7Ask, and it will be given you.
> Seek and you will find.
> Knock, and the door will be opened to you.

8‘For everyone who asks receives, and everyone who seeks
finds, and to everyone who knocks it will be opened. 9Or is there
among you a man who, when his son asks him for bread, gives him
a stone instead? 10Or one who gives him a serpent when he asks
him for a fish? 11When even you, who are yet so far from the Good,
are able to give your children good things, will not your Father in
the heavens all the more give what is good to those who ask HIM?
12Everything which you want men to become able to do, that you
should first do to them yourselves. That is the essential meaning of
the Law and the prophets.

13‘Enter through the narrow gate. Only that road which leads
into the abyss is wide and comfortable. And many are they who
travel along it. 14But narrow is the gate and full of hardship the path
which leads to the higher life, and it is only a few who find it.

15‘Be on your guard against those who make themselves tools of
deceiving spirits. Disguised as lambs they come to you, although
inwardly they are rapacious wolves. 16You can recognize them by
their fruits. Can grapes be harvested from a thorn bush, or figs from
thistles? 17A good tree will always bear good fruits and a rotten tree
bad fruits. 18A good tree cannot bear bad fruits and a rotten tree
cannot bear good fruits; 19and every tree that does not bear good
fruits has to be felled and burnt. 20So you will recognize them by
their fruits.

21‘Not everyone who says “Lord, Lord” to me will gain entry
to the realm of the heavens, but he who acts according to the will
of my Father in the heavens. 22On that day many will say to me,
“Lord, Lord, did we not prophesy through your power, and drive

out demons through your power, and carry out many deeds of the
spirit through your power?” [23]And I will speak to them emphatically and say, “I have never known you. Leave my presence; you
have caused nothing but chaos with your work.”

[24]‘Whoever hears these my words and acts accordingly will
be like a prudent man who built his house on rock. [25]Now heavy
rain fell and the rivers rose and the winds blew and the house was
exposed to the elements; yet it did not collapse. For it had the rock
as its foundation.

[26]‘But whoever hears these words, and does not act accordingly,
will be like a foolish man who built his house on sand. [27]And when
the heavy rain fell and the rivers rose and the winds blew and the
house was exposed to the elements, then it collapsed and its doom
was sealed.’

[28]And it happened: When Jesus had completed this teaching,
great excitement arose among the people, [29]for he taught as one in
whom the creating powers themselves are at work; not in the usual
style of the scribes.

8 *Healing a leper*

As he came down from the mountain, great crowds followed him.
[2]And see, a leper came up to him, fell down before him and said,
‘Lord, if only you will you can make me clean.’ [3]And he stretched
out his hand, touched him, and said, ‘It is my will; be clean!’ And at
once he was cleansed of his leprosy. [4]Then Jesus said to him, ‘Take
care that you speak to no one about this. But you should go to the
priests and show yourself to them. Make the gift of offering which
Moses prescribes, as a proof to them.’

The Roman officer from Capernaum

[5]When he came to Capernaum a Roman officer approached him;
he asked for his help [6]and said, ‘Lord, my boy is lying in the
house paralysed, suffering terribly.’ [7]He answered him, ‘I will
come and heal him.’ [8]Then the officer answered, ‘Lord, I am not
worthy to have you enter my house. Speak just one word, then

my boy will be healed. 9I, too, am a man with people above me;
and I have soldiers subordinate to me. If I say to one: Come!
then he comes; and to another: Go! then he goes. And when I say
to my servant: Do this! then he does it.' 10Jesus heard this with
amazement and said to those who followed him, 'Certainly it is
true, in no Israelite have I yet found such power of faith. 11It has
to be said:

> Many will come from far away, from the East and
> from the West and have their place in the kingdom
> of the heavens with Abraham, Isaac and Jacob; 12but
> the sons of the kingdom will find that they have been
> thrust out into the darkness of external existence where
> human beings live, wailing and grinding their teeth.'

13And, turning to the officer, Jesus said, 'Go now; according to your
faith, so let it be.' And in the same hour the boy was healed.

Peter's mother-in-law

14After this Jesus went to Peter's house and saw his mother-in-law
lying with a fever. 15He touched her hand, and the fever left her. And
she got up and served him.

16When it was evening, many who were possessed were brought
to him, and through the power of his word he drove out the demons
and healed all the sick. 17So the word of the prophet Isaiah was
fulfilled:

> He has taken our sickness from us,
> he has borne all our infirmities.

Two enquiries

18When Jesus saw the crowd which surrounded him, he asked them
to get ready to sail to the other side of the sea. 19Then a scribe
came up to him and said, 'Master, I will follow you wherever you
go.' 20Jesus answered him, 'Foxes have their holes and the birds of
heaven have their nests, but the Son of Man has nowhere to lay his
head.'

21And another of his followers said to him, 'Lord, permit me

first to go and bury my father.' 22But Jesus answered, 'Follow me,
and let the dead bury their dead.'

Calming the storm

23Then he got into the ship, and his disciples followed him. 24And
see, there was a great swell and movement in the sea, so that the
ship was quite swamped by the waves. But he slept. 25Then they
came to him, woke him and said, 'Lord, help! We are perishing.'
26He said to them, 'How full of fear you are, and how weak is your
faith!' Then he rose and commanded the winds and the sea; and
there was a great calm. 27And they said, full of wonder, 'What kind
of Being is this, that even the winds and the sea obey him?'

Healing two demon-possessed Gadarenes

28When he came to the other side of the sea, to the country of the
Gadarenes, two men who were possessed by demons came out of
the tombs and stood in his way. They were exceedingly dangerous,
so that no one could pass along that road. 29And see, they called
out loudly: 'What is this power between us and you, Son of God?
Have you come here to discipline us before the time is fulfilled?'
30Far from them a large herd of pigs was feeding. 31And the demons
begged him, 'If you cast us out, send us into the herd of pigs.' 32And
he said to them: 'Depart.' And they fled and went into the pigs.
And see, the whole herd rushed down the steep incline into the sea
and perished in the waters. 33The herdsmen fled into their town and
reported everything, also what had happened to the men possessed
by the demons. 34And see, the whole town came out to meet Jesus,
and when they saw him, they begged him to travel on and leave
their country.

9 *Healing a paralysed man*

And he boarded the ship and went across the sea again and came to
his own town.

2And see, they brought to him a paralysed man, lying on a
stretcher. And Jesus saw the faith which moved them, and he said

to the paralysed man, 'Take courage, my son, your sins are taken
from you.' 3And see, some of the scribes said to themselves, 'He
presumes to claim divine powers for himself.' 4But Jesus saw what
they were thinking, and he said, 'Why do you have thoughts of evil
in your hearts? 5Which is easier to say: Your sins are taken from
you, or Stand up and walk? 6With your own eyes you shall see that
the Son of Man has the authority to forgive sins on earth.'

And he said to the paralysed man, 'Stand up, take your bed and
go to your house.' 7And he got up and went to his house.

8The crowd which saw it was awe-struck and praised the revelation of God who gives such authority to men.

The call to Matthew

9As Jesus walked on, he saw a man called Matthew sitting at the tax
office; and he said to him, 'Follow me!' And he got up and followed
him.

10And as he sat at table in the house, see, many tax-collectors
and outcasts came and shared in the meal with Jesus and his disciples. 11When the Pharisees saw this, they said to his disciples,
'How can your teacher eat with the tax-collectors and outcasts?'
12He heard the question and said, 'Those who are strong do not need
a physician, but rather those who are sick. 13Go now, and learn to
understand this word: "My concern is what lives in the heart, and
not the service of sacrifice." I have not come to call to me those who
are blameless, but those suffering from sin.'

About fasting

14At that time the disciples of John came to him and said, 'What is
the purpose of the asceticism which we and the Pharisees practise,
whilst your disciples do not?' 15Jesus answered, 'Should the wedding guests mourn as long as the bridegroom is with them? The
days will come when the bridegroom will be taken from them. Then
they may take up asceticism. 16No one puts a patch of new, hard
cloth on an old garment. Because it is firmer, it tears away from the
garment and the tear becomes worse.

17‘Neither does anyone pour new wine into old wineskins; otherwise the skins burst, the wine spills out and the skins are also of
no further use. New wine must be put into new skins, then both are
preserved.’

The woman with a haemorrhage and raising Jairus’ daughter

18While he was thus speaking to them, see, a ruler came to him, fell
at his feet and said, ‘My daughter has just died. But if you come
and lay your hand on her, she will waken to life again.’ 19And Jesus
got up and followed him, together with his disciples. 20And see,
a woman who had suffered from a haemorrhage for twelve years
came up behind him and touched the hem of his garment; 21for she
said to herself: If I only touch his garment, I shall be healed. 22Then
Jesus turned, looked at her and said, ‘Take courage, my daughter,
your faith has healed you.’ From that hour the woman was well.
23And Jesus came into the house of the ruler. When he saw the flute
players and the crowd of wailing mourners, 24he said, ‘You may go;
the girl is not dead, she is asleep.’ And they laughed at him. 25When
the crowd had been removed, Jesus went in and took the girl by
the hand. Then the girl arose. 26And the report of this event spread
through the whole country.

Healing two blind men

27Jesus walked on, and he was followed by two blind men who kept
calling: ‘Have mercy on us, Son of David.’ 28When he got home
to his house, the blind men came to him, and Jesus said to them,
‘Do you have the trust that I can do this?’ They answered, ‘Yes,
Lord.’ 29Then he touched their eyes and said, ‘According to your
faith, so let it be.’ 30And their eyes were opened. Jesus spoke to
them with emphasis: ‘Take care that no one gets to know what has
happened.’ 31But they went away and talked about him through the
whole country.

Healing a dumb man
[32]When they had gone, see, a man was brought to him who was
dumb and possessed by a demon. [33]He drove out the demon, and
the dumb man could speak again. And the crowd said, full of
amazement: Never has anything like it happened in Israel. [34]But
the Pharisees said: He drives out demons with the power of the
Prince of Demons. [35]And Jesus wandered through all towns and
villages and taught in their synagogues and proclaimed the message of healing from the heavenly kingdom and healed all sicknesses and infirmities. [36]And when he saw the crowd, he was filled
with great compassion for the people, for they were exhausted
and scattered like sheep that have no shepherd. [37]And he said to
his disciples, 'The harvest is great, but the reapers are few. [38]Pray
the Lord of the harvest that HE send out reapers to gather in HIS
harvest.'

10 *The calling and mission of the twelve disciples*
And he called together his twelve disciples and gave them authority
to drive out unclean spirits and to heal all diseases and infirmities.
[2]These are the names of the twelve apostles:
The first is Simon who was given the name Peter. Then come
Andrew, his brother, and James the son of Zebedee and John, his
brother; [3]Philip and Bartholomew, Thomas and Matthew the tax-collector, James the son of Alphaeus, and Thaddaeus, [4]Simon the
Cananaean, and Judas Iscariot who betrayed him.
[5]These twelve Jesus sent out, and for their journey he instructed
them: 'Do not go astray on the ways of the foreign peoples, and
do not join the community of the Samaritans; [6]but rather seek the
way to the lost sheep of the house of Israel. [7]Go out and proclaim
the message: "The kingdom of heaven has come close." [8]Heal the
sick, awaken the dead, cleanse the lepers, drive out the demons.
You have received a free gift, now give freely. [9]Do not acquire gold
or silver or copper for your own pocket. [10]You do not need a bag
on the journey, nor a second coat, nor shoes or a staff. Whoever is
active deserves to receive what he needs.

11‘When you come to a town or a village, discover who in it is worthy – then stay with him until you travel on. 12When you enter a house, give greeting. 13And if the house is worthy, then your peace will come upon it. But if it is not worthy, then your peace shall return to you. 14Wherever they do not receive you or listen to your words, leave that house or that town and shake the dust from your feet. 15Yes, I tell you, on the day of the great decision, the destiny of Sodom and Gomorrah shall be more bearable than that town’s. 16See, out of the power of my own Being I send you out as lambs among the wolves. Strive to have the intelligence of serpents and the purity of doves. 17Be on your guard against men. They will take you to the law courts; in their synagogues they will scourge you. 18You will be dragged before governors and kings because my Being lives in you, but you will be a proof of the spirit to them and to the peoples. 19When they take away your liberty, do not be anxious about how you should speak and what you should say. At the right hour it will be given to you what you are to say; 20for it will not be you who speak: The Spirit, which the Father, the Ground of the World, gives you, speaks through you.

21‘Brother will hand over brother to death, and the father his child. Children will rise up against parents and kill them. 22And you will be hated by everyone for the sake of my name. But he who endures until the aim is reached will attain salvation. 23If they persecute you in one town, escape to another. Yes, I say to you, you will not come to the end of the towns in Israel before the Son of Man comes.

24‘No pupil is above his teacher, and no servant is above his master. 25Let it be enough for the pupil to become like his teacher and the servant like his master. If they have called the master of the house a satanic spirit, all the more will they malign the members of his household. 26But do not be afraid of them. There is nothing shrouded which will not be unveiled, and nothing secret which will not become accessible to knowledge. 27What I say to you in the dark, tell it in the light; and what you hear whispered, proclaim from the housetops.

28‘Do not fear those who can kill the body but not the soul.
Rather be afraid of him who can destroy both soul and body in the
life after death. 29Are not two sparrows sold for a few pennies? And
yet not one of them falls to the ground without your Father’s will.
30Even the hairs on your head are all numbered. 31So have no fear.
You are worth more than many sparrows. 32Everyone who confesses
to my Being before men, I also will acknowledge before my Father
in the heavens; 33but whoever denies me before men, I also will
deny before my Father in the heavens.

34‘Do not think that I have come to bring a trite peace on earth.
I do not bring peace, but a sword. 35I have come to separate a
man from his father and a daughter from her mother and a bride
from her husband’s mother. 36A man’s relations will become his
enemies. 37Whoever loves father and mother more than me is not
worthy of me. And whoever loves son or daughter more than me
is not worthy of me, either. 38And whoever is not prepared to bear
his cross and follow me is not worthy of my Being. 39Whoever
finds his soul will also lose it; but whoever loses his soul for
my sake will truly find it. 40Whoever receives you receives me,
and whoever receives me receives HIM who sent me. 41Whoever
receives a prophet for the sake of his prophetic power will himself receive a share of the prophetic power. And whoever receives
a good man for the sake of the goodness that lives in him will
himself receive a share of that goodness. 42And whoever gives a
refreshing drink to a disciple because he is aware of the germi-
nating power of the higher being in him will not remain without
a share of that power himself.’

11 And when Jesus had completed this teaching of his twelve disciples, he went on from there, teaching and proclaiming in the towns
of that country.

The Baptist’s question

2At that time John heard in prison about the deeds of Christ; he
sent his disciples to him 3to ask, ‘Are you he who is to come, or
are we to expect another?’ 4And Jesus answered them, ‘Go and tell

John what you hear and what you see. 5The blind become seeing, the lame walk. Lepers are cleansed, the deaf hear, the dead are raised and those who have become poor receive the message of salvation. 6And all those are blessed who do not stumble over my Being.'

7When the messengers had gone again, Jesus began to speak to the crowd about John: 'What was it you wanted to see when you went out into the desert? A reed swaying in the wind? 8Or was it something else you wanted to see? A man wearing fine clothes? See, it is in kings' houses that you find those who wear fine clothes. 9What was it you wanted to see? A prophet? Yes, I tell you, he is more than a prophet. 10He it is of whom scripture says:

> See, I send my angel before you,
> he shall prepare your way,
> that your Being may be revealed.

11'Yes, I tell you: Among all who were born of earthly mothers, none is greater than John the Baptist. And yet the least of the beings in the heavenly world is greater than he. 12From the days of John the Baptist, and even more now, the kingdom of heaven is found through the will; those who exert their will can freely grasp it. 13The books of the prophets and the Law are words of the spirit which were valid until John. 14And if you are willing to accept it: He is Elijah, whose return men are expecting. 15He who has ears, let him hear!

16'To what shall I compare people of the present time? They are like a group of boys, sitting in the market place and calling to one another: 17We played the flute for you, but you did not dance; we sang mournful songs, but you did not weep. 18John came, but he did not eat and did not drink, and so they said: He is possessed by a demon. 19The Son of Man came and ate and drank. And now they say: See, a man who gives himself up to eating and wine-drinking, a friend of tax-collectors and outcasts. Thus, those who owe their existence to the divine wisdom sit in judgment upon it.'

20And he began to speak reproachful words about the towns where most of his spiritual deeds had taken place and which had

not found the way to a change of heart and mind: 21'Woe to you,
Chorazin, woe to you, Bethsaida! If the deeds done in you had
been done in Tyre and Sidon, they would long ago have signi-
fied their change of heart and mind with mourning garments and
ashes. 22And so I say to you: On the great day of decision the destiny of Tyre and Sidon shall be more bearable than yours. 23And
you, Capernaum, have you not been exalted to heaven? You shall
descend to the realm of shadows. If the deeds done in you had
been done in Sodom, that town would be standing to this day.
24And so I say: The land of Sodom will have a more bearable
destiny than you on the great day of decision.'

25At that time Jesus lifted up his soul and said, 'To you I confess
and give praise, O Father, Lord of heaven and earth. You have hidden your secrets from the wise and the clever, but you reveal them
to childlike souls. 26Yes, Father, it is your will that men should thus
stand before your countenance. 27All secrets have been entrusted to
me by my Father, and no one can know the Son except the Father,
and no one can know the Father except the Son and with him those
to whom the Son chooses to reveal HIM. 28Come to me, all who have
hardships and heavy burdens to bear. I will give you new forces
of life. 29Take my yoke upon you and learn from my Being: In me,
courage and humility of heart are combined. You shall find sources
of new life-forces for your souls; 30for my yoke is gentle, and my
burden is light.'

12 *Disputes about the Sabbath and the Son of Man*

At that time Jesus went through the cornfields one Sabbath day.
His disciples were hungry and began to pick ears of corn and to
eat them. 2The Pharisees saw this and said to him, 'Look, your
disciples are doing what is not allowed on the Sabbath.' 3He
answered them, 'Have you not read what David did when he and
those with him were hungry? 4How he entered the house of God
and ate the shewbread which is only for the priests and which was
forbidden him and those with him? 5And have you not read in the
book of the Law that in the temple-service the priests may break

the sabbath-rest without committing a sin? 6And I say to you: Something greater than the Temple is here. 7If you had understood the word:

> My concern is with the stirring of the heart and not with sacrifices,

you would not condemn those who in reality are without guilt. 8The Son of Man is lord of the Sabbath.'

9He went on from there and entered their synagogue. 10And see, there was a man with a withered hand. And they asked him, 'Is it permitted to heal on the Sabbath?' They were looking for a reason to accuse him. 11He said, 'Is there a man among you with one sheep, who, if it falls into a pit on the Sabbath, will not lift it out at once? 12Is not a human being much more than a sheep? So surely it must be allowed to do a good deed on the Sabbath.' 13And he said to the man, 'Stretch out your hand.' And as he stretched it out it was restored and was healthy like the other. 14But the Pharisees went out and debated how they could proceed against him to destroy him. 15When Jesus perceived this, he left that district. Many people followed him, and he healed them all 16and impressed upon them not to reveal his secret. 17The word of the prophet Isaiah was to be fulfilled:

> 18See, that is my Son whom I have chosen,
> whom I love and in whom my soul is revealed.
> I will pour out my Spirit upon him
> that he may proclaim to the peoples the turning-point of time.
> 19He will cause neither quarrels nor uproar,
> his voice will not be heard in the streets.
> 20He will not break a swaying reed
> nor extinguish a glimmering wick
> until he has brought the time of decision to victory.
> 21And the peoples will place their hope in his name.

22Then they brought to him a blind and dumb man who was possessed by a demon. And he healed him, so that he became able to speak and see again. 23And the crowd of people, as if out

of themselves, said, 'Is that not the Son of David?' 24When the
Pharisees heard that, they said, 'He is only able to drive out
demons because he does it through the power of Beelzebub, the
Prince of Demons.' 25But he perceived their thoughts and said to
them, 'Every kingdom that is divided destroys itself. No town
and no house community that is divided can continue to exist.
26And if one satanic power drives out another, then Satan is
divided against himself; how then can his kingdom remain? 27If I
drive out demons with the power of Beelzebub, with what power
do your sons do it? Your own sons shall be your judges. 28But
the truth is that I drive out the demons with the power of the
Spirit of God, and thus the Kingdom of God makes itself known
among you. 29Or can anyone enter a strong man's house and rob
him of his weapons, unless he first fetters the strong man? Only
afterwards can he enter his house to carry off the loot. 30Whoever
is not with my Being, is against my Being; and those not able
to find the inner harmony which is created through my Being,
they serve disunity. 31Therefore I say to you: Every weakness
and failing and every hostile word can be taken from men, but
enmity against the spirit cannot be taken from them. 32The word
which someone speaks against the Son of Man can be forgiven
him; but if he directs it against the Holy Spirit, it cannot be forgiven him, neither in the present nor in the future cycle of time.

33'Either you plant a noble tree and harvest noble fruits from it,
or you plant a common tree and harvest common fruits. The value
of the tree can be seen by its fruits. 34You sons of the serpent, how
can you believe that what you say is good when you yourselves are
evil?

'When the mouth speaks, it reveals what is in the heart. 35A good
man distributes goodness out of the good treasure. An evil man distributes evil out of the evil treasure. 36I tell you that on the great
day of decision, men will have to give account of every loveless
word which they have spoken. 37Your share of the true Being will
be according to your words; your share of the transitory world will
be according to your words.'

[38]Then some of the scribes and Pharisees said to him, 'Master,
we wish to see a deed performed by you which will prove your
power of spirit.' [39]But he answered them, 'Only a humanity which
has become degenerate and unfaithful to the holy order of life
craves for a wonder. But no other wonder will be given to it, except
the sign of the prophet Jonah. [40]As Jonah was three days and three
nights within the fish, so the Son of Man will lie for three days and
three nights in the heart of the earth. [41]On the day of decision the
people of Nineveh will arise against the people of today and will be
their stern judges, since *they* changed their hearts and minds after
the proclamation of Jonah. And see, here is something greater than
Jonah. [42]The queen of the South will arise on the day of decision
against the people of today and will be their stern judge; for she came
from the ends of the earth to hear the wisdom of Solomon. And see,
here is something greater than Solomon. [43]When an impure spirit
has left a man it wanders through waterless places and seeks for
peace without finding it. [44]Then it says: I will return to the dwelling
from which I went out. And when it comes it finds the house empty,
cleaned and adorned. [45]And now the spirit goes and joins with seven
other spirits even worse than itself, and they enter and dwell there.
And in the end it is worse for that man than before. So it shall also
be for the degenerate humanity of today.'

New human relationships

[46]While he was still speaking to the crowd, see, his mother and his
brothers stood outside and wished to speak with him. [47]And someone said to him, 'See, your mother and your brothers are standing
outside and wish to speak with you.' [48]And he replied to the man
who was speaking to him, 'Who is my mother and who are my
brothers?' [49]And he stretched out his hand towards his disciples and
said, 'See, my mother and my brothers. [50]Whoever acts out of the
will of my Father in the heavens is my brother and my sister and
my mother.'

13 *Seven parables about the kingdom of heaven*
On that day Jesus went out of the house to the sea and there he
sat down. 2Then a great crowd of people streamed towards him,
until he eventually had to get into a boat and sit down in it; and the
whole crowd stood on the shore. 3And he said many things to them
in parables.

He said: 'See, the sower went and sowed. 4As he was sowing, a portion of the seed fell on the path and the birds came
and ate it up. 5Another portion fell on rocky ground where there
was little earth. And because the earth had no depth, the plants,
although they sprouted quickly, 6soon dried up when the sun
rose higher, since they were not able to take root. 7Others fell
among the thorns, and the thorns grew up and choked them.
8Another portion fell on good earth and bore fruit, some a hundredfold, some sixtyfold, and some thirtyfold. 9Whoever has
ears, let him hear!'

10Then the disciples came to him and said, 'Why do you speak
to them in parables?' 11He answered, *'You* have the gift of being
able with your thinking to understand the mysteries of the kingdom
of the heavens. They do not have this gift. 12To him who has it will
more be given, so that he will have abundance. From him who does
not have will be taken even that which he has. 13That is why I speak
to them in pictures; for they have eyes and yet they do not see. They
have ears and yet they do not hear; they do not have the power of
understanding through thought. 14The word of the prophet Isaiah is
fulfilled in them:

> You hear with your ears, but do not understand,
> You see with your eyes, but do not perceive.
> 15The hearts of men have become lifeless and dull,
> Their ears are hard of hearing,
> And their eyes are tired.
> In spite of their eyes they do not see,
> In spite of their ears they do not hear,
> They can no longer understand with the .
> Only if they change the direction

of their inner life will
I be able to heal them.
[16]Blessed are your eyes, for they see, and your ears, for they hear.
[17]Yes, I say to you: Many prophets and men of God have longed to
see what you see, and did not see it, and to hear what you hear, and
did not hear it.

[18]'You have heard the parable of the sower. [19]Whoever hears
the word of the inner kingdom and yet does not take it into his
consciousness, to him comes the power of evil and robs him of
the seed in his . That is the seed which fell on the path. [20]As for
the seed that fell on rocky ground, that means those who hear the
word and at once receive it enthusiastically. [21]But it cannot take
root in their being and only lives for a short time. When such a
person has to endure hardships and challenges on account of the
word, at once his inner power fails. [22]As for the seed which fell
among the thorns, that means those who hear the word but in
whom it is choked and made sterile by anxieties about what is
temporal, and also by the illusory element within earthly possessions. [23]And as for the seed which fell on good earth, that means
those who hear the word and take it into their consciousness
and in whom it bears fruit, in the one a hundredfold, in another
sixtyfold, in yet another thirtyfold.'

[24]And he placed another picture before them: 'The kingdom
of the heavens can be compared with a man who sowed good
seed in his field; [25]but while everyone was asleep his enemy came
and sowed weeds among the wheat and went away again. [26]Now
when the plants sprouted and bore fruit, then the weeds also
appeared. [27]Then the servants of the master of the house came to
him and said, "Master, did you not sow good seed in your field?
So where do the weeds come from?" [28]He answered, "A man who
is our enemy has done this." Then the servants said, "If you want
us to, we will go and gather the weeds." [29]He said, "Do not do
that, otherwise when you gather the weeds you will tear up the
wheat also. [30]Let both grow until the harvest. And when harvest
time has come, I will say to the reapers: Gather the weeds first

and bind them in bundles to be burnt, but gather the wheat into
my barn".'

[31]Again he placed another picture before them: 'The kingdom of
the heavens is like a grain of mustard which a man takes and plants
in his field. [32]It is the smallest of all seeds, but when it grows it is
soon taller than the herbs and becomes a tree in whose branches the
birds of the air build their nests.'

[33]And he told them another parable: 'The kingdom of the heavens is like leaven which a woman took and mixed with three measures of flour until all the flour was leavened.'

[34]Jesus spoke to the people in parables in this way, and he spoke
to them only in parables. [35]The word of the prophet was to be fulfilled:

In pictures will I speak,
so that I can uncover everything
which has been hidden
since the foundation of the earth.

[36]And he dismissed the crowd and went into the house. And his
disciples came to him and said, 'Explain to us the parable of the
weeds in the field.' [37]He answered, 'He who sowed the good seed
is the Son of Man. [38]The field is mankind. The good seeds are the
sons of the kingdom. The weeds are the sons of the evil power,
[39]and the enemy who sowed the weed is the Tempter himself. The
harvest is the completion of the cycle of time, and the reapers are
the angels. [40]Just as the weed is gathered and burnt in the fire, so
will it be at the completion of the cycle of time. [41]The Son of Man
will send out the angels who serve him, and out of his kingdom
they will gather all obstacles to the true self and all those who are
in the service of anarchy and chaos, [42]and hand them over to the
world fire.

'Those concerned must endure an existence of lamentation and
gnashing of teeth. [43]But those who serve the Good will shine like
the sun in the kingdom of their Father. He who has ears, let him
hear!

[44]'The kingdom of the heavens is like a treasure hidden in a

field. A man found it and hid it and went, full of joy, to sell everything
that he owned in order to acquire the field.

45‘The kingdom of the heavens is also like a merchant in search
of fine pearls. 46And when he found a particularly valuable pearl, he
sold all his goods and bought the pearl.

47‘Lastly, the kingdom of the heavens is like a net which was
cast into the sea and all kinds of fish were caught in it.

48‘When it was full, the fishermen drew it ashore and sat down
around it and gathered the good fish into containers, but the useless
ones they threw out. 49So it will be at the completion of the cycle
of time. The angels will go forth to separate out all those who have
given themselves over to evil from those who bear the Good within
them. 50They will be handed over to the world fire and must endure
an existence of lamentation and gnashing of teeth.

51‘Have you understood all this?’ They answered, ‘Yes.’ 52And
he said, ‘Every student of the scriptures who has been taught by
the kingdom of the heavens itself is like a man who is master of his
house and knows when to bring out what is new and when what is
old from his treasures.’

Rejection in Nazareth

53And it happened: When Jesus had finished this series of parables
he went on 54and came to his home town. There he taught in the
synagogue in such a way that the people were beside themselves
with amazement and said, ‘From where does he get this wisdom
and the power for such deeds? 55Is he not the carpenter’s son, and is
not his mother called Mary? Are not James and Joseph and Simon
and Judas his brothers, 56and are not his sisters all well known to us?
From where does he get the power for all this?’ 57His way of being
caused confusion amongst the people. But Jesus said to them, ‘A
prophet is nowhere less accepted than in his home town and in his
own house.’ 58And he was not able to do many deeds of the spirit
there, for the hearts of the people were weak.

14 *The death of John the Baptist*
At that time Herod the tetrarch heard what the people said about
Jesus, 2and he said to those around him, 'He is John the Baptist who
has been raised from the dead; that is why such powers of the spirit
work through him.' 3For Herod had ordered John to be arrested,
bound and imprisoned because Herodias, the wife of his brother
Philip, wanted it. 4John had said to him, 'You have no right to have
her as your wife.' 5He dared not have him killed for fear of the
people, for they regarded him as a great prophet. 6Then, on Herod's
birthday the daughter of Herodias danced before the guests, and so
pleased Herod 7that he solemnly promised to give her whatever she
might demand. 8But she had been instructed by her mother beforehand and so she said, 'Give me here the head of John the Baptist
on a platter.' 9The King was shocked, but because he had sworn it
before his guests he commanded that her request should be granted,
10and he had John beheaded in the prison. 11And so John's head was
brought in on a platter and given to the girl who brought it to her
mother. 12And his disciples came and took the body and buried it
and told Jesus what had happened.

Feeding the five thousand
13When Jesus heard their report he went away from there and, in
order to be by himself, he went by ship to an isolated, lonely place.
When the people heard of it they followed him on foot from the
towns. 14And when he came and saw the great crowd of people he
had compassion on them and healed those among them who were
sick.

15When evening came, the disciples came to him and said,
'Lonely is the place and the day is over, let the people now go, so
that they can buy food for themselves in the villages.' 16But Jesus
said, 'They need not go away; you give them something to eat.'
17They said, 'We have nothing here except five loaves and two fish.'
18He said, 'Bring them here to me.' 19And he told the crowd to sit
down on the grass. Then he took the five loaves and the two fish,
lifted up his soul to heaven, spoke the words of blessing, broke the

bread and gave it to the disciples. And the disciples gave it to the
people. 20And all ate and were satisfied, and when the remaining
fragments were gathered up, it was twelve full baskets. 21Those
who were fed were five thousand men, besides the women and the
children.

Walking on the sea

22And immediately he urged the disciples to get into the ship and
sail before him to the other side, while he dismissed the crowd.
23And he left the crowd and went up on the mountain by himself to
pray. Late in the evening he was still there alone.

24The ship was already many stadia from the land and was
being beaten by the waves, for the wind was against them. 25And
in the fourth watch of the night he came to them, walking on the
sea. 26And when the disciples saw him walking on the sea they
were frightened and cried out with fear: 'It is a ghost!' 27But at
once he spoke to them: 'Take heart, it is I; have no fear!' 28Then
Peter answered him, 'Lord, if it is you, bid me come to you over
the water.' 29He said, 'Come!' And Peter got out of the ship and
walked on the water and came to Jesus. 30But when he felt the
wind he became afraid and began to sink, and he cried out: 'Lord,
save me!' 31And at once Jesus reached out his hand and drew him
near and said, 'How weak is your heart! Why did you become
unsure?' 32And they got into the ship and the wind ceased. 33And
those in the ship fell down before him and said, 'You are truly
God's Son.'

34When they had crossed over, they came to land at Gennesaret.
35And when the people there recognized him, they made it known
in all that region, and all who were sick were brought to him, 36and
they asked him to be allowed only to touch the hem of his garment.
And those who touched it were completely healed.

15 *True purity*

Then Pharisees and scribes came to Jesus from Jerusalem and said,
2'Why do your disciples disregard the traditions of the priests?

They do not wash their hands before eating bread.' [3]He answered,
'And why do you yourselves disregard the divine commandments
of your traditions? [4]The word of God says:

Honour your father and your mother

and

Whoever curses his father or his mother must die.

[5]But you say, "Whoever says to his father or mother: I will make an
offering to God of what I owe to you" he need no longer honour his
father and mother. [6]So, for the sake of your human traditions, you
have made void the word of God. [7]You hypocrites! It was of you
that Isaiah prophesied when he said:

[8]Only with their lips do men honour me,
Their heart is far from my Being;
[9]They think to serve me with empty ritual
and only teach human doctrines and commandments.'

[10]And he called the crowd of people together and said, 'Listen
and understand my words! [11]A human being cannot be degraded by
what goes into the mouth; but what comes out of the mouth, that
may degrade him.'

[12]Then the disciples came to him and said, 'Do you know that
the Pharisees are beside themselves because of what you said?' [13]He
answered, 'Every plant which my heavenly Father has not planted
will be uprooted one day. [14]Disregard them! They are blind guides
of the blind. If a blind man leads a blind man, both will fall over
the precipice.'

[15]Then Peter said, 'Explain the parable to us.' [16]He answered,
'Do you still understand so little? [17]Do you not know that everything
which enters a human being through the mouth is taken into the
entrails of the body until the body casts it out as waste? [18]But what
goes forth from the mouth comes from the heart, and it is this
which can degrade a human being; [19]for it is from the heart that
evil thoughts come: Enmity against the lives of others, impurity
in human relationships, uncleanliness of soul, greed for the possessions of others, misuse of speech against other human beings,
misuse of speech against the world of the spirit. [20]All these degrade

a human being; but it does not degrade him if he eats without the
washing of hands.'

Healing a Canaanite woman

21And Jesus went on and came to the region of Tyre and Sidon.
22And see, a Canaanite woman from that region came up to him
and called out: 'Have pity on me, Lord, Son of David. My daughter
is tormented by demons.' 23He answered her not a word. Then his
disciples came and urged him, 'Send her away, for she keeps calling
out after us.' 24And he answered, 'I have been sent only to the lost
sheep of the house of Israel.' 25Then she threw herself at his feet
and said again, 'Lord, help me!' 26He said, 'It is not right to take
the children's bread and give it to the dogs.' 27She said, 'Yes, Lord,
and yet the dogs eat the crumbs that fall from their master's table.'
28Then Jesus said to her, 'O woman, the power of your faith is great.
What you wish for shall happen.' And in the same hour her daughter
was healed.

Healings

29And Jesus went on and came again to the Sea of Galilee. And
he went up on the mountain and sat down. 30And great crowds of
people flocked to him and brought with them many who were lame
or crippled or blind or dumb, and many with other diseases. They
threw themselves at his feet and he healed them. 31Great amazement
came over the crowd when they saw that the dumb could speak,
the crippled were healed, the lame walked and the blind could see
again. And they praised the God of Israel.

Feeding the four thousand

32And Jesus called his disciples together and said, 'I have compassion on the people. They have now been with me for three days,
and have nothing to eat. I do not want to send them away hungry,
because they may become weak on the way.' 33Then the disciples
said to him, 'Where in the desert can we get enough bread to satisfy so great a crowd?' 34Jesus said to them, 'How many loaves

have you?' They answered, 'Seven, and a few small fish.' [35]Then
he made the people sit down on the ground [36]and took the seven
loaves and the fish, spoke the words of blessing, broke the bread
and gave it to the disciples. And the disciples gave it to the people.
[37]And all ate and were satisfied. And when the remaining fragments
were gathered up, it was seven full baskets. [38]The number of those
who were fed was four thousand men, as well as the women and
the children. [39]After this he dismissed the crowd, boarded the ship
and came to the region of Magadan.

16 *Signs of the times*
Pharisees and Sadducees came to him to test him. They demanded
of him that he should justify himself before their eyes by a deed of
supernatural power. [2]But he said to them, 'In the evening you say,
"It will be good weather, for the sky is red," [3]and in the morning:
"Today it will be stormy, for the sky is red and threatening." So you
know how to interpret the changing appearance of the sky; but the
signs of the times you do not recognize. [4]Only a humanity which
has become degenerate and unfaithful to the holy order and harmony of life demands a wonder. But no other sign will be granted
it except the sign of the prophet Jonah.' And he left them standing
and went away.

[5]And when they came to the other side of the lake, the disciples had forgotten to bring any bread. [6]Then Jesus said to them,
'Take care, beware of the leaven of the Pharisees and Sadducees.'
[7]And they pondered this; and then it occurred to them that they had
forgotten to bring bread. [8]But Jesus perceived what went through
their minds and said, 'Why are you so preoccupied with the fact
that you have no bread? How weak is your faith! [9]Are your hearts
and minds still not open? Do you not remember the five loaves
among the five thousand and the number of the baskets that you
filled? [10]And the seven loaves among the four thousand, and again
the number of the baskets? [11]Do you not understand that I am not
speaking to you about earthly bread? Beware of the leaven of
the Pharisees and the Sadducees.' [12]Then they understood that he

was not speaking of ordinary leaven, but of the teaching of the
Pharisees and Sadducees.

Peter's confession

13And Jesus came to the district of Caesarea Philippi. There he asked
his disciples, 'Who do men say that the Son of Man is?' 14They
answered, 'Some say John the Baptist, others say Elijah, and yet
others say Jeremiah or one of the other prophets.' 15He said, 'And
who do you say that I am?' 16Then Simon Peter answered, 'You are
the Christ, the Son of the Living God.' 17And Jesus said, 'Blessed
are you, Simon, son of Jona; you have not received this revelation
from the world of the senses but from the world of my Father in the
heavens. 18And I say to you: You are Peter, the Rock. On this rock
I will build my congregation and the gates of the abyss shall not
swallow it up. 19To you I will give the keys to the kingdom of the
heavens. What you bind on the earth shall also be considered bound
in the heavens, and what you loose on earth shall also be considered
loosed in the heavens.' 20And with emphasis he told his disciples to
tell no one that he was the Christ.

First foretelling of death and resurrection

21From then on Jesus Christ began to tell his disciples that he must
go to Jerusalem, that much suffering from the elders and high priests
and scribes lay before him, that he must be killed and that he would
be raised on the third day.

22Then Peter took him aside and began to remonstrate with him,
'I mean well, Lord; do not allow this to happen to you.' 23Then he
turned to Peter and said, 'Leave me, power of Satan. Your aim is to
alienate me from my purpose. You are no longer thinking heavenly
thoughts; now you are only thinking as earthly Man.'

Conditions of discipleship

24And Jesus said to his disciples, 'Whoever would follow me must
practise denial of self and bear his cross. Only so can he follow
me. 25Whoever is concerned about saving his soul will lose it, but

whoever loses his soul for my sake will truly find it. 26What use is
it to a human being to acquire the whole world, if in the process his
soul becomes stunted? Does a human being have anything which
he can give to regain his soul? 27The Son of Man will come in the
light-revelation of the Father, the Ground of the World, accompanied by the angels who serve him. To each individual human being
he will give the destiny which corresponds to his deeds.

28'Yes, I tell you: Among those who are standing here there are
some who, before they taste death, will see the Son of Man as he
comes in his kingdom.'

17 *The Transfiguration*

And after six days Jesus took Peter and James and John his brother,
and led them, as an intimate group, up on a high mountain. 2And
he was transformed before them. His countenance shone like the
sun, and his garments became shining white like light itself. 3And
see, Moses and Elijah appeared to them, in conversation with him.
4And Peter said to Jesus, 'Lord, it is good that we are here. If
you wish it, I will build three shelters here, one for you, one for
Moses and one for Elijah.' 5And while he was still speaking, see,
a shining cloud overshadowed them, and see, a voice spoke out of
the cloud:

'This is my Son whom I love. In him I have been revealed. Hear
his word!'

6When the disciples heard this, they fell on their faces. They
trembled at the nearness of the spirit. 7Then Jesus came to them,
touched them and said, 'Stand up, have no fear!' 8And when they
raised their eyes they saw no one except Jesus by himself.

9During the descent from the mountain Jesus urged them, 'Do
not speak to anyone of what you have seen, until the Son of Man
is raised from the dead.' 10And the disciples asked him, 'What is
meant when the scribes say that first Elijah must come again?' 11He
answered, 'Elijah does indeed come and prepare everything. 12And
I tell you: Elijah has already come, and human beings did not recognize him but treated him according to their whim. The Son of

Man will also have to suffer this from them.' [13]Then the disciples
understood that he was speaking to them of John the Baptist.

Healing the moonstruck boy

[14]When they came to the crowd, a man approached them, fell on
his knees before him and said, [15]'Lord, have pity on my son; he is
moonstruck and suffers greatly. Often he falls into fire and often
into water. [16]I brought him to your disciples, but they could not heal
him.' [17]Then Jesus said, 'How weak are the hearts of men, and how
distorted the image of Man has become in them. How long must I
still be with you? How long must I still bear you? Bring him to me.'
[18]And Jesus spoke sharply to him, and the demon left him. From
that hour the boy was healed.

[19]When they again were together in their intimate circle, the
disciples asked Jesus, 'Why could we not drive the demon out?'
[20]He said, 'Because the power of your faith is too weak. Yes, I tell
you, if you had faith as a mustard seed, you would be able to say to
this mountain: Move from here to over there. And at once it would
move. Nothing would be impossible for you.'

Second foretelling of death and resurrection

[22]Now while they were still living in Galilee, Jesus said to them,
'The Son of Man will be delivered into the hands of men, [23]and
they will kill him, and on the third day he will be raised.' Then they
became deeply sorrowful.

The Temple tax

[24]When they came to Capernaum, the collectors of the Temple
tax went up to Peter and said, 'Does your teacher pay the tax?'
[25]He said, 'Yes.' And when he came home, Jesus anticipated him
by asking, 'What do you think, Simon? From whom do the kings
of the earth take toll and tax? From their sons or from strangers?'
[26]He answered, 'From strangers.' Jesus went on, 'So therefore the
sons are free. [27]But we will not give them any cause to become
agitated; therefore go to the sea and cast a line. Take the first fish

you pull up, and when you open its mouth you will find a coin in it. Take that and give it to them for me and for you.'

18 *Living as brothers*

In that hour the disciples came to Jesus and said, 'Who is the greatest in the kingdom of the heavens?' [2]And he called a child to him,
put him in their midst [3]and said, 'Yes, I say to you, if you do not turn
about inwardly and reawaken the pure forces of childhood within
yourselves, you will not find access to the kingdom of the heavens. [4]The more a person can humbly enliven this Being of the child
within himself, the greater he is in the kingdom of the heavens.
[5]Whoever immerses himself in the being of such a child, trusting
in me, will find me through the child. [6]But whoever hinders the
delicate beginnings in Man of that which grows through faith in me,
it would be better for him to have a millstone hung about his neck
and be sunk to the depths of the sea. [7]Woe to mankind because of
the hindrances to inner growth! It is true that these hindrances are
a necessity of destiny, but woe to that human being through whom
they arise.

[8]'If your hand or your foot separates you from your own higher
being, then cut it off and cast it away from you. It is better for you
to find access to the true life crippled or lame than to be consigned
to the cosmic fire with two hands and two feet. [9]And if your eye
blinds you to your own higher being, then pluck it out and cast it
away from you. It is better for you to find true life, one-eyed, than
to be lost to the fiery abyss with two eyes.

[10]'See that you do not despise these delicately growing capac-
ities in Man. I tell you that the angels, who guide all child-nature,
unceasingly behold the countenance of my Father who is in the
heavens.

[12]'What do you think? If a man has a hundred sheep, and one of
them goes astray, will he not leave the ninety-nine in the mountains
and set out to look for the one that is lost? [13]And when he has found
it, yes, I tell you, he will be more delighted with it than with the
ninety-nine that did not stray. [14]So it is not the will of your Father

in the heavens that one of these developing higher beings, however
small, should be lost.

[15]'If your brother does you an injustice, go and talk to him about
it in private. If he listens to you, you have gained a true brother.
[16]If he does not listen to you, then take one or two others with you,
so that every word can be confirmed by the mouth of two or three
witnesses. [17]If he still refuses to listen, then turn to the congregation. And if he will not listen to the congregation either, then regard
him as a stranger or as a tax-collector. [18]Yes, I say to you, what you
bind on earth shall also be considered bound in the world of spirit,
and what you loose on earth shall also be considered loosed in the
spiritual world.

[19]'Furthermore I say to you, when two of you are in accord on
earth when asking for something, it shall be fulfilled for them in the
kingdom of my Father in the heavens. [20]For where two or three are
gathered in the name of my Being, there I myself am in the midst
of them.'

Mutual forgiveness

[21]Then Peter came to him and said, 'Lord, how often must I forgive
my brother when he does me an injustice? Up to seven times?'
[22]Jesus answered, 'Not seven times, but seventy times seven times.
[23]The kingdom of the heavens can actually be compared to a man,
a king, who wished to settle accounts with his servants. [24]As he
began the reckoning, a debtor was brought to him who owed ten
thousand talents. [25]Since he could not pay the debt, the lord ordered
that he, his wife, his children and everything that he had should
be sold so that the account could be settled. [26]Then the servant fell
on his knees and said, "Have patience with me, and I will pay you
everything." [27]Then the lord had pity on the servant, released him
and forgave him the debt. [28]Afterwards this servant met a fellow
servant who owed him a hundred denarii. He took hold of him to
throttle him and said: "Pay your debt!" [29]The fellow servant fell
on his knees and begged: "Have patience with me, I will pay you
everything." [30]But he refused and threw him into prison until he

should pay the debt. [31]When his fellow servants saw what was
done to him they became very sad. They went to their lord to tell
him what had taken place. [32]Then the lord sent for the servant and
said: “You are a wicked servant! I forgave you your whole debt
because you pleaded with me; [33]could you not also be generous to
your fellow servant, as I was generous to you?” [34]And in anger the
lord handed him over to be punished until he had given back all
that he owed.

[35]‘So also my heavenly Father will treat you if each one of you
does not forgive his brother from his heart.’

19 *Journey to Judea*

And when Jesus had completed this teaching, he left Galilee and
went to the region of Judea beyond the Jordan. [2]And a great crowd
of people followed him, and he healed there also.

Questions about divorce

[3]Then Pharisees came to him to test him and said, ‘Are there reasons
which can justify a divorce?’ [4]He answered, ‘Have you not read that
in the very beginning the Creator made human beings male-female,
[5]and that HE said:

> For this reason a man shall leave his father and
> mother to be united with his wife. And even as regards
> their physical being they will form a unity.

[6]So the two are physically actually no longer two, but one. And what
the divine world has united should not be parted by Man.’ [7]Then
they said to him, ‘Why then did Moses decree that a divorce is possible on condition that a documented disclaimer is made?’ [8]He said,
‘Because your hearts are rigid and hardened, Moses allowed you to
divorce. In the very beginning it was not so. [9]I say to you: Whoever
divorces his wife, except for unchastity, breaks the marriage when
he marries another woman.’ [10]Then his disciples said to him, ‘If that
is how it is between man and woman, it is better not to marry.’ [11]But
he said to them, ‘What I say now will not be understood by everyone; but those for whom it is intended will understand it. [12]There

are human beings who have been asexual from birth. And there are some who become so by the influence of other human beings. And lastly there are those who raise themselves above what is sexual through their striving for the kingdom of the heavens. He who can understand this, let him grasp it.'

Blessing the children

13And children were brought to him, that he might lay his hands on
them and pray for them. But the disciples rebuffed them. 14Then
Jesus said, 'Let the children be, do not hinder them from coming to
me; for the kingdom of the heavens belongs to those who are like
them.' 15And he laid his hands on them and went on.

The rich young man

16And see, one came up to him and said, 'Master, what good deeds
must I do to attain to timeless life?' 17He said, 'Why do you ask me
about the Good? Only One there is who is the Good. If you desire
entrance to the true life, then take the commandments to heart.' 18He
said, 'Which ones?' Jesus answered, 'Those which say:

> You shall not kill, you shall not break marriage, you
> shall not steal, you shall not slander, 19honour your
> father and mother;

and,

> Love your fellow man as you love yourself.'

20Then the young man said, 'I have observed all this; what do I still
lack?' 21Jesus said, 'If you desire to reach the highest aim, then
go and sell what you possess and give the proceeds to the poor.
By doing that you will acquire a treasure in the heavens. And then
come and follow me!' 22When the young man heard this word he
went away, sad; for he had many possessions.

23And Jesus said to his disciples, 'Yes, I tell you, whoever is rich
will not easily find access to the kingdom of the heavens. 24Again
I tell you: A camel will more easily go through the eye of a needle
than a rich man will enter the kingdom of God.'

25When the disciples heard this they were very alarmed and said,

'But then who can find salvation?' [26]Jesus looked up and said, 'It
is not possible out of what is merely human in you, but for the
divine in Man everything is possible.' [27]Then Peter said to him,
'See, *we* have given up everything and have followed you. What
will that mean for us?' [28]Jesus answered, 'Yes, I say to you, in the
sphere of new birth where the Son of Man sits on the throne of
his light-revelation, you who have followed me will also sit on
twelve thrones and be the guides of destiny for the twelve tribes of
Israel. [29]Everyone who leaves houses or brothers or sisters or father
or mother or children or fields in order to win recognition for my
name, will receive in manifold abundance, and will be granted life
which endures through all cycles of time. [30]Many who now are first
will be last, and many who are last will become first.'

20 *Parable of the vineyard*
'The kingdom of the heavens is like a human being, a master of his
house, who went out early in the morning to hire workers for his
vineyard. [2]After agreeing with the workmen on a wage of a denarius a day, he sent them into the vineyard. [3]About the third hour he
went out and saw other workmen standing idle in the market place,
4and he said to them, "You, too, go into the vineyard, and I will
give you a fair wage." And they went. [5]And about the sixth and the
ninth hour he went and did the same. [6]When he went out about the
eleventh hour he saw yet others standing there; and he said to them,
"Why do you stand here idle all day?" [7]They said, "Because no
one has hired us." He said, "You, too, go into the vineyard." [8]And
when the evening came, the master of the vineyard said to his steward, "Call the workmen and give them their wages; begin with the
last, then the others until you come to the first." [9]So those who had
been hired about the eleventh hour came forward, and each of them
received a denarius. [10]When it was the turn of the first, they thought
they would receive more. But they, too, received a denarius each.
[11]They took it, but they grumbled at the master of the house [12]and
said, "They came last and have only worked one hour, yet you have
made them equal to us who have borne the burden and the heat the

whole day long.” 13Then he said to one of them, “Friend, I am not
doing you an injustice. Did we not agree on a wage of a denarius?
14Take what belongs to you and go. I wish to give to these last as
I give to you. 15Am I not free to do as I wish with what belongs to
me? Do you give me an evil look because I am good? 16Thus the last
will be first, and the first last”.’

17Jesus prepared to go up to Jerusalem; he took the twelve aside
for an intimate conversation and said to them on the way, 18‘See, we
are going up to Jerusalem. The Son of Man will be handed over to
the power of the chief priests and scribes; he will be condemned to
death 19and committed into the hands of the foreign peoples to be
mocked and scourged and crucified. But on the third day he will be
raised.’

The request of the mother of James and John

20Then the mother of the sons of Zebedee came up to him with
her sons and knelt before him to plead with him. 21He said to her,
‘What is it you want?’ She said, ‘Promise that these two sons of
mine will have their place next to you in your kingdom, one on
your right and the other on your left.’ 22Jesus answered, ‘You do
not know what it is you are asking. Are you able also to drink the
cup which I must drink?’ They said, ‘Yes.’ 23Then he said, ‘You
will indeed drink my cup; but the place on my right and on my
left is not for me to give. That is for those for whom it has been
prepared by my Father.’ 24When the other ten heard this, they were
indignant at the two brothers. 25Then Jesus called them to him
and said, ‘You know that the rulers of the world have power over
their people and that great men exercise authority over them. 26It
shall not be like that among you; whoever among you wants to
be a great man, let him be your servant, 27and whoever among
you wants to be first, let him be your slave. 28The Son of Man has
not come to be served but to serve and to offer up his soul for the
salvation of many.’

Healing of the blind men of Jericho

29As they were leaving Jericho, a great crowd followed them. 30And
see, two blind men sat by the wayside. And as they heard that Jesus
was passing by, they called out loudly: ‘Lord, have pity on us, Son
of David!’ 31The crowd rebuked them and told them to be quiet. But
they only called out even more loudly: ‘Lord, have pity on us, Son
of David!’ 32Then Jesus stood still and called to them: ‘What do
you want me to do for you?’ 33They said, ‘Lord, that our eyes may
be opened.’ 34And Jesus felt compassion for them and touched their
sight, and at once they could see again and followed him.

21 *The entry into Jerusalem*

And they approached Jerusalem and came to Bethphage by the
Mount of Olives. Then Jesus sent two disciples ahead 2and said to
them, ‘Go to the village which you see before you. There you will
straight away find an ass tied, and a colt with her. Untie them and
bring them to me. 3And if anyone says anything to you, then say:
The Lord needs them. Then he will let you take them at once.’ 4The
word of the prophet was to be fulfilled:

> 5Say to the daughter Zion:
> See, your king comes to you in majesty.
> He rides on an ass and on the foal of the beast of burden.

6The disciples went and did what Jesus had told them; 7they
brought the ass and the colt and laid their garments on them and he
sat on them. 8Many in the crowd spread their clothes on the road,
others cut branches from the trees and strewed them on the road.
9And the crowds which went before him and followed him called
out loudly:

> Hosanna, sing to the Son of David!
> Blessed be he who comes in the name of the Lord!
> Sing to him in the highest heights!

10As he entered Jerusalem in this way, the whole town was
stirred and said, ‘Who is he?’ 11And the crowd said, ‘It is Jesus, the
prophet from Nazareth in Galilee.’

Cleansing the Temple
[12]And Jesus went into the Temple and drove out all who sold and
bought in the Temple. He overturned the tables of the money-
changers and the stands of the pigeon-sellers, [13]and he said to
them, 'Scripture says:

> My house shall be a house of worship;
> but you make it a den of robbers.'

[14]And the blind and the lame came to him in the Temple, and he
healed them. [15]When the chief priests and the scribes saw the wonderful things he did, and when they heard the children in the Temple
call out: Sing to the Son of David! they were indignant [16]and said
to him, 'Do you hear what they are saying?' Jesus answered, 'Yes.
Have you never read:

> By the mouth of children and new-born infants I am praised?'

[17]And he left them standing and went out of the town to Bethany
and stayed there overnight.

The fig tree
[18]In the morning, as he was returning to the town, he felt hunger.
[19]And see, a single fig tree stood by the road. He went up to it, and
found nothing but leaves on it. Then he said, 'Never again shall
fruit ripen on you in all ages.' And the fig tree withered at once.
[20]When the disciples saw it, they were amazed and said, 'How
could the fig tree wither at once?' [21]Jesus answered, 'Yes, I say to
you, if you have the power of faith without wavering, then you
will not only bring forth the fruit of the fig tree, but you will be
able to say to this mountain: Rise up and throw yourself into the
sea, and it will be so. [22]Whatever you shall ask in the power of
faith, you will receive it.'

The question of authority
[23]And he went into the Temple and taught. Then the chief priests
and elders of the people came and said, 'By whose authority are
you working? Who has given you your task and your ordination?'

[24]Jesus answered, 'Let me ask you something; if you give me the
answer to it, then I will tell you by what authority I do what I do.
[25]By whose commission did John baptize? Was he given this task
from God or from men?' They deliberated and said to themselves: If
we say, 'From God,' he will ask us, 'Then why did you not believe
him?' [26]And if we say, 'From men,' we must fear the people. For all
regarded John as a prophet. [27]And so they answered Jesus, 'We do
not know.' Then he said, 'Then I also will not say by what authority
I act.'

Two parables about the vineyard

[28]'What do you think? A man had two sons. He went to the first
and said, "Son, go and work in the vineyard today." [29]He answered,
"Yes, sir." But he did not go. [30]Then he went to the second and
said the same to him. He answered, "I will not." Later, however,
he regretted his answer and went after all. [31]Which of the two did
the will of the father?' They said, 'The second.' Jesus said, 'Yes, I
say to you, the tax-collectors and the harlots will find access to the
kingdom of God more readily than you. [32]John came to you in the
way of God's order and harmony, but you would not listen to him.
Yet the tax-collectors and the harlots opened their hearts to him.
You saw it, and even then you did not change your hearts and minds
and respond to him.

[33]'Hear another parable: There was a man, the master of a
house. He planted a vineyard and surrounded it with a fence and
dug a winepress in it and built a tower. Then he handed it over to
the vine-growers and went away to another country. [34]When the
grape-season came, he sent his servants to the vine-growers to
receive his fruit. [35]But the vine-growers took hold of the servants;
they beat one, killed another and stoned the third. [36]Then he sent
out servants anew, a greater number than the first time. But they
treated them in the same way. [37]Lastly he sent his son to them,
because he said to himself: My son they will respect. [38]But when
the vine-growers saw the son, they said to themselves: This is
the heir. Come, let us kill him, then we will have his inheritance.

39 And they took him and threw him out of the vineyard and killed
him. 40 Now when the lord of the vineyard comes, what will he
do to those vine-growers?' 41 They said, 'He will repay evil with
evil and destroy them. And the vineyard he will give to other
vine-growers, who will deliver to him the fruits of the vineyard at
harvest time.' 42 And Jesus said to them, 'Have you never read this
passage in the scriptures:

> The stone which the builders regarded as useless has
> become the corner stone. The LORD HIMSELF so shaped
> it, and our eyes see it with wonder?

43 Therefore I tell you: The kingdom of God will be taken away from
you and be given to a people who allow the fruits of the kingdom
to ripen. 44 And whoever runs against this stone will be dashed to
pieces; and he on whom it falls will be crushed.'

45 When the chief priests and the Pharisees heard his parables,
they knew that he was speaking about them. 46 And they tried to get
him into their power, but they were afraid of the people, for all held
him to be a prophet.

22 *Parable of the royal marriage feast*

And Jesus continued to speak in parables to them: 2 'The kingdom of
the heavens is like a human being, a king, who prepared a marriage
feast for his son. 3 And he sent out his servants to call the guests
who had been invited to the marriage, but they would not come.
4 Then he again sent out other servants and said, "Say to those who
have been invited, see, I have prepared my banquet, the oxen and
the other fatted beasts have been slaughtered; everything is ready.
Come to the wedding." 5 But they disregarded it and went off, one
to his field, another to his business. 6 The others took hold of the
servants, maltreated them and killed them. 7 Then the king grew
angry; he sent out his army, destroyed the murderers and set fire to
their town. 8 Then he said to his servants, "Although the marriage
feast is prepared, the guests have not proved themselves worthy of
it. 9 Now therefore go to the remotest roads and invite to the wedding whoever you find." 10 And the servants went into the streets

and gathered all whom they found, bad and good. And the wedding hall was filled with guests. [11]Then the king came in to see the
guests, and among them he noticed a man who was not dressed in
the wedding garment. [12]And he said to him, "My friend, how did
you get in here, since you are not wearing a wedding garment?"
And he was speechless. [13]Then the king said to the servants, "Bind
him hand and foot and cast him out into the darkness of external
existence where human beings live, lamenting and gnashing their
teeth." [14]For the call goes to many, yet only a few make themselves
real bearers of higher life.'

Paying taxes

[15]Then the Pharisees consulted with one another how they might
ensnare him in his own words. [16]And they sent their own disciples
as well as those of the Herodians to him to ask him, 'Master, we
know that you are truthful and that you teach the way of God in
truth. You are beholden to no one, for you do not regard the outer
standing of men. [17]Now tell us your opinion: Is it right to pay tax to
Caesar, or not?' [18]But Jesus saw through their evil intent and said,
'Why do you want to put me to the test, you hypocrites? [19]Show me
the tax coin.' And they brought him a denarius. [20]He said, 'Whose
likeness and inscription is this?' [21]They said, 'Caesar's.' Then he
answered, 'Then give to Caesar what belongs to Caesar and to God
what belongs to God.' [22]They were amazed by this answer and they
left him and went away.

Dispute with the Sadducees

[23]On the same day Sadducees, who deny resurrection, came to him
and asked him, [24]'Master, Moses said:

> If someone dies without children, his brother should marry the widow and let descendants be born to his brother.

[25]Now among us there were once seven brothers. The first married
and died. Since he had no children, he left his wife to his brother.
[26]But the second brother also died and the third, until eventu-

ally all seven had died. 27Last of all the woman died. 28Now in
the resurrection, to which of the seven brothers will the woman
belong, since they were all married to her?' 29Jesus answered,
'You are caught up in error. You understand neither the scriptures nor how God works. 30In the sphere of resurrection, no-one
marries and no-one is given in marriage. There human beings are
without gender, like the angels of heaven. 31Have you not read
the word of God which was spoken to you about the resurrection
of the dead:

> 32I am the God of Abraham and the God of Isaac and
> the God of Jacob?

But the Being of God does not live in the dead, but in the living.'

33The people listening were beside themselves at his teaching.

The greatest commandment

34When the Pharisees heard that he had reduced the Sadducees to
silence, they assembled, 35and one of them, a specialist in the Law,
put him to the test and asked, 36'Master, which commandment is the
greatest in the Law?' 37He answered:

> 'Love the Lord who is your God with all the power of
> your heart, your soul and your thoughts.

38That is the great and first commandment. 39But the second is like
it:

> Love your fellow Man as you love yourself.

40In these two commandments is contained the whole Law and the
books of the prophets.'

41And Jesus asked the assembled Pharisees, 42'What do you
think of the Christ? Whose son is he?' They answered, 'The son
of David.' 43He said to them, 'How then can David, inspired by the
Spirit, call him his Lord:

> 44The LORD of existence said to my Lord:
> You shall sit at my right hand;
> I will subdue your enemies
> and place them beneath your feet.

45Since David calls him his Lord, how then can he be his son?'

[46]No one could answer him, and from that day on no one dared to ask him any more.

23 *Woe to the Pharisees*
Then Jesus spoke to the crowd and to his disciples: [2]The scribes and
the Pharisees sit on the seat of Moses. [3]Take to heart and observe
everything that they tell you. But do not let your actions be guided
by what they do; for they do not act according to their own words.
[4]They bind together heavy burdens and lay them upon men's shoulders; but they themselves are not willing to lift a finger to carry
this burden. [5]Everything that they do is only a show before men.
They wear great amulets and broad and long tassels on their garments. [6]They love to sit at the head of the table and to sit in the
most important seat in the synagogue. [7]In the street they want to be
greeted by everyone and be addressed as great teachers. [8]But you,
do not address them as great teachers. You have one teacher only,
and you are all brothers. [9]You should give the name of Father to no
one on earth. You have one Father only, and HE is in the heavens.
[10]Nor should you yourselves be called 'leaders,' for your leader is
the Christ. [11]Whoever among you is great, let him prove it by serving you. [12]Whoever exalts himself shall be humbled, and whoever
humbles himself shall be exalted.

[13]'Woe to you, you scribes and Pharisees, you hypocrites! You shut the kingdom of the heavens against men. You cannot find entrance yourselves, and so you want to bar the entrance to those who can find it.

[14]'Woe to you, you scribes and Pharisees, you hypocrites! You devour house and home of widows and make out that you have many prayers to attend to. You load grievous destiny upon yourselves.

[15]'Woe to you, you scribes and Pharisees, you hypocrites! Restlessly you roam over land and sea to win just one follower. And when you have him, you turn him into a son of the abyss, twice as bad as yourselves.

[16]'Woe to you! You are blind guides when you say: It is point-

less to call upon the power of the Temple; an oath is only of use when it is sworn by the gold of the Temple. 17How foolish and blind you are! What is greater, the gold or the Temple through which alone the gold is made sacred? 18And furthermore you say: It is pointless to call upon the power of the altar; an oath is only of use when it is sworn by the gifts on the altar. 19You blind men! Which is greater, the offering or the altar by which alone the offering is made sacred? 20Whoever calls upon the power of the altar at the same time calls upon the power of that which is on the altar. 21And whoever calls upon the power of the Temple at the same time calls upon him who dwells in it. 22And whoever calls upon the power of the heavens at the same time calls upon the heavenly throne and upon HIM who sits on it.

23'Woe to you, you scribes and Pharisees, you hypocrites! You take a tithe of the herbs, of mint, dill and cummin, but that which is weighty in the Law you neglect: Self-knowledge, love and a compassionate heart. These ought to be actively striven for, the other need not be neglected. 24Blind guides you are. You strain off the gnat in your cup, but you swallow the camel.

25'Woe to you, you scribes and Pharisees, you hypocrites! You cleanse the cup and the plate on the outside, but inside they are full of greed and poison.

26'You blind Pharisee, first cleanse the inside of the cup; only then does it make any sense for it to be clean outside.

27'Woe to you, you scribes and Pharisees, you hypocrites! You are like whitewashed tombs. From outside they are beautiful, but inside they are full of dead men's bones and all kinds of uncleanness. 28You are like that. From outside you appear before men as though devoted to the Good, but inwardly you are full of hypocrisy and discord.

29'Woe to you, you scribes and Pharisees, you hypocrites! You build monuments to the prophets and adorn the memorials to the men of God 30and you say: If we had been there in the days of our fathers we would not have taken part in shedding the blood of the prophets. 31However, you merely prove thereby that you are sons of those who killed the prophets, 32and so you fill the measure of your fathers.

33'You serpents and sons of the serpent! How can you avoid the fall into the abyss when the great decision comes? 34See, I will send prophets and wise and learned men to you. Some of them you will kill and crucify, the others you will scourge in your synagogues and persecute from town to town. 35But in time revenge must be taken upon you for the shedding of innocent blood on the earth, from the blood of Abel who was devoted to God, to the blood of Zechariah the son of Barachiah, whom you killed between the sanctuary and the altar. 36Yes, I say to you: Revenge shall be taken upon present-day mankind for all this. 37Jerusalem, Jerusalem, you killed the prophets and stoned the messengers who came to you. How often have I wanted to call your children together as a hen gathers her chicks under her wings. But you did not want to come. 38See, your house shall stand deserted. 39I say to you: From now on you will not see me again until you say:

Blessed be he who comes in the name of the Lord.'

24 *Apocalyptic words on the Mount of Olives*

As Jesus came out of the Temple his disciples gathered around him and drew his attention to the buildings of the Temple. 2Then he said to them, 'You see all this in its outer appearance now; but I must tell you: Here not one stone will be left upon another; everything will be destroyed.'

3Then as he sat on the Mount of Olives his disciples came to him for an intimate gathering and said, 'Tell us when these events will happen and by what signs we shall recognize your spiritual coming and the completion of the cycle of time.' 4Jesus answered:

'See that no one leads you onto a wrong path. 5Many will come and make use of my name. They will say: "I am the Christ." And they will lead many astray. 6You will become aware of the tumult of war and the cries of battle; see that you do not fail in inner courage. It is necessary that all this should happen, but that is not yet the fulfilment of the aim.

7‘One part of humanity will rise against another, one kingdom against the other. Everywhere there will be famines and earthquakes; 8and yet these are just the birth-pangs of the new world.

9‘You will have to endure great suffering and distress; you will be put to death; the hatred of all peoples will be turned against you because my Being is in you. 10Then many people will falter inwardly, they will treacherously fight one another and bear burning hatred against one another. 11Many will appear who will make themselves mouthpieces for deceiving spirits; they will lead many astray. 12And as the chaos grows ever worse, the capacity for love will grow cold in many. 13Only he who endures until the aim has been achieved can find salvation. 14This message of the heavenly kingdom will be proclaimed to the whole of humanity, a testimony to all peoples. Then the goal is near.

15‘And when you see the hideous forms which arise when the true self of Man errs – the prophet Daniel says that they will arise in the Holy Place (he who reads this, let him grasp the meaning) 16then those who are in Judea should flee to the mountains. 17And whoever is on the roof let him not first go down to gather up what is in the house. 18And whoever is out in the field let him not turn round to fetch his garment. 19Woe to those who are pregnant and those who are breast-feeding in those days! 20Pray that your flight may not be in the storms of winter or during the stern day of the Sabbath. 21A crushing burden will rest upon souls, such as has not been from the very beginning of the world until the present time, and as it will never again be in the future. 22And if those days were not shortened, then everything that is incarnated on earth would be subject to total destruction. But because of those who take the higher being into themselves, the days will be shortened.

23‘If then someone says to you, “See, here is the Christ,” or “See, there!” do not listen. 24For certain people will appear, calling themselves Christ, but they are not; and also prophets who are not so in reality. They will call up great visions and will work wonders, in order to lead human beings on the wrong path, if possible also those in whom the higher being is already living. 25See, I have told you this in advance.

26'If you are told: "See, he is in the loneliness of the desert," do not go there. And when you are told: "See, he is in his inner room," do not believe it. 27For the spiritual coming of the Son of Man will be like the lightning which flashes up in the East and shines out as far as the West. 28Wherever the carcase is, there the vultures will gather.

29'Immediately after the trials of those days, the sun will grow dark, the moon will no longer shine, the stars will fall from heaven, and the Beings of Power in the heavenly spheres will stir. 30Then the sign of the Son of Man will light up in the spiritual world; in the midst of their cries of woe all the peoples on the earth will behold the Son of Man as he comes in the ether-cloud realm, mightily empowered through the Spirits of Movement, radiantly surrounded by the Spirits of Revelation. 31And he will send out his angels and the great trumpet will sound, and they will gather together all those who are united with him as bearers of the higher being, from all four directions of the universe, from one end of the heavens to the other.

32'Learn from the parable that the fig tree provides. When the sap streams through its branches and its leaves appear, then you know that summer is near. 33So also, when you see all this approaching, you should know that it is near, before the very doors. 34Yes, I tell you: Before the time of this generation shall have come to an end, the first signs will appear. 35The heavens and the earth will pass away, but my words will not pass away. 36About that day and hour no one knows anything, neither the angels in the heavens, nor the Son, but only the Father. 37The time in which the Son of Man reveals himself will be like the days of Noah. 38Just as in the days before the flood, when they ate and drank, married wives and husbands until Noah entered the ark, 39and just as they did not recognize how things stood until the great flood broke in upon them and swept everything away, so shall it be when the Son of Man appears. 40Two men will be out in the field; one will be touched by it, the other left alone. [41]Two women will be grinding at the mill; one will be touched by it, the other left alone.

Call to wakefulness

[42]'So be alert, for you do not know on which day your Lord comes. [43]Clearly you realize: If the master of the house knew at what hour of the night the thief would come, he would keep awake and not permit his house to be broken into. [44]So therefore be prepared, for the Son of Man comes at an unexpected hour.

Parable of the good and bad servant

[45]'Imagine a faithful and wise servant whom his master has put in charge of the household, and who gives everyone their food at the proper time. [46]Blessed is this servant if the lord, when he comes, sees him carrying out his appointed task. [47]Yes, I tell you, he will entrust him with all his goods. [48]But if he is a bad servant he says to himself: "My master is a long time coming." [49]And if he begins to torment his fellow servants and to eat and drink with drunkards, [50]then the master of the servant will come on a day when he does not expect him and at an hour which he does not know. [51]It will be for him as if he were cut in pieces with a sword; like everything which is untrue and false, he will be banished to a world in which there is only wailing and grinding of teeth.

25 *Parable of the ten maidens*

'Then the kingdom of the heavens will be like ten maidens who took their lamps and went out to meet the bridegroom. [2]Five of them were dull of soul, five were alert and prudent. [3]The foolish indeed took their lamps, but they forgot the oil. [4]The sensible ones took flasks of oil for their lamps. [5]Now, because the bridegroom was a long time coming, they all became tired and fell asleep. [6]But in the middle of the night the call went up: See, the bridegroom is coming, go out to meet him! [7]Then all the maidens rose and trimmed their lamps. [8]And the foolish said to the prudent, "Give us some of your oil, for our lamps are going out." [9]But the prudent said, “No, the oil would not be enough for us and for you as well. You had better go to the dealers and buy oil for yourselves.” 10And while they were away, buying, the bridegroom came; and those who were ready to receive him went with him into the wedding hall, and the doors were closed.

11‘Afterwards the other maidens came also and said, “Lord, Lord, open to us!” 12But he replied, “I tell you once for all, I do not know you.”

13‘So be alert of soul, since you do not know the day or the hour.

Parable of the talents

14‘It is like a man going on a journey; he called together his servants and entrusted his property to them. 15To one he gave five talents, to another two, to another one, to each according to his ability. Then he left the country. 16And he who had received the five talents at once began to work with them and gained another five. 17So also he who had been given two gained another two. 18But he who had been given one, went and hid his master’s silver by burying it in the earth. 19When a long time had gone by, the master of the servants returned and settled accounts with them. 20First the one who had been given five talents came forward, bringing five more. He said, “Lord, five talents you gave me; see, I have gained another five.” 21Then the master said, “You have done well, you good and faithful servant; you have faithfully tended a little, now I will make you a steward over much. You shall have a share of the joy of your master.”

22‘Then the one who had been given two talents came forward and said, “Lord, two talents you gave me; see, I have gained another two.” 23Then the master said to him, “You have done well, you good and faithful servant; you have faithfully tended a little, now I will make you a steward over much. You shall have a share of the joy of your master.”

24‘Then the one who had been given one talent also came forward and said, “Lord, I know that you are a hard and stern man; you reap where you did not sow, you gather in where you did not

distribute. 25I was afraid, and so I buried your money in the earth.
See, here you have what is yours back again." 26Then the master
answered, "You bad and idle servant! You claim to know that I reap
where I did not sow and that I gather in where I did not distribute?
27Should you then not all the more have taken my money to the
money-changers, so that, on my return, I could receive my property
together with the interest on it? 28Take the talent from him and give
it to the one who has ten talents." 29To him who has shall be given,
and he shall have in abundance; from him who has not, even what
he has will be taken. 30Cast the worthless servant out into the darkness of external existence where there is only wailing and gnashing
of teeth.

Judgment upon the world
31'When the Son of Man comes, illumined by the light of revelation,
surrounded by all angels, then he will ascend the throne of the kingdom of his revelation. 32He will gather before his countenance all
the peoples of the world, and he will cause a division among them,
as a shepherd separates the sheep from the goats, 33the sheep on the
right and the goats on the left.

34'Then, as king, he will say to those standing at his right hand:
"Come, you who are blessed by my Father, you shall receive as
your own the kingdom which has been intended for you from the
creation of the world. 35I was hungry and you gave me to eat; I was
thirsty, and you gave me to drink; I was a stranger, and you made
me a welcome guest; 36I was naked, and you clothed me; I was ill,
and you visited me; I was in prison, and you came to me."

37'And they, who are devoted to God, will answer: "Lord, when
did we satisfy your hunger or thirst? 38When did we receive you
when you were a stranger or clothe you when you were naked?
39When did we visit you when you were ill or in prison?" 40And the
king will say to them, "Yes, I say to you, what you did for the least
of my brothers, that you did for me."

41'And then he will speak to those standing at his left hand,
"You will not remain near me. You are subject to the burning fire

in which the aeon is consumed and in which dwells the Adversary
with his angels. [42]I was hungry and you did not give me to eat; I
was thirsty, and you did not give me to drink; [43]I was a stranger,
and you did not welcome me; I was naked, and you did not clothe
me; I was ill and in prison, and you did not visit me."

[44]'And they will answer, "Lord, when did we see you hungry
and did not give you to eat, or thirsty and did not give you to drink,
or a stranger or naked or ill or in prison and did not help you?"
[45]And he will say to them, "Yes, I say to you, what you neglected to
do for the least of my brothers, you failed to do for me."

[46]'And they will become subject to the aeon of anguish, whereas
those devoted to God shall find the aeon of life.'

26 And it happened: When Jesus had spoken all these words and
had completed his teaching, he said to his disciples, [2]'You know
that it will be Passover festival in two days' time. The Son of Man
will be betrayed and crucified.'

Anointing in Bethany

[3]And the chief priests and the elders of the people gathered in the
hall of the high priest Caiaphas [4]and made a resolution to get Jesus
into their power by treachery and to kill him. [5]They said to themselves, however: It had best not be during the festival, in case there
should be an uprising among the people.

[6]When Jesus was in Bethany in the house of Simon the leper, [7]a
woman came up to him with an alabaster jar of the most precious
ointment; and she poured it on his head as he sat at table. [8]When
the disciples saw it, they were indignant and said, 'Why this
waste? [9]It could have been sold for a large sum and the proceeds
given to the poor.' [10]But Jesus perceived their thoughts and said,
'Why do you plague the woman? She has done a good deed to me.
[11]The poor you will always have with you, but you will not always
have me. [12]By anointing my body she has prepared me for burial.
[13]Yes, I say to you, wherever in the whole world this Gospel is
proclaimed, what she has done will be told and her memory will
be honoured.'

Betrayal by Judas

14 Then one of the twelve, Judas Iscariot, went to the chief priests
15 and said, 'What will you give me if I deliver him into your hands?'
And they offered him thirty pieces of silver. 16 From then on he
sought an opportunity to betray him.

The Last Supper

17 On the first day of the Unleavened Bread the disciples came to
Jesus and said, 'Where do you want us to prepare the Passover
meal?' 18 He said, 'Go into the town, you know to whom, and say to
him, "The Master says: My time is near. With you will I celebrate
the Passover festival with my disciples".' 19 And the disciples carried out the directions Jesus had given them, and they prepared the
Passover meal.

20 And in the evening he sat down to the meal with the twelve
disciples. 21 And while they were eating he said, 'Yes, I tell you, one
of you will betray me.' 22 Then they became very sad and asked him
one after another, 'Is it I, Lord?' 23 He answered, 'He who dips the
bread with me in the dish will betray me. 24 The Son of Man must
die, as the scriptures also say about him. But woe to that man by
whom the Son of Man is betrayed! For that man it would be better
if he had never been born.' 25 Then said Judas who betrayed him, 'Is
it I, Master?' And Jesus said, '*You* said it.'

26 And while they were eating, Jesus took the bread, blessed it,
broke it and gave it to the disciples and said, 'Take and eat, this is
my body.' 27 And he took the cup, blessed it and gave it to the disciples and said, 'Drink of it, all of you, 28 for this is the blood of the
covenant; it is shed for many for the overcoming of the sickness of
sin. 29 And I say to you: From now on I will no longer drink of this
gift of the vine until the day when I, in renewed form, drink it with
you in the realm of my Father.'

Prayer in Gethsemane

30 And when they had sung the hymn, they went out to the Mount
of Olives. 31 And Jesus said to them, 'In this night you will all lose

your faith in me and lose your inner certainty. For the scripture
says:

I will strike the shepherd,
and the sheep of the flock will be scattered.

32But after my resurrection I will lead you to Galilee.' 33Then Peter
said to him, 'Even if all lose their faith in you, yet I will never
lose my faith.' 34Jesus said to him, 'Yes, I say to you: In this night,
before the cock-crow you will deny me three times.' 35And Peter
said, 'And if I had to die with you, never would I deny you!' And
all the disciples said likewise.

36And Jesus came with them to the place called Gethsemane,
and he said to his disciples, 'Rest here, I will go over there to pray.'
37And he took with him Peter and the two sons of Zebedee. And he
was filled with grief, and his strength began to fail. 38And he said to
them, 'My soul is deeply sorrowful, to the very brink of death. Stay
here and keep awake with me.'

39And he went a few steps forward, and fell on his face. And he
prayed: My Father, if it be possible, then let me be spared this cup.
Yet not my will, but Thine be done. 40And he comes to the disciples
and finds them sleeping and he says to Peter, 'Could you not keep
awake with me one hour? 41Keep awake and pray that you do not
fall into temptation! The spirit of Man is willing, but the physical
body is weak.'

42And he went away a second time to pray: My Father, if it be
possible, let me not have to drink this cup. Thy will be done. 43And
again he came and found them sleeping, for their eyes were heavy.

44And he left them and went and prayed for the third time and
said the same words. 45And he came to the disciples and said, 'Must
you always tire and fall asleep? See, the hour has come when the
Son of Man is given into the hands of men alienated from God.
46Stand up and let us go. See, my betrayer is approaching.'

Jesus' arrest

47And while he was still speaking, see, Judas came, one of the
twelve, and with him a great crowd with swords and clubs, sent

out by the chief priests and the elders of the people. [48]The betrayer
had told them how they would know him: the one I shall kiss is
the man; seize him. [49]And at once he came up to Jesus and said,
'Greeting, Master!' And kissed him. [50]Jesus said to him, 'Friend,
do that for which you have come.' Then they came forward and
laid hands on Jesus and took him prisoner. [51]And see, one of those
who were with Jesus stretched out his hand and drew his sword
and struck the servant of the High Priest and cut off his ear. [52]Then
Jesus said to him, 'Put your sword back into its place. For all who
reach for the sword will also perish by the sword. [53]Or do you
think I could not ask my Father for help? He could send me at
once more than twelve legions of angels. [54]But then how could the
scriptures be fulfilled that everything must happen in this way?'

[55]In that hour Jesus said to the crowds, 'Why have you come
out with swords and clubs to capture me like a robber? Every day
I sat in the Temple teaching, and you did not seize me. [56]All this
has taken place so that the scriptures of the prophets should be
fulfilled.'

Then all the disciples left him and fled.

Accusation before the High Priest

[57]Those who had captured Jesus led him to Caiaphas the High
Priest, where the scribes and elders were gathered. [58]And Peter
followed at a distance as far as the court of the High Priest. He
went inside and sat down with the servants to see what the outcome would be.

[59]The chief priests and the whole council sought after false
testimony against Jesus so that they could condemn him to death.
[60]But they found no grounds, although many false witnesses came
forward. At last, two came forward [61]and said, 'He said: "I can
destroy the Temple of God and build it up again in three days".'

[62]Then the High Priest stood up and said to him, 'Have you no
answer to what these men say against you?' [63]But Jesus was silent.
And the High Priest went on: 'I exhort you by the living God that
you tell us whether you are the Christ, the Son of God.' [64]Then

Jesus said to him, '*You* must say it. I tell you: From now on you
will see the Son of Man sitting at the right hand of power, coming
in the ether-cloud realm of the heavens.'
[65]Then the High Priest tore his garment and said, 'He has spoken a blasphemy. Do we still need further witnesses? Now you
have heard the blasphemy. [66]What is your view?' They said: 'He
deserves death.' [67]And they spat in his face and struck him. Some
hit him in the face [68]and said, 'Prophesy to us, Christ, who was it
that hit you?'

Peter's denial

[69]And Peter was sitting outside. Then a maid came up to him and
said, 'You also belong to that Jesus from Galilee.' [70]He denied it,
so that everyone heard it when he said, 'I do not know what you
are talking about.' [71]As he was going out and came to the gate,
another maid saw him and said to those who were standing there,
'This man was also with that Jesus of Nazareth.' [72]And he denied
it again, and swore, 'I do not know the man.' [73]Soon after, those
standing by came up to Peter and said, 'You are definitely one of
them, for your accent gives you away.' [74]Then he began to curse
and to swear: 'I do not know the man.' At that moment the cock
crowed. [75]Then Peter suddenly remembered the words of Jesus:
Before cock-crow you will deny me three times. And he went out
and wept bitterly.

27 *Judas' repentance*

When morning came, the chief priests and elders of the people
gathered in council to condemn Jesus to death. [2]And they bound
him and led him to Pilate, the Roman governor, and handed him
over to him.
[3]Then Judas, who had betrayed him, realized that he was condemned. He recognized his error and gave the thirty pieces of
silver back to the chief priests and the elders [4]and said, 'I have
done great wrong; I have betrayed innocent blood.' But they
answered, 'What has that got to do with us? See to it yourself.'

[5]Then he threw the pieces of silver into the Temple and went and
hanged himself. [6]And the chief priests took the silver coins and
said, 'It will not do to put them into the Temple treasury, since
they have been paid for blood.' [7]And they consulted together and
used them to buy a potter's field as a burial place for foreigners.
[8]That is the reason why that field to this day is called the Field of
Blood. [9]And so the word of the prophet Jeremiah was fulfilled:

> They took thirty pieces of silver, that was the price of
> him who was sold, whom they bought from the sons
> of Israel. [10]And they gave them for the potter's field,
> as the Lord has shown me.

Interrogation before Pilate

[11]And Jesus was placed before the governor. And the governor
asked him, 'Are you the King of the Jews?' And Jesus said, '*You*
must say it.' [12]And when the chief priests and elders accused him,
he made no answer. [13]Then Pilate said to him, 'Do you not hear all
this that they are saying against you?' [14]But he made no answer,
not even to a single one of their accusations, so that the governor
was amazed.

[15]At the Passover festival the governor usually released to the
people a prisoner of their choice. [16]At that time there was a man
in prison who was known as Barabbas, [17]and Pilate said to the
assembled crowd: 'Whom shall I release for you, Barabbas or
Jesus who is called Christ?' [18]For he realized that they had handed
him over to the court out of envy. [19]As he was sitting on the Seat
of Judgment, his wife sent word to him: 'Do not be drawn into the
destiny of this man of God. Because of him I have suffered much
this night in a dream.' [20]The chief priests and the elders incited
the crowd to demand the release of Barabbas and the death of
Jesus. [21]Then the governor spoke to them again, 'Which of the
two shall I release for you?' And they said, 'Barabbas.' [22]Pilate
returned, 'What then shall I do with Jesus who is called Christ?'
They all said, 'Let him be crucified.' [23]He said, 'But what evil has
he done?'

But they shouted all the louder: 'Crucify him!' [24]When Pilate saw that he was gaining nothing, but rather that the uproar was getting ever greater, he took water and washed his hands before the crowd and said, 'Innocent am I of this blood. Let it be your responsibility.' [25]And the people said, 'Let his blood be a burden upon us and our children.' [26]Then he released Barabbas for them. But Jesus he had scourged and led away to be crucified.

Crowning with thorns

[27]And the soldiers of the governor took Jesus and led him into the barracks of the Roman bodyguard, and gathered the whole battalion around him. [28]And they stripped him, put a purple robe on him [29]and plaited a crown of thorns and put it on his head and gave him a rod in his right hand. Then they kneeled before him, mocking him, and said: 'Greetings, King of the Jews!' [30]And they spat on him, took the rod and struck his head with it. [31]And when they had finished their sport with him, they stripped him of the robe and put his own clothes on him again and led him away to be crucified. [32]On the way they came upon a man from Cyrene, by name Simon. Him they forced to carry his cross.

The Crucifixion

[33]And they came to the place which is called Golgotha, the place of a skull. [34]And they gave him wine mixed with gall to drink. But when he tasted it he would not drink. [35]And they crucified him and shared his garments by casting lots for them. [36]Then they sat down to keep watch over him. [37]Above his head, where the reason for the sentence was usually placed, was written: THIS IS JESUS THE KING OF THE JEWS. [38]With him they crucified two criminals, one on the right and one on the left. [39]The passers-by shook their heads and hurled words full of hate at him: [40]'You would destroy the Temple and build it new in three days; now save yourself if you are the Son of God, and come down from the cross!' [41]The chief priests and scribes and elders also mocked him: [42]'He helped others, but he cannot help himself. He is the King of Israel; very

well, let him come down from the cross and we will believe in
him. 43He trusted in God; let HIM rescue him if HE wants him.
After all, he did say: I am the Son of God.' 44The criminals who
were crucified with him reviled him with similar words.

The hour of death

45From the sixth hour until the ninth, darkness spread over the whole
land. 46And about the ninth hour Jesus called out with a loud voice:
'Eli, Eli, lama sabachthani?' That means: My God, my God why
have you forsaken me? 47Some of the bystanders who heard it said,
'He is calling Elijah.' 48And one of them at once ran and fetched
a sponge soaked in vinegar, put it on a rod and gave him to drink.
49The others said, 'Let us see whether Elijah will come to rescue
him.' 50And again Jesus called out with a loud voice, then he gave
up his spirit.

51And see, the curtain in the Temple was torn in two, from top
to bottom, and the earth shook and the rocks split, 52and the tombs
opened and many of the dead who had sanctified themselves, arose.
53They left the tombs, and after his resurrection they came into
the holy city and were seen by many. 54And the Roman centurion
and his men who were keeping watch over Jesus were awestruck
when they saw the earthquake and everything that happened, and
they said, 'This really was the Son of God.' 55Many women stood
there and looked on from a distance. They had followed Jesus
from Galilee in order to serve him. 56Among them were Mary from
Magdala and Mary the mother of James and Joseph, and the mother
of the sons of Zebedee.

The burial

57When it was evening there came a rich man from Arimathea,
named Joseph, who also was a disciple of Jesus. 58He went to
Pilate and asked him for the body of Jesus. And Pilate ordered it
to be given to him. 59And Joseph took the body, wrapped it in pure
linen 60and laid it in his new tomb which he had had hewn in the
rock. And he rolled a great stone before the entrance to the tomb

and went away. [61]And Mary Magdalene and the other Mary were
there; they were sitting opposite the tomb.

[62]And on the next day, the day after the day of preparation,
the chief priests and Pharisees gathered before Pilate [63]and said,
'Sir, we remember that this imposter said, while he was still alive:
After three days I will rise again. [64]Therefore order the tomb to be
securely guarded until the third day, in case the disciples come and
steal him away and tell the people: He has risen from the dead.
This last fraud would be even worse than the first.' [65]Pilate said,
'You shall have a guard; go and make everything as secure as you
can.' [66]And they went to put a guard on the tomb and they sealed
the stone.

28 *The Resurrection*
When the Sabbath was over, in the early morning light of the first
day of the week, Mary of Magdala and the other Mary came to see
to the tomb. [2]And see, there was a great earthquake, the angel of
the Lord descended from heaven, came and rolled the stone away
and sat upon it. [3]His appearance was like lightning, and his garment
was shining white like snow. [4]His presence terrified the guards; they
trembled and fell down as if dead.

[5]And the angel said to the women, 'Have no fear. I know that
you seek Jesus who was crucified. [6]He is not here. He has risen,
as he himself said. Come and see the place where he lay. [7]Now go
quickly to his disciples and say to them: He has risen from the dead
and will lead you to Galilee where you will behold him. See, that is
what I have to say to you.'

[8]Quickly they left the tomb, filled with both fear and joy, and
they ran to take the message to the disciples. [9]And see, Jesus came
to meet them and said: 'Greetings!' And they went up to him and
took hold of his feet and fell down before him. [10]Then Jesus said to
them, 'Have no fear! Go and give my brothers the message that they
are to go to Galilee. There they will behold me.'

[11]While they were going, see, some of the guard went into the
town and reported everything that had happened to the chief priests,

[12]who then assembled together with the elders, and conferred. They
gave the soldiers a substantial sum of money [13]and said, 'Tell people that his disciples came in the night and stole him away while
you were asleep. [14]And if it comes to the governor's ears, we will
talk with him and see to it that nothing happens to you.' [15]And they
took the money and did as they were told, and this version has been
handed down among the Jews to this day.

Sending out the disciples

[16]And the eleven disciples went to Galilee, to the mountain where
Jesus had appointed them to their task. [17]And they beheld him and
fell down before him. But some of them were only able to open a
part of their consciousness to him.

[18]And Jesus came to them and said, 'Now all creative power in
heaven and on the earth has been given me. [19]Go forth and be the
teachers of all peoples and baptize them in the name and with the
power of the Father, and of the Son and of the Holy Spirit. [20]And
teach them to hold fast the spiritual aims which I have given you.
And see, I am in your midst all the days until the completion of
earthly time.'

The Gospel of Mark

1 *John the Baptist*

The new word from the realms of the angels sounds forth through
Jesus Christ. [2]Fulfilled is the word of the prophet Isaiah:

See, I send my angel before you;
he is to prepare your way.
[3]The voice of one calling in the loneliness:
'Prepare the way for the Lord,
make sure that his paths are straight!'

[4]John the baptizer was in the desert. He proclaimed baptism,
the way of a change of heart and mind, which frees Man from sin.
[5]And they went out to him from all of Judea and Jerusalem and
received baptism from him in the river Jordan and confessed their
sins.

[6]John wore a garment of camels' hair and a leather belt around
his waist. Hard fruits and wild honey were his food. [7]And he
proclaimed:

'After me comes one who is mightier than I.

'I am not worthy to bend down before him and undo the straps
on his shoes. [8]I have baptized you with water, but he will baptize
you with the Holy Spirit and with fire.'

Baptism and Temptation of Jesus

[9]In those days it happened: Jesus came from Nazareth in Galilee
and was baptized by John in the Jordan. [10]And suddenly, as he
stepped up out of the water, he saw how the heavens were torn
open and the Spirit in the form of a dove descended upon him.
[11]And a voice sounded from the heavens: 'You are my beloved
Son, in you I am revealed.'

12 And suddenly he felt himself driven by the Spirit into the
desert, 13 and he remained in the loneliness of the desert for forty
days, tempted by the Adversary. And he was among wild animals,
and the angels served him.

The first disciples

14 After John had fallen into the hands of his enemies, Jesus came
to Galilee and proclaimed God's message of salvation. 15 His words
were: 'The time is fulfilled, the Kingdom of God is near. Change
your hearts and minds and fill yourselves with the power of the
Gospel.'

16 And as he walked along the shore of lake Galilee he saw
Simon and Andrew, the brother of Simon. They were casting their
nets into the sea, for they were fishermen. 17 And Jesus said to
them, 'Come and follow me; I will make you fishers of men.'
18 And at once they left their nets and followed him. 19 And when he
had gone a short distance further he saw James the son of Zebedee
and John his brother, who were preparing their nets in their ship.
20 And at once he called them and they left their father Zebedee
who was in the ship with their hired men and they followed him.

First healings: Healing a man possessed by a demon

21 And they came to the town Capernaum, and as it was a Sabbath
he went straight away into the synagogue and taught. 22 And they
were taken out of themselves by his teaching, for he taught them
like someone in whom a creative power lives, and not like the
scribes. 23 And suddenly there was in their synagogue a man with
an unclean spirit; 24 he cried out: 'What is between us and you,
Jesus, you Nazarene? You have come to destroy us. I know who
you are, you are the Holy One of God.' 25 Then Jesus raised his
hand threateningly against him and said, 'Be silent and leave him!'
26 And the unclean spirit threw the man this way and that; then it
left him with loud shouts and cries. 27 And all were amazed and
asked one another, 'What is this? A new teaching with creative
authority? He commands the unclean spirits and they obey him.'

[28]And at once the news about him spread through all the regions surrounding Galilee.

Peter's mother-in-law

[29]And at once, as he left the synagogue, he went into the house of Simon and Andrew with James and John. [30]Simon's mother-in-law lay ill with a fever and at once they told him about her. [31]And he came, took her by the hand and raised her up. And the fever left her, and she served them.

[32]It was already getting late, the sun was setting, and they brought to him all who were sick and possessed. [33]And in the end the whole town was gathered before the door. [34]And he healed many people of the most varied illnesses and drove out many demons; and he did not allow the demons to speak, because they knew him.

[35]And in the morning, so early that it was still like night, he arose and went out of the house and went to a lonely place to pray. [36]And Simon and those who were with him went after him [37]and found him and said, 'Everyone needs you and is seeking you.' [38]And he answered them, 'Let us go somewhere else into the nearby towns. I will also proclaim the message there; for that is why I have come.' [39]And, proclaiming, he went to their synagogues in all Galilee and drove out the demons.

Healing a leper

[40]Once a leper came to him and begged him on his knees: 'If you only will, you can heal me.'

[41]The sight moved him and he stretched out his hand, touched him and said, 'I will; be healed!' [42]And at once the leprosy left him and he was healed. [43]Jesus was deeply stirred in soul and spirit and sent him away [44]and said:

'Take care that you speak to no one about it; but rather go and show yourself to the priest and make the offering which you are to give according to the instruction by Moses for your healing, as a proof for them.' [45]But he went and began to be very active proclaiming and spreading the word, so that Jesus could no longer openly enter a town. So he remained outside in lonely places. And people flocked to him from all directions.

2 *Healing a paralysed man*
After some days he went to Capernaum again, and it become known
that he was in the house. 2Then so many flocked together that there
was no room left, not even in front of the door; and he proclaimed
the word to them. 3Then a paralysed man was brought, carried by
four men. 4And, since they could not bring him close to him because
of the crowd, they uncovered the roof over the place where he was
standing, opened it up and let down the stretcher on which the paralysed man was lying. 5And when Jesus saw their deep trust he said
to the paralysed man, 'My child, you are free from the burden of
your sins.' 6There were also some scribes sitting there who objected
inwardly: 7'How can he say that! That is a blasphemy. Who can
free someone from sin except the one and only God?' 8Jesus perceived at once in his spirit what kind of objection they were making
inwardly, and he said, 'Why do you allow such thoughts to live in
your hearts? 9Which is easier, to say to the paralysed man: You are
free from your sins, or: Stand up, take your stretcher and walk?
10But you shall see that the Son of Man has the creative power to
free Man from the burden of sin on the earth.' And so he said to
the paralysed man, 11'I say to you, stand up, take your stretcher and
return to your house.' 12And suddenly he was able to stand upright,
and he took his stretcher and before their very eyes he walked out.
And they were all lifted out of themselves with wonder and they
praised the revelation of God and said, 'Never have we seen anything like this!'

The call to Levi (Matthew)
13And he left the house and went again along the shore of the
lake, and the whole crowd of people came to him and he taught
them. 14And as he went on he saw Levi the son of Alphaeus sitting
at the tax desk and said to him: 'Follow me!' And he stood up

and followed him. [15]Once Levi was sitting at table in his house
and many tax-collectors and despised people were sitting at table
together with Jesus and his disciples, for there were many who
followed him. [16]And the scribes among the Pharisees saw that he
was eating with despised people and tax-collectors, and they said
to his disciples, 'How can he eat with tax-collectors and those we
despise?' [17]Jesus heard this, and he said to them, 'Those who are
healthy do not need a physician, whereas those who are sick do.
I have not come to call the righteous but those who have gone
astray, to change their heart and mind.'

First disputes: Fasting and keeping the Sabbath holy

[18]The disciples of John and the Pharisees practised asceticism. And
they came to him and said, 'Why do the disciples of John and the
disciples of the Pharisees fast, but your disciples do not?' [19]Jesus
answered, 'The sons of the marriage feast, can they fast when the
bridegroom is in their midst? As long as the bridegroom is in their
midst they cannot fast. [20]But there will come times when the bridegroom will be taken from them; on that day they may fast. [21]No one
puts a piece of new, stiff material as a patch on an old garment; otherwise the new patch pulls away from the old garment and the tear
becomes even worse. [22]Nor does anyone pour new wine into old
wineskins; otherwise the wine bursts the skins and both the wine
and the skins go to waste. New wine belongs in new skins.'

[23]On a Sabbath he went beside the cornfields and while they
were walking his disciples began to pick ears of grain. [24]Then the
Pharisees said to him, 'Look, how can they do what is not allowed
on the Sabbath?' [25]And he answered them, 'Have you never read
what David did when he was in need and when he and those who
were with him were hungry? [26]How he went into the house of God
to Abiathar the High Priest, and how he ate the shewbread which of
course only the priests may eat, and how he also shared it with those
who were with him?' [27]And he said to them, 'The Sabbath is there
for the sake of Man, and not Man for the Sabbath. [28]So is the Son of
Man lord of the Sabbath.'

3 *Crowds from the outlying regions*

And again he went into the synagogue. And there was a man who had a withered hand. [2]And they watched him closely to see if he would perform a healing on the Sabbath, for they were looking for a reason to accuse him. [3]Then he said to the man with the withered hand, 'Stand here in the middle!' [4]And then he said to them, 'What is it permissible to do on the Sabbath? To do what is good or what is evil? To heal the soul or to kill it?' And they were silent. [5]And he looked around at them with anger, but also full of sorrow at how unbending were their hearts. Then he said to the man, 'Stretch out your hand.' And he stretched his hand out and it was restored. [6]And at once the Pharisees hurried out and consulted with the Herodians how they might do away with him.

[7]And Jesus withdrew with his disciples to the sea. And a great crowd followed him from Galilee, from Judea, [8]Jerusalem and Idumea, and also from beyond the Jordan and from the region of Tyre and Sidon; many flocked to him because they heard abut his deeds. [9]And he told his disciples to have a boat ready for him so that he could avoid the crush of people; [10]for he healed many, and so all who had a disease pressed him to lay his hand on them. [11]And the unclean spirits threw themselves on the ground before him when they saw him and cried out: 'You are the Son of God.' [12]And he told them emphatically not to make him known.

Calling the twelve

[13]And he went up on to the mountain and called to him those whom he had chosen, and they came to him. [14]There were twelve whom he chose to be always with him. They were to be sent out to proclaim [15]and to be given the creative power to drive out demons. [16]Thus he founded the circle of the twelve and gave Simon the second name Peter. [17]The others were James the son of Zebedee and John the brother of James. He gave them the name Boanerges, that means the sons of the thunder. [18]The remaining ones were Andrew and Philip and Bartholomew and Matthew and Thomas

and James the son of Alphaeus, and Thaddaeus and Simon the
Cananaean, [19]and Judas Iscariot who later betrayed him.

Dispute about working out of the spirit

And he went to his home, [20]and again so many flocked together
that they could not even eat their bread. [21]And his own relations
heard about it and went to take him in; they said that he was out
of his mind. [22]And the scribes who had come from Jerusalem said,
'He is possessed by Beelzebub, and with the Prince of Demons he
drives out demons.' [23]And he called them together and said to them
in pictures: 'How can one satanic being drive out another satanic
being? [24]If a kingdom is divided and fights against itself, it cannot
last. [25]And if a house is divided and comes into conflict with itself,
it will not remain. [26]And so also the satanic might cannot remain in
power when it is divided and fights itself; it comes to the end of its
power. [27]No one can enter the house of a powerful person to rob him
of his goods if he does not first overpower and fetter the powerful
one; only then can he plunder his house. [28]Yes, I say to you: All
transgressions can be forgiven the sons of men, even the misuse of
the Word, insofar as they are able actually to make wrong use of
the Word. [29]But whoever makes wrongful use of the Holy Spirit can
not receive forgiveness in this aeon; he is guilty of a transgression
which goes beyond this aeon.' [30]For they had said that he worked
out of an unclean spirit.

New human relationships

[31]Then his mother and his brothers came and remained standing outside and sent a messenger to call him. [32]A great crowd was sitting
around him; and they said, 'Look, your mother and your brothers
and sisters are standing outside, wanting you.' [33]But he answered,
'Who is my mother, and who are my brothers?' [34]And he looked
around on all who sat in a circle about him and said, 'See, these are
my mother and my brothers! [35]Whoever acts in accordance with the
will of God is my brother, my sister and my mother.'

4 *Three parables about the Kingdom of God*

He began to teach again by the sea shore. And a great crowd gathered by him so that he had to get into a ship. And he sat in it on the sea, whilst the crowd was on land, looking out on the sea. 2And he taught them many things in parables, and this was his teaching: 3‘Listen! See, the sower went to sow. 4And as he scattered the seeds a portion fell by the wayside, and the birds flew down and devoured it. 5And another portion fell on rocky ground where there was not much earth. Quickly it sprang up, because it could not root deeply in the earth. 6And as the sun rose higher it was scorched, and it withered because it had no root. 7And another portion fell among thornbushes, and when the thorns grew taller they choked it and it bore no fruit. 8And another portion fell into good earth and bore fruit as it sprang up and grew, and yielded thirtyfold and sixtyfold and a hundredfold.’ 9And he said, ‘Whoever has ears to hear, let him hear!’

10And when he was alone with them, those who were about him as well as the twelve asked him about the meaning of the parables. 11And he said to them, ‘To you the mystery of the Kingdom of God has been given; but those who are outside receive it in the form of parables. 12They have to go through that state of soul in which they see with their eyes and yet do not see; hear with their ears and yet do not understand. They must not be set back in the development of their consciousness; but neither should they lose the fruits of their path.’ 13And he said to them, ‘Do you not understand this parable? How then shall you understand the whole wealth of parables?

14‘The sower sows the word. 15And when the word is sown along the path it falls among those to whom, when they hear it, the Adversary comes at once to snatch to himself what has been sown in their soul. 16The seed which falls on rocky ground is a picture for those who at once take up with enthusiasm the word that they hear, 17but who are not firmly rooted in life, and are inconstant. Then when difficult destiny or persecutions have to be endured for the sake of the word they give up at once. 18Yet others are meant when the parable says that the seed fell among thornbushes. When they have heard the word [19]and then return to the cares of earthly life and come under the influence of the temptations of wealth and the other cravings of the soul, then the word is choked and it bears no fruit. [20]But those among whom the seed falls into good earth are those who hear the word and really take it into themselves. They bear fruit, thirtyfold, sixtyfold and a hundredfold.'

[21]And he said to them, 'Surely the purpose of the coming of the light is not that it be put under a vessel or under a bed? Should it not rather be placed on a stand? [22]There is nothing hidden which shall not be revealed, and nothing kept secret which is not to be made known to all. [23]Whoever has ears to hear, let him hear!' [24]And he continued: 'Pay close attention to what you hear. According to the measure by which you give, you in turn will receive, and you will be given still more. [25]For to him who has will be given, and from him who has not will be taken away even what he thinks he has.'

[26]And he said, 'The Kingdom of God is like when a man sowed seed on the ground [27]and then lay down to rest and got up again, night after night, day after day; and meanwhile the seed sprouts and grows tall without him knowing it. [28]Out of its own forces the earth brings forth its fruit, first the green blade, then the ear and lastly the fullness of the grain in the ear. [29]And then, when the fruit is ripe, he comes with the sickle: Harvest has come.'

[30]And he said, 'With what shall we compare the Kingdom of God, with what parable can it be described? [31]It is like a mustard seed which, when it is sown on the earth, is smaller than all seeds on earth. [32]But once it has been sown it grows up and becomes greater than all herbs and produces large branches, so that the birds of the air can build their nests in its shadow.'

[33]With many such parables he proclaimed the word to them as they were able to receive it.

[34]And he did not speak to the people except in parables. And in intimate conversation he explained everything to his disciples.

Calming the storm

[35]On that day he said to them when evening had come, 'Let us
cross the lake.' [36]And they withdrew from the crowd and when
he had boarded the ship they took him into their midst. Other
ships were also nearby. [37]Then a violent whirlwind arose and the
waves crashed together over the ship so that it quickly filled with
water. [38]He himself was in the stern of the ship and was asleep on
a pillow. Then they woke him up and said, 'Master, are you not
concerned that we are perishing?' [39]And he stood up and raised
his hand against the wind and spoke towards the sea: 'Quiet! Be
silent.' And the wind dropped and there was a great calm. [40]And
he said to them, 'Why are you so fearful? Why have you no faith?'
[41]But they were even more afraid and said to one another, 'What
kind of a Being can this be? Even the wind and the sea obey him.'

5 *Healing the demon-possessed Gerasene*

And they came to the other shore of the lake, to the district of
the Gerasenes. [2]And as he came out of the ship, suddenly a man
with an unclean spirit came towards him out of the tombs. [3]He
had made his dwelling in the tombs, and no one had been able
to restrain him any longer, not even with chains. [4]He had often
been bound with fetters and chains, but always he had broken the
chains and sawed through the fetters; no one had the strength to
subdue him. [5]He wandered among the tombs and mountains, night
and day, shouting and striking himself with stones. [6]When he saw
Jesus in the distance he came running, threw himself down before
him [7]and cried out with a loud voice: 'What is between me and
you, Jesus, you Son of the highest God? I adjure you by God, do
not torment me!' [8]For Jesus had said to him, 'You unclean spirit,
leave this man!' [9]And he asked him, 'What is your name?' And he
answered, 'My name is Legion, for we are many.' [10]And the spirits
begged him earnestly not to drive them out of the country. [11]And
a great herd of pigs was feeding there on the hillside; [12]and they
begged him: 'Send us into the pigs.' [13]And he permitted it. And the
unclean spirits came out and entered the pigs, and the herd threw

itself over the edge into the sea. About two thousand animals were
drowned in the sea. [14]And the herdsmen fled and reported it in the
town and in the fields. And everyone came hurrying to see what
had happened.

[15]And they came to Jesus and saw the possessed man sitting
there, dressed and in his right mind, he who had been possessed
by the legion of demons. And they were alarmed. [16]And those
who had seen it told them what had happened with the possessed
man and the herd of pigs. [17]Then they asked Jesus to leave their
district. [18]And as he entered the ship, the man who had been possessed asked to be allowed to be with him. [19]But he did not allow
it; instead, he said to him, 'Go to your house to your own people
and proclaim to them what the Lord has done for you and what
love HE has shown you.' [20]And he went and began to proclaim in
the district of the Ten Towns what Jesus had done for him, and
everyone was amazed.

The woman with a haemorrhage and raising Jairus' daughter

[21]When Jesus again had crossed over the lake, a great crowd gathered about him, and he stayed a while on the shores of the lake.
[22]Then one of the leaders of the synagogue, by name Jairus, came;
and when he saw Jesus he fell at his feet [23]and begged him to help:
'My little daughter is near to death; come and lay your hands on
her, then she will become well and continue to live.' [24]And he set
off with him.

A great crowd followed him, so that he was in a crush of people.
[25]And there was also a woman who had suffered from a haemorrhage for twelve years. [26]She had had to endure much from a
great number of physicians, and had already spent all that she had
without getting any better; on the contrary, she was getting worse.
[27]Since she had heard much about Jesus she approached him
through the crowd and touched his garment from behind. [28]She
said to herself: Even if I only touch his garment, I shall become
well. [29]And at once the source of her bleeding dried up and she
felt in her body that she was healed of her disease. [30]Then Jesus

suddenly became aware inwardly that power had gone forth from
him, and he turned round in the crowd and said, 'Who touched my
garments?' 31Then his disciples said to him, 'You can see the crush
of people around you; how can you ask: Who touched me?' 32And
he looked around to see who had done this. 33Then the woman
was afraid and began to tremble, for she was well aware what had
happened to her. She came and fell down before him and told him
the whole truth. 34And he said to her, 'My daughter, your heart's
faith has healed you. Go on your way in peace and be healed of
your disease.'

35And while he is still speaking, messengers come to the leader
of the synagogue and say, 'Your daughter has died. Why do you
still trouble the Master?' 36Jesus heard these words, and he says to
the leader of the synagogue, 'Have no fear, only have trust.' 37And
he allowed no one to go with him except Peter, James and John,
the brother of James. 38And they come to the house of the leader
of the synagogue, and he sees the helplessness and confusion and
the women weeping and lamenting loudly. 39And going in he says
to them, 'Why are you making a noise and weeping? The child is
not dead; she is only sleeping.' 40And they ridiculed him. Then he
drives them all out of the house, and he takes the child's father
and mother and those who are with him and enters the room where
the child lay. 41And he takes the girl by the hand and says to her,
'Talitha coumi;' that means: 'Young maiden, I say to you, arise!'
42And at once the girl was able to get up and walk about. She was
twelve years old. And suddenly they were overcome with great
wonder. 43And he impressed upon them that no one must know of
this. Then he said that she should be given something to eat.

6 *Rejection in Nazareth*

And he left that place and came to his home town, and his disciples
followed him. 2On the next Sabbath he went into the synagogue
and began to teach. And the many who were listening were beside
themselves with astonishment and said, 'How has he come by all
this? What kind of wisdom is this that reveals itself to him? And

how is it that such world-powers work through his hands? [3]Is he not the carpenter, the son of Mary and the brother of James and Joses and Judas and Simon? And are not his sisters living here amongst us?' And they were scandalized by him. [4]Then Jesus said to them, 'Nowhere is a prophet regarded less than in his own country, among his blood relations and in his own house.' [5]It was impossible for him to do anything out of a higher power there. He only healed a few sick people by laying his hands on them. [6]The lethargy of their hearts amazed him.

Sending out the twelve disciples

[7]And he went through the surrounding villages, teaching. Then he called the twelve to him and began to send them out in pairs; he gave them authority over the unclean spirits; [8]and he instructed them: 'On your way take nothing with you except a staff; no bread, no bag, no money in your belt. [9]But you are to wear sandals on your feet. Nor should you put on two coats.' [10]And he went on: 'When you have entered a house, stay there until you leave that place again. [11]And if you come to a place where you are not received, and where they do not hear you, then when you move on, shake off the dust which has clung to your feet. Let them learn from that.' [12]And they went out and by their proclamation they called on the people to change their hearts and minds, [13]and they drove out many demons and anointed many sick people with oil and healed them.

[14]And King Herod heard of it, for Jesus' name had become known, and he said, 'John the Baptist has risen from the dead, that is why such world-powers work through him.' [15]Others said, 'He is Elijah;' yet others said that he was a prophet or like one of the prophets. [16]But when Herod heard that he said, 'He whom I beheaded, John, has risen.'

Death of the Baptist

[17]For Herod had sent messengers to seize John, and had thrown him, fettered, into prison because of Herodias, the wife of his

brother Philip whom he had married. [18]John had said to Herod, 'It
is not right for you to marry your brother's wife.' [19]Then Herodias
burned with hate against him and wanted to kill him, but she could
not; [20]for Herod was in great awe of John; he knew that he was a
man who was devoted to the Good and filled with the spirit. He
guarded him well and listened to him, although it often made him
uneasy; yet he liked listening to him.

[21]Then came a day of celebration. For the festivities on the day
of his birth Herod invited the most important people in his kingdom and the commanders of his army and the princes of Galilee
to the banquet. [22]Now when the daughter of Herodias came in
and danced, she pleased Herod and his guests very much. Then
the king said to the girl, [23]'Ask of me whatever you want; I will
give it to you.' And he vowed to her: 'Whatever you ask I will
give it you, even half my kingdom.' [24]She went out and said to her
mother, 'What shall I ask for?' Herodias said, 'The head of John
the Baptist.' [25]And eagerly, she at once hurried back in again to
the king and said, 'I want you immediately to give me the head
of John the Baptist on a dish.' [26]Then the king was appalled and
saddened, but because of his oath and because of his guests he did
not want to break his word to her. [27]And so the king at once sent
an executioner and ordered him to bring the head. He went and
beheaded him in the prison [28]and brought his head on a dish and
gave it to the girl, and the girl gave it to her mother. [29]And when
his disciples learnt of it they came and took his body and laid it
in a tomb.

Feeding the five thousand

[30]And the apostles gathered around Jesus again and told him
everything that they had done and taught. [31]And he said to them,
'Come with me now to an intimate gathering in a lonely place
where you can come to rest a little.' For there were many coming
and going, and they could not even find time to eat. [32]So they went
by ship to a lonely place to be by themselves.

[33]But many saw and recognized them as they set off, and they

hurried there on foot from all the towns, and even overtook them.
34And as he disembarked he saw the great crowd, and he was moved
by compassion at the sight; for they were like sheep who have no
shepherd, and he began to teach them many things.

35And since it was already late, his disciples came to him and
said, 'The place is lonely, and it is already late. 36Let them go, so
that they can still go to the farms and villages round about and buy
themselves something to eat.' 37But he answered, '*You* give them
to eat.' They said, 'Should we go and buy bread worth two hundred
denarii and give them to eat?' 38He said, 'How many loaves have
you? Go and see.' And when they had found out, they said, 'Five,
and two fish.' 39Then he told them to make them all settle down
on the green grass as if sitting at table. 40So they all sat down in
groups of a hundred and of fifty. 41And he took the five loaves and
the two fish, lifted up his soul to the Spirit, blessed and broke the
loaves and gave them to the disciples, so that they should share
them out to the people. And he also shared the two fish among
them all. 42And they all ate and were satisfied. 43And when the
remaining fragments were gathered up, there were twelve baskets
full. And there was some fish left over also. 44It was five thousand
men who ate of the loaves.

Walking on the sea

45And at once he made his disciples board the ship and go across
the lake to Bethsaida; meanwhile he would send the people off.
46After he had told them to do this, he went on to the mountain to
pray. 47And when evening had come, the ship was in the middle
of the lake, and he alone was on the firm ground. 48And he saw
that they were labouring at their oars, for the wind was against
them. Then, about the fourth watch of the night, he comes to them,
walking on the sea. And he wanted to pass by them. 49When they
saw him walking on the sea they thought it was a delusion, and
they cried out aloud. 50They had all seen him, and there was great
confusion among them. But then he spoke to them at once, 'Take
courage, it is I; have no fear.' 51And he got into the ship with them,

and the wind dropped. They were completely and utterly out of
themselves because of this. 52They had not awoken to insight
through their experience with the loaves, their hearts were still
hardened.

53And when they had crossed the lake and had reached land again,
they came to Gennesaret and moored at the shore. 54And when they
disembarked, the people recognized him, 55and everywhere in the
district they quickly set out and carried the sick people to him on
stretchers, wherever they heard that he was. 56And everywhere he
went, into villages, towns or farms, they laid the sick in the market
places and asked him at least to let them touch the hem of his garment. And all who touched him were healed.

7 *True purity*

Once the Pharisees and some of the scribes came to him from
Jerusalem 2and saw that some of his disciples ate the bread with
their hands just as they were, without the prescribed washing. 3For
the Pharisees and all Jews only eat after repeated washings of their
hands, in strict adherence to the tradition of their forebears. 4Also,
when they come in from the street they only eat after completing
the ritual of sprinkling. And there are many other traditional rules
which they follow, among them solemn washing of chalices, jugs
and bronze vessels. 5And the Pharisees and scribes asked him,
'Why do your disciples not follow the traditions from the time of
the Patriarchs, but eat the bread with unwashed hands?' 6He said to
them, 'It was about you, you hypocrites, that Isaiah prophesied a
true word:

> Only with their lips do men honour me,
> Their heart is far from me,
> 7They try to serve me with empty forms,
> Their teaching is empty of all but human notions and doctrines.

8'You abandon the aims of God, all the more to cling to the
human traditions which prescribe for you the washing of jugs and
chalices and many other such things.' 9And further he said to them,

'It's splendid the way that you nullify the commandment of God in
order to enforce your own traditions! 10Moses says:

> Honour your father and your mother,

and:

> Whoever uses evil words against father or mother shall be subject to death.

11But you say: "When someone says to his father or his mother:
Corban – that means I will make a gift of offering instead of what
I owe to you – 12then he is relieved of all obligations to father and
mother." 13In this way you make the tradition which you have
received superior to the divine word. And you do much the same
with many other things.'

14And again he called the people together and said, 'Hear me, all
of you, and pay attention to the meaning of my words: 15A human
being is not defiled by what enters him from outside. It is only by
what proceeds from him that he can be degraded. 16Whoever has
ears to hear, let him hear!'

17And as he turned away from the crowd and went into the
house his disciples asked him about the meaning of the parable.
18And he said to them, 'Are you also without understanding? Are
you not aware that nothing of that which enters Man from outside
can degrade him? 19For it does not enter his heart but his stomach, and leaves him again by the natural process which cleanses
him of all food.' 20And he went on: 'What proceeds from Man
can degrade Man. 21In the innermost part of the human heart lies
the source of the bad soul impulses. From there come indecency,
theft, murderous intent, faithlessness in marriage, 22greed, malice,
deceit, licentiousness, envy, slander, arrogance, indolence. 23All
these base stirrings of the soul come from within. It is by them
that Man is defiled.'

Healing the Syrophoenician woman

24And he set off and went on to the region of Tyre. And he went into
a house and did not want anyone to know about his presence. But
he could not remain hidden. 25Straight away a woman heard of him;

her daughter was possessed by an unclean spirit. She came and fell
at his feet. [26]She was Greek, a Syrophoenician by birth. She begged
him to free her daughter from the demon. [27]And he said to her, ‘First
let the children be fed. It is not right to take the bread from the
children and throw it to the dogs.’ [28]But she answered, ‘Yes, lord,
but the dogs under the table also eat the children’s crumbs.’ [29]And
he said to her, ‘For the sake of this word, go your way; the demon
has left your daughter.’ [30]And she went into her house and found the
child lying on the bed, freed of the demon.

Healing a deaf and dumb man

[31]And as he left the region of Tyre again, he went through Sidon to
the Sea of Galilee via the region of the Ten Towns.

[32]Then they brought to him a man who was deaf and who spoke
only with difficulty. And they asked him to lay his hand on him.
[33]And he took him aside by himself, away from the crowd, and he
put his fingers into his ears and moistened his finger with spittle
and touched his tongue. [34]Then he lifted up his soul to the spirit, and
with a deep sigh he said to him: ‘Ephphatha – be opened!’ [35]And
his hearing was opened and his tongue was suddenly released and
he could speak properly. [36]And he told them to say nothing to anyone about it. But the more he forbade it, the more they proclaimed
it. [37]They were beside themselves beyond all measure and said,
‘He has done great deeds; to the deaf he gives their hearing, to the
dumb he gives their speech.’

8 *Feeding the four thousand*

In those days a great crowd had gathered again, and they had nothing to eat. Then he called his disciples to him and said to them,
[2]‘The sight of the crowd touches my heart; they have already been
with me three days and have nothing to eat. [3]If I send them home
hungry they will be faint with exhaustion on the way, and some
are from far away.’ [4]But his disciples answered, ‘Where can one
get bread in the desert to feed them?’ [5]Then he asked them, ‘How
many loaves have you?’ They said, ‘Seven.’ [6]And he told the

crowd to sit down on the ground. And he took the seven loaves,
blessed them, broke them and gave them to his disciples so that
they should share them out, and they gave them to the crowd.
7They also had a few small fish, and he blessed them so that they,
too, should be shared out. 8And they ate and were satisfied and
took up the remaining fragments, seven baskets full. 9There were
about four thousand people. 10And he sent them away, and at once
he boarded a ship with his disciples and came to the region of
Dalmanutha.

The Pharisees demand a sign

11And the Pharisees came out and began to argue with him. In
order to test him, they demanded of him a demonstration of supernatural power. 12Then his spirit was deeply wounded, and he said,
'Why does this kind of human being crave for a wonder? Yes, I
say to you: No such wonder shall be granted to them.' 13And he
left them standing, entered the ship again and went across the
lake. 14They had forgotten to bring bread, and had only a single
loaf with them in the ship. 15And he told them, 'Be alert, and
beware of the leaven of the Pharisees and of the leaven of Herod.'
16But they were preoccupied with the fact that they had no bread
with them. 17When he became aware of that he said to them, 'Why
are you so concerned that you have no bread? Are your thinking
and your understanding still not awake? Are your hearts still hardened? 18You have eyes and yet you do not see, and you have ears
and yet you do not hear. Do you not remember 19how I broke five
loaves for the five thousand, how many baskets full of fragments
remained for you?' They answered, 'Twelve.' 20'And when I broke
seven loaves for the four thousand how many full baskets did you
take up?' They said, 'Seven.' 21And he went on, 'Has your understanding still not awoken?'

Healing a blind man

22And they came to Bethsaida. Then they brought to him a blind
man and begged him to lay his hand upon him. 23And he took the

blind man by the hand and led him outside the village, moistened
his eyes with spittle and laid his hands upon him. Then he asked
him, 'Do you see anything?' 24And the blind man opened his eyes
and said, 'I see people as though they were walking trees.' 25And
he laid his hands upon his eyes again, and now when he looked
about him he was completely restored and saw everything in clear
outlines. 26And he sent him home and said, 'Do not go into the
village, and speak to no one about it.'

Peter's confession

27And Jesus went on with his disciples into the region of Cacsarea
Philippi. And on the way he asked the disciples, 'Who do people
say that I am?' 28They answered, 'Some take you to be John the
Baptist, others Elijah, yet others a prophet.' 29Then he asked them,
'And you, who do you say that I am?' Then Peter answered: 'You
are the Christ.' 30And he told them most earnestly not to speak about
him to anyone.

The first foretelling of death and resurrection

31And he began to teach them: 'The Son of Man must suffer much
and be rejected by the elders and the chief priests and the scribes;
and he will be killed and will rise again after three days.' 32He
said this quite openly and freely. Then Peter took him aside and
began to make objections. 33But he turned round and looked at
his disciples, warded Peter off and said, 'Withdraw from me, the
Adversary is speaking through you; your thinking is not divine
but merely human in nature.'

Conditions of discipleship

34And he called the crowd together, including his disciples, and said,
'Whoever would follow me must practise self-denial and take his
cross upon him; only thus can he follow me.

35'For whoever is only concerned about his soul's salvation will
lose it; but whoever is prepared to lose his soul, because he wants to
serve me and the Gospel, will find the salvation for his soul. 36What

use is it to a human being to gain the whole world and yet be impoverished in his soul? [37]What could a human being give as a ransom for his soul? [38]Whoever in present humanity, which has broken its marriage to the spirit and has given itself up to the powers of the abyss, scorns my Being and my words, him the Son of Man will also spurn when he becomes visible in the revealing light of his Father in the midst of the holy angelic spheres.'

9 *The Transfiguration*
And he said to them, 'Yes I say to you: Among those who are standing here there are some who will not taste death before they have seen the Kingdom of God powerfully breaking through.'

[2]And after six days Jesus took Peter and James and John aside and took them up with him onto a high mountain to be together, intimately alone. And his appearance was transformed before their eyes, [3]and his garments shone radiantly, a shining white, bright beyond all measure, whiter than anyone on earth would be able to make them. [4]And there appeared to their seeing souls Elijah and Moses, conversing with Jesus. [5]This made Peter say to Jesus, 'Master, it is good that we are here; let us build three shelters, one for you, one for Moses and one for Elijah.' [6]But he was unaware of what it was he was saying; for they had been shaken and were deeply awed. [7]Then a cloud formed which overshadowed them, and out of the cloud sounded a voice: 'This is my beloved Son, hear him!' [8]And suddenly, as they looked about them, they saw no-one any more, only Jesus who was with them.

[9]And as they again descended from the mountain he told them to say nothing to anyone about what they had seen, before the Son of Man should have risen from the dead. [10]This saying remained with them and they discussed amongst themselves how this resurrection from the dead was to be understood. [11]And they asked him, 'Why do the scribes say that first Elijah must come again?' [12]He answered, 'It is right that first Elijah must come again and set everything to rights. That is in accordance with scripture and is the preparation for the coming of the Son of Man who will have

to endure many stages of suffering and of humiliation. [13]But I say
to you: Elijah has already come and men treated him according to
their whim as scripture says of him.'

Healing the boy possessed by a demon

[14]And when they again came to the other disciples, they saw a great
crowd gathered around them, including scribes who were conversing with them. [15]Suddenly, with amazement the crowd saw him
and hurried towards him to greet him. [16]And he asked them, 'What
are you discussing with them?' [17]And one of the crowd answered,
'Master, I have brought my son to you who is possessed by a dumb
spirit. [18]And when it seizes him, it tears him this way and that and
he foams and grinds his teeth and then he is as though exhausted.
And I turned to your disciples for them to drive out the demon, but
they could not.' [19]Then he said to them, 'How weak is the inner
power of human beings in this age! How long must I still be with
you? How long must I still bear with you? Bring him here to me!'
[20]And they brought the boy to him. And suddenly when the spirit
saw him, the cramps came on again and the boy fell to the ground
and rolled about and foamed at the mouth. [21]And he asked the father
of the boy, 'How long has he been suffering this?' And he answered,
'From childhood. [22]Often it throws him into the fire and often into
the water to destroy him. If you have the power, help us and have
compassion on us.' [23]And Jesus said to him, 'Oh, if only you had
the power yourself! For him who has the power of faith all things
are possible.' [24]And suddenly the father of the boy burst out, 'I have
faith, help my lack of faith!' [25]Jesus saw how the crowd was gathering hurriedly and he raised his hand against the unclean spirit
and said to it, 'You spirit without speech and without hearing, I
command you, leave him and do not enter him again!' [26]And with
screams and convulsions it left him. And the boy lay there as if
dead, so that many said, 'He has died.' [27]But Jesus took him by the
hand and raised him up and life returned to him.

[28]When they arrived home the disciples asked him in intimate
conversation, 'Why did we not have the power to drive it out?'

29 He answered, 'This kind can only be overcome by the power
which is won through prayer and through fasting.'

The second foretelling of death and resurrection

30 And they went on and came through Galilee, and he did not want
anyone to recognize him; 31 for he was teaching his disciples and
saying to them, 'The Son of Man will be delivered into the hands of
men and they will kill him; but after three days he will rise again.'
32 But they did not understand the saying, and they dared not ask him
about it.

Ambition and true community

33 And they came to Capernaum. And in the house he asked them,
'What were you speaking about on the way?' 34 They were silent;
for on the way they had talked to each other about who was the
greatest. 35 And he sat down and called the twelve together and said,
'Whoever wants to be the first must be the last of all and the servant
of all.' 36 And he took a child and placed him in the middle of the
circle, caressed him and said, 37 'Whoever takes the being of such a
child into himself and does so in my name, he takes me into himself; and whoever takes me into himself takes in not only me but
also HIM who sent me.'

38 Then John said, 'Master, we saw someone who was driving out
demons in your name; but he does not belong to those who follow
us. So we stopped him doing it because he does not follow us.' 39 But
Jesus said, 'Do not stop him. Someone who does powerful deeds in
my name will not lightly begin to speak evil about me. 40 Whoever
is not against us is for us.

41 'If someone gives you a drink of water because your being is
filled by the Being of Christ, yes, I say to you: The progress of his
destiny will not be hindered. 42 And someone who causes another
to stumble whose inner power is yet small because the faith is only
just beginning to grow in him, for him it would be better to have a
millstone hung about his neck and to be thrown into the sea.

43 'If your hand is a stumbling block to your inner development,

cut it off. It is better to find access to the true life as a cripple than
with two hands to succumb to the powers of the abyss where burns
the fire that is never extinguished. [45]And if your foot causes you to
stumble inwardly, cut it off. It is better to find the true life lame than
to fall into the abyss with two feet. [47]And if your eye causes you
to go astray inwardly, pluck it out. It is better to find access to the
Kingdom of God with one eye than with two eyes to succumb to the
powers of the abyss [48]where the creeping worm of their fallen being
never ends and where burns the fire that is never extinguished.'

[49]Everyone must be salted with fire. [50]Salt is good, but if salt
loses its saltness how will you season it again? Have salt in yourselves and cultivate peace with one another.

10 *Journey to Judea and a question about divorce*

And he set off and came to the region of Judea and beyond the
Jordan. And again large crowds flocked to him and he taught them
as his custom was. [2]And Pharisees came to him and asked him
whether it was lawful for a man to divorce his wife; they wanted
to test him with this question. [3]He said, 'What commandment did
Moses give you?' [4]They said, 'Moses allowed divorce on the condition of a written annulment.' [5]Then Jesus said to them, 'This commandment was given to you because of your hard-heartedness.' [6]In
the primeval beginnings of creation Man was created male-female.
[7]Therefore he will leave his father and his mother and join himself
to his wife. [8]And the duality shall one day again become a physical
unity, so that there will no longer be two kinds, but only one kind
of physical body.

> [9]Now what God has joined together, Man shall not sepa-
> rate.

[10]And at home the disciples again asked him about this. [11]And he
said to them, 'Whoever leaves his wife and takes another to wife,
he breaks his marriage to her; [12]and when a woman who has left her
husband takes another man, then she breaks the marriage.'

Blessing the children

[13]And they brought children to him, that he might touch them.
But the disciples prevented them. [14]When Jesus saw that, he was
indignant and said to them, 'Let the children come to me and do
not hinder them; for they bear the Kingdom of God within themselves. [15]Yes, I say to you, whoever does not take up the Kingdom
of God in himself like a child, he will not find access to it.' [16]And
he caressed the children and blessed them, laying his hands upon
them.

The rich young man

[17]As he went on his way he was overtaken by someone who came
running, kneeled before him and asked him, 'Good Master, what
must I do to attain to timeless life?' [18]Jesus said to him, 'Why do
you call me good? No one is good except one: God. [19]You know the
commandments:

> 'You shall not kill, you shall not break marriage, you
> shall not steal, not slander, not defraud, honour your
> father and mother.'

[20]And he answered, 'Master, all this I have observed meticu-
lously from my youth.' [21]Then Jesus looked at him, had to love him,
and said to him, 'You still lack one thing. Go and sell everything
that you have and give the proceeds to the poor. For that you will
win a treasure in the spiritual worlds. And then come and follow
me!' [22]But he was not pleased by this saying and went away saddened, for he had many possessions.

[23]And Jesus looked around and said to his disciples, 'How
difficult it is for human beings who are rich to find access to the
Kingdom of God!' [24]And the disciples were astonished at his
words. But Jesus went on, 'How difficult it is altogether to find
access to the Kingdom of God. [25]It is more possible for a camel
to pass through the eye of a needle than for someone who is rich
to find entrance to the Kingdom of God.' [26]They were very much
taken aback and said to one another, 'Who then can find salvation?' [27]Then Jesus looked at them and said, 'For that in us which

is merely human much is impossible, which for the God in us is
possible. Everything is possible for God.'

[28]Then Peter said to him, 'We have left everything behind and
have followed you.' [29]Jesus said, 'Yes I say to you: No one leaves
house and brothers and sisters and mother and father and children
and fields to serve me and the new angelic word [30]without receiving back a hundredfold what he has sacrificed, in physical, earthly
existence, houses and brothers and sisters and mothers and children and fields, even in the midst of persecutions; and in the future
world-existence the life which continues through all cycles of time.
[31]Many who now are first will be last; and many who now are last
will be first.'

The third foretelling of death and resurrection

[32]They were on their way up to Jerusalem. Jesus went before them
and they were astonished by him. The longer they followed him the
more they were filled with a strange foreboding. And again he took
the twelve aside and began to speak of his coming destiny: [33]'See,
we are going up to Jerusalem, and the Son of Man will be betrayed
to the chief priests and the scribes, and they will condemn him to
death and leave him to the mercy of the peoples of the world; [34]and
they will mock him and spit in his face and scourge him and kill
him, and after three days he will rise again.'

James' and John's request

[35]Then James and John, the sons of Zebedee, hurried forward to
him and said, 'Master, we want you to do what we ask of you.'
[36]He said, 'What is it that you want me to do for you?' [37]They
answered, 'Grant that we may find our place at your side when
you are raised up to the light of the spirit; one on your right, the
other on your left.' [38]But Jesus said to them, 'You do not know
what it is you are demanding. Can you drink the cup that I must
drink, and can you also be baptized with the baptism which I am
to receive?' [39]They said, 'We can.' And Jesus said to them, 'You
shall drink the cup that I drink, and receive the baptism which I

shall receive. [40]But to sit at my right hand and at my left is not in my power to grant. That is only granted to those in whose destiny it lies.' [41]When the other ten heard that, they were indignant about James and John. [42]And Jesus called them together and said, 'You know that those who are supposed to be the rulers have power over their people, and that their great men exercise this might. [43]It shall not be like that among you. Whoever among you wants to be great, let him be your servant; [44]and whoever among you wants to be the first, let him be a slave to all. [45]For the Son of Man also has not come to be served but to serve, and to give his life for the deliverance of many.'

Healing the blind man of Jericho

[46]And they come to Jericho. And as he came out of Jericho with his disciples and a great crowd, Bartimaeus, a blind beggar, the son of Timaeus, was sitting by the roadside. [47]And when he heard that Jesus of Nazareth was going past he began to call out loudly: 'Son of David, Jesus, have compassion on me!' [48]And many threatened him and told him to be silent. But he only called out all the more: 'Son of David, have compassion on me!' [49]Then Jesus stopped and said, 'Call him here.' And they called the blind man and said to him, 'Courage, stand up, he is calling you!' [50]Then he threw off his cloak, sprang to his feet and hurried to Jesus. [51]And Jesus said to him, 'What do you want me to do for you?' The blind man said, 'Master, grant that I may see again.' [52]And Jesus said, 'Go your way, your faith has healed you.' And suddenly he could see again and followed him on the way.

11 *The entry into Jerusalem*

And when they came near to Jerusalem, to Bethphage and Bethany at the Mount of Olives, he sent out two of his disciples, [2]and said to them, 'Go into the place which you see before you, and immediately as you enter it you will find the colt of an ass tied there, on which no one has ever yet sat. Untie it and bring it here. [3]And if anyone asks you why you are doing that, say, 'The Lord has need of

it; and at once he will send it here to me.' 4And they went and found
the colt out in the street, tethered at a door, and they untied it. 5And
some of the men who were standing there said to them, 'Why are
you untying the colt?' 6And they answered as Jesus had told them.
Then they let them do it. 7And they brought the colt to Jesus, placed
their cloaks on it and he sat on it. 8Many spread their cloaks on the
road, others strewed branches which they had cut from the trees
in the fields. 9And those who went ahead and those who followed
called out:

Hosanna, sing to him!
Blessed be he who comes in the name of the Lord of the
World.
10Blessed be the kingdom of our father David
which is now being fulfilled.
Sing to him in the highest heights!

11And hc entered Jerusalem and went into the Temple. There he
viewed everything all around him, and when evening had come he
set out with the twelve on the way to Bethany.

The fig tree

12And on the next day when they left Bethany again, he felt hunger.
13And from a distance he saw a fig tree in full leaf, and he went to
see if he could find fruits on it. And when he came up to the tree he
found nothing but leaves; and indeed it was not the season for figs.
14And in response he said to the tree, 'Never again in any age to
come shall anyone eat of your fruits!' And his disciples heard these
words.

Cleansing the Temple

15And they came to Jerusalem. And he went into the Temple and
he began to drive out those who sold and those who bought in the
Temple; he overturned the tables of the money-changers and the
chairs of those who sold doves, 16and he did not allow vessels to
be carried through the Temple. 17And he taught them and said, 'Is
it not written:

> My house shall be called a house of prayer among all peoples?

But you have made it a den of robbers.' 18When the chief priests and the scribes heard this, they wondered how they might destroy him. They were afraid of him because all the people were enraptured by his teaching. 19And when evening came he went out of the town.

20In the morning when they passed by they saw that thc fig tree had withered right down to its roots. 21Then Peter remembered and said to him,' Master, see! The fig tree which you cursed has withered.' 22And Jesus said to them, 'Through the power of faith you can unite with God. 23Yes, I say to you: Whoever then shall say to this mountain: Rise up and throw yourself into the sea, and has no doubt in his heart but rather is confident that his word will be effective, he will experience that it will happen. 24Therefore I say to you: Everything towards which you direct the power of prayer in your inner striving will be granted to you, if only you have full confidence that you can achieve it.

25'But when you prepare to pray, if you are holding a grudge in your heart against anyone, first forgive; then your Father who is in the heavens can also forgive you your strayings.'

The question about authority

27And again they came to Jerusalem. As he was walking in the Temple, the chief priests and the scribes and the elders came up to him 28and said to him, 'By what authority do you act? Or who has given you authority to do your deeds?' 29And Jesus said to them, 'Let me, too, put a question to you, for you to answer. Then I will tell you by what authority I act. 30Did John baptize by divine authority or by human authority? Answer me!' 31And they debated with one another: 'If we say: By divine authority, he will ask: Then why did you not believe in him? 32So shall we say: By human authority?' This they dared not say for fear of the people who all had really held John to be a prophet. 33And so they answered Jesus, 'We do not know.' Then Jesus said to them, 'Then neither will I tell you by what authority I act.'

12 *The parable of the vine-growers*
And he began to speak to them in parables: 'A man planted a
vineyard and surrounded it with a hedge and dug a winepress
and built a tower. Then he let it out to vine-growers and left the
country. 2And when the time had come he sent a servant to the
vine-growers to receive his share of the fruit of the vineyard from
them. 3But they took hold of the servant and beat him and sent him
away empty-handed. 4And again he sent a servant to them; they
beat him about the head and humiliated him. 5And yet once more
he sent out a servant, and him they killed. And they did the same
with many others; some they beat, the others they killed. 6Now, he
still had one other: His beloved son. Finally he sent him, too, to
them, thinking: They will respect my son. 7But those vine-growers
said to one another: This is the heir, come, let us kill him; then the
inheritance will belong to us.

8'And they took hold of him, killed him and threw his body
out of the vineyard. 9Now what will the lord of the vineyard do?
He will come and destroy the vine-growers and give the vineyard
to others.

10'Have you not read this in the scriptures:

> The stone which the builders called useless has
> become the corner stone. 11The Lord has brought it
> about and our eyes see it with wonder?'

12They were determined to get him in their power; but they were
afraid of the people. For they had clearly understood that in this
parable he was referring to them. So they left him alone and took
themselves off.

Paying taxes
13And they sent some of the Pharisees and Herodians to set a trap
for him with words. 14And they came and said to him, 'Master, we
know that you speak the truth and are not influenced by the personal status of anyone. You do not look at the outer circumstances
of people; you teach the divine path with absolute integrity. Now,
is it permitted to pay the tax to Caesar or not? 15Shall we pay it,

or shall we not pay it?' But he saw through their hypocrisy and
said to them, 'Why do you want to trap me? Bring me a denarius
to look at.' 16They brought it. Then he said, 'Whose picture and
inscription is this?' They answered, 'Caesar's.' 17Then Jesus said,
'Give to Caesar what belongs to Caesar, and give to God what
belongs to God.' They were dumbfounded by him.

The dispute with the Sadducees

18And Sadducees, who deny the resurrection, came to him and
asked him, 19'Master, from Moses we have the commandment:
When a man's brother dies and leaves a wife but no children, then
the brother must marry the woman and raise up offspring for his
brother. 20Now once there were seven brothers. The first took a
wife and died, leaving no children. 21Then the second married the
woman and also died without children. With the third the same
thing happened, 22and in the end all seven were without descendants. Last of all, the woman also died. 23Whose wife will she be
in the resurrection when they all return to life, since all seven
had her as wife?' 24Jesus answered, 'You are on the wrong track.
You know neither the scripture nor the way God guides destiny.
25When the resurrection of the dead comes, human beings will
neither marry nor be given in marriage, for then they are of similar
nature to the angels in the spiritual worlds. 26But that the dead
rise again, have you not read it in the Book of Moses, in the story
of the thornbush, when the voice of God said, "I am the God of
Abraham and the God of Isaac and the God of Jacob"? 27But HE is
not God of the dead but of the living. You are quite wrong.'

The most important commandment

28Then a scribe came to him; he had heard them arguing and had
observed how well he answered them. And he asked him, 'Which
is the most important of all the commandments?' 29And Jesus
answered, 'The first is this:

> Hear Israel, the Lord our God is the only Lord, 30and
> you shall love the Lord your God with all your heart,

with all your soul, with all your powers of thinking
and with all your powers of will.
31 The second is this:
Love your neighbour as yourself.
There is no commandment greater than these.' 32 Then the scribe
said, 'Good Master, you have spoken the truth: HE is One and
beside HIM there is no other. 33 And what matters is that one loves
HIM with the whole heart, with all powers of thinking and with all
powers of will. Also that one loves one's neighbour as oneself.
That is more than all burnt offerings, more than all offerings
altogether.'
34 When Jesus saw that he answered with real insight he said
to him, 'You are not far from the Kingdom of God.' Then no-one
dared to ask him any more questions.

About the scribes, and the widow's offering

35 And Jesus continued to teach in the Temple: 'How can the scribes
say that the Christ is the son of David? 36 After all, David himself,
inspired by the Holy Spirit, says:
The divine LORD said to my Lord:
You shall sit at my right hand,
while I will overthrow your enemies
and put them under your feet.
37 'If David calls him his Lord, how then can he be his son?'
The great crowd of people enjoyed listening to him. 38 And in
his teaching he said, 'Beware of the scribes who walk about in
ceremonial garments and want to be saluted in the streets. 39 In
the synagogues they want to have the chief seats and at meals the
places of honour. 40 They feed off widows' houses and claim they
have endless prayers to attend to. They burden themselves with a
grievous destiny.'
41 And he was sitting opposite the Temple collection box and saw
how the people put money into it. Many rich people gave large
sums. 42 Then came a poor widow and put in two lepta, that is about
one penny. 43 And he called his disciples together and said to them,

'Yes, I say to you, this poor widow has given more than all the
others who put something in the collection box. [44]They all gave
out of their abundance; but she, although she is in need, has given
everything that she had, all she had left for her living.'

13 *Apocalyptic words on the Mount of Olives*
And as he came out of the Temple one of his disciples said, 'Look,
Master, what magnificent stones, what wonderful buildings!' [2]And
Jesus said to him, 'Do you now see the magnificence of this edifice?
There will not be one stone left upon another, everything will be
destroyed.'

[3]And he sat down on the Mount of Olives, opposite the Temple.
There Peter, James, John and Andrew asked him in intimate conversation, [4]'Tell us when that will happen, and by what sign will it be
known when all this will be fulfilled?'

[5]Then Jesus began to speak to them, 'Take care that no one leads
you astray. [6]Many will come as though they came in my name, and
they will say: I am he. And they will lead many astray. [7]And so
when you hear the noise of war and cries of battle, let it not distract
you. It is necessary that all this should happen, but that is not yet
the fulfilment of the aim. [8]One people will rise against another and
one ideology against another. Everywhere the earth will be shaken,
and there will be famines; yet these are only the birthpangs of a new
age. [9]Look to yourselves; you will be accused and handed over and
dragged before the courts and into the synagogues. You will have
to stand before rulers and kings to defend yourselves because of
my Being with which you are united. But you shall be a proof of
the Spirit to them. [10]First, the proclamation of the new angelic word
must have reached all peoples.

[11]'If you are carried off and handed over, do not be anxious
about what you shall say. In that hour you shall speak out of what
will be given to you; for it is not you who speak, but the Holy
Spirit speaks through you. [12]Then one brother will hand over
another to his death and the father his child; children will rise up
against parents and will bring death upon them. [13]And you will be

hated by all because of my name. But he who endures until the goal has been reached, will share in the salvation.

14‘Then, when you see the aberration of the human self set up, a hideous form, where it should not be (let the reader penetrate what he reads with his thinking), let all those who are in Judea seek refuge in the mountain heights. 15And whoever is on the roof, let him not go down to fetch something from his house; 16and whoever is out in the field, let him not go back to what is behind him to fetch his garment.

17‘Woe to those who are with child and to nursing mothers in those days. 18Pray, so that all this will not come upon you in a wintry world. 19Such times will burden souls as in no age since the very beginning of creation, when God made the world, until the present time; nor will it ever be like that again in the future. 20And if the Lord of the ages had not shortened the days, then not one Being in the physical world would be able to partake of salvation. But because of those human beings who take HIM into themselves and whom HE thereby can raise up out of humanity, HE has shortened the days.

21‘Then, if someone says to you, “See, here is the Christ, look, there!” do not waste your faith on that. 22For false Christs and false prophets will arise who will even perform signs and wonders in order, if possible, also to lead astray those in whom the higher self is already awakened. 23So look to yourselves. I have told you everything beforehand. 24In the days after those hardships the sun will be darkened, the moon will no longer give its light, 25the stars will be falling from heaven and the powers of the heavenly spheres will be thrown off course. 26Then the coming of the Son of Man will be visible in the realm of the clouds, invested with power, illumined by the light of revelation of the world of spirit. 27And he will send out the angels to gather in all those who feel themselves united with him, from all four winds, from the ends of the earth to the ends of heaven.

28‘Learn from the parable of the fig tree: When the sap rises through its branches and it puts forth its leaves, then you see that

summer is near. 29So also, when you see these things coming about,
you shall be aware that the revelation of the Son of Man is near, at
the very door. 30Yes, I say to you: Even before the time of human
beings now living shall have come to an end, all this will begin.
31Heaven and earth will pass away, but my words will not pass away.
32No one knows anything about that day or that hour, not even the
angels in heaven, nor the Son, but only the Father.

33'Be observant and be awake; for you do not know when the
time will be. 34It is like when a man goes on a journey and leaves
his house. He gives his servants authority, gives each one his task
and tells the door-keeper to be alert. 35So you too be alert. You do
not know when the master of the house will come, whether in the
evening or at midnight or at cockcrow or in the morning. 36Take
care that he does not find you sleeping if he comes suddenly. 37And
what I say to you applies to all human beings: Be alert!'

14 *The anointing in Bethany and betrayal by Judas*

It was two days before the Passover and the feast of Unleavened
Bread. The high priests and the scribes were determined to get him
into their power by stealth and to kill him. 2For they said, 'It had
better not be during the feast, otherwise there will be an outcry
amongst the people.'

3And as he was sitting at table in Bethany as a guest in the house
of Simon the leper, a woman came with an alabaster phial of ointment of pure nard; she broke the phial and poured it over his head.
4Some of those present were indignant about it and said to themselves, 'Why this waste of the precious ointment? 5Could not this
ointment have been sold for more than three hundred denarii, and
the proceeds given to the poor?' And they turned on her angrily,
6but Jesus said, 'Leave her be! Why are you worrying her? She has
done a good deed for me. 7The poor you always have with you;
you can do good to them whenever you like. But me you do not
always have with you. 8She has given what she had. She has carried
out, before my burial, the anointing of my body. 9Yes, I say to you:
Wherever the new angelic word will be proclaimed, which is to

permeate the whole world, her deed will be spoken of and she will be remembered.'

10 And Judas Iscariot, one of the twelve, went to the chief priests to betray him to them. 11 When they realized what his intention was, they were delighted and promised him money. From now on he watched for an opportunity to betray him.

The Last Supper

12 And on the first day of the feast of Unleavened Bread, when it is the custom to slaughter the Passover lamb, his disciples asked him, 'Where shall we prepare the Passover meal for you?' 13 And he sent two of his disciples out and said to them, 'Go into the town. There a man carrying a jar of water will meet you. Follow him, 14 and where he enters, say to the head of the house, "The Master asks you, Where is the room set aside for me where I can celebrate the Passover meal with my disciples?" 15 And he will show you a large upper room which is furnished with cushions. There prepare everything for us.' 16 And the disciples set out, came to the town, and found everything as he had told them, and they prepared the Passover meal.

17 And when it was evening he came with the twelve. 18 And as they were sitting at table, eating, Jesus said, 'Yes, I say to you: One of you who is sharing the meal with me will betray me.' 19 Then they were very distressed and asked him one after the other, 'Is it I?' 20 And he said to them, 'It is one of the twelve. He who is dipping the morsel with me in the dish. 21 For the Son of Man must fulfil his destiny as it is described in scripture. But woe to the man by whom the Son of Man is betrayed. It would be better for him if he had never been born.'

22 And as they were eating, he took the bread, spoke the words of blessing and broke it and gave it to them and said, 'Take it, this is my body.' 23 And he took the cup, spoke the word of consecration and gave it to them; and they all drank of it. 24 And he said to them:

'This is my blood, the seal on the covenant with God; it is poured out for many. 25 Yes, I say to you: I will no longer drink of

the juice of the vine until the day comes when I shall drink of it in
a new way in the Kingdom of God.'

The prayer in Gethsemane and arrest

26And when they had sung the hymn they went out to the Mount of
Olives. 27And Jesus said to them, 'You will all stumble because of
me, for scripture says:

I will strike the shepherd, and the sheep will be scattered.

28But when I have risen I will go before you to Galilee.' 29Then
Peter said to him, 'Even if they all go astray, I will not.' 30But Jesus
said to him, 'Yes, I say to you: This very night, before the cock
crows for the second time, you will deny me three times.' 31But he
said all the more vehemently, 'Even if I have to die with you, I will
never deny you.' And all the others said the same.

32And they come into the garden which is called Gethsemane,
and he says to his disciples, 'Sit down here, while I go to pray.'
33And he takes Peter and James and John with him. Then he begins
to shudder, he is overtaken by profound weariness 34and he says,
'My soul is overshadowed by anguish even unto the abyss of
death. Stay here and remain watchful.' 35After a few steps he fell
to the ground, and he prayed that, if it were possible, he might last
through this hour, 36and he said, 'Abba, Father, everything is in
your power, take this cup from me; but let happen not what I will,
but what you will.' 37And he came and found them deeply asleep.
And he said to Peter, 'Simon, are you sleeping? Do you lack the
strength to be awake with me for even one hour? 38Be watchful
and pray, so that you are not overcome by temptation. The spirit
in Man has the intentions and the will, but the physical body is
weak.' 39And again he went away to pray. And he spoke the same
words. 40And again, when he came, he found them deeply asleep;
their eyes were very heavy and they did not know what to answer
him. 41And he came for the third time and said to them, 'You are
sleeping and are still inactive. Now it is here: The hour has come.
See, the Son of Man is betrayed into the hands of the enemies of
God. 42Stand up. Let us go! See, my betrayer is here.'

43And suddenly, while he was still speaking, Judas came up,
one of the twelve, in the midst of a whole crowd with swords
and clubs, sent by the chief priests and scribes and elders. 44The
betrayer had agreed with them on a sign: The one whom I shall
kiss is the man. Seize him and take him into custody. 45And all at
once he stepped forward and said: 'Master!' and kissed him. 46And
they laid hands on him and took him prisoner. 47But one of those
who stood by drew his sword and struck the servant of the High
Priest and cut off his ear. 48And Jesus said to them, 'You have
come out with swords and clubs as against a criminal to capture
me. 49Day after day I have been in the Temple with you, teaching,
and you did not touch me; but scripture had to be fulfilled.' 50Then
they all deserted him and fled.

51And there was a youth there who followed him. He was clad
only in a white linen cloth next to the skin. They tried to seize him,
52but he left the linen cloth behind and fled naked.

Accusation before the High Priest

53They led Jesus before the High Priest. All the chief priests and
elders and scribes assembled there. 54And Peter followed him at
a distance right into the courtyard of the High Priest. There he sat
with the servants and warmed himself at the fire.

55The chief priests and the whole assembly sought testimony
against Jesus, so that they could condemn him to death; but they
found none. 56However, many false witnesses appeared, but their
evidence did not tally. 57Eventually some others stood up to give
false evidence against him by saying, 58'We ourselves heard him
say: I will tear down this Temple built with hands and, in three
days, build another, not made with hands.' 59But not even in this
did the evidence tally.

60Then the High Priest stood up, stepped into their midst and
asked Jesus, 'Have you no answer to what these men are saying
against you?' 61But he was silent and answered not a word. Then
the High Priest asked him again, 'Are you the Christ, the Son of
the One we worship?' 62And Jesus said, 'I am; and you will see the

Son of Man sitting on the throne at the right hand of the Might of the World, coming with the clouds of heaven.'

[63]Then the High Priest tore his garment and said, 'Do we need further witnesses? [64]You have heard the blasphemy. What is your opinion?' And they all declared him guilty and condemned him to death. [65]Some began to spit on him and to cover his face and to strike him, and then they said, 'Now show us if you can prophesy.' And the guards struck him in the face.

Peter's denial

[66]Peter was below in the courtyard. Then one of the maids of the High Priest comes by, [67]and, when she sees Peter who is warming himself by the fire, she looks him in the face and says, 'You were also with that Nazarene, Jesus.' [68]But he denied it and said, 'I do not know him, and I don't understand what you mean.' And he went out into the forecourt. At that moment the cock crowed. [69]And again the maid saw him, and said to the bystanders, 'He is one of them.' [70]But he denied it again. And after a little while, the bystanders said to Peter, 'You are definitely one of them, for you are a Galilean.' [71]And with cursing and swearing he insisted: 'I do not know the man you are talking about.' [72]And at that moment, the cock crowed for the second time. Then Peter remembered the word that Jesus had spoken to him: 'Before the cock crows for the second time, you will deny me three times.' And he burst into tears.

15 *Interrogation before Pilate*

The moment day broke, the chief priests conferred with the elders, the scribes and the whole Sanhedrin. Then they led Jesus away fettered and handed him over to Pilate. [2]Pilate asked him, 'Are you the King of the Jews?' He answered, '*You* say it.' [3]And the chief priests brought serious charges against him. [4]Then Pilate asked him again, 'Have you no answer to make? Do you hear the accusations they are making against you?' [5]But Jesus did not answer any more, so that Pilate was surprised.

[6]Every year, for this festival, he used to release to the people

a prisoner, whichever one they asked for. [7]At that time there was a prisoner called Barabbas. He had taken part in a rebellion and in a murder which the rebels had committed. [8]And the people came up and demanded that also this time he should do what he usually did. [9]Pilate said to them, ‘Do you want me to release for you the King of the Jews?’ [10]For he was well aware that it was out of envy that the chief priests had handed him over. [11]But the chief priests stirred up the crowd to have him release Barabbas to them instead. [12]Then Pilate turned to the people once more and said, ‘Then what shall I do with the one whom you call the King of the Jews?’ [13]And they yelled: ‘Crucify him!’ [14]And Pilate said, ‘But what crime has he committed?’ But they only shouted even louder: ‘Crucify him!’ [15]So in the end Pilate decided to do their will, and he released Barabbas for them. And he ordered that Jesus be scourged and taken to be crucified.

Crowning with thorns

[16]The soldiers took him inside the hall which is called the praetorium and they called the whole cohort together. [17]Then they dressed him in a purple cloak and plaited a crown of thorns and put it on him. [18]Then they began to make obeisance to him: ‘Greetings, King of the Jews!’ [19]And they struck him over the head with a reed and spat on him and kneeled before him as though they wanted to worship him. [20]And after they had mocked him in this way, they stripped him of the purple cloak and put his own clothes on him again.

Then they led him out to crucify him. [21]And they forced a passer-by, Simon of Cyrene who was coming home from the field, the father of Alexander and Rufus, to carry his cross.

The Crucifixion

[22]And they led him to the place called Golgotha (translated, that means: Place of the skull), [23]and they offered him wine mixed with myrrh, but he did not take it.

[24]And they crucified him and divided his garments, having

decided the share for each one by casting lots. [25]It was the third
hour when they crucified him. [26]The inscription which was to
declare the charge against him read: THE KING OF THE JEWS.
[27]And with him they crucified two criminals, one on his right,
and one on his left.

[29]And those who went past hurled hate-filled words at him. They
shook their heads and said, 'Bah – so you are the one who was
going to tear down the Temple and build it again in three days!
[30]Why don't you help yourself and come down from the cross?'
[31]And the chief priests mocked him likewise by saying to each other
and to the scribes, 'He healed others, but he can't heal himself.
[32]You, Christ, King of Israel, why don't you come down from the
cross so that we may see it, revere you and believe in you!' And
those who were crucified with him also mocked him.

The hour of death

[33]And when the sixth hour had come, deep darkness descended
upon the whole earth until the ninth hour. [34]And in the ninth hour
Jesus called out with a loud voice: 'Eloi, Eloi, lama sabachthani?'
Translated that means: My God, my God, why are you leaving me?
[35]And some of those who were standing there and heard it said, 'See,
he is calling Elijah.' [36]Then one of them ran and filled a sponge with
vinegar, put it on a reed and gave him to drink and said, 'Wait, let
us see if Elijah will come to take him down.' [37]And Jesus uttered a
loud cry and breathed out his spirit.

[38]And the curtain of the Temple was torn in two from above
down.

[39]And when the centurion who stood facing him saw him die
he said, 'This man really was the Son of God.' [40]There were also
women looking on from a distance, among them Mary of Magdala
and Mary the mother of James the younger and of Joses, and
Salome, [41]who had followed him and served him when he was
still in Galilee, and also many others who had wandered with him
up to Jerusalem.

The burial
42When it was already late in the day – it was the Day of Preparation,
the day before the Sabbath – 43Joseph of Arimathea, a respected
member of the council, who also lived in the expectation of the
coming of the Kingdom of God, took courage and went in to Pilate
and asked for the body of Jesus. 44Pilate was surprised that he could
be dead so soon, and he summoned the centurion and asked him if
he had already been dead a long time. 45And when he had heard the
centurion's report, he granted the body to Joseph. 46And he bought
linen and took him from the cross, wrapped him in the linen and laid
him in a tomb which had been hewed out of the rock; and he rolled a
stone against the entrance to the tomb. 47And Mary Magdalene and
Mary the mother of Joses saw where he laid him.

16 *The Resurrection*
And when the Sabbath was over, Mary Magdalene, Mary the mother
of James, and Salome bought aromatic spices and took them to the
tomb to anoint him.

2And at dawn on the first day of the week they came to the tomb,
just as the sun was rising. 3And they said to one another, 'Who will
roll away the stone for us from the entrance to the tomb?' 4And as
they looked up, they saw that it had been rolled back; and the stone
was very large.

5And they went into the tomb. There they saw a young man
sitting on the right side, clad in a shining white garment. And they
were beside themselves with amazement. 6Then he said to them,
'Do not be startled! You seek Jesus of Nazareth, the crucified one.
He is risen and is not here. See, there is the place where they laid
his body. 7Now go and say to his disciples and to Peter: "He will
lead you to Galilee." There you will see him as he promised you.'

8And they fled from the tomb in great haste, for they were trembling with agitation, and their souls were as if transported, and,
being awestruck, they were unable to say anything to anyone about
what they had experienced.

The appearance of the Risen One

[9]When he had risen, early on the first day of the week, he appeared first to Mary of Magdala, from whom he had driven out seven demons. [10]And she went and proclaimed it to those who had walked with him and who were now sunk in tears and lamenting. [11]When they heard: He lives and she has seen him, their hearts could not grasp it. [12]After this he revealed himself, transformed in appearance, to two of them on the way as they were walking over the fields. [13]And they came and proclaimed it to the others; but they could not open their hearts to their words either.

[14]Finally he appeared to the eleven themselves as they were celebrating the meal. And he reprimanded them for their lack of openness and for their hardness of heart, because they had not wanted to believe those who had seen him, the Risen One.

[15]And he said to them, 'Go out into all the world and proclaim the new message from the realms of the angels to all creation. [16]Whoever unites his heart with it and receives the baptism will attain to the salvation. But whoever closes himself against it will meet his downfall. [17]Spiritual powers will stand by those who unite themselves with it and will attend their path. Through the power of my Being they will drive out demons, they will speak in new languages; [18]they will raise up serpents, and poisons which they are given to drink will not harm them; they will lay their hands on the sick and give healing forces to them.'

[19]And when Jesus, the Lord, had thus spoken to them, his Being grew wide, expanding into the spheres of the heavens, where he sits on the throne at the right hand of God, as the fulfiller of HIS deeds. [20]And the disciples went forth and proclaimed the message everywhere, and the Lord worked with them and gave weight to their words by the revelations of spiritual power which attended their way.

The Gospel of Luke

1 *Introduction*

Many have already set themselves the task of describing in the right sequence and stages the events which have been fulfilled among us. 2The tidings have been passed on to us from those who, from the very beginning, have become self-seers and servants of the Word. 3And so I, too, must write down in the right order what has shown itself to me, now that I have carefully and exactly trodden the steps of the path from its beginning. I do this for you, honoured Friend of God: 4By your own insight may you now win through to certainty in all that you have come to know through the teaching you have received.

Annunciation to Zechariah

5It was at the time when Herod was king of Judea. There was a certain priest named Zechariah who served as a member of the division of Abijah. His wife was of the daughters of Aaron and was called Elizabeth. 6They were both devoted to the Good; the eye of the spiritual world rested upon them, and with pure souls they walked in the ways of God. 7They had no child, because Elizabeth was barren, and both were advanced in years.

8Now when it was his turn in the division to serve at the altar before the countenance of God, 9it fell to him by lot, according to the priestly custom, to enter and offer incense in the Temple of the Lord; 10meanwhile, the whole multitude of the people were praying outside at the hour of the censing.

11Then he saw the angel of the Lord standing at the right side of the altar where the smoke was rising. 12And Zechariah was alarmed at the sight; the nearness of the Spirit bore

fearfully on his soul. [13]But the angel said to him, 'Do not be
afraid, Zechariah, for your prayer has been heard; your wife
Elizabeth will bear you a son, and you shall call him John.
[14]You will be filled with joy and gladness; many will rejoice
because of his birth. [15]Great will he be in the sight of the Lord.
He will drink no wine nor anything intoxicating, and even from
his mother's womb will he be filled with the Holy Spirit. [16]He
will turn many sons of the people of God to the Lord their
God again. [17]He will be his forerunner and will pave his way,
bearing within him the spirit and the power of Elijah, to change
men's hearts so that fathers shall rediscover the meaning of
childhood, and those who have become alienated from God
shall find the meaning of the Good again. So shall he make a
well-prepared people ready for the Lord.'

[18]And Zechariah said to the angel, 'How can I understand this;
I am old, and my wife is also advanced in years?' [19]The angel said,
'I am Gabriel, who stand before the countenance of God. I was sent
to speak to you and to proclaim this message of salvation to you.
[20]See, you will be silent and unable to speak until the day when
these things shall be fulfilled, because you do not trust in my words
which will be fulfilled in their time.'

[21]The people stood outside and waited for Zechariah and wondered at how long he stayed in the Temple. [22]But when he came out
he was unable to speak, and they realized that he had seen a vision
in the Temple. He could only communicate with them through
signs; his mouth remained dumb.

[23]And when his days of priestly service were over, he went to his
home. [24]After these days his wife Elizabeth conceived, and she hid
herself for five months and said, [25]'What a great wonder the Lord
has done for me in these days! HIS eye rests upon me, and HE takes
away my shame before men.'

Annunciation to Mary

[26]In the sixth month the angel Gabriel was sent from God to a town
in Galilee called Nazareth, [27]to a maiden who was betrothed to a

man named Joseph, of the house of David; and the maiden's name
was Mary.

[28]The angel came to her and said, 'Hail, O blessed one, the Lord
HIMSELF is with you. Graced are you among all women!' [29]Mary was
filled with consternation by these words. How was she to understand this greeting? [30]Then the angel said to her, 'Have no fear,
Mary. Full of grace, the Spirit of God is coming upon you. [31]See,
you will conceive in your body and bear a son. You shall give him
the name Jesus. [32]He will be great, he will be called the Son of the
Highest God. The Lord God will give him the throne of his father
David, [33]so that he will be the eternal king of the house of Jacob,
and his kingdom will be without end.'

[34]Then Mary said to the angel, 'How will this be, since I have
never known a man?'

[35]The angel said, 'Holy Spirit will come upon you; the power
of the Highest God will overshadow you, and the holy being to
be born of you will be called Son of God. [36]And see, Elizabeth
who is related to you, in spite of her age she also has conceived
a son. She is carrying him now in the sixth month, although
she is regarded as barren. [37]No word is spoken in the worlds
of spirit which does not have the power to become reality on
earth.'

[38]Then Mary said, 'See, I am the handmaid of the Lord. May
your word be fulfilled upon me.' And the angel departed from
her.

Meeting of Mary and Elizabeth

[39]In those days Mary set out and went with haste into the hill
country, to a town in Judea. [40]And she came to the house of
Zechariah and greeted Elizabeth. [41]And when Elizabeth heard
the greeting of Mary, the babe leaped in her womb. And the Holy
Spirit filled Elizabeth [42]and she spoke with solemn and mighty
words:

> Blessed are you among all women, blessed is the fruit of
> your body.

[43]How is it that I am so highly honoured that the mother of my Lord should come to me?
[44]For see, when my ear heard the sound of your greeting, the babe leaped for joy in my womb.
[45]Blessed is she who has trust that the divine promise spoken to her will be fulfilled.
[46]And Mary said:
My soul grows great in praising you, O Lord of life.
[47]My spirit rejoices before you, O bringer of healing.
[48]You have turned your gaze upon me, your lowliest maid.
See, all future generations shall call me blessed.
[49]HIS power lives in me, HE has made me great, holy is HIS name.
[50]HIS goodness flows through all generations of mankind,
and it reaches those who feel HIS greatness.
[51]HIS arm has done great deeds;
HE has scattered those who thought themselves the greatest in their proud hearts.
[52]HE has overthrown the mighty from their thrones,
HE has raised up those of lowly birth.
[53]HE fills the hungry with good things and sends the rich empty away.
[54]HE has turned again to HIS child Israel.
Goodness springs new in HIS heart,
[55]as once HE spoke to our fathers, to Abraham and his descendants.
HE bears us through all ages of the earth.

[56]And Mary stayed with her for three months. Then she returned to her home.

The birth of John

[57]Now the time was fulfilled for Elizabeth to give birth, and she
bore a son. [58]And when her neighbours and relations heard how
great a good fortune the Lord had granted her, they all rejoiced with
her. [59]And on the eighth day they came for the rite of circumcision

of the child, and they wanted to call him Zechariah, his father's
name. 60But his mother said, 'No, he is to be called John.' 61And
they replied, 'There is no one among your relations who is called
by that name.' 62Then they made signs to his father and asked what
he wanted him to be called. 63And he asked for a writing tablet and
wrote on it: John is his name. And they were all amazed. 64At that
moment his mouth was opened, his tongue was loosed and he began
to praise God. 65All the neighbours were filled with great inner tur-
moil, and these events were spoken of throughout the mountainous
region of Judea. 66All who heard of it pondered the question in their
hearts: What will this child become? And the hand of the Lord was
with him.

Zechariah's song of praise

67And his father Zechariah began to speak prophetically, filled with
the Holy Spirit:

68All praise be to God, the guiding lord of HIS people,
Israel.
With a mild gaze HE has turned towards HIS people,
HE brings them redemption.
69HE has raised up for us a cornucopia of salvation
in the house of HIS son David,
70and thus is fulfilled what HE said through all ages
by the mouth of HIS holy prophets:
71Redeemed shall we be from the powers of the enemy,
and we shall be set free from the tyranny of the powers of
hate.
72The heritage of the fathers shall not die,
it shall be protected by the grace of God.
The meaning of the holy covenant with God is renewed in
spirit,
73the oath which once HE swore to our father Abraham:
74Freed from all fear, delivered from all powers of
enmity,

our whole lives shall, from now on, be only service
before the countenance of God,
75with purity of soul and with a truthful heart.
76You, child, will be called the herald of God Most High.
You go before HIS countenance to prepare the ways for
HIM.
77You bring knowledge of salvation to HIS people,
you show them the power which heals all sickness of
sin:
78the depths of mercy of our God bestowing upon us
a new dawn from the heights.
79A bright light shines for the souls in the darkness
of the realm of the shadow of death.
May this light guide our feet and lead us on the path of
peace.

80And the child grew and became strong in spirit and lived in the
loneliness of the desert until the day when he appeared before the
people of Israel.

2 *The birth of Jesus*

In those days a proclamation went out from Caesar Augustus that
a census of the people should be taken over the whole earth. 2It
was the first time that such a census had taken place. It came at the
time when Quirinius was governor of the province of Syria. 3And
everyone set out to be enrolled, each to his ancestral town.

4And so Joseph also set off from Nazareth in Galilee to Judea,
to the town of David which is called Bethlehem; for he was of the
house and lineage of David. 5He went to be enrolled together with
Mary, his betrothed. And Mary was with child. 6When they came
to their destination, the time was fulfilled for her to be delivered,
7and she gave birth to a son, her first-born, and she swaddled him
in linen and laid him in a manger, because there was no place for
them in the inn.

8And in that neighbourhood there were shepherds in the field.
They guarded and protected their flocks through the night. 9All at

once, the angel of the Lord stood before them, and the light of the revelation of God shone about them. Great fear came upon them, [10]but the angel said, 'Have no fear. See, I proclaim a great joy to you, which shall be for all mankind. [11]Today the bringer of healing is born to you in the town of David: Christ, the Lord. [12]And this is the sign by which you will know him: You will find a child swaddled in linen, lying in a manger.'

[13]And suddenly the fullness of the heavenly, angelic choirs was around the angel; their song of praise sounded forth to the Highest God:

> [14]God be revealed in the heights
> and peace on earth
> to men of good will.

[15]And as the angels withdrew from them, entering again into the heavenly spheres, the shepherds said to one another, 'Let us go to Bethlehem to see the fulfilment of the word which the Lord has made known to us.' [16]And they went with haste and found Mary and Joseph and the babe which was lying in the manger. [17]And when they saw it they made known what they had been told about the child. [18]And all who heard it were astonished at the words of the shepherds. [19]But Mary kept these words safe and contemplated them in her heart. [20]And the shepherds returned home; heavenly light shone forth from the words with which they praised God, the Ground of the World, for all that they had heard and seen. What they had been told had really been fulfilled.

[21]After eight days it was time for the circumcision of the child, and he was given the name Jesus according to the words of the angel, spoken before his conception.

Presentation in the Temple

[22]Then came the days of purification as prescribed by the Law of Moses. And the parents brought the child to Jerusalem to consecrate him to the Lord, [23]because the Law says:

> Every first-born male shall be considered consecrated to God.

[24]They also had to make the gifts of offering decreed by the
Law:

A pair of turtledoves, or two young pigeons.

Simeon and Anna

[25]And see, there was in Jerusalem a man named Simeon. He was
devout, entirely dedicated to the Good, and lived in expectation of
him who was to bring the consolation of the Spirit to the people of
God. The Holy Spirit was upon him, [26]and through the power of
the Holy Spirit it had been revealed to him that he would not die
before he had seen Christ, the Lord. [27]Inspired by the Spirit he went
into the Temple, just as the parents brought in the child to fulfil the
custom of the Law. [28]And he took the child in his arms, praising the
divine Ground of the World, and said:

[29]Now, you let your servant depart in peace, O Master,
according to your word.
[30]For now my eyes have seen your healing deed
[31]which you have prepared before all peoples:
[32]A light which leads the peoples of the world to revelation
and makes your own people shine in the spirit.

[33]And his father and mother were amazed that such words were
spoken about him. [34]And Simeon blessed them and said to Mary,
his mother:

See, he will cause the fall of many among his people,
but he will also let them rise again.
He is a being who will call up dissent;
[35]a sword will pierce your soul, too.
Through him the thoughts and ponderings of many hearts
will be revealed.

[36]There was also a prophetess, Anna, a daughter of Phanuel of
the tribe of Asher. She was of great age. After her girlhood she had
lived seven years with her husband, [37]and, now a widow, she was
eighty-four. She never left the Temple and served day and night
with inner work on her soul and with prayer. [38]In that hour she also
came and offered up her thanks to the heavenly world; and she

spoke of the child to all in Jerusalem who lived in expectation of
the salvation.

[39]And when they had completed everything that the Law of
the Lord demands, they returned home to Galilee, to their town
Nazareth. [40]And the child grew, maturing in his spirit-filled soul;
divine grace was upon him.

The twelve-year-old Jesus in the Temple

[41]Every year his parents went to Jerusalem for the feast of the
Passover. [42]And when he was twelve years old they took him with
them. [43]Now when they had gone there and had fulfilled the custom
of the Law during the days of the feast, they set off on their way
home; but the boy Jesus stayed behind in Jerusalem. His parents
did not know this; [44]they thought he was among the company of
travellers. After a day's journey they missed him and looked for
him among their friends and relations. [45]As they did not find him,
they returned to Jerusalem to look for him there. [46]And after three
days they found him in the Temple. He was sitting in the midst of
the teachers, listening to them and asking them questions. [47]And
those who heard him did not know what to think about the mature
understanding revealed in his answers. [48]And when they saw him
they were taken aback, and his mother said to him, 'My child, why
have you done this to us? See, your father and I have been looking
for you anxiously.' [49]And he said to them, 'Why did you look for
me? Do you not know that I must be in my Father's house?' [50]And
they did not understand what he said to them. [51]And he went down
with them and came again to Nazareth and was guided willingly by
them in all things. And his mother kept all words in her heart with
care. [52]And Jesus progressed in wisdom, in maturity and in grace in
the sight of God and men.

3 *John the Baptist*

It was in the fifteenth year of the reign of Tiberius Caesar; Pontius
Pilate was governor of Judea, Herod was tetrarch of Galilee, his
brother Philip tetrarch of Ituraea and Trachonitis, and Lysanias

tetrarch of Abilene. 2Annas and Caiaphas were High Priests. Now the word of God came to John the son of Zechariah in the loneliness of the desert.

3And he wandered through the whole country by the Jordan and called upon men to be baptized to change their hearts and minds and to become free of their sins. 4And thus was fulfilled what is written in the book of the prophet Isaiah:

> The voice of one calling in the loneliness says:
> Prepare the way of the Lord,
> make his paths straight.
> 5Fill every valley
> and level all mountains and hills;
> let all that is crooked be made straight;
> let every steep incline be made into level road.
> 6Then all earthly beings shall behold the healing deed of God.

7Great crowds went out to be baptized by John. And he said to them, 'You are sons of the serpent yet. Who has led you to believe that you can avoid the decline of the old ways of the soul? 8Let your endeavour be to produce true fruits of the change of mind and heart. Do not look for excuses by saying to yourselves: We have Abraham as our father. I say to you: The Father in heaven can just as well raise up sons of Abraham from these dead stones. 9Already the axe is laid to the root of the trees, and every tree that does not bear good fruit is felled and thrown into the fire.'

10And the crowd asked him, 'What shall we do?' 11And he answered, 'Let him who has two garments share with him who has none, and let him who has food act similarly.' 12And tax-collectors also came to him to be baptized, and they said, 'Master, what shall we do?' 13He said, 'Keep strictly to what you have been authorized to do; do not go beyond that.' 14And soldiers also asked him, 'And what shall *we* do?' And he said, 'Avoid looting and every kind of unnecessary violence, and be content with your wages.'

15The people were full of keen expectation, and all questioned

in their hearts whether perhaps John might be the Christ. 16 But John
said to them all, 'I baptize you with water; but One is coming who
is mightier than I, and I am too insignificant even to untie the strap
of his shoes. He will baptize you with the Holy Spirit and with
fire. 17 Already he has the winnowing fork in his hand to clear his
threshing floor. He will gather the wheat into his barn, but the chaff
he will burn in a fire that is never quenched.'

18 And many other admonishing words did he speak as a messenger of the spirit. 19 But eventually it happened that Herod the
tetrarch, who had been reproved by him because of Herodias, his
brother's wife, and because of all the other evil things that Herod
had done, 20 now added this to them all, that he locked John up in
prison.

Baptism and genealogy of Jesus

21 While John still worked as Baptist among the people, Jesus also
was baptized. While he prayed, the heavens were opened, 22 and the
Holy Spirit descended upon him, formed like the bodily image of a
dove. And a voice sounded out of the heavenly heights: You are my
beloved Son, in you will I reveal myself.

23 At this moment of new beginnings, Jesus was thirty years old.
He was, so thought everyone, a son of Joseph,

> of Heli, 24 of Matthat, of Levi,
> of Melchi, of Jannai, of Joseph,
> 25 of Mattathias, of Amos, of Nahum,
> of Esli, of Naggai, 26 of Maath,
> of Mattathias, of Semein, of Josech,
> of Joda, 27 of Joanan, of Rhesa,
> of Zerubbabel, of Shealtiel, of Neri,
> 28 of Melchi, of Addi, of Cosam,
> of Elmadam, of Er, 29 of Jesus,
> of Eliezer, of Jorim, of Matthat,
> of Levi, 30 of Simeon, of Judas,
> of Joseph, of Jonam, of Eliakim,
> 31 of Melea, of Menna, of Mattatha,

of Nathan, of David, [32]of Jesse,
of Obed, of Boaz, of Sala,
of Nahshon, [33]of Amminadab, of Admin,
of Arni, of Hezron, of Perez,
of Judas, [34]of Jacob, of Isaac,
of Abraham, of Terah, of Nahor,
[35]of Serug, of Reu, of Peleg,
of Eber, of Shelah, [36]of Cainan,
of Arphaxad, of Shem, of Noah,
of Lamech, [37]of Methusela, of Enoch,
of Jared, of Mahalaleel, of Cainan,
[38]of Enos, of Seth, of Adam
who was of God.

4 *The Temptation*
And Jesus left the Jordan valley, his soul filled with the Holy Spirit.
And he followed the guidance of the Spirit into the loneliness of the
desert. [2]There he remained for forty days, during which he had to
withstand the temptation by the Adversary.

During this time he took no food at all, and when the days came
to an end he felt hunger. [3]Then the Adversary said to him, 'If you
are the Son of God, speak to this stone so that it becomes bread.'
[4]But Jesus answered him, 'Scripture says:

Man does not live by bread alone.'

[5]And the Adversary led him up, showed him all realms of the
world in one single moment, [6]and said to him, 'I will give you
power over everything that you see, the earthly and even the forces
beyond the earthly. For the power belongs to me, and I can give it to
whom I will. [7]If you will kneel in worship of me, the whole world
shall be yours.' [8]But Jesus replied, 'Scripture says:

Let all your worship be for the divine Lord,
let your service be for HIM alone.'

[9]Then he removed him to Jerusalem and set him on the parapet
of the Temple and said to him, 'If you are the Son of God, throw
yourself down from here. [10]For it says in the scriptures that HE has

commanded HIS angels to protect you 11and bear you up on their
hands so that not even your foot shall strike against a stone.' 12But
Jesus answered him, 'Yet it also says:

> You shall not make your heavenly Lord become a
> servant of your arbitrary wishes.'

13And when the Adversary had put him through all temptation,
he departed from him to bide his time.

Teaching in the synagogues and rejection in Nazareth

14And Jesus, empowered by the Spirit, returned to Galilee. His fame
spread through the whole region. 15He appeared as teacher in the
synagogues, and everyone praised his spirit.

16And he came to Nazareth where he had spent his childhood.
And here, too, he went to the synagogue on the Sabbath day, as was
his custom. And when he stood up to read aloud, 17he was handed
the book of the prophet Isaiah. He opened it and found the place
where it says:

> 18The Spirit of the Lord is upon me.
> He anoints me to bring the message of the spirit to the poor;
> he sends me to proclaim liberation to the captives
> and new sight to all the blind.
> I am to lead on the way of salvation those who have been crushed;
> 19I am to proclaim a new world-hour
> in which we shall come to know the grace of God.

20When he had closed the book he gave it to the attendant and sat
down. The eyes of all in the synagogue were fixed on him. 21Then
he began to speak: 'Today this word of scripture is fulfilled in your
hearing.' 22And everyone approved of him, and they were full of
wonder at the spiritual grace of his words. But at the same time they
asked themselves, 'Is this not Joseph's son?' 23And he said to them,
'You will respond to me with the proverb:

> Physician, first heal yourself.

The deeds which we hear you have done in Capernaum, do

here also in your home town.' [24]And he said, 'Yes, I tell you, no prophet is accepted in his home town. [25]It is the truth I tell you: At the time of Elijah, when the sky was closed up for three and a half years and there was a great famine in all the earth, there were many widows in Israel; [26]and yet Elijah was sent to none of them. Rather, he was sent to the widow of Zarephath in the land of Sidon. [27]And there were also many lepers in Israel at the time of the prophet Elisha, and none of them was healed; only Naaman the Syrian.'

[28]At these words, all in the synagogue became furious. [29]They sprang up, pushed him out of the town and led him to the brow of the hill on which their town was built. They wanted to throw him over the precipice, [30]but he went through the midst of their ranks and disappeared.

First healing: Healing a man possessed by a demon

[31]And he went down to Capernaum, the Galilean town. And there, too, he taught on the Sabbath. [32]And the people were beside themselves because of his teaching, for his word worked with spiritual power. [33]In the synagogue there was also a man who was possessed by an unclean demon; it cried out with a loud voice: [34]'What is it that binds us to you, Jesus of Nazareth? Have you come to destroy us? I know who you are: You are the Holy One of God!' [35]Jesus raised his arm against it and said, 'Be silent and leave him!' Then the demon threw the man to the floor in their midst and departed from him without harming him. [36]Thcy were all amazed and said to one another, 'What powerful words! He speaks with such command to the unclean spirits that they must give way to him, as though all creative power and the might of worlds were in him.' [37]And reports of him spread through the whole surrounding countryside.

Peter's mother-in-law

[38]And he set off, leaving the synagogue, and entered Simon's house. Simon's mother-in-law was suffering from a high fever, and they

asked him to help her. 39And he went and stood by the head of her
bed and commanded the fever to cease, and she was freed of it. At
once she arose to serve them.

40And while the sun was setting, many people came to him.
They brought the sick who were suffering from all kinds of disease.
And he laid his hands on each one and healed them all. 41Demons
departed from many and cried out, 'You are the Son of God!' But
he raised his arm against them and ordered them not to say that they
had recognized the Christ in him.

42And when it was day again he went out and came to a lonely
place. But the crowd looked for him, and when they found him
they clung to him and would not let him go again. 43Then he said to
them, 'I must also take the message of the Kingdom of God to the
other towns, for that is why I was sent.' 44And he preached in the
synagogues in all of Galilee.

5 *The first disciples; Peter fishing*

Once the crowd was pressing him hard, wanting to hear the word of
God from him. He was standing on the shore of Lake Gennesaret.
2Then he saw two boats on the beach; the fishermen had got out
and were washing their nets. 3And he stepped into one of the boats
which belonged to Simon, and asked him to row a little distance out
from the shore.

And he sat down and spoke to the crowd from the boat and
taught them. 4Then he stopped speaking and said to Simon, 'Put
out into the deep and let down your nets there for a catch.' 5Simon
answered, 'Master, we worked all night and caught nothing; but
because you say so I will cast the nets.' 6And when they did this
they caught a great shoal of fish, so that their nets were being torn.
7And they beckoned to their partners in the other boat to come and
help them. And they came, and so they filled both boats which
almost sank under the weight. 8When Simon Peter saw this, he fell
on his knees before Jesus and said, 'Lord, depart from me, I am a
sinful man.' 9For great alarm had overwhelmed him and also the
others who were with him, because of the catch of fish which they

had made. [10]James and John, the sons of Zebedee, who were
partners with Simon, had the same experience. And Jesus said
to Simon, 'Do not be afraid, from now on you will be a fisher of
living men.' [11]And they brought the boats to land, left everything
and followed him.

Healing a leper

[12]Once when he came to one of the towns he was met by a man who
was completely covered in leprosy. When he saw Jesus he fell on
his face and implored him: 'Lord, you can heal me if you only will.'
[13]Then he stretched out his hand, touched him and said, 'I will; be
clean!' And at once the leprosy left him. [14]But he commanded him
to say nothing to anyone about it. Instead, he said to him, 'Go and
show yourself to the priest and make the offering which the Law of
Moses prescribes for your healing, as a proof to them.'

[15]Reports of him spread ever further, and great crowds flocked
together to hear him and to be healed of their infirmities through
him. [16]But he withdrew to lonely places and was absorbed in
prayer.

[17]One day he was teaching, and among the listeners were also
Pharisees and experts in the Law who had come from all the villages of Galilee and Judea and from Jerusalem. The mighty power
of the Lord HIMSELF worked through him and enabled him to heal.

Healing a paralysed man

[18]And see, some men brought on a stretcher a person who was
paralysed. They tried to carry him into the house to place him
before him. [19]But, since they could not bring him in through the
dense crowd, they went up on the roof and lowered him and the
stretcher down between the tiles so that he came to rest in the
middle, in front of Jesus. [20]When he saw their deep trust he said,
'Man – the burden of sin is taken from you.' [21]Then the scribes
and the Pharisees began to say to themselves, 'Who is this man
who dares to speak such blasphemy? Who can forgive sins but
the one and only God?' [22]But Jesus perceived their thoughts and

said to them, 'What thoughts are these, stirring in your hearts?
[23]Which is easier to say: You are freed from your sins, or: Stand
up and walk? [24]But you shall see that the Son of Man has the
power to release Man from sin here on the earth.' And so he said
to the paralysed man, 'I say to you, stand up, take your stretcher
and go home.' [25]And at once he stood up in the sight of them
all, took the pallet on which he had been lying and went home,
praising God. [26]And an ecstasy came over them all. They praised
God and, deeply moved, they said, 'Today we have seen a great
wonder.'

The call to Levi (Matthew); the banquet in his house

[27]As he went on after this he saw a tax-collector called Levi sitting
at his tax office. And he said to him, 'Follow me!' [28]And he left
everything, got up and followed him. [29]And at his house Levi prepared a great banquet in his honour, and many tax-collectors and
others were sitting at table together. [30]Then the Pharisees and the
scribes in that district said accusingly to his disciples, 'How can
you eat and drink with tax-collectors and sinners?' [31]And Jesus
said to them, 'Healthy people do not need a physician, but the
sick do. [32]I have not come to call upon the righteous to change
their hearts and minds, but rather those who are suffering from the
burden of sin.'

About fasting and keeping the Sabbath holy

[33]Then they said to him, 'The disciples of John practise all kinds
of asceticism and say many prayers, and so do the pupils of the
Pharisees. Your disciples, however, eat and drink.' [34]Jesus answered,
'Surely the wedding guests should not fast as long as the bridegroom
is in their midst. [35]But the days will come when the bridegroom will
be taken from them; then let them turn to fasting.' [36]And he told
them a parable, 'No one cuts a piece out of a new garment to use it
as a patch on an old garment. He would only ruin the new garment,
and the piece from the new would not match the old. [37]Nor would
anyone pour new wine into old wineskins; the new wine would

only ruin them. The wine would spill out, nor could anyone use the
wineskins any more. [38]New wine belongs in new wineskins. [39]But
whoever is used to drinking old wine does not want the new, and he
says: The old wine is milder.'
6 Once he was walking through the cornfields on a Sabbath; his
disciples plucked some ears and ate the grain which they had rubbed
loose with their hands. [2]Then some of the Pharisees said, 'Why are
you doing something which is not allowed on the Sabbath?' [3]And
Jesus answered, 'Have you not read what David did when he and
his companions were hungry? [4]How he entered the house of God
and took the altar bread and ate of it and also gave some to his
companions, although no one except the priests are allowed to eat
it?' [5]And he said to them, 'The Son of Man is Lord of the Sabbath.'
[6]On another Sabbath he entered the synagogue and taught. There
was a man there whose right hand was withered. [7]And the scribes
and Pharisees watched him intently to see if he would heal on the
Sabbath, for they were looking for a reason to accuse him. [8]But
he saw their thoughts and said to the man with the withered hand,
'Get up, and stand in the middle!' And he stood up and stepped
forward. [9]And Jesus said to them, 'I ask you, what is permitted on
the Sabbath? To do good or do harm, to save life or to destroy it?'
[10]And he looked round at each one of them. Then he said to the man:
'Stretch out your hand!' He did so, and his hand was healthy once
more. [11]Then their fury knew no bounds, and they discussed among
themselves what action they should take against Jesus.

Calling the disciples

[12]In those days he went onto the mountain to pray. He spent the
whole night in prayer, turned towards God. [13]And when day came
he called his disciples to him and chose from them twelve and called
them apostles: [14]Simon, whom he named Peter, and Andrew his
brother, James and John, Philip, and Bartholomew, [15]and Matthew,
and Thomas, and James the son of Alphaeus, and Simon who was
called the Zealot, [16]and Judas the son of James, and Judas Iscariot
who later became a traitor.

The Sermon on the Plain

17Then he came down with them until he was standing on a level
place. A great number of his disciples surrounded him, together
with a large crowd from the whole of Judea and Jerusalem and from
the coastal regions of Tyre and Sidon who had come to hear him
and to be healed of their diseases. 18Those who were plagued by
unclean spirits were also cured. 19And the whole crowd yearned to
touch him because living power radiated from him, and he healed
them all.

20Then he turned his gaze upon his disciples and said:

'Blessed are you, the poor; the Kingdom of God is within
you.

21'Blessed are you, you who are hungry now; you shall be satisfied.

'Blessed are you, you who are weeping now; you shall have
laughter.

22'Blessed are you, you who are hated, shunned and reviled by
men, whose names are despised as being nothing but evil, if you
suffer this for the sake of the Son of Man. 23You can be joyful and
dance for happiness, for see, you shall be richly compensated in the
world of spirit. Their fathers treated the prophets in just the same
way.

24'But woe to you, the rich; for you have forfeited your comfort
of the spirit.

25'Woe to you, you who are satisfied now; for you shall become
hungry.

'Woe to you, you who are laughing now; for you shall become
sad and weeping.

26'Woe to you, when all men speak pleasing words to you; that
is what their fathers also did to the false prophets.

27'But to you hearing me I say: Love your enemies; do good to
those who hate you; 28bless those who curse you; pray for those who
insult you. 29To him who strikes you on the cheek, offer the other
also. From him who takes your coat do not withhold your cloak
either. 30Give to everyone who asks you; and do not ask for the

return of what is taken from you. [31]As you want men to treat you, do so to them.

[32]'If you love those who love you, do you deserve thanks for that? Sinners, too, love those who love them. [33]And if you do a good deed to those who do good deeds to you, do you deserve thanks for that? Sinners, too, do that. [34]And if you make gifts only in the hope of being given gifts in return, do you deserve thanks for that? Sinners, too, make gifts in order to receive in return.

[35]'So love your enemies, do good deeds, and be generous without hoping for reward. Only then will your reward be great in reality; you will be sons of the highest divine Being. For the highest Being also bows down in HIS goodness to ungrateful men, and to those lost in evil. [36]Be compassionate as your Father is compassionate.

[37]'Do not set yourselves up as judges, then you will also not be judged. Do not condemn, then you will also not be condemned. Forgive one another, then your debts will also be forgiven you. [38]Be of those who give, then you will also be among those who receive. A good measure, pressed down, shaken and full to the brim will be poured into your lap. The measure you use will be the measure you receive.'

[39]And he told them a parable: 'Can a blind man guide a blind man? Will they not both fall into the pit? [40]A pupil is not greater than his teacher; but everyone should strive to acquire the wisdom and experience that his teacher has.

[41]'Why do you see the speck in your brother's eye, since you do not see the beam in your own eye? [42]How can you say to your brother: Brother, let me take out the speck that is in your eye – since you yourself do not see the beam in your own eye? You hypocrite, first remove the beam from your own eye, and then see if you can remove the speck from your brother's eye.

[43]'No good tree bears bad fruit, and no sick tree bears good fruit. [44]Every tree can be recognized by its fruits. Figs cannot be gathered from thistles, nor can grapes be picked from brambles. [45]A good man produces what is good from the good treasury of his heart,

and a bad man what is bad from the bad. The mouth speaks of that
which fills the heart.

46‘Why do you continually call me Lord when you do not go by
what I say? 47A person who comes to me and hears my words and is
guided by them, I will show you whom he is like. 48He is like a man
building a house who digs deep and lays the foundation upon rock.
Then, when the floods burst through and the stream surges violently
against the house, it nevertheless is not shaken; for it has been well
built. 49But whoever hears my words, yet does not follow them, he
is like a man who builds a house on the ground without laying a
foundation. When the stream surges against it, it immediately col-
lapses and only a great pile of rubble is left.’

7 *The centurion of Capernaum*
When he had finished this speech, to which the people also listened,
he went to Capernaum. 2There, the servant of a centurion lay sick
and was near to death; the centurion valued him greatly. 3When the
centurion now heard of Jesus, he sent the elders of the Jews to him,
asking him to come and save his servant’s life. 4They came to Jesus
and asked him earnestly and said, ‘He deserves your help, 5for he
loves our people, and he built the synagogue for us.’ 6And Jesus set
off with them. And when he was already near the house, the centurion sent his friends to meet him with the message, ‘Lord, do not
trouble yourself; I am not worthy to have you enter my house, 7and
therefore I also did not presume to come to you myself. Speak only
a word, then my boy will be healed. 8I, too, am a man subject to
higher authority, and I, in turn, have soldiers under me, and when I
say to one: Go; then he goes, and to another: Come; then he comes.
And when I say to my servant: Do this, then he does it.’ 9When
Jesus heard this, he was amazed; he turned to the crowd following
him and said, ‘I tell you, nowhere in Israel have I found such a
power of trust.’ 10And when the messengers returned to the house,
they found the servant well.

Raising the young man of Nain
11Soon afterwards his way led him to the town Nain. His disciples
and a great crowd followed him. 12And as he approached the gate of
the town, see, a dead man was being carried out, the one and only
son of his mother who was a widow. And many people from the
town went with her. 13And when the Lord saw her, he was deeply
moved, and he said to her, 'Do not weep!' 14And he came up and
touched the bier so that the bearers stood still. And he said: 'Young
man, I say to you, stand up!' 15And the dead man sat up and began
to speak. And he gave him to his mother. 16Fear took hold of them
all. But then they praised the revelation of God and said, 'A great
prophet has risen among us, God is turning to HIS people again.'
17These words about him spread through the whole of Judea and all
the neighbouring regions.

The Baptist's question
18John's disciples told him of all that had happened. 19Then John
called to him two of his disciples and sent them to the Lord with
the question: 'Are you the One who is to come, or must we wait for
another?' 20And the men came to him and said, 'John the Baptist
has sent us to you to ask: Are you the One who is to come, or must
we wait for another?' 21In that hour he was at work, healing many
of their diseases and illnesses and evil spirits, and he gave new
sight to many who were blind. 22And so he replied, 'Go and report
to John what you have seen and heard: The blind see, the lame
walk, lepers are healed, the deaf hear, the dead are awakened and
the poor receive the message from God. 23Blessed is he who finds
himself in me without stumbling.'

24When John's messengers had gone again, he began to speak
to the people about John, 'What was it you wanted to see when
you went out into the desert? A reed swaying in the wind? 25Or
was it something else you wanted to see? Did you want to see a
man dressed in resplendent garments? See, those who dress in
splendid and sumptuous clothes are in kings' palaces. 26Or was
it something different you went to see; maybe a prophet? Yes, I

tell you, he is more than a prophet. [27]He is the one about whom scripture says:

> See, my angel I send before you.
> He is to go before your countenance and prepare the way
> for you.

[28]'I say to you, among all those who are born of women there is none who is greater than John. And yet the lowliest Being in the Kingdom of God is greater than he.' [29]All the people who heard him, including the tax-collectors, recognized the aims of God and were baptized by John. [30]The Pharisees and the Law-experts, however, rejected the divine will by scorning the baptism of John.

[31]'To whom shall I compare the human beings of this time, whom are they like? [32]They are like children who sit in the market place and call to one another: We played the flute for you, and you did not dance; we sang mournful songs, and you did not weep. [33]John the Baptist came and ate no bread and drank no wine, and you said: He is possessed. [34]And now the Son of Man comes and eats and drinks, and you say: Look, he is a glutton and a drunkard, a friend of tax-collectors and sinners. [35]In this way, the divine wisdom is put on trial by all her children.'

Meal with Simon; anointing by the woman who had sinned

[36]Once, a Pharisee invited him to eat with him. And he went to the Pharisee's house and sat at table. [37]And see, in that town there lived a woman who was regarded as a sinner. When she learned that he was a guest in the Pharisee's house, she brought an alabaster vessel of ointment, [38]and standing behind him at his feet she wept and began to wet his feet with her tears and to wipe them with her hair. And she kissed his feet and anointed them with the ointment.

[39]When the Pharisee who had invited him saw this, he said to himself: If he were a seer, he would know what sort of woman it is who is touching him. He would be able to see that she is a sinner. [40]Then Jesus said to him, 'Simon, I have something to say to you.' And he replied, 'Teacher, say it!' [41]'A creditor had two debt-

ors; one owed him five hundred denarii, the other fifty. [42]Since they could not pay their debt, he forgave them both. Which of the two will now love him more?' [43]Simon said, 'I suppose, he whom he forgave the greater debt.' And he said, 'You have judged rightly.'

[44]Then he turned towards the woman and said to Simon, 'Look at this woman. I came to your house, and you did not wash my feet; but she has wet my feet with her tears and wiped them with her hair. [45]You gave me no kiss; but all the time she has been in the house she has not ceased kissing my feet. [46]You did not anoint my head with oil; but she has anointed my feet with precious ointment. [47]And therefore I say to you: Her many sins are forgiven her, for she has shown much love. But he who is forgiven little also loves little.' [48]And he said to her, 'You are released from your sins!'

[49]The other guests began to say to themselves, 'Who is this, who even forgives sins?' [50]And he said to the woman, 'The power of your trust has helped you. Go in peace!'

8 *The women following*

And in the time after this he went through the towns and villages, preaching and proclaiming the message of the spirit from the Kingdom of God. The twelve were with him, [2]as well as some women whom he had healed of evil spirits and diseases: Mary from Magdala whom he had freed from seven demons, [3]Joanna, the wife of Chuza, a steward in Herod's service, Susanna and many others. They provided for them out of their means.

The parable of the sower

[4]A great crowd went along, and there were ever more coming from the towns. Then he spoke to them in a parable: [5]'Once, a sower went out to sow the seed. And as he sowed, a portion of the seed fell on the path and was trodden on, and the birds of the sky ate it up. [6]Another portion fell on the rock, and the sprouting green withered because it lacked moisture. [7]Yet another portion fell in the midst of

thorns which grew up with it and choked the sprouting seed. [8]And
lastly, a portion of the seed fell into good earth and grew and bore
fruit, a hundredfold.' And with a loud voice he added: 'Whoever
has ears to hear, let him hear!'

[9]His disciples asked him what this parable might mean. [10]And he
said, 'You have the gift of being able to understand the mysteries
of the Kingdom of God; but to the others they must be spoken of in
pictures, for they see and yet do not see, and hear, although they do
not understand with their thinking.

[11]'And this is the meaning of the parable: The seed is the word
of God. [12]Those on the path are those who indeed hear the word,
but from whose hearts the adversary powers take it away again,
so that they shall not find salvation through the power of faith.
[13]Those on the rock are those who receive the word joyfully when
they hear it, but then do not take root; for a while the power of the
word lives in their hearts, but then, when other influences rise up,
they go off on other ways. [14]Those in the thorns, they are the ones
who indeed hear the word but in whom it is choked and prevented
from bearing fruit by their concern about earthly belongings and
by the cravings and wishes of earthly life. [15]Those in the good
earth, they are the ones who receive the word with a harmonious
and good heart and keep it alive and patiently tend it there until it
bears fruit.

[16]'No one lights a lamp only to cover it with a vessel or to place
it under the bed. Rather, it is put on a stand, so that all who enter
may see the light. [17]There is nothing hidden which shall not be
revealed, and there is nothing kept secret which shall not be made
accessible to understanding and be brought to light. [18]So pay heed
to how you listen. For to him who has will be given; but from him
who has nothing will be taken even what he thinks he has.'

[19]Once, his mother and his brothers came to him, but could
not reach him because he was surrounded by a crowd of people.
[20]He was told: 'Your mother and your brothers are standing outside, wishing to see you.' [21]Then he answered, 'My mother and my
brothers are those who hear the word of God and act on it.'

Calming the storm

22On one of those days he boarded a ship with his disciples, and he
said to them, 'Let us go across to the other side of the lake.' And
they cast off, 23and while they were sailing he fell asleep. Then a
great storm arose over the lake. The waves broke over them so
that they were in great danger. 24Then they went to him, woke him
and said, 'Master, Master, we are perishing!' And he arose and
raised his hand against the wind and the tumultuous waves. Then
the elements ceased raging, and there was a great calm. 25And he
said, 'Where is your faith?' And, overwhelmed by fear and astonishment, they said to one another, 'Who can this be who commands
the wind and the water, and they obey him?'

Healing the demon-possessed Gerasene

26When they had crossed over the lake they came to the region of
Gerasa, which is opposite Galilee. 27And when he stepped ashore
there, he was met by a man from the town who was possessed by
demons. He kept no garment on him for long, nor did he remain
in any house, but lived among the tombs. 28When he saw Jesus he
cried out, fell down before him and shouted, 'What is it that binds
me to you, Jesus, you Son of the Highest God? I beg of you: Do
not torment me!' 29And he commanded the unclean spirit to leave
that human being. For a long time it had thrown him this way and
that with great force, and so he had been fettered with chains and
shackles and kept in custody. But he had burst the fetters and had
been driven into the desert by the demon. 30And Jesus asked him,
'What is your name?' He answered, 'Legion.' For he was possessed by many demons. 31And they begged him not to command
them to depart into the depths of the abyss. 32Now a large herd of
pigs were feeding there in the mountains. And they asked him to
allow them to enter these. And he allowed it. 33Then the demons
left the man and entered the pigs, and the whole herd ran over the
precipice into the lake and was drowned.

34When the herdsmen saw this, they fled and brought the news
to the town and the fields. 35And people went out to see what had

happened. And when they came to Jesus, they found the man who
had been possessed by the demons sitting at the feet of Jesus,
clothed and in his right mind. And they took fright at this. 36Those
who had seen it told them how the possessed man had been healed.
37Then all the inhabitants of the region of Gerasa asked him to
leave their country, so great was their fear. And he boarded the
ship to sail home. 38And the man who had been possessed asked
him to be allowed to stay with him; but Jesus told him to go, and
said, 39'Return home to your house and proclaim what God has
done for you.' And he went and proclaimed in the whole town
what Jesus had done for him.

The woman with a haemorrhage and raising Jairus' daughter

40When Jesus returned, the crowd welcomed him, for they were all
waiting for him. 41And see, a man called Jairus came to him, the
leader of the synagogue. He fell at Jesus' feet and begged him to
come to his house; 42for he had a child, his one and only daughter,
twelve years old, and she was dying.

As they went on their way, he was hemmed in by the crowd.
43And a woman who had suffered from a flow of blood for twelve
years and whom no one had been able to heal, 44came up to him
from behind and touched the hem of his garment; and at once the
flow of blood ceased. 45Then Jesus said, 'Who was it that touched
me?' And when all denied it, Peter said, 'Master, how can you ask
that, seeing how the crowd presses and jostles you?' 46But Jesus
said, 'Someone touched me; I felt a power going forth from me.'
47And when the woman saw that she could not remain unrecog-
nized, she came forward, trembling, and fell down before him.
Then, before all the people, she explained why she had touched
him and how she had been healed immediately. 48And he said to
her, 'Daughter, the power of your faith has helped you. Go in
peace.'

49While he was still speaking, one of the elders of the synagogue came and said, 'Your daughter has died, do not trouble the
Master any further.' 50When Jesus heard this, he said, 'Have no

fear, but have trust, then she can be saved.' 51And he went into the house, but allowed no one to come in with him, except Peter and John and James and the father and mother of the child. 52And all were weeping and lamenting over her already. But he said, 'Do not weep, she is not dead, she is sleeping.' 53And they laughed at him, for they knew that she was dead. 54And he took her by the hand and called: 'Maiden, arise!' 55And her spirit returned, and at once she sat up. And he gave directions that she should be given something to eat. 56The parents of the child were beside themselves with amazement. And he told them not to speak to anyone about what had happened.

9 *Sending out the twelve disciples*
He called the twelve together and passed on to them potent authority and formative power, so that they could work against all demonic mischief and heal all sickness. 2And he sent them out to proclaim the Kingdom of God and to heal, 3and he said to them, 'On the path upon which you are now entering you should not be dependent on anything, neither staff nor purse, neither bread nor money, nor should you have a second garment. 4When you have entered a house, remain there until you are travelling on again. 5Wherever you are not received, leave the town and shake the dust from your feet as a testimony against them.' 6And they set out and wandered through the villages; everywhere they proclaimed the Gospel and healed.

7Now Herod the tetrarch heard about what was happening, and when some said that John had risen from the dead, he was bewildered. 8Others said that Elijah had appeared, and yet others that one of the prophets of old had risen again. 9Then Herod said, 'John I beheaded; so who is this about whom I hear so much?' And he very much wanted to see him for himself.

10And the apostles returned and told him of all that they had been able to do. And he called them to himself and withdrew to the town Bethsaida to be alone with them. 11But the crowds heard about it and followed him. Then he made them welcome and spoke to them about the Kingdom of God, and healed all who had need of healing.

Feeding the five thousand

12 And the day began to decline. Then the twelve came to him and said, ‘Send the crowd away, so that they can go to the villages and farms around here and find places to rest and food and drink; for here we are in a lonely place.’ 13 And he said to them, *‘You* give them to eat.’ They replied, ‘We have no more than five loaves and two fish – unless we go and buy food for the whole crowd.’ 14 There were about five thousand men. Then he said to his disciples, ‘Let them sit down in groups of fifty each.’ 15 They did this, and made them all sit down. 16 Then he took the five loaves and the two fish, and lifting up his soul to the spirit he blessed them, broke them and gave them to his disciples to share among the people. 17 And all ate and were satisfied, and when the remnants were gathered up there were twelve baskets full of pieces.

Peter’s confession and the first foretelling of suffering

18 On one occasion he had withdrawn to devote himself completely to prayer. Then he asked the disciples who were with him, ‘Who do the people say that I am?’ 19 They answered, ‘Some think you are John the Baptist, others Elijah, yet others believe that one of the prophets from olden times has risen from the dead.’ 20 Then he said to them, ‘And you – who do you say that I am?’ And Peter said, ‘You are the Christ of God.’ 21 And he told them strictly not to tell this to anyone. 22 And he went on and said, ‘The Son of Man must suffer much and be scorned and killed by the elders and chief priests and scribes; but then, on the third day, he will be awakened to life.’

Conditions of discipleship

23 And speaking to all he said, ‘Whoever would follow me must learn to deny himself and take his cross upon himself daily. Only so can he follow me. 24 Whoever is only concerned about the salvation of his soul will lose it; but whoever is prepared to lose

it for the sake of my Being, he will find salvation for his soul.
25What use is it to a human being to win the whole world, and
lose or corrupt himself in the process? 26Whoever does not unite
himself with my Being and with the words that I speak, with him
the Son of Man will not unite, either, when he reveals himself in
his spiritual radiance and in the radiance of the Father and all the
realms of the angels.

27'I tell you the truth: Some of those who are standing here will
not taste death without having seen the Kingdom of God.'

The Transfiguration

28And it was about eight days after these words that he took Peter
and John and James with him and ascended the mountain to pray.
29And while he was still deep in prayer, the appearance of his
countenance changed and his garment became gleaming, radiant
white. 30And see, two men were speaking with him: Moses and
Elijah. 31They became visible in the supersensible light, and they
spoke of the fulfilment that his earthly life was about to reach in
Jerusalem. 32Peter and the others who were with him sank into
deep sleep. But when they awoke they beheld the radiance of the
spiritual light that shone from him and the two men who were
standing by him. 33And as the two figures were parting from him,
Peter said to Jesus, 'Master, how good it is for us that we are here!
Let us build three tabernacles, one for you, one for Moses and one
for Elijah.' But he did not know what he was saying. 34And while
he was speaking, a cloud came and overshadowed them. They
were troubled when they saw the figures vanishing in the cloud.
35Then a voice spoke out of the cloud: 'This is my Son, the Chosen
One, hear him!' 36And while the voice was still speaking, they saw
Jesus alone standing before them. And they kept silence and told
no one in those days anything about what they had seen.

Healing of the epileptic boy

37As they came down from the mountain the next day, a great crowd
came towards them. 38And see, a man from the crowd called out:

'Master, I beg you, attend to my son, he is my one and only son, [39]and see, often he is seized by a spirit and then he suddenly cries out aloud, he is convulsed and foams at the mouth and the power that has him in its grip only slowly desists. [40]I asked your disciples to drive out this spirit, but they could not.' [41]Then Jesus said to them all, 'How weak is the inner power of faith in you, and how distorted is your true being! How long must I remain with you and bear with you? Bring your son here!' [42]And as he came near, the demon threw him this way and that, and he was convulsed. And Jesus raised his hand against the unclean spirit and healed the boy and gave him back to his father. [43]And they were all overcome with wonder at the greatness of God which had been revealed.

The second foretelling of suffering

While everyone was full of admiration for all that he did, he said to his disciples, [44]'Write these words upon your hearts: The Son of Man must be delivered into the hands of men.' [45]But they did not understand his words, the significance was hidden from them and so their feelings were not touched either; nor did they dare ask him what he meant by these words.

[46]Once, they began to argue about who among them was the greatest. [47]Jesus saw what thoughts lived in their hearts, and he took a child and put him by his side [48]and said to them, 'Whoever receives such a child in my name receives me. And whoever brings my Being to life within himself, receives HIM who sent me. Whoever among you is least in this sense, he is the one who is great in reality.'

[49]Then John said, 'Master, we know a man who drives out demons and claims that he is doing it in your name. We forbade him, because he does not follow you as we do.' [50]But Jesus said to him, 'Do not forbid him; for whoever is not against you is for you.'

Journey to Jerusalem begins: Rejection in Samaria

[51]When the time came near for him to depart from earthly life, he set his inner eye steadfastly on his goal and began the journey

to Jerusalem. 52He sent messengers ahead to prepare the way for
the fulfilment of his will. And they set off and came to a village
in Samaria. There they wanted to find lodging for him, 53but the
people refused to receive him; they opposed the will of his spirit
which was urging him on towards Jerusalem. 54When the disciples
James and John saw it, they said, 'Lord, do you want us to make
fire fall from heaven through the power of our word and destroy
them, as Elijah did?' 55Then Jesus turned, raised his hand against
them and said, 'Do you not know which spirit it is you serve?'
56And they went on to another village.

Three new disciples

57And as they progressed along the road, someone said to him, 'I
will follow you wherever you go.' 58But Jesus said to him, 'The
foxes have their holes and the birds of the air have their nests; but
the Son of Man has nowhere to lay his head.' 59And to someone
else he said, 'Follow me!' But he replied, 'Allow me first to go and
bury my father.' 60And he said, 'Let the dead bury their dead, but
you: go and proclaim the Kingdom of God!' 61And another said, 'I
will follow you, Lord, but allow me first to say farewell to those
at my home.' 62But Jesus said, 'Whoever has put his hand to the
plough but then looks back is incapable of serving the Kingdom
of God.'

10 *Sending out of seventy disciples*

After this, the Lord appointed seventy others and sent them on
ahead of him, two by two, to prepare for him in every town and
place where he himself was about to come. 2And he said to them,
'The harvest is plentiful, but the reapers are few; pray the Lord
of the harvest to send reapers to gather in the harvest. 3Go your
way; see, I send you as lambs among the wolves. 4On this path
carry no purse, nor bag, nor sandals. You need salute no one.
5When you enter a house, first say: Peace be to this house! 6And
if a son of peace lives there, your peace shall be transferred as a
power to him; but if not, it shall return to you. 7And remain in the

same house, eating and drinking what they provide, for the worker deserves his wages; do not go from house to house. [8]Whenever you enter a town and they receive you, eat what is set before you; [9]heal the sick there and say to the people: The Kingdom of God is near to you.

[10]'But when you come to a town where they do not receive you, go into the streets and say: [11]Even the dust of your town that clings to our feet, we wipe it off before your eyes; you, too, will have to recognize that the Kingdom of God is near. [12]I tell you, the destiny of Sodom shall be more bearable on the great Day of decision than the destiny of that town. [13]Woe to you, Chorazin! Woe to you, Bethsaida! For if the mighty spiritual deeds done in you had been done in Tyre and Sidon, the people there would have changed their ways long ago and have shown it by wearing sackcloth and ashes. [14]It shall be more bearable on the great Day of decision for Tyre and Sidon than for you. [15]And you, Capernaum, have you not been exalted to heaven? Now you shall fall into the abyss of death. [16]He who hears you hears me, and he who rejects you rejects me, and he who rejects me rejects HIM who sent me.'

[17]The seventy returned and said joyfully, 'Lord, even the demons obey us through the power of your name!' [18]And he said, 'I saw the satanic power fall like lightning from heaven into the depths. [19]See, I have given you the spiritual power which enables you to tread upon serpents and scorpions and to triumph over all the might of the enemy. There is no power which can defeat you. [20]Nevertheless, do not rejoice in this, that the demons obey you; but rejoice that your names have been written into the world of the spirit.'

[21]In that hour he was filled with the exultation of the Holy Spirit, and he said, 'I give praise to you, O Father God, Lord of heaven and earth, because you keep these things hidden from those who consider themselves wise and intelligent, and reveal them to those who are youthful of soul. Yes, Father, that is the blessing which streams forth in the revelation of your will from your countenance.

[22]'All things have been entrusted to me by my Father, and no one knows the nature of the Son except the Father, and no one knows

the nature of the Father except the Son and those to whom the Son chooses to reveal it.'

23And he turned to his disciples and spoke to them in intimate conversation: 'Blessed are the eyes which see what you see. 24I tell you: Many prophets and kings longed to see what you see, and did not see it, and to hear what you hear, and did not hear it.'

The good Samaritan

25Then a teacher of the Law stood up to dispute with him and said, 'Teacher, what must I do to win a share in the eternal life?' 26And he said, 'What is written in the Law, what have you read there?' 27He answered, 'Love the Lord your God with all your heart and with all your soul and with all your strength and with all your thinking, and love your neighbour as you love yourself.' 28And he said to him, 'You have given the right answer; act in accordance with it, and you will find life.'

29But he wanted to justify himself and said to Jesus, 'And who is my neighbour?'

30Then Jesus answered, 'Once, a man was going down from Jerusalem to Jericho and he fell into the hands of robbers. They robbed him of his clothes, beat him half dead and left him lying there helpless, and ran off. 31And it so happened that a priest was going down that same way. When he saw him he walked on past him. 32So, too, a Levite who was on that road walked past him when he saw him lying there. 33But then a Samaritan came by. When he saw him he had compassion on him, 34went up to him, bandaged his wounds, pouring on oil and wine, set him on his own beast, took him to an inn and looked after him. 35And the next day he took out two denarii, gave them to the innkeeper and said, "Take care of him, and any expenses you have I will refund you when I come back." 36Which of these three, do you think, proved neighbour to him who had fallen into the hands of the robbers?' 37He answered, 'The one who showed compassion on him.' And Jesus said to him, 'Go and do likewise.'

Mary and Martha

38On his journey he once came to a village, and a woman called
Martha received him into her house. 39She had a sister named Mary
who sat down at the Lord's feet and listened to his words. 40But
Martha hurried busily through the house so as not to neglect her
work of serving. And she went to him and said, 'Lord, does it not
annoy you that my sister is leaving me to do all the serving by
myself? Do tell her to help me!' 41But the Lord answered her,
'Martha, Martha, you are anxious and troubled about so much;
42however, what is needed is not preoccupation with many things,
but one thing only. Mary has chosen well: The one thing which
shall not be taken away from her.'

11 *Question about prayer*

Once, he was absorbed in prayer in a quiet place. And when he
paused, one of his disciples said to him, 'Lord, teach us the way of
prayer, as John also taught it to his disciples.' 2And he said to them,
'When you pray, say this:

Father,
may your name be hallowed,
may your Kingdom come to us;
3give us each day our daily bread,
4forgive us our sins, as we forgive all those who are
indebted to us,
and lead us not into temptation.'

Parable of the friend who asks

5And he said to them, 'Imagine that one of you has a friend who
comes to him in the middle of the night and calls: "Dear friend,
lend me three loaves, 6for a friend of mine has come to me after
a long journey, and I have nothing to set before him." 7Now, will
the one indoors say, "Do not bother me, the door is already shut
and my children and I have gone to bed; I cannot get up and
give you anything?" 8I say to you, if he does not get up and give

to him because he is his friend, yet he will awake and give him
what he needs because of the boldness of his plea.'

[9]And so I say to you, 'Ask, and you will receive; seek, and you
will find; knock, and the door will be opened to you. [10]Whoever
asks receives; whoever seeks finds, and to him who knocks will
be opened. [11]What father among you, if his son asks for bread, will
give him a stone; or give him a serpent when he asks for a fish [12]or a
scorpion when he asks for an egg? [13]When you, who are so far from
the Good, nevertheless can give good gifts to your children, will not
the Father in the heavens all the more give the Holy Spirit to those
who draw near to HIM in prayer?'

Driving out a dumb demon: Working out of the spirit

[14]Once he was driving out a demon from a man who had no speech.
And when the demon went out of him, the dumb man was able to
speak. The crowd was amazed at this, [15]and some said, 'He drives
out demons with the power of Beelzebub, the Prince of demons.'
[16]Others wanted to test him and tried to get him to work a magical
wonder. [17]But he knew their thoughts and said, 'Every kingdom
that is divided within itself will soon be laid waste, one house after
another will fall down. [18]Now, if Satan divides his powers within
himself, how will his kingdom be able to remain? You have not
considered this when you claim that I drive out demons with the
power of Beelzebub. [19]If I drive out demons with the power of
Beelzebub, with what power do your sons do it? Your sons will be
your judges. [20]But since, in fact, I encounter the demons with the
authority of God's hand, it follows from this that the Kingdom of
God has already come to you.

[21]'When a powerful man in full armour guards his own palace,
what he owns is in peace. [22]But if someone who is even stronger
than he comes and throws him down, then he loses his armour
which he relied upon, and the victor divides the spoils.

[23]'Whoever does not unite with my Being is against me and my
Being. And whoever does not work for inner composure, he divides
and scatters.

24 ‘When an impure spirit leaves a Man, whilst his inner being is
still weak, then the spirit roams through waterless places, seeking
rest and not finding it. Then he says: I will return to the dwelling
which I have left. 25 When he comes to this dwelling, he finds it
cleaned and adorned. 26 Then he goes and brings seven spirits who
are even worse than himself; and they enter and dwell in that Man.
And in the end, it is worse for the Man than before.’

27 As he was saying this, a woman in the crowd raised her voice
and said, ‘Blessed is the body that bore you, blessed the breasts that
nourished you!’ 28 But he said, ‘Truly blessed are those who hear the
divine word and keep it in their hearts!’

The proof of the spirit

29 As the crowds thronged around him ever more, he said, ‘People
in these times are a corrupt generation. They look for materialistic
evidence of the spirit; but they will be given no other proof of the
spirit than the sign of Jonah. 30 As Jonah became a proof of the spirit
for the inhabitants of Nineveh, so shall the Son of Man be for this
age. 31 On the great Day of decision, the queen of Sheba will arise
and judge the people of this age; for she came from the ends of the
earth to hear the wisdom of Solomon, and see: Something greater
than Solomon is here. 32 And the inhabitants of Nineveh will arise
in the days of decision and judge the people of this age; for they
changed their hearts and minds at the proclamation of Jonah, and
see: Something greater than Jonah is here.

33 ‘No one takes a light to put it in a hidden place or under a
vessel. He will put it on the stand, so that all who come in see
the light. 34 The light of the body is your eye. And when your eye
is clear and pure, the life of your whole body will be illumined;
but if your eye is clouded, then the life of your body, too, will be
full of darkness. 35 Therefore take care that the light is not turned
into darkness in you. 36 And when your whole body is completely
illumined so that there is no room for darkness any longer, then
there will be a shining radiance in you, as if a bright light shines
within you.’

Meal with a Pharisee

[37]While he was still speaking, a Pharisee invited him to a meal. And he went to his house and sat at table. [38]When the Pharisee saw this, he was very surprised that he did not wash before the meal. [39]And the Lord said to him, 'You Pharisees cleanse the outside of cup and dish, but inside you are full of greed and malice. [40]You fools! Did not HE who made the outside also make the inside? [41]Lay open what is within you in a free deed of love, then your whole being is pure.

Woe to the Pharisees and teachers of the Law

[42]'But woe to you Pharisees! You demand tithes on every spice, on rue and on all other herbs; but you forget to examine yourselves and you neglect the love of God. It is necessary to strive actively for these things, and the others do not have to be given up for that reason.

[43]'Woe to you Pharisees because the most prominent seat in the synagogue and the salutations of the people in the streets are of such importance to you. [44]Woe to you, you are like graves which have become unrecognizable and which people walk over without knowing it.'

[45]And one of the teachers of the Law answered, 'Master, with these words you are insulting us, too.' [46]And he said, 'Woe to you also, you teachers of the Law! You burden the people with loads which they can hardly bear; but you yourselves do not so much as lift a finger to carry this burden.

[47]'Woe to you who build memorials to the prophets whom your fathers killed; [48]thereby you confirm the deeds of your fathers and approve them. In the past, they killed them, now you are building memorials to them. [49]And so the divine wisdom spoke the truth: "I will send prophets and apostles to mankind; and they will kill some and persecute others." [50]But in the end there will be a reckoning for the blood of all the prophets which has been shed since the creation of the world, [51]from the blood of Abel onwards to the blood of Zechariah who perished between the altar and the

sanctuary. Yes, I tell you: This present generation will have to
account for it.

52‘Woe to you, you teachers of the Law! You have stolen the
key of knowledge. You yourselves can no longer find entry into the
worlds of spirit, and so you want also to hinder those who could
find it.’

53When he had hurled these words at them, the scribes and the
Pharisees began to press him hard. They raised all kinds of questions, 54in an attempt to trap him through his own words and to find
a reason to charge him.

12 *Courage to confess the spirit*
While the people were flocking to him in such vast numbers that
they almost trampled one another, he began to speak, addressing
his disciples first: ‘Beware of the leaven of the Pharisees which is
nothing but hypocrisy. 2There is nothing hidden which cannot be
revealed, and nothing secret that cannot become known. 3All that
you say in the dark shall be heard in the light, and what you whisper
to one another in your own rooms shall be proclaimed loudly from
the housetops.’

4I say to you who are my friends: ‘Do not fear those who kill
the body but have no power to do anything more. 5I will show you
whom you should fear: Fear him who, after he has killed the body,
has the power to cast the soul into the abyss. Yes, I say to you, you
may well be afraid of him! 6Are not five sparrows sold for two
pennies? And yet none of them has been forgotten or been lost to
the sight of God. 7So, too, each hair of your head has been counted.
Do not fear! For you are much more than the sparrows.

8‘I tell you, when someone acknowledges before other human
beings that he lives in my Being, the Son of Man will also make
it known that he lives in him, and this he will acknowledge in
the sight of all angels of God. 9But whoever rejects me before
other human beings will also be rejected before all angels of God.
10If someone speaks against the Son of Man, he can be forgiven.
But if he directs hostile words against the Holy Spirit, he cannot

be forgiven. [11]When you are dragged before the synagogues and
before the rulers and those who wield higher authority, do not be
concerned about how you shall defend yourselves and what you
shall say. [12]At the right moment, the Holy Spirit will teach you
what you are to say.'

Anxiety about external things: Parable of the rich farmer

[13]One of the crowd said to him, 'Teacher, tell my brother to share
the inheritance with me.' [14]But he answered, 'O man, who has made
me a judge or divider over you?' [15]And he said to them all, 'Beware
and guard against all cravings for earthly goods, for no one wins
life by a surfeit of earthly possessions.'

[16]And he told them a parable: 'Once there was a rich man whose
fields yielded a particularly plentiful harvest. [17]And he thought to
himself: Now what shall I do, for I have nowhere to store this surplus? [18]And he said: I know what I will do: I will pull down my
barns and build larger ones; and there I will store all my grain and
my goods. [19]Then I shall say to my soul: My soul, now you have
many goods stored up, which will last for many years; be at ease,
eat, drink, be merry. [20]But God spoke to him: You fool! This very
night they will demand your life; and the things you have collected,
whose will they be?

[21]'It will be like that for everyone who lays up earthly goods for
himself but has no riches which endure before God.'

[22]And he said to his disciples, 'Therefore I say to you, let not
care enter your soul about what you shall eat or about how you shall
clothe the body. [23]For the soul is more than food, and the body is
more than clothing. [24]Learn from the ravens; they neither sow nor
reap, they have neither dwelling nor barn, and yet God feeds them.
And are you not much more than the birds?

[25]'Which of you can increase his stature by so much as a cubit,
however much he worries? [26]If worrying cannot bring about even
so insignificant an effect as that, why then do you give yourselves
so many worries? [27]Learn from the lilies: They do not spin or
weave; but I tell you, even Solomon in his great splendour was not

arrayed like a single one of them. 28If God clothes the grass and flowers of the field which are magnificent today and are thrown into the stove tomorrow, will HE not all the more clothe you? How weak is your faith! 29So therefore you should not be concerned about what you shall eat and drink, nor should you be striving after high honours. 30Let that be the concern and striving of those human beings who have given themselves over to mere external existence. Your Father knows what your needs are. 31Let your striving be towards the Kingdom of God, then everything else will be yours as well. 32Have no fear, little flock, it is the intention of the revealing will of your Father that you should be given a share in the Kingdom of God.

33'Sell what you possess and make gifts of offering. Acquire imperishable possessions, gather treasure in the spiritual worlds which cannot be lost, which no thief can steal from you and no moth can damage. 34Where you have gathered your treasure, there your heart will also carry you.

Call to wakefulness: Parable of two servants

35'Let your loins be girded and your lamps burning. 36Be like men who are expecting their master back from the marriage feast, so that they can open the door to him at once when he comes and knocks. 37Blessed are the servants whom the master finds awake when he comes! Yes, I tell you, he will put on an apron himself and show them to the table and serve them. 38And if he does not come until the second or third watch of the night, and yet finds them awake: Blessed are the servants! 39You know: If the master of the house knew at what hour the thief comes, he would not let his house be looted. 40So be ready; the Son of Man comes at an hour that you had not thought.'

41Then Peter said, 'Lord, are you telling us this parable, or is it for all human beings?' 42And the Lord answered, 'Imagine a reliable and competent steward whom his master appoints to be in charge of the whole staff, to give to each one what he is entitled to. 43Blessed is that servant if the master comes and finds him carrying out his duties. [44]I tell you, he will entrust him with all his goods without further ado. [45]But if the servant says in his heart, "My master will not be coming all that soon," and begins to maltreat the other servants and the maids, himself all the while eating and drinking and becoming intoxicated, [46]then the master of that servant will come on a day when he does not expect him, and at an hour that he does not know. The master will virtually tear him to pieces; he will treat him as those deserve who have not proved faithful.

[47]'A servant who knows his master's will but does not act according to it and so does not carry out his will, deserves the severest punishment. [48]If he does not know the master's will and then does something that deserves punishment, he will escape more lightly. From one who has many gifts, much will also be expected; and from one who has been entrusted with much, more will also be demanded.

Signs of the times

[49]'I have come to cast fire on the earth; I have no other wish than to see it burning already. [50]But first I have to go through a baptism, and I am so constrained until it is accomplished! [51]Do you think I have come to establish peace on earth? No, I tell you: Nothing but division comes about through me. [52]From now on, five who are in a house together will separate from one another. Three will separate from two and two from three, [53]father from son and son from father, mother from daughter and daughter from mother, mother-in-law from the bride and the bride from her mother-in-law.'

[54]And to the crowd he said, 'When you see a cloud rising in the west, you say at once: It is going to rain; and it happens. [55]And when you notice that the south wind is blowing, you say: It is going to be hot; and that also happens. [56]Your hearts and minds are all awry! You know how to interpret the appearance of the earth and sky; but the signs of our times, why do you not interpret them?

[57]'And why do you not trust yourselves to judge what is or is not right? [58]When you go with your adversary before the court of law,

make an effort to come to an agreement with him while you are still
on the way. Otherwise it could happen that he drags you before the
judge and the judge hands you over to the warder and the warder
throws you into prison. [59]I tell you, you will not get out until you
have paid your debt to the very last penny.'

13 *Questions about guilt*

At that time people came to him and told him about the Galileans
whose blood Pilate had mingled with the blood of their own sacrificial animals. [2]And he said to them, 'Do you think that those Galileans
were worse sinners than the other people in Galilee, because they
suffered such a fate? [3]No, I tell you: If you do not change your heart
and mind, you will all perish likewise. [4]Or remember those eighteen
who were crushed and killed when the tower of Siloam collapsed;
do you think that they were more guilty than the other inhabitants
of Jerusalem? [5]No, I tell you: If you do not change your heart and
mind, you will all perish likewise.'

Parable of the fig tree

[6]Then he told them this parable: 'Once, a man had planted a fig tree
in his vineyard. And when he came looking for fruit, he found none.
[7]Then he said to the gardener of the vineyard, "Look, for three years
now I have been coming, and have looked in vain for fruit on this
fig tree. Cut it down; why should it go on using up the earth?" [8]But
the gardener answered, "Sir, leave it for just one more year. I will
dig the earth all around it and give it some manure. [9]If it then bears
fruit, well and good; if not, you can cut it down".'

Healing the woman bent over

[10]Once, he was teaching in a synagogue on the Sabbath. [11]And
see, there was a woman who had been suffering from an illness
for eighteen years: She was bent over and could not stand up
straight. [12]When Jesus saw her, he called her to him and said to
her, 'Woman, you are released from your illness!' [13]He laid his
hands upon her, and at once she was able to straighten up. And

she praised the power of God. [14]Then the leader of the synagogue,
indignant because Jesus had healed on the Sabbath, said to the
people, 'There are six days for doing work; on those days you
can come and let yourselves be healed – but not on the Sabbath.'
[15]But the Lord replied: 'You hypocrites! Does not every one of
you untie his ox or his ass from the manger on the Sabbath and
lead it away to the water-trough? [16]This daughter of Abraham was
held bound by the dark might of the Enemy for eighteen years;
should she then not be released from her bondage on the day of the
Sabbath?' [17]All his opponents were put to shame by these words,
and the people rejoiced over all the signs of spiritual power which
happened through him.

Two parables of the Kingdom of God

[18]And he said, 'What is the Kingdom of God like, to what shall I
compare it? [19]It is like a grain of mustard which a person took and
threw into his garden, and it grew until it became like a tree in
whose branches the birds of the sky build their nests.'

[20]And he went on: 'To what shall I compare the Kingdom of
God? [21]It is like leaven which a woman took and mixed into three
measures of flour, until the whole dough was leavened.'

The question about attaining to the Kingdom of God

[22]Travelling on, on his way to Jerusalem, he went through towns
and villages, and taught. [23]And once someone asked him: 'Lord,
is it really so that only a few will attain to salvation?' He said,
[24]'Exert all your strength to find entry through the narrow gate.
I tell you: Many want to find that entry, but they do not have the
necessary strength. [25]The time will come when the master of the
house will arise and shut the door, and you will stand outside and
knock on the door and call: "Lord, open to us!" And he will reply:
"I do not know where you come from." [26]And again and again
you will say, "But we ate and drank before your eyes, and you
taught in our marketplaces!" [27]And he will reply: "I do not know
you. Go – do not come near me, you all serve the Adversary!"

28There will be lamentation and gnashing of teeth among you
when you see Abraham, Isaac and Jacob and all the prophets in
the Kingdom of God while you yourselves are excluded. 29And
from east and west, from north and south people will come and be
guests at table in the Kingdom of God. 30See, the last will be first,
and the first last.'

Enmity of Herod
31In that hour some Pharisees came to him and said, 'Flee from here,
for Herod wants to kill you!' 32He answered, 'Go and tell that fox:
Today and tomorrow I still drive out demons and heal people, but
on the third day I reach my aim. 33Today and tomorrow and on the
day after I must still continue on my way until its end; for it cannot
be that a prophet should perish away from Jerusalem.

34'Jerusalem, Jerusalem, you have killed God's messengers and
stoned those who were sent to you. How often I have wanted to
gather your children about me, as a hen gathers her chicks under
her wings. But you did not wish it. 35See, your house will become
deserted. And I tell you, you will not see me until the day when
you say:

Blessed be he who comes in the name of the Lord!'

14 *Meal with a Pharisee and healing a man with dropsy*
On one Sabbath he went to the house of a leading Pharisee to eat
the bread with him, and they were all watching him carefully.
2And see, a man stood before him who was suffering from dropsy.
3And Jesus said to the teachers of the Law and the Pharisees, 'Is
it allowed to heal on the Sabbath, or not?' 4And they were silent.
And he took care of him, healed him and let him go. 5Then he said
to them, 'If one of you has a child or an ox fall into the well, will
you not pull it out at once, even on a Sabbath day?' 6And they had
no answer to that.

7And he told the guests a parable, because he noticed how
they all had their eye on the places of honour at the table. He said,
8'When you are invited by someone to a marriage feast, do not sit in

the most important seat. Someone entitled to a greater honour than you may have been invited, 9and then his and your host would come and say to you, “Give your seat to this man;” and with shame you would have to sit in the last place. 10But rather, when you are invited take the lowest place; then he who invited you will say to you, “Friend, go up higher;” and you will be honoured in the presence of all the guests. 11Whoever exalts himself will be humbled, and whoever humbles himself will be exalted.’

12And he said to his host, ‘When you give a meal, whether in the morning or in the evening, do not invite your friends and brothers and relatives nor your rich neighbours; for they will also invite you and give you back what you gave them. 13Rather, when you give a meal, invite the poor, the cripples, the lame and the blind. 14Then you will be blessed. They have nothing to pay you back with, and so your recompense will come to you in the realm in which everything good is resurrected.’

15When one of the guests at the table heard these words, he said to him, ‘Blessed is he who eats the bread in the Kingdom of God!’

Parable of the great banquet

16And he said, ‘A man once gave a great banquet and invited many; 17and when the hour for the banquet had come, he sent his servant to say to those who had been invited, “Come, for everything is now ready.” 18But one after another they made excuses. The first said, “I have bought a field and must go out and see it; please excuse me.” 19And another said, “I have bought five pairs of oxen and am just going to try them out; please excuse me.” 20And yet another said, “I have just got married and cannot come.” 21And the servant returned and reported this to his master. And the master of the house became angry and said to his servant, “Go at once into the streets and alleys of the town and bring here the poor, the cripples, the blind and the lame!” 22And the servant came and said, “Sir, I have carried out your orders, but there is still room.” 23And the master said to the servant, “Go out onto the roads and to the hedges and urge all whom you find there to come in, so that my

house can be filled. [24]I tell you, none of those who were invited
first shall share in my meal".'

Conditions of discipleship

[25]Great crowds of people were wandering with him. And he turned
to them and said, [26]'If someone comes to me but cannot free himself from his father and his mother, from his wife and his children,
from brothers and sisters, yes, even from his own soul, he cannot
be my disciple. [27]Whoever does not take his cross upon himself
and follow me on my way, he cannot be my disciple. [28]Who among
you, intending to build a tower, does not first sit down and cal-
culate all the costs to see if he has enough to complete it? [29]If he
does not do that, he is mocked by all who see that he is not able
to complete the building, although the foundation is already in
place, [30]and they say, "This person began to build, and was unable
to complete it." [31]Or which king will engage in a war with another
king without first deliberating whether he is able to counter him
who is marching towards him with twenty thousand men with at
least ten thousand? [32]If he does not have that strength, he will send
an ambassador to his opponent while he is still far off and ask for
peace terms. [33]And so this applies to every one of you: Whoever
is not prepared to renounce everything that belongs to him cannot
be my disciple.

[34]'Salt is good. But when once it has lost its salting power, there
is no way of restoring it. [35]It is of no use for the soil nor for the
dunghill; it must be thrown away. He who has ears to hear, let him
hear!'

15 *Three parables: The lost sheep, lost coin, lost son*

A great crowd of tax-collectors and other despised people gathered
round to hear him. [2]Then the Pharisees and scribes said indignantly,
'He receives sinners and sits at table with them.' [3]So he told them
this parable:

[4]'If one of you has a hundred sheep and loses one of them, will
he not leave the ninety-nine in the wilderness and search for the

one which is lost until he finds it? [5]And when he finds it, he lays
it on his shoulders, full of joy, [6]and goes home. He calls friends
and neighbours together and says to them: Be happy with me, for
I have found the lost sheep. [7]I say to you: Just so is the joy in the
heavenly worlds greater over one sinner who changes heart and
mind than over ninety-nine righteous persons who think that they
need not change.

[8]'Or think of a woman who owns ten silver coins. If she loses
one coin, does she not light a lamp and sweep the house and search
diligently until she finds what was lost? [9]And when she has found it,
she calls her friends and neighbours together and says, "Be happy
with me, I have found the silver coin which I had lost."

[10]'I say to you: Just so there will be joy among the angels of God
over one sinner who changes heart and mind.'

[11]And he went on: 'There was a man who had two sons, [12]and
the younger of them said to his father, "Father, give me the share
of the property that falls to me." So he divided his estate between
them. [13]A few days later the younger son took the whole of his
share and left home for a distant country, where he wasted his
substance in reckless living. [14]And when he had spent everything,
a severe famine arose in that country and he began to be in need.
[15]So he went and joined himself to one of the citizens of that country who sent him on to his farm to feed the pigs. [16]He would gladly
have fed on the husks that the pigs were eating, but no one gave
him anything.

[17]'Then he came to himself and said: How many of my father's
hired servants have more food than they can eat and here am I,
starving to death! [18]I will arise and go to my father and I will say
to him, "Father, I have sinned against heaven and before you – [19]I
am no longer worthy to be called your son, treat me as one of your
hired servants." [20]And he arose and came to his father. But while
he was still a long way off, his father saw him and had compassion
on him. He ran to meet him, embraced him and kissed him. [21]And
the son said to him, "Father, I have sinned against heaven and
before you. I am no longer worthy to be called your son." [22]But

the father said to his servants, “Quick, fetch a robe, my best one,
and put it on him, and put a ring on his hand and shoes on his
feet. [23]Bring the fatted calf and kill it, and let us have a feast to
celebrate the day, [24]for this my son was dead and is alive again, he
was lost and is found.”

‘And they began to make merry. [25]Now his elder son was in the
field; and as he came and drew near to the house, he heard music
and dancing. [26]And he called one of the servants and asked what
this meant. [27]And he said to him, “Your brother has come, and
your father has killed the fatted calf for joy that he has received
him safe and sound.” [28]But he was angry and would not go in. His
father came out and invited him, [29]but he said to his father, “Look,
I have served you for many years, and I have never disobeyed
one of your commandments; yet you never gave *me* a kid so that I
might make merry with my friends.” [30]But when this son of yours
comes, who has wasted your property with harlots, for him you
kill the fatted calf! [31]But he said to him, “My child, you are always
with me, and all that is mine is yours. [32]You should rejoice and be
glad, for this your brother was dead and is alive; he was lost and
is found”.’

16 *Parable of the unjust steward*
And he said to the disciples, ‘A rich man had a steward of whom
he heard that he was squandering his property. [2]He sent for him
and said to him, “What is this that I hear about you? Give account
of your house-management; you shall not remain in your post
any longer.” [3]Then the steward said to himself: What shall I do
if my master takes my job from me? I am not able to do manual
work, and I am ashamed to beg. [4]I know what I will do, so that
people will take me into their homes when I am removed from
my post. [5]And he called all those who were in debt to his master
to him, one at a time; and he said to the first, “How much do you
owe my master?” [6]He answered, “A hundred kegs of oil.” And
he said, “Here, take your bill, sit down and quickly write fifty.”
[7]Then he asked another, “How much do you owe?” He answered,

"A hundred measures of wheat." And he said, "Here is your bill,
write eighty." 8And the master pointed out how cleverly the dis-
honest steward had acted, and he said, "The sons with earthbound
minds are cleverer in their way than the sons of the light." 9I say
to you: Use to make friends for yourselves those merely earthly
goods which have been hoarded unjustly, so that when they are all
used up you will be received into the eternal dwelling-places of
the spirit.

10'Whoever proves trustworthy in small things is also trustworthy in great things; and whoever does wrong in small things also
does wrong in great things. 11And if you do not prove trustworthy
in your dealings with merely earthly goods, unjustly hoarded, will
you then be entrusted with the true riches? 12If you do not prove
trustworthy with things which are essentially foreign to you, will
anyone then give you that which concerns us here? 13No servant
can serve two masters simultaneously; either he will hate the one
and love the other, or he will be attached to the one and despise
the other. You cannot serve both God and the powers of all merely
earthly existence at the same time.'

The Pharisees and the Law

14The Pharisees, who were greedy for money, heard these words,
and they made fun of him. 15And he said to them, 'You put yourselves forward as moral examples before people; but God sees into
your hearts. What is highly regarded among human beings may be
hideous in the sight of God.

16'The Law and the prophets were valid until John came. From
now on, the Gospel of the Kingdom of God takes effect, and everyone can enter it through inner effort. 17And yet it is more possible
for heaven and earth to pass away than for even one dot of the
Law to become invalid. 18Everyone who leaves his wife and marries
another breaks a marriage. And whoever marries a woman who has
been left by her husband also breaks a marriage.

The rich man and Lazarus

19‘Once there was a rich man, dressed in purple and fine linen. Every day he held splendid and merry feasts. 20And a poor man named Lazarus lay in front of his entrance hall, covered with sores, 21and begged for the scraps from the rich man’s table to still his hunger. And the dogs came and licked his sores. 22Now the poor man died and was carried by angels to Abraham’s bosom. And the rich man also died and was buried. 23And in the realm of shadows, where he had to endure great suffering, he lifted up his eyes and saw Abraham from afar, and he saw Lazarus in his bosom. 24And he called out: “Father Abraham, have mercy on me and send Lazarus to dip his fingertip in water and cool my tongue with it, for I am suffering in this flame!” 25But Abraham said, “My son, remember that you had goods in your earthly life; but Lazarus only had what was bad. Now he is receiving comfort for his soul here, and you are suffering. 26And what is more, a great chasm separates us from you; no one wanting to cross from here to you is able to do so, nor can anyone pass from there to us.” 27Then he said, “Then I beg you, father, to send him to the house of my father, 28for I have five brothers. I want him to be a witness to the truth for them, so that they do not also come to this place of torment.” 29But Abraham said, “They have Moses and the prophets; let them hear them.” 30He replied, “No, father Abraham, if someone rises from the dead and comes to them, then they will change their hearts and minds.” 31But he said, “If they do not heed Moses and the prophets, neither will they heed one who rises from the dead”.’

17 *Obligations of inner growth: Parable of the servant’s duty*

And he said to his disciples, ‘It is not possible for all hindrances to inner growth to be avoided. But woe to him through whom they come. 2It would be better for him if a millstone were hung round his neck and he were thrown into the sea, than that he should be the cause of disruption in inner growth for even one single, delicately burgeoning human Self.

[3]'Take heed to yourselves! If your brother has done you an injustice, reproach him with it. And if he changes his heart and mind, forgive him. [4]And even if he treats you unjustly seven times a day and turns to you seven times and says, "I have changed my heart and mind," you should forgive him.'

[5]And the apostles said to the Lord, 'Strengthen our faith!' [6]And the Lord said, 'If you had faith as a mustard seed, you could say to this sycamine tree: Be uprooted and be planted in the sea! And it would obey you.

[7]'Who of you who has a servant for ploughing or for herding sheep will say to him when he comes home from the field, "Come at once and sit down at table?" [8]Rather, he will say, "Prepare the meal for me, put on your apron and wait on me while I eat and drink; afterwards you can eat and drink, too." [9]Does the servant deserve thanks for doing his duty? [10]Think of yourselves like that; when you have done all that you have been told to do, then say: We are feeble servants, we have only done what we were obliged to do.'

Healing ten lepers and the grateful Samaritan

[11]And he went on, on his way to Jerusalem, right through Samaria and Galilee. [12]And once, as he came to a village, he was met by ten lepers. They stood at a distance [13]and called with raised voices: 'Jesus, Master, have mercy on us!' [14]When he saw them he said to them, 'Go and show yourselves to the priests.' And as they went they were healed. [15]But one of them turned back when he became aware that he had been healed, praised the revelation of God with a loud voice, [16]fell on his face at Jesus' feet and thanked him. And he was a Samaritan. [17]Jesus said, 'Were not ten healed? Where are the other nine? [18]Are they not returning to praise the power of God? Why is it only this foreigner who does that?' [19]And he said to him, 'Stand up and go your way; your faith has helped you.'

The coming of the Kingdom and foretelling the suffering
[20]At that time the Pharisees asked him, ‘When will the Kingdom
of God come?’ And he answered, ‘The Kingdom of God does not
come in a form which is outwardly perceptible. [21]Nor does it come
in such a way that one can say: Look, here it is, or there. Behold –
the Kingdom of God is within you.’ [22]And he said to the disciples,
‘There will come times when you will long to experience even
one of the days of the Son of Man, and you will not experience it.
[23]Then they will say to you: Look – there! or Look – here! Do not
follow this call, do not go on this path. [24]For the Son of Man in
his day will be like the lightning which flashes up in one part of
the sky and yet instantly pours out its bright light over the whole
firmament. [25]But first he must suffer much agony and be rejected
by this present humanity. [26]As it was in the days of Noah, so will
it be in the days when the Son of Man will reveal himself: [27]They
ate and drank, they came together in marriage as man and wife,
until the day when Noah entered the ark and the great flood broke
over them and destroyed everything. [28]It was the same in the days
of Lot: They ate, drank, bought, sold, planted, built, [29]until Lot left
Sodom, and fire and sulphur rained from heaven and everything
perished. [30]It will be like that, too, in the days when the Son of
Man will reveal himself.

[31]‘When that time comes, let him who is on the roof of his
house, having left his goods in the house, not go down to fetch
them. And let him who is out in the open field not go back to what
he has left behind. [32]Remember Lot’s wife! [33]For whoever tries to
preserve his soul unchanged will lose it, and whoever is prepared
to lose it, will in truth find himself in the life of the spirit. [34]I tell
you: Then there will be two sleeping at night in one bed; one is
gripped by it, the other is left empty-handed. [35]Two women will
be grinding at one mill: One is deeply stirred, the other is left
empty-handed.’ [37]And they said to him, ‘Where shall we turn our
gaze, Lord?’ And he answered, ‘Become aware of your life-body,
and you will see the eagles which are gathering.’

18 *Parable of the widow who asked*
And he told them a parable to show them the importance of a continuous and untiring life of prayer: [2]'In a town there lived a judge,
without reverence for God and without any regard for other human
beings. [3]And there was a widow in the town who kept coming to
him and saying, "Get me justice against my accuser!" [4]For a long
time he would not; but then he said to himself: Though I have no
reverence for God and no regard for human beings, [5]yet I will see
that this widow gets justice because she will not leave me in peace.
Otherwise she will end up by wearing me out.'

[6]And the Lord said, 'Notice what the godless judge said. [7]And
will God not all the more give justice to HIS chosen ones when
they call upon HIM night and day? Will HE not be magnanimous
towards them? [8]I tell you: HE will give them their justice at once.
But the Son of Man – when he comes, will he find the necessary
inner strength in human beings living on the earth?'

Parable of the Pharisee and the tax-collector
[9]To some who had a great deal of self-assurance and considered
themselves perfect whilst despising other people, he told this
parable: [10]'Two men went up into the Temple to pray. One was a
Pharisee, the other a tax-collector. [11]The Pharisee stood there, and
whilst praying he said to himself: God, I thank you that I am not
like other human beings, robbers, evil-doers and marriage-breakers,
or like this tax-collector. [12]I fast twice a week, and I give tithes of
all that I receive. [13]But the tax-collector stood far off and dared not
lift up his eyes to heaven. He beat his breast and said: God, have
compassion on me, sinner that I am. [14]I tell you: When that man
went down into his house again, he had been justified more than
the other. Whoever exalts himself will be humbled, and whoever
humbles himself will be exalted.'

Blessing the children
[15]And the people brought their tiny children to him so that he might
lay his hands on them. When the disciples saw this, they wanted to

stop them. [16]But Jesus called them to him and said, 'Let the children come to me and do not hinder them. They have the Kingdom of God in their very being. [17]Yes, I tell you: Whoever does not take the Kingdom of God into himself as a child has it within him, he will never find the way into it.'

The rich leader of the people

[18]Once, one of the leaders of the people asked him, 'Good Master, what must I do to attain to eternal life?' [19]And Jesus said to him, 'Why do you call me good? No one is good, except the divine Father only. [20]Do you know the commandments: You shall not corrupt marriage, you shall not kill, you shall not steal, you shall not bear false witness, honour your father and mother?' [21]He said, 'All that I have kept from my youth.' [22]When Jesus heard this answer, he said, 'Then there is one thing more for you to do. Sell all your goods and give the proceeds to the poor; thereby you will acquire a treasure in the spiritual worlds; and then come and follow me!' [23]These words made him very sad, for he was extremely rich.

[24]Jesus saw it and said, 'How hard it is for those who have earthly riches to find entry into the Kingdom of God! [25]It is easier for a camel to go through the eye of a needle than for a rich man to enter into the Kingdom of God.' [26]Those who heard this asked, 'Then who can find salvation?' [27]And he answered, 'What is impossible for human strength will become possible through the power of God.'

[28]Then Peter said to him, 'See, we have left all that was ours behind us and have followed you.' [29]And he said to them, 'Yes, I say to you, everyone who leaves a house or a wife or brothers or parents or children for the sake of the Kingdom of God [30]will receive much more in this earthly existence, and, in the coming aeon, deathless life.'

Foretelling death and resurrection

[31]And he took the twelve aside and said to them, 'See, we are going up to Jerusalem, and everything written in the books of the

prophets will be done to the Son of Man and so be fulfilled. 32He
will be betrayed to the peoples of the world; be mocked, maltreated, spat on; 33and when they have scourged him, they will
kill him. But then he will rise again on the third day.' 34But they
understood nothing. His words were hidden from them, they did
not grasp their meaning.

Healing the blind man of Jericho

35As he approached Jericho, a blind man was sitting by the wayside,
begging. 36And hearing a crowd going by, he asked what this meant.
37They told him, 'Jesus of Nazareth is passing by.' 38And he called
out: 'Jesus, Son of David, have compassion on me.' 39And those
who were in front scolded him, telling him to be quiet; but he cried
out all the more: 'Son of David, have compassion on me.'

40And Jesus stopped and let him be brought to him. And when he
came near, he asked him, 41'What do you want me to do for you?'
He said, 'Lord, let me receive my sight again.' 42And Jesus said to
him, 'Receive your sight; your faith has healed you.'

43And immediately he saw again, and he followed him, praising
the revelation of God. And all the people saw it and gave praise to
God.

19 *Meal with the chief tax-collector Zacchaeus*

And he came to Jericho and went through the town. 2See, there was
a man called Zacchaeus; he was a chief tax-collector, and a rich
man. 3He wanted to see Jesus to know who he was; but because
he was small of stature, he could not see him in the great crowd.
4So he ran on ahead and climbed up into a mulberry-fig tree to
see him, for he had to come past there. 5And when Jesus came to
the place he looked up to him and said, 'Zacchaeus, come down
quickly, for today I must be a guest in your house!' 6And he came
down hurriedly and made him welcome in his house with great
joy. 7All who saw it became indignant and said, 'He has gone in to
be a guest in the house of a sinner.' 8Then Zacchaeus stood before
the Lord and said, 'Lord, see, half of all that I have I give to the

poor, and if I have taken too much from someone, I give it back to
him fourfold.' [9]And Jesus said to him, 'So today healing has come
to this house. This man, too, is a true son of Abraham, [10]and the
Son of Man has come to seek and to save what was lost.'

Parable of the silver pounds

[11]He also told a parable to those who were listening; for he was
already near Jerusalem, and they thought that the Kingdom of
God must reveal itself any moment now. [12]He said, 'There was
once a man of noble birth; he went to a distant country to win
the royal crown and then return home. [13]He called ten of his servants, gave them ten pounds of silver money and said to them,
"Work with these until I come!" [14]But the citizens of his country
hated him and sent a delegation after him to say, "We do not want
him to be our king." [15]Now when he returned, having won the
royal crown, he sent for those servants to whom he had given
the money. He wanted to see what each one had achieved with it.
[16]The first one came and said, "Lord, your pound has gained ten
pounds more." [17]And he said, "I will praise you, you are an able
servant; you have proved yourself in a small matter, you shall
have authority over ten towns." [18]And the second came and said,
"Your pound, Lord, has made five pounds." [19]And he answered,
"And so you shall rule over five towns." [20]And another came and
said, "Lord, here is your pound. I kept it wrapped up in a cloth,
[21]for I was afraid of you; you are a severe man, and you take
where you did not give, and you reap where you did not sow."
[22]And he answered him, "My judgment upon you is taken from
your own words. You are a bad servant. Since you knew that I am
a severe man and take where I did not give, and reap where I did
not sow, [23]why did you not take my money to the money-changers
so that I could have reclaimed it with interest when I came back?"
[24]And he said to those who were standing there, "Take the pound
from him and give it to him who has been given the ten pounds."
[25]And they said to him, "Lord, he already has ten pounds!" [26]I tell
you, "To him who has will be given, and from him who has not

will be taken away even what he has. [27]But as for my enemies who
did not want me to be their king, bring them here and kill them
before my eyes".'

The entry into Jerusalem

[28]After these words he continued on his way up to Jerusalem. [29]And
when he came near to Bethphage and Bethany, to the hill which is
called the Mount of Olives, he sent two of his disciples ahead [30]and
said, 'Go into the village that lies before us. When you get there,
you will find the colt of an ass tied, on which no human being has
yet sat. Untie it and bring it here. [31]And if anyone asks you why
you are untying it, you must say, "Its Lord needs it".' [32]And the two
who were sent went and found everything as he had told them. [33]As
they were untying the colt, those to whom it belonged said, 'Why
are you untying the colt?' [34]And they answered, 'Its Lord needs
it.' [35]And they brought it to Jesus, laid their garments on the colt
and set Jesus upon it. [36]So he travelled on, and the people spread
their garments on the way. [37]Now he was close to the place where
the way leads down from the heights of the Mount of Olives into
the valley, and great joy came over the crowd of disciples and they
began to sing a song of praise. Remembering all the spirit – deeds
that they had seen, [38]they called out with a loud voice:

> Blessed be he who comes,
> the King, in the name of the Lord.
> Peace in the heavens
> and revelation in the heights!

[39]Some of the Pharisees who were in the crowd said, 'Master,
tell your disciples to stop it!' [40]But he answered, 'I tell you, if they
are silent, the stones will speak all the more loudly.'

[41]And when he came close and saw the town, he wept over it
and said, [42]'If only you could still recognize what this day means
for you and what could make for peace for you! But everything is
concealed from your eyes. [43]There will come days upon you when
your enemies will build a rampart about you and besiege you and
harass you from all sides. [44]And they will level you to the ground,

together with all your children. They will not leave one stone upon
another in you, because you did not recognize the moment when the
eye of destiny was upon you.'

Cleansing the Temple

[45]And he went into the Temple and began to drive out all the traders,
[46]and he said to them, 'Scripture says:

> My house shall be a house of worship,
> but you have made it a den of robbers.'

[47]And every day he was in the Temple, and taught. The chief
priests and the scribes, as well as the leaders of the people, were set
on doing away with him; [48]but they could not find an opportunity,
for all the people hung upon his words.

20 *The question about authority*

On one of those days, when he was teaching the people in the
Temple and proclaiming the heavenly message to them, the chief
priests, the scribes and the elders came up to him [2]with this question:
'Tell us, by what authority do you act; who has given you this task
and this authority?' [3]Jesus answered, 'Let me also ask you something. Tell me, [4]did John baptize by divine or by human authority?'
[5]They thought about it and said to themselves, 'If we say: By divine
authority, he will ask: Then why did you not believe him? [6]But if we
say: By human authority, the whole people will stone us, for they
are all convinced that John was a prophet.' [7]And so they answered,
'We do not know.' [8]Then Jesus said to them, 'Then neither will I tell
you by what authority I act.'

Parable of the vine-growers

[9]And he turned to the people and told them this parable, 'A man
planted a vineyard and let it out to vine-growers. Then he went to
another country for a long time. [10]And when the time had come, he
sent a servant to the vine-growers, so that they should give him a
portion of the harvest of the vineyard. But the vine-growers maltreated the servant and sent him back empty-handed. [11]And again he

sent a servant; but they beat and cursed him, too, and sent him away
empty-handed. 12And for the third time he sent a messenger; on
him, too, they inflicted wounds, and they threw him out. 13Then the
lord of the vineyard said, "What shall I do? I will send my beloved
son; perhaps they will respect him." 14But when the vine-growers
saw him, they debated with one another and said, "This is the heir.
Let us kill him, then we will get the inheritance." 15And they threw
him out of the vineyard and killed him. Now what will the lord of
the vineyard do to them? 16He will come and put the vine-growers
to death and entrust the vineyard to others.'

When they heard that, they said, 'May that never happen!' 17But
he looked at them and said, 'What then might be the meaning of this
word of scripture:

> The stone which the builders regarded as useless has
> become the corner stone?

18'Whoever runs against this stone will be smashed to pieces,
and if it falls on anyone he will be ground to dust.'

Paying taxes

19In that very hour the scribes and the chief priests tried to get their
hands on him, but they were afraid of the people. They had understood that they were the ones he meant when he told the parable.
20So they observed him closely and sent spies to watch him, who
pretended to be sincerely striving people. They wanted to catch him
through one of his pronouncements, so that they could then hand him
over to the judgment and jurisdiction of the governor. 21So they asked
him, 'Master, we know that you speak and teach frankly and honestly
and are not concerned with anyone's personal standing. You are truly
teaching the way of God. 22Is it right for us to pay the tax to Caesar,
or not?' 23But he saw through them and was aware of their falseness,
and he said, 24'Show me a denarius. Whose likeness and inscription
is on this coin?' They answered, 'Caesar's.' 25And he said, 'So give
to Caesar what belongs to Caesar, and give to God what belongs to
God.' 26They were not able in the presence of the people to catch him
by his words. They were amazed by his answer and became silent.

Dispute with the Sadducees

[27]Then there came to him some of the Sadducees who deny that
there is resurrection, [28]and they asked him, ‘Master! Moses, of
course, stipulated for us that if a man’s brother dies, who had a
wife but no children, then the man must marry the woman and
bring descendants into the world for his brother. [29]Now there were
once seven brothers, and the first took a wife and died without
children. [30]And the second [31]and the third took her to wife, and in
the end all seven. But they all died without leaving any children.
[32]Finally the woman also died. [33]Whose wife, then, will she be in
the resurrection, seeing that all seven had her as wife?’ [34]Jesus
answered them, ‘The sons of this earthly era marry and are given
in marriage; [35]but those who are held to be worthy to attain to the
future aeon and to the resurrection of the dead do not marry and
are not given in marriage. [36]There, they have no mortal bodies,
they are of like nature as the angels; they are sons of God, being
sons of the resurrection. [37]That the dead are raised, Moses showed
when, by the thornbush, he described the divine I AM as the God of
Abraham and the God of Isaac and the God of Jacob. [38]The Divine
Being lives, not in the dead but in the living. All who bear this
Being within themselves live because of it.’ [39]Then some of the
scribes said, ‘Master, you have answered well.’ [40]And they dared
not ask him any further questions.

[41]And he said to them, ‘How can anyone say that the Christ is
David’s son, [42]since David himself says in the Book of Psalms:

> The Lord of life said to my Lord,
> you shall sit at my right hand.
> [43]I will make your enemies subject to you
> and put them under your feet.

[44]If David calls him his Lord, how can he be his son?’

Beware of scribes

[45]And in the hearing of all the people he said to his disciples,
[46]‘Beware of the scribes! They love to go about in ceremonial garments; they like being greeted respectfully in the market places,

they want the leading position in the synagogues and the place of
honour at banquets. 47But they consume house and home of widows
under the pretext that they have endless prayers to attend to. They
burden themselves all the more with grievous destiny.'

21 *The widow's offering*
As he looked up, he saw the people putting their gifts into the col-
lection-box for the treasury. They were rich. 2But he also saw a
poor widow who put in two lepta, 3and he said, 'I tell you in truth,
this poor widow has given more than all of them. 4For all the others
gave of their surplus; but she out of her poverty has given all that
she had for her living.'

Apocalyptic words
5Some were speaking about the Temple, how beautifully adorned it
was with precious stones and gift-offerings. 6Then he said, 'You are
only considering what you can see with eyes. But there will come
times when not one stone will be left upon another; everything will
become subject to destruction.'

7And they asked him, 'Master, when will this be? And by what
sign shall we know that it is coming close?' 8He said, 'Take care
that no one leads you onto a wrong path. Many will come and,
speaking in my name, will say: I am! and: The time has come! Do
not follow them. 9Then you will hear noise and tumult of war and
revolution: Let it not give rise to fear in you. It is necessary for all
this to happen. But the ultimate aim is yet far off.'

10And he went on: 'One part of humanity will rise against the
other, and one kingdom against another. 11There will be great
earthquakes, epidemics and famines in many places; great and
alarming phenomena will be seen in the sky. 12But before this
you will be seized and persecuted; you will be handed over to
the teaching authorities and the prisons, and you will be dragged
before kings and rulers for my name's sake. 13Then it will be for
you to bear witness. 14But imprint it on your hearts that you shall
not be anxious about how to defend yourselves. 15From me you

will receive both the words and the wisdom which none of your
adversaries will be able to withstand or even contradict. [16]And
you will also be betrayed by parents and brothers, relatives and
friends. Some of you will be put to death, [17]and you will be hated
by everyone for my name's sake. [18]But not a hair of your head
shall be lost. [19]Through patient power of endurance you will then
truly find yourselves.

[20]'So when you see Jerusalem surrounded by armies, then know
that the time of its destruction has come. [21]Then all who are in
Judea should flee to the mountains, and those who are in the town
should leave, and those who are in the open country should not
enter the town. [22]For then the days of higher justice have come, and
everything written in the scriptures will be fulfilled. [23]Woe to those
who are pregnant and the mothers who are breast-feeding when that
time comes! For the distress of a grievous destiny is coming upon
the earth, cosmic wrath will be discharged upon this people. [24]Many
will fall by the edge of the sword and be dragged away into slavery
among all the peoples of the world. And Jerusalem will be overrun
and trampled upon by the heathen peoples until the time of the heathen peoples, too, is fulfilled.

[25]'And signs will appear in sun, moon and stars, and there will
be distress among the peoples of the earth and helplessness in the
face of the surging sea and its mighty waves. [26]And human beings
will lose their heads for fear and expectation of what is breaking
in upon the whole earth. And even the forces of the heavens will
be shaken. [27]Then the Son of Man will appear to seeing souls in
the clouds of the sphere of life, borne up by the might of the World
Powers, radiant with the glory of revelation. [28]And when all this
begins to happen, straighten yourselves, stand upright and raise
your heads, for then your redemption is drawing near.'

[29]And he told them a parable: 'Look at the fig tree and all the
other trees; [30]when they begin to come into leaf, you know from
that that summer is near. [31]So also, when you see all that begin to
happen, you can know that the Kingdom of God is near. [32]Yes, I
tell you, even before the time of people living now shall have come

to an end, all that will begin to happen. 33The heavens and the earth
will pass away, but my words will not pass away.
34'Take care that your hearts do not become unresponsive
through dissipation and intoxication and the cares of material existence; otherwise the breaking of the Day will come upon you suddenly like a snare. 35For that Day will come upon all who live on
the earth. 36So be of wakeful spirit at all times, school your souls
in prayer, so that you may become strong to live through all that is
coming without being harmed, and to be able to stand before the
revelation of the Son of Man.'
37He spent the days teaching in the Temple, but at night he left
the town and stayed on the Mount of Olives. 38And already early
in the morning all the people flocked to him to hear him in the
Temple.

22 *Betrayal by Judas*
The feast of unleavened bread was coming, which is called the
Passover. 2The chief priests and the scribes were looking for ways
and means to destroy him. But they feared the people. 3Then a
satanic possession came over Judas, whose other name was Iscariot
and who was one of the twelve. 4He went and negotiated with the
chief priests and the commanding officers how he could betray
him to them. 5They were delighted and promised him money as a
reward. 6He agreed, and from then on he sought for a favourable
opportunity to betray him to them without the people noticing.

The Last Supper
7Then came the day of the unleavened bread, on which the Passover
lamb was killed. 8And he sent Peter and John and said, 'Go and
prepare the Passover meal for us.' 9They said, 'Where are we to prepare it?' 10And he answered, 'See, when you enter the town you will
be met by a man carrying a water-jar. Follow him into the house
which he enters, 11and say to the master of the house: The Master
says to you: Where is the guest room where I can celebrate the
Passover meal with my disciples? 12Then he will show you a large

upper room furnished with carpets and cushions. Prepare the meal
there.' 13And they went and found everything as he had said, and
they prepared the meal.

14And when the hour had come, he sat down at the table, and the
apostles with him. 15And he said to them, 'I have waited with great
longing to eat the Passover with you, before my path of suffering
begins. 16I tell you: I will eat it no more until it comes to fulfilment in the Kingdom of God.' 17And he took the cup and blessed
it and said, 'Take this and share this draught among you. 18For I
tell you: From now on I shall no longer drink of the juice of the
vine until the Kingdom of God has appeared.' 19And he took the
bread, blessed it, broke it and gave it to them and said, 'Take this,
it is my body which is given for you. And always when you do
this, make my Being come alive within you.' 20And after the meal
he also took the cup and said, 'This cup is the new covenant with
God, established through my blood which is shed for you. 21But
see, the hand of my betrayer is with mine on the table. 22Certainly,
the Son of Man must fulfil the way which has been determined for
him; but woe to that human being by whom he is betrayed.' 23Then
they began to discuss among themselves which of them might be
capable of doing such a thing.

Conversation with the disciples

24And an argument began among them about which of them
might be the greatest. 25But he said to them, 'The kings of the
heathen peoples lord it over them, and the rulers let themselves
be proclaimed as benefactors. 26It shall not be like that with you.
27Whoever among you wants to be great, let him become as the
youngest, and whoever wants to be the leader, let him serve others. So who is greater, the one who sits at table or the one who
serves? You think: The one who sits at table. But I am in your
midst as one who serves.

28'You are those who have remained with me through all my
trials. 29And so I pass on to you the kingdom as my Father has given
it to me. 30You shall eat and drink at my table in this kingdom that I

bring; you shall sit on the twelve thrones as guides of the destiny of
the twelve tribes of the people of God. [31]Simon, Simon, see, Satan
is trying hard to get you all; he will shake you through the sieve just
like wheat is sifted. [32]For you, Simon, I have prayed, that your inner
strength may not fail. When you have come to yourself again, you
shall strengthen your brothers.' [33]And Peter said, 'Lord, I am ready
to go with you into captivity and death.' [34]But he answered, 'I tell
you, Peter, before the cock crows today you will have denied three
times that you know me.'

[35]And he said to them, 'When I sent you out without money
and bag and shoes, did you ever go short of anything?' They said,
'Never.' [36]And he went on, 'But now, let him who has purse and bag
hold them in readiness, and whoever has nothing, let him sell his
garment and buy a sword. [37]For I tell you that this scripture must be
fulfilled in me:

> He will be numbered among the criminals.

My path is now at its goal.' [38]And they said, 'See, Lord, here are two
swords.' And he said, 'It is enough.'

The Prayer in Gethsemane and arrest

[39]And he left the house and went to the Mount of Olives as was
his custom. And the disciples followed him. [40]And when he came
to the place he said to them, 'Pray, so that you may not enter into
temptation.' [41]And he withdrew from them about a stone's throw.
And he knelt and prayed: [42]'Father, if it be your will, then let me be
spared this cup. But not my will, but your will be done.' [43]Then an
angel from heaven appeared to him and gave him strength. [44]And as
he was in the throes of death he prayed with even greater intensity.
And his sweat became as drops of blood which fell to the earth.
[45]Then he rose from prayer; but when he came to the disciples, he
found that they had fallen asleep for sorrow, [46]and he said to them,
'Why are you sleeping? Rise through prayer, so that you may not
enter into temptation.'

[47]And while he was still speaking, see, a crowd came up, led by
that same Judas who was one of the twelve. He went up close to

Jesus and kissed him. 48But Jesus said to him, 'Judas, with a kiss
do you betray the Son of Man?' 49When those who were around
him saw what was coming, they asked, 'Lord, shall we strike with
the sword?' 50And one of them struck the servant of the High Priest
and cut off his right ear. 51But Jesus said, 'Stop – no more!' And
he touched the ear and healed him. 52And Jesus said to the crowd
that was coming and to the chief priests, the officers of the Temple
guard and the elders, 'You have come out as if against a robber,
with swords and clubs. 53Was I not with you in the Temple day after
day, and you did not stretch out your hands after me? But this is
your hour: Darkness rules.'

Peter's denial

54And they seized him and led him into the High Priest's house.
Peter followed at a distance. 55They lit a fire in the middle of the
courtyard, and Peter was among those who sat down by the fire.
56As the light of the fire fell on him, a maid looked at him intently
and said, 'This man was also with him.' 57But he denied it and said,
'Woman, I do not know him.' 58Soon afterwards someone else saw
him and said, 'You are one of them.' But Peter replied, 'Man, I
am not.' 59And after about an hour still another said emphatically,
'This man was definitely also with him, for he is a Galilean.' 60But
Peter said, 'Man, I do not understand what you are saying.' And
the moment he said that, the cock crowed. 61And the Lord turned
and looked at Peter. Then Peter remembered the word that the Lord
had spoken, 'Before the cock crows today, you will deny me three
times.' 62And he went and wept bitterly outside.

Accusation before the Sanhedrin

63The men who were guarding Jesus made mock of him. They covered his face, 64struck him and asked, 'Now show us your visionary
ability and say who it was that struck you.' 65And they hurled many
other abusive words at him.

66At dawn, the assembly of the elders of the people, the chief
priests and the scribes gathered together and led him before their

Sanhedrin and said, [67]'If you are the Christ, tell us.' He answered,
'Whatever I tell you, you will not believe me. [68]And whatever I ask
you, you will give me no answer. [69]From now on the Son of Man
will be exalted to the right hand of the divine power.' [70]Then they
all said, 'So, are you the Son of God?' And he answered, 'It is you
who say that I am.' [71]And they said, 'What further evidence do we
need? We have heard it ourselves from his own lips.'

23 *Interrogation before Pilate and Herod*

Then the whole assembly stood up and led him before Pilate. [2]And
they accused him and said, 'We caught this man inciting our people
and speaking against the tax to Caesar. He also called himself the
Christ, and claims to be a king.' [3]Then Pilate asked him, 'Are you
the King of the Jews?' He answered him, '*You* must say it.' [4]And
Pilate said to the chief priests and the people, 'I find no guilt in this
human being.' [5]They, however, intensified their accusations and
said, 'He stirs up the people to revolt through his teaching which
he is now spreading through the whole of Judea, having begun
in Galilee.' [6]On hearing this, Pilate asked if he were a Galilean;
[7]and when he learned that he belonged to the area under Herod's
jurisdiction, he sent him to Herod who was also in Jerusalem at
that time.

[8]When Herod saw Jesus, he was delighted, for he had wanted
for a very long time to see him because of all that he had heard
about him. He hoped to see him do some kind of magic feat. [9]And
so he asked him many questions, but he gave him no answer.
[10]Meanwhile, the chief priests and the scribes stood by and brought
the most violent accusations against him. [11]Then Herod began to
despise him. He and all his soldiers mocked him, and he robed him
in a cloak of shining white and sent him back like that to Pilate.
[12]On that day, Pilate and Herod became friends after having been
enemies before.

[13]And Pilate called together the chief priests and the leaders
[14]and the people and said to them, 'You brought this person to me as
though he were an instigator of rebellion among the people. I have

questioned him in your presence and have not found him guilty of
the charges you bring against him; 15nor did Herod, and therefore
he sent him back to us. See, he has done nothing deserving death;
16therefore I will chastise him and then release him.' 18Then they all
shouted with one voice: 'Kill him and set Barabbas free for us!' 19He
was a man who had been thrown into prison because of an insurrection in the town and for murder. 20Pilate addressed them once more,
wanting to set Jesus free. 21But they interrupted him and shouted:
'Crucify, crucify him!' 22And for the third time he said to them, 'But
what evil has he done? I have found nothing in him deserving death.
I will chastise him and then release him.' 23But they pressured him
with loud shouts and demanded that he be crucified. In the end, they
won the day with their shouting. 24Pilate decided that their demand
should be granted. 25He set free the man who was in prison because
of insurrection and murder, whose liberty they were demanding;
but Jesus he handed over to their will.

Bearing the cross

26And as they led him away, they stopped Simon, a man from
Cyrene, who was just coming from the field. They laid the cross
on him, to carry it behind Jesus. 27A great crowd of people followed him, among them many women who intoned laments and
wept over him. 28Then Jesus turned to them and said, 'Daughters of
Jerusalem, do not weep for me; but rather weep for yourselves and
your children! 29For see, there will come times when mankind will
say: Blessed are the barren, blessed the bodies that have not given
birth and the breasts that have never nursed. 30And they will say to
the mountains: Fall on us! and to the hills: Bury us! 31For if such
things are possible while the tree is yet green, what may not happen
when it is dry?'

The Crucifixion

32There were also two others who were led out with him to be exe-
cuted as criminals. 33And when the procession arrived at the place
called the Skull, they crucified him and the criminals, one on the

right and one on the left. [34]And Jesus said, 'Father, forgive them;
for they know not what they do.' And they cast lots to divide his
clothing among themselves. [35]And the people stood by and looked
on. And the leaders of the people jeered at him and said, 'He helped
others; now let him help himself if he is the Christ of God, the
Chosen One!' [36]The soldiers also mocked him, came up and offered
him vinegar [37]and said, 'If you are the king of the Jews, save yourself!' [38]Above him was written this inscription: THIS IS THE KING OF
THE JEWS.

[39]One of the criminals who were hanged sneered at him, 'Are
you not the Christ? Then save yourself and us!' [40]Then the other
replied reproachfully, 'Have you absolutely no respect for God?
You and I are both condemned, [41]and justly so; for we are receiving what we have brought on ourselves by what we have done.
But he has done nothing wrong.' [42]And he went on, 'Jesus, bear
me in mind when you enter into your Kingdom!' [43]And Jesus said
to him, 'Yes, I say to you, this very day you will be with me in
Paradise.'

The hour of death

[44]It was now about the sixth hour. Then darkness came upon the
whole earth until the ninth hour. [45]The sun failed. And the curtain
in the Temple was torn down the middle. [46]And Jesus called with a
loud voice: 'Father, into your hands do I direct my spirit.' And when
he had said this he breathed his last.

[47]The officer who saw this praised the revelation of God and
said, 'He was really a good and holy man.' [48]And the crowds of people who had flocked together to see this spectacle beat their breasts
when they saw what happened, and then returned home. [49]And all
who knew him stood at a distance and looked on, among them also
the women who had followed him from Galilee.

The burial

[50]And see, there was a man called Joseph, a member of the council, a noble and upright man; [51]he had not agreed with either their

decision or their actions. He was from the town of Arimathea in
Judea and lived in expectation of the Kingdom of God. [52]He went
to Pilate and asked for the body of Jesus. [53]And he took it down,
wrapped it in fine linen and laid him in a tomb cut into the rock,
in which no one had yet been laid. [54]It was the day of Preparation,
and the Sabbath was about to begin. [55]The women who had accompanied Jesus from Galilee had come, too. They saw how his body
was laid in the grave, [56]and went home to prepare ointments and
aromatic spices. During the Sabbath they were at rest, as the commandment decrees.

24 *The Resurrection*
But on the first day of the week, at the very first glimmering of
dawn, they came to the tomb with the aromatic extracts that they
had prepared. [2]And they found the stone rolled away from the
tomb, [3]but when they went into the tomb they did not find the
body of Jesus, the Lord. [4]And while they stood there, completely
at a loss, suddenly two men were standing before them in raiment
which shone like continuous lightning. [5]They were overcome by
terror and they bowed their faces to the ground. Then those beings
said to them, 'Why do you seek the Living One among the dead?
He is not here, he has risen. [6]Remember the words that he spoke
while he was still in Galilee: [7]The Son of Man must be betrayed
and delivered into the hands of sinful men and be crucified; but
on the third day he will rise.' [8]And they remembered his words
[9]and returned home from the tomb and proclaimed all this to the
eleven and the others who belonged to his circle. [10]It was Mary of
Magdala and Joanna and Mary the mother of James; they and the
other women who were with them told this to the apostles. [11]But it
seemed to them like empty talk; they did not believe them.

The walk to Emmaus
[13]And see, on that day two of them were on their way to a place
called Emmaus which is sixty stadia from Jerusalem. [14]And they
talked to each other about all that had happened. [15]And while they

were conversing this way and that, Jesus himself came near and
accompanied them on the way. 16But their eyes were kept from
recognizing him. 17And he said to them, 'What words are these
that you are exchanging while you walk?' And, sorrowfully, they
stood still. 18And one of them, named Cleopas, said, 'You must be
the only one among all the inhabitants of Jerusalem who does not
know what has happened here in these days.' 19He said, 'What do
you mean?' And they replied, 'The things that happened to Jesus
the Nazarene; he was a prophet of great power in word and deed
before God and all men. 20Our chief priests and leaders condemned
him to death and crucified him. 21And we had hoped that he was
the long-expected redeemer of Israel. Today is the third day since
all those things happened. 22And now some women of our circle
have caused us great excitement: They were at the tomb at dawn
23and did not find his body there; they came back saying that they
had seen a vision of angels, who said to them that he lives. 24Then
some of our friends went to the tomb and found everything as
the women had said; but him they did not see.' 25Then he said to
them, 'How unenlightened is your thinking and how slow your
heart, that all that the prophets said is not living in your souls!
26Was it not necessary for the Christ to suffer all this so that he can
reveal his light-form on earth?' 27And he explained to them all the
words of scripture which are about him, beginning with Moses
and through all the books of the prophets.

28Meanwhile they were getting near to the place where they
were going, and he made as if to go on. 29But they urged him and
said, 'Stay with us, for it is near evening and the day is now drawing to an end.' And he went in and stayed with them. 30And when
he had sat down at table with them, he took the bread, blessed it,
broke it and gave it to them. 31Then their eyes were opened and
they recognized him; but then he vanished from their sight. 32And
they said to each other, 'Did not our hearts already burn within us
when he spoke to us on the way and laid open the meaning of the
scriptures to us?'

The appearance of the Risen One in Jerusalem
[33]In the same hour they set out and returned to Jerusalem. There
they found the eleven gathered together with the others, and they
were received by them [34]with the words, 'The Lord really has risen
and has appeared to Simon!' [35]Then they also told what they had
experienced on the way and how he made himself known to them
in the act of breaking the bread.

[36]And while they were still saying this, he himself stood in their
midst. [37]They were alarmed and frightened because they thought
that they were seeing a ghost. [38]And he said to them, 'Why are you
so bewildered? Why do so many doubting thoughts arise in your
hearts? [39]Look at my hands and my feet: It is really I. Touch me and
look at me: A spirit-vision has not flesh and bones as you see on
me.' [41]As they still could not fathom it for sheer joy and amazement,
he said, 'Have you anything here to eat?' [42]They gave him a piece of
broiled fish, [43]and he took it and ate before their eyes.

[44]And he said to them, 'That was the meaning of the words
which I spoke to you while I was still with you: Everything written about me in the Law of Moses and in the books of the prophets
and in the Psalms must be fulfilled.' [45]Then he opened their understanding for the scriptures [46]and said, 'You see, scripture foretells
that the Christ will suffer and will rise from the dead on the third
day, [47]and that the change of heart and mind which leads to release
from the sickness of sin shall be proclaimed from Jerusalem in his
name to all peoples. [48]You are the witnesses. [49]And see, I pour out
that power upon you which is spoken of in my Father's promise.
Remain in the town until you have been clothed with this power
from out of the heights.'

[50]And he led them out to near Bethany and raised his hands and
blessed them. [51]And while he was blessing them, he vanished from
their sight. [52]And they returned to Jerusalem with great joy [53]and
were continually in the Temple, giving praise to God.

The Gospel of John

1 *Prologue*

In the very beginning was the Word,
and the Word was with God,
and the Word was a divine Being.
2He was in the very beginning with God.
3All things came into being through him,
and nothing of all that has come into being was made
except through him.
4In him was life,
and the life was the light of human beings.
5And the light shines in the darkness;
and the darkness has not accepted it.
6There came a man,
sent from God,
his name was John.
7He came to bear witness,
to witness to the light
and so to awaken faith in all hearts.
8He himself was not the light,
he was to be a witness to the light.
9The true light that enlightens all human beings
was to come into the world.
10It was in the world,
for the world came into being through it,
yet the world did not recognize it.
11It came to men of individual spirit,
but those very individuals did not accept it.
12To all, however, who did accept it,

it gave the free power to become children of God.
They are the ones who trustingly take its power into themselves.
13They receive their life, not out of blood,
nor out of the will of the flesh,
and not out of human willing;
for they are born of God.
14And the Word became flesh
and lived among us.
And we have beheld his revelation,
the revelation of the only Son of the Father,
full of grace and truth.
15John bears witness to him
and proclaims loudly:
'This is he of whom I said:
After me comes he who was before me,
for he is greater than I.'
16Of his fullness have we all received grace upon grace.
17The Law was given through Moses.
Grace and truth have come into being through Jesus Christ.
18No human being has ever seen the divine Ground of the World with eyes.
The only Son, who was in the bosom of the Father, he has become the guide in such seeing.

John the Baptist

19This is the testimony of John, when the Jews sent priests and
Levites from Jerusalem to ask him, 'Who are you?' 20Freely and
openly he made confession. He confessed: 'I am not the Christ.'
21Then they asked him, 'Who are you then? Are you Elijah?' And
he said, 'I am not.' – 'Are you the prophet?' He answered, 'No.'
22Then they said, 'Who are you? What answer are we to give those
who sent us? What do you say about yourself?' 23He said, 'I am the
voice of one crying in the loneliness:

Prepare the way for the Lord!
That is what the prophet Isaiah proclaimed.' [24]And those who had
been sent by the Pharisees [25]asked him, 'Why do you baptize if you
are neither the Christ, nor Elijah, nor the prophet?' [26]John answered
them, 'I baptize with water. But in your midst already stands one
whom you do not know, [27]who comes after me although he was
before me. I am not worthy even to untie the strap of his shoes.'
[28]This took place in Bethany near the mouth of the Jordan where
John was baptizing.

[29]The next day he sees Jesus coming to him, and says, 'See, the
Lamb of God who takes the sin of the world upon himself. [30]He it
is of whom I said: After me comes one who was before me, for he
is greater than I. [31]I did not know him; but for this I have come,
and have baptized with water, so that human souls in Israel might
become able to experience the revelation of his being.' [32]And John
testified: 'I saw how the Spirit descended like a dove from heaven
upon him and remained united with him. [33]I did not know him, but
HE who sent me to baptize with water said to me, "He on whom you
see the Spirit descend, so that it remains united with him, he it is
who baptizes with the Holy Spirit." [34]And I saw this, and so I testify
that this is the Son of God.'

The first disciples

[35]The next day John was again standing there, and two of his
disciples were with him. [36]And as he saw Jesus walking past,
he said, 'See, the Lamb of God.' [37]The two disciples heard him
say this, and they followed Jesus. [38]Then Jesus turned and saw
them following and said to them, 'What are you seeking?' They
answered, 'Rabbi (translated, that means Teacher), where do you
live?' [39]He said, 'Come and see!' And they came and saw where
he lived and stayed with him all that day. It was about the tenth
hour. [40]Andrew, the brother of Simon Peter, was one of the two
who had followed him because of what John had said. [41]The first
one he met was his brother Simon, and he said to him, 'We have
found the Messiah (which translated means Christ).' [42]And he

led him to Jesus. Jesus looked at him and said, ‘You are Simon,
the son of Jonah. Your name shall be Cephas (which translated
means Peter, the Rock).’
43The next day he wanted to set out for Galilee. And he finds
Philip and says to him, ‘Follow me!’ 44Philip was from Bethsaida,
the town of Andrew and Peter. 45Philip finds Nathanael and says
to him, ‘We have found him of whom Moses in the Law and also
the prophets wrote. It is Jesus, the son of Joseph from Nazareth.’
46Then Nathanael said to him, ‘Can good come out of Nazareth?’
Philip says to him, ‘Come and see.’ 47When Jesus saw Nathanael
coming towards him, he said of him: ‘He really has reached the
stage of an Israelite in whom there is no untruth.’ 48Then Nathanael
says to him, ‘From where do you know me?’ And Jesus replied,
‘Before Philip called you, when you were under the fig tree, I saw
you.’ 49Then Nathanael said, ‘Master, you are the Son of God, you
are the spiritual leader of Israel.’ 50And Jesus answered, ‘Because
I said to you, I saw you under the fig tree, have you found confidence in me? You will experience greater things than this.’ 51And
he said to him, ‘Yes, I say to you all: You will see heaven opened,
and the angels of God ascending and descending above the Son
of Man.’

2 *The first sign: The marriage at Cana*
And on the third day a wedding was celebrated at Cana in Galilee.
The mother of Jesus was there, 2and Jesus and his disciples were
also invited to the marriage feast. 3As the wine ran short, the
mother of Jesus says to him, ‘They have no more wine.’ 4And
Jesus answers her, ‘Pay heed, O woman, to the power which flows
between me and you. My own hour has not yet come.’ 5Then his
mother says to the servants, ‘Do whatever he tells you.’ 6Six stone
jars were standing there, for the Jewish ritual of purification. Each
of them held two or three measures. 7And Jesus says to the servants, ‘Fill the jars with water.’ And they filled them up to the brim.
8Then he says to them, ‘Now draw some and take it to the master
of the feast.’ And they did so. 9The master of the feast did not

know where what he was given had come from; only the servants
who had drawn the water knew that. And as he tasted the water
which had become wine, he calls the bridegroom [10]and says to
him, 'Everyone usually serves the good wine first, and then, when
the guests have drunk much, the poorer kind. But you have kept
the good wine until now.' [11]This, the very beginning of his signs,
Jesus fulfilled at Cana in Galilee. Thereby he made manifest the
radiating power of his being, and deep trust in him was awakened
in his disciples.

The first Passover: Cleansing the Temple

[12]After this he went down to Capernaum, he himself and also his
mother and his brothers and his disciples. They only stayed there
for a few days. [13]The Passover festival of the Jews was approaching. And Jesus went up to Jerusalem. [14]In the Temple he found the
dealers who were selling oxen, lambs and pigeons, and also the
money-changers at their tables. [15]And he made a whip of cords
and with it he drove them all out of the Temple, as well as the
lambs and oxen. He poured out the coins of the money-changers
and overturned their tables. [16]And to those selling pigeons he said,
'Take those away, and do not make my Father's house a place of
trade!' [17]Then his disciples recalled the word of the scriptures:

> Zeal for your house consumes me.

[18]And the Jews approached him with this question: 'What sign
can you do to prove that you have the right to act like this?' [19]Jesus
answered, 'Demolish this temple, and in three days I will raise it
up anew.' [20]Then the Jews said, 'It has taken forty-six years to con-
struct this Temple, and will you build it in three days?' [21]But he was
speaking of the temple of his body. [22]Later, when he had risen from
the dead, his disciples remembered these words; the scripture and
the word which Jesus had spoken lent certainty to their faith.

Conversation with Nicodemus by night

[23]While he was staying in Jerusalem at the Passover festival, many
found confidence in his name through seeing the signs that he did.

24But Jesus did not entrust himself to them. 25He had insight into
all human beings and had no need for anyone to show him the
nature of Man. To his awareness, what is within Man was clearly
apparent.

Now there was a man who was a member of the order of the
Pharisees; his name was Nicodemus. He held high rank among the
Jews. 2He came to him during the night and said to him, 'Master,
we know that you have come as a teacher from God; for no human
being can do such signs of the spirit as you do, unless God HIMSELF
works into his deeds.' 3Jesus answered, 'Yes, I tell you: Whoever
is not born anew from the heights cannot see the Kingdom of
God.'

4Then Nicodemus said, 'How can a person be born when he
is already old? Can he return to his mother's womb to be born
again?' 5Jesus answered, 'Yes, I tell you this: Whoever does not
come to a new birth through the formative power of the water and
the breath of the Spirit cannot gain entrance into the Kingdom of
God. 6That which is born of the element of earth is itself earthly
in nature; but that which is born of the breath of the Spirit is itself
wafting spirit. 7Do not wonder at this, that I said to you: You must
all be born anew from the heights. 8The wind blows where it will.
You hear its sound, but you do not know where it comes from or
where it is going. So also is everyone who is born of the breath of
the Spirit.'

9Then Nicodemus said, 'How can one attain to this?' 10And
Jesus answered, 'You are a teacher among the leaders of the people, and you do not know this? 11I tell you truly: We speak of what
we know, and we testify to what we have seen. But none of you
accepts our testimony. 12When I spoke to you about earthly matters, you did not have any faith in me; how will you believe me if
I speak to you about heavenly matters? 13No one has ascended into
the world of spirit who has not also descended out of the world of
spirit; that is the Son of Man. 14And as Moses lifted up the serpent
in the wilderness, so must the Son of Man be lifted up, 15so that
all who feel his power in their hearts may win a share of the life

that is beyond time.' [16]The Father showed HIS love for the world
through this, that HE offered up HIS only Son. From now on, no
one shall perish who fills himself with his power; indeed, he shall
win a share of the life that is beyond time. [17]It was not to judge the
world that the Father sent the Son into the world, but to save the
world. [18]Whoever becomes filled with his power is not put before
a judge; but whoever closes himself off from his power is already
judged, because he has not trusted the being and the power of
the only begotten Son of God. [19]This is already a judgment upon
the world, that the light has come into the world and that human
beings loved darkness more than light; for their deeds served the
powers of evil. [20]Everyone who devotes himself to the transitory
part of existence through his deeds, becomes an opponent of the
light. He does not turn to the light, in case the true nature of his
deeds should be exposed. [21]But whoever serves the true nature of
existence through his deeds, comes to the light. By their shining
radiance his deeds reveal that they have concrete reality in the
realm of the Spirit.

The last witnessing by the Baptist

[22]After this Jesus and his disciples came to the land of Judea.
There he stayed with them and baptized. [23]John also baptized; he
was at Aenon near Salim, because there was much water there,
and people came to him and were baptized. [24]John had not yet
been imprisoned. [25]Then a dispute arose between the disciples of
John and the Jews about the path of purification. [26]And they came
to John and said to him, 'Master, he who came to you beyond the
Jordan, to whom you bore witness – see, he baptizes, and everyone is going to him.' [27]John answered, 'No human being can grasp
for himself anything which is not given to him from the higher
worlds. [28]You yourselves can testify that I said: I am not the Christ,
but I have been sent before him. [29]He who has the bride, he is the
bridegroom. But the friend of the bridegroom, who stands by and
listens to him, he is filled with great joy at the bridegroom's voice.
This joy of mine is now fulfilled. [30]He must increase, but I must

decrease.' [31]He who comes from above, towers above all. He who
is of the earth, his being is earthly and his words are earthbound.
The One who comes from the heavenly world exceeds all others.
[32]What he has seen and heard, to that he testifies; but no one accepts
his testimony. [33]But whoever does receive his testimony thereby
sets his seal to this: that God is Truth. [34]For he who has been sent by
God speaks words which are spirit-filled. He does not bestow the
spirit in sparing measure. [35]The Father loves the Son and has given
all existence into his hand. [36]Whoever places his faith in the Son has
timeless existence. Whoever does not trust in the Son will not see
the true life. The wrath of God remains on him.

4 *Conversation with the Samaritan woman*

At this time, the Lord became aware that it was rumoured among
the Pharisees that Jesus was finding and baptizing more disciples than John [2](although Jesus himself did not baptize, though
his disciples did). [3]Therefore he left Judea and went again to
Galilee. [4]He had to pass through Samaria, [5]and he came to a
Samaritan town called Sychar, near the area which Jacob gave
to his son Joseph. [6]Jacob's well was also there. Jesus was weary
with travelling, and he sat down by the well. It was about midday, the sixth hour.

[7]Then a Samaritan woman came to draw water. And Jesus says
to her, 'Give me to drink!' [8]His disciples had gone away into the
town to buy food. [9]Then the Samaritan woman says to him, 'How
can you, a Jew, ask a drink of me, a Samaritan woman?' For the
Jews avoided all contact with the Samaritans. [10]Jesus replied, 'If
you knew something of the power that God gives us, and if you
knew him who is saying to you: Give me to drink, you would ask of
him and he would give you the water of life.' [11]Then she says, 'Sir,
you have nothing to draw with, and the well is deep. From where
will you take the living water? [12]Or are you, perhaps, greater than
our father Jacob, who gave us this well and drank from it himself,
he and his sons and his herds?' [13]Jesus answered her, 'Every one
who drinks of this water will become thirsty again. [14]But whoever

drinks of the water that I give him, his thirst shall be quenched
during this aeon of time. The water that I give him will become in
him a spring of the water flowing into true life.' 15Then the woman
says to him, 'Sir, give me this water, so that I may never be thirsty
again and never need come here again to draw.'

16He says to her, 'Go, call your husband, and then come back
here.' 17Then the woman said, 'I have no husband.' Jesus says,
'You are right in saying that you have no husband. 18Five husbands
have you had, and he whom you have now is not your husband.
So you have told the truth.' 19Then the woman says to him, 'Sir,
now I see that you are a prophet. 20Our fathers worshipped on
this mountain; but you Jews say that in Jerusalem is the place for
worship.' 21Jesus answers, 'Woman, have faith in me: The hour is
coming when your worship of the Father will be neither on this
mountain nor in Jerusalem. 22You worship a Being who eludes
your consciousness. Our divine service is at one with our conscious awareness. That is why salvation for mankind had to be
prepared for among the Jews. 23The hour will come, and it has
come, when the true worshippers of God will worship the Father
with the power of the Spirit and in awareness of the truth. And the
Father yearns for those who worship HIM in such a way. 24God is
Spirit, and those who worship HIM must do so with the power of
the Spirit and in awareness of the truth.' 25Then the woman says to
him, 'I know that Messiah is coming, who is called Christ. When
he comes, he will proclaim everything to us.' 26Jesus says to her,
'I AM he, speaking to you.'

27Just then his disciples came back; they were surprised that he
was talking with the woman. But no one asked, 'What do you want
from her, and why are you talking with her?' 28Then the woman left
her water jar standing, went into the town and said to the people,
29'Come, I will show you a man who was able to tell me everything
I have done. Could he be the Christ?' 30And they all flocked out of
the town to him.

31Meanwhile his disciples urged him: 'Master, eat!' 32But he
answered them: 'I have food to sustain me which is not known

to you.' [33]Then the disciples said to one another: 'Has someone
perhaps brought him something to eat?' [34]Jesus replied, 'My nourishment is to work out of the will of HIM who sent me and to fulfil
HIS deeds. [35]Do you not say that in four months it will be time for
the harvest? See, I say to you, lift up the eyes of your souls! You
will see the fields, shining white already and ripe for harvesting.
[36]Already now it is worthwhile for the reaper to gather the fruits
which bear timeless existence within them. Together they shall
rejoice, he who sowed and he who reaps. [37]That is the true meaning of the word: One sows and the other reaps. [38]I sent you out to
gather in a harvest for which you have not worked. Others did the
work, and now you enter into their work.'

[39]Many Samaritans from that town had confidence in him
because of the way the woman spoke for him with the words:
'He was able to tell me everything I have done.' [40]So when the
Samaritans came to him, they asked him to stay with them. And
he stayed there two days. [41]And ever more people believed him
because of his teaching, [42]and they said to the woman, 'Now we
no longer base our trust only on your words. Now we have heard
him for ourselves, and we know: He really is the Christ, who
brings salvation to the whole world.'

The second sign: Healing the son of a courtier

[43]After the two days he went on to Galilee. [44]Jesus himself confirmed that a prophet is not appreciated in his own homeland. [45]Now
when he came to Galilee, he was welcomed by the Galileans who
had witnessed his deeds in Jerusalem when they had been there
for the festival.

[46]And he came again to Cana in Galilee, where he had made
the water wine. There was a courtier whose son was lying ill in
Capernaum. [47]When he heard that Jesus had come from Judea
to Galilee, he went to him and asked that he would come down
and heal his son who was already near death. [48]Jesus said to him,
'Unless you see signs and wonders, you have no trust.' [49]Then the
courtier said to him, 'Sir, come down before my child dies!' [50]Then

Jesus said, 'Go now, your son lives!' And the man put his faith in
the word that Jesus spoke to him, and he went. 51While he was on
his way, his servants came to meet him to tell him that his boy was
living again. 52When he asked them the hour when he began to get
better, they answered him, 'Yesterday at the seventh hour the fever
left him.' 53Then the father realized that it was the same hour in
which Jesus said to him, 'Your son lives.' And he was filled with the
power of faith, he himself and all his household. 54This, the second
of his signs, Jesus did when he had come from Judea to Galilee.

5 *The third sign: Healing a paralysed man*
It was near to a Jewish festival, and Jesus went up to Jerusalem.
2By the Sheep Gate in Jerusalem there was a pool, called Bethesda
in Hebrew, with five porches. 3In them lay many invalids, blind,
lame, crippled and weak, waiting for the water to come into movement. 4For at certain times a powerful angelic being descended
into the pool, so that the water surged up. Then, whoever was first
to step in after the surge of the water, was healed, no matter from
what disease he was suffering. 5Now among the invalids was a
man who had been ill for thirty-eight years. 6When Jesus saw him
lying there and became aware that he had been ill for so long, he
said to him, 'Have you the will to become whole?' 7Then the sick
man answered, 'Sir, I have no one to carry me down to the pool
when the water surges up. And by the time I get there by myself,
someone else always steps in before me.' 8Jesus said to him, 'Stand
up, take your pallet and walk!' 9And at once the man was healed;
he took up his pallet and walked.

Now that day was a Sabbath, 10and so the Jews said to the man
who was healed, 'Today is Sabbath, and it is not allowed for you to
carry your pallet.' 11But he replied, 'He who healed me said to me:
Take up your pallet and walk!' 12And they asked him, 'Who is the
man who said to you: Take and walk?' 13But the man who had been
healed did not know who it was. Jesus had withdrawn from the
crowd which was gathered in that place. 14Later, Jesus found him
in the Temple and said to him, 'See, you have become well. Sin no

more, that your destiny will bring you nothing worse.' 15Then the
man went and told the Jews that it was Jesus who had healed him.
16From then on, the Jews persecuted Jesus because he did this on
a Sabbath.

The working of the Father and of the Son

17Then he himself countered them and said, 'My Father works
until now, and I also work.' 18Then the Jews sought all the more to
kill him; now he had not only profaned the Sabbath, but had even
called God his own Father and made himself equal to God. 19And
Jesus stood before them and said, 'Yes, I tell you: The Son can do
nothing out of himself, but only what he sees the Father doing.
Whatever the Father does, that the Son does, in his turn. 20For the
Father loves the Son and shows him all that HE is doing, and HE
will show him even greater deeds, so that you will be amazed.
21For as the Father raises the dead and gives them life, so also
the Son gives life to whom he will. 22The Father does not make
the decision about any one; rather, HE has passed on all the decisions of destiny to the Son. 23All human beings should honour
the Son, as they honour the Father. And whoever does not honour
the Son, does not honour the Father who sent him. 24Yes, I say to
you: Whoever hears the word that I speak, and places his trust
in HIM who sent me, he has life beyond the cycles of time. The
great decision of destiny does not apply to him, for he has already
passed from death to life. 25Yes, so it is: The hour is coming – it
has already come – when the dead will hear the call of the divine
Son, and those who hear him will be bearers of true life. 26As the
Father bears the life of the world in HIS being, so HE has also given
the Son the power to bear the life of the world in his being. 27And
thereby – because he is also the Son of Man – HE has given him
authority to make the decisions about destiny. 28Do not wonder at
this: The hour is coming when all who are in the tombs will hear
his call. 29Those who have worked for the Good will come forth
to the resurrection of life; but those whose deeds were unusable,
to the resurrection of judgment. 30I can do nothing out of myself;

I base my judgment on what I perceive in the realm of spirit, and
my judgment is just; for I do not seek to satisfy my own will, but
the will of HIM who sent me.

Witnessing for the Son

[31]'If I were only appearing as my own witness, my testimony would
be without truth; [32]but there is another who bears witness to me, and
I know that the testimonial HE gives me is the full truth. [33]You sent
messengers to John, and he gave valid testimony. [34]But human testimony is not enough for me, for I want you to find salvation through
my word. [35]He was the burning and shining lamp, and you wanted
nothing more than to bathe for a while in that light. [36]A weightier
testimony is at my disposal than that of John. The deeds which the
Father has given me to accomplish, the deeds which I fulfil, they
testify for me that the Father has sent me. [37]And so the Father who
sent me HIMSELF testifies to me. You have never heard HIS voice or
seen HIS form; [38]the Word which proceeds from HIM does not live
in your souls, for you do not open yourselves to him whom HE has
sent. [39]You pore over the scriptures, because you think that in them
you have the power of eternal life. They do, indeed, bear witness
to me; [40]but your will does not lead you to me, where you can find
true life.

[41]'I do not depend on the opinion of human beings. [42]I have
found for myself that there is no love of God in your souls. [43]I have
come in my Father's name, and you do not receive me. But when
someone else comes in his own name, then you will receive him.
[44]How can you find the faith, so long as you feel more need for the
mutual approval you exchange with one another than for the light-
form of your higher being which can only be found in the heavenly
world?

[45]'Do not think that it is I who accuse you before the Father.
Your accuser is Moses, on whom you set your hope. [46]If you really
put your faith in Moses, you would also have confidence in me, for
it was about me that he wrote. [47]But if you have no confidence in his
writings, how will you have confidence in my words?'

The fourth sign: Feeding the five thousand

After this Jesus went away to the Sea of Galilee by Tiberias. 2A
great crowd of people followed him because they had seen the
signs of the spirit which he did on those who were ill. 3And Jesus
went up on a mountain, and there he sat down with his disciples.
4The Passover, the festival of the Jews, was near. 5Now when Jesus
lifted up his eyes, seeing in the spirit, and beheld a great crowd of
people streaming towards him, he said to Philip, 'Where can we
buy bread so that they may eat?' 6He asked him this to put him to
the test. He himself knew what he would do. 7Philip answered,
'Two hundred denarii would not buy enough bread for them, even
if each of them were only to get very little.' 8Then one of his disciples, Andrew, the brother of Simon Peter, said to him, 9'Here is a
lad who has five barley loaves and two grilled fish; but what does
that amount to among so great a crowd?' 10Jesus said, 'Let the
people sit down!' Now there was much green grass in that place.
And so the men sat down, in number about five thousand. 11Jesus
then took the loaves, spoke the words of blessing over them and
shared them among those who were seated; he did the same with
the fish – all received as much as they wanted. 12When they were
satisfied, he said to his disciples, 'Gather up the fragments left
over, so that nothing be lost!' 13And they gathered up twelve baskets of fragments which had been left over when the five barley
loaves were eaten. 14Now when the people saw the sign that he had
done, they said, 'This really is the prophet who is to come into the
world.' 15When Jesus became aware that they were about to seize
him and proclaim him king, he withdrew again to the mountain,
alone by himself.

The fifth sign: Walking on the sea

16When evening came, his disciples went down to the shore,
17boarded the ship and began the voyage over the sea to Capernaum.
Darkness had fallen by now, and Jesus had not yet come to them.
18The sea began to be churned up by a strong wind. 19When they had
gone about twenty-five or thirty stadia, they saw Jesus walking on

the sea and coming near to the ship. And they were full of fear. [20]But
he said to them, 'I AM, have no fear!' [21]Now when they wanted to
take him into the ship, immediately the ship was at the land, at the
place to which they wanted to go.

I AM the bread of life

[22]On the following day, the people who were still standing on the
other shore saw that in that place there was no other ship but the
one. They knew that Jesus had not boarded the ship with the disciples and that the disciples had set off alone. [23]But then other ships
from Tiberias came near to the place where the meal had taken
place with the bread blessed by the Lord. [24]Now when the people
saw that neither Jesus was there, nor his disciples, they boarded
their ships and sailed to Capernaum to seek Jesus. [25]And they
found him on the other side of the sea and said to him, 'Master,
when did you come here?' [26]Jesus answered them, 'Yes, I say to
you: You are not seeking me because you saw deeds of spiritual
power, but because you ate of the loaves and were satisfied. [27]Do
not put your efforts into acquiring the perishable nourishment,
but the nourishment which endures and leads to imperishable life.
The Son of Man will give it to you; the Father God has set HIS
seal upon him.' [28]Then they said to him, 'What must we do, in
order that our deeds may work with the working of God?' [29]Jesus
answered, 'This is the working of God, that you have faith in him
whom HE has sent.' [30]And they asked further: 'By what sign that
you do shall we be able to see your essential nature and come to
believe in you? What is your working? [31]Our fathers ate the manna
in the desert, as it says in scripture:

Bread from heaven he gave them to eat!'

[32]Jesus answered them, 'Yes, I say to you: It was not Moses who
gave you the bread from heaven; rather, it is my Father who gives
you the bread, spiritually-real, from heaven. [33]It is the bread of God,
it descends from heaven and gives true life to the world.' [34]Then
they said, 'Lord, give us this bread always.'

[35]Jesus replied, 'I AM the bread of life. Whoever comes to me

will hunger no more, and whoever has faith in me will thirst no
more. [36]But I have already told you: You have seen me, and yet your
hearts remained closed. [37]All whom the Father gives me will find
the way to me. And him who comes to me I will not reject. [38]I have
descended from heaven, not to do my will, but the will of HIM who
sent me. [39]And this is the will of HIM who sent me, that I should lose
nothing of all that HE has given me, but that I should impart to it
the power of resurrection at the end of time. [40]This is the will of the
Father, that every one who sees the Son and has faith in him should
have a share in the imperishable life; and I will give him the power
of resurrection at the end of time.'

[41]Then the Jews became indignant at him, because he had said,
'I AM the bread which descends from heaven.' [42]And they said
to each other, 'Is this not Jesus, the son of Joseph, whose father
and mother we know? How can he say: I have descended from
heaven?' [43]But Jesus faced them and said, 'Do not grumble among
yourselves! [44]No one can find the way to me, unless the Father
who sent me causes him to feel drawn to me; and I give him the
power of resurrection at the end of time. [45]In the books of the
prophets it says:

> They shall all become pupils of God himself.

Everyone who has received the word and the teaching from the
Father will find the way to me. [46]No one has ever seen the Father
except he who himself comes from the Father; he has seen the
Father. [47]Yes, I say to you: Whoever has faith has imperishable
life. [48]I AM the bread of life. [49]Your fathers ate the manna in the
wilderness, and they died. [50]This is the bread which descends from
heaven. Whoever eats of it will not die. [51]I AM the life-giving bread
which descends from heaven. Whoever eats of this bread will live
through all cycles of time. And the bread which I shall give – that
is my earthly body which I shall offer up for the life of the world.'
[52]Then the Jews argued among themselves and said, 'How can he
give us his earthly body to eat?' [53]Jesus answered, 'Yes, I tell you:
If you do not eat the earthly body of the Son of Man and drink his
blood, you have no life in you. [54]Whoever eats my body and drinks

my blood has life beyond the cycles of time, and I give him the
power of resurrection at the end of time. [55]For my flesh is the true
sustenance, and my blood is the true draught. [56]Whoever truly eats
my flesh and drinks my blood remains in me and I in him. [57]As the
life-bearing Father sent me, and as I bear the life of the world by
the will of the Father, so also he who makes me his sustenance will
have life within him through me. [58]This is the bread which descends
from heaven. It will no longer be as it was with the fathers who ate
of it and died. Whoever eats this bread will live through the whole
cycle of time.' [59]He said this in his teaching in the synagogue in
Capernaum.

Division in the circle of the disciples

[60]Many of his disciples who heard this said, 'These are hard and
difficult words; who can bear to hear them?' [61]Jesus was aware that
his disciples could not come to terms with this, and he said to them,
'Do you take offence at this? [62]What will you say when you see
the Son of Man ascending again to where he was before? [63]It is
the Spirit that gives life; the physical by itself is of no avail. The
words that I spoke to you are spirit and are life. [64]But there are some
among you who have no faith.' For Jesus knew from the beginning
who would have faith in him and who would betray him. [65]And he
went on: 'This is why I said to you: No one can find the way to me
unless it is given him by the Father.' [66]On hearing this, many of his
disciples drew back and no longer walked with him.

Peter's confession

[67]Then Jesus said to the twelve, 'Will you also leave me?' [68]And
Simon Peter answered him, 'Lord, to whom could we go? You
have words full of unending life. [69]We have perceived with our
hearts and recognized with our thinking that you are the Holy
One of God.' [70]And Jesus said to them, 'Did I not choose you, as
the twelve? And yet one among you is an adversary.' [71]He meant
Judas, the son of Simon Iscariot. It was he, one of the twelve, who
intended to betray him.

Journey to Jerusalem
After this Jesus wandered through Galilee. He avoided Judea,
because the Jews wanted to kill him. 2The Jewish festival of
Tabernacles was close. 3Then his brothers said to him, 'Now go
up to Judea and let your disciples see openly the deeds you do. 4It
is pointless for someone to be working in obscurity if he wants to
be in the public eye. Since you are doing such deeds, then show
yourself to the world!' 5His brothers spoke like that because they
did not believe in him. 6But Jesus answered them, 'My time has
not yet come. For you, any time is as good as any other. 7People
cannot hate you, but me they hate; for through me it becomes
apparent that their activity and bustle serve the Adversary. 8You
may go up to the festival; but I am not yet going up to this festival, because for me the time is not yet fulfilled.' 9So saying, he
remained in Galilee.

10Now when his brothers had gone up to the festival, he also
went up, not outwardly visible, however, but unseen. 11The Jews
looked for him at the festival and said, 'Where is he?' 12And there
was much whispering about him in the crowd. Some said, 'He is
good.' But others said, 'No, he leads the people astray.' 13No one,
however, dared to speak publicly about him, for fear of the Jews.

His working at the festival
14When the middle of the festival week had come, Jesus went
up into the Temple and taught. 15The Jews were taken aback and
said, 'How does he come by his expertise in the scriptures when
he has never studied?' 16Then Jesus replied to them, 'The teaching which I proclaim is not from me, but from HIM who sent me.
17Anyone whose willing and doing is filled by HIS will can know
whether the teaching comes from a divine source, or whether I
am merely speaking out of myself. 18Whoever merely speaks out
of himself is seeking to glorify himself. And only he who seeks
to reveal the being of HIM who sent him is a bringer of truth, and
in him there is no falsehood. 19Did not Moses give you the Law?
And yet none of you really acts according to the Law. Why are

you wanting to kill me?' [20]Then the crowd answered, 'You are possessed by a demon! Who wants to kill you?' [21]And Jesus went on: 'One single deed I did, and you are amazed by it. [22]Moses gave you the circumcision – I do not mean that it stems from Moses, for of course it goes back to the fathers – and so you circumcise a man on the Sabbath. [23]Now if a man receives circumcision on the Sabbath, so that the Law of Moses may not become invalid, why are you outraged that I made a human being entirely whole on the Sabbath? [24]Do not judge by outer appearances, but rather look at things in depth and then form your judgment.'

[25]Then some from Jerusalem said, 'Is that not the one they want to kill? [26]Look, he is speaking openly, and no one opposes him. Have the authorities perhaps concluded that he is the Christ? [27]But we know him and know where he comes from. Yet when the Christ comes, no one knows where he is from.' [28]Then Jesus, teaching in the Temple, raised his voice and called out: 'You say that you know me and that you know where I come from. But I have not come for my own purposes; HE who is Truth itself has sent me. You do not know HIM. [29]But I know HIM, for I come from HIM; HE has sent me.' [30]Then they tried to seize him; but no one could lay hands on him, because his hour had not yet come.

Chief priests and Pharisees plan his arrest

[31]Many in the crowd believed in him; they said, 'Can the Christ, when he comes, do greater spirit-deeds than he?' [32]The Pharisees heard that this is what was thought and said about him amongst the people, and the chief priests and the Pharisees sent their servants to get him into their power. [33]Then Jesus said, 'Only a short time shall I still be with you; then I go to HIM who sent me. [34]You will seek and not find me. Where I am you cannot come.' [35]And the Jews said to one another, 'Where could he go so that we would not be able to find him? Perhaps he intends to go to the Jews in the Greek lands and teach the Greeks themselves. [36]What does he mean by those words: You will seek and not find me; where I am you cannot come?'

37On the last, the great, day of the festival Jesus stood there
and called out loudly: 'Whoever thirsts, let him come to me and
drink! 38Whoever fills himself with my power through faith, from
his body shall flow streams of life-bearing water, as scripture
says.' 39He said this to indicate the Spirit which those were to
receive who unite with him in faith. But this Spirit was not yet
working, for Jesus had not yet revealed his spirit-form. 40Some of
the people who heard these words said, 'He really is the prophet.'
41Others said, 'He is the Christ.' Still others said, 'How can the
Christ come from Galilee? 42Does not scripture say that Christ is
to come from the seed of David and from Bethlehem, the town
of David?' 43And so there was a division about him among the
crowd. 44Some wanted to seize him, but no one laid hands on him.

Division of the Sanhedrin

45Now when the servants returned to the chief priests and
Pharisees, they were asked, 'Why have you not brought him?'
46The servants answered, 'Never yet did a man speak like this man
speaks.' 47Then the Pharisees said, 'So you, too, have already been
led astray? 48Did ever anyone of the leaders of the people or the
Pharisees join him? 49Only this mob who know nothing of the Law
– let them be damned!' 50Then Nicodemus, who had already come
to him once and who belonged to their circle, said, 'Does our Law
judge a man without first giving him a hearing and establishing his
guilt?' 51And they answered, 'Are you perhaps from Galilee, too?
Search, and you will see that no prophet can rise from Galilee.'
52Then they all went home.

8 *The adulteress*

And Jesus went to the Mount of Olives. 2But as soon as the next
day dawned he was already in the Temple again, and the people
flocked to him, and he sat down and taught them. 3Then the scribes
and the Pharisees brought a woman who had been caught in adultery, and they placed her in the middle. 4Then they said to him,
'Master, this woman has been caught in the act of adultery. 5In the

Law, Moses commands us to stone such women. What do you
say about it?' 6They said this to test him, and to find a reason for
accusing him. But Jesus only bent down and wrote with his finger
in the earth. 7When they continued pressing him with questions,
he straightened up and said, 'Whoever among you is free of sin,
let him throw the first stone at her.' 8And again he bent down and
wrote in the earth. 9When they had heard his words, they went out,
one by one, beginning with the eldest. In the end, he alone was
left, and the woman was still standing in the middle. 10Then Jesus
straightened up and said to her, 'Woman, where are they? Has no
one condemned you?' 11She said, 'No one, Lord.' Then Jesus said,
'I do not condemn you, either. Go, and from now on do not sin
any more!'

I AM the light of the world

12And Jesus began to speak to them again: 'I AM the light of the
world; he who follows me will not walk in darkness but will have
the light in which there is life.'

13Then the Pharisees said to him, 'How can you be your own
witness? Your testimony is not valid.'

14Jesus answered them, 'Even if I do bear witness to myself, my
testimony is valid, for I know from where I come and where I am
going. But you do not know whence I come and where I am going.
15You judge according to the physical aspect of Man, but I judge no
one. 16Yet even if I did judge, my judgment would be valid; for I am
not alone, but HE who sent me is with me. 17In your Law it says that
the testimony of two persons is valid. 18I bear witness to myself, and
the Father who sent me also testifies to me.'

19Then they said, 'Where is your Father?' And Jesus answered,
'You know neither me nor my Father. If you knew me, you would
know my Father also.' 20These words he said as he was teaching in
the treasury of the Temple. And no one seized him, because his hour
had not yet come.

Descent from above and from below
21And he went on: ‘I go away now, and you will seek me, and in
your sin you will be subject to death. Where I am going you cannot
come.’ 22Then the Jews said, ‘Will he perhaps kill himself, since
he says: Where I am going you cannot come?’ 23And he said to
them, ‘You come from below, I AM from above. You belong to this
world which perishes, but I do not come from this world. 24That
is why I said to you: You will be subject to death in your sins. If
you do not fill yourselves with the power of my being, you will
be subject to death in your sins.’ 25Then they said to him, ‘Who
are you?’ And Jesus answered, ‘Why do I still talk to you at all?
26There are many things which I could say about you, and many
things to judge. But HE who sent me is Truth itself, and so I speak
out into the world what I have heard from HIM.’ 27But they did not
understand that he was speaking to them of the Father. 28And Jesus
went on, ‘When you lift up the Son of Man, then you will know
that I am the I-AM. I do nothing out of myself, but I proclaim what
the Father teaches me. 29HE who sent me works in my working.
HE does not leave me on my own; what I do is always in accord
with HIM.’

Abraham and Christ
30Because of these words many found trust in him. 31And Jesus
spoke to the Jews who had found trust in him: ‘If you can live
and find permanence in my word, then you really are my disciples, 32and you will recognize the truth, and the truth will
lead you to freedom.’ 33Then they answered him, ‘We are
Abraham’s seed. Never have we been slaves to anyone. How
then can you say, “You will become free”?’ 34Jesus answered,
‘Yes, I say to you: Everyone who sins is a slave to sin. 35But
a slave does not really belong to the house lastingly; it is the
son who really belongs lastingly to the house. 36When the Son
gives you freedom, then you will be really free. 37I know that
you are Abraham’s seed, but you want to kill me because my
word finds no dwelling in you. 38What I have seen with my

Father, that I proclaim. You also act according to what you
have received from your father.'
[39]Then they answered him, 'Abraham is our father.' And
Jesus said, 'If you are sons of Abraham, then do the deeds that
Abraham did! [40]But now you are wanting to kill me, one who
has proclaimed and spoken the truth to you as I have received it
from God. Abraham did not do this. [41]Now, do the deeds which
your father did!' Then they said, 'We were not born of an impure
union; actually we only have one Father: God HIMSELF.' [42]Jesus
replied, 'If God were your Father, you would love me. For I have
come forth from God and continue to come from HIM. I did not
come for my own purposes, but HE sent me. [43]Why then do you
not understand my way of speaking? You are unable to open your
hearing to my word. [44]You are descended from the father of the
Adversary, and your will is to act according to the desires of this
father of yours. From the very beginning his desire has been to
destroy Man. He has no part in true existence, because the true
being is not in him. When he proclaims deceiving appearances,
he is speaking out of his own being; for he is the bringer and the
father of deceit. [45]Me, who proclaim to you true existence, you do
not trust; [46]yet who among you can convict me of error? Why do
you not trust in me, since I am proclaiming the true existence to
you? [47]Whoever is of God receives the words of God. The reason
why you do not receive them is that you are not of God.'
[48]The Jews countered: 'Are we not right when we say that you
are a Samaritan and are possessed by a demon?' [49]Jesus said, 'I
have no demon within me; nothing but reverence for the Father
lives in me; but you dishonour me. [50]I am not striving for transfiguration and revelation of my own being; but there is One who
wills it, and through it HE will bring about decisions. [51]Yes, I say
to you: Whoever keeps my word in his heart is free of the sight
of death through all earthly time.' [52]Then the Jews said, 'Now we
know for sure that you are possessed by a demon. Abraham died,
and all the prophets died; and you say: Whoever keeps my word
will not taste death for all time. [53]Are you greater than our father

Abraham, who died? Or the prophets, who also died? Who do
you think you are?' 54Jesus answered, 'If it were my own aim to
reveal my being, such a revelation would be worthless. But it is
the Father who reveals me; and although you call HIM "our God,"
55you do not know HIM. But I know HIM. If I were to say that I
did not know HIM, I would be deceived as you are. But I do know
HIM and I bear the power of HIS word within me. 56Abraham, your
father, rejoiced that it was to be granted him to see the coming
down of my being. And he saw it and was filled with joy.' 57Then
the Jews said to him, 'You are not yet fifty years old and you
claim to have seen Abraham?' 58And Jesus answered, 'Yes, I tell
you: From the days before Abraham was born, I existed as the
I-AM.' 59Then they picked up stones to hurl at him. But Jesus was
concealed from them and left the Temple.

9 *The sixth sign: Healing a man born blind*

As he passed by, he saw a man who had been blind from birth. 2And
his disciples asked him, 'Master, who sinned, this man himself or
his parents, that he was born blind?' 3Jesus answered, 'The blind-
ness does not stem from his sin nor from his parents; but rather,
through it the working of the divine in him is to become manifest.
4Through our deeds we must serve the deeds of HIM who sent me,
as long as it is day. Night comes, when no one can work. 5As long
as I am in the world of mankind, I AM a light for that world.' 6When
he had said these words, he mixed his spittle with earth and made a
paste out of it; this he put on the man's eyes 7and said to him, 'Go
and wash in the pool Siloam!' Translated, that means: Sent out. And
he went and washed and came back seeing.

8Then the neighbours and those who had seen him before as a
blind beggar, said, 'Is that not the man who used to sit and beg?'
9Others said, 'Yes, it is.' And yet others said, 'No, he only looks
like him.' Then he himself spoke, 'I am that man.' 10And they
asked him, 'Then how were your eyes opened?' 11He answered,
'The man whom they call Jesus made a paste of earth and anointed
my eyes with it and said to me: Go to the pool Siloam and wash.

And as I went and washed, I received my sight.' [12]Then they asked
him, 'Where is he?' And he answered, 'I do not know.'

[13]Then they took to the Pharisees the man who had been blind;
[14]for the day on which Jesus had opened his eyes with the paste
of earth was a Sabbath. [15]Therefore the Pharisees asked him how
he had received his sight. He answered, 'He put a paste of earth
on my eyes, and I washed. Since then I can see.' [16]Then some
of the Pharisees said, 'This man is not sent from God, otherwise
he would keep the Sabbath holy.' But others said, 'Can a sinful
human being do such deeds of the spirit?' So there was a division
among them. [17]And they again turned to the man who had been
blind and asked, 'What do you say about him, since he opened
your eyes?' And he answered, 'He is a prophet.'

[18]The Jews would not believe that he had been blind and had
received his sight; so they called the parents of him who had
become seeing [19]and asked them, 'Is that your son, and do you
confirm that he was born blind? Then how is it that he can now
see?' [20]His parents answered, 'Certainly we know that he is our
son and that he was born blind. [21]But how it comes about that he
can see now, that we do not know. We do not know who opened
his eyes. Ask him; he is of age and can tell you about it himself.'
[22]His parents said this because they were afraid of the Jews. For
the Jews had already decided that anyone who confessed to him as
the Christ would be excluded from their community. [23]That is why
his parents said, he is of age, ask him.

[24]So for the second time they called the man who had been
blind, and said to him, 'We now ask you before God. We know
that this man is a sinner.' [25]He replied, 'Whether he is a sinner, I
do not know. But one thing I do know: I was blind and now I see.'
[26]And they asked further, 'What did he do to you? How did he
open your eyes?' [27]He answered, 'I have already told you, but you
did not listen. Why do you want to hear it again? Do you also want
to become his disciples?' [28]Then they shouted at him: 'You are his
disciple. We are disciples of Moses. [29]We know that the voice of
God has spoken to Moses; but we do not know out of what spirit

this man works.' 30The man who had been healed said, 'It is rather
strange that you do not know out of what spirit he works, since he
did open my eyes. 31After all, we know that God does not listen to
sinners; but he hears those who are devout and who act according
to the divine will. 32Never in our age has it been heard of that
anyone opened the eyes of one born blind. 33If he were not sent by
God, he would not have the power to do such a deed.' 34But they
answered, 'You were wholly born in sin, and you dare to instruct
us?' And they threw him out.

35Jesus heard that they had thrown him out, and he found him
and said to him, 'Do you trust in the Son of Man?' 36He answered,
'Tell me who he is, Lord, so that I may place my trust in him.'
37Then Jesus said, 'You have seen him. He it is who is speaking to
you.' 38And he said, 'I believe, Lord.' And he fell down before him.

39And Jesus said, 'To bring about a separation I have come into
this world. Those who do not see are to become seeing, and those
who are seeing are to become blind.' 40These words were heard
by some of the Pharisees who were with him, and they asked him,
'So, are we also blind?' 41And Jesus answered, 'If you were blind
you would be free of sin; but now you claim to be seeing, and so
your sin remains.'

10 *I AM the door*
Yes, I say to you, 'Anyone who does not go in to the sheep
through the door but breaks into the fold somewhere else, he is a
thief and a robber. 2He who enters through the door is a shepherd
of the sheep. 3To him the doorkeeper opens, and the sheep hear
his voice and he calls each one by name and leads them out. 4And
when he has brought them out, he goes before them, and the sheep
follow him, for they know his voice. 5A stranger they will not
follow; they flee from him, for they do not know the stranger's
voice.' 6Jesus used this picture-language with them, but they did
not understand what he was saying to them. 7And Jesus went on:
'Yes, I say to you: I AM the door to the sheep. 8All who came
before me are thieves and robbers. But the sheep did not listen to

them. 9I AM the door. He who enters through me will find salvation. He learns to cross the threshold from here to beyond, and
from there to here, and he will find nourishment for his soul, as
the sheep find pasture in the field. 10The thief comes only to steal
and kill and destroy. But I – I have come so that they may have
life and overflowing abundance.

I AM the good shepherd

11'I AM the good shepherd. The good shepherd lays down his life
for the sheep. 12A hired man who is not a real shepherd and does
not care about the sheep, abandons the sheep and runs away when
he sees the wolf coming; and the wolf snatches them and scatters
them. 13He is a hireling, he cares nothing for the sheep. 14I AM the
good shepherd, and I know who belongs to me; and those who are
mine know me, 15as the Father knows me and I know the Father. I
offer my life for the sheep. 16And I havc other sheep that are not of
this fold. I must also lead them, and they will listen to my voice, and
then there will be one flock, one shepherd. 17That is why the Father
loves me, because I lay down my life, that I may take it up anew.
18No one can take my life from me; but in full freedom I myself
offer it up. I have the power to give it away, and also the power to
receive it anew. That is the task given to me by my Father.'

19Then there was again a division among the Jews because of
these words. 20Many of them said, 'He is possessed by a demon and
completely out of his mind. Why do you listen to him?' 21Others
said, 'These are not the words of one who is possessed. After all,
can a demon open the eyes of the blind?'

Further attacks by the Jews

22It was just at the time of the festival of the Dedication of the
Temple in Jerusalem. 23It was winter. Jesus walked in the Temple,
in the portico of Solomon. 24Then the Jews gathered round him and
said, 'How long will you hold our soul in suspense? If you are the
Christ, tell us plainly.' 25Jesus answered, 'I have spoken to you, but
you did not open yourselves to my words. The deeds that I do in my

Father's name, they bear witness to me. [26]But you do not accept this
testimony, for you do not belong to my sheep. [27]My sheep listen to
my voice, and I know them, and they follow me, [28]and I give them
true life. They shall not perish in this age, and no one shall tear
them out of my hand. [29]My Father, who has given them to me, is
greater than all else, and no one can ever tear them out of the hand
of the Father. [30]I and the Father are one.'

[31]Then the Jews again picked up stones to stone him. [32]But Jesus
said to them, 'By many healing deeds have I shown that I work out
of the power of the Father. For which of these deeds do you want
to stone me?' [33]Then the Jews answered, 'We are not stoning you
because of a work of healing, but because of blasphemy. You are a
human being and are making yourself a god.' [34]But Jesus replied, 'Is
it not written in your Law:

I said: You are gods?

[35]Now when scripture which is unchangeable calls them gods
to whom the word of God is addressed, [36]how can you say to him
whom the Father has hallowed and sent into the world, "You are
blaspheming!" because I said, "I am a Son of God?" [37]If it is not the
works of my Father that I do, then your hearts may remain closed to
me. [38]But if I am doing them, at least open your hearts to my deeds if
you are not able to trust me myself. Then you will realize ever more
that the Father is in me and that I am in the Father.' [39]And again they
tried to seize him, but he slipped away, out of their hands.

[40]And again he went to the region beyond the Jordan, to the
place where John baptized in the beginning. There he remained.
[41]And many came to him; and they said, 'John did no signs, but
everything that John said about him is true.' [42]And there were many
who found faith in him there.

11 *Lazarus*

A man was ill: Lazarus from Bethany, the home of Mary and her
sister Martha. [2]This was the Mary who had anointed the Lord
with precious ointment and had wiped his feet with her hair. Her
brother Lazarus fell ill. [3]Then the sisters sent word to him: 'Lord,

see, he whom you love is ill.' [4]When Jesus heard this, he said,
'This illness does not lead to death but to the revelation of God;
the creative might of the Son of God shall be revealed through it.'
[5]Jesus loved Martha and her sister and Lazarus. [6]Now when he
heard of his illness, he remained for two days in the place where
he was. [7]Then he said to his disciples, 'Let us go to Judea again.'
[8]The disciples said, 'Master, now, when the Jews were after you
to stone you, you want to go there again?' [9]Jesus said, 'Does not
the day have its measure – twelve hours? Whoever walks his way
in the day, he does not stumble, for he sees the light of this world.
[10]But whoever walks his way in the night, he stumbles because
no light shines for him.' [11]Thus he spoke to them. Then he went
on, 'Lazarus, our friend, sleeps; but I go to awaken him.' [12]Then
the disciples said to him, 'Lord, if he is sleeping, he will recover.'
[13]But Jesus had spoken of his death, and they thought he was
speaking of sleep. [14]Then Jesus spoke to them openly, 'Lazarus
has died. [15]And I am glad for your sake that I was not there, so that
your faith may awaken. But now let us go to him.' [16]Then Thomas,
who was called the Twin, said to his fellow disciples, 'Yes, let us
go, that we may die with him.'

[17]When Jesus got there, he found that he had already been in
the tomb for four days. [18]Bethany was near Jerusalem, about fifteen
stadia away. [19]Many Jews had come to Martha and Mary to con-
sole them about their brother. [20]When Martha heard that Jesus was
coming, she went to meet him. But Mary remained within. [21]And
Martha said to Jesus, 'Lord, if you had been here, my brother would
not have died. [22]But I know that God fulfils whatever you ask of
him.' [23]Jesus answered her, 'Your brother will rise again.' [24]Martha
said to him, 'I know that he will rise again in the great resurrection
at the end of time.'

I AM the resurrection and the life

[25]Then Jesus said to her, 'I AM the resurrection and the life. Whoever
fills himself with my power through faith, he will live even when
he dies; [26]and whoever takes me into himself as his life, he is set

free from the might of death in all earthly cycles of time. Do you
feel the truth of these words?' [27]And she said, 'Yes, Lord. With my
heart I have recognized that you are the Christ, the Son of God,
who is coming into the world.' [28]When she had said this, she went
and called her sister Mary and said to her privately, 'The Master
is here and is asking for you.' [29]When Mary heard this, she got up
quickly and went to him; [30]Jesus had not yet entered the town. He
had stayed in the place where Martha had met him. [31]When the
Jews who were with her in the house, consoling her, saw Mary get
up quickly and go out, they followed her. They thought she was
going to the tomb to weep there. [32]But Mary came to the place
where Jesus was, and when she saw him, she fell at his feet and
said to him, 'Lord, if you had been here, this brother of mine would
not have died.'

The seventh sign: The raising of Lazarus

[33]When Jesus saw how she and the Jews coming with her were
weeping, he aroused himself in spirit and, deeply moved, [34]he
said, 'Where have you laid him?' They answered, 'Come, Lord,
and see.' [35]Jesus wept. [36]Then the Jews said, 'See how he loved
him.' [37]But some of them said, 'Could not he who restored the
sight of the blind man keep this man from dying?' [38]And again
Jesus, deeply moved within himself, went up to the tomb. It was
a cave, and a stone lay across it. [39]And Jesus said, 'Take away the
stone!' Then said Martha, the sister of him whose life had reached
completion, 'Lord, he has already begun to decompose, for this is
the fourth day.' [40]But Jesus said, 'Did I not say to you that if you
had faith you would see the revelation of God?' [41]Then they took
away the stone. And Jesus lifted up his eyes to the spirit and said,
'Father, I thank you that you have heard me. [42]I knew that you
always hear me; but because of the people standing here I say it,
so that their hearts may know that you have sent me.' [43]Then he
called with a loud voice: 'Lazarus, come out!' [44]And the dead man
came out, his feet and hands bound with strips of linen, his face
covered with a veil. And Jesus said, 'Unbind him, and let him go!'

The Sanhedrin decides to kill him

[45]Many of the Jews who had come to Mary and saw this deed found trust in him. [46]But some went to the Pharisees and reported to them what Jesus had done. [47]Then the chief priests and the Pharisees called a meeting of the Sanhedrin and said, 'What shall we do? This man does many signs. [48]If we leave him in peace, everyone will eventually follow him, and then the Romans will come and take both country and people from us.' [49]Then one of them, Caiaphas, who held the position of High Priest that year, said to them, [50]'You are ignorant, otherwise you would see that it is better for you that one man dies for the people, than that the whole people perishes.' [51]He did not say this out of himself, but, being the High Priest of that year, he foresaw prophetically that Jesus would die for the people, [52]and not only for the people, but for those, scattered among all mankind, who have the potential to become children of God and to become one through him. [53]From that day on, they stood firm in their decision to kill him.

The last Passover

[54]Now Jesus no longer appeared in public among the Jews, but went away to the region at the edge of the desert, to the town Ephraim; there he stayed with his disciples. [55]The Passover festival of the Jews was close, and many people went up to Jerusalem from the country before the festival to sanctify themselves. [56]They looked for Jesus there, and while they were standing in the Temple they said to one another, 'What do you think; will he be coming to the festival?' [57]The chief priests and the Pharisees had given orders that if anyone knew where he was he must report it to them, so that they could capture him.

12 *Anointing in Bethany*

Six days before the Passover festival, Jesus went to Bethany, where Lazarus was, whom he had awakened from the dead. [2]There they prepared a meal for him. Martha served at the table, and Lazarus was one of those who sat at table with him. [3]Then Mary took a

vessel with precious oil of nard and anointed the feet of Jesus and
wiped his feet with her hair. And the whole house was filled with
the fragrance of the oil. [4]Then said Judas Iscariot, one of his disciples who was intending to betray him, [5]'Why was this oil not
sold for three hundred denarii and the proceeds given to the poor?'
[6]But he did not say this because he was concerned about the poor,
but because he laid claim to what did not belong to him. He kept
the accounts and had charge of the donations. [7]But Jesus replied,
'Leave her be; what she has done shall count on the day of my
burial. [8]The poor you always have with you, but you do not always
have me.'

[9]A great crowd of Jews had discovered that he was there, and so
they came; but they did not only come to see Jesus, but also to see
Lazarus whom he had awakened from the dead. [10]The chief priests
had decided also to kill Lazarus, [11]for because of him many Jews
went there and found faith in Jesus.

The entry into Jerusalem

[12]The next day a great crowd of people who were coming to the
festival heard that Jesus was on his way to Jerusalem. [13]And they
took branches from the palm trees, went out to meet him and
called:

> Hosanna!
> Blessed be he who comes in the name of the Lord.
> He is the King of Israel.

[14]And Jesus found the foal of an ass and sat upon it, in accordance with the word of scripture:

> [15]Fear not, Daughter Zion!
> See, your king is coming,
> sitting on the colt of the beast of burden.

[16]At first, the disciples did not grasp what was happening. But
later, when the spirit-form of Jesus had been revealed, they remembered that this had already been foretold by scripture, and that they
themselves had helped to fulfil the prophesy. [17]The people who had
been there when he called Lazarus out of the tomb and awakened

him from the dead now testified and confessed to him. [18]That was
also the reason why the people went out to meet him: They had
heard about the sign which he had done. [19]But the Pharisees said
to one another, ‘Now you can see that all our efforts are in vain.
Look, all the world is following him.’

Meeting with Greeks

[20]Among those who were going up to worship at the festival there
were also some Greeks. [21]They approached Philip, who was from
Bethsaida in Galilee, and asked him, ‘Sir, we should like to see
Jesus.’ [22]Philip went and spoke with Andrew, and so Andrew and
Philip came to Jesus to speak to him. [23]And Jesus said to them,
‘The hour has come for the Son of Man to be revealed in his spirit-form. [24]Yes, I tell you: Unless a grain of wheat dies when it falls
into the earth, it remains as it is. But if it dies, it bears much fruit.
[25]Whoever loves his own soul will lose it; but whoever hates that
in his soul which belongs to the transient world will save it for
true, deathless life. [26]Whoever would serve me, must follow me on
my way. Where I am, there also must he be who would serve me;
and my Father will honour him who serves me. [27]Now my soul is
deeply disturbed. What shall I say? Father, save me from this hour?
But it was for this purpose that I came to this hour. [28]Father, reveal
your name!’ Then a voice sounded from heaven: ‘I have revealed
it, and I will reveal it anew.’ [29]The crowd standing by and listening
said, ‘It thundered.’ Others said, ‘An angel spoke to him.’ [30]But
Jesus said, ‘This voice was not heard for my sake, but for yours.
[31]This is the hour of decision for the whole world. The ruler of
this world will be cast out. [32]And when I have been exalted above
earthly existence, I will draw all human beings to me.’ [33]He said
this to indicate the death towards which he was going. [34]Then the
people answered him, ‘When we were taught the Law we always
heard that the Christ remains and leads over into the coming aeon;
so how can you say that the Son of Man must be raised up? Who
is this Son of Man?’ [35]And Jesus answered, ‘For a short time yet
the light is in your midst. Tread your path while you have the light,

so that the darkness does not overcome you. Whoever walks in
darkness does not know where he is going. [36]While you still have
the light, open your hearts to the light, so that you may become
sons of light.'

The unbelief of the Jews

When Jesus had spoken these words, he went away and kept himself concealed from them. [37]However many signs of the spirit he
had done before their eyes, they still could not find the strength to
trust in him. [38]The word of the prophet Isaiah had to be fulfilled:

> Lord, who receives our message?
> And to whom is revealed the creating arm of the Lord?

[39]They really could not open their hearts, and so Isaiah says in
another place:

> [40]He has made their eyes blind and hardened their
> hearts, so that, in spite of their eyes, they do not see,
> and in spite of their hearts, they do not perceive; they
> are not to return to the old spiritual powers. But in
> time I will heal them.

[41]This Isaiah said because he beheld his spirit-form and therefore could already speak of him. [42]Although some of the rulers of
the people could relate to him, for fear of the Pharisees they dared
not confess it, in case they should be excluded from the synagogue.
[43]They loved human prestige more than the divine revelation.

[44]But Jesus called out aloud: 'Whoever has faith in me, has faith
not in me, but in HIM who sent me. [45]And whoever sees me sees
HIM who sent me. [46]I have come as a light into the world, so that
every one who unites with me may become free of the spell of the
darkness. [47]If any one hears my words and does not keep to them,
I do not judge him. I have not come to judge human beings, but to
heal them. [48]If any one rejects me and gives no room in himself to
my words, he already has a judge. The word that I have spoken will
itself be his judge at the end of time. [49]For I have not spoken only
out of myself. The Father who sent me has HIMSELF given me as
spirit-aims what I should say and what I should proclaim. [50]And I

know that HIS spirit-aim is the true life of our cycle of time. What
I proclaim, I proclaim as the Father HIMSELF has spoken it to me.'

13 *Washing the feet of the disciples*
The Easter festival was approaching. In his spirit, Jesus perceived
that the hour had come for him to pass from the earthly world to the
world of the Father. He loved all those who had become his own from
out of mankind, and he sustained this love to its fulfilment. 2When
the meal began, the Adversary had already put the thought that he
would betray him into the heart of Judas, the son of Simon Iscariot.
3Jesus knew that the Father had given everything into his hands,
now that he, who had come from the heavenly world, was to return
to the heavenly world. 4So he got up from the meal, laid aside
his outer garments and bound an apron around himself. 5Then he
poured water into the bowl which was there for the ritual washing
and began to wash the disciples' feet and to wipe them with the
apron which he was wearing. 6Then he came to Simon Peter. And
he said, 'Lord, do *you* wash my feet?' 7Jesus answered, 'What I am
doing, you do not yet understand; but later you will grasp it.' 8And
Peter said, 'You shall not wash my feet, neither now nor in times to
come.' Then Jesus answered him, 'If I do not wash you, you have
no part in me.' 9And Simon Peter said, 'Lord, not only my feet
but also hands and head.' 10Jesus replied, 'Whoever receives this
washing has only need of the washing of the feet, for that purifies
his whole being. You are all now clean, although not every one of
you.' 11For he knew who would betray him; that is why he said:
Not all of you are clean.
12When he had washed their feet, he took his garment and sat
down with them again and said, 'Do you understand what I have
now done for you? 13You call me Master and Lord, and you are
right, for so I am. 14If then I, your Lord and Master, have washed
your feet, you owe it to each other to wash one another's feet. 15I
have given you an example, so that you may do for one another what
I have done for you. 16Yes, I say to you: A servant is not greater than
his master, and the messenger is not greater than he who sent him.

[17]If you understand this, blessed are you if you do it. [18]Not about all
of you can I say: I perceive the higher being of those whom I have
chosen. But the scripture must be fulfilled:

He who eats my bread treads on me with his feet.

[19]I say this to you now, before it happens, so that when it takes
place you may know with certainty that it is I. [20]Yes, I say to you:
Whoever receives one whom I send receives me; and whoever
receives me receives HIM who sent me.'

Indicating the traitor

[21]When he had said this, his spirit was stirred profoundly, and he
bore witness: 'Yes, I tell you, one of you will betray me.' [22]The
disciples looked at one another, at a loss to know whom he meant.
[23]Now one of his disciples was at the table, lying close to the
breast of Jesus, the disciple whom Jesus loved; [24]so Simon Peter
beckoned to him and said, 'Ask who it is of whom he speaks.'
[25]Then he who was lying so close to the breast of Jesus asked him,
'Lord, who is it?' [26]And Jesus answered, 'It is he to whom I shall
give the morsel when I have dipped it.' And he dipped the morsel
and gave it to Judas, the son of Simon Iscariot. [27]And after he had
taken the morsel, the power of Satan entered into him. And Jesus
said to him, 'What you are about to do, do it soon!' [28]But none
of those at the table understood why he said that to him. [29]Some
thought that, because Judas was in charge of the money, Jesus
was saying: Buy what we need for the festival, or that he should
give something to the poor. [30]So, after receiving the morsel, he
immediately went out. And it was night.

Foretelling Peter's denial

[31]When he had gone out, Jesus said, 'Now the Son of Man is
revealed; the divine in him has been revealed. [32]And since God
has been revealed in him, then God will also reveal him in HIM-
SELF, and soon now will HE reveal him. [33]Little children, only for a
short time longer am I with you, and then you will seek me. And
as I said to the Jews: Where I am going you are not able to come,

so I now also say it to you. 34A new task and aim I give you: Love
one another! As I have loved you, so you should love one another.
35By this everyone shall recognize you as my disciples, that you
have love for one another.'

36Then Simon Peter said to him, 'Lord, where are you going?'
And Jesus answered, 'Where I am going you cannot follow me
now; but later you will follow me.' 37Peter said, 'Lord, why cannot I
follow you now? I will lay down my life for you.' 38Jesus answered,
'You will give your life for me? Yes, I tell you: Even before the
cock crows you will deny me three times.'

14 *I AM the way and the truth and the life*

'Let your hearts not become troubled. Have faith in the power
which leads you to the Father and which leads you to me. 2In my
Father's house there are many dwellings; otherwise I would not
have said to you: I go there to prepare a place for you. 3And when
I go to prepare a place for you I will come to you anew, and I
will take you to myself so that where I am you may be also. 4And
where I am going, you know the way.'

5Then Thomas said to him, 'Lord, we do not know where you
are going; how can we know the way?' 6Jesus answered, 'I AM the
way and the truth and the life. No one finds the way to the Father
but through me. 7If you had recognized me, you would also have
known my Father. From now on you know HIM, for you have seen
HIM.'

8Then Philip said to him, 'Lord, show us the Father, then we
have all that we need.' 9Jesus answered, 'I have now been with
you so long, and yet you have not known me, Philip? He who has
seen me has also seen the Father – how can you still say, "Show
us the Father"? 10Do you not believe that I am in the Father and
the Father is in me? The words that I speak to you I do not speak
out of myself. The Father who lives in me fulfils HIS deeds through
me. 11Believe me that my Self lives in the Father and the Father
lives in me. If you cannot trust me, at least build your faith on
these deeds.

12‘Yes, I say to you: Whoever takes me into himself will also be
able to do the deeds that I do – and greater deeds he will do, because
I go to the Father. 13What you pray for in my name, I will fulfil it, so
that the Father will be revealed in the deeds of the Son. 14Everything
which you pray for in my name: I will fulfil it.

The promise of the Holy Spirit

15‘If you truly love me, you will take my aims into your will. 16And
I will pray the Father, and HE will send you another Comforter,
the giver of spirit-courage, who will be with you for this whole
earthly aeon, 17the Spirit of Truth. Not all people can receive HIM.
They do not see HIM and do not recognize HIM. But you know
HIM, for HE guides you as a higher being above you, and HE will
enter your innermost heart.

18‘I will not leave you as orphans. I shall come to you. 19Yet a
short time and the world will see me no more; but you will perceive
me. I live, and you shall share in this life. 20On that day you will
recognize: I in the Father, and you in me and I in you. 21Whoever
knows my aims and takes them into his will, he it is who truly
loves me. And he who loves me will be loved by my Father, and I
will love him and reveal myself to him.’

22Then Judas (not Iscariot) said to him, ‘Lord, for what reason will you reveal yourself to us but not to all people?’ 23Jesus
answered, ‘Whoever truly loves me bears my word in himself, and
my Father will love him, and we will come to him and dwell with
him for ever. 24Whoever does not love me does not bear my word
in himself. And the word that you perceive is not from me but
from the Father who sent me. 25I have said this to you because I
am still with you. 26The Comforter, the giver of spirit-courage, the
Holy Spirit whom the Father will send in my name, HE will teach
you everything and awaken your memory of all that I said to you.

27‘I leave you the peace; my peace I give to you. I do not give it
as the world gives. Let your hearts not grow troubled and fearful.
28You have heard that I said: I go away, and yet I come to you. If
you really loved me you would rejoice that I go to the Father, for

the Father is greater than I. [29]And now I have told you before it happens, so that your souls shall be secure when it happens. [30]I shall not speak much more with you. Already the master of this world is coming, but he cannot touch me. [31]I fulfil the task that the Father has given me, so that the world shall know that I love the Father. Be prepared – then we can leave this place.

15 *I AM the true vine*
'I AM the true vine and my Father is the vinedresser. [2]Every branch of mine that bears no fruit HE takes away, and every branch that does bear fruit HE makes pure, that it may bear more fruit. [3]You have already been purified by the power of the word which I have spoken to you. [4]Abide in me and I in you. As the branch cannot bear fruit by itself unless it is given life by the vine, neither can you unless you stay united with me. [5]I AM the vine, you are the branches. He who remains united with me and I in him, he bears much fruit, for apart from me you can do nothing. [6]If a man does not remain united with my being, he withers like a branch that is cut off – such branches are gathered, thrown into the fire and burned.

[7]'If you abide in me and my words live on in you, pray for that which you also *will,* and it shall come about for you. [8]By this my Father is revealed, that you bear much fruit and become ever more my disciples.

[9]'As the Father has loved me, so I have loved you – live on in my love. [10]If you take my aims into your will, then you will live on in my love, just as I have taken the aims of my Father into my will and live on in HIS love. [11]These words I have spoken to you that my joy may be in you, and that your joy may be complete.

[12]'This is the task I put before you, that you love one another as I have loved you. [13]No man can have greater love than this, that he offer up his life for his friends. [14]You are my friends if you follow the task I give you. [15]No longer can I call you servants, for the servant does not know what his master is doing, but I call you friends because I have made known to you all that I have heard from my Father. [16]You did not choose me, but I have chosen you

and appointed you that you should go and bear fruit and that your
fruit should live on after you, so that what you ask the Father in
my name HE should give it to you. 17This I say to you out of the
fullness of my power – love one another.

The world's hatred

18'If people hate you, remember that they hated me before you. 19If
you belonged to people in general, they would love you as belonging to them, but because you do not belong to them since I chose
you out of mankind, people hate you. 20Remember the word that
I spoke to you: "A servant is not greater than his master." If they
have persecuted me, they will also persecute you. If they have held
on to my word, they will hold on to yours, too. 21Everything that
they do to you, they will do as though they did it to me, for they do
not know HIM who sent me. 22If I had not come and had not spoken
to them, they would be without sin, but now they have no excuse
for their sin. 23He who hates me, hates my Father also. 24If I had not
done deeds among them such as no one else has ever done, they
would be without guilt. But now they have seen me and have still
hated both me and my Father. 25But it was to fulfil the word that is
written in their Law:

They hated me without a cause.

The working of the Holy Spirit

26'But when the Comforter comes, the Spirit of Truth who proceeds
from the Father, HE will bear witness to me. 27And you will also be
my witnesses, because you have been united with me from the very
beginning.

16 *Reunion with the disciples*

'These words I have spoken to you so that you may not go astray.
2They will exclude you from their society, and the hour will come
when those who kill you will think that they are doing God a service. 3They will do all this because they have recognized neither
me nor the Father. 4I have said this to you, so that when the time

comes you will remember that I told you about it. In the beginning
I did not need to say such things to you for I was with you. 5But
now I go to HIM who sent me; and none of you asks me, "Where
are you going?" 6Now that I have said these things to you, sorrow
enters your hearts. 7But I tell you the truth: It is for your salvation and healing that I leave you. For if I did not go away, the
Comforter, the giver of spirit-courage, would not come to you.
When I now go away I will send HIM to you. 8When HE comes, HE
will call mankind to account for the decline into sinfulness, for the
working of Man's higher being and for the great world-separation.
9For the decline into sinfulness, because they do not fill themselves with my power; 10for the working of Man's higher being,
because I go to the Father and you see me no more; 11for the great
world-separation, because the decision has already been made
about the ruler of this world.

12'I have yet much to say to you, but you cannot bear it now.
13But when the Spirit of Truth comes, HE will be your guide on the
way to the all-embracing truth. HE will not speak out of HIMSELF,
but what HE hears HE will speak, and HE will proclaim to you what
is to come.

14'HE will reveal me; for what HE draws from my being HE will
proclaim to you. 15Everything that the Father has is also mine. That
is why I said: He will draw upon my being and proclaim to you.

16'Yet a short time and you will see me no more; and again a
short time and you will see me.' 17Then some of his disciples said
to one another, 'What does he mean: A short time and you will
not see me and again a short time and you will see me; and: I go
to the Father?' 18And so they said, 'What is meant by "a short
time"? We do not understand his words.' 19Jesus knew that they
wanted to ask him, and he said, 'You are wondering that I said:
A short time and you will not see me, and again a short time and
you will see me. 20Yes, I tell you; you will weep and lament, while
other people will be happy. You will be sorrowful, but your grief
will be turned into joy. 21A woman giving birth must suffer pain;
for her hour has come. But when she has borne the child, she no

longer considers the anguish for joy that a human being is born
into the world. 22So you have to suffer pain now. But I will see
you again, and then your hearts will be filled with joy, and no one
can take that joy from you. 23On that day you will have no need to
ask me anything. Yes, I say to you: From now on, what you ask
from the Father HE will give you in my name. 24Up to now you
have not yet prayed in my name. Pray from the heart, and it will
be given to your heart, so that your joy may be fulfilled.

Speaking openly about the Father

25'I have said all this to you in imagery. But the hour is coming
when I will no longer speak to you in pictures. Then I will speak
openly and plainly to you about the Father. 26On that day you will
pray in my name. I do not say that I will pray the Father for you;
27for the Father HIMSELF loves you because you have loved me and
have believed that I come from the Father. 28I went forth from the
Father and came into the earthly world; and now I leave the sense-
world again and go to the Father.' 29Then his disciples said, 'See
– now you are speaking plainly and openly and not in pictures.
30Now we recognize that everything has been revealed to you. You
do not need anyone to question you. And so our hearts confess that
you come from the Father.'

31And Jesus answered, 'Do you now feel my power in your
hearts? 32See – the hour is coming, it has already come, when you
all will be scattered, each one into his own loneliness. Then you
will also leave me alone; but I am not alone, for the Father is with
me. 33I have said these words to you, so that in me you may find
the peace. In the world you have much hardship; but take courage;
I have overcome the world.'

17 *The High Priestly prayer*

When he had said this, Jesus raised his vision to the spirit and
said, 'Father, the hour has come; reveal the being of your Son,
so that your Son may reveal your being. 2You have made him
the creating power in all earthly human bodies, that he may give

true life to all who came to him through you. [3]And the true life is
this, that they recognize you as the one true Ground of the World,
and Jesus Christ as the one whom you have sent to them. [4]I have
revealed your being on the earth and have fulfilled the task which
you have given me to do. [5]And now, Father, Ground of the World,
let my being be revealed in the light which shone about me in
your presence, before the world yet was. [6]I havc made manifest
your name to those human beings who have come out of the world
to me through you. Yours they were, and you have given them to
me, and they have kept your word in their inmost being. [7]Thus
they have recognized that everything which you have given me
is from you; [8]for all the power of the word which you have given
me, I have brought to them. They have taken it into themselves
and have recognized in deepest truth that I come from you, and
they have come to believe that I have been sent by you. [9]I pray
to you for them as individual human beings, not for mankind in
general. Only for the human beings which you have given me,
because they belong to you. [10]Everything that is mine is yours,
and what is yours is mine, and the light of my being can shine in
them. [11]I am now no longer in the world of the senses; but they
are still in the world of the senses. And I am coming to you. Holy
Father, keep, through the power of your being, those who came
to me through you, so that they may become one, as we are one.
[12]As long as I have been with them, I have kept and sheltered,
through the power of your being, those who came to me through
you, and none of them has been lost except he who was born to be
an instrument of destruction; and so scripture has been fulfilled.
[13]Now I am coming to you, and I am saying these words while
I am still among humankind, so that my joy may be fulfilled in
them. [14]I have brought them your word; but other people have
hated them because they are not of their world, as I, also, am
not of their world. [15]My prayer is not that you should take them
out of the earthly world, but that you protect them from the evil.
[16]They are not of the earthly world, as I, also, am not of that world.
[17]Hallow them through the truth. Your word is Truth. [18]As you sent

me into the world, so now I have sent them into the world. 19And
I consecrate myself for them, so that they may be consecrated in
truth. 20And not only for them do I pray to you, but also for those
who will unite with me through their proclamation, 21so that they
may all be one; as you, Father, are in me and I in you, so they shall
be one in us, so that the world may come to believe that you have
sent me. 22I have given them the power of revelation which you
have given me, so that they may be one, as we are one. 23I am in
them, and you are in me, and so they are consecrated to become
perfectly one, so that the world may recognize that you have sent
me and that you love them as you love me.

24'Father, Ground of the World, that is my will: That those whom
you have given me may ever be with me where I am and that there
they will behold the revelation of my being which you, in your
love, have given me before the world was. 25Exalted Father, earthly
human beings have not recognized you; but I have recognized you,
and these have recognized that you sent me. 26I have revealed your
name to them, and I will continue to reveal it, so that the love with
which you have loved me may remain in them and so my being may
be revealed in them.'

18 *The arrest*

After these words Jesus left the house with his disciples and
crossed over the Kidron brook. On the other side there was a garden which he and his disciples entered. 2This place was also known
to Judas who betrayed him; for Jesus had often gathered his disciples around him there. 3And so Judas took a unit of the cohort and
also some of the servants of the chief priests and the Pharisees,
and came with torches and lanterns and weapons. 4Jesus saw in
the spirit all that was about to happen to him, and so he stepped
forward and said to them, 'Whom do you seek?' 5They answered,
'Jesus of Nazareth.' He said, 'I AM he!' Judas who betrayed him
was standing there with them. 6Now when he said to them: I AM
he, they reeled back and fell to the ground. 7And once more he
asked them, 'Whom do you seek?' Again they answered, 'Jesus of

Nazareth.’ 8And Jesus said, ‘I said to you that I am he. If you are
seeking me, let these others go their way.’ 9The word was to be
fulfilled which he had spoken: Of those which you gave me I let
not one be lost.

10Simon Peter had a sword. He drew it and attacked the High
Priest’s servant and cut off his right ear. The servant’s name was
Malchus. 11Then Jesus said to Peter, ‘Put your sword into its sheath!
Shall I not drink the cup which the Father has given me?’ 12Then
the soldiers, the officer and the servants of the Jews seized Jesus,
bound him 13and led him first to Annas. He was the father-in-law
of Caiaphas who held the position of High Priest that year. 14It was
Caiaphas who had advised the Jews that it was good that one man
should die for the people.

Peter’s denial and Jesus before the High Priest

15Simon Peter followed Jesus, and so did another disciple. This
disciple was an acquaintance of the High Priest, and he went with
Jesus into the court of the High Priest’s residence. 16Peter stood
outside at the gate. Then the other disciple, the acquaintance of the
High Priest, went and spoke to the maid who kept the door, and
brought Peter in. 17Then the maid keeping the door said to Peter,
‘Are not you also one of this man’s disciples?’ He answered, ‘I am
not.’ 18The servants and attendants were standing about; they had
made a charcoal fire to warm themselves, for it was cold. Peter
stood next to them and warmed himself.

19Meanwhile the High Priest questioned Jesus about his disciples and his teaching. 20Jesus answered him, ‘I have spoken publicly before all the world. I have always taught in the synagogue
and in the Temple where all the Jews come together. I have not
said anything in secret. 21Why do you ask me? Rather, ask those
who heard what I spoke to them. See, they know what I have proclaimed.’ 22When he said this, one of the attendants standing by
gave Jesus a slap in the face and said, ‘How dare you answer the
High Priest like that?’ 23Jesus said to him, ‘If I have said something
wrong, then prove that it was wrong. But if I have said what is

right, then why do you hit me?' [24]Then Annas sent him bound to Caiaphas the High Priest.

[25]Simon Peter was still standing there, warming himself. And they said to him, 'Are you not also one of his disciples?' He denied it and said, 'I am not.' [26]Then said one of the servants of the High Priest, a relation of the one whose ear Peter had cut off, 'Did I not see you in the garden with him?' [27]Again Peter denied it, and at that moment the cock crowed.

Interrogation before Pilate

[28]From Caiaphas they led Jesus to the Roman courthouse. It was early morning. They did not themselves enter the courthouse so as not to become unclean, but be able to eat the Passover. [29]So Pilate came out to them and said, 'What charge are you bringing against this person?' [30]They answered, 'If he were not doing anything wrong we would not have brought him before you.' [31]Then Pilate said, 'Take him yourselves and try him according to your own Law.' But the Jews said, 'We have no authority to execute anyone.' [32]The word of Jesus was to be fulfilled by which he indicated the kind of death he would suffer. [33]Then Pilate went inside the courthouse again, called Jesus and said to him, 'Are you the King of the Jews?' [34]Jesus answered, 'Are you saying that out of yourself, or have others said it to you about me?' [35]Pilate said, 'Am I a Jew? Your own people and the chief priests have handed you over to me. What have you done?' [36]Jesus answered, 'My kingdom is not of this world. If my kingdom were of this world, my servants would have fought and would not have let me fall into the hands of the Jews. But my kingdom is not from here.' [37]Then Pilate asked, 'Are you a king, then?' Jesus answered, '*You* must say whether or not I am a king. I descended and was born into the earthly world to testify to the truth. Everyone who is of the world of truth hears my voice.' [38]Then Pilate said to him, 'What is truth?' And when he had said this, he went out to the Jews again and said to them, 'I find no guilt in him. [39]But you have the custom that I release a prisoner for you at the Passover festival. If you wish it,

I will release for you the King of the Jews.' [40]But they shouted back: 'Not him, but Barabbas!' And Barabbas was a murderer.

19 *Crowning with thorns*

Then Pilate took Jesus and had him scourged. [2]And the soldiers plaited a crown of thorns and put it on his head and threw a purple cloak round him, [3]walked up to him and said, 'Hail, King of the Jews!' And they struck him in the face. [4]And again Pilate went out and said to them, 'See, thus I bring him out to you, so that you may know that I find no guilt in him.' [5]And Jesus came out, wearing the crown of thorns and the purple cloak. And he said to them, 'See, this is Man.' [6]When the chief priests and the Temple attendants saw him, they shouted: 'Crucify, crucify him!' Then Pilate said to them, 'Take him yourselves and crucify him, for I find no guilt in him.' [7]Then the Jews replied, 'We have a law, and according to that law he must die, because he has made himself a Son of God.'

The judgment

[8]When Pilate heard these words, he was even more alarmed, [9]and he again went into the courthouse and said to Jesus, 'From where have you received your mission?' But Jesus gave him no answer. [10]Then Pilate said to him, 'You will not speak to me? Do you not know that I have the power to release you and also to crucify you?' [11]Jesus answered, 'You would not have power over me unless it had been given you from on high. Therefore the greater burden of destiny falls upon him who handed me over to you.' [12]Upon this, Pilate wanted to set him free. But the Jews shouted: 'If you release him, you are no longer a friend of Caesar; for everyone who makes himself a king is against Caesar.' [13]When he had heard these words, Pilate led Jesus out and sat down on the judgment seat in the place called The Pavement; in Hebrew, Gabbatha. [14]It was the Day of Preparation of the Passover festival, about midday. And he said to the Jews, 'See, this is your King.' [15]But they shouted: 'Away with him, away with him, crucify him!'

Pilate asked them, 'Shall I crucify your King?' And the chief
priests answered, 'We have no king but Caesar.' [16]Then he handed
him over to them to be crucified.

The Crucifixion

[17]And they seized Jesus and, carrying his own the cross, he went
out to the Place of a Skull, in Hebrew called Golgotha. [18]There
they crucified him, and with him two others, one on the one side,
the other on the other side, and Jesus in the middle. [19]Pilate had
written a title and fixed it on the cross. It read: JESUS OF NAZARETH,
THE KING OF THE JEWS. [20]This title was read by many Jews, for
the place where Jesus was crucified was near the city. It was written in Hebrew, in Latin and in Greek. [21]Then the chief priests of
the Jews said to Pilate, 'Do not write: "The King of the Jews,"
but "This man said: I am the King of the Jews".' [22]But Pilate
answered, 'What I have written I have written.'

[23]Now when the soldiers had crucified Jesus they took his garments and divided them into four parts, one for each soldier. Then
they also took the cloak. This cloak was seamless, woven in one
piece from top to bottom. [24]Then they said to one another, 'Let
us not tear it, but cast lots to see whose it shall be.' The word of
scripture was to be fulfilled:

> They divided my clothes among them,
> and for my cloak they cast lots.

[25]Therefore the soldiers did this.

Standing by the cross of Jesus were his mother and his mother's
sister, Mary the wife of Clopas, and Mary of Magdala. [26]Now when
Jesus saw his mother standing there and the disciple whom he loved,
he said to his mother, 'Woman, see, that is your son.' [27]And then he
said to the disciple, 'See, that is your mother.' And from that hour
the disciple took her to himself.

The death

[28]After this Jesus perceived in spirit: Everything is now nearing its
goal and fulfilment, and, so that the word of scripture should be

accomplished, he said, 'I thirst.' 29There was a jar of vinegar standing there. And they soaked a sponge in vinegar, fixed it around a hyssop branch and held it to his mouth. 30And when Jesus had taken the vinegar, he said, 'It has been fulfilled.' Then he bowed his head and breathed out his spirit.

31Since it was the Day of Preparation, the Jews did not want the bodies to remain on the cross, for that Sabbath was a great festival day. So they asked Pilate that their legs might be broken and that they should be taken down from the cross. 32And so the soldiers came and broke the legs of first the one, and then the other, who had been crucified with him. 33When they came to Jesus and saw that he had already died, they did not break his legs. 34But one of the soldiers thrust a lance in his side, and at once blood and water flowed out. 35He who saw it has testified to it, and his testimony is true. And he knows that he is speaking the truth, so that you also may find the way of faith. 36All this happened so that the scripture should be fulfilled:

> His bones shall not be broken

37and also the other place in the scriptures:

> They shall look on him whom they have pierced.

The burial

38Then Joseph of Arimathea went to Pilate and asked him for permission to take down the body of Jesus from the cross. He was a disciple of Jesus, but kept it secret for fear of the Jews. Pilate gave him permission. And so he came and took down the body. 39Nicodemus came also, who had first come to Jesus in the realm of night, and he brought about a hundred pounds of a mixture of myrrh and aloes. 40And they took the body of Jesus and wrapped it in strips of linen soaked with the balsam spices, according to the burial custom of the Jews. 41At the place of the crucifixion there was a garden, and in the garden there was a new tomb where no one had ever been buried. 42They laid Jesus there because of the Jewish Day of Preparation, for the tomb was near.

0 *The Resurrection*

On the first day after the Sabbath at the first breaking of the day,
Mary of Magdala comes to the tomb and sees that the stone has
been taken away. 2And she runs and comes to Simon Peter and to
the other disciple whom Jesus loved, and says to them, 'They have
taken the Lord out of the tomb, and we do not know where they
have laid him.' 3And so Peter and the other disciple set off towards
the tomb. 4They both ran, and the other disciple ran faster and
overtook Peter and came to the tomb first. 5He bent forward and
saw the linen cloths lying there, but he did not go in. 6Then Simon
Peter, who was following him, also came, and he went straight
into the tomb. And he beheld the linen cloths lying there 7and
the veil which had been over his head; it was, however, not lying
with the cloths but bundled up in one particular place. 8Then the
other disciple also went in, he who had come first to the tomb; and
he understood, and faith entered his heart, giving certainty to his
soul. 9For as yet they had not grasped the meaning of the word of
scripture, that he would rise from the dead. 10And the disciples
went again to their house.

Appearance before Mary of Magdala

11But Mary stood outside before the tomb and wept. And weeping
she bends forward into the tomb 12and sees two angels in shining white garments sitting there, one at the head and the other at
the feet where the body of Jesus had lain. 13And they say to her,
'Woman, why are you weeping?' She answers, 'They have taken
away my Lord, and I do not know where they have laid him.'
14And saying this, she turned and sees Jesus standing, but is not
aware that it is Jesus. 15And Jesus says to her, 'Woman, why are
you weeping? Whom are you seeking?' He appears to her to be
the gardener, and she says to him, 'Sir, if you have taken him
away, tell me where you have laid him, so that I can take him
back.' 16Jesus says to her, 'Mary!' And again she turns and says to
him in Hebrew, 'Rabboni;' that means: Master. 17But Jesus says to
her, 'Do not touch me, for I have not yet ascended to the Father.

Now go to my brothers and say to them: I ascend to the Father
who gives existence to me and to you and who lives as a divine
power in me and also in you.' [18]Then Mary of Magdala goes and
tells the disciples the message, 'I have seen the Lord and he spoke
these words to me.'

Appearance before the disciples

[19]On the evening of that day, the first day after the Sabbath, the
disciples had locked the doors of the room where they were, for
fear of the Jews. Then Jesus came and stood in the midst and
said to them, 'Peace be with you!' [20]And while he said this, he
showed them his hands and his side. Full of joy the disciples
recognized the Lord. [21]And again he said, 'Peace be with you! As
the Father has sent me, so I send you.' [22]And when he had said
this, he breathed on them and said, 'Receive Holy Spirit! [23]Whom
you release from sin, they shall be released, and whom you leave
in their sin, they shall remain in it.'

[24]Thomas, one of the twelve, who was called the Twin, was not
there when Jesus came. [25]Later, the other disciples said to him, 'We
have seen the Lord.' But he replied, 'Unless I see in his hands the
mark of the nails and place my finger in the place where the nails
were, and place my hand in his side, I cannot believe it.'

Appearance before Thomas

[26]And eight days later the disciples were again gathered in the inner
room, and Thomas was there. The doors were locked. Then Jesus
came, stood in the midst and said, 'Peace be with you!' [27]And then
he said to Thomas, 'Stretch out your finger and see my hands, and
stretch out your hand and place it in my side. Be not rigid in your
heart; but rather feel my power in your heart.' [28]Then Thomas said to
him, 'You are the Lord of my soul, you are the God whom I serve.'
[29]And Jesus said to him, 'Have you found my power in yourself
because you have seen me? Blessed are those who find my power
in their hearts, even when their eye does not see me.'

[30]Many other signs were done by Jesus before the eyes of his

disciples. They are not recorded in this book. [31]But what is in this
book has been written so that you all may come to certain faith in
your souls that Jesus is the Christ, the Son of God. And when you
have come to that faith, you will find true life through the power of
his name.

21 *The early meal by the sea*
After this Jesus revealed himself anew on the shores of the Sea
of Tiberias. And this is how he revealed himself: [2]Simon Peter,
Thomas called the Twin, Nathanael from Cana in Galilee, the
sons of Zebedee and two others of his disciples were together.
[3]Simon Peter says to them, 'I will go and cast out the nets.' And
they answer, 'We will go with you.' And they left the house and
got into the boat. But in that night they caught nothing. [4]Just as
day was breaking, Jesus stood on the shore; yet the disciples did
not recognize that it was he. [5]Then Jesus says to them, 'Children,
have you nothing to eat?' They answer him, 'No.' [6]And he says to
them, 'Cast your net out on the right side of the boat, and you will
find.' When they threw out the net they were hardly able to haul it
in, so great was the abundance of fish. [7]Then that disciple whom
Jesus loved said to Peter, 'It is the Lord!' When Peter heard: It is
the Lord, he flung on his cloak and tied it round himself, for he
was naked, and threw himself into the sea. [8]The other disciples
followed in the boat. They were only about two hundred cubits
from the land and were hauling the net with the fish. [9]When they
got out on land, they see a coal fire there, with fish lying on it, and
bread. [10]And Jesus says to them, 'Bring some of the fish that you
have just caught.' [11]Then Simon Peter went up and drew the full
net ashore with one hundred and fifty-three large fish. Despite the
great number, the net did not tear. [12]And Jesus says to them, 'Come
to the meal!' None of the disciples dared to question him: 'Who are
you?' They saw, and they recognized that it was the Lord. [13]And
Jesus comes and takes the bread and gives it to them, and likewise
the fish. [14]This was already the third time that Jesus revealed himself to the disciples as the One risen from the dead.

The tasks of Peter and the beloved disciple

[15]When the meal was over, Jesus says to Simon Peter, 'Simon, son of John, do you love me more than the others?' He answers, 'Yes, Lord, you know that you are dear to me.' And he says to him, 'Feed my lambs.' [16]And he asks him a second time, 'Simon, son of John, do you love me?' And he answers, 'Yes, Lord, you know that you are dear to me.' And he says to him, 'Be a shepherd to my little sheep.' [17]The third time he asks him, 'Simon, son of John, am I dear to you?'

Then Peter was grieved that on the third occasion he asked him, 'Am I dear to you?' And he answered, 'Lord, you know all things, you know that you are dear to me.' And Jesus says to him, 'Feed my sheep. [18]Yes, I tell you: when you were young you tied your own belt and followed aims you had set yourself; but when you reach maturity of age you will stretch out your hands, and someone else will gird you and lead you to aims you do not set yourself.' [19]With these words he showed him in a picture by what death the divine in him should be revealed. And he says to him, 'Follow me.'

[20]Then Peter turned and saw that the disciple whom Jesus loved was following. He was the one who had lain close to his breast at the meal and had said: Lord, who is it who betrays you? [21]When Peter sees him, he says to Jesus, 'Lord, what is *his* task?' [22]Jesus answers him, 'If I choose for him to remain until my coming, it does not concern you: Follow me!'

[23]Because of this it was said among the brothers that this disciple would not die. But Jesus did not say to Peter: He will not die. Rather, he said, 'If I choose for him to remain until my coming, that does not concern you.' [24]This is the disciple who bears witness to all this. He wrote it down, and we recognize that his testimony is the truth. [25]Jesus also did many other things, but if they were all written down one after another, I do not think that the world itself could contain the books that would have to be written.

The Acts of the Apostles

Prologue

My first word, O Friend of God, concerned all that which Jesus created by his deeds and by his teaching; [2]until the day when he was taken up after he had shown his chosen apostles the Way through the power of the Holy Spirit. [3]By many manifestations of his being he had shown himself as the victor over death after his passion. For forty days he revealed himself to their seeing souls and spoke to them of the mysteries of the Kingdom of God.

Ascension

[4]And while he was thus in their midst, he directed them not to leave Jerusalem: 'Wait here for the fulfilment of the Father's promise which you have sensed through me. [5]John baptized you with water, but you are to be baptized with the Holy Spirit. Not many more days will pass before then.' [6]Then they all gathered closely together and asked him, 'Lord, will you then also restore the kingdom to the people of Israel?' [7]And he said to them, 'It is not your task to discern the times and moments which the Father has decided upon out of HIS rightful, almighty power. [8]But you will receive the power which descends upon you: the power of the Holy Spirit; and then you will be my witnesses in Jerusalem and in all Judea and Samaria and to the very end of the earth.' [9]And as he said this he was lifted up before their eyes, a cloud received him and they saw him no longer. [10]And while they still directed their gaze upwards after him into heaven, see, suddenly two men in white garments stood by them [11]and said, 'You men from Galilee, why do you stand there looking up to heaven? This Jesus, who has been taken up before you into heaven, will come again, revealed

in the same kind of way as you have now seen him pass into the
heavenly sphere.' 12Then they returned to Jerusalem from the
heights of the Mount of Olives which is near Jerusalem, a Sabbath
day's journey away.

Choosing Matthias

13And they entered the house and went up into the upper room
in which they usually gathered: Peter and John and James and
Andrew, Philip and Thomas, Bartholomew and Matthew, James the
son of Alphaeus and Simon the Zealot and Judas the son of James.
14In unity of soul they devoted themselves to prayer, together with
women and with Mary the mother of Jesus, and with his brothers.

15It was in those days that Peter once got up and stood in the
midst of the brothers – about a hundred and twenty names had
gathered – and said, 16'Men and brothers, the word of scripture
had to be fulfilled which the Holy Spirit spoke through the mouth
of David, indicating Judas who showed the captors of Jesus the
way. 17He was one of our number and had received the same task
of destiny as we. 18With the reward which he received for his mis-
deed he bought a field. There, after he had hanged himself, he fell
into the abyss and burst open so that all his entrails gushed out.
19This became known to all the people in Jerusalem, so that they
called this field Akeldama in their language, that is Field of Blood.
20For it is written in the book of Psalms:

> His dwelling-place shall be desolate and lonely,
> no-one shall live there.

And:

> Let his task as leader pass to someone else.

21Therefore, one of the men who walked with us during the time
when the Lord Jesus shared his life with us, 22from the baptism of
John until the day when he was taken up – one of these men must
become a witness with us to his resurrection.' 23And two were put
forward: Joseph, whose second name was Barsabbas and who was
called the Just, and Matthias. 24And, praying, they said, 'Lord, you
who know the hearts of all, show us which one of these two you

choose, [25]so that he may take the place in service and apostleship
which Judas deserted to go his own ways.'
[26]And they cast lots for them, and the lot fell on Matthias; thus
he was enrolled with the circle of the eleven apostles.

2 *The Pentecost event*

And as the time of the fifty days neared its fulfilment they were
waiting with shared devotion for the beginning of the Pentecost festival. [2]Then suddenly a sound came from the spiritual heights like
the rushing of a mighty wind, and it filled the whole house in which
they were gathered. [3]And to their seeing there appeared tongues of
fire, like flames which divided until they came to rest on each one of
them. [4]And they were all filled by the Holy Spirit and began to speak
in foreign tongues; each uttered what the Spirit gave him to say.
[5]In those days there were Jews living in Jerusalem from every
nation under heaven, men who were devoted to the spirit. [6]When
that voice sounded, they hurriedly gathered in great numbers, and
each one was filled with consternation because he heard them speak
in his own language. [7]Beside themselves with amazement they said,
'See, are not all these who are speaking Galileans? [8]How can it
be that each one of us hears them speak in his native language:
[9]Parthians and Medes and Elamites and inhabitants of Mesopotamia,
Judea and Cappadocia, Pontus and Asia, [10]Phrygia and Pamphylia,
people from Egypt, Libya and Cyrene, Romans who live here, Jews
and proselytes, [11]Cretans and Arabs? We all hear them proclaim the
great deeds of God in our own language.' [12]They were all beside
themselves and could not grasp what was happening. And one said
to another, 'What is to become of this?' [13]But others said mockingly,
'They are drunk on sweet wine.'

Peter's Pentecost address

[14]But Peter stood up, together with the other eleven apostles, raised
his voice and addressed the people: 'Jewish men, and all of you
who live in Jerusalem, let this be known to you, hear my words!
[15]These men are not drunk, as you suppose; after all, it is only the

third hour of the day. 16But rather, the word of the prophet Joel is
being fulfilled:

> 17In the last days, so speaks God, I will pour out my
> Spirit upon all earthly life. Then your sons and your
> daughters shall begin to speak words of the spirit, your
> young men shall awaken to seeing in the spirit and your
> elders shall dream enlightened dreams. 18Ycs, truly, in
> those days I will pour out my Spirit upon those who
> serve me, men and women, and the gift of prophesy
> will awaken in them. 19I will cause wonders to happen
> above in the heavens and signs on the earth below:
> blood and fire and clouds of smoke. 20The sun shall
> become dark and the moon like blood. All this comes
> before the great Day of the Lord. 21Whoever then calls
> on the name of Christ will find a share in the salvation.

22'Men of Israel, hear my words! Jesus of Nazarcth, whom the
divine Ground of the World himself has accredited to you by deeds
of higher powers, by wonders and by signs which, as you know, the
divine world did through him in your midst, 23he was offered up in
accordance with the previously resolved will of God and with the
foreknowledge of the divine world. With unworthy hand you crucified him and killed him. 24But God raised him again by unbinding
the pangs of death; it was not possible for him to be held by the
might of death. 25The word of David refers to him:

> The eye of my soul beholds the LORD before me at all times.
> HE stands on the right of me that I may not be shaken.
> 26Therefore my heart rejoices and my tongue exults.
> My earthly body, too, may hope for new existence.
> 27You do not let my soul sink into the abyss.
> You do not let him whom you hallow become prey to corruption.
> 28You have shown me the path of life.
> You fill my heart with joy when I behold your countenance.

29‘Men and brothers, let me speak frankly to you about the
patriarch David. He died and was buried; and his grave is here to
this day, here where we stand. 30Since he was a prophet and was
aware that God had sworn with an oath that an offspring of his
seed would one day sit on his throne, 31he saw into the future and
spoke of the resurrection of Christ: for he neither sank into the
abyss of death, nor did his earthly body become prey to corruption. 32This Jesus, about whom we are speaking, was raised up by
God; of that we all are witnesses. 33He has been raised up to be
on the right hand of God, and the promise of the Holy Spirit has
been passed to him by the Father. That is how he has poured out
the forces which you see and hear. 34David was not raised up into
the spheres of heaven, but he said:

> The Lord of all existence said to my Lord: You shall
> sit at my right hand. 35I will make your enemies sub-
> ject to you and put them beneath your feet.

36‘Therefore let all the house of Israel know for certain that God
has made this same Jesus, whom you crucified, the Lord and the
Messiah, the Anointed One.’

The first congregation

37Those who heard this felt how the words penetrated their hearts,
and they said to Peter and the other apostles, ‘Men and brothers,
what shall we do?’ 38Peter answered, ‘Change your hearts and
minds, and then let each one of you be baptized in the name and
the power of Jesus Christ, so as to be healed from the might of sin;
and you will receive the gift of the Holy Spirit. 39For the promise
is to you and your children and also to all those who live in the
widths of the world and perceive the call of our Lord from out
of the divine realms.’ 40And for a long time he continued to bear
witness and to urge them: ‘Seek release and healing from the mis-
representations of our times!’ 41And those who opened themselves
to his word let themselves be baptized. About three thousand souls
were added that day.

Life in the congregation
[42]And devoutly they tended the teachings of the apostles, the celebration of communion, the breaking of bread and the prayers.
[43]All souls were filled by the awareness of the nearness of God.
Many wonders and signs were done through the apostles. [44]And
all who found the faith practised community in all things. [45]They
sold their belongings and shared the proceeds among each other,
according to the needs of each individual. [46]They determined
to be together in the sanctuary day by day. They tended the
breaking of bread from house to house and received the gift
with rejoicing and inwardness of heart. [47]They praised God and
carried the touch of the Spirit further to all people. And the Lord
allowed the community to grow, day by day, of those who were
touched by his healing power.

3 *Healing a paralysed man*
Once, Peter and John were going up to the Temple at the ninth
hour, the hour of prayer. [2]And a man who had been lame from
his mother's womb was being carried up. Every day they put him
down at that door of the Temple which was called the Beautiful
Portal, so that he could ask for alms of those who entered the
Temple. [3]When he saw Peter and John who were about to go into
the Temple, he also asked them for alms. [4]Peter looked at him
together with John and said, 'Look at us!' [5]And he turned towards
them, expecting to receive a gift from them. [6]But Peter said, 'I own
no silver or gold, but what I have, that I will give you: in the name
of Jesus Christ the Nazarene, walk!' [7]And he grasped him by the
right hand and lifted him upright. And at once strength flowed into
his feet, and his ankles became firm. [8]He jumped up and was able
to stand and walk, and he entered the Temple with them, walking
and jumping for joy and praising God. [9]And all the people saw him
walking about and heard him praising God. [10]They recognized him
as the one who had sat and begged at the Beautiful Portal of the
Temple; they were filled with wonder and beside themselves with
amazement at what had happened to him. [11]As he now clung to

Peter and John, all the people ran together expectantly to them in
the portico which is called Solomon's.

[12]When Peter saw this, he began to speak to the people, 'Men
of Israel, why do you wonder about this, and why do you stare at
us as though we had made this man able to walk through our own
powers and piety? [13]The God of Abraham, Isaac and Jacob, the God
of our fathers, revealed the true being of HIS Son Jesus, whom you
betrayed and denied before Pilate, when Pilate was about to give
judgment that he should be set free. [14]You denied the Holy and Just
One, and asked instead for the release of a murderer. [15]You killed
the Founder and Guide of life; but God raised him from the dead.
We are witnesses to his resurrection. [16]And because this man, whom
you see and know, trusted in his name, this name has become a
power in him, and the inner connection with him has brought him
renewed health before the eyes of you all. [17]But now, brothers, I
know that you acted in ignorance, as did your leaders. [18]But thus
the Ground of the World made that to be fulfilled which HE had
proclaimed in advance by the mouth of all the prophets: that Christ
must suffer. [19]Now change your hearts and minds and turn to where
you can be released from your sin. Then there will come a time
when you will be ensouled anew before the countenance of the
Lord; [20]when he will be sent to you, too, who is to come to you:
the Christ Jesus. [21]The sphere of the heavens must shelter him until
the time when all existence is led back to its origins. For aeons,
God has already spoken about this through the mouth of the holy
prophets. [22]Moses said:

> The Lord God will make a prophet like me come forth
> from among your brothers. Hear him in everything
> that he shall speak to you. [23]Those souls, however,
> who do not listen to his word shall be torn from their
> people and given over to destruction.

[24]All the prophets from Samuel onwards, the whole series of those
who have spoken to us, have spoken of *our* time. [25]You are the sons
of these prophets and of the covenant which God made with your
fathers when HE said to Abraham:

In your seed shall all branches of humanity on the
earth be blessed.

26You were to be the first when God raised HIS Son. HE sent him
in order to bless you, insofar as each one frees himself from his
entanglement in the might of the evil.'

4 *The apostles are arrested*

While they were still speaking to the people, the priests, the captain of the Temple and the Sadducees came up to them. 2They were
annoyed because they were teaching the people and, by speaking
about Jesus, were proclaiming the resurrection of the dead. 3They
laid hands on them and placed them in custody until the next day,
for it was already evening. 4But in many of those who had heard
their word, the power of faith had come alive. The number came
to about five thousand men.

5Next morning the rulers and elders and scribes gathered in
Jerusalem, 6together with Annas the High Priest, Caiaphas and John
and Alexander – in short, all who were of the highpriestly family.
7They placed them in their midst and put the question to them: 'By
what power and in whose name did you do this?' 8Then Peter, filled
with the Holy Spirit, said, 'Rulers of the people and elders, 9if today
we are on trial because of the good deed done to this sick man
and must say by what power he has been healed, 10then let it be
proclaimed before you and all the people of Israel: he stands before
you, healed, through the being and the power of Jesus Christ, the
Nazarene, whom you crucified and whom God raised from the
dead. 11He is the stone which you builders rejected as unusable, but
which nonetheless has become the corner-stone. 12In no one else is
salvation to be found; there is no other name under heaven in the
human realm which could lead us to salvation.'

13When they observed Peter's frankness, and also that of John,
they were surprised, since they had thought them to be uned-
ucated laymen. Now they became aware that they had belonged
to the circle around Jesus. 14Then, as they saw the man who had
been healed standing with them, they did not know what to say in

opposition. [15]They ordered them out of the council and conferred
with one another: [16]'What shall we do with these men? Through
them a clear sign of the spirit has been performed which is plain
to all the inhabitants of Jerusalem and which we cannot deny.
[17]But so that it does not draw even more people, let us forbid
them to speak any more to anyone about this name.' [18]And they
called them in again and forbade them strictly to speak or teach
about the name of Jesus. [19]But Peter and John answered, 'Is it better, before the countenance of God, to listen more to you than to
God HIMSELF? Judge for yourselves. [20]We cannot be silent about
what we have seen and heard.' [21]And they threatened them and
let them go, because they could find no way to punish them, and
also because of the people; for everyone praised God for what
had happened, [22]all the more so as the man on whom this sign of
healing had been performed was already more than forty years
old.

Return to the congregation

[23]When they were released they came to their own people and
reported what the chief priests and elders had said. [24]When they
had heard it, they raised their voice in prayer with one accord
and said, 'Ruler of the world, who created heaven and earth and
the sea and all creatures in them, [25]you have spoken through the
mouth of our father David, your servant filled by the Holy Spirit:

> Why do the peoples rage and forge futile plans? [26]The
> kings of the earth assemble and the rulers gather
> against the highest LORD and against the Christ whom
> HE has sent.

[27]'Truly, in this city these men got together against Jesus, your
holy servant whom you anointed as Christ: Herod and Pontius
Pilate together with the peoples of the world and the tribes of
Israel, [28]so that they might fulfil what had already been decided
upon by your hand and your will. [29]And now, Lord, look upon their
threats and give your servants the strength to proclaim your word
with courage. [30]Stretch out your hand and let deeds of healing,

signs and wonders be performed in the name and in the power of Jesus, your holy servant.'

[31]While they were praying thus, the place where they were gathered was shaken, and they were all filled by the Holy Spirit and proclaimed the word of God courageously.

Property held in common in the Jerusalem congregation

[32]Those who found the faith were, in their great multitude, one heart and one soul. No longer did anyone regard his possessions as his personal property; they had everything in common. [33]And with great power the apostles gave their testimony to the resurrection of the Lord Jesus. Rich blessing was upon them all. [34]There was no one among them who was in want. For those among them who owned lands or houses sold them, [35]and brought the proceeds to lay at the apostles' feet. Then a distribution was made to each one, according to his need. [36]Joseph, too, who had been given the name Barnabas by the apostles, which means Son of Consolation when translated, a Levite from Cyprus, [37]sold a field which belonged to him and brought the proceeds and laid the money at the apostles' feet.

5 *Ananias and Sapphira*

And a man named Ananias with his wife Sapphira sold a piece of property; [2]but with his wife's knowledge he kept back some of the proceeds, and brought only a part to lay at the apostles' feet. [3]Then Peter said, 'Ananias, why have you let Satan enter your heart, and why do you deceive the Holy Spirit by keeping back a part of the price of the land? [4]Why did you not just keep the field? And even after it was sold, were you not free to dispose of it as you yourself wished? How did this plan enter your heart? You have not defrauded men but God.' [5]When Ananias heard these words, he broke down and died. Great fear came upon all who heard it. [6]The young men arose, lifted him onto a bier and carried him out to bury him.

[7]After about three hours his wife came in, not knowing what had happened. [8]Peter said to her, 'Tell me whether you sold the land

for this price.' She answered, 'Yes, that was the price.' 9And Peter
said, 'Why did you agree together to put the Spirit of the Lord to the
test? See, you hear the footsteps at the door of those who have buried your husband. They will carry you out, too.' 10And in the same
moment she fell down at his feet and died; and when the young
men came in they found her dead, too, and they carried her out and
buried her beside her husband. 11Great fear came upon the whole
congregation and all who heard of it.

Healings in the Temple portico

12Through the hands of the apostles many signs and wonders
happened among the people. They always met in unity of soul in
Solomon's portico. 13None of the others dared to push himself into
their midst, but the people held them in high honour. 14Ever more
found the way to Christ through the faith, multitudes of men and
women. 15They even carried the sick people into the streets on beds
and stretchers, in order that, when Peter came by, his shadow might
fall on them. 16Many also flocked together from the towns around
Jerusalem, bringing the sick and those who were tormented by
unclean spirits; and all were healed.

The apostles are arrested for the second time

17But now the High Priest intervened, together with those around
him and those who belonged to the party of the Sadducees. They
were filled with jealousy 18and took hold of the apostles and threw
them into the common jail. 19But in the night an angel of the Lord
opened the doors of the prison, led them out and said, 20'Go and
stand in the Temple before all people and proclaim the full message
of the higher life.' 21And when they had heard this, they entered the
Temple at daybreak and began to teach.

Now the High Priest and those around him called together the
Sanhedrin and the full council of the sons of Israel. Then messengers were sent to the prison to fetch the apostles. 22But the servants did not find them in the prison. They returned and reported,
23'We found the prison securely locked and the guards standing at

the doors, but when we opened the gate we found no one inside.'
[24]When the captain of the Temple and the chief priests heard this
they were at a loss; they could not understand what had happened.
[25]Then a man came and reported, 'See, the men whom you threw
into jail are standing in the Temple and teaching the people.' [26]The
captain of the Temple went with his servants to fetch them; but they
did not dare use violence for fear of being stoned by the people.
[27]They brought them and put them up before the Sanhedrin.

The High Priest turned to them [28]and said, 'We ordered you
strictly not to speak about this name any more, and see, you have
filled the whole of Jerusalem with your teaching. You intend to
call up this man's blood upon us.' [29]Then Peter in the gathering
of the apostles answered, 'God is to be obeyed more than men.
[30]The God of our fathers raised up Jesus whom you nailed to a
cross and killed. [31]God has exalted him to be the highest guide
and bringer of healing, to be the fulfiller of HIS deeds, so that the
way is opened for Israel to a change of heart and mind and to
forgiveness of sin. [32]We ourselves are witnesses to what we say,
and the Holy Spirit witnesses with us, whom God gives to those
who follow HIS will.' [33]When they heard these words they burned
with rage and wanted to kill them.

[34]Then one of the Sanhedrin stood up, a Pharisee named
Gamaliel, a teacher of the Law who was famous and popular with
all the people. He ordered the men to be sent out for a short while.
[35]Then he said, 'Men of Israel, consider carefully what you are
about to do with these men. [36]Some time ago we had the rebellion
of Theudas who thought himself significant. He had a following
of about four hundred. When he was killed, his whole retinue dispersed and the entire affair came to nothing. [37]After that, Judas
the Galilean arose in the days of the census and many people followed him. He, too, perished, and all his followers were scattered.
[38]Therefore I now advise you: leave these men alone and set them
free. Either their will and work comes from human resources, in
which case they will fail. [39]Or else it proceeds from the will of
God: then you will not be able to destroy them. You will end up

as men who fight against God.’ 40They agreed with him, called the
apostles in again, had them beaten and forbade them to speak about
the name of Jesus. Then they let them go.

41When they left the meeting of the Sanhedrin they were full of
joy that they had been found worthy to suffer disgrace for the name
of Christ. 42And they did not cease to teach every day in the Temple
and in the houses and to proclaim Christ Jesus as the content of the
Gospel.

Choosing the seven deacons

In these days the number of the disciples grew rapidly, and indignation arose among the Greek-speaking against the Hebraic members because their widows were overlooked in the daily hand-outs.
2Then the twelve called the full number of the disciples together
and said, ‘It is not good that we neglect the divine word for the
service at the tables. 3Therefore, dear brothers, look for seven
men among you who have proved themselves as bearers of the
Spirit and of wisdom. We will appoint them to this task, 4and then
we will devote ourselves entirely to prayer and the service of the
word.’ 5This suggestion seemed good to them all, and so they chose
Stephen, a man who was filled with the power of faith and the Holy
Spirit, and also Philip, Prochorus, Nicanor, Timon, Parmenas and
Nicolaus, a proselyte from Antioch. 6These were presented to the
apostles who, praying, laid their hands on them. 7And the divine
word grew, and the number of disciples in Jerusalem increased
greatly. A great number of priests, too, followed the call on the
path of the faith.

The work of Stephen and his address

8And Stephen, filled with the touch of the Spirit and with divine
power, performed great deeds and signs of the Spirit among the
people. 9Then some of those who belonged to the synagogues of
the Libertines, of the Jews from Cyrene, Alexandria, Cilicia and
Asia began to argue with Stephen. 10But they could not withstand
the wisdom and spirit of his words. 11Then they put forward men

who were to say: 'We heard him speak derogatory words against
Moses and against God.' [12]Thus they stirred up the people and the
elders and the scribes; finally they went up to him, overpowered
him and led him before the Sanhedrin. [13]They put up false witnesses
who said, 'This man never ceases to revile the Holy Place and the
Law. [14]We have heard him say, "Jesus the Nazarene will destroy
this place and change the customs which Moses gave us".' [15]Then
all who sat in the Sanhedrin looked at him, and they saw his face,
shining like the face of an angel.
7 The High Priest said, 'Is this so?' [2]And he answered, 'Men,
brothers and fathers, listen! The God of revealing light appeared to
our father Abraham when he was in Mesopotamia, before he settled
in Haran. [3]And HE said to him:

> Depart from your country and your blood-relations
> and move to the country which I will show you.

[4]Then he left the country of the Chaldeans and lived in Haran. And
after the death of his father, God led him further and he came to this
country in which you now live. [5]But God gave him no inheritance
in it, not even a foot's length. HE only promised to give it to him in
possession eventually, and after him to his seed. Yet at that time he
had no son. [6]And God said:

> Your seed shall live as strangers in a strange land.
> They will be enslaved and harassed for four hundred
> years. [7]But I will judge the people whom they must
> serve.

And HE went on:

> After that they shall leave that country and shall wor-
> ship me in this place.

[8]And HE gave him the divine covenant, the seal on which is the
circumcision.

'And so Abraham fathered Isaac and circumcised him on the
eighth day. And Isaac fathered Jacob, and Jacob the twelve patriarchs. [9]And the patriarchs were jealous of Joseph and sold him into
Egypt; but the divine power was with him [10]and led him out of all
trials and gave him gracefulness and wisdom before Pharaoh, king

of Egypt, who made him governor over Egypt and over all his
house. [11]Then a famine and severe afflictions of destiny came upon
all Egypt and Canaan, and our fathers could find no sustenance any
more. [12]But Jacob heard that there was grain in Egypt, and so he sent
out our fathers for the first time. [13]On the second visit Joseph made
himself known to his brothers, and thus Joseph's family became
known to Pharaoh. [14]And Joseph sent and called to him Jacob his
father and all his kindred; there were altogether seventy-five souls.
[15]And Jacob went down to Egypt, and he and our fathers died [16]and
were carried back to Shechem and laid in the tomb which Abraham
had acquired by buying it with a sum of silver from the Sons of
Hamor in Shechem.

[17]'Now when the time drew near for the fulfilment of the promise which God had made to Abraham, the people increased in
Egypt and became great in number [18]till another king ruled over
Egypt who knew nothing of Joseph. [19]He deceived our people
and tormented our fathers and forced them to expose their infants
that they might not live. [20]At this time Moses was born; he was
a favourite of God. He was brought up for three months in his
father's house. [21]But then, when he had been exposed, the daughter
of Pharaoh took him to herself and brought him up as her own son.
[22]So Moses was instructed in all the wisdom of the Egyptians and
proved himself powerful in word and deed.

[23]'When he had reached forty years, the thought arose in
his heart to go and see his brothers, the sons of Israel. [24]And he
saw how one of them was being treated unjustly; he came to his
assistance and avenged the one being maltreated by killing the
Egyptian. [25]He thought that his brothers would now recognize him
as the one through whose hand God was to bring them deliverance. But they did not recognize him. [26]On the following day he
appeared before them as they were fighting. He wanted to reconcile them and spoke peaceably to them, "Men, remember that you
are brothers. Why do you maltreat each other?" [27]But the one who
had offended his neighbour pushed him aside and said, "Who has
appointed you to be a ruler and judge over us? [28]Do you want to

kill me, too, as you killed the Egyptian yesterday?" 29At this word
Moses fled and lived as a stranger in Midian, where two sons
were born to him.

30'When forty years had again passed, an angel appeared to
him in the desert of Mount Sinai, in the fiery flame of the burning
thorn bush. 31Moses was filled with wonder at the vision he was
granted. As he approached nearer to discern more exactly, the
voice of the Lord sounded:

> 32I am the God of your fathers, the God of Abraham,
> Isaac and Jacob.

Then Moses felt fear and did not dare look up any more. 33And the
Lord spoke to him:

> Loosen the shoes from your feet, for the place where
> you are standing is holy ground. 34I have seen the suf-
> fering of my people in Egypt and I have heard their
> groans, and have come down to free them; and so I
> now send you to Egypt.

35'This same Moses, whom they had rejected with the words
"Who has appointed you to be a ruler and judge?" him God HIMSELF
sent as ruler and deliverer by the hand of the angel who appeared
to him in the thorn bush. 36Thus he became the one who led them
out, and who performed signs and wonders in Egypt, by the Red
Sea and in the desert for forty years. 37This Moses spoke to the
sons of Israel: "God will make a prophet like me come forth from
among your brothers." 38He it is who worked in the congregation
of the people in the desert as mediator between the angel who
spoke to him on Mount Sinai and our fathers. He received living
words to give to us. 39But our fathers would not listen to him nor
follow him. They thrust him aside, and in their hearts they turned
to Egypt again.

40'So they said to Aaron, "Make for us gods who will go before
us. We do not know what has happened to this Moses who led us
out of Egypt." 41In those days they made a statue of a bull and
brought offerings to this image and rejoiced in the work of their
hands. 42Then God turned away from them and let them become

servants of the host of the star-spirits, as it is written in the book of the prophets:

> You who are of the house of Israel, did you ever slaughter and bring me an offering during the forty
> years in the desert? [43]You have claimed the sanctuary of Moloch for yourselves and have served the star of the god Rephan; you have served the images which you yourselves have made. I will banish you even beyond Babylon.

[44]'In the desert our fathers had the tabernacle, the tent of God's presence. Thus it was ordained by HIM who said to Moses that he should build it according to the archetypal image which he had
seen. [45]After they had made this tabernacle their own, our fathers, together with Joshua, carried it into the land which was in the possession of foreign, heathen peoples. God drove these peoples out from there before our fathers until the days of David. [46]To
David it was granted to stand before the countenance of God, touched by HIS Spirit, and he asked leave to build a dwelling for the God of Jacob. [47]But it was Solomon who built the house.
[48]However, the highest divine Being does not live in a house which could be built with human hands. That is the meaning of the prophetic word,

> [49]Heaven is my throne
> and the earth my footstool.
> What house would you build for me,
> says the Lord,
> or what place can you show me where I might rest?
> [50]Has not my hand created all this?

[51]'You stubborn people, uncircumcised in heart and ears, always you obstruct the way for the Holy Spirit. As your fathers did, so
do you. [52]Which of the prophets did your fathers not persecute? They killed those who foretold the coming of the bringer of goodness, whose betrayers and murderers you now have become. [53]You
received the Law through the mediation of angels, but you have not kept it.'

Death of Stephen and persecution of the congregation
[54]While they were listening, their hearts swelled in great agitation,
and they ground their teeth. [55]Stephen, filled with the Holy Spirit,
looked up to heaven and saw the light of the revelation of God,
and Jesus standing at the right hand of God. [56]And he said, 'See,
the heavens are opened to my beholding. I see the Son of Man at
the right hand of God.' [57]Then they cried out with a loud voice,
covered their ears and rushed upon him all together; [58]they drove
him out of the city and stoned him. And the witnesses laid down
their garments at the feet of a young man named Saul. [59]And as
they were stoning him, Stephen said, 'Jesus, Lord, receive my
spirit!' [60]And he fell to his knees and called out with a loud voice:
'Lord, do not hold this sin against them.' And when he had said
this, he breathed his last.

8 But Saul took pleasure in all that happened when they killed
him. On that same day a great persecution began against the congregation in Jerusalem. Everyone except the apostles scattered
into the region of Judea and Samaria. [2]Devout men buried Stephen
and made long lamentations over him. [3]But Saul raged against the
congregation, burst into all the houses, dragged men and women
out and had them thrown into prison.

Philip in Samaria
[4]Now those who had fled in all directions travelled through the land
and proclaimed the word. [5]Thus Philip came to the city of Samaria
and proclaimed the Christ to the inhabitants. [6]Great crowds heard
Philip's words. They were of one heart and one soul when they
listened to him and when they saw the signs of the spirit which he
performed. [7]With loud cries, the unclean spirits came out of many
who were possessed, and many who were lame in the body or the
feet were healed. [8]There was great joy in that city.

Simon the magician
[9]Before this, a man named Simon had had a certain influence. He
practised magic, was able to put the people of Samaria into ecstasy

and claimed to be one of the great leaders of humanity. 10Everyone
clung to him, from the least to the greatest, and said, 'He is the
embodiment of a higher spiritual power.' 11The reason why they
had been his adherents for so long was that he had put them into
ecstasy by magical means. 12When now Philip came with his proclamation of the Kingdom of God and of the name of Jesus Christ,
many were moved by it, and men and women were baptized.
13Even in Simon the faith stirred, and so he also was baptized, and
he attached himself to Philip, deeply moved by the great signs and
deeds which he performed.

14When the apostles, who had remained in Jerusalem, heard that
Samaria had received the divine word, they sent Peter and John
there. 15They went down and prayed for the people that they might
receive the Holy Spirit. 16Until then, the Holy Spirit had not yet
descended upon any of them. Through the baptism they had only
been united with the name and the power of Jesus, the Lord. 17But
those on whom they now laid their hands received the Holy Spirit.

18When Simon saw that the Spirit was bestowed by the laying
on of the apostles' hands, he brought them money 19and said, 'Give
me also a share in this power, so that anyone on whom I lay my
hands may receive the Holy Spirit.' 20But Peter said to him, 'Your
money perish with you, because you thought that God's gift of
grace could be bought like that! 21Your being is alien to the Spirit
of God, and you will have no share in this word, for your heart is
not pure before the countenance of God. 22Change your heart and
mind and free yourself from the falseness of your being. Pray to
the Lord that the deceitfulness of your heart may be forgiven you.
23I see that you are full of bitter gall and entangled in the snare of
untruth.' 24Then Simon answered, 'Pray for me to the Lord, that the
destiny of which you have spoken may not strike me!'

25They continued to witness and proclaim the word of the Christ,
and then returned to Jerusalem. On the way, they carried the message to many villages of Samaria.

Philip and the Ethiopian
26Once, an angel of the Lord spoke to Philip: 'Arise and go south-
ward on the road that leads down to Gaza from Jerusalem!' This
road goes through the desert. 27And he arose and went. And see, an
Ethiopian, a eunuch and a dignitary of the court of the Ethiopian
queen Candace, who was in charge of the whole treasury of the
queen, had travelled to Jerusalem to worship there. 28Now he was
on his way home. He sat in his chariot and read in the book of
the prophet Isaiah. 29Then the Spirit spoke to Philip: 'Go and follow this chariot!' 30Philip hurried forward and heard him reading
the words of the prophet Isaiah, and said, 'Do you understand the
meaning of these words?' 31He answered, 'How am I to understand,
since no one guides me?' And he invited Philip to get in and sit
next to him. 32The passage of scripture he was reading was this:

> Like a sheep he was led to the slaughter,
> and, like a lamb which is silent before its shearer,
> he did not open his mouth.
> 33By his humility he undoes the judgment which is laid
> upon him.
> Who can describe his history?
> His life is exalted above the earthly plane.

34Then the eunuch said to Philip, 'Please tell me: about whom
is the prophet speaking here? Is he speaking about himself or about
someone else?' 35And Philip, beginning with this word of scripture,
began to proclaim to him the message about Jesus.

36As they travelled on they came to a watercourse, and the
eunuch said, 'See, here is water: what is to prevent my being
baptized?' 38And he ordered the chariot to stop, and they both
entered the water, Philip and the eunuch, and he baptized him.
39When they again came out of the water, Philip was borne away
by the Spirit. The eunuch saw him no more and travelled on, full
of joy. 40Philip emerged again in Azotus, and, passing through all
the towns as far as Caesarea, he proclaimed the Gospel everywhere.

Saul before Damascus

Saul was still full of passionate hatred and destructive urges against
the disciples of Christ. He applied to the High Priest 2and asked him
for orders to the synagogues in Damascus. He wanted to bring those
he would meet on the way, men and women, bound to Jerusalem.
3As he was on the way and came near to Damascus, suddenly a
light from heaven shone around him. 4He fell to the ground and
heard a voice saying to him, 'Saul, Saul, why do you persecute
me?' 5He said, 'Who are you, Lord?' And he received the answer:
'I am Jesus, whom you are persecuting. 6Now arise and go into the
town. There you will be told what you are to do.' 7The men who
were travelling with him stood speechless. Although they heard a
voice, they saw nobody. 8Saul arose from the ground; but when he
opened his eyes, he could see nothing. So they led him by the hand
and brought him into Damascus. 9For three days he was blind, and
took neither food nor drink.

10In Damascus lived a disciple called Ananias. The Lord
appeared to him in spirit and said, 'Ananias.' He answered, 'See,
here am I, Lord.' 11And the Lord said to him, 'Arise and go to
the street called "straight," and enquire in the house of Judas for
Saul of Tarsus. See, he is deep in prayer 12and has just perceived
in a vision that a man named Ananias will come to him and lay
his hands on him and give him back his sight.' 13Then Ananias
said, 'Lord, I have heard many speak about this man, how much
suffering he has brought to your holy ones in Jerusalem. 14And
now he has come here with authority from the chief priests to
imprison all who call upon your name.' 15But the Lord answered
him, 'Go to him, for he is my chosen instrument. He is to carry
my name before the peoples and the kings and the sons of Israel.
16And I will also show him what sufferings he will have to take
upon himself in the service of my name.' 17Then Ananias set out,
went into the house and laid his hands upon him and said, 'Saul,
my brother, the Lord has sent me: Jesus, whom you beheld on
your way. May you become seeing again, may the Holy Spirit fill
you.' 18At that moment something like scales fell from his eyes, he

could see again. He arose, was baptized, 19took food and regained
his strength.

He stayed for some days with the disciples in Damascus. 20And
straight away he began to proclaim in the synagogues that Jesus
is the Son of God. 21All who heard him were astonished and said,
'Is this not the same man who persecuted everyone in Jerusalem
who confessed to this name? And has he not come here to bring
them bound before the chief priests?' 22But Saul developed all the
more power of word and caused great confusion among the Jews of
Damascus by demonstrating that Jesus is the Christ. 23After some
days, the Jews decided to kill him, 24but Saul learnt of their plan.
They watched the gates day and night in order to catch him. 25But in
the night the disciples let him down over the wall in a basket.

Saul in Jerusalem and his return to Tarsus

26When he had arrived in Jerusalem, he tried to join the circle of
disciples, but they were all afraid of him and could not believe that
he now was also a disciple. 27Then Barnabas approached him, led
him to the disciples and told them how on the way he had seen
Christ, and how Christ had spoken to him. He also told them that
he had stood up bravely for the name of Jesus in Damascus. 28So he
went in and out among them in Jerusalem, 29proclaimed the name
of Christ courageously and openly, and spoke and argued with
the Greek-speaking Jews. Then they tried to kill him. 30When the
brothers became aware of it they brought him to Caesarea and sent
him on to Tarsus. 31Now the congregation in the whole of Judea,
Galilee and Samaria had a time of peace during which it could
devote itself to consolidation and the nurturing of reverence on
the path of Christ. It grew by the inner power which it received
through the Holy Spirit.

Peter's work near the Mediterranean Sea

32At that time, Peter, who was visiting the congregations
everywhere, also came to the circle of those in Lydda who had
turned towards the salvation. 33There he found a man called

Aeneas, who had been paralyzed and bedridden for eight years.
34And Peter said to him, 'Aeneas, through the power of Jesus
Christ you can be healed. Stand up and make your own bed!'
And at once he stood up. 35All the inhabitants of Lydda and
Sharon saw him, and they turned to the Christ.

36At Joppa lived a disciple called Tabitha, which translated
means Gazelle. She never tired of doing good works and helping deeds of love. 37In those days she became ill and died. They
washed her and laid her out in the upper room, the room of the
meal. 38Since Lydda is near Joppa, and the disciples heard that
Peter was there, they sent two men to him and asked him, 'Come
to us without delay!' 39And Peter rose and went with them. When
he arrived, they led him to the upper room. There all the women
crowded around him, weeping and showing him the clothes and
garments which Tabitha had made while she was still living.
40Then Peter showed them all out, knelt down and prayed; then he
turned to the body and said, 'Tabitha, arise!' And she opened her
eyes, and when she saw Peter she sat up. 41He gave her his hand
and let her stand up. Then he called the brothers and the women
in and led her to them, alive. 42This became known throughout
Joppa, and many felt united with Christ through the faith. 43And
it came about that Peter stayed a number of days in Joppa in the
house of Simon, a tanner.

10 *Peter and the Roman centurion*
In Caesarea there lived at that time a man called Cornelius, a
centurion of the so-called Italian regiment. 2He was devout and
godfearing with all his household. He did many deeds of love
among the people and was in constant communication with the
divine world through prayer. 3Once, at about the ninth hour of the
day, he had a clear visionary experience: an angel of God came
to him and said to him, 'Cornelius!' 4He looked at him, became
frightened and said, 'What is it, Lord?' He said to him, 'Your
prayers and your deeds of love have risen up to where they are
written into the consciousness and memory of a higher world

before the countenance of God. [5]Now send men to Joppa and
bring Simon here, whose other name is Peter. [6]He is a guest of
Simon the tanner whose house is by the sea.' [7]After these words
the angel vanished again. And Cornelius called two members of
his household and a devout soldier from among those who were in
his charge, [8]told them everything and sent them to Joppa.

[9]On the following day, as they were on their way and were
already near to the town, Peter went up on the housetop to pray.
It was about the sixth hour. [10]He was hungry and wanted to eat.
While the meal was already being prepared, an ecstasy came upon
him. [11]He saw how the heavens opened and a vessel descended. It
was like a great cloth which was let down to the earth by the four
corners. [12]In it were all kinds of animals of the earth, quadrupeds,
reptiles, and birds of the air. [13]And a voice said to him, 'Stand up,
Peter, slaughter and eat!' [14]But Peter said, 'No, Lord; for I have
never eaten anything unholy or unclean.' [15]And the voice spoke
to him again: 'What God has cleansed, do not profane it.' [16]This
happened three times; then the vessel was taken up at once into
heaven.

[17]While Peter was still quite unsure about the meaning of this
vision, see, there came the men who had been sent by Cornelius.
When they had found Simon's house they entered the porch [18]and
asked loudly whether Simon Peter lived there. [19]Peter was still pondering in his soul about the vision. Then the Spirit said to him,
'See, here are two men who are looking for you. [20]Arise, go down
and go with them without misgivings, for I have sent them.' [21]Then
Peter went down and said to the men, 'See, I am the one whom
you seek. What is the reason for your coming?' [22]They answered,
'The centurion Cornelius, a devout and godfearing man who is also
highly thought of by the whole Jewish people, has received a revelation through a holy angel that he is to call you to his house and
listen to your word.' [23]Then he asked them into the house.

The next day he set off with them. Some of the brothers from
Joppa accompanied him. [24]On the following day he came to Caesarea.
Cornelius was expecting them and had gathered his relations

and close friends about him. [25]When Peter came to the entrance
of the house, Cornelius went to meet him and fell at his feet with
deference. [26]But Peter lifted him up and said, ‘Stand up; I am a
human being like you.’ [27]And in conversation with him he entered
the house. When he found so great a gathering in there [28]he said
to them, ‘You know that Jews are not allowed to associate with
people of other races or to enter their houses. But God has shown
me that no human being should be called unholy or unclean. [29]That
is why I came without objection when I was sent for. And so now
I ask why you called me here?’ [30]Then Cornelius said, ‘Four days
ago I was praying in my house. Suddenly, at about the ninth hour,
a Being in shining white garments stood before me [31]and said,
“Cornelius, your prayer has been heard and your good deeds have
ascended to the consciousness of the divine world. [32]Now send
messengers to Joppa and let Simon Peter be called, who is a guest
of Simon the tanner in his house by the sea.” [33]Thereupon I sent
for you at once, and it is good that you have come. Now we are all
gathered here in the sight of the divine world, to hear what tasks
you have been given by the Lord.’

[34]Then Peter began to speak: ‘Only now is it becoming actual
experience for me that outer differences among people are of no
account before God. [35]HIS divine pleasure rests upon anyone in
all the peoples who approaches HIM with devotion and who serves
the Good. [36]HE sent the Word to the sons of Israel as the embodiment of the message of peace: through Jesus Christ, who is Lord
of all human beings. [37]You have heard of the working of the Word
which, beginning in Galilee, penetrated the whole of Judea. After
John’s call to baptism came Jesus of Nazareth. [38]He was anointed
by God with the Holy Spirit and with great power. You know how
he went through the land, helping and bringing healing to all who
had fallen into the power of the Adversary. The power of God was
with him, [39]and we all are witnesses to all the deeds which he performed in Judea and Jerusalem. They killed him by nailing him to
the cross. [40]But God raised him on the third day and enabled him
to be revealed, [41]not to all people but to the witnesses prepared

by God, to us who ate and drank with him after his resurrection
from the dead. [42]To us he gave the task to proclaim him to the
people, testifying that he has been ordained by God to assess and
order the destinies of the living and the dead. [43]He it is, about
whom all the prophets said that everyone who unites with him
will find release from sin through the power of his being.'

[44]While Peter was speaking thus, the Holy Spirit descended upon
all who heard him. [45]The Christians who were of Jewish descent,
and who had come with Peter, were utterly astounded because the
gift of the Holy Spirit was also poured out on non-Jewish peoples.
[46]They heard them speaking in tongues and praising God. Then
Peter said, [47]'Who now could deny them the water of baptism, since
they have received the Holy Spirit just as we have?' [48]And he gave
them the directive that they should be baptized in the name and the
power of Jesus Christ. And they asked him to stay with them for
some days.

11 *Justification before the apostles in Jerusalem*

The apostles and the brothers in Judea heard that the non-Jewish
peoples had also received the word of God. [2]So when Peter returned
to Jerusalem, the adherents of the circumcision criticized him [3]and
reproached him, 'You went into the houses of the uncircumcised
and sat at table with them.'

[4]Then Peter began to tell them everything from the beginning:
[5]'I was staying in the city of Joppa and was deep in prayer when,
in an ecstasy, I had a visionary experience. I saw a vessel like a
great unfolded sheet descend from heaven by its four corners. It
came down to me. [6]When I looked into it I saw all kinds of animals
of the earth, quadrupeds, wild animals and reptiles, and also the
birds of the air. [7]Then I heard a voice which spoke to me, "Get up,
Peter, slaughter and eat!" [8]But I replied, "No, Lord, no – for nothing unconsecrated or unclean has ever entered my mouth." [9]And
the voice sounded anew from heaven: "What God has cleansed, do
not profane it!" [10]This happened three times, and then everything
was drawn up again into heaven. [11]And see, at that very moment

three men stood before the house in which we were staying, sent
to me from Caesarea. 12And the Spirit told me to go with them
without hesitation. These six men here accompanied me, and we
entered the man's house. 13And he announced to us how in his
house he had seen the angel who said to him, "Send messengers
to Joppa and let Simon Peter come to you. 14He will speak words
to you which will show you and all your house the way of salvation." 15When I then began to speak, the Holy Spirit descended
upon them, just as we ourselves experienced it at our beginning.
16Then I remembered the word of the Lord: "John baptized with
water, but you will be baptized with the Holy Spirit." 17If then God
gives them the same gift as HE gave to us, after they had united
themselves in faith with the Lord Jesus Christ, how could I offer
resistance to the divine will?'

18When they heard this, they ceased disputing with him. They
praised the divine Ground of the World and said, 'Then for the
heathen peoples, too, does God clear the way for a change of heart
and mind which leads to true life.'

Antioch, where the term 'Christians' was first used

19Those who had dispersed into the world after the fate of Stephen,
came as far as Phoenicia, Cyprus and Antioch; at first they brought
the word to the Jews only. 20But some of them, men from Cyprus
and Cyrene, came to Antioch and began to speak to the Greeks
also and brought them the message of Jesus, the Lord. 21And the
hand of Christ worked into their working, and great was the number of those who found the faith and turned to Christ. 22News of
this reached the congregation in Jerusalem, and they sent Barnabas
to Antioch. 23When he arrived there and saw the divinely blessed
spiritual life, he was full of joy. He encouraged them all to remain
united with Christ with absolute devotion, 24for he was a man full
of goodness, filled with the Holy Spirit and the power of faith.
Thus a great number found the way to Christ. 25And Barnabas set
off for Tarsus to seek Saul; 26when he found him he took him with
him to Antioch. For a whole year they worked in the congregation

there and taught many people. In Antioch, the disciples were called
'Christians' for the first time.
[27]At that time certain prophets came from Jerusalem to Antioch.
[28]One of them named Agabus described, through spiritual inspiration, how a great famine threatened the whole of mankind. This was
in the reign of the Caesar Claudius. [29]Then the disciples gathered
gifts, each as much as he was able, which were to be sent as aid to
the brothers in Judea. [30]And they did so, and they were delivered to
the elders by the hand of Barnabas and Saul.

12 *Persecution in Jerusalem and death of James*
At this same time Herod the king set about making trouble and
disaster for certain personalities from the congregation. [2]James, the
brother of John, he killed with the sword; [3]and when he saw that
he pleased the Jews thereby, he proceeded to arrest Peter. This was
during the very days of Unleavened Bread; [4]he had him seized and
thrown into prison, where he was handed over to four squads of
four soldiers each to guard him. After the Passover he intended to
bring him before the people.

Peter's arrest and escape
[5]Now while Peter was locked up in prison, the congregation sent
prayers for him unceasingly to the divine world. [6]In the night
before his public presentation by Herod to the people, Peter had to
sleep in double chains between two soldiers. Before the door were
sentries who were guarding the prison. [7]And see, suddenly the
angel of the Lord stood before him and light filled the room. The
angel struck Peter in the side, woke him and said, 'Get up quickly!'
And the chains fell off his hands. [8]Then the angel said to him, 'Gird
yourself and put on your shoes!' And he did so. Then the angel
went on: 'Wrap yourself in your mantle and follow me!' [9]And he
followed him, but he did not know that what the angel did was
real. He thought it was merely an imagined experience. [10]When
they had passed through the first and the second guard, they came
to the iron gate which led into the city. It opened to them of its

own accord; they went out into the open and entered a street. And
suddenly the angel vanished from him. 11And when Peter came
to himself again he said, 'Now I know that the Lord really sent
his angel to rescue me from the power of Herod and from all the
dangers which threaten me from the Jewish people.'

12And when he looked about him, he was standing outside the
house of Mary, the mother of John whose other name was Mark. In
this house many were gathered and were praying. 13He knocked at
the gate of the entrance-porch, and a maid named Rhoda came to
listen. 14When she recognized Peter's voice, in her joy she forgot
to open the gate; she ran into the house and announced that Peter
was standing outside. 15But they said to her, 'You are out of your
mind.' But she insisted that it really was so. They said, 'It is his
angel.' 16But Peter continued knocking at the gate. When at last
they opened up to him they were beside themselves with amazement when they saw him. 17Then he indicated with his hand that
they should be quiet, and he told them how the Lord had led him
out of the prison. And he added, 'Tell this to James and the brothers.' Then he departed and went to another place.

18When the day dawned there was great confusion among the
soldiers. They did not know what had become of Peter. 19Herod
instigated a search for him, but he could not be found. When he
had interrogated the sentries, he commanded that everything be
made ready for departure. He went down from Judea to Caesarea
and stayed there, 20for he was planning a war against the inhabitants of Tyre and Sidon. But they came to him with one mind and,
having won over Blastus, the king's chamberlain, they asked for
peace. Their lands depended for their existence upon the king's
territories. 21On a specially appointed day Herod put on his royal
robe, ascended to the throne and made a public speech. 22The people shouted: 'Here speaks a god, and not a man!' 23Immediately
afterwards the angel of the Lord struck him, because he claimed
for himself the glory which belongs to God only. Eaten up by
worms, he died.

24But the word of Christ grew and spread. 25Barnabas and Saul

returned, having fulfilled their task in Jerusalem, and they took
John Mark with them.

13 *Mission through the Holy Spirit*
In the congregation in Antioch these men were active as prophets
and teachers: Barnabas, Symeon who was also called Niger, Lucius
of Cyrene, Manaen the school-companion of Herod the tetrarch,
and Saul. 2They were devoting themselves to the sacramental life
and their soul-exercises, when the Holy Spirit said to them, ‘Set
Barnabas and Saul free for the work to which I have called them!’
3Then, disciplining their souls and praying, they laid their hands on
them and let them go.

Paul’s first journey: in Cyprus
4Escorted by the Holy Spirit they came to Seleucia, and from there
they sailed to Cyprus. 5When they arrived in the town of Salamis
they proclaimed the divine word in the Jewish synagogues. John
was with them as their helper. 6Then they travelled across the
whole island as far as Paphos; there they came upon a Jewish
magician and false prophet named Bar-Jesus. 7He was one of the
company around the proconsul Sergius Paulus, a sensible man; he
summoned Barnabas and Saul and wanted to hear the word of God
from them. 8But they were opposed by Elymas the magician – for
that is how his name is translated – whose endeavour it was to
distract the proconsul from the way of the faith. 9But Saul, who
was also called Paul, filled with the Holy Spirit, looked him in the
face 10and said, ‘You are full of pretence and superficiality, a son
of the Adversary and an enemy of the Good. When will you stop
distorting the clear paths of Christ? 11See, the hand of the Lord is
over you; you shall become blind and unable to see the sun for
a time.’ And at once he was engulfed by darkness and became
benighted; he groped about, needing someone to lead him by the
hand. 12When the proconsul saw this, his heart was stirred and he
opened himself completely to the teaching of Christ.

In Pamphylia and Pisidia
13As they set sail from Paphos, Paul and his companions came
to Perga in Pamphylia. There John left them and returned to
Jerusalem. 14From Perga they went through the country and came
to Antioch in Pisidia. And on the Sabbath day they went into the
synagogue and sat down in the gathering there. 15After the reading
from the books of the Law and the prophets, the rulers of the
synagogue sent word to them: 'Men and brothers, if you wish to
speak a word to strengthen the soul of the people, do so.'

16Then Paul stood up, gestured with his hand and said, 'You
men of Israel, and you of the circle of the devout, listen! 17The
God of the people Israel chose our fathers; he let Israel reach its
full development in the foreign land of Egypt. Then, with the arm
of highest divine power, he led them out of the foreign land 18and
kept them alive in the desert for forty years. 19Then he destroyed
seven nations in the land of Canaan and divided the land between
them. So it was for four hundred and fifty years. 20Then he gave
them judges until the time of the prophet Samuel. 21At that time
they clamoured for a king, and God gave them Saul, the son of
Kish, of the tribe of Benjamin. That lasted forty years. 22When he
had taken him from them again, he awakened David to be their
king, of whom he himself testified:

> I have found David the son of Jesse, a man after my
> heart; he will be the fulfiller of my will.

23From his seed the Father, the Ground of the World, has brought
forth Jesus, in accordance with HIS promise, as the bringer of healing to the people of God. 24John, who came to prepare the way,
had proclaimed the baptism which leads to a change of heart and
mind to the whole people of Israel. 25And when John reached the
aim of his life he said, "I am not the one whom you take me to be;
but see, after me comes One the sandals of whose feet I am not
worthy to untie."

26'Men and brothers, sons of the lineage of Abraham, and you
of the circle of the devout: to us was sent the bringer of healing, the
divine Word. 27Those who live in Jerusalem and their leaders did

not recognize this. By the judgment they made, they themselves
fulfilled the words of the prophets which are read on Sabbath after
Sabbath: 28although they found no guilt deserving death in him,
yet they demanded of Pilate that he should have him put to death.
29And when they had thus fulfilled all the prophecies which are
written about him in the holy scriptures, they took him down from
the cross and laid him in the grave. 30But God raised him from the
dead. 31For many days he appeared to those who had accompanied
him on his way from Galilee up to Jerusalem. They are now his
witnesses before the people. 32And so we, too, proclaim to you that
the promise made to our fathers 33has been fulfilled by God to us
children. HE has raised Jesus, as it is written in the second psalm:

> You are my son, today I have begotten you.

34'That HE would raise him, so that decay should have no power
over him any more, HE expresses like this:

> I will give to you the redemption in which David trusted.

35And he says in another place:

> You will not let your Holy One become prey to corruption.

36When David had served God's will during his own time, he fell
asleep and was united with his fathers; and he became subject to
decay. 37But the One whom God raised up is not subject to decay.
38You should know, therefore, men and brothers: in him is proclaimed to you the release from sin 39and from all bonds of the Law
of Moses to which you are unable to do justice. In him, everyone
who unites with him finds the true existence. 40Beware, that there
does not come upon you what the prophets foretold:

> 41See, you scoffers, be amazed and put to shame!
> I fulfil a deed in your days,
> and when you are told of it, you will not believe it.'

42As they were leaving the synagogue, the assembled people
asked them to speak to them again on the next Sabbath. 43And when
the assembly dispersed, many Jews and devout proselytes followed
Paul and Barnabas; and they talked to them and urged them to keep
alive the touch of the divine Spirit which they had felt.

44On the next Sabbath almost the whole town gathered to hear
the word of God. 45But when the Jews saw the great crowds they
became jealous; they contradicted Paul's words and made them
seem ridiculous. 46Paul and Barnabas said frankly, 'The divine
word had to be spoken first to you. But since you reject it and
consider yourselves not needy of timeless life, see, we turn to the
heathen peoples. 47For this is our task which we have been given
by the Lord:

I have set you to be a light for the peoples.
You shall be the salvation of mankind unto the ends of the earth.'

48When the non-Jews heard this, they were glad and praised the
word of Christ. Faith came alive in all who were touched by this
word, and they felt the timeless life. 49The word of Christ spread
through the whole land. 50But the Jews were successful in inciting
certain aristocratic women, belonging to the circle of the devout,
and the leading men of the city. They instigated a persecution
against Barnabas and Paul and drove them out of their district.
51But they shook off the dust from their feet before them, and came
to Iconium. 52The disciples were filled with joy and with the Holy
Spirit.

14 *Mistaken for gods in Lycaonia*
Now while they were in Iconium, they held gatherings in the
Jewish synagogue and spoke in such a way that a great number
of Jews and Greeks were touched to the heart by it. 2But the Jews
who were unable to follow stirred up enmity against the brothers
in the minds of the non-Jews. 3They continued for a considerable
time to proclaim the Christ freely and openly, and he proved to
be present when the word of his gracious will was proclaimed,
and he caused revelations and deeds of the spirit to be done by
their hands. 4Eventually there was a schism among the people of
the town; some sided with the Jews, and some with the apostles.
5At last, the storm broke, both among the non-Jews and the Jews
and their rulers. They were about to assault and stone the apostles, 6when they became aware of the danger and fled to the towns

Lystra and Derbe in Lycaonia, and to the neighbouring districts.
[7]There they settled and proclaimed the Gospel.

[8]In Lystra there lived a man who had no strength in his feet and
therefore always had to sit. He was lame from birth and had never
been able to walk. [9]He was one of the audience when Paul was
speaking. Paul looked at him and recognized that he was full of
trust in the healing power of the Spirit. [10]And he said to him with a
loud voice, 'Get up and stand upright on your feet!' And he sprang
up and walked about. [11]When the crowd saw what had been done
through Paul, the people lifted up their voice and called out in
Lycaonian: 'The gods have taken on the likeness of men and have
descended to us.' [12]And they called Barnabas Zeus, and Paul –
because he was the bearer of the word – they called Hermes. [13]The
priest of the Zeus temple in front of the town brought oxen and
garlands to the gates of the town and wanted to begin a great feast
of sacrifice with the people. [14]But when the apostles Barnabas and
Paul heard this, they tore their garments, stormed at the people
and called: [15]'Men, what do you mean by this? We are just as
much mortal human beings as you are, and it was just this that
we wanted to achieve with our proclamation: that you should turn
away from empty images to the life-bearing God who has created
heaven and earth and the sea and all the creatures in them. [16]In
bygone epochs HE let all peoples walk their own ways. [17]And certainly HE did not fail to reveal himself: HE dispensed the forces of
good actively, HE gave you rain from heaven and fruitful times;
HE filled your hearts with nourishment and joy.' [18]And with these
words they were barely able to restrain the people from offering
sacrifice to them.

[19]But then Jews came from Antioch and Iconium, turned the
people against the apostles and stoned Paul; thinking he was dead,
they dragged him out of the town. [20]But as his disciples stood in a
circle about him, he stood up again and went into the town. On the
next day he set off with Barnabas for Derbe [21]and proclaimed the
Gospel there.

Return journey

When they had won a considerable number of disciples, they
returned to Lystra, Iconium and Antioch, 22and everywhere they
strengthened the souls of the disciples and urged them to stand fast
in the faith, since it is only through many trials that we find entry
into the realm of God. 23And everywhere in the congregations they
lent a helping hand with the appointment of elders, with prayer and
soul-discipline, and organized their working for Christ, with whom
they had united in their hearts.

24When they had passed through Pisidia they came to Pamphylia
25and proclaimed the word in Perga. Then they went down to Attalia
26and, finally, they sailed to Antioch, where they had been given the
task, now completed, by the touch of the divine Spirit. 27There they
now gathered the congregation together and reported everything
which God had done through them, and also that the door of faith
had been opened for them to the non-Jewish peoples. 28And they
stayed in the circle of the disciples for an extended period.

15 *Paul and Barnabas in Jerusalem*

Now some men came down from Judea and taught the brothers:
'If you do not let yourselves be circumcised, as it was laid down
by Moses, you cannot find salvation.' 2This caused great agitation,
and Paul and Barnabas had to argue vehemently with them. In the
end it was decided that Paul and Barnabas and some others should
go up to Jerusalem to the apostles and elders in order to resolve
this dispute. 3Escorted by the congregation they set off and went
through Phoenicia and Samaria. Everywhere they spoke about the
conversion of the heathen peoples, and thereby they gave great joy
to all the brothers.

4When they arrived in Jerusalem they were received by the
congregation and the apostles and the elders, and they told of the
deeds which God had done through them. 5Then some who, from
being Pharisees had became Christians, countered them and said,
'They have to be circumcised and be obliged to keep the Law of
Moses.'

Peter's and James' address at the council in Jerusalem

6And the apostles and the elders gathered together to come to a view on this question. 7As a violent argument developed, Peter got up and said, 'Men and brothers, you know that already a long time ago the divine world itself willed it that non-Jews should hear the word of the Gospel from my mouth and find the way of the faith. 8And God, the knower of the heart, bore witness to them and gave them the Holy Spirit, just as HE did to us. 9HE made no distinction between us and them, and HE purified their hearts through the power of faith. 10Now why do you want to put the divine world to the test again, by putting so heavy a yoke on the shoulders of the disciples as neither our fathers nor we ourselves have been able to bear? 11Through the gracious goodness of the Lord Jesus the faith lives in us and leads us to salvation; and their path is exactly the same.'

12Then the whole gathering was silent and listened to Paul and Barnabas, who related what signs and deeds of the spirit God had done through them among the non-Jewish peoples.

13As they all remained silent, James said, 'Men and brothers, hear me! 14Simon has shown how God has begun to turn to the heathen peoples to win a people from among them which can be a bearer of HIS name. 15This is also in accord with the words of the prophets which we can read in the scriptures:

> 16After this I will turn again
> and rebuild the sanctuary of David
> which has fallen.
> I will restore its ruins.
> It shall be set up anew.

17For the other human beings shall also seek the Lord, all peoples of the world:

> My name shall sound over them.

18Thus speaks the Lord, who now fulfils what has been in HIS mind for aeons.'

19'Therefore my decision is that those of the non-Jewish peoples who turn to God should not have unnecessary burdens laid upon

them. [20]They should only be asked to commit themselves to abstain
from the cult of idols, from immorality and from ceremonies in
which blood is used. [21]From the very beginning Moses has had
those who proclaim for him; in every town and on every Sabbath
his words are read in the synagogues.'

The council's decision and conveying it to Antioch

[22]Then it seemed right to the apostles and elders of the whole
congregation to choose men from their midst and send them to
Antioch with Paul and Barnabas: Judas, also called Barsabbas, and
Silas, leading men among the brothers. [23]The following letter was
sent by them: 'The apostles, elders and brothers send their greeting to the non-Jewish brothers in Antioch, Syria and Cilicia. [24]We
have heard that some of us have caused confusion and unclarity in
your souls by their teaching, although they had received no commission from us. [25]On hearing this, we unanimously decided to
choose men to send you with our beloved brothers Barnabas and
Paul [26]who are engaging their whole soul for the name and being of
Jesus Christ, our Lord. [27]Therefore we have asked Judas and Silas
to give you the same message by word of mouth. [28]It is the will of
the Holy Spirit and ours, too, that no burdens should be laid upon
you, except for the absolute essentials: [29]that you keep away from
the sacrifices to idols, from ceremonies in which blood is used and
from immorality. If you keep yourselves from these, then you do
what is right. Farewell!'

[30]They took their leave and came to Antioch. There they gathered the congregation together and delivered the letter. [31]When
it was read out, it gave them joy, inner confidence and certainty.
[32]Judas and Silas, who also had the gift of prophecy, offered the
brothers great spiritual comfort and strengthened them. [33]After they
had worked in this way for a time, they took their leave with the
peace-greeting from the brothers and returned to those who had
sent them. [34]Silas, however, decided to remain, and so Judas went
on without him. [35]Paul and Barnabas stayed in Antioch, teaching
and proclaiming the Gospel and many other words of the Lord.

Paul's second journey: separating from Barnabas
36After a time Paul said to Barnabas, 'Let us depart and visit the
brothers in all the towns where we proclaimed the word of the
Lord. Let us see how they are.' 37Barnabas also wanted to take
John Mark with them on the journey. 38But Paul was of the opinion that they could not take someone with them who had deserted
them from Pamphylia onwards and who had not gone with them
to the work. 39It came to a sharp conflict between them, so that
they finally separated from each other. Barnabas took Mark with
him and set off for Cyprus. 40Paul chose Silas as his companion
and departed, commended to the gracious will of the Lord by the
brothers. 41And he travelled through Syria and Cilicia and brought
new strength to the congregations.

16 *Paul in Galatia*
And he came to Derbe and from there to Lystra. And see, in that
town there was a disciple named Timothy, the son of a Jewish
woman who had become a Christian, and of a Greek father. 2He
was highly regarded by the brothers in Lystra and Iconium. 3Paul
wanted Timothy to accompany him on his journey, and he performed the circumcision on him. He did this out of consideration
for the Jews in those towns; for everyone knew that his father was a
Greek. 4Travelling from town to town they urged the congregations
to keep to the directives which had been arrived at by the apostles
and the elders in Jerusalem. 5And the congregations were strengthened anew in their faith, and increased in numbers daily.

6But as they then travelled through Phrygia and Galatia, they
were prevented by the Holy Spirit from proclaiming the word in
Asia. 7And as they came to the region of Mysia and were preparing
to travel on to Bithynia, the spirit of Jesus did not allow it. 8Then
they passed by Mysia and went down to Troas. 9There, a vision
appeared to Paul in the night; a Macedonian stood before him and
asked, 'Come over to Macedonia to help us!'

Paul in Macedonia: entering Europe
[10]Since he had had this vision, it at once was our endeavour to
travel to Macedonia; for we were sure that the divine world itself
had called us to proclaim the Gospel there. [11]So we set sail from
Troas and had a straight voyage to Samothrace and on the following day to Neapolis. [12]From there we came to Philippi, which
is the capital of Macedonia, a Roman colony. We remained in
this town for several days. [13]On the next Sabbath we went out
before the gate of the town to the river, where we supposed there
was a place of prayer. We sat down and spoke to the women who
gathered there. [14]Among those who listened to us was a devout
woman named Lydia, a seller of purple garments, from Thyatira.
The Christ opened her heart so that she professed to what Paul
spoke of. [15]When she and her household had received the baptism,
she turned to us with the request: 'If you believe that in my heart I
have united myself with Christ, then come to my house and stay!'
And she pressed us.

[16]Once, as we were going to the place of prayer, we came upon
a servant girl who had a spirit of soothsaying; she brought her
masters a large income by her oracular sayings. [17]She constantly
followed Paul and us about and called out: 'These men are servants of the Highest God, they are proclaiming to you the way of
salvation!' [18]She did this for many days. At last, Paul could bear
it no longer; he turned around and said to the spirit, 'I command
you in the name of Jesus Christ to come out of her.' And at once it
came out of her. [19]When her masters saw that their hope of profit
had gone, they seized Paul and Silas and dragged them to the
market place to the rulers; [20]they brought them before the magistrates and said, 'These people are causing a disturbance in our
town. They are Jews, [21]and they are proclaiming a code of morals
which we, as Romans, may neither accept nor practise.' [22]And the
crowd became agitated against them, and the magistrates tore the
garments off them and gave orders that they should be flogged.
[23]And when they had received many blows, they were thrown
into jail. The jailer was ordered to guard them securely, [24]and he

thereupon locked them in the innermost cells of the prison and
secured their feet in the stocks. 25At about midnight Paul and Silas
began to praise God in prayers and hymns, and the other prisoners
were listening to them. 26Suddenly there was a great earthquake,
so that the foundations of the prison shook. In a moment all the
doors sprang open, and the fetters fell off all the prisoners. 27The
jailer awoke with a start and saw the doors of the prison standing
open. Then he drew his sword to kill himself, because he thought
the prisoners had escaped. 28But Paul called out with a loud voice:
'Do not harm yourself, for we are all here!' 29Then he let lights
be brought and hurried in. Trembling with fear he threw himself
down before Paul and Silas, 30led them out and said, 'Gentlemen,
what must I do to attain to salvation?' 31They said, 'Place your
trust in Jesus the Lord, and you and your house will find salvation.'
32And they proclaimed the divine word to him and to all who were
in his house. 33And in the same hour of the night he took them in,
washed their wounds and let himself and all who belonged to him
be baptized. 34Then he brought them up to his dwelling, set food
before them and rejoiced with all his family that he had found the
faith in God.

35When it was day, the magistrates sent their messengers with
this directive: 'Let these men go free!' 36And the jailer reported
these words to Paul and said, 'The magistrates have sent messengers; you are to be set free. So therefore go in peace.' 37But Paul
said, 'They have beaten us publicly without trial and thrown us
into prison, although we are Roman citizens. And now we are to
be set free secretly? No! Let them come themselves and escort us
out.' 38The messengers reported this to the magistrates. When they
heard that they were Romans they became frightened 39and went
and apologized to them, led them out and asked them to leave the
town. 40And so they left the prison and went to Lydia's house. And
when they had seen the brothers and given them new courage, they
travelled on.

7 *Paul in Thessalonica*
They went through Amphipolis and Apollonia and came to
Thessalonica where there was a synagogue of the Jews. [2]Paul went
in to them, as was his custom, and on three Sabbath-days he discussed with them words from the scriptures. [3]He explained and
demonstrated to them that it was necessary for the Christ to suffer
and to rise from the dead, and he said, 'This Jesus, about whom I
am speaking to you, is the Christ.' [4]Some of them were persuaded
and joined Paul and Silas. Of the Greeks who belonged to the circle of the devout, a much greater number was won. Among them
were many distinguished women. [5]Then the Jews became jealous,
employed some dissolute fellows from the marketplace and instigated a riot, stirring the town up to a furious uproar. Then they went
to the house of Jason to look for them and bring them out before
the people. [6]When they did not find them, they dragged Jason and
some of the brothers before the city authorities and called out:
'These men, who have turned the world upside down, have arrived
here in our town; [7]Jason has taken them in. They act against all
the decrees of Caesar and say that there is another king, namely
Jesus.' [8]And with these words they managed to confuse both the
city authorities and the crowd. [9]But when Jason and the others had
stood surety, they let them go.

Paul in Beroea
[10]Without delay, the brothers set Paul and Silas by night on the
way to Beroea. When they arrived there, they went into the
Jewish synagogue. [11]Here the people were of nobler mind than
in Thessalonica. They received the word with great openness and
studied the scriptures daily to test what they had heard.

[12]And many of them found the faith, both distinguished Greek
women and a great number of men. [13]When the Jews in Thessalonica
learned that Paul proclaimed the divine word in Beroea also,
they came there too and stirred the people up and incited them.
[14]Then the brothers immediately sent Paul on by sea; but Silas and
Timothy remained behind. [15]Those who were accompanying Paul

brought him as far as Athens, and, after receiving instructions for Silas and Timothy to join him there as soon as possible, they took their leave.

Paul in Athens

[16]While Paul was waiting for them in Athens, his spirit was powerfully stirred when he saw how completely the town was given up to the idols. [17]And so he began to speak in the synagogue with the Jews and the devout people. And he did the same in the marketplace every day before those who happened to be passing by.

[18]Once, some philosophers of the Epicurean and the Stoic schools were arguing with him. Some said, ‘What does this word-sower actually mean with his speeches?’ Others said, ‘It appears that he wants to bring a message of new gods.’ For he proclaimed Jesus and the resurrection. [19]And they took him with them and led him to the Areopagus and said, ‘May we know what this new teaching is which you are presenting? [20]For your words sound strange to our ears; we wish to know what these things mean.’ [21]For all the Athenians and the foreigners who lived there spent their time in nothing except telling or hearing something new.

[22]Paul stood in the middle of the Areopagus and said, ‘Athenians, I see that you are devoted to the gods in every respect. [23]I have gone through your town and have looked at your shrines, and I found an altar with the inscription: TO THE UNKNOWN GOD. The one whom you revere, without knowing him, he it is whom I proclaim to you. [24]The divine Being who created the Cosmos and all beings who are within it, the Lord of heaven and earth, does not live in temples built with hands. [25]Nor is the service which is HIS due performed with human hands. How should HE need anything from Man, since HE gives life and breath and all existence to all men? [26]With creative power, HE caused the whole human race to proceed from one Being; and now mankind inhabits the whole face of the earth. And for their dwelling-places HE has limited and structured space and time, [27]so that they must seek for the divine Being and long for HIM, to sense HIM and find HIM. HE is not far

from each one of us, 28for in HIM we live and weave and have our
being. That has also been expressed by some of your poets: "We
are his offspring." 29Now, since we are the offspring of God, we
should not imagine that God is like an image of gold, silver or
stone which has been shaped by the art and the spirit of Man.
30The divine world no longer looks upon the times of unknowing.
But from now on it demands a change of heart and mind of all
people in all places. 31One day – thus it has been decided by God
– the moment had to come when mankind must find the direction
towards the Being of the Divine. This was to come about through a
human being. Through him, the way to the faith is open to all men.
God has raised him from the dead.'

32When they heard of the resurrection of the dead, some began to
scoff; but others said, 'We want to hear more from you about this.'
33So Paul went out from their midst. 34A few joined him and were
filled with the power of faith. Among them were also Dionysius the
Areopagite and a woman named Damaris and some others.

18 *Paul in Corinth*

After this, Paul left Athens and came to Corinth. 2There he found a
Jew named Aquila, a native of Pontus. He had recently come from
Italy with his wife Priscilla; this was because Claudius had commanded that all Jews must leave Rome. 3Paul came and worked
with them, for they were also tentmakers by trade. 4Every Sabbath
he spoke in the synagogue and won over both Jews and Greeks.

5When Silas and Timothy arrived from Macedonia, the Word
pressed upon Paul and he was urged to testify before the Jews that
Jesus is the Christ. 6But when they were hostile to him and scorned
his proclaiming he shook out his garments and said to them, 'Your
blood be upon your heads! I am now clean and free and can turn
fully to the foreign peoples.'

7And he went away and came to the house of a man named
Titius Justus who belonged to the circle of the devout. His house
was next door to the synagogue. And the leader of the synagogue,
8Crispus, became a Christian, together with all his household;

and many Corinthians were touched to the heart when they heard the word, and were baptized. [9]One night Christ spoke to Paul in a vision: 'Have no fear – speak, and do not be silent; [10]for I am with you, and no one shall lay hands on you and hurt you. In this town there are many more who are mine.' [11]And he remained there a year and six months and instructed those who heard him in the word of God.

[12]When Gallio became proconsul of Achaia, the Jews set upon Paul in a concerted attack, brought him before the seat of judgment [13]and said, 'This man is teaching people a form of divine worship which is contrary to the Law.' [14]But when Paul was about to speak, Gallio retorted to the Jews, 'If it were a matter of a crime or an evil deed, I would hear you out, you Jews. [15]But since you come about a dispute over words and names and over the Law which is valid among you, you must see to it yourselves how you arrive at justice. I will not be a judge in such questions.' [16]And he sent them away from the judgment seat. [17]Then they all set upon Sosthenes, a ruler of the synagogue, and beat him in front of the judgment seat. But Gallio paid no attention to this.

Return journey

[18]Paul remained there for a considerable time. Then he took leave of the brothers and sailed for Syria. Priscilla and Aquila accompanied him. In Cenchreae he had his hair shorn because he had made a vow. [19]And they came to Ephesus. There he left them to themselves and went into the synagogue and spoke to the Jews. [20]And they asked him to stay for a longer period; he declined, [21]but on taking leave of them he said, 'I must be in Jerusalem for the coming festival, but if God wills it I will return to you.' And so he left Ephesus [22]and came to Caesarea; he went up and greeted the congregation and then returned to Antioch.

The third journey: Apollos in Ephesus

[23]After a short interval he began a new journey and visited Galatia and Phrygia and strengthened all the brothers.

24At that time a Jew named Apollos came to Ephesus. He was
a native of Alexandria, a man of the word, knowledgeable and
learned. 25He had been instructed in the way of Christ and spoke
and taught thoroughly and with burning spirit about the life of
Jesus. But he only knew the baptism of John. 26He began to speak
openly in the synagogue. When Priscilla and Aquila heard him,
they took him aside and explained to him the way of God more
exactly. 27When he then wanted to go to Achaia, the brothers
wrote to the disciples there and urged them to receive him. When
he got there he was a great help to those who had come to the
faith through the touch of the Spirit. 28He repeatedly overcame
the Jews by publicly proving by the scriptures that Jesus is the
Christ.

19 *Paul in Ephesus*
While Apollos was in Corinth, Paul travelled through the high
country and came to Ephesus. There he found a group of disciples,
2and he spoke to them, 'Did you receive the Holy Spirit after you
had found the faith?' They replied, 'We have never heard anything
about the Holy Spirit.' 3And he asked, 'So which baptism did you
receive?' And they said, 'The baptism of John.' 4Then Paul said,
'John baptized with the baptism which leads to a change of heart
and mind; when he spoke to men he did it to direct them towards
the One who was to come after him, namely Jesus. 5Thus he led
them to the faith.' When they heard this they were baptized in
the name and in the power of Jesus the Lord. 6And as Paul laid
his hands upon them, the Holy Spirit came down upon them, and
they spoke with the tongues of the Spirit and prophesied. 7It was
a circle of twelve men. 8And he entered the synagogue, and for
three months he openly proclaimed his message there: with great
power of word and conviction he spoke of the Kingdom of God.
9But when certain hardened people, not open to the spirit, mocked
the divine Way before all the listeners, he withdrew from them,
gathered only the circle of the disciples about him and spoke to
them daily in the school of Tyrannus. 10This continued for two

years, so that all the residents of the province Asia were able to
hear the word of Christ, the Jews as well as the Greeks.

[11]The divine world gave extraordinary proofs of higher powers
by the hands of Paul. [12]When the cloths and garments which he had
worn next to his skin were taken and laid on those who were sick,
they were healed and the evil spirits left them.

[13]Some of the travelling Jews tried to use the name of Jesus
the Lord as a spell for those who were possessed by evil spirits.
They said, 'I exorcize you in the name of the Jesus whom Paul
proclaims.' [14]Seven sons of a Jewish high priest named Sceva were
doing this. [15]However, the evil spirit answered them, 'I know Jesus,
and Paul I know; but who are you?' [16]And the man who was possessed by the evil spirit attacked them, overpowered them and used
all his strength on them, so that they fled out of the house, naked and
wounded. [17]This soon became known to all the Jews and Greeks in
Ephesus, and they were all afraid. The name of the Lord Jesus grew
in might and esteem. [18]Many came and confessed to the faith and
reported what they had been doing. [19]And many who had occupied
themselves with magical practices brought their books and burned
them publicly; and when the value of the books was estimated, a
sum of fifty thousand silver coins was arrived at. [20]So the word of
Christ grew mightily in greatness and power.

[21]After all these events Paul formed the plan in spirit to travel
through Macedonia and Achaia and then go to Jerusalem, and he
said, 'When I have been there, I must also see Rome.' [22]And he sent
two of his helpers, Timothy and Erastus, to Macedonia. He himself
remained in Asia for a while.

The riot in Ephesus

[23]At this time a great stir arose about questions to do with the Way.
[24]A silversmith named Demetrius, who made silver Artemis temples
and thereby brought considerable income to the craftsmen, [25]called
his people together and all those who were in the same trade and
said, 'Men, you know that we get good profit from our business.
[26]Now you see and hear how this Paul speaks to great crowds, not

only in Ephesus, but almost everywhere in the province of Asia,
and brings people over to his side by telling them that true gods are
not made with hands. [27]That is not only a danger for us as regards
our trade, but also because thereby the temple of the great goddess
Artemis is brought into disrepute. Her divine greatness is in danger
of being brought to nought, she who is revered in all Asia and by
all mankind.'

[28]These words caused a great stir among the listeners; they all
shouted, 'Great is Artemis of Ephesus!' [29]The town was filled with
tumult, everyone rushed forward in the same direction towards
the theatre. And they dragged along Gaius and Aristarchus, Paul's
travelling companions from Macedonia. [30]Paul wanted to go in
among the crowd, but the disciples would not let him. [31]Some of
the leaders of the province who were his friends sent to him and
urged him not to venture into the theatre. [32]There, some shouted
one thing, some another. The whole crowd was in uproar, yet most
of them had no idea why they had gathered. [33]Some in the crowd
took hold of Alexander whom the Jews were pushing forward.
And Alexander motioned with his hand and wanted to justify himself before the people. [34]But when they recognized that he was a
Jew, they began to shout for two hours with one voice: 'Great is
Artemis of Ephesus!'

[35]Eventually the town clerk managed to quieten the crowd. He
said, 'Men of Ephesus! There can be no one who does not acknowledge that the town of Ephesus is the temple-guardian of the great
Artemis and of her image, sent down from Zeus. [36]Since this cannot be denied, it is for you to remain calm and not do anything rash.
[37]You have brought these men here who have neither profaned the
temple nor blasphemed against our goddess. [38]If Demetrius and
his craftsmen have a complaint against any one, let them bring the
case to court. What are proconsuls for? Let them take their quarrel
there. [39]If you then have further wishes they can be dealt with in
the regular assembly. [40]As it is now, we are in danger of being
charged with rioting, and we have no excuse to give to justify this
commotion.' [41]With these words he dismissed the crowd.

20 *Journeying through Greece and Macedonia*
When the uproar had ceased, Paul sent for the disciples, spoke
words of encouragement to them and took leave of them; then he
began the journey to Macedonia. [2]He went through all those parts,
and gave much strength to the congregations everywhere through
his word. Eventually he came to Greece, [3]where he remained for
three months. When he was about to set sail for Syria, a plot
against him by the Jews became known to him, and he decided
to return through Macedonia. [4]Accompanying him were Sopater,
the son of Pyrrhus of Beroea, Aristarchus and Secundus of
Thessalonica, Gaius of Derbe as well as Timothy; also Tychicus
and Trophimus of Asia. [5]They went on ahead and waited for us in
Troas. [6]After the Days of Unleavened Bread we sailed away from
Philippi, and after a voyage of five days we came to them in Troas.
There we stayed for seven days.

In Troas
[7]On the first day of the week we gathered together for the celebration of the breaking of bread, and Paul spoke to the gathering, as
he was intending to depart on the following day; he continued his
words until midnight. [8]There were many torches in the upper room
where we were gathered. [9]Now a young man named Eutychus
was sitting in the window. As Paul continued to speak still longer
he sank into a deep slumber, and, being overcome by sleep, he
fell down from the third floor. When he was picked up he was
as though dead. [10]Then Paul went down, threw himself on him,
embracing him closely, and said, 'Do not be alarmed, for his soul
is in him.' [11]And he went up once more, broke bread and ate of it;
then he continued with his discourse until daybreak. Then he took
his leave. [12]The lad they led home, alive, with a feeling of great
inner strength.

Continuing to Miletus and farewell to Asia
[13]We went ahead by ship to Assos. From there on we were to travel
together with Paul; for so he had arranged it, intending himself to

travel on foot. 14When he caught up with us in Assos, we took him
on board and came to Mitylene. 15On the next day we came opposite
Chios, and on the following day we reached Samos. On the day after
that we came to Miletus. 16For Paul had decided to sail past Ephesus,
so as not to lose time in Asia. He was hurrying to be in Jerusalem, if
possible, for the Pentecost festival.

17But from Miletus he sent messengers to Ephesus and called
to him the elders of the congregation. 18When they arrived he said
to them, 'You know how I lived among you all the time from the
first day that I set foot in Asia, 19serving the Christ with all humility and devotion and with tears and many trials which befell me
through the plotting of the Jews. 20You also know that I did not
withhold from you anything which could be of benefit to you, and
that I did not tire of speaking to you and teaching you, publicly
and from house to house. 21I wanted to testify to both Jews and
Greeks about the change of heart and mind before God and about
the faith in Jesus, our Lord. 22And see, now I go to Jerusalem as
one bound in the spirit, not knowing what will happen to me. 23I
only know, because it has been shown to me through the Holy
Spirit in town after town, that chains and severe trials await me.
24But I do not let myself be shaken by that, nor do I attach any
great value to my life, if only I may complete my path and the task
I received from Jesus the Lord, which is to testify to the Gospel
of God's goodness. 25And see, I know that all you among whom
I have wandered, proclaiming the Kingdom of God, will see my
face no more. 26Therefore I solemnly testify this day before you
that I am clean of all blood. 27In my proclaiming I did not withhold
anything from you of the will of the divine world.

28'Therefore take heed to yourselves and to all the flock, in
which you have been placed as guardians through the Holy Spirit;
you are to be shepherds of the congregation of God. By his blood
he has acquired it as his own. 29I know that after my departing fero-
cious wolves will burst in among you; they will show no mercy
to the flock. 30Out of your own midst men will arise and proclaim
falsehoods in order to lead the disciples astray and to win them for

themselves. [31]Therefore be alert, and remember that for three years
I did not tire of showing everyone the inner ways with tears, night
and day.

[32]'And now I commend you to the power of Christ and to the
word in which his merciful will is perceptible and which has the
power to build up and to pass on the spiritual inheritance to all those
who give themsclves to be sanctified. [33]Silver and gold and apparel
I did not covet. [34]You know that these my hands by their service
themselves made what was needed for me and also for those who
were with me. [35]Always I wanted to show you that it is right to help
the needy through effort and work. I wanted to imprint on your
memory the words of the Lord Jesus, who said, "It is more blessed
to give than to receive".'

[36]And after these words he knelt down and prayed with them
all. [37]Deep sorrow filled their hearts. And they embraced Paul and
kissed him. [38]Thc greatest grief was because of his words that they
would see his face no longer. And they accompanied him to the
ship.

21 *From Miletus to Tyre, Ptolemais and Caesarea*
When we had taken our leave of them and set sail, we came by a
straight course to Cos, on the following day to Rhodes and from
there to Patara. [2]And when we had found a ship which was going
directly to Phoenicia, we went aboard and set sail. [3]Cyprus was
sighted; we kept it on our left and sailed on to Syria where we
landed at Tyre. There the ship was to unload its cargo. [4]We stayed
for seven days with the disciples we found there. Because of certain spiritual experiences they said to Paul that he should not go up
to Jerusalem. [5]When the time of our stay was over, we departed;
and they all, with women and children, accompanied us till we
were outside the town. There we knelt down on the beach and
prayed. We bade one another farewell, [6]then we went on board the
ship, and they returned home.

[7]The voyage took us from Tyre on to Ptolemais. There we
greeted the brothers and stayed with them for one day. [8]The next

day we departed again and came to Caesarea where we went to
the house of Philip the evangelist, who was one of the seven, and
stayed with him. [9]He had four daughters, unmarried women who
could prophesy. [10]We stayed there several days. Then a prophet
named Agabus came down from Judea. [11]He visited us and took
Paul's belt, bound his own feet and hands with it and said, 'The
Holy Spirit says: "So will the Jews in Jerusalem bind the man
to whom this belt belongs and deliver him into the hands of the
peoples of the world".' [12]When we heard this, we and the people
there urged him not to go up to Jerusalem. [13]But Paul answered,
'Why are you weeping? Why do you make my heart heavy? I am
prepared to give up not only my freedom but my life in Jerusalem
for the name of the Lord Jesus.' [14]As he could not be persuaded,
we gave up our efforts and said, 'The will of the Lord be done.'

Paul before the apostles in Jerusalem

[15]After these days we prepared ourselves and went up to Jerusalem.
[16]Some of the disciples from Caesarea went with us, among them
also Mnason from Cyprus, an early disciple with whom we were
to stay. [17]In Jerusalem we were joyfully received by the brothers.
[18]On the following day Paul came with us to James where all the
elders were gathered. [19]He greeted them and related in detail what
the divine world had done among the peoples through his ministry. [20]When they had heard him, they praised God. Then they
said to him, 'Brother, you see how many thousands of the Jews
have come to the faith, and yet have remained zealous for the Law.
[21]Now they have heard that you teach the Jews who live among
the heathen peoples to turn away from Moses, and that you say
the newborn should not be circumcised and the old customs need
not be kept any more. [22]What will happen? They will soon learn
that you are here. [23]Now do what we say: among us are four men
who have taken a vow. [24]Take these men with you and purify yourself along with them. Give them the necessary money so that they
can have their heads shorn. Then everyone will know that there is
nothing to the rumours that are circulating about you, but that you

actually follow the way of the Law carefully. 25As regards the non-Jews who come to the faith, we have already stated our decision in writing: they are to keep away from the sacrifices to the idols, from blood sacrifices, from the secret, magical cults and from unchastity.'

26Then Paul took the men with him and purified himself with them. On thc following day he went with them into the Temple and gave notice when the days of purification would be fulfilled, namely when the offering had been presented for each one of them.

Paul's arrest

27When the seven days were almost over, Jews from Asia saw him in the Temple and stirred up the whole crowd 28and called out, 'Men of Israel, help! This is the man who is spreading a teaching everywhere which is against the people, against the Law and against this Holy Place. He has also brought Greeks into the Temple and profaned this Holy Place.' 29For they had previously seen Trophimus the Ephesian with him in the town and assumed that Paul had brought him into the Temple. 30The whole town became agitated, a great crowd gathered. They took hold of Paul and dragged him out of the Temple, and at once the gates were shut behind him. 31As they tried to kill him, word went to the commander of the cohort that the whole of Jerusalem was in a tumult. 32At once he took a unit of soldiers and their officers and stormed into the crowd. When they saw the commander and the soldiers, they stopped beating Paul. 33Then the commander stepped forward, took him and ordered him to be bound with double chains. Then he inquired who he was and what he had done. 34All the people shouted at once; and, since he could not learn the facts because of the uproar, he ordered him to be taken into the fortress. 35When they came to the steps, the soldiers actually had to carry him to protect him from the violence of the people, 36for the mob ran behind, shouting: 'Kill him!'

Address to the Jews
37As Paul was about to be taken into the fortress, he asked the
commander, ‘May I say something to you?’ And he said, ‘Do
you speak Greek? 38Are you not the Egyptian, then, who recently
stirred up a revolt and led four thousand murderers into the
desert?’ 39Paul replied, ‘I am a Jew from Tarsus in Cilicia, a citizen of a respected town. I request permission from you to speak
to the people.’ 40He gave him permission, and Paul went onto the
steps and beckoned to the people with his hand. A great silence
descended, and Paul began to speak to them in the Hebrew
language:
2 ‘Men, brothers and fathers, hear the defence with which I come
before you.’ 2When they heard that he spoke to them in Hebrew,
they became even more quiet. And he went on:
3‘I am a Jew, born in Tarsus in Cilicia, but brought up in this
town where I received my education at the feet of Gamaliel and
learned all the exact details of the Law of the fathers and became
just such a zealot for God as you all are today. 4I went on on this
path until I was face to face with death. I bound both men and
women and delivered them to prison. 5The High Priest and the
whole council of elders will bear me witness. From them I was
given the authority and went to the brothers in Damascus, because
I also wanted to take them all bound to Jerusalem to receive their
punishment. 6As I was travelling and came near to Damascus, a
bright light from heaven suddenly flashed about me in the midday
hour. 7I fell to the ground and heard a voice say to me: “Saul,
Saul, why do you persecute me?” 8And I answered, “Who are you,
Lord?” He said to me, “I am Jesus the Nazarene whom you are
persecuting.” 9Those who were with me saw the light, but the voice
speaking with me they did not hear. 10And I said, “What shall I do,
Lord?” And the Lord said to me, “Rise, and go into Damascus.
There you will be told everything that has been ordained for you
to do.” 11Since I could no longer see because of the radiant power
of that light, my companions led me by the hand into Damascus.
12There Ananias came to me, a man devout in the sense of the Law

and one highly regarded by all the Jews who lived there. 13He
stood before me and said, "Saul, brother, lift up your eyes!" And
at once I raised my eyes and saw him. 14He said, "The God of our
fathers has chosen you to know HIS will. You shall see the Lord
of the higher life and shall hear his voice. 15And you are to be his
witness to all men and to proclaim what you have seen and heard.
16Why do you still hesitate? Rise to be baptized and cleansed of
sin, and call upon his name!" 17And when I returned to Jerusalem
and was praying in the Temple 18it came to pass that I saw him in
my ecstasy, and he said to me, "Make haste and leave Jerusalem
quickly, for here your testimony about me will not be accepted."
19And I said, "Lord, they know that in every synagogue I beat and
imprisoned those who have united themselves with you through
faith. 20And when the blood of Stephen your witness was shed, I
also was standing by and took pleasure in what was happening,
and I looked after the garments of those who killed him." 21And
he answered me, "Go on your way. I will send you far away to the
peoples of the world".'

The effect of his address

22Up to these words they had listened to him, but then they raised
their voices and shouted, 'Away with him from the earth! He must
not live any longer.' 23And they called out loudly and tore their garments and threw dust into the air. 24Then the commander ordered
that he be brought into the fortress and gave instructions that he
be interrogated by scourging, to find out why they shouted thus
against him. 25As they were stretching him out with the thongs,
Paul said to the captain who was standing by, 'Is it lawful for you
to scourge a Roman citizen without due trial?' 26When the captain heard that, he hurried to the commander and said, 'What are
you doing? This man is a Roman citizen.' 27Then the commander
came and said to him, 'Tell me, are you a Roman citizen?' He
said, 'Yes.' 28The commander said, 'I had to pay a large sum to
acquire this citizenship.' And Paul said, 'But I was actually born
a citizen.' 29At once those who were about to interrogate him let

him be. And the commander was afraid when he realized that he
had bound him although he was a Roman citizen.

Paul before the Sanhedrin

30The next day he determined to find out more precisely why the
Jews accused him. He released him and commanded that the chief
priests and the whole Sanhedrin should meet. Then he led Paul in
before them.

3 And Paul looked the members of the Sanhedrin in the eye and
said, 'Men, brothers, to this day I have walked in the sight of God
with the consciousness of being on the right path.'

2Then the High Priest Ananias commanded those who stood
by him to strike him on the mouth. 3But Paul said to him, 'God
will strike you, you whitewashed wall! You sit in judgment on me
according to the Law, and yet contrary to the Law you order me to
be struck?' 4Those who stood by said, 'You dare to revile God's
High Priest?' 5Paul answered, 'I did not know, brothers, that he is
the High Priest. For it is written:

> Do not speak evil against a ruler of your people.'

6Now Paul knew that some of them were Sadducees and the
rest were Pharisees; so he called out to the Sanhedrin: 'Men, brothers, I am a Pharisee and the son of a Pharisee, and I am on trial
with respect to the hope and the resurrection of the dead.' 7When
he had said this, an argument arose between the Pharisees and the
Sadducees, and the assembly was divided. 8For the Sadducees deny
the resurrection and also the existence of angels and the spirit,
whereas the Pharisees acknowledge them both. 9A great clamour
arose, and some of the scribes of the Pharisees' party stood up and
threw these words into the debate: 'We do not find any evil in this
man. Maybe the spirit or an angel did speak to him.' 10As the tumult
grew ever worse, the commander became afraid that Paul would be
torn to pieces by them, and he ordered the cohort to go down and
take him out of their midst and bring him into the fortress.

Murder plot against Paul

[11]In the following night the Christ came to him and said, 'Be of good courage; as you have testified about me in Jerusalem, so shall you do also in Rome.'

[12]When it was day, the Jews plotted and swore neither to eat nor drink till they had killed Paul. [13]There were more than forty who made this conspiracy. [14]They went to the chief priests and the elders and said, 'We have solemnly sworn to eat nothing till we have killed Paul. [15]Now, you go with the Sanhedrin to the commander and request that Paul be brought before you once more, so that you can investigate his case more thoroughly. We are ready, then, to kill him before he gets near.'

[16]Now the son of Paul's sister heard of this planned ambush; he went to the fortress and told Paul about it. [17]Then Paul called one of the officers and said, 'Take this young man to the commander, for he has something to report to him.' [18]So he took him and brought him to the commander and said, 'The prisoner, Paul, called me and asked me to bring this young man to you, as he has something to say to you.' [19]Then the commander took him by the hand, led him to one side and asked him privately, 'What is it that you have to tell me?' [20]He answered, 'The Jews have decided to ask you to bring Paul before the Sanhedrin tomorrow, as though to investigate his case more thoroughly. [21]Do not agree to it; for more than forty of them will be lying in ambush for him. They have sworn neither to eat nor drink till they have killed him. They are ready armed, and are only waiting for your consent.' [22]Then the commander dismissed the young man and told him, 'Do not mention to anyone that you have informed me of this.'

[23]Then he called two officers and said, 'Get ready two hundred soldiers, seventy horsemen and two hundred spearmen; they are to set off at the third hour of the night to march to Caesarea. [24]Have horses standing by, too. They are to carry Paul unharmed to Felix the governor.' [25]And he wrote a letter as follows:

[26]'Claudius Lysias extends greetings to his Excellency the governor Felix. [27]This man was seized by the Jews; they were

about to kill him when I took charge with the soldiers and rescued him, having learned that he was a Roman citizen. [28]I wanted to know the charge on which they were accusing him, so I put him before their Sanhedrin. [29]I found that he was accused because of arguments to do with their Law. They were not making accusations which might have led to the death penalty or imprisonment. [30]I was informed that an ambush was planned against him; therefore I sent him to you at once, and told his accusers to present their case against him before you.'

Paul protected by the Romans and moved to Caesarea

[31]As ordered, the soldiers took Paul and led him by night to Antipatris. [32]The next day they returned to the fortress, while the horsemen went on with him. [33]When they came to Caesarea, they delivered the letter to the governor and presented Paul to him. [34]When he had read the letter, he asked which province he came from. When he learned that he was from Cilicia [35]he said, 'I will question you when your accusers arrive.' And he gave orders that he should be kept under guard in Herod's praetorium.

24 *Interrogation before the governor Felix*

After five days the High Priest Ananias went down with some of the elders and the orator Tertullus to present their case against Paul before the governor. [2]When Paul had been called, Tertullus began for the prosecution:

'Thanks to you we have been enjoying peace for a long time, and through your forethought, most excellent Felix, this people has benefitted from many reforms. [3]We acknowledge this in every respect and with deep gratitude. [4]But now, so as not to inconvenience you more than absolutely necessary, I would ask you, please, to hear us briefly. [5]We regard this man as a pest, an agitator among all the Jews of the world. He is a ringleader in the sect of the Nazarenes [6]and has tried to profane the Temple. We seized him and intended to judge him according to the Law, [7]but commander Lysias interfered, removed him by force out of our hands [8]and ordered that his accusers should turn to you. Now you will be able to form your own opinion and judgment about everything of which we accuse him.'

[9]The Jews agreed with his speech and confirmed that all this was so. [10]And when the governor had given him the sign that he might speak, Paul answered, 'I know that for many years you have been judge over this nation, and so I will defend myself before you with confidence and courage. [11]You can easily ascertain that I only came to Jerusalem twelve days ago to pray. [12]And I was not found to be instigating a revolt or stirring up a crowd, either in the Temple or in the synagogues or anywhere else in the town. [13]They can give you no proof of the accusations they bring against me. [14]But to this I confess before you, that on the Way, which they call sectarian, I serve the Father God and hold to everything which is written in the Law and in the prophetic books. [15]In looking up to the divine world I am filled with the same hope as they: that there will be a resurrection of those who serve the Good as well as of the enemies of goodness.

[16]'That is why I always strive to be able to have a clear conscience before God and before men. [17]After many years I have now come to fulfil my duty of love to my people and to bring my offering. [18]I was about to purify myself in the Temple for this service when they found me. I was neither part of a crowd, nor was there any disturbance. It was some Jews from Asia who saw me there. [19]They ought to appear before you and make their accusation, if they have anything against me. [20]Or else let these men here say what wrongdoing they found when I stood before the Sanhedrin. [21]They will only be able to point to one thing which I called out as I stood in their midst: I am on trial before you today with respect to the resurrection of the dead.'

[22]Then Felix referred them to a later time, for he knew a good deal about the Way. He said, 'When commander Lysias comes, I will decide your case.' [23]And he gave the captain orders that he should be kept in custody but otherwise left in peace, and that none of his friends should be prevented from attending to his needs.

[24]After some days Felix came with his wife Drusilla, who was a

Jewess; he sent for Paul and listened as he spoke to him about the
inner life that grows out of union in faith with Christ Jesus. [25]But
when Paul spoke about Man's true being, about self-control and
about the coming world-decision, Felix became afraid and said,
'That is enough for today. When I next have an opportunity I will
send for you.' [26]But he was also hoping that Paul would give him
money, so he sent for him often and conversed with him.
[27]After two years, Felix was succeeded by Porcius Festus; and to
prove his favour to the Jews, Felix left Paul in prison.

5 *Paul before the new governor Festus*
Three days after Festus had taken office in his territory, he went up
to Jerusalem from Caesarea. [2]There the chief priests and the leaders of the Jews spoke against Paul [3]and asked Festus as a favour
to have him sent to Jerusalem; for they were planning an ambush
to kill him on the way. [4]However, Festus replied that Paul must
remain in Caesarea, since he himself would shortly return there.
[5]He added: 'Then let those among you who are able come down
with me, and there voice their accusation if there is anything wrong
about this man.' [6]He did not stay there more than eight or ten days;
then he returned to Caesarea. On the following day he went up
to the judgment-seat and ordered that Paul be brought. [7]When he
appeared, the Jews who had come from Jerusalem surged round
him and levelled many serious accusations against him, none of
which, however, they were able to substantiate.

Paul's appeal to Caesar
[8]In his defence Paul said, 'I have sinned neither against the Jewish
Law, nor against the Temple, nor against Caesar.' [9]Festus wanted
to show favour to the Jews, so he asked Paul, 'Are you prepared
to travel up to Jerusalem and there be questioned by me about
these matters?' [10]Paul answered, 'I am standing before Caesar's
judgment seat, and it is there that I ought to be tried. I have done
no wrong to the Jews, as you know very well. [11]If I have committed a crime for which I deserve to die, I do not seek to escape

death; but if there is nothing in the accusations they bring against
me, then neither can anyone hand me over to them. I appeal to
Caesar.' [12]Festus conferred with the council; then he said, 'You
have appealed to Caesar; to Caesar you shall go.'

[13]After some days, King Agrippa and Bernice (his sister) came
to Caesarea to greet Festus. [14]And as they stayed there several days,
Festus laid Paul's case before the king. He said, 'There is a man
here, whom Felix left behind in prison. [15]When I was in Jerusalem,
the chief priests and the elders of the Jews appeared before me
because of him, demanding that he be sentenced. [16]I answered them
that it is not the custom of the Romans to condemn a man as a
favour to somebody, before the accused has met his accusers face
to face and has had the opportunity to defend himself against the
accusation. [17]When therefore they came here, I did not delay, but
went up to the judgment-seat the very next day and ordered the
man to be brought. [18]When the accusers stood around him, however, they actually had nothing to put forward that I could have
accepted. [19]There were points of dispute about their religion and
about a certain Jesus, who is dead, but about whom Paul says that
he is alive. [20]Since I am not well versed in these questions, I asked
him if he was willing to go to Jerusalem and there stand trial. [21]But
Paul appealed and demanded to be kept in custody to await his
majesty's decision. And so I ordered him to be held until I could
send him to Caesar.' [22]Then Agrippa said to Festus, 'I would also
like to hear this man myself.' And he answered, 'Tomorrow you
shall hear him.'

Paul before King Agrippa

[23]The next day Agrippa and Bernice came with great pomp and
entered the audience hall with the officers and the most prominent
men of the town. By command of Festus Paul was brought in.
[24]And Festus said, 'King Agrippa and all you men gathered here
with us, here you see a man, because of whom a great number of
Jews in Jerusalem and here have come to me, shouting that he
ought not to live any longer. [25]But I have found that he has done

nothing deserving death. Now he has appealed to his imperial majesty, and I have decided to send him there. [26]However, I know
nothing definite to write to the sovereign about him. That is why I
have brought him before you, especially before you, King Agrippa,
so that, after we have examined him, I shall know what to write.
[27]It seems pointless to me to send a prisoner without being able to
indicate the charges against him.'

26 Then Agrippa said to Paul, 'You have permission to speak for
yourself.' And Paul stretched out his hand and began his defence:
[2]'I consider myself fortunate, King Agrippa, that today I can
answer to you for all the things I am being accused of by the Jews,
[3]for you are very knowledgeable about all the customs and areas
of dispute among the Jews; and so I ask you to hear me with magnanimity. [4]All the Jews know that my life from my youth onwards
has been rooted in my people in Jerusalem. [5]Those who know me
from earlier days can testify, if only they are willing, that I have led
my life according to the laws of the strictest party of our religion,
namely as a Pharisee. [6]And now I am on trial here because of hope
in the fulfilment of the divine promise made to our fathers. [7]The
twelve tribes of our people perform the holy service day and night
with devotion and perseverance because they long for the fulfilment
of this hope. Because of that hope I am accused by the Jews, O
King! [8]Do you find something absurd about God raising the dead?
[9]I myself was once convinced that I had to fight vigorously against
the name of Jesus the Nazarene, [10]and indeed I did so in Jerusalem.
Many saints I imprisoned by the authority I had been given by the
chief priests. And when they were to be put to death, I cast my vote
for it. [11]In all the synagogues I urged passionately that they should
be forced to recant through punishments. I raged against them to
excess, and I even pursued them to towns outside the country. [12]On
one such occasion I was travelling to Damascus with the authority
and commission of the chief priests, [13]when in the midday hour, O
King, I saw on the way a light from heaven, brighter than the sun
itself, which shone around me and my companions. [14]We all fell
to the ground, and I heard a voice saying to me in Hebrew: "Saul,

Saul, why do you persecute me? All your struggling will not free
you from the goad." [15]And I said, "Who are you, Lord?" The Lord
answered, "I am Jesus whom you are persecuting. [16]Now arise and
stand on your feet. I have appeared to you to make you a servant
and a witness to what you have seen and what I will reveal to you
in the future. [17]I shall make you free of your people and of all the
non-Jewish people to whom I send you. [18]Open their eyes, so that
they may turn from darkness to light, from the Satanic power to
God. They are to have a share in the overcoming of the sickness of
sin and in the inheritance which spirit-filled men receive through
faith in me." [19]King Agrippa, I did not resist the heavenly vision;
[20]beginning in Damascus, then in Jerusalem and in the whole of
Judea and beyond that among the non-Jewish peoples, I proclaimed
the need for a change of heart and mind, for devotion to God and
for deeds which follow from such an inner change. [21]That is why
the Jews seized me in the Temple and tried to kill me. [22]However,
through the divine help which I have experienced to this day, I can
stand here and testify before both the lesser and the great. And I am
saying nothing but what the prophets and Moses foretold: [23]that the
Christ was destined to suffer, and, being the first to rise from the
dead, he would proclaim a light to both the people of Israel and the
non-Jewish peoples.'

[24]As he was thus making his defence, Festus called out loudly:
'You are out of your mind, Paul, your deep knowledge is driving
you out of your mind!' [25]But Paul said, 'I am not raving, most
excellent Festus; I am speaking words of sober truth. [26]The king
understands what I am saying. I turned to him with perfect frankness; I am convinced that nothing of it was obscure to him, for
it did not happen in some hidden corner. [27]King Agrippa, do you
believe the prophets? I know that you believe them.' [28]Agrippa said
to Paul, 'It would not take much for you to make me a Christian
through your words.' [29]Paul replied, 'My prayer to God is that,
whether much or little would be needed, not only you but all who
have heard me today might become as I am, except for my chains.'

[30]Then the king rose, and the governor, Bernice and those who

had been sitting with them; [31]and they withdrew, saying to one
another, ‘This man is not doing anything that deserves death or
imprisonment.’ [32]And Agrippa said to Festus, ‘He could be released
if he had not appealed to Caesar.’

27 *The way to Rome: journey from Caesarea to Crete*
As it had now been decided that we should sail for Italy, Paul and
some other prisoners were handed over to a captain of Caesar’s
regiment, named Julius. [2]We boarded a ship from Adramyttium,
which was bound for the coastal ports of Asia, and set sail.
Aristarchus, a Macedonian from Thessalonica, was with us. [3]Next
day we came to Sidon. Julius was very kind to Paul and allowed
him to go to his friends to be taken care of. [4]As our voyage went
on we had to sail close to Cyprus, because the wind was against
us. [5]We sailed across the sea off Cilicia and Pamphylia and came
to Myra in Lycia. [6]There the captain found an Alexandrian ship
bound for Italy, and made us transfer to it. [7]For a number of days
we only progressed slowly and arrived with difficulty off Cnidus
because the wind hindered our voyage. We sailed close to Crete
by Salmone [8]and only with a struggle did we reach a place called
Good Harbour. It was near the town of Lasea.

Paul gives warning
[9]Now, it was getting late in the year and the voyage was becoming dangerous; the time of the fast had already passed, and Paul
warned them [10]and said, ‘Men, I see that we shall not be safe from
accident and harm on this voyage; not only the cargo and the ship
are at risk, but our very lives.’ [11]But the captain paid more attention to the helmsman and the master of the ship than to what Paul
said. [12]As the harbour was unsuitable for wintering in, the major-
ity decided that the voyage should continue, if possible to get to
Phoenix and winter there. That is a harbour serving Crete which
is sheltered from both sea and land winds. [13]As the south winds
sprang up just then, they thought they could realize their intention,
weighed anchor and sailed on along the coast of Crete.

Shipwreck

[14]But quite soon the weather changed, and a whirlwind arose,
called Euraquilo. [15]The ship was driven off, and it was impossible
to hold out against the wind; so we gave way and let the ship
drift along. [16]When we came under the lee of a small island called
Clauda, we managed only with great difficulty to get control of
the lifeboat. [17]We hauled it on board and took the prccaution of
undergirding the ship. For fear of being driven on the Syrtis, they
lowered the rigging and let the ship be driven along like that. [18]As
we were in the grip of a violent storm, on the following day we
threw some cargo out, [19]and on the third day we even threw all the
equipment of the ship overboard with our own hands. [20]For days
we saw neither sun nor stars. The storm drove us with great force,
and we gave up all hope of being saved.

[21]No one had eaten for a long time; then Paul stood in their
midst and said, 'Men, you should have listened to me and not have
set sail from Crete, then we would have been spared this disaster
and harm. [22]But now I urge you not to lose heart. None of you will
lose his life; only the ship is lost. [23]For this night there appeared to
me an angel of the God to whom I belong and whom I serve, [24]and
he said, "Do not be afraid, Paul! You shall stand before Caesar,
and see, God grants you the lives of all those who sail with you."
[25]So take heart, men! I place my trust in God: it will be as I have
been told. [26]We must run on some island.'

[27]In the fourteenth night of our drifting on the Adriatic Sea,
about midnight, the sailors realized that they were nearing land.
[28]They sounded, and measured twenty fathoms. A little farther on
they sounded again, and measured fifteen. [29]Since they now feared
that we might run on to a rocky shore, they dropped four anchors
from the stern, and longed for daybreak. [30]Then the sailors tried
to escape from the ship; they began to lower the boat into the sea,
under pretence of dropping anchors from the bow of the ship. [31]But
Paul said to the captain and the soldiers, 'Unless these men stay in
the ship, you cannot be saved.' [32]Then the soldiers cut through the
ropes by which the boat hung, and let it go.

[33]When dawn came at last, Paul urged them all to take some
food. He said, 'This is the fourteenth day that you have spent hungry and anxiously waiting, without eating anything. [34]Therefore I
advise you: take some nourishment, it is necessary if you are to
be saved. For not a hair is to perish from the head of any of you.'
[35]When he had said this, he took the bread, and in the presence of
all he looked up to the divine world, spoke the words of thanks and
blessing over the bread, broke it and began to eat. [36]Then they all
felt new courage and also took food. [37]In all, we were two hundred
and seventy-six souls on the ship. [38]When they were satisfied, they
lightened the ship by throwing the cargo of grain overboard.

[39]When it was day, they did not recognize the land before which
we were. However, they noticed a bay with a flat beach, on which
they planned if possible to run the ship ashore. [40]So they cut the
anchors free and left them in the sea; at the same time they undid
the lashings which secured the rudder, hoisted the foresail to the
wind and steered for the beach. [41]But they struck a spit of land, and
the ship grounded. The bow dug itself in and became immovable,
while the stern was broken up by the force of the waves. [42]The
soldiers intended to kill the prisoners, so that none of them should
escape by swimming; [43]but the captain wanted to save Paul and
prevented them from carrying out their plan. He ordered those who
could swim to jump overboard first and make for the land. [44]The
others must reach the shore on planks or wreckage from the ship.
And so it came about that all reached land alive.

28 *Stay on Melite*
After we had been saved we learned that the island was called
Melite. [2]The foreigners showed us extraordinary kindness. They
made us welcome and lit a fire, because it was cold and had begun
to rain. [3]But when Paul gathered a bundle of sticks and put them
in the fire, a snake, awakened by the heat, crept out and fastened
on his hand. [4]When the natives saw the creature hanging from his
hand, they said to one another, 'This man must be a murderer: he
has just escaped from the sea, but now the avenging spirit does not

permit him to go on living.' 5He, however, shook off the creature
into the fire and suffered no harm. 6They expected him to swell
up or suddenly drop dead; but when they had waited a long time
and saw that nothing untoward happened to him, they revised their
opinion and said that he must be a god.

7In that district the governor of the island had an estate. His name
was Publius. He received us and entertained us most hospitably for
three days. 8It happened that the father of Publius lay sick with
fever and dysentery. Paul went to him, prayed, laid his hands on
him and healed him. 9Thereupon the other sick people on the island
also came and were healed. 10And they showed us great honour, and
when we were leaving they brought us whatever we needed.

Continuing the journey via Sicily

11After three months we set sail in an Alexandrian ship which
had wintered by the island. In its coat of arms it had the sign of
Gemini, the Twins. 12We came to Syracuse and stayed there for
three days. 13From there we sailed across to Rhegium. After one
day a south wind sprang up, and so we got to Puteoli in two days.
14There we found brothers who asked us to stay with them for
seven days. And so we reached Rome.

Arrival in Rome

15When the brothers there heard about us they came as far as
Forum Appii and Tres Tavernae to meet us. On seeing them, Paul
offered a prayer of thanks to God and took heart. 16When we
entered the city of Rome, Paul was given permission to arrange
for a place of his own to stay, together with the soldier who was
guarding him.

17After three days Paul called together the leaders of the Jews.
When they came, he said to them, 'Men, brothers, although I have
done nothing against the people or the customs of the fathers,
yet in Jerusalem I was handed over as a prisoner to the Romans.
18They wanted to set me free after the interrogation, because I was
not guilty of a capital crime. 19But the Jews objected, and I was

obliged to appeal to Caesar, though I had no intention of bringing
a charge against my people. [20]That is the reason why I asked you
to come to me, and why I have spoken to you. It is because of the
hope of Israel that I bear this chain.' [21]Then they answered him,
'We have received no letters from Judea about you; nor have any
of the brothers come to us with evil reports or accusations against
you. [22]But we would like to hear what your thoughts are, for all we
know about this sect is that it meets with opposition everywhere.'

[23]They appointed a day for him, and came to him in his lodging in great numbers. He explained and testified to the nature of
the Kingdom of God, spoke to them with convincing power about
Jesus and referred to the Law of Moses and to the prophets. This
lasted from morning till evening. [24]Some were convinced by what
he said, others closed their minds to it. [25]Finally they began to
quarrel with one another, and went away after Paul had made one
particular statement: 'How truly did the Holy Spirit say to your
fathers through the prophet Isaiah:

> [26]Go to this people and say:
> You shall hear with your ears yet not understand,
> and you shall see with your eyes and yet not perceive.
> [27]Dead is the heart of this people,
> their ears are hard of hearing, and their eyes are closed.
> In spite of their eyes they shall not see,
> and in spite of their ears not hear,
> and in spite of their hearts be uncomprehending
> and find it hard to change their heart and mind
> and to find healing through me.

[28]So let it be known to you: the salvation of God has been sent to
the peoples of the world; *they* will listen to the message.'

[30]For two whole years he lived in the lodging he had rented,
and received all who came to him, [31]and proclaimed the Kingdom
of God, and taught about Jesus Christ, the Lord, quite openly and
unhindered.

The Letter of Paul to the Romans

1 *Greeting to the congregation*
Paul, in the service of Christ Jesus, an apostle by calling, by
spiritual destiny a proclaimer of the message of healing from God
[2]of which we have foreknowledge through the prophets in the holy
scriptures.
[3]It is the message about the Son. In his body he is descended
from the family of David. [4]But by the saving Spirit which proceeds from him we recognize in him the spiritual figure of the Son
of God, on the strength of his resurrection from the dead. That is
Jesus Christ, our Lord. [5]Through him we have received the grace
and the task to awaken faith – that is, hearing with the heart – in
all peoples in his name, his being and his power. [6]To you also,
who have been called by Jesus Christ, have I been sent; [7]to you all
who live in Rome, beloved by God, destined for salvation. May
grace be yours and peace from God our Father, and from Jesus
Christ the Lord.

Thanks, and his intention to visit
[8]Firstly, I send my thanksgiving prayer for you all to the Father,
the Ground of the World, in the power of Jesus Christ; for the
tidings of your faith has already reached the whole world. [9]God
HIMSELF, whom I serve with all the power of my spirit in the proclamation of the Gospel of HIS Son, is my witness that I bear you
in my thoughts without ceasing and include you in my prayers at
all times. [10]My prayer is that it may become possible to come to
you on the ways of destiny on which I am guided by God's will.
[11]I wish so much to see you, to let you share in the gift of the
touch of the Spirit which strengthens your souls, [12]or, better still:

I wish to be strengthened myself, too, in your midst and be filled
with comfort by the interchange between your faith and mine.

[13]I will not disguise it from you, dear brothers: often I have
undertaken to come to you, but until now I have always been prevented. It was my wish that the fruits of my work should ripen
among you also, as it has been granted me to experience among
other peoples. [14]I feel myself to be in debt to both the Greeks and
the non-Greeks; to those who strive for wisdom, as well as to those
who follow powers of the soul other than the intelligence. [15]That
is why I feel the urge to come to Rome, in so far as it is within my
power, and there proclaim the Gospel also in your midst.

[16]I do not feel lowered in my own self because of living completely for the Gospel, for in it lives a power of God which heals the
souls of all who unite with it in faith. It is meant first for the Jews,
but also for the Greeks. [17]For through it, the true being is revealed
and made apparent, the justice of God which proceeds from faith
and leads to faith. As it is said:

> The true being is his, for whom faith becomes a
> source of life.

God's anger over the non-Jews

[18]The divine world must reveal itself from the heights as a sphere of
wrath to a humanity which has become separated from God and the
true being, and which perverts the truth into untruth and injustice.
[19]Within men, the ability still lives to perceive the divine in the
truth. In the past, the divine was fully visible to them.

[20]Ever since the creation of the world, the supersensible nature
of the divine Being has been spiritually perceptible in the kingdoms of creation: HIS eternal creative power and HIS divine greatness. Therefore there is no excuse for those human beings who fail
to relate to the divine world with reverence, praise and gratitude,
[21]since they are still able to perceive that world. In their thinking
they have ended up with a void, and therefore their hearts have
become blind and darkened. [22]They make out that they are wise,

but they have become foolish 23and have lost sight of the shining
glory of the imperishable divine Being. They see only the world
of mere images; their sight only takes in the perishable form of
earthly man and of the birds, the four-legged and the creeping
animals.

24That is why God has let them become prey to the desires of
their own hearts, through which they lose their purity, so that they
ultimately enter into an irreverent relationship even to their own
bodies. 25Out of themselves they pervert divine truth into deceptive
appearance, and give more respect and service to what has been
created than to the Creator, to whom we send our song of praise
from aeon to aeon. Amen.

26Therefore God has let them sink into unworthy passions, so
that the females among them have perverted natural habits of life
into unnatural. 27And the males among them have lost their natural conduct towards the female sex; instead, they have allowed
violently erupting passions to arise between them, men between
men, so that they offend against every good and ordered behaviour. But they have had painfully to experience in themselves the
results of their strayings. 28Since they no longer attached any value
to taking the divine Being into their consciousness, God let them
fall prey to degenerate thinking, so that their actions no longer
relate to the meaning of existence, either. 29Their being has become
filled with moral weakness and degeneracy, with selfishness and
corruption. They are full of negation of the being of others and the
life of others; they are quarrelsome and hinder each other. There is
nothing good left in their relationships with other human beings.
30They chatter instead of being silent, they lie instead of speaking
the truth. They blaspheme against the divine instead of revering
it. They are arrogant instead of striving upwards; they are haughty
instead of humble. Empty phrases are in their mouths instead of the
pure word. They take their inspiration from evil rather than good
spirits. Without respect, they despise the generations that have gone
before. 31Thoughtless, faithless, loveless and without feeling have
they become. 32And yet with all this they still have an awareness

of the divine order of the world and ought to know that death enters the being of those who let themselves go in such ways. Not only do they behave like that themselves, they take pleasure in seeing others doing the same.

God's anger over the Jews

Never, O Man, whoever you are, do you have reason or excuse when you make yourself a judge over others. For with the judgment you pass upon others you judge yourself. You make yourself a judge of what you also do yourself. 2We do know that the divine world responds according to the truth, to the deeds of men which are in contradiction to the divine laws. 3Do you not consider, O Man, when you judge others because of deeds which you also do yourself, that you, neither, will be able to avoid the reaction of the divine world? 4You despise the wealth of possibilities that arise out of God's goodness, patience and great-heartedness, and therefore you do not recognize that the goodness of God is to lead you, too, to a change of heart and mind. 5Through the hardness of your nature and the incorrigible rigidity of your heart you store up cosmic wrath for yourself on the day of the great world-storm and the revelation of the divine world-judgment. 6Then each one will be given what corresponds to his deeds. 7Those who have served the Good and have striven after the deathless life with patient endurance will be given radiance of being, dignity and death-conquering power. 8But those who have not been open to the truth but only to untruth and injustice in their turbulent opposition, will fall prey to the divine wrath and the burning fire of their cravings. 9Oppression and anxiety must take hold of every human soul who has served the evil. In the first place this applies to the Jews, but also to the Greeks. 10Radiance of being, dignity and peace will be to him who has worked in the service of the Good. That, too, applies to the Jews, but also to the Greeks. 11Before the countenance of God, differences of personality lose their significance.

12Those who serve sin without the Law will also be drawn into the decline without the Law. Those who serve sin with the Law, already receive their judgment by the Law. [13]Before the countenance of God, it is not those who hear the Law who are right, but those who actively fulfil it. [14]And when the peoples who do not have the Law act by nature in accordance with the Law, then they, who do not have the Law, are a law to themselves. [15]It becomes apparent that it is written in their hearts to act in accordance with the Law. They can trust the inner witness of their consciencc, and so they can find their way through the conflicts of accusing and defending thoughts. [16]This applies to the spiritual dawn, when God gives the innermost part of man its direction through Jesus Christ. This is in accordance with the Gospel that is proclaimed by me.

[17]You call yourself a Jew; you rely on the Law and boast of your relation to God. [18]You know HIS will, and, because you have been educated in it, you know all the details of the Law. [19]And now you imagine that you are a guide to the blind, a light to those who walk in darkness, [20]a teacher of those without knowledge, an cducator of the immature. You think that in the Law you possess the embodiment of knowledge and truth. [21]But why do you who teach others not teach yourself? Why do you preach, 'You shall not steal' and yourself steal? [22]Why do you thunder against immorality and are immoral yourself? Why do you damn idols but yourself profane what is holy? [23]Why do you boast of the Law but despise God by breaking the Law? [24]It is as the scripture says:

> The name of God is desecrated among the heathen
> peoples because of you.

[25]Circumcision is meaningful, if you follow the Law in all your deeds. But if you break the Law, you are like the uncircumcised, despite your circumcision. [26]If, however, someone who is not circumcised fulfils the meaning of the Law, does not then his uncircumcision become circumcision for him? [27]He who is uncircumcised by nature but who fulfils the Law will be your judge, because you break the Law in spite of the letter of the Law and your circumcision. [28]For he is not a real Jew who is one outwardly only, and real circumcision is not something physical only. [29]He is a true Jew who is one inwardly; and true circumcision is of the heart,

done in the spirit, not merely according to the letter. What counts here is not acknowledgment by men but by God HIMSELF.

So what advantage do the Jews have? What is the value of circumcision? [2]Much in every respect; in the first place they have been entrusted with the revelation of the divine Word. [3]What does it matter if some of them did not open their hearts to it? Does their lack of trust destroy the trust of God? [4]By no means! It is still so that God is truth, even if all human beings live a lie. As the scripture says:

> True being lives in the revelation of your word;
> victorious, you overcome every trial.

[5]But if what is false and unjust in us serves to bring God's justice and truth to light, can we then ask if God does not make HIMSELF unjust when – to speak in human terms – HE becomes angry with men? [6]It is wrong to ask thus, for how else would it be possible for God to be the world judge! [7]And yet we ask: If the truth of God only appears in its full light-glory because of what is false and wrong in me, why am I still condemned as a sinner? [8]Why should I not do what is alleged about us maliciously: that we say, 'Let us do evil, so that good may come about'? Truly, this would be worthy of condemnation. [9]Therefore we ask once more: Do we have any advantage? And now we answer: Absolutely not. We have already shown that both the Jews and the Greeks are under the power of sin. [10]The scripture is true:

> There is no one who is righteous, no, not one;
> [11]and there is no one who has real insight,
> no one who really seeks God.
> [12]They have all turned aside and no longer fulfil their purpose;
> there is no one who acts out of true goodness, not one.
> [13]Their gullet is an open grave,
> with their tongues they practise deceit,
> snake venom is under their lips,
> [14]their mouths are full of curses and bitterness.

[15]Their feet are swift when blood is to be shed,
[16]ruin and misery follow their paths,
[17]they do not know the way of peace,
[18]there is no fear of God in the look of their eye.

[19]We know that what the Law says, it says to those who belong to the Law. But the meaning of its speaking is that before it every mouth should become silent, and the whole world should feel itself in the wrong before God. [20]It follows from this that

no human being incarnated on the earth can attain to true
being before God

by carrying out works in order to comply with the Law. Through the Law, only the consciousness of sin is awakened.

Redemption through faith

[21]But now, true being, the divine righteousness, has appeared beyond the Law, as it has already been foretold by the Law and the prophets: [22]that true, divine being which Man can attain when he unites himself in faith with Christ. The way is open to all who have faith. In that, there is no distinction. [23]All human beings are under the curse of sin and have lost the light-glory of God. [24]But the way to the true being is also open again to all human beings, without their merit, purely as a gift of grace from God: through the salvation which has come about through Christ Jesus. [25]God has made him a source of healing and atonement.

Faith opens the heart to the power of his blood, and so the true higher being and life can prove its work through him. The load of sin which had been heaped up in the world was wiped out by the power of divine patience. [26]And so the new revelation of God's justice shines forth in our present world aeon: Christ appears as bearer and giver of the true higher life which opens up through faith in Jesus.

[27]What then becomes of Man's fame? It is extinguished. By what law? By the law of works? No, but by the law of faith. [28]It is our conviction that Man finds the true divine being through faith, quite apart from the works of the Law. [29]Is God only God of the Jews?

Is HE not also the God of the heathen peoples? Yes, also of those
peoples. 30He is the same one Godhead who opens the true being
to those who have the circumcision – through faith, and to those
who do not have the circumcision – also through faith. 31Are we
thereby overthrowing the Law in favour of faith? By no means.
We are only now getting to understand the true significance of the
Law.

4 *Abraham – the father of faith*
We can learn something important from what was granted to our
father Abraham as regards his earthly-bodily life. 2If Abraham had
reached fulfilment of his life through the works that he did, then he
would indeed have deserved to be praised; but before the countenance of God, matters appear differently. 3What does scripture say
about this?

> Abraham had trust and faith in God, and therefore he
> was counted as righteous.

4To someone who works, his wages are not awarded as a favour,
but because he is owed them. 5But as well as the way of works
there is also another: when someone opens himself in faith and
trust to the power of him who can restore true being to those who
have become alienated from God, for such a man his faith becomes
the cause of fulfilment of his being by God. 6This is also what
David means when he calls that man blessed, whom God grants the
true being without asking about his works:

> 7Blessed are those whose strayings are forgiven
> and whose sins are covered by the mantle of love.
> 8Blessed is the man, whose sin is no longer regarded by
> the Lord.

9Now, is this blessing only for those who have the circumcision,
or is it also for those who do not have it? We have said, 'Abraham
had trust and faith in God, and therefore he was counted as righteous.' 10How is this to be understood? Did it happen when he had
already received the circumcision or when he was still uncircumcised? It was not because of his circumcision, but while he was

still uncircumcised. [11]He received the sign of circumcision as a seal of the fulfilment which had been granted him through his faith while he was yet uncircumcised. Abraham was to be the father of all those who reach faith, and thereby the fulfilment of their being, without circumcision. [12]And he was also to be the father of those who have circumcision, but who do not rely on that alone, but tread the path of faith as our father Abraham also did before he had the circumcision.

[13]The promise that was given to Abraham and his descendants, that they should be bearers of mankind's future: this promise did not come from the Law. It was the fruit of fulfilment of being through the faith. [14]If the men of the Law were the bearers of the inheritance, then faith would be without significance and the promise without content. [15]The Law can only cause divine wrath; for where the Law is not, there can also not be transgression of the Law.

[16]That is why faith is the source of the true future. It makes space for grace, and that is what constitutes the power and validity of the promise that has been made to all generations, not only to those who belong to the people of the Law, but also to those who are sons of the faith of Abraham. He is the father of us all [17]according to the word of scripture:

> I have chosen you to be the father of many peoples.

With faithful trust he turned to that divine power which gives life to what is dead and calls into being what is not in being. [18]Out of his faith he found hope, even where there was nothing to hope for any more, and so he became the father of many peoples according to the word:

> Your seed shall be as great as the world.

[19]He did not waver in his faith, for he did not regard the mortality of his body, although he was near to a hundred years old; nor did he regard the mortality of Sarah's womb. [20]He had no doubts through lack of trust in the divine promise; rather, he let himself be carried by the strong power of faith, and gave praise to the revelation of God [21]with absolute conviction that God has the

power to make HIS promises into reality. [22]Therefore the fulfilment of his life was awarded him and

he was counted as righteous.

[23]Yet the scripture does not only mean him when it says it was awarded
him. [24]It also means us, for it will also be awarded to us when we
unite in faith with HIM who raised Jesus our Lord from death, [25]he
who was given in offering because we have fallen, and who has been
called to life so that we may find the true being and life.

5 *The Fall of Adam and Christ's deed of grace*

Therefore, since we have found a share in the higher life through
the activity of faith, we can be at peace with the divine world. This
can be, thanks to Jesus Christ our Lord, [2]through whom we can
find access to the realm which now lets us stand in such a stream
of grace. And we feel exalted by the hope of growing into the light
of the divine revelation. [3]But that is not all. We can also be proud
of all hardships that we have to endure. We know that all suffering
strengthens the power to bear. [4]Patience proves to be worthwhile,
and gives us the right to look forward to the future with joy. [5]That
kind of hope will not be disappointed, for the love of God has been
poured out in our hearts through the Holy Spirit which has been
given us.

[6]While we were yet bowed down by weakness, at the right
world-hour Christ took death upon himself for humanity which
had become alienated from God. [7]For someone who does not fall
short of perfection no one needs to die; but to bring about the Good
it is worth staking one's life. [8]God has shown HIS love to us in
this, that Christ died for us while we were yet under the spell of
sin. [9]Since now we have found a share in the higher life through
the blood of Christ, may we not all the more hope that he will
redeem us from a form of existence which must turn the love of
God into wrath? [10]Since we have been transformed back towards
God through the death of HIS Son while we were still against God,
will we not all the more share in this redeeming transformation
through his life? [11]Not only are we inwardly sure of this; we may

be proud of it before the countenance of God through Jesus Christ,
our Lord, who now causes this transformation in us.

[12]Now it is like this: through one man sin came into the world,
and through sin death. Death has become the destiny of all human
beings because they all live in a condition of sin. [13]And already
before the Law existed there was sin in the world, only – before
the Law was there, there was no consciousness of sin yet. [14]Death
already reigned from Adam to Moses, also over those who did
not yet have any consciousness of sin; it reigned over them too,
because the original transgression of Adam spread to all. And yet
Adam is also the archetype of one who is to come. [15]Over against
the Fall there is the great deed of grace. On the one hand: through
the Fall of the one, many became subject to death. How great,
on the other hand, must be the freely given grace of God which
is offered in its full richness to many human beings through the
sacrifice of the one human being, Jesus Christ.

[16]Therefore, matters are not the same with regard to the gift of
grace and the sin of one. Through the lapse of the one, the catastrophe of the Cosmic Fall was initiated, but the deed of grace prepares
the way again out of the welter of strayings towards true being. [17]If
death has become the ruler through the Fall of the one and through
that one, will not those who have received the riches of the freely
given grace, and thereby their true being, share all the more in the
reign of life which has been instituted by the One, Jesus Christ?
[18]Just as all became caught up in the decline through the Fall of the
one, so also the restitution of life was initiated for all through the
sunlike truthfulness of being of One. [19]Just as many became prey
to sin through the deafness to God of the one human being, so also
the true word and being were opened again to many through the
new hearing of God by the One. [20]The Law was only brought in to
complete the Fall. But when sin has reached its fullest extent, then
grace has become all the greater. [21]Just as sin has ruled through
death, so grace will reveal its power all the more through the true
higher being that leads to deathless life: through Jesus Christ, our
Lord.

Sin and holiness

May we now say, ‘We will remain in sin so that grace may
appear in its full greatness’? 2By no means. How can we still
live in a condition to which we have died? 3For of course you
know that when we became united with Christ Jesus through
baptism we were also particularly drawn into his death. 4We are
laid in the grave, since our baptism connected us with his death.
The meaning of this is that as Christ was awakened from death
by the light-glory of the Father, so we, too, walk on our further
ways with renewed powers of life. 5As we have been united so
closely with him that we bear an image of his death in us, so we
also grow towards an image of his resurrection. 6We know: our
old self has also been crucified, so that our bodily nature, ruled
as it is by sin, should no longer be able to compel us and we no
longer should be under the tyranny of sin. 7Whoever has died to
its might, for him the way to the true being has been cleared. 8If
we have died with Christ, then our faith lets us share in his life.
9We know that Christ who rose from the dead does not die again;
death has lost its power over him. 10Through his death he died
out of the realm of sin once for all; through his life he lives in
the life of God.

11From now on, you, too, should think of yourselves like this:
feel yourselves to be dead as regards sin, but as living through
the share in the life of God which you have through Jesus Christ.
12Then sin shall no longer be the ruler of your mortal body; it
shall no longer compel you to follow base desires. 13No longer
lend the members of your body to sin as instruments to pervert
existence, but rather place yourselves in the service of God as
human beings who have won through death to life, and make
your members into instruments and weapons of the true being
before HIM. 14No longer shall sin be your master. You are no
longer under the Law, but under grace. 15But it does not follow
that, because we are no longer under the Law but under grace, we
therefore can sin without a care. 16For you do know: when you
enter into the service of a master and promise him obedience, then

you also owe him your service and obedience. Either you submit yourselves to the rule of sin, which leads into death, or else you place yourselves with listening, open hearts in the service of the higher life. [17]Let us thank God for the course of your becoming. Once you were slaves of sin, but now, in willing obedience you have opened your hearts to the archetypal image which is shown to you by your education into the divine. [18]Now that you are freed from the tyranny of sin, you have become helpful to the true higher being.

[19]I must speak to you in human pictures because your earthly-bodily nature keeps the spiritual in you weak. As once you put the members of your body in the service of impurity and lawlessness which brings forth ever more lawlessness, so now make them of use to the true being for the sanctification of life. [20]When you were the slaves of sin, the true being could not work upon you. [21]What fruits did your life bring forth in those days? Today you are ashamed of them. They all led only to death. [22]Now that you are freed from the spell of sin and have entered the service of God, you bring forth fruits of healing and holiness. They lead to deathless life. [23]The wages of sin is death. The gracious gift of God is eternal life through Jesus Christ, our Lord.

7 *Living under the Law*

Do you not know, dear brothers – for I am, of course, speaking to experts on the Law – that the Law only rules over a person as long as he is living in a physical body? [2]A married woman is bound by the Law to her husband as long as he lives. When the man dies, the Law that has bound her to the man loses its validity. [3]As long as the man is living, she is regarded as an adulteress if she becomes the wife of another man. But if the man dies, she is freed from the Law and is not regarded as an adulteress if she marries another man. [4]In the same way, dear brothers, you have died to the ties of the Law through your share in the body of Christ; you are able to unite with someone else: with him who has risen from the dead.

From now on we may bear fruit for God. [5]When we were bound to our mortal bodily nature, it was the sinful desires, awakened in the members of our body by the Law, which made us bear fruits of death. [6]Now we are freed from the spell of the Law; we have died to that which held us captive. Now we serve the new world which is born out of the spirit, no longer the old world which has become like fixed letters.

[7]What shall we say? That the Law itself is sin? By no means. But I would have no consciousness of sin without the Law. I would not be conscious of what 'coveting' is as such, if the Law did not say: you shall not covet! [8]Sin found an impetus in the commandment of the Law and was thus able to awaken all kinds of desires in me. Without the Law, sin would not have awakened from its deathlike sleep. [9]Once I lived without the Law. Then, when the commandment of the Law came, sin came to life and I became permeated with forces of death. [10]Thus the commandment which should have served life became death to me, [11]for sin seduced me through the impetus which it derived from the commandments and made me a prey to death. [12]As such, the Law is sacred, and the commandments are sacred, just and good, too. [13]Does this mean that something which is good has become the cause of my dying? By no means. Rather, because sin as such has become conscious in me, that which is good in itself has caused my dying. Sin had to become an excess of sin through the commandments.

[14]We know that the Law is of spiritual origin. My human nature as I am now, however, is made of substances of the earth and is enslaved to sin. [15]My insight and awareness do not keep pace with my actions, for I do not do what I want, but what I detest – that is what I do. [16]Now when I do what I myself do not want, then a voice within me agrees with that of the Law and I must admit that it is good. [17]Really it is not I myself at all who acts like that, but sin which dwells within my being. [18]Therefore it is clear that the Good does not dwell in me, that is to say, in my physical body. It has been given to me to want the Good, but not how to fulfil it. [19]I

do not do the good that I want, but the evil that I do not want, that
I do. [20]But if I do what I do not want, then it is not I myself who
acts; it is the power of sin which dwells within my being. [21]Thus
I find within myself a law which compels me to do evil, although
I want to do good. [22]My innermost self joyfully accepts the Law
of God, [23]but I become aware that another law is at work in the
members of my body, a law which conflicts with the Law which
my thinking respects: it holds me captive in the law of sin which
is in my members.

[24]O, wretched man that I am! Who will free me from this body
of death? [25]I thank God through Jesus Christ who is our true Lord.
So I in my true self can serve the Law of God with my understanding, even though the law of sin works in my physical body.

8 *Living in the spirit*

For those who are in Christ there is no death sentence. [2]For the
Law of the life-spirit which began by working in Jesus Christ has
made us free from the law of sin and death. [3]When the Law began
to lose its power – for it was weakened by the growing might of
matter – God intervened and sent HIS Son in earthly form into
the world which was permeated by sin; thus HE halted the might
of sin in earthly existence. [4]The meaning of the Law was to be
fulfilled through us, so that we no longer need to have the physical as the central fact in our existence but may seek that in the
spiritual. [5]Those who live exclusively in earthly matter have a
way of thinking which only understands the material; those who
live in the spirit can also understand the spiritual. [6]Materialistic
thinking produces death, spiritual thinking engenders life and
peace. [7]For this reason, thinking which is caught in materialism
is hostile to God, because it does not follow the order of the
divine world, indeed it does not have the strength to do it. [8]God's
eye does not rest with pleasure on those who live only in earthly
matter.

[9]But you do not live in the physical, you live in the spiritual
in so far as the Spirit of God dwells in you. Anyone who does not

take the Spirit of Christ into himself has no part in him. [10]But if Christ is in you, even though death may dwell in your body through sin, your spirit can create new life out of the sphere of true being, the righteousness of God. [11]If the Spirit of HIM who awakened Jesus from the dead lives in you, then HE who raised Christ Jesus from the dead will create life for your death-riddled bodies also. He does that, because HIS Spirit dwells in you.

[12]Therefore, dear brothers, it is our sacred duty not to allow the world of matter to become our master, even though we live in an earthly body. [13]If you become taken up with earthly matter, you will find nothing but death. But if you raise yourselves to the spirit in order to master what is dead, then you will, in truth, advance to life. [14]Those in whom the Spirit of God works as the impetus of life: they are sons of God. [15]You have not come under a spirit of servitude which chases you from one fear to another: you have been given the Spirit of sonship. He gives us the right to call to God as *Father.* [16]This Spirit confirms it to us, in agreement with our own spirit, that we are born of God. [17]If we are children, then we are also heirs. And if we are heirs of God, then we are fellow heirs with Christ. If we share in his suffering, we will also share in his transfiguration.

The future hope for creation

[18]I consider that all difficulties and sufferings of the present age are trivial compared with the light-power of the world of spirit which will reveal itself. [19]All around us creation waits with great longing that the sons of God shall begin to shine forth in mankind. [20]Creation has become transitory, not through its own doing, but because of him who, becoming transitory himself, dragged it down with him, and therefore everything in it is full of longing for the future. [21]For the breath of freedom will also waft through the kingdoms of creation; the tyranny of transitory existence will cease. When the sphere of the Spirit grows bright, unfreedom will be replaced by the freedom which is intended for all God's offspring. [22]We know that the whole of creation suffers and sighs in the pangs of a new

birth until the present day. [23]And not creation alone; although we
have received the first fruits of the new Spirit, we, too, are painfully waiting for the secret of sonship which is to bring redemption
right into our bodily nature.

[24]The salvation which is given us works in us as a germ for
the future and counts on our hope remaining alive. Hoping for
something which is already before our eyes is no true hope. How
can anyone direct his hope towards something which is already
before his eyes? [25]Since we have to hope for something that is only
to become and grow and be fulfilled in the future, let us wait for
it with patience. [26]Then the Spirit will stand in for us where our
strength fails. Out of ourselves we cannot know what we may pray
for; the Spirit stands in for us with wordless sighing. [27]And he who
can read in the heart knows the Spirit's thought-life; he knows that
the Spirit speaks in a right and godly way for those who devote
themselves to him. [28]We know that all things help those who love
God to come nearer to the aim of the Good. That is true for all
who have been called according to the original divine intentions,
[29]for to whom HE has given being through HIS knowing, HE has
also given form of being. They are to become of the same form of
being as the Son who then will become the first-born among many
brothers. [30]And to those to whom HE gave form of being HE also
gave their own, individual being through the call. And for those
who have been called, higher life and higher consciousness, justice
and glory are foreplanned.

[31]What is there still to say? If God plans for our salvation, what
opposing power can still threaten us with disaster? [32]As HE did not
spare HIS own Son but gave him for us all, how should HE not
give us HIS full grace with him? [33]Who can appear as prosecutor
against those who have become fit to be chosen by the divine?
[34]Who will condemn him whom God HIMSELF has given true being?
Christ Jesus who took death upon himself, yes, who won through
to resurrection and has become the fulfiller of the deeds of God: he
intercedes for our higher being. [35]What could ever separate us from
the love of Christ? What distress or trouble, what outer or inner

need, what defencelessness or danger, what violence? [36]The word
of scripture says:

> In everything that the day brings we must die in order
> to come to you. We are regarded as sacrificial animals
> who are led to the slaughter.

[37]In all these trials we are triumphant conquerors through him
who offers us his love. [38]I know from experience: neither the forces
of death nor the forces of life, neither angels nor Mights, neither
things present nor things to come, not the World-Powers themselves, [39]neither heights nor depths nor any other thing or Being in
creation can separate us from the love of God which took on body
in Christ Jesus, our Lord.

The divine will in Israel

What I want to say now is a truth which I do not only speak out of
myself but out of my life in Christ, and so it is free of illusion; it
is also in accord with what the Holy Spirit speaks in me through
the voice of conscience. [2]Because of it, I have great sorrow and
unceasing anguish in my heart. [3]How I wish that I could take the
curse upon myself which arises because my brothers and relations
by physical descent, the people of Israel, do not find the way to
Christ. [4]To them as a race the secret of sonship and the divine revelation was given, as well as the giving of the Law, the rituals of
worship and the promises. [5]They were the people of the Fathers,
and from them proceeded the physical body for the Christ, he who
is the highest of all divine Beings, whose praise we offer through
all aeons. Amen.

[6]It is not so that the word of God has proved to be wrong, only
we must not simply take those who are bodily descendants of Israel
for the true Israel. [7]Not all who are of Abraham's seed are therefore
children in the true sense. It is said:

> Through the call your true seed will arise in Isaac.

[8]That means that it is not simply those who are children
through physical descent who are children in the sense of God's
intention. Rather, those must be regarded as the true seed

who are children in the sense of the promise. [9]The promise
was:

When the time for it has come, I will come to you,
and Sarah will bear you a son.

[10]And so it happened, not only then, but also when Rebecca bore
the one true son by our father Isaac. [11]The validity of the divine
resolves, then, which cause a selection to be made within mankind, is not dependent upon the deeds of men, but arises from
divine guiding of destiny. [12]That is why it was said to this matri-
arch:

The greater will serve the lesser,

even before her sons had done anything good or bad; [13]as the
scripture also says:

Jacob I loved, Esau I loved not.

[14]Now what are we to say to this? Does it mean that there is
injustice in the divine world? Certainly not. [15]To Moses was
said:

I will have mercy on him to whom I give my mercy;
my compassion is for whom I give my compassion.

[16]The decision, then, does not lie with the one who exerts himself
or strives, but with the loving will of God: [17]as the scripture says
about the Egyptian Pharaoh:

This is the reason why I have placed you in the fore-
front of events, so that the power of my being should
be shown through you and so my Name be proclaimed
over the whole earth.

[18]We have to understand: who is to relate to HIS goodness, and who
will be allowed to fall prey to hardening of their nature, that comes
from HIS will for the future. [19]Now you might object: does it then
make any sense at all to blame somebody, if nobody can counter
the will that is imposed upon him? [20]O Man, who are you that you
dare to counter God with your arguments? Can what is moulded
say to its moulder: ‘Why have you made me like this?’ [21]Is not the
potter free to make out of the same clay one vessel for noble use
and another for menial purpose? [22]Although the will of God could

only appear as sternness and anger to a humanity which had separated itself from HIM – and thus HIS power became very apparent
– yet HE bore with

the vessels formed through wrath, destined for decline
with great patience. [23]But through the vessels which HIS mildness
could fashion, he wanted the full richness of the revealing glory of
HIS being to appear, since they were predisposed for this kind of
translucence. [24]To this aim we, too, have been called by HIM, and
that means not only those who are Jews by descent but also those
from the heathen peoples.

[25]HE has already indicated this through the words of Hosea:

> I will call to be my people those who are not of
> my people, and to be my beloved she who was not
> beloved. [26]And in the very place where it was said
> to them, 'You are not my people,' there they will be
> called to be the sons of the living God.

[27]And Isaiah cries out about Israel:

> Though the number of the sons of Israel be as the
> sand of the sea, only a remnant of them will find
> salvation: [28]for the Lord will bring into effect on the
> earth the word which leads to fulfilment and deci-
> sion.

[29]And Isaiah also predicted:

> If the Lord of hosts did not leave something of our
> seed, we would be like Sodom, and as Gomorrah we
> would be.

Israel has not reached the goal of its Law

[30]What shall we say, then? Clearly, righteousness is also intended
for the heathen peoples; that is, fulfilment of their being through
faith, even though they have not walked the path of righteousness.
[31]Israel, however, which pursued the Law of righteousness, has
not reached the goal of its Law. [32]Why? They did not walk the
path of faith, but of works. And so they have run up against the
stumbling-block, [33]as scripture has already said:

See, I will raise up a stone in Zion which men will
stumble over, and a rock which will cause them to
fall. But whoever goes towards his goal with faithful
trust will not be thrust back.

10 Dear brothers, the dearest wish of my heart and my prayer to
God for them is that they still will find salvation. 2I can vouch for
them that they are zealous for God, but they lack insight. 3They do
not know the true higher being, the divine righteousness. They only
think about their own human righteousness. They do not submit to
the true higher being which is in God.

4For in Christ, the Law has reached its aim and its end. Now
every one can find the true being on the path of faith. In a word of
scripture, 5Moses speaks of the righteousness which is found on the
path of the Law:

He who fulfils it by his deeds will have life in it.

6But the righteousness which is found through faith says:

Do not say in your heart: 'Who is able to ascend into
heaven?' That would be nothing less than wanting
first to bring Christ down to the earth. 7Nor should
you say, 'Who is able to descend into the abyss?'
That would be nothing less than wanting first to bring
Christ up from the realm of the dead.

8So what does it really say?

God's speaking is very near to you; it is in your mouth
and in your heart.

That is the word which we proclaim to you. 9When your mouth
confesses Jesus as the Lord, and when the faith of your heart
knows that God has awakened him from death, then you will find
salvation. 10The faith of the heart leads to true being, the confession of the mouth to healing power. 11That is the meaning of the
scripture:

He who unites with him through faith can no longer
be put to shame.

12In that, there is no difference between Jews and Greeks. It is the
same Lord for all. He bestows his richness on all who call upon him.

13 Everyone who calls upon the name of the Lord finds
his healing power.
14 But how are they to call upon him rightly if they are not turned
towards him in faith? And how are they to believe in him if they
have not heard of him? And how are they to hear of him if he is not
proclaimed? 15 And how can they proclaim if they are not sent out?
Scripture says about this:
Winged are the feet of the messengers who proclaim the
Good!
16 But not all have opened the ears of their souls to the Gospel.
Isaiah says:
Lord, who has received our proclamation with faith?
17 Faith is born out of hearing, but the speaking of Christ himself
awakens the hearing. 18 And now I must ask, 'Did they not hear it?'
The answer would be:
Their sound has reached unto all lands,
their words reached the remotest parts of the world.
19 And so I ask further, 'Did Israel not understand?' Moses was the
first to say it:
I will cause your displeasure over a people
that ceases to be a people;
I will provoke you to anger with a people
whose spiritual purpose dies.
20 And Isaiah dares to say:
I have let myself be found by those who did not seek me.
I appeared to those who did not ask for me.
21 But to Israel he says:
All day long I hold out my hands
to a disobedient and contrary people.

11 *Through grace, a remnant of Israel may become worthy*

And so I ask, 'Has God rejected HIS people?' That is out of the
question. I am, after all, an Israelite myself, of the seed of Abraham
and a member of the tribe of Benjamin. 2 God has not rejected
HIS people, for already from the very beginning HE gave it its

purpose. Do you not remember what scripture says about Elijah?
As accuser of Israel he stands before God:

> [3]Lord, they have killed your prophets and demolished
> your altars.
> I alone am left, and now they also seek my life.

[4]But what answer do the words of God give him?

> I have kept for myself a remnant:
> the seven thousand who did not bow the knee to Baal.

[5]So, too, there is a remnant in our time. It is formed when the selection by destiny comes about under the influence of grace. [6]If grace
is working, then it cannot be achievement in the sphere of works
that is the cause; otherwise grace would no longer be grace. [7]What
does this now mean? What Israel strove for, it has not been granted
completely. Those who found their way through to become the elect,
to them it has been granted. The others became prey to hardening of
their nature. [8]That is what the word of scripture means:

> God gave them a spirit of torpor,
> so that, in spite of their eyes, they cannot see
> and, in spite of their ears, they cannot hear.
> That is so to the present day.

[9]And David says:

> At their table they shall be like prisoners and like
> bewitched men, like animals who have been caught in
> a snare. Thus shall they find their deserved fate. [10]Their
> eyes shall be darkened so that they no longer see with
> them; bend their backs towards the earth forever.

The heathen peoples are the spur for Israel

[11]Does that then mean that they have stumbled so as to fall? By no
means. What made them fall led the heathen peoples to the path of
salvation. And now they can be spurred on by them. [12]As their fall
helped all of humanity forwards so much, and their defeat helped
the heathen peoples in particular, how much better it would be if
they now also could reach fulfilment themselves. [13]And now I speak
to those of you who have come from the heathen peoples. I have

become an apostle to the heathen peoples and I am thankful for the task that has been given me. [14]Maybe I will yet be able to shake up those who are of my nation and help some of them towards salvation. [15]For if their falling helps towards the restoration of humanity, would it then be anything other than new life wresting itself from death if they were to connect again?

[16]If the leaven is consecrated, then so is the whole loaf because of it. And if the root is holy, then so are the branches. [17]If now some branches have been broken off, and you, who were a wild olive tree, have been grafted in and can share in the sap from the same root as the fine olive tree, [18]then do not look askance at the other branches. If you consider yourself better than them, then remember that it is not you who support the root, but the root supports you. [19]Maybe you will say:

> The branches have been broken off so that I could be grafted in.

[20]Very well, the reason why they were broken off was their unbelief, and the reason why you are standing in their place is your faith. And yet, be not arrogant, but devout and modest. [21]If God did not spare the branches which were noble by nature, HE will also not spare you. [22]Recognize the goodness and also the severity of God. HIS severity is towards those who have fallen, HIS goodness is towards you if you remain near to HIM, otherwise you, too, will be cut off from the tree. [23]And even the others, if they do not persist in their unbelief, can be grafted in again; God is very well able to plant them in again. [24]For as you were cut from an olive tree which is wild by nature and were planted, contrary to nature, into a fine olive tree, all the more easily can those who belong to the olive tree by nature be planted into it again.

[25]I will not hide this mystery from you, dear brothers, so that you do not regard yourselves as anything special. A part of Israel has succumbed to hardening of its nature for a certain time, namely until the full number of the other peoples have found the way in. [26]Thus, in spite of everything, the way to salvation is open to all Israel. That is what the scripture means:

> The deliverer will come from Zion; he will turn
> Jacob's alienation from God to the Good. 27This is my
> covenant with them, that in time I will take the burden
> of sin from them.

28As regards the Gospel they appear as enemies of God for
your sakes. But according to HIS will for election they are loved by
God for the sake of the fathers. 29God does not vary in HIS grace
or in the calling which proceeds from HIM. 30As there once was a
time when you, too, did not give ear to God – and yet you have
now found the forgiving goodness of God, in spite of that unbelief
– 31so they are now in the condition in which they close themselves
off from the divine goodness which you have met, until in time
they, too, will be open to this goodness. 32For although God has
let them fall under the spell of unbelief, HE nevertheless intends
HIS goodness to be for them all, too. 33Oh, what inexhaustibly
rich depths there are in the wisdom and knowledge of God! How
unfathomably deep are HIS resolutions and untraceable HIS ways!

> 34Who has measured the thoughts of the Lord with his
> thoughts? Or who has ever been HIS adviser? 35Or who
> has given HIM something, that he might receive a gift
> in return?

36From HIM and through HIM and towards HIM are all things. May HE
be revealed through all aeons! Amen.

12 *Make your personal life holy*

I appeal to you, dear brothers: open yourselves to the all-embracing
mercy of God by giving yourselves fully in offering, right into your
bodily nature, as a living, holy sacrifice, well-pleasing to God. Let
that be your right service to God, according to the divine Word.
2Do not allow the outer circumstances of the age to enter into you
in such a manner that they dictate your way of being. Rather, strive
for a transformation of your soul through constant renewal of your
awareness, so that you develop perception for what is God's will,
for the Good, for what is harmonious and the aim of consecration
of the world.

[3]By virtue of the touch of the Spirit which has been granted
me I say to each one of you: take care not to let your self-assurance grow beyond bounds. Guide your self-assurance by
wise self-denial, as God has given it to each one of you to be
able to do through his measure of faith. [4]As each one of us has
many members of his one body, and in fact each member has
a different function from the others, [5]so we, though many, are
yet one body in Christ; and among each other we are also members of one another. [6]The different gifts of grace are distributed
among us according to the grace we have received. If someone
has the gift of prophecy, then let him use it in conjunction with
the power of faith. [7]Let him who devotes himself to serving do
it in a true spirit of service. Let him who has the gift of teaching be completely at one with his teaching. [8]Let him who has
the gift of spiritual counselling be fully open to the call of the
Spirit. Whoever distributes gifts, let him do it with all simplicity.
Whoever is to lead, let him call up his full inner strength to do
it. And whoever does deeds of mercy, let him do them with a
cheerful soul.

[9]Let love be genuine; shrink from the evil; hold close the Good.
[10]Let the brotherly love which you practise in your circle come
from the heart. Outdo one another in devotion. [11]Do not become
lame in your zeal. Let your spiritual being be like a flame. Place
yourselves in the service of him who is the true guide. [12]Show that
hope makes the soul glad. Patiently bear what is hard. Do not cease
from regular prayer. [13]Together carry the hardships of those who
belong to your congregation. Practise hospitality. [14]Bless those
who persecute you; bless, and do not curse. [15]Be glad with those
who are happy, weep with those who weep. [16]Practise unity of
mind among each other. Do not indulge yourselves with pre-
tentious thoughts, but take trouble over the simplest things. Do
not be proud of your cleverness. [17]Do not repay evil with evil, but
rather go out to meet everyone with good thoughts. [18]As far as it
depends upon you, whenever it is at all possible live in peace with
all human beings. [19]Do not think that you have to judge and pun-

ish one another, my beloved brothers; leave a space for the great
wrath. As the scripture says:

> 'The judging power of destiny is *mine;*
> *I* will create the compensation of destiny,' says the Lord.

20Rather:

> When your enemy is hungry, give him food,
> and when he is thirsty, give him to drink.
> If you do that, you heap burning coals upon his head.

21Let not the evil conquer you, but overcome the evil with
good.

13 *Subordination to the God-given order*

Let every soul subordinate itself to the higher powers which are
above it. For there is no authority which does not originate in the
spiritual world. Where there are authorities, they are elements of
the divine order. 2Therefore whoever offends against them does
not only resist some power or other, he resists the divine order.
And thus those who oppose attract the corresponding blows of
destiny unto themselves. 3The guiding powers are not there in
order to arouse fear where good is being done, but where evil is
done. If, therefore, you want to face the higher powers without
fear, then serve the Good actively, and you will not fail to receive
their recognition. 4To you, they are servants of God for your good.
But if you serve the evil, then you have reason to live in fear of
them, for they do not bear the sword in order not to use it. They
are servants of God, enforcers of the world-wrath over those who
do evil deeds. 5Therefore it is necessary that you subordinate yourselves, not only to escape the wrath, but also for the sake of your
conscience. 6That is the reason why you also must pay taxes. The
higher authorities have constantly and carefully to be aware that
they are performers of the divine will.

7Give to everyone what you owe him, taxes to him who
has the right to demand them; revenue to the tax-collector, respect
to whom respect is due, honour to whom honour is due. 8Among
yourselves, you do not owe one another anything, except that you

love one another. Whoever loves his neighbour fulfils the rest of the
Law. [9]For the commandments:

> You shall not commit adultery, you shall not kill, not
> steal, not follow your base desires

and all the other commandments of that kind are summed up in the
word:

> Love your neighbour as yourself.

[10]Love does not inflict harm on a neighbour. Love is the fulfilment
of the Law.

[11]We say that, because we know the urgent mystery of the
time. The hour has come to awaken from sleep. Already salvation
has come closer to us than it was at the beginning of our faith.
[12]The night draws to an end, the day breaks! So let us cast off
the works of darkness and put on the weapons of light. [13]As befits
the day, our life shall be worthy of its light: not in obscenity and
self-indulgent cravings, not in cantankerous self-seeking. [14]Put on
the Being of Jesus Christ, the Lord. And when you attend to the
needs of the body, do it so that your needs and cravings do not bind
you to it.

14 *Weakness of the individual and strength of community*

Let the supportive strength of your community benefit those especially whose power of faith is still weak, so that they do not get
caught up in the mere 'for and against' of intellectual thinking.
[2]One person believes that he can eat anything, another, who feels
himself to be weak, confines himself to vegetable food. [3]But then,
he who eats must not feel superior and despise him who does not
eat. Nor must he who does not eat denigrate the one who does;
the only thing that matters, surely, is that God says yes to him.
[4]For who are you that you think you can criticize someone who
lives a different life to you? He must find out for himself whether
he stands or falls before his Lord. And he will be upheld; and,
of course, the Lord is able to lift him up. [5]One person considers
certain days to be especially important; to another they are all
alike. Let each one be fully convinced of his opinion. [6]He who

gives precedence to certain days does it, after all, as someone who
wants to serve the Lord. And he who eats anything also does it
to serve the Lord and sends his prayer of thanks to God. It is just
the same with him who does not eat certain things; he, too, sends
his prayer of thanks to God. [7]None of us lives for himself, and no
one dies for himself. [8]If we live, our life belongs to the Lord, and
when we die, then especially we die into him. In life or in death
we belong to the Lord. [9]To this end Christ died and became alive
again, that he might become the higher being of the dead and of
the living.

[10]What makes you criticize your brother? Indeed, how can you
despise your brother? We shall all stand before the divine seat of
judgment; [11]for this is what the scripture says:

> I am the Life, says the Lord,
> before me every knee shall bow,
> and every tongue shall confess to God.

[12]So every one of us has responsibility for himself before God.
[13]Then let us no longer pass judgment on one another. Rather, put
your minds to never being a stumbling-block to a brother, let alone
being the cause of his fall. [14]I know with absolute certainty which is
grounded in Jesus the Lord that nothing is common as such. Only
for him who considers it common does it become common. [15]If
your brother has difficulties because of the food which you eat,
then, already, love is no longer the guideline of your life. You may
not, of course, bring ruin to a human being for whom Christ died,
because of what you eat. [16]Be careful that your highest good is not
brought into disrepute. [17]The Kingdom of God is not in food and
drink but in the higher forces of life, in a soul filled with peace
and in the joy which the Holy Spirit gives. [18]Whoever serves Christ
with these aims in view can be sure of the pleasure of God and the
approbation of men. [19]Therefore let us strive for peace and building
a true community among one another.

[20]Do not hinder the working of God for the sake of a particular
diet. Everything is pure, but it can still cause harm to someone
who only eats it with inner difficulties. [21]It is better not to eat meat

and drink wine than to do this or anything else which becomes
an obstacle for your brother. [22]If you have the power of faith,
then protect it in your innermost being before the countenance of
God. Blessed is he who does not war with himself in his convic-
tions. [23]Whoever eats something, whilst reproaching himself for
it, he does harm to himself, because he does not act out of faith.
Everything that does not come from faith is sin.

5 We who are inwardly strong have a duty to bear the weaknesses
of those who are not so strong, but without being self-satisfied
about it. [2]Let each one of us be a cheerful example to his neighbour
so that he is strengthened by it. In this way we serve to build up
the congregation rightly. [3]For Christ also was not self-satisfied,
but rather he could say with the scripture:

> Every humiliation to which you are subjected falls on me.

[4]Everything that has been foretold in the holy scriptures serves
for our instruction; from the carrying power and the word of the
Spirit which stream towards us from the scriptures we are to win
true hope. [5]May the God of endurance and spiritual comfort give
you unity of heart and mind in your community. That is in accord
with the nature and being of Christ Jesus, [6]so that you may praise
God, the Father of Jesus Christ, in unity and as if with one voice.
[7]Therefore care for one another, as Christ cares for you, in order to
reveal God.

[8]For I can say: Christ came to the people of the Law and
the circumcision as one who serves, in order to make true the
words of God and to confirm the promises which were made to
the Fathers. [9]The heathen peoples can only praise God for HIS
freely given, merciful love. That is what is meant by the word of
scripture:

> Therefore I will confess to you among the foreign peoples,
> and sing the praise of your name.

[10]And further:

> Rejoice, you heathen peoples, together with the people of God.

[11]And:
Praise the Lord, you heathen peoples.
All peoples of the earth shall praise HIM.
[12]And Isaiah says:
The root of Jesse shall burgeon, and he who comes forth from it
shall guide all peoples; all peoples shall place their hope in him.
[13]May the God of hope fill you with all joy and peace because
of your faith, so that your souls may overflow with trusting hope
through the power of the Holy Spirit.

Looking back, and announcing a visit to Rome
[14]When I unite with you in soul, my brothers, then I know with
absolute certainty that you are full of goodness and are endowed
with spiritual insight in great fullness, so that you yourselves
surely will be able to help one another along the way. [15]And yet
I have dared to write to you about certain things which I wanted
to call to your mind once more. I have been sent out, by the grace
which God has granted me, [16]to serve Christ Jesus in priestly fashion among the heathen peoples. There I am to fulfil the Gospel
like a holy act, in order that the offering which the heathen peoples
will make hereafter shall be pleasing to God, being hallowed by
the Holy Spirit. [17]And therefore I have reason to be proud of the
power of Christ Jesus before the countenance of God. [18]I would
not dare to speak of it, if Christ himself did not speak through
me for the awakening of spiritual hearing among the peoples.
He works through me in word and deed, [19]he works through me
with a power which creates signs and wonders, he works through
me with the power of the Holy Spirit. Thus it was granted me to
spread the Gospel of Christ from Jerusalem into wide surroundings, as far as Illyricum. [20]In doing this, I was always concerned
to proclaim the Gospel in places where the name of Christ was not
yet known. I did not want to build on a foundation which others
had laid already, [21]but I wanted to follow the word of scripture:

They shall see him who have not yet heard about him,
they shall understand him who have not yet received tidings of him.
22That was also the reason why it so often became impossible for
me to come to you.
23But now, since there is no room left for me to work in these
regions, I hope that the wish to come to you, which I have had for
many years, will be fulfilled; 24for I plan to travel to Spain, and I
hope to see you as I pass through and then to be sped on my journey
there by you, once I have enjoyed being with you for a while. 25At
present, however, I am going to Jerusalem to do the congregation
there a service. 26For the friends in Macedonia and Achaia have
joyfully collected a donation for the poor in the congregation in
Jerusalem. 27They were pleased to do it, and, indeed, they also owe
it to the friends, for when people of other nations are allowed to
share in their spiritual riches, then it is no more than just that they
should now also support them with earthly wealth. 28When this
has been done, when I have handed the proceeds of the collection
safely over to the friends, I shall set off to come to you and then to
Spain. 29I am certain that if it is granted me to come to you, then
I will come in the fullness of Christ's blessing.
30I call upon you, dear brothers, in the name of Jesus Christ our
Lord, and by the love of the Spirit, to help me in my striving with
the prayers which I send to God, 31that I may escape the dangers
which the enemies of the faith are preparing for me in Judea, and
that I will be able to serve the congregation in Jerusalem suffi-
ciently well. 32Then, if God wills it, I will come to you with joy
and be refreshed in your company. 33The God of peace be with you
all. Amen.

16 *Greetings to individual members*
I commend to you our sister Phoebe. She serves the congregation
in Cenchreae. 2Receive her in the name of the Lord, as befits those
who have a share in the salvation. Help her with whatever she may
need, for she has been a great support to many and to me also.

[3]Greet Prisca and Aquila, my fellow workers in the service of
Jesus Christ, [4]who risked their necks for my life. And so, not only
I but all the congregations within the heathen peoples owe them
a debt of gratitude. [5]Greet also the congregation that gathers in
their house. Greet my dear friend Epaenetus. He was the first one
from Asia to find his way to Christ. [6]Greet Mary who has taken
so much trouble for your sakes. [7]Greet Andronicus and Junias
my kinsmen and my fellow prisoners; they are highly esteemed
among the apostles and, of course, they found Christ even before
I did. [8]Greet Ampliatus, with whom great love in Christ unites me.
[9]Greet Urbanus, our fellow worker in the service of Christ, and my
beloved Stachys. [10]Greet Apelles who has proved himself in Christ.
Greet also the people of the household of Aristobulus, [11]and greet
my kinsman Herodion, and also those of the house of Narcissus
[12]who are united with the Lord. Greet Tryphaena and Tryphosa who
achieve so much in the service of the Lord. Greet the beloved Persis
who also has done so much. [13]Greet Rufus, eminent in Christ, and
his and my mother. [14]Greet Asyncritus, Phlegon, Hermes, Patrobas,
Hermas and the brothers who belong with them. [15]Greet Philologus
and Julia, Nereus and his sister and Olympas, and everyone who is
with them, striving for the salvation. [16]Greet one another with the
holy kiss. All the congregations of Christ greet you.

Beware of fraudulent teachers

[17]Just one more word of warning, dear brothers: keep an eye open
for those who take pleasure in creating schisms and annoying mis-
representations of the teaching into which you have been educated.
Avoid them; [18]they do not, in reality, serve Christ our Lord. They
are driven by urges which arise out of their own bodily nature.
By using fine words and pompous speech they lead the hearts of
the guileless astray. [19]Your openness and your good will is known
everywhere. I rejoice over you and wish that you may find the good
way in wisdom, immune to all evil. [20]The God of peace will soon
crush the satanic power under your feet. The grace of Jesus, our
Lord, be with you!

Greetings from the fellow workers, and concluding adulation
21Timothy, my fellow worker, greets you; so do my close friends
Lucius, Jason and Sosipater. 22And I also greet you, I Tertius, to
whom it was granted to write down this letter in the service of the
Lord. 23Gaius, who has been so hospitable to me and the whole
congregation, Erastus, the city treasurer, and our brother Quartus
greet you.

25We lift up our hearts to him who has the power to give
you strength through the Gospel which I serve and through the
proclamation of Jesus Christ, and also through the mystery which
is now being revealed after it had remained in silence for aeons.
26Now it is being disclosed through the fulfilment of the prophetic
scriptures, in accordance with the intention of the eternal Godhead
which awakens the hearing to the faith through this revelation
among all peoples. 27The Father, the Ground of the World, who
alone is the source of all wisdom, may HE be revealed in HIS light-
glory through all aeons to come. Amen.

The First Letter of Paul
to the Corinthians

1 *Greeting to the congregation*

Paul, through God's guiding of destiny called to be an apostle of Christ Jesus, and Sosthenes, our brother, [2]to the congregation of God in Corinth and to all who strive for holiness in the power of Christ Jesus in that they, through their vocation, have been shown the way of sanctification; together with all who call upon the name of Jesus Christ our Lord in all places there and here:

[3]The grace be with you and the peace from God our Father, and from Jesus Christ, our Lord.

Words of thanks

[4]At all times I offer up thanks for you to the divine Father because of the grace of God which has been given to you in Christ Jesus. [5]In him all wealth of soul is granted you, all power of the Word and all spiritual insight: [6]the testimony of the Being of Christ has found firm ground in you, [7]and none of the particular spiritual gifts is missing among you. So you may confidently look towards the new revelation of Jesus Christ, our Lord.

[8]He it is who grants you inner certainty and, without letting you stumble, guides you to the goal: to the dawning of the Day of Jesus Christ, our Lord.

[9]The divine Ground of the World is faithful; through your vocation HE has taken you into the community of HIS Son, Jesus Christ, our Lord.

Partisanship

[10]Dear brothers, in the name of Jesus Christ, our Lord, I send you this word of admonition: cherish unity of the Word among one another, so that no divisions arise amongst you. Let unity of mind and unity of inner understanding be restored amongst you. [11]For it has come to my ears, dear brothers, through Chloe's circle, that quarrels have arisen amongst you. [12]I mean this, that amongst you some are saying: I belong to Paul, I to Apollos, I to Peter, I to Christ. [13]Is Christ divided in pieces? Or was Paul crucified for you? And were you baptized in the name of Paul? [14]I am grateful to the guidance of destiny that I have not baptized any of you except Crispus and Gaius. [15]Thus no one can say that you have been baptized in my name.

[16]Furthermore I baptized the house community of Stephanas. I know of no one else whom I have baptized.

[17]The content of the apostolic task which has been given me by Christ is not that I should baptize, but that I should proclaim the Gospel. And I am not to do that as though it were a matter of gems of wisdom: the cross of Christ shall not be divested of its historic reality.

Proclamation works either as foolishness or as wisdom

[18]The word of the cross is a nonsense to those who belong to the world that perishes; but to us who experience the salvation, it is a divine world power.

[19]Scripture says:

> I will let the wisdom of the wise perish;
> the understanding of the clever I will topple from its height.

[20]For where are the wise? Where are the learned? Where are those who are skilled in thinking, in our times? Has not God HIMSELF let the wisdom of the world lose its content? [21]Humanity, which once lived within divine wisdom, has lost the wisdom by which it could perceive the divine world. For this reason it was God's will for salvation, through the paradoxical nature of the Christ proclamation, to grant the salvation to those in whose hearts the faith lives.

[22]Whereas the Jews demand that a wonder shall happen, and
whereas the Greeks concern themselves with the old wisdom, [23]we
proclaim the crucified Christ, over which the Jews stumble and
which for non-Jews only means that foolishness has taken the place
of wisdom. [24]But to those who sense the call of the Spirit, be they
Jews or Greeks, we proclaim Christ as a divine power and as the
source of a new divine wisdom. [25]What in God is foolishness is yet
wiser than human beings, and what is weakness in God is yet more
powerful than human beings.

[26]In yourselves you can see, dear brothers, to whom the call
goes. There, there are not many who count as wise in the world, not
many who wield power, not many of noble birth. [27]The divinity has
chosen those without wisdom amongst men in order to let the glory
of the wise fade; it chose the weak among men in order to put the
strong to shame; [28]and it chose those of low birth and the despised
among men, those of no account, in order to bring to nought the
inner being of those who count for something. [29]Every reason for
the earthly world to praise itself shall be taken away in the face of
the divine world.

[30]Through the will of God it comes about that you are members of the Being of Christ Jesus. Through the divine Father *he* has
become our wisdom; *he* is the very essence of the Good, the power
of penetration by spirit, the redemption of souls.

[31]And so the word of scripture is fulfilled:

Whoever would praise himself,
let him praise what he has become through the Lord.

2 When I came to you, dear brothers, I did not come in order
to proclaim the personal testimony of God to you with forceful
words and superior wisdom. [2]I did not come among you with the
opinion that I was knowledgeable, except for one thing: that I
knew about Jesus Christ, namely him who was crucified. [3]I came
to you in weakness, in uncertainty and agitation. [4]My working
with the word and my proclamation did not consist of words of
a wisdom which persuades through thinking; the essential thing
was that the spiritual and the higher power showed themselves as

immediately present. 5Your faith was not to rest on human wisdom, but on divine power.

6And yet what we proclaim is also wisdom: namely the wisdom which lives in the circle of those who have been consecrated.
It is not the wisdom which belongs to the present aeon, nor that
belonging to the leaders of this aeon, who are already becoming
powerless. 7What we speak comes out of the divine wisdom of the
mysteries which has lived in secret after having been preformed
through the divine Ground of the World already before all cycles
of time, in order to be revealed to us.

8None of the leaders of the present cycle of time recognized this
wisdom. If they had recognized it they would not have nailed him
to the cross who is Lord of the revelation.

9Scripture says it like this:

> What no eye has ever seen, and no ear has ever heard,
> what never has become conscious in the heart of a
> human being, that God has prepared for those who
> love HIM.

10And now to us the divine Ground of the World has revealed it
through HIS Spirit.

The Spirit penetrates everything with its insight, also the depths
of the Godhead. 11Who would be able to understand the being of
Man if the spirit of Man were not in him? In the same way, the
being of God can only be understood through the Spirit of God.

12The Spirit which we have received is not the spirit of the world
of the senses, but the Spirit which proceeds from God HIMSELF, so
that we shall clearly perceive what has been bestowed on us by
God.

13So also what we speak is more than such words as human wisdom has taught us: they are words which the Spirit itself teaches
us. We comprehend the spiritual through thoughts bestowed on
us by the Spirit.

14A man who is only soul cannot take into himself what streams
forth out of the divine Spirit. For him it is foolishness; he cannot
understand it, for it can only be comprehended in a spiritual way.

15The spiritual man, however, is capable of understanding
everything, even if he himself is understood by no one.

16Who has ever perceived the thoughts of the Lord;
who could ever be HIS adviser?

But to us are given the thoughts of Christ.

3 *Partisanship renders the proclamation ineffectual*

Dear brothers, I could not yet speak to you as to men of the Spirit.
I had to speak to you as to men who are still caught up in their
physical being and who are not yet of age as regards the way of
Christ. 2Milk I gave you to drink, I could not yet give you solid
food; you did not yet have the strength for it. Even now you do not
have the strength for it. 3You are still caught up in what is earthly.
For there is even strife and jealousy among you. Does this not
show that you are still caught up in earthly things, and are walking
on merely human ways?

4When the one says: I belong to Paul, and the other: I belong to
Apollos, is that not a sign that you remain caught in merely human
things? 5For what is Apollos, what is Paul? They are servants
through whom you have come to the faith, and each of them has
worked as the Lord gave it to him.

6I planted, Apollos watered what had been planted, but God
caused the growth. 7Whether someone plants or whether he waters
is of equal value. 8Each one will receive his reward according to
the work that he has done. 9We are fellow workers with God; you
are the field of God and God's building.

10Out of the power which the divine grace has given me I first
laid the foundation as a wise master-builder should; some one else
has built further on it. Now let each one attend to how he also can
build further. 11No other foundation, however, can be laid by anyone, except the one that has already been laid: and that is Jesus
Christ.

12Whether anyone builds on the foundation with gold or silver or
precious stones, or with wood or rushes or reeds, 13in each case the
building will show who has built it. The great dawning of the Day

will reveal everything. In fire, everything loses its external layers: by the test of fire the value of what each has created shows itself.
[14]If what someone has built remains, then he will be rewarded for
it. [15]Anyone whose work is destroyed by the fire will, himself, also suffer harm, even though his true being, going through the fire, still can find the salvation.

[16]Do you not know that you are a temple of God and that the
Spirit of God would live in you? [17]Whoever destroys the temple of
God, on him will also come destruction from out of the Godhead. For the temple of God is holy, and you are that temple.

[18]Let no one be deceived; if someone among you counts as wise
according to the standards of the present age, he must first become
foolish before he can be truly wise. [19]For the wisdom of this world
is foolishness before the divine world.

Scripture says:

> He lets it become clear that the wise only have cleverness left.

[20]And in another place:

> The Lord sees through the thoughts of the wise, which have become without content.

[21]So, among men, no one can assess his own worth.

[22]Everything is there for your sakes: be it Paul or Apollos or
Peter, be it the whole world, life or death, be it what is present or
what is to come, everything belongs to you; [23]but you belong to
Christ, and Christ belongs to the Father.

4 We would wish that men should look upon us as servants of
Christ, as stewards of the divine mysteries. [2]And of a steward only
one thing is expected: that he is found faithful.

[3]For me it is not of consequence what judgment you make
about me or what judgment otherwise is made about me on the day
of a human decision. Nor do I judge about myself. [4]I am not aware
of anything which should compel me to do so. Now, that is not to say that I stand justified in all things. The only one who is entitled to a judgment about me is the Lord.

[5]Therefore, do not come prematurely to a judgment. When the

Lord comes, he will bring light into the darkness of all hidden things and reveal what the nature of the will is which rules the hearts. Then every single one will find his due acknowledgement from the divine world.

[6]This, dear brothers, I would wish you to apply to me and to Apollos. Through us you shall learn to keep within the bounds given to you by scripture. No one shall so enthuse in a subjective way for the one that he thereby turns against the other. [7]Who has given you such importance? What do you have that you have not first been given? But if you have been given it, then how can you boast of it as though you had not first received it?

[8]You are already filled and already rich. In your dignity you feel as though you do not need us any more. I could wish that you had really risen so high, so that we could partake of your greatness and dignity.

Personal experiences

[9]I think God wanted to make it clear that we, the least among the apostles, are marked for death. For our destiny has become a spectacle for the whole world, for angels and for men. [10]For the sake of Christ we have become fools, but for you Christ has become the source of insight. We are weak, but strength streams to you. You stand in glory, whereas we are despised. [11]Right up to the present hour we are suffering hunger and thirst and are without garment, beaten and homeless; [12]we take pains with the work which we carry out with our own hands.

We are reviled, but we bless; we are persecuted, but we stand firm; [13]words filled with hatred are flung at us, but we speak words of comfort. We have become an annoyance to the whole world, the scum of humanity. That is how it stands with us now.

[14]I do not write this to you in order to shame you, but to show you, as my children, the right direction for your thoughts. [15]For even if you have ten thousand teachers on the way of Christ, yet you do not have several fathers. For I have conceived you in the Being of Christ Jesus through the proclamation of the Gospel.

16So I call upon you to walk the path which I also walk. 17In order to encourage you in this, I have sent Timothy to you. He is my beloved and devoted child in the Lord. He is to keep alive in you the remembrance of the paths which I walk, united with the Christ, and which I teach everywhere in all congregations.

18During the time when I could not come to you, some have given themselves up to illusions about themselves. 19But I will soon come to you, if the Lord wills it. Then I will test not the words but the strength of those who have lost themselves in illusions.

20The Kingdom of God does not consist of words, but of power. 21Which do you choose? Shall I come with the rod of the teacher to you, or in love and in the spirit of the consecrating power of souls?

5 *Moral strayings in the congregation*

Ever and again one hears that there are abhorrent sexual practices among you, such as there have not been even in the pagan cults: namely that someone has entered into a union with his father's wife. 2And you give yourselves up to complacent illusions, instead of feeling the seriousness of things and keeping anyone who is entangled in such deeds away from your circle.

3I, who am absent in body but present in spirit, have already had to form a judgment about him who has done this, exactly as though I were in your midst. 4I have formed this judgment in the name of Jesus, the Lord, and I make it known in your gathering in which I am present in spirit, with the power of Jesus, our Lord: 5the physical body of such a one shall be given over to the destroying, satanic power, so that his spiritual being nevertheless can reach salvation in the dawning of the Christ-Day.

6Your reputation is not good. Do you not know that a small amount of leaven is sufficient to leaven the whole dough? 7Throw out the leaven of the old way of being, so that you can become the leaven of new being, since you also still have some unleavened in you.

Our Passover lamb has been killed: that is Christ. 8So let us celebrate the Easter Festival, not with the old leaven, not with the leaven

of forces which have become bad and evil, but with the unleavened bread of purity and truth. [9]In my letter I wrote to you that, in
your circle, you should have nothing to do with those who still live
in the impure cults. [10]You cannot, of course, avoid every contact
with those within present humanity who still are involved with the
impure movements, nor with those who live in egotism, in greed
and in the service of idols; for otherwise you would have to leave
the world altogether.

[11]Therefore, when I wrote to you that you should have nothing
to do with such persons, what I meant is this: if someone bears the
name of brother and yet still lives in the impure cults, in egotism,
in the service of idols, in the misuse of the word, in intoxication
and in greed, then do not any longer include him in the community
of the meal.

[12]Why should I pass judgment about those who are outside the
circle? At least you can form a clear judgment about those who are
within the circle! [13]Those outside are subject to the judgment of the
Divinity. Whoever falls into the power of the evil, drive him out
of your circle.

6 *The effect of our bearing on the world, the angels, the future*
When one of you has a grievance against another, how does he
come to seek justice from those who do not know the true good,
instead of from those who belong to the congregation? [2]Do you not
know that the bearers of salvation will decide the destiny of the
whole world? But if the destiny of the world is decided through
you, then why do you not trust yourselves to make decisions in
small cases?

[3]You also know that even the destiny of the angels is decided
through us; how should we then not find what is right in the affairs
of human life? [4]If you have to decide about questions relating to
practical life, why then do you set those up as judges who count
for nothing in the congregation?

[5]That I have to say this to you is bad. Is there not one single one
among you who is wise enough to reach a just verdict about his

brothers' affairs? [6]As it is now, one brother actually fights with another and, on top of that, allows himself to be judged by those to whom the faith is foreign.

[7]It is really bad enough that you have law cases among one another at all. Why do you not rather accept injustice? Why do you not rather let yourselves be hurt? [8]Instead of this, you yourselves behave unjustly and cause hurt even within the circle of the brothers. [9]For you must know that those in whom the true good does not live cannot be heirs to the Kingdom of God. Do not be deceived. Those who live in the impure cults and in the service of idols, those who sin against marriage, those who are wayward in their souls, those who misuse the male reproductive powers, [10]those who appropriate the goods of others, those who are greedy and given to intoxication, those who treat the Word with lack of seriousness and allow themselves to be driven by greed: all of these exclude themselves from the Kingdom of God. [11]Some of you have strayed in this way. But now you are washed clean, you are hallowed, and have taken up the essence of the Good in the being and in the power of Jesus Christ the Lord and through the Spirit of the divine Ground of the World to whom we belong.

[12]Everything is possible for me, but not everything brings me forward. Everything is possible for me, but I may not let myself be mastered by anything. [13]Food is for the physical-material body and the physical-material body is for the food. God allows both to perish.

The body is not there for the sexual desires: the body for the Lord and the Lord for the body. [14]The divine Ground of the World, who let the Christ rise again, will also guide us to resurrection through HIS mighty power.

[15]Do you not know that your bodies are limbs of Christ? How then dare I make limbs of indecency out of the limbs of Christ? That shall not be.

[16]You do know that anyone who joins himself to a prostitute becomes one body with her. For, as it is said:

> The two shall become one at the physical level.

[17]But whoever joins himself to the Lord becomes one spirit with him.
[18]Turn away from the world of sexual cults completely. In every
other sinful behaviour, the human being leaves his life-body out of
account. But whoever behaves with indecency carries sin directly
into his life-body.
[19]Do you not know that your body is a temple of the indwelling
Holy Spirit in you? You have received it from God: you do not
belong to yourselves.
[20]Your freedom was bought for you for a high price. So now let
your body become a revelation of God.

7 *Being single or married*
To what you wrote I would answer: it would be good for the human
being if he could be freed from sexual contact. [2]But, in order not
to fall into impure relationships, let each have a woman belonging
to him and each woman a man belonging to her. [3]Let the man
strive to do justice to the woman, and likewise the woman to the
man. [4]The feminine human does not have complete access to her
bodily nature without the masculine element. In the same way,
neither does the masculine human being without the feminine.
[5]The two shall not desert one another, unless their separation
comes about by agreement for a certain time, perhaps in order,
once in a while, to be able to live completely in the practice of
prayer. But then you shall find one another again, so that the temptation of the Adversary does not gain power over you as a result
of your lack of self-control. [6]I say this as advice and opinion, not
as a firm rule. [7]I would wish that all human beings should keep
it as I keep it. But of course each one has received his individual
gifts from God, and so life takes quite different forms for each
individual person.
[8]Of the unmarried and the widowed I say: it would be good if
they can remain as they are and can be at peace within themselves.
I, too, belong to these. [9]If, however, they do not have the strength
of self-control, then they should marry. It is better to enter upon a
marriage than to consume oneself in fire.

[10]To the married I give the following guidance – it comes not from me but from the Lord himself: the woman shall not separate from the man. [11]If, however, she has nevertheless separated from him, then she shall remain unmarried or else be reconciled with the man again. On the other hand, the man shall not allow that the woman leaves him.

[12]To the others I speak in my own, not in the Lord's name: if a brother has a wife who is not one of us, but who nevertheless consents inwardly to live in community with him, then he shall not separate from her. [13]And if a woman has a husband who does not belong to the faithful, but who nevertheless wishes to live with her, then she shall not separate from her husband. [14]For the non-Christian man may be brought into the realm of sanctification through the woman, as also may the non-Christian woman through the brother. Otherwise, your children would still be in the unrefined, earthly condition, whereas in fact they are in the realm of sanctification.

[15]If the separation is brought about by the non-Christian, then let it happen. In such cases the brother or sister should not become unfree. Do not risk the peace which we have through the divine call. [16]Can you, as a woman, know whether you are able to guide the man to salvation; and are you, as a man, certain to be able to make the woman a partaker of the salvation?

[17]Only let each one form his life according to the gifts which the Lord has granted him, and according to his call through the divine Ground of the World. I desire that this should be the rule in all congregations.

[18]If the call of the Spirit has gone to someone who has been circumcised, he shall not become unfaithful to the way of the circumcision. If someone who is uncircumcised has been called, he shall not let himself be circumcised. [19]Circumcision is unimportant and uncircumcision is also not important.

What matters is only that we follow the divine world-aims. [20]Let each one walk further on the way on which he was when the call reached him. [21]If you experienced the call as a slave, do not let that trouble you. However, if you can become free, then make use of this possibility with joy. [22]The slave to whom the Christ call has gone is a freed man of the Lord. In the same way, someone who was free when he was called is a slave of Christ. [23]A high price has been paid for you. Do not become slaves of men anew. [24]Let each one remain faithful, dear brothers, to the way which the divine world has shown him through the call.

[25]About virginity I have not received any explicit guidance from the Lord. I give you my opinion as someone who has found inner certainty through the merciful goodness of the Lord. [26]I mean, that in view of the stresses of the present times it is good for the human being to be virginal. [27]If you are connected to a woman, then do not strive for a loosening of this connection. But if you are free, then do not seek for a wife. [28]If you marry nevertheless, then you are not doing anything wrong. Even if a virginal being marries, it does not mean sin.

But certainly those who do this will encounter great difficulties of earthly-bodily life, from which I would gladly save you.

[29]Dear brothers, it has to be said: our times are full of high tensions. In any case, those who are married shall be as though they were not; [30]those who weep shall be as though they did not, and those who are joyful shall also be as though they were not. Those who buy shall be as though they were without possessions, [31]and those who use worldly things shall not make ill use of them. The form which the earthly world has now is in the process of transition.

[32]I would that nothing should trouble you. He who is unmarried only has cares as regards the Lord; he wants to find his approval in everything. [33]He who is married also has worldly cares; he wants to please the woman [34]and so is divided within himself. The unmarried woman or girl, too, can give her care entirely to the affairs of the Lord and so strive for the hallowing of her bodily and her spiritual nature. The married woman, however, also has worldly cares and wants to please the man.

[35]I say all this in order to be helpful to you, not in order to catch you in a snare. To me, what matters is the healthy ordering of life and the continual turning to Christ.

[36]If someone thinks that virginity is not appropriate for him any more – since he reached maturity long ago and now things ought to be different – then let him do what he wants. He does not become sinful by marrying.

[37]But whoever has fought through to firmness and power in his heart, and does not feel under any compulsion since he is master of his will, he does well if he reaches the decision in his heart to preserve his virginity. [38]So that he who gives up his virginity in favour of marriage does what is right, but he who does not give it up does better still.

[39]A woman is bound to her husband by the Law as long as he lives; but if the husband dies, the woman is free and may marry whom she wishes. However, she should do it only out of her connection with the Lord. [40]In my opinion she behaves more correctly spiritually, if she remains as she is and is able to be at peace within herself. That is my opinion, and I do believe that I also have a share of the Spirit of God.

About eating meat from sacrifices to idols

Regarding the worship of idols, this is how things stand: we may assume that we all nowadays are in possession of intellectual understanding. Mere intellectual understanding, however, puffs us up, whereas love builds us up inwardly. [2]Even when someone believes that he has grasped something through his intellect, he has not grasped it in his true being. [3]But whoever lovingly looks up to the divine world stands within the stream of divine recognition.

[4]Now as regards the eating of sacrificial food offered to idols, we know that in the whole universe no divine image or divine Being has reality except the One. [5]Although there are Beings in the heavenly worlds and also on the earth which are called gods, so that one really can speak about many gods and many guiding spirits, [6]we nevertheless turn only to one Father God; everything comes from HIM, and in HIM we see our ultimate goal. And we turn also only to the one Lord: to Jesus Christ. Through him everything came into being, and also our 'I' lives through him.

7This knowledge, however, is not living in all men. Some are
still caught up in the earlier customs of divine worship, to which
belong also the eating of sacrificial food. And precisely through
this, their conscience, which is still weak, becomes blurred. 8For
us, the food which we eat is of no importance in our relationship
to the spiritual world. We neither lose by not eating, nor do we
gain anything when we eat. 9Only, you must take care that this
inner freedom which you have does not become a stumbling block
to those who are weak. 10If anyone sees you, who are a man of
insight, at the communal table of idol-worship, will not his conscience, being weak, become strengthened in its inclination to eat
sacrificial food of the idols? 11In this way the weak man can suffer
severe harm through you, who have insight; and yet he is also one
of the brothers for whom Christ died. 12If you sin against your
brothers by making stumbling blocks for their weak consciences,
then you sin against Christ himself.

13Therefore, I would rather never again eat meat so as not to
cause harm to my brother, if my eating can be enough to cause his
ruin.

9 *The apostle's freedom*

Am I not a free human being? Am I not an apostle? Have I not
beheld Jesus, our Lord? Are you not the workmanship which it
is granted me to complete in the power of the Lord? 2Even if I do
not count as an apostle for others, yet for you I count as such. In
the being of the Lord, you are the seal on my apostolic task. 3That
is my justification against those who think that they must test me
first. 4May we not eat and drink what we wish because of our inner
freedom? 5And have we not the freedom to have a sister with us
as wife like the other apostles and brothers of the Lord, and like
Peter? 6Or is it only Barnabas and I who do not have the freedom
to do something else besides the work? 7What soldier fights at his
own expense? What owner of a vineyard cultivates it, but may not
eat of its fruits? Or what herdsman looks after his flock without
receiving his share of the milk? 8Is this said only in human terms,

or do not the books of the Law say the same thing? [9]In the Law of
Moses it is said:

Do not muzzle the ox when threshing.

Does God speak thus in order to care for the oxen? [10]Or does HE
not rather say this for our sakes?

What scripture says, is said for us. He who guides the plough
should do it with hope; and he who threshes the grain should also
do it in the expectation of his share of the crop. [11]We have sowed
the spiritual seed among you; is it now so outrageous if we harvest earthly things from you? [12]If others have a claim on your
possessions, why should we not have all the more right to a share?
In fact, we have never made use of this freedom; rather, we bear
everything in order not to place any kind of obstacle in the way
of the Gospel of Christ. [13]Do you not know that those who serve
in the Temple live on the gifts of offering? And that those who
serve at the altar have a share of the gifts for the altar? [14]That is
also how the Lord wishes it to be: those who proclaim the Gospel
shall have what they need for their living, through their service to
the Gospel.

[15]I myself did not need to make any of these claims, and so I
am not writing all this so that it shall be applied to me. I would
rather die than allow anyone to destroy the fulfilment of my life.
[16]Yet when I proclaim the Gospel, that is not to my own credit. In
doing so, I follow an inner compulsion. Woe to me if I did not proclaim the Gospel! [17]If I do it with joy, that in itself is my reward.
If I do it unwillingly, I am still carrying out the task that has been
entrusted to me. [18]What then is my reward? It is the proclaiming of
the Gospel, and so I place the Gospel into the world as a free gift
and do not fall into the danger of misusing the freedom and the
right which I have through my service to the Gospel.

[19]It is out of the very freedom which I have, that I have made
myself a servant of all human beings, in order to win as many as
possible. [20]To the Jews I have become a Jew, in order to win the
Jews. To those who are caught up in the Law, I let myself also be
ensnared, although I had already become free, in order to win those

who were caught up. 21To those who live without law, I became as
one without laws, in order to win those who are free of it, although
I am not without law before God, being a bearer of the law of
Christ. 22To the weak I became weak, in order to win the weak. I
became all things to all men, so that I might show at least some
out of all these groups the way to salvation. 23Everything that I do,
I do for the Gospel that I may have part in it.

24Do you not know how it is at the race-track: everyone takes
part in the race, but only one wins the prize? So make every effort,
as though to win the prize. 25Everyone who takes part in the contest practises all kinds of abstinence. They all do it in order to win
the perishable wreath; we are striving for the imperishable wreath.
26The reason that I run my race like this is that the goal is well
known to me. I appear as a fighter, because I know that my blows
do not fall on the air. 27And, because I do not want to appear before
men as a herald before I have proved myself, I control my body
from out of the spirit and so make it my tool.

10 *The dangers of taking part in ritual meals of sacrifice*

I will not leave you, dear brothers, in ignorance about what it
means that our fathers were all under the cloud and passed through
the sea. 2Through the cloud and the sea they all received the baptism of Moses. 3They also all ate the same spiritual food, 4and
drank the same spiritual drink. For they drank from the spiritual
rock which accompanied their way, and this rock was the Christ.

5Many of them, however, did not fulfil the divine expectation
and met their end in the desert.

6All these are picture events for us: we should not fall under
the domination of destructive passions as they did. 7Do not allow
yourselves to be led astray into the kind of idolatrous conduct
which a number of them did. This is what scripture indicates with
the words:

> When the people sat down, it was in order to eat or
> drink;
> when they arose, it was in order to play.

[8]We will beware of the strayings of immorality into which they
fell, so that in one day twenty-three thousand fell. [9]Nor will we
blaspheme with magical means against the selfhood power given
by the Lord, as some of them did who then perished through the
snakes. [10]Do not, grumbling, oppose the progress of events as some
of them did, who then, however, became victims of the destructive
power of the Adversary.

[11]These historical events were at the same time archetypal images
and were written down in the scriptures, so that we, who feel the goal
of the aeons to be near, can be shown the way in our hearts.

[12]Let him who believes himself to be standing, take care that
he does not fall. [13]You have not yet been led into a temptation
which went beyond human power to bear. The divine Ground of
the World keeps HIS faith with you; HE does not let any temptation
approach you which is beyond your power. In every danger HE
will make it possible that you will be able to bear the destinies
springing forth out of the temptation.

[14]Therefore, my beloved, leave the way of the worship of idols.
[15]I speak to such as have understanding; you are able to form a
judgment about what I say.

[16]The cup of blessing, over which we speak the words of consecration, does it not offer the communion of the blood of Christ?
The bread which we break, does it not offer the communion of
the body of Christ? [17]Because it is one bread, therefore we are all
together one body, for we all share in the one bread.

[18]Look at the historical Israel. Is it not so, that those who eat
of the sacrifice are taken into the community of the altar? [19]What
am I trying to say? Am I trying to give importance to idolatrous
sacrifices? Or even to the idols themselves? [20]What is sacrificed
there is sacrificed to demonic powers, and not to the divine Power
of the World. I do not wish that you should be drawn into the
community of the demons.

[21]No one can drink, at the same time, of the cup of the Lord
and of the cup of the demons. Nor can you, at the same time, be
partakers of the table of the Lord and of the table of the demons.

[22]Or would we set ourselves against the selfhood power given by the Lord? Or are we, perhaps, stronger than he?

[23]We have the freedom for everything, but not everything brings us forward. We have the freedom for everything, but not everything builds us up. [24]Let no one be only concerned with his own interests; let each one strive for the good of the other.

[25]Everything which is sold in the meat market you may eat, but you should not undertake a special examination of conscience because of it.

[26]The earth with all its fullness belongs to the Lord.

[27]If you are invited by someone outside the circle, and you want to take up the invitation, then you may eat everything that is put before you without making special enquiries because of your conscience. [28]Only if someone says to you: take, this is holy sacrificial food, then do not eat of it. You must do this for the sake of him who speaks thus to you, for what matters is the consciousness with which we relate to things. [29]By this I mean not your own consciousness, but that of the other.

For why should my freedom be determined by the consciousness of someone else? [30]If I have a share in the grace, why should I allow the prayer of blessing that I speak to be belittled?

[31]So, whether you eat or drink, or whatever else you do, do everything in such a way that the divine can be revealed through it. [32]Do not give offence to the Jews, nor to the Greeks, nor to the congregation of God. [33]I, too, take pains to do justice to everyone in everything. I will not seek for my own advantage but that of the many, so that many may find the way to salvation.

11 Tread the path that I also tread; but I tread the path of Christ.

The conduct of men and women at worship

[2]I must praise you that you remember me in all things and keep the traditions in the way in which you received them from me. [3]I would wish that you take the following into your thinking: for all masculine nature, Christ is the head. Feminine nature has its head in the masculine, and the head of Christ is the divine Ground of the

World. 4If a man prays or prophesies with his head covered, it is
a devaluation of his head-forces. 5The same applies to a woman
if she prays or prophesies with her head uncovered, for that is the
same as if her hair had been cut off. 6If a woman wants to remain
with her head uncovered, then her hair may as well be cut off. And
if she feels her nature to have become distorted because her hair
has been cut off or cropped, then let her decide to cover her head.
7A man shall not cover his head, because he is the image and revelation of the divine Being. But woman reveals the soul-nature of
man. 8For the masculine did not come forth out of the feminine,
but the feminine out of the masculine. 9And the masculine was not
created for the sake of the feminine, but the feminine for the sake
of the masculine. 10That is why the feminine being should care for
the forming forces around her head, in order to create the right
relationship to the angels.

11Nevertheless, in Christ there is neither the feminine only
without the masculine, nor is there the masculine only without the
feminine. 12Just as it is true that the feminine came forth out of the
masculine, so it is equally true that the masculine owes its existence to the feminine. And everything has its origin in the divine
Ground of the World.

13You can judge for yourselves whether it can be right that a
woman should stand with uncovered head to pray to God. 14Does
not nature itself teach you that long hair lowers the dignity of a
man, 15whilst it reveals the true being of a woman? The woman
has been given the long hair like a covering. 16If anyone wishes to
argue about this, let him take note that this is not customary with
us nor in the congregations which are dedicated to God.

Worthy celebration of the Christ-meal

17Now, what I still have to say to you is this: regrettably, your gatherings are becoming weaker rather than growing. 18First of all, this:
I hear that the divisions among you are carried right into your congregation gatherings. Up to a point, I can well imagine this, 19for
there must be different streams among you in order that those whose

'I' has been proved, stand out clearly. [20]When you come together, it is not primarily to celebrate the Christ-meal. [21]Everyone makes his own individual meal out of it. The one remains sober, the other becomes intoxicated with wine. [22]Do you not have houses where you can eat and drink? Or do you think yourselves superior to the congregation of God and want to shame those who have no special wants? What shall I say to you? Shall I praise you? For this I cannot praise you.

[23]I received these words, as I handed them on to you, from the Lord himself. In the night in which he was betrayed, Lord Jesus took the bread [24]and spoke words of blessing over it and broke it and said, 'Take this, it is my body! From now on do this to make my Being present.' [25]In the same way he also took the cup after the bread had been eaten and said, 'This cup is the new covenant with God through my blood. Do this, whenever you drink from it, to make my Being present.'

[26]So, every time you eat this bread and drink from this cup, you proclaim the sacrificial death of Christ and prepare for his coming. [27]And whoever eats the bread and drinks from the cup of the Lord without the right attitude of soul becomes an accomplice against the body and the blood of the Lord. [28]Only after stern self-examination may men eat of this bread and drink from this cup. [29]Whoever eats and drinks without considering the exalted mystery of this body, causes grievous destiny to fall upon himself by so eating and drinking. [30]That is why so many among you are weak and ill and asleep. [31]If we strive for true self-knowledge, we are not subject to the judgment of others. [32]When we place ourselves under the judgment of the Lord, it becomes an education of our soul which frees us from the decay of the world of the senses. [33]So each one of you, dear brothers, keep all the others in his heart when you gather for the meal. [34]If anyone wants to satisfy his hunger, let him do it at home, so that you do not call a judgment of God upon you by your gathering.

Everything else I will arrange as soon as I come.

2 *The organism of the congregation*
As regards the different spiritual gifts I will not leave you, dear
brothers, without information. [2]When you were still heathens, you
were drawn, as you know, to the false gods who lack the power of
the word. This was in accordance with the direction in which you
were guided. [3]Now I must say to you: no one in whom the Spirit
of God begets the word can say, 'Jesus be cursed!' But neither can
any one say, except that the Holy Spirit also speaks in his word:
'Jesus the Lord!'

[4]There are the most varied gifts of grace, but they all have their
origin in one and the same Spirit. [5]There are the most varied ways
of serving, but they all relate to one and the same Lord. [6]And there
are the most varied forces, but it is the same Divinity which is the
all-including force of all these others.

[7]It is given to each and every one to make the working of the
Spirit apparent in his own way, always in a positive and furthering
sense. [8]To the one is given the word of wisdom out of the Spirit,
to another the word of spiritual insight out of the same Spirit, [9]to
a third the power of faith, once more out of the same Spirit.

In the one, the one Spirit works as healing, [10]another is able
to let cosmic forces work through him, another has the gift of
prophecy, yet another the gift of being able to distinguish between
spirits. The one has the gift of speaking in tongues, the other the
art of interpreting what is spoken in tongues.

[11]All this is caused by the same one Spirit who wills to endow
each one with his individual abilities. [12]For as the body is one, and
yet has many members, and all the members of the body, though
many, form one body, so it is in the Christ Being.

[13]We have all been baptized with one Spirit and thereby have
become one body with one another, whether we are Jews or
Greeks, slaves or free men; and so also the same draught of the
Spirit is offered to us all.

[14]The body does not consist of one member, but of many. [15]If
the foot were to say, 'I am not the hand, therefore I do not belong
to the body,' it does not therefore belong any the less to the body.

[16]And if the ear were to say, 'I am not the eye, therefore I do not
belong to the body,' it does not therefore belong any the less to the
body.

[17]If the whole body were eye, where would be the hearing? If it
were all hearing, where would be the sense of smell?

[18]Now the divine Ground of the World has placed the members
according to HIS world aims, each one for the particular task which
it has in the body.

[19]If the whole were only a member, would it then be a body?
[20]But now the members have manifoldness as their characteristic;
the body, oneness.

[21]The eye cannot say to the hand, 'I do not need you;' nor
can the head say to the feet, 'I do not need you.' [22]But rather,
those members which appear to us to be the weaker, are precisely
the most necessary for the body, [23]and those which we regard as
insignificant prove to be particularly important. Whatever in us is
not beautiful is adorned with particular care; [24]whatever in us is
well formed does not need this.

The divine Ground of the World has joined the body together
out of such different elements, and has accorded the unassuming
members all the greater significance [25]in order that there should be
no division in the body, and that all members should work harmoniously together and care for one another.

[26]If one member suffers, then all the members suffer, and if
one member shines in the light of the Spirit, then all the members
rejoice.

[27]Now you are the body of Christ; each according to his portion
is a member of it.

[28]The divine Ground of the World has placed all in the congregation: the first as apostles, the second as prophets. Thirdly, as
teachers; then follow the bearers of particular powers, those who
possess the gift of healing, the shepherds of souls, those who guide
and order, those skilled in speaking in tongues.

[29]Are all apostles? Are all prophets? Are all teachers? Are all
able to let particular powers work through them? [30]Have all the gift

of healing? Are all skilled in speaking in tongues? Are all able to
interpret what is spoken in tongues?
[31]Strive to make the best out of the gifts of grace working
together.

The Hymn to Love

Yet I will show the way which is higher than all others.

13 If I speak out of the Spirit with the tongues of men and of
angels: if I am without love, then my speaking remains as sounding brass or tinkling cymbal. [2]And if I had the gift of prophecy
and could speak of all mysteries and could impart all knowledge
and, further, had the power of faith which removes mountains; if
I am without love, then I am nothing. [3]And if I were to give away
everything that is mine, and lastly were to give away even my
body for burning, if I am without love, then all is in vain.

[4]Love makes the soul great
Love fills the soul with healing goodness
Love does not know envy,
It knows no boasting,
[5]It does not allow of falseness,
Love does not harm that which is decent,
It drives out self-seeking,
Love does not allow the inner balance to be lost,
It does not bear a grudge,
[6]It does not rejoice over injustice,
It rejoices only in the truth.
[7]Love bears all things,
Is always prepared to have faithful trust,
It may hope for everything and is all-patient.

[8]If love is truly present it cannot be lost. The gift of prophecy
must one day be extinguished, the wonder of languages cease,
clairvoyant insight come to an end. [9]Our insight is incomplete,
incomplete is our prophecy.

[10]But one day the perfect must come, the complete consecration-
aim; then the time of the incomplete is over.

[11]When I was still a child, I spoke as a child, and I felt and thought as a child. When I became a man, I put childish ways behind me.

[12]Now we still see everything in dark outlines, as in a mirror. Some day we will see everything face to face. Now my insight is incomplete, but then I shall stand in the stream of true insight, in which recognizing and being recognized are one.

[13]We find permanence which bears all future within it in the exalted triad:

In faith
In hope,
And in love.

But the greatest of these is love.

14 *Speaking in tongues and speaking prophecy*

Let love be your way and your aim. Cultivate the gifts of the Spirit with enthusiasm, but practise the gift of prophecy above all. [2]Whoever speaks in tongues speaks not to men but to the heavenly world. He speaks out mysteries in the Spirit, but no one understands him. [3]But he who practises the gift of prophecy speaks to men; he gives them upbuilding power, brings the call of the Spirit near to them and encourages their souls. [4]He who speaks in tongues edifies himself, he who speaks through the gift of prophecy builds up the congregation. [5]Now, it would please me if you all could speak in tongues, but it would please me even more if you all had the gift of prophecy. He who has the gift of prophecy is above him who can speak in tongues, unless he also can interpret what he speaks, so that the congregation is furthered through him.

[6]How would it help you, brothers, if I were to come to you speaking in tongues, and did not speak to you as prophet or teacher, whether out of spiritual sight or spirit-knowledge? [7]Would that not be the same as with lifeless things which can sound, for example, a flute or zither? If I do not place clear intervals between the tones, how can one recognize what is being played on the flute or zither? [8]And if I play an indistinct sound on a bugle will anyone then

put on his armour? [9]So it is with you. If you practise speaking in tongues and do not speak intelligible words, how can anyone understand what is being spoken? What you speak will be spoken into the air.

[10]There are countless kinds of voice in the world. There is actually nothing that does not have a voice. [11]But if I do not know what the voice wants to make known, I stand as a stranger before the speaking Being, and the speaking Being remains dark and foreign to me. [12]Encourage one another with this! When you strive for the gifts of the Spirit, consider also that the congregation must be furthered thereby and that inner wealth should grow among you.

[13]Therefore, he who practises speaking in tongues should strive in his life of prayer for the ability to interpret for himself.

[14]For although, when I pray in tongues, my spiritual nature prays, it is nonetheless so that my conscious understanding remains barren. [15]What am I trying to say? Of course I want to pray with my spiritual nature, but I also want my conscious understanding to take part in the prayer. When I sing psalms I want to do it with my spiritual nature and at the same time also with my waking consciousness. [16]When you speak the words of blessing in spiritual ecstasy, how can he who represents the congregation say Amen to your blessing of thanksgiving? For he does not understand your words. [17]Maybe you speak the blessing rightly and well for yourself, but he is not helped thereby. [18]I thank God that I can speak in tongues better than you all: [19]but in the congregation I would rather speak five words with waking consciousness than ten thousand words in tongues. Only thus can I be a teacher to others.

[20]Dear brothers, do not sink back to the stage of childhood in your consciousness. In learning evil you may remain children, but with your consciousness you must strive for the highest aim. [21]In the book of the Law it is written:

> In foreign languages and with foreign sounds will I
> speak to this people, but even then they will not learn
> to listen to my word, says the Lord.

[22]Thus, speaking in tongues shall not show those who already

have found the faith the way to the Spirit, but those who do not yet believe. But the gift of prophecy shall serve those who have the faith, not those who do not have it. [23]If the whole congregation is gathered in spirit and then all were to begin speaking in tongues, would not the outsiders and strangers who enter ask if you are out of your minds? [24]If, on the other hand, all had mastered prophesying, an outsider or stranger who entered could be assessed and judged by everyone. [25]What lay hidden in his heart would become apparent, and he would fall on his face to worship God and exclaim: It is true, in you is God, he is present among you.

[26]What I want to say is this, dear brothers: When you gather, let each one seek for his part in the singing of psalms, in the teaching, in the revelation, in the speaking in tongues and the interpretation thereof; and all this in such a way that it serves the upbuilding of everything. [27]If someone wants to speak in tongues he should do it before two, or, at most, three others; and he should speak in short passages which are then interpreted each time. [28]If there is no one there who can interpret it, then he who speaks in tongues shall be silent in the congregation; he may speak silently to himself and to God in this language. [29]Of those who have mastered prophesying let two or three speak; the others may then weigh what has been said. [30]If then one of those who have been listening receives a revelation, the first speaker shall be silent. [31]Thus you all can speak through the gift of prophecy, one after another, and all can learn through it and gain inner encouragement. [32]Those who have mastered the gift of prophesying are able to direct their spiritual nature consciously. [33]Thereby it is seen that God does not foster confusion, but peaceful harmony.

Keep to this, as it is in all the congregations of those who strive for holiness: [34]that which is of a specifically feminine nature shall be silent in the congregation. It is not good if these forces hold forth; they should subordinate themselves, as already stated in the Law. [35]If the feminine desires to follow the way of discipleship, it should, of its own accord, turn to the corresponding masculine with its questions. It is not right if the feminine speaks out in the

congregation. 36For did the divine Word proceed from you, or has
it come only to you?
37If anyone thinks that he has the gift of prophecy, or another
gift of the Spirit, then let him strive to understand what I write to
you, for it is written as a commission from the Lord. 38Whoever
prefers to remain in ignorance may do so. 39So strive for the gift of
prophecy, dear brothers, without therefore becoming opponents of
speaking in tongues. 40Only see to it that everything that happens
is done becomingly and in good order.

5 *About the resurrection of the dead*
Dear brothers, I would imprint deeply on your understanding
consciousness the Gospel which I have proclaimed to you, which
you have made the content of your soul, which gives your being
firmness 2and which fills you with healing power. Bring to remembrance the words with which I proclaimed it to you. For certainly you have kept them, unless it should be that your faith has
lost its power.
3First of all I brought you the message as I received it myself:
that Christ, in accordance with ancient scriptures, suffered death for
our sickness of sin, 4that he was laid in the grave and rose again on
the third day, as the old scriptures already have said.
5Then he appeared to Cephas, thereafter to the twelve; 6then
more than five hundred brothers saw him at the same time, of whom
most are still living; others, however, have already died. 7Thereafter,
he appeared to James and then to all the apostles. 8Last of all
he appeared to me also, who am one born prematurely.
9I am the least among the apostles. Actually, I am not worthy of
the name apostle, since I persecuted the congregation of God. 10By
the grace of God I am what I am, and this grace which fills me as
a power has not remained without fruit. I have taken more pains
than all others, yet it was not I but the grace of God which was
active in my work. 11And it makes no difference whether they have
achieved more, or I: our proclamation flowed out of this power; out
of it your faith wakened.

12But now if Christ is proclaimed as him who rose from death,
how can there still be some amongst you who deny the resurrection
of the dead? 13If there is no resurrection of the dead, then, also,
Christ did not rise from the dead. 14And if Christ did not rise again,
then our proclamation is without content, and the power of faith
in your hearts is an illusion. 15We are revealed as false witnesses
of God. Our testimony – that God has raised Christ again – would
be turned against God, since HE cannot have raised him if there is
no resurrection of the dead.

16If there is no resurrection of the dead, then also Christ has not
risen. 17But if Christ has not risen, then your faith is an illusion and
you are still subject to the tyranny of your sin. 18And also those
who have fallen asleep, feeling themselves sheltered in Christ, are
subject to the decline of the world. 19If we may only hope for the
power of Christ for our life between birth and death, then we are
the most to be pitied of all human beings.

20But now it is a fact that Christ has risen from the dead. He
is the beginning of the new life among the souls who have fallen
asleep.

21For as death came into the world through a human being, so
also the resurrection has come into the world through a human
being. 22As in Adam all men have become subject to death, so they
are called to life in Christ.

23And everyone will follow the order which corresponds to
the nature of his true self. Christ forms the very beginning. Those
who have joined themselves to him follow him in his coming in
spirit. 24Then comes the goal, when he gives the world which has
united itself with him to the divine Father, and brings to nought the
Mights, the Revealers and the World Powers.

25He must be the Lord of destiny until he has forced all enemies under his feet. 26As the last enemy, death is brought to nought,
27then he really has subjected the whole cosmos to the tread of his
foot. When it is said that everything has become subject to him,
clearly there is yet a power that is not subject to him, namely the
One who has subjected everything to him.

[28]When everything has become completely subject to him,
then he himself, the Son, will subordinate himself to the One who
has made everything subject to him, so that God is everything in
everything. [29]What would become of those who have been baptized
over the dead? If there is no kind of resurrection of the dead, what
meaning has the baptism over the graves?

[30]And what is the sense in risking our life hour by hour? [31]Day
by day I die; that causes the intensification of life for you which
I experience in oneness with Christ Jesus our Lord. [32]When I,
thrown back only on myself as a human being, fought with the
wild beasts in Ephesus, what sense did that have? If there is no
resurrection, then the word is true:

Let us eat and drink, for tomorrow we will be dead.

[33]Do not deceive yourselves. Frivolous gossip spoils the best way
of life. [34]Strive with all might for truth, and avoid sin. Some have
already become completely without organs for the divine world.
Let my words guide you to your right senses again.

[35]Now someone may ask, 'How will the resurrection of the dead
take place? What sort of body is it that they have?'

[36]You foolish man. Whatever you may sow, nothing will awake
to life if it does not die. [37]Whatever you may sow, never can you
sow the body that is yet to come. You only sow the naked seed,
whether it be of wheat or of some other fruit of the field.

[38]The Ground of the World gives the corn the living body in
accordance with HIS divine will. And to each single seed HE gives
its own life-body.

[39]Nor is any one physical body like any other physical body.
Rather, the physical body of Man is different, that of the animals
is different, the physical body of the birds is different, that of the
fishes is different.

[40]And there are supersensible-heavenly bodies and there are
earthly bodies. And the supersensible-heavenly bodies have a
different light-form, the earthly bodies different again.

[41]The light-form of the sun is different
The light-form of the moon is different

The light-form of the stars is different
and every star is different from all others in its light-form.

[42]This is the world in which the resurrection of the dead takes place.

The seed is sown in the realm of decay, the life is awakened in the realm in which there is no decay.

[43]The seed is sown in the realm of worthlessness, the life is awakened in the realm of the revealing life-forms.

The seed is sown in the realm of weakness, the life is awakened in the realm of the World Powers.

[44]The seed that is sown is the soul-body, the life that is awakened is the spirit-body. Wherever there is a soul-body there will also be a spirit-body.

[45]This is also what is said in the holy scriptures:

The first human being, Adam, took on body in a
life-bearing soul-sheath; the last Adam in a life-creat-
ing spirit-form.

[46]But it is not the spirit-body that is put on first, but the soul-body, thereafter the spirit-body.

[47]The first Adam received his form from the earth as an earthly
form, the second Adam from the heavens as a heavenly form. [48]As
the Man formed in an earthly way, so all earthly men are formed.
As the Man formed in a supersensible-heavenly way, so also all
supersensible-heavenly men are formed. [49]And as we bear the
earthly form, so we should also bear the form of the supersensible-heavenly.

[50]This I speak out clearly, dear brothers: if we were only physical beings of flesh and blood, we could not become partakers of the Kingdom of God. The perishable cannot, out of itself, become a partaker of the realm in which there is no decay.

[51]See, I speak out a mystery: we shall not all sleep; but we shall
all go through a great transformation, [52]when space becomes an
atom and time becomes as a flash of lightning at the sound of the last trumpet.

At the sound of the trumpet the dead shall be called to life as

imperishable beings, and we shall all be transformed; [53]for that
which now bears decay must clothe itself with imperishable being,
and that which now bears mortality must clothe itself with immor-
tal being. [54]But when that which now bears decay has been clothed
with imperishable being, and when that which is mortal now has
been clothed with immortality, then the word will be fulfilled
which is written:

Death is destroyed by the victory of life.
[55]Death, where is your victory?
Death, where is your sting?

[56]The sting of death is sin, and sin exercises its power through the Law.

[57]Let us thank the divine Power of the World. HE has given us the victory of life through Jesus Christ, our Lord.

[58]So then, my beloved brothers, stand secure and firm. Do not waver. Stand in the fullness of the working of Christ at all times. You know that your labour in Christ is not in vain.

16 *Appeal for a collection*

I still want to say something about the collecting of gifts for the
congregation in the Holy Place. You ought to do this in the same
way as I have arranged it in the congregations in Galatia. [2]Let each
one of you put something aside for it on the first day of the week
and so, according to his discretion, collect a sizeable amount. Then
it will not be necessary only to collect when I come. [3]When I have
arrived among you, I will send those whom I have decided upon
to Jerusalem with letters, that they may take your thanks-offering
there. [4]If it seems advisable that I should travel there myself, then
they may accompany me.

The travel plans of Paul and his fellow workers

[5]I will come to you on my journey through Macedonia. I have to
travel through Macedonia, [6]and it may be that I will stay with you
a fair length of time, perhaps during the winter. You will then give
me travel-companions on my further journeys. [7]This time I would

like to visit you not just in passing, and so I hope to remain some
time with you, if it is in accordance with the will of the Lord.
[8]Until Pentecost I will stay in Ephesus. [9]There a great gate has been
opened to me, which gives me many possibilities for work. On the
other hand, I also have many opponents there.

[10]When Timothy comes, make sure that he can feel at ease
among you. He, like I, is deeply involved in the work for Christ.
[11]Let no one think badly of him. Then speed him on his way with a
peaceful heart, so that he may come to me. I am expecting him in
the circle of the brothers. [12]As regards Apollos, our brother, I have
often asked him to go to you with the other brothers. However,
he definitely did not want to come now; he will come as soon
as he finds a favourable opportunity.

Final advice and greetings

[13]Be watchful, be firm in the faith, be manly and strong. [14]Let all
that happens among you be done in love.

[15]I have one more request of you, dear brothers. You know the
household of Stephanas. They were the beginning of the Christian
life in Achaia and devoted themselves completely to serving those
who dedicate themselves to God. [16]Subordinate yourselves willingly to them, as well as to anyone who works with them and shares
their effort! [17]I am glad that Stephanas and Fortunatus and Achaicus
are with you now. They have completed what was still missing
among you. [18]They have re-enlivened my spirit and yours. Strive to
meet them with the right understanding!

[19]The congregations in Asia send you greetings. Many greetings come to you also from Aquila and Prisca, living in the Lord,
together with the whole congregation that gathers in their house.
[20]All brothers greet you. Greet one another with the holy kiss of
brotherhood!

[21]I, Paul, write this greeting with my own hand. [22]Whoever does
not love the Lord excludes himself from the true existence. *Marana
tha!* [23]The grace of Jesus the Lord be with you. [24]My love streams
to you all out of our closeness to Christ Jesus.

The Second Letter of Paul to the Corinthians

Introduction

Paul, through God's guiding of destiny an apostle of Christ Jesus,
and Timothy our brother, to the congregation of God in Corinth
together with all those in the whole of Achaia who have found a
share in the salvation:
[2]The grace be with you and the peace from God our Father and
from Jesus Christ, the Lord.

Words of thanks

[3]With words of blessing let us praise God, the Father of Jesus
Christ, our Lord. HE is the fount of all mercy, the divine origin
of all spiritual comfort. [4]HE gives us courage through all our
afflictions, so that we are able to give courage to others in their
troubles, by virtue of the spiritual comfort with which HE fills our
souls. [5]Just as the share we have in the sufferings of Christ grows
constantly, so the comfort of the Spirit increases constantly in us
through Christ. [6]If trials are laid upon us, it is to strengthen your
spiritual courage and for the salvation of your souls. If we are
strengthened inwardly by the Spirit, that is also to strengthen your
spiritual courage which shows itself in patient strength to bear the
same sufferings which are laid upon us. [7]We think about you with
well-founded confidence in the future, because we know that you
not only share in the common sufferings but also in the common
comfort of Spirit.

Rescue from the danger of death

[8]We will not hide from you, dear brothers, the desperate straits
we were in, in Asia. There, tremendously heavy burdens were laid
upon us, far beyond our strength, so that we feared for our lives.
[9]We had already prepared ourselves inwardly for death and no
longer placed any confidence in ourselves, but only in the divine
Father who leads the dead to resurrection. [10]But HE, in whom we
place our hope, delivered us from this peril of death and is always
at our side. We hope for HIS protection in the future also, [11]espe-
cially since we know that you strive to help us through your prayer.
We are certain that prayers of thanksgiving are rising out of many
hearts for the blessing which has come upon us.

Defence against being reproached for untruthfulness

[12]We may praise ourselves for this – and the voice of conscience in
us confirms it for us – that our ways of working in the world were
not guided by worldly thoughts, but by divine grace in all our
striving for holiness and purity. That is especially so as regards
our work among you. [13]We are not writing anything to you that
you are not able to read and understand; and I hope that you will
understand to the end [14]what you have already grasped in part,
namely that we have become a praiseworthy enhancement of your
lives, as you also will show yourselves to be an enhancement of
our lives at the great breaking of the Day: the Day of Jesus, our
Lord.

[15]My soul was full of this confidence when recently I wanted to
come to you. You were to experience the grace of the Spirit anew.
[16]From you I wanted to travel to Macedonia and then return to
you, so that you might give me travel-companions to Judea. [17]Did
I make these plans too quickly and too lightly? Or was I caught up
in earthly matters when I made them? Is it not true that for me Yes
remains Yes, and No remains No? [18]God HIMSELF will vouch for
it: the word that we have given you does not mean both Yes and
No at the same time. [19]For Christ Jesus, the Son of God, whom we
proclaimed among you, Silvanus and Timothy and I, is not at the

same time Yes and No. In him, only the Yes has become reality.
[20]Whatever promises God has made: in him is the fulfilling Yes.
That is why his Being sounds forth towards God as the Amen
which praises HIS revelation, and in which we should join. [21]HE is
the source of our and your firmness in oneness with Christ. [22]HE
has anointed us and put HIS seal upon us and planted the germ of
the Spirit in our hearts.

[23]I call to God; HE will testify to my soul that it was only to
spare you that I postponed my journey to Corinth. [24]We do not
want to make ourselves lords over your faith; rather, we are the
helpers of your joy in which you live through the faith.

2 I have decided not to come to you again as long as there is anything between us which causes pain. [2]For if I have to cause you
pain, can then any one of you make my soul glad, unless it be one
who has been hurt by me previously?

[3]And so I have written to you, so that those do not cause me
grief, when I come, who should give me joy. I have confided so
completely in you that I believe my joy to be alive in you all, too.
[4]Out of heavy afflictions and pain-filled heart I wrote to you with
many tears; not that I wanted to cause you pain, but rather that I
wanted to show you the superabundant love which I have for you.

[5]If someone has been the cause of pain, then he has not only
hurt me, but – to put it carefully – in a way, all of you. [6]It is enough
if such a person is corrected from many sides at the same time.
[7]Now you should rather be concerned to lighten and encourage
him again, so that he does not ultimately become submerged by an
excess of sorrow. [8]Therefore I call upon you: let him now above all
experience your love. [9]I have written you this, because I want to
discover whether you remain true, and whether you are prepared to
serve in all things.

[10]To whomsoever you show forgiving goodness, to him I will
also show it. And when I forgive someone, in so far as I have
anything to forgive anyone, I do it for your sakes before the countenance of Christ. [11]The Satanic powers shall not make capital
out of us; the thoughts of these powers are not unknown to us.

Experience in Troas
12When I came to Troas to proclaim the Gospel of Christ, a door
was opened for me so that I could work for the Lord, 13but my
spirit could not rest because I did not find my brother Titus there.
And so I took my leave from the friends and journeyed on to
Macedonia.

14Our thanks are due to the divine Ground of the World who
enables us to carry the victory in Christ at any time; it is HIS doing
that the fragrance of spiritual insight which reveals him is spread
to all places, through us.

15We are the aroma of Christ before God, both amongst those
who belong to the new life, as also among those who belong to the
declining world. 16To the one we bring the scent of death which
causes death, to the other the scent of life which gives life.

Who can think himself able to cause such things out of himself?
17We are not like the many who peddle the word of God like cheap
goods. We will proclaim it out of purified souls in the power of
Christ as coming from God and in the presence of God.

3 *The immediacy of the new revelation*
Are we now beginning to commend ourselves again? Or do we,
like others, need letters of recommendation to you or from you?

2You yourselves are our letter. It has been written into our hearts
and can be recognized and read as such by all men. 3What you are,
is openly perceptible to all eyes. You are a letter of Christ; we
were the ones who had to deliver it. It is written, not with ink, but
with the spirit of the divine life; not on tablets of stone, but on the
tablets of the heart of flesh and blood.

4Through Christ we live with so great a trust in the divine
Ground of the World. 5Our foundation is not that we think we
are able to do anything of any consequence out of ourselves, or
even to form thoughts of any import out of our own powers. What
we are able to do, we owe to the divine world; 6it is this world
that makes us worthy to be servants and guardians of the New
Covenant. No longer do we serve the written code, but the Spirit.

The written code leads into death, but the Spirit gives new life.

7But if the priestly ministry that led into death (symbolized by the letters carved on stone) already then was fulfilled in the light of revelation – for the sons of Israel were not able to look upon the face of Moses because of the light of revelation that shone from it, although it was already fading – 8then how much more must the priestly ministry which serves the living Spirit radiate in the revealing light! 9If the ministry that was for the time of descent had spiritual radiance, then the ministry of the ascending higher being must be all the more overflowing with spiritual radiance.

10The light of the earlier revelation must pale in comparison with this abundance of spiritual radiance. 11When even that which was decaying shone in the Spirit, how great must be the spiritual radiance of that which leads into the future!

12Filled with such hope for the future, we may step forward with joyous courage. 13The time of Moses is over. He had to cover his face, so that the sons of Israel should not see the fulfilment of that which was in a process of decline. 14In those days the minds of men became hardened.

Right up to the present day the book of the Old Covenant has remained covered with this veil for the reader. The veil was not drawn aside; only Christ takes it away. 15Right up to the present day, everyone who reads in the Books of Moses has this covering veil over his heart. 16Only for those who turn to the Lord is the veil removed.

17The Lord is Spirit, and where the Spirit of the Lord is, there is freedom. 18So the revealing light of the Lord is reflected in us all who have unveiled faces. And we become transformed into the image that we see, from one stage of clear shining-power to another, shining in the light that rays out from the Lord who is the Spirit.

4 Since we have been given the new priestly task out of merciful goodness, we will be untiring. 2We have renounced all double standards, we steer clear of the path of cunning and deceit which falsify the divine word. In the presence and power of God we address the full consciousness of men, proclaiming the truth freely and openly. [3]If there are still veils which cover the Gospel as proclaimed by us, they are in the souls of those who belong to the declining world. [4]In them, the spirit of the present age has made the spiritual senses blind through the deadness of their hearts. They are not able to see the revealing light that lives in the Gospel, radiating from the revealing spirit-form of Christ, who is the image of God.

Overcoming the forces of decline
[5]We are not proclaiming ourselves, we proclaim Christ Jesus, the Lord. In the service of Jesus, we serve you. [6]God HIMSELF, who spoke the word:

Out of the darkness let the light shine forth!

HE has lit the light in our hearts. It leads us to illumination through insight into the world of light of the divine revelation which streams towards us from the countenance of Christ.

[7]That is the costly treasure that we possess; but we keep it in fragile earthly vessels. It must be clear that the truly great power belongs to God, and does not come from us. [8]The weight of worlds rests on us in all things, but we do not succumb to fear. We feel empty, but the desolation of our soul does not gain power over us.
[9]We are persecuted, but we are not deserted. We are cast out, but the abyss does not swallow us up. [10]At all times we are clothed in our bodily existence with the death of Jesus, so that the power of life of Jesus also may become shiningly revealed in our bodily nature. [11]Although we live, yet we are constantly exposed to the powers of death through our share in the Being of Jesus, so that the power of life of Jesus may be revealed in our physical body, although it is subject to death. [12]So the power of death works in us; but in you there is already the newly given life.

[13]We stand in the unity of spirit-existence through faith. Scripture says:

I believed, and therefore I spoke.

So it is with us: since we have faith, we have also been given the
authority to speak. [14]We know that HE who raised the Lord Jesus
will also lead us to resurrection with him and will make us and you
a part of the new existence. [15]All this is for your good, in order
that the working of grace, which is fulfilled in a shared sacramental life, will lead ever deeper into the richness of the revealing,
divine light. [16]That is why we do not become tired; and even if our
outer nature falls prey to destruction, yet our inner nature is revital-
ized on every new day. [17]How passing and easy is everything that
afflicts us, since it opens to us the weighty sphere of the light-body
in surpassing fullness which shall outlast the cycles of time! [18]Let
us then not fix our gaze upon the world of the senses, but on that
of the supersensible. The sense world is subject to decay; but the
supersensible world is eternal.

5 *The earthly and the heavenly dwelling*
We know: if the dwelling falls apart in which we live on earth as
in a tent, we have a building from God, a dwelling which is not
made with hands, but which is eternal and belongs to the realm of
the heavens. [2]Towards this our longing and desire is directed; to be
clothed with this tabernacle which is given us out of the spiritual
worlds, [3]so that we may be covered and not be naked. [4]As long as
we live in the earthly tent we have hard trials to endure; we do not
desire to be unclothed but clothed, what is mortal in us must be
taken up completely into the true life. [5]The God who has created
this aim for us has given us the first gift of the Spirit.

[6]So we are always full of confidence. We know: as long as
we live in the body, we are still far from the Lord – [7]we are still
walking in faith and not yet seeing. [8]But we are full of confidence, we would rather be without the covering of the body, if
only we can be near the Lord. This is what our heart strives after:
[9]whether we are in the body or out of the body, we desire that he
should look upon us with favour. [10]For it will be the destiny of us
all to be completely uncovered in the place where Christ sits, on
the threshold of testing, in order that each one shall receive the

consequences of his life, what is good as well as what is evil,
imprinted on his bodily nature.

[11]We know that however we speak to men about the fear before
the Lord, before the eye of God we stand revealed completely.
And I hope that we are also recognized by your most inward consciousness for what we really are. [12]Not that we once more want
to commend ourselves to you, but we want to make it possible for
you to be proud of us. For by this you stand more securely against
those who judge according to the outer standing of the personality rather than according to the value of the heart. [13]When we are
in a state of consciousness which is free of the body, we become
serving members of the divine world; but in level-headed, ordinary
consciousness we serve you.

[14]The love of Christ lays upon us a duty to follow this pointer;
since One has died for all, then all have died, [15]and he died for
all so that the living should no longer live only for themselves.
From now on, their life is a part of the life of him who died and
rose for them. [16]Therefore, in future our knowledge of Man no
longer rests on what is physical. And even if we had known
Christ in his physical form, such knowledge is no longer the
decisive thing: [17]whoever is in Christ, in him begins the new
creation. All that is old has passed away; see, something new has
come into being.

[18]All this has been caused by God who has transformed us
back towards HIMSELF in Christ, and has commissioned us to carry
out the priestly service of transformation. [19]God worked through
Christ and, transforming it, HE raised the world back to HIMSELF.
No longer did HE look upon its errors, but in our midst HE instituted
the creative Word of transformation.

The task of the apostle in troubled times

[20]In the service of Christ we carry out our priestly task, in that God
speaks through us. On behalf of Christ we ask you: strive on the
way of transformation towards God! [21]God made him, who did not
know sin, into a part of the world of sin for us, so that we might

become members of righteousness, of true being, through him in God.

As workers with Christ we admonish you: take care that you
have not taken the power of God's grace into your being in vain.
2The word of God says:

At the right time I heard you;
on the day of salvation I sent you help.

Observe: the right and good time is now here, the day of salvation has come. 3We intend to work in such a way that no obstacle
is placed in anyone's path by us.

No shadow shall fall on the priestly ministry. 4We will show
ourselves in all things to be true servants and tenders of the divine
by our willingness to bear great burdens

in the daunting weight of the times,
against the sternness of destiny,
through all anxieties,
5through all blows of fate,
in every dungeon,
through all confusions,
through all troubles,
through all renunciation of peace and sleep,
through all renunciation of bodily nourishment.

6We will cherish

purity of soul,
clarity of insight,
openness of heart,
healing goodness,
the wielding of the Holy Spirit,
an honest soul-mood of love,
7the truth-bearing divine Word,
the wielding of the divine power of the world.

We will put on the armour of the higher powers of life on our right and on our left

8whether we are honoured or held in contempt,
whether we are rejected or praised.

Even if we are considered to be seducers,
yet we are bearers of the truth.
9Even if we are unknown, yet we are known by the
Spirit.
We are dying men, and see, the true life is ours.
We suffer hard trials, but death wins no power over us.
10We become sad, and yet are always filled with joy.
We are poor, yet we make many rich.
We have nothing, yet the whole world belongs to us.

Keeping apart from those without faith

11Our mouth has been opened to you, Corinthians, and our heart
is wide open to you. 12In us, you are not constricted. If you are
constricted, it is in your own inner being. 13So return like for like.
I speak to you as to my children. Open your hearts, you also!

14Do not fall under the foreign yoke of those who do not have
the faith. For what has higher existence to do with meaningless-
ness, what is there in common between light and darkness? 15What
concord is there between Christ and Belial? How can we regard
him who has the faith in the same way as him who does not?
16Is the temple of God the same as that of the idols? You are the
temple of the Divinity which gives true life.

God HIMSELF speaks it:

I will live within them and move among them. I
will be their God, and they shall be my people.
17Therefore, leave their circles, separate yourselves
from them, says the Lord. Do not touch anything
unclean. Then I will receive you. 18I will be your
Father, and you shall be my sons and daughters. So
speaks the Lord, to whom belongs all power.

7 Since, then, we have been given such significant promises, let
us, my beloved, strive for purification from all pollution of the
body and of the spirit; let us feel, full of reverence, the earnestness
of the divine and stride forwards on the way of holiness. 2Give us
room in your hearts: we have done no one an injustice, we have

harmed no one and we have exploited no one. [3]I do not say this
in order to blame you; for, as I have already said, you live in our
hearts. We are united in dying together and living again together.
[4]Great is my confidence when I think of you, and great my joyful
pride in you. Comforting spiritual encouragement fills my soul, my
joy is over-brimmingly full, it carries me through all our afflictions.

Joy over the change of heart of the Corinthians

[5]When we came to Macedonia, it was not a peaceful time from the
physical point of view. We were beset by one difficulty after another.
Our outer life was battle, our inner life was unsettled. [6]But God,
who helps and comforts the afflicted, also comforted us through the
arrival of Titus. [7]But it was not only his presence, but above all the
spiritual comfort which he had found with you. He told us about
your longing, your pain and about the enthusiastic efforts that you
take upon yourselves for me. I was overjoyed about that.

[8]For even if I made you unhappy by my letter, yet I do not
regret having written it. Of course I was sorry to see that the letter
made you sad for a while; [9]but now I am glad, not because of your
sadness, but because this sadness has helped you to change your
hearts and minds. Your sorrow was in accord with the divine will;
and it can be no part of the divine will that you should suffer harm
through us. [10]Sorrow that is in accord with God's will leads to a
transformation of being, which we do not regret, because it leads
to salvation. Sorrow that comes from the earthly world can only
lead to the death of the soul. [11]See how this sorrow which is in
accord with God has woken inner striving in you; also what new
self-assurance, what indignation, what rousing, what longing to
go forward, what enthusiasm and what readiness to atone! You
have proved in every respect that you are purely concerned about
the cause itself. [12]I wrote to you neither because of those who
have been unjust, nor because of those who had suffered injustice.
Rather, I wished that it should become clear, also to you yourselves, with what enthusiasm you exert your wills for us before the
countenance of God. [13]We are now full of confidence in this.

The wonderful certainty that we felt made it even more joyful
for us to share the joy of Titus. His spirit was revived by you all. [14]I
had praised you to him, and I have not been disappointed by you.
Just as I always spoke the truth when I spoke to you, so the praise
of you which I spoke to Titus has shown itself to be true. [15]His
soul feels deeply attached to you. He remembers the openness
which he found in all of you, as well as the awe and respect with
which you received him. [16]I am happy that I can rely on you thus
in all things.

8 *Report of the collecting of gifts in Macedonia*
Dear brothers, I want to speak to you about the divine grace which
has come to the congregations in Macedonia. [2]It became a source
of brimming joy for them that they withstood many trials; and
their deep poverty has become richness through the wealth of their
selfless giving. [3]They gave gladly, according to what lay within
their power; indeed, I must stress, beyond their power. [4]Tirelessly
and urgently they asked us to establish a gift of gratitude for the
community, intended for the service in the hallowed circle. [5]What
we had not dared to hope for, they at once made available for the
Lord and for us. [6]And so we have asked Titus to complete the
collecting of the thanks-offering among you also, which he began
to do earlier. [7]Just as you are rich in everything, in the faith, in the
gift of the Word, in spiritual insight, in enthusiastic work and in
the love that unites you and us, so also now show yourselves great
in this thanks-offering.

[8]What I say should not be regarded as a command. I only wish
that your love should not seem to be less strong than the enthusiasm of the other congregations. [9]You know the self-sacrificing
giving of Jesus Christ our Lord. For your sakes he became poor,
he who was rich, in order that you should become rich through his
poverty. [10]I tell you what my opinion is; you can draw the practical
conclusions from it.

After all, you began only a year ago, and then not yet with work,
but with the will to work. [11]Now crown your will with work. May

you be successful in changing that to which your will inclines into
deeds according to your strength. [12]Where there is good will, what
it has to give is prized; what it does not have is disregarded. [13]It
is not meant that you should suffer hardship so that others may be
well off. [14]For the sake of compensation, your affluence at present
can even out the shortages among the others; another time your
shortage may be evened out from surplus of the others, and so,
gradually, an equalization will be prepared, [15]about which scripture
says:

> Where there is much, there shall be no surplus,
> where there is little, no shortage.

[16]We thank God who has awakened such a strong striving in the
heart of Titus to be active for you. [17]He was open to the call, but
because his own joy in doing was greater still, he set out to come
to you by his own decision. [18]We have also sent with him another
brother who is highly regarded in all congregations because of
his proclamation of the Gospel. [19]The congregations even decided
themselves that he should travel with us when they handed over
the thanks-offering, which is to serve the continuing revelation of
the Lord and the furthering of our good will. [20]We take great care
that no one should be able to find fault with the way we serve this
rich gift. [21]We want to ensure that everything happens in a good
and right way, not only before the countenance of the Lord, but
also in the eyes of men. [22]Together with those two, we also send
that brother who has shown himself particularly enthusiastic on
many occasions, and who is now driven by a particularly powerful
impulse because he feels especially strongly drawn to you. [23]Both
about Titus, who is my friend and my colleague among you, and
also about the brothers who come as messengers from the congregations, I can say that the revealing light of Christ is with them.
[24]Therefore, show them your love, justify to them the high opinion
we have of you. What you do to them is done in the sight of all
congregations.

9 *Encouragement towards generosity*
I do not really need to write any more to you about the thanks-offering for the service in the hallowed circle; 2for I know your
willingness to help. I praised you to those in Macedonia for it, and
I said that Achaia had been ready for action for a year. Your readiness to help has spurred on many. 3I have sent the brothers, so
that the words of praise we have said about you for this shall not
be empty words. It will be seen that you are prepared, as I have
said. 4When the Macedonians come with me to you, they shall not
find you unprepared; otherwise, we would have to be ashamed
of the whole thing – to say nothing about you. 5And so I have
thought it necessary to ask the brothers to go on to you, so that
they can help to make the blessing that you already have promised,
become reality. For in what happens, a real blessing should be
revealed, and not self-interest.

6What I mean is this: he who holds back when he is sowing
can only reap sparingly; and he who sows with blessing can also
reap with blessing. 7Let everyone give as his heart is inclined, not
unwillingly and not out of compulsion: he who can give with a
joyful soul is loved by God. 8God is able to pour over all of you the
gifts of grace so that you always, and in all respects, have amply
enough and can draw on the abundance for every good work.

9As scripture says:

> He has scattered HIS gifts and given to the poor;
> HIS justice will endure beyond the cycle of time.

10He who gives the seed to the sower will also give the bread
for food, and will multiply the seed which you scatter, and let
the germ of goodness grow in you. 11You will receive manifold
richness through your rich willingness to give, which makes our
gift-offering into a thanks-offering to God. 12What we intend is a
solemn, holy service which is not only for meeting the needs of
those who are striving for consecration.

It is to become mighty through many prayers of thanksgiving
which rise up to God. 13As you prove yourselves in this service,
they will praise God for the way in which you place yourselves in

the right way under the power of the Gospel of Christ, and bring
generous goodness to life within yourselves as the power of true
community. Then you are not only united with those to whom the
gift is made, but also with all others. [14]They have already united
themselves in prayer with you, full of longing, for the sake of the
divine grace that flows to you in superabundance. [15]Let us thank
God for HIS gift which transcends anything that can be said in
words.

0 *Justification against reproaches by Jewish Christians*
I, Paul, am addressing this call to you personally, filled with the
goodness and gentleness of the Christ Being, bowed down towards
us. When I am personally present in your midst, I am retiring; from
a distance I appear before you with frankness. [2]I would wish that
I do not have to appear forceful when I am with you; of course, I
could confidently deal with those who hold the opinion that we are
pursuing material aims.

[3]Although we tread our path in physical bodies, yet we are not
fighting a physical battle. [4]The weapons of our battle are not of a
physical kind: it is divine strength that fills us. [5]It is able to dissolve
what has become hardened and what stems from merely human
thinking. It can overcome every barrier that is erected against true
knowledge of God. It can oblige human thinking to acknowledge
the greatness of the Christ Being; [6]it can even cause just consequences of destiny to overtake those who do not acknowledge it.
This strength will also fill you, when your openness has become
complete.

[7]Look around you among men. If anyone relies on belonging
to Christ, then he should also bear in mind that we, too, belong to
Christ. [8]I hope it will not be misinterpreted when I felt that I must
indicate quite unequivocally the authority which the Lord has
given us for your furtherance, not for your exclusion. [9]For it must
not seem that I wanted to frighten you with my letters. [10]It is said
about us that, although our letters are full of weight and strength,
yet our personal presence is weak and our working with the word

is of no significance. [11]Whoever says that, has yet to recognize that we are exactly the same in the words of the letters which we write when we are absent, and in what we do when we are present.

[12]We do not presume to count ourselves among those who consider themselves important, let alone thinking ourselves their equal. But they only ever compare themselves with themselves, and are foolish enough only to measure themselves against themselves.

[13]If we speak well of ourselves, it is not because we do not have the proper yardstick; rather, we use the measure which God has given us for guidance. We also use this measure when we are concerned with our relationship to you. [14]We do not strive immoderately in all directions, as though we did not need to have any regard for you; we did, after all, really come to you and proclaim the Gospel of Christ to you. [15]We also took great care not to praise ourselves where others had done the work. We are confident that we will grow with the increase in your faith, so that one day we will have the standing among you which corresponds to the measure of our being. [16]Then we shall be able to carry the Gospel on from you, without interfering with the rights of others, and without making claims on anything other than what is ours. [17]Whoever wants to find the value of his own being, let him seek it in the Lord. [18]No one has yet found his own worth by speaking on his own behalf, but he can find it when Christ speaks for him.

11 *Justification on the basis of the Gospel*

I ask you to tolerate my perhaps rather tempestuous manner, and, of course, you do tolerate it. [2]I enthuse about you, but this enthusiasm stems from a divine driving force. When I led you to Christ, it was as if I married a pure bride to her husband. [3]But I fear that, just as Eve once was led astray by the cunning serpent, your hearts and minds might be spoiled and taken away from the pure devotion to Christ. [4]For perhaps you would readily accept it if someone were to come and show you another Jesus-figure than the one we have proclaimed to you, or if you were to receive another spirit than the one you have received, or another gospel than the one you have

accepted from us. [5]I do not think that I am in any way inferior to
those who are considered greater apostles than all others. [6]I may
be unskilled in the art of dealing with words, but I am not so in
spiritual insight. But, of course, you know our being very well.

[7]Was it an error on my part when I abased myself so that you
might be raised, when I proclaimed the divine Gospel to you without you making a corresponding effort? [8]I even neglected other
congregations, and accepted support from them, in order to work
among you. [9]When I was with you and in want, I did not become
a burden to anyone. My need was met by the brothers who had
come from Macedonia. In every way I took care not to be bur-
densome to you, and I will continue to take such care. [10]The truth
of Christ is in me. Of that I can be proud; and no one in Achaia
can take that from me. [11]Why do I say that? Out of lack of love
for you? God knows how things truly stand in that respect.

[12]What I do, and what I will be doing, I do to fend off those
who seek for opportunities to take our place by praising themselves.
[13]They are false apostles, deceiving fellow workers who only pre-
tend to be apostles of Christ. [14]That is not to be wondered at, since
even Satan makes himself out to be an angel of light. [15]Therefore
it is not difficult either for those who are in his service to make
themselves out to be servants of the true Gospel. Their destiny will
correspond to their deeds.

Justification on the basis of his being persecuted

[16]I say it again: let no one think that I have lost my inner calm. If,
once in a while, it should seem so, then tolerate my impulsiveness
when I praise myself a little. [17]What I say now, I do not say in the
name of the Lord, I say it impetuously, as it were, in that I dare
to praise myself. [18]When so many people out there in the world
praise their own worth, why should I not also be permitted to do it
in my own way? [19]Since you are wise people, you will gladly also
let the foolish count for something once in a while. [20]After all, you
tolerate it when you are made unfree, exploited and deported, and
when you are provoked and struck in the face. [21]When I say that,

it is most certainly not meant as praise. Do you suppose *we* were
too weak for that?

If anyone dares to speak a bold word – now I really speak
completely without reservation – then it is I! 22Are they Abraham's
seed? So am I. 23Are they servants of Christ? I am bold enough
to say that I am one to a greater degree. I have taken on greater
difficulties; I have borne heavier chains; I have endured more
suffering, often I was in danger of my life. 24By the Jews I was
sentenced to thirty-nine lashes on five occasions, 25three times
I have been scourged, once I was stoned; three times I had to
endure shipwreck. I have spent nights and days in the depths of
the abyss. 26I have travelled many roads, I have withstood the
dangers on the rivers, among robbers, persecutions from the Jews
and the pagans, dangers in the towns, in the desert, on the ocean
and among false brothers. 27Difficulties and burdens I have borne,
watched through many nights, suffered hunger and thirst, fasted
many days, exposed to frost and unprotected. 28As well as all this,
there are the daily demands, the concern for all the congregations.
29Is someone ill, without my being ill with him? Is injustice being
done to someone, without my feeling heated about it? 30If I have
to praise myself, then I will praise myself for my weakness. 31God
HIMSELF, the Father of Jesus the Lord, who is to be praised with
words of blessing through all aeons, HE knows that I am not lying.
32What happened in Damascus was this: the governor under King
Aretas ordered that the city should be closely guarded, in order to
seize me; 33but I was let down in a basket through a window in the
wall, and so was able to escape his hands.

12 *Justification on the basis of his visions*

Since we are speaking of things about which one may praise
oneself – actually I do not expect much to be gained by that –
then I must also speak of the visions and revelations in which the
Lord has shown himself to me. 2I know a man, living in Christ;
fourteen years ago – whether in the body or in a condition freed
of the body, I do not know; God knows it – 3he was transported

into the third heavenly sphere, and about this same man I know – whether he was in the body, or in a condition freed of the body, I do not know, God knows it – 4he was transported into Paradise and perceived unspoken words which may never be spoken by human mouth. 5On behalf of this man I will praise myself. If I look to my earthly, personal nature, I can only praise my weakness.

6It would by no means be foolish of me if I wanted to praise myself. I speak the truth. But I refrain from it, so that no one should have a better opinion of me than he can form for himself by what he sees and hears of me. That also applies to the wealth of revelations which I have been granted.

The thorn in the body

7So that I should not myself become presumptuous because of it, a thorn has been given me in my physical body. An angel of the satanic power is active there, whose blows strike me, so that I should not presume too much. 8Because of it I have already asked the Lord three times to cause it to leave me. 9But he said to me, 'Be content with the grace that flows to you from me. The higher power completes what is lacking in human weakness.' Therefore I would rather praise myself for my weaknesses, so that the power of Christ can be with me. 10I will be cheerful in my weaknesses, whether the events of my life lift me up or force me down, whether they drive me into the widths or into confinement: everything for the sake of Christ. Whenever I feel my weakness, immediately great strength fills me.

11I have let myself be carried away! You forced me to it. The right thing would have been for you to stand up for me. For in nothing am I inferior to those apostles who are considered greater than all others, even if I am nothing. 12The signs of the apostolic calling have been fulfilled in all patience in your midst: through picture-revelations, through spiritual events and through deeds filled with power. 13Is there anything wherein you are less favoured than the other congregations, except that I never became a burden to you? Forgive me for this injustice.

Announcing another visit
[14]See, I am prepared to come to you a third time. And I will also
this time not be a burden to you. I do not seek your goods, but you
yourselves. For the children do not need to collect treasures for
their parents, but the parents for the children. [15]I will gladly give
everything, yes, I will give myself for your souls. Since I have so
great a love for you, do I then deserve to be loved so little by you?

[16]So, one thing is certain: I did not become a burden on you.
But, since I am so clever, perhaps I have outwitted you? [17]Have I
made you over-privileged because of one of those whom I sent to
you? [18]For I asked Titus and the brother whom I sent with him. Has
Titus made you over-privileged? Do we not both strive in the same
spirit? Do we not tread the same path?

[19]I suppose you have been thinking for a long time that we want
to justify ourselves to you? Yet we are speaking in the power of
Christ before the countenance of God, and, indeed, everything that
we say is to help your inner upbuilding, beloved. [20]I fear that, when
I come, I may not find you as I would wish; and perhaps you may
then also not find me as you would wish. For it could be that there
is cantankerousness and jealousy among you, alienation and division in the soul, slander and gossip, conceit and animosity. [21]May
the divinity which guides me not let me lose heart over you again
when I come, and become sad that many remain in their sinful
nature, instead of recognizing, through a change of heart, in what
impurity, wastefulness and impropriety they still are caught up.

13 So, I am coming to you for the third time. Then every case shall
be confirmed through the mouths of two or three witnesses. [2]I said
it to you when I was with you for the second time, and I repeat
it now when I am far from you – and I am not only addressing
those who have belonged to the impure movements, but also all
others: when now I come to you again, I will spare no one. [3]For
you demand proof that Christ speaks through me. His will is not
to work in the form of weakness among you, but as power. [4]Out of
human weaknesses it came about that he was nailed to the cross;
but through the world-power of God he won life. We do not cease

being weak when we are united with him, but we also have a share in his life which enables us to work among you out of the world-power of God.

[5]Test yourselves to see whether you stand firm in the faith; prove your inner power. Or are you not able to recognize whether Christ Jesus is in you? Has your inner strength not yet become firm? [6]I hope that you will recognize that we are not lacking in inner value. [7]We pray to the divine Ground of the World that no evil may happen through you. Not in order that our achievements shall become apparent, but that good may come about through you, even if we then are left standing, unproven. [8]Against the truth we can do nothing, we can only work for the truth. [9]We will be glad of our weakness, if only you are strong. This is our prayer: that right order will come about among you.

[10]I am writing this while I am still far from you; when I am with you I do not want to have to make stern use of the authority which the Lord has given me, and which is to serve your inner upbuilding, not destruction.

Greeting and words of blessing

[11]So now, dear brothers, be glad! Order your life of soul, be open to the strength-giving Word, live in unity of heart and mind and in peace. And the God of love and of peace will be with you. [12]Greet one another with the holy kiss of brotherhood. [13]All those who have become partakers of the salvation greet you.

[14]The grace of Jesus Christ the Lord, the love of God and the fellowship of the Holy Spirit be with you all.

The Letter of Paul to the Galatians

1 *Prologue*
Paul, an apostle who did not receive his task from human beings
or through human beings, but who was sent out through Jesus
Christ himself and the divine Father who awakened him from the
dead, [2]and with me all the brothers; to the congregations in Galatia:
[3]Grace be with you, and peace from God our Father and from
Jesus Christ the Lord, [4]who gave himself for the healing of our sin,
to wrest us from the spell of the present aeon which has become
subject to the power of evil. This was the will of God who is our
Father. [5]May HE be revealed through all future aeons! Amen.

Reason for writing: the true Gospel is under threat
[6]I am amazed how quickly you have let yourselves be led away
from HIM who called you through the grace of Christ. Now you
incline your minds to a different gospel, [7]and yet of course there
is no other. There are only people who want to make you waver
by distorting the Gospel of Christ. [8]Even if you were to receive a
message through us, or through an angel from the spiritual world,
contradicting the one which has already been proclaimed to you
by us: it would be deserving of condemnation. [9]It is as we have
already told you – I say it once again: if someone brings you a
message which contradicts the one which you have received, he is
to be condemned.
[10]So am I actually following the will of human beings or the will
of God? Am I seeking the approval of human beings? If I were out
to be praised by human beings, I would not be a servant of Christ.
[11]I want to make it clear to you, dear brothers, that the Gospel
which I have proclaimed to you does not originate with human

beings. [12]I did not receive it from human beings through any kind
of teaching, but through the spirit-revelation of Jesus Christ.

The stages of becoming an apostle to the foreigners

[13]You have, of course, heard how once I trod the ways of Judaism,
and how I persecuted and hurt the congregation of God without
mercy. [14]On this Jewish way, I soared above many of my contem-
poraries who were my own people; with boundless fanaticism I
upheld the traditions of the fathers. [15]But then it was the good
pleasure and will of HIM, who, from my mother's womb, had set
me special aims, and had called me through HIS grace: [16]to reveal
HIS Son in me. I was to be his herald among the peoples of the
world. I did not immediately confer with human beings, [17]nor did I
go to Jerusalem to those who were apostles before me, but I withdrew initially into Arabia, from where I returned to Damascus.

[18]Only three years later did I go to Jerusalem to get to know
Peter, and I stayed two weeks with him. [19]I saw none of the other
apostles, with the exception only of James, the brother of the Lord.
[20]What I write to you is spoken before the countenance of God; HE
knows that I speak no untruth. [21]After that I went into the regions
of Syria and Cilicia. [22]To the congregations which had been formed
in Judea in the name of Christ I was unknown by sight. [23]They only
knew from hearsay: he who once persecuted us has now become
the herald of the faith against which he once raged. [24]And so they
praised God for the revelation which had been granted to me.

2 *Meeting with the first apostles in Jerusalem and Antioch*

Later, after fourteen years had passed, I went up once more to
Jerusalem with Barnabas, and I also took Titus with me. [2]It was
because of a spiritual vision that I went. I wanted to ask those
working there what they thought about the way I was proclaiming
the Gospel to the heathen peoples. I had a confidential conversation with the leading personalities; for I did not wish that my
work should be – or have been – in vain. [3]But it was not even
demanded of Titus, my companion, who was after all a Greek, that

he should be circumcised. 4Difficulties only arose through a number of people passing themselves off as brothers, who interfered.
They had crept in to set themselves up as overseers and critics of
the freedom which we have in Christ Jesus; they wanted to make
us dependent on them. 5Not for one moment, however, did we
yield to their lust for power; and so the truth of the Gospel was not
compromised for you in any way. 6But those who were regarded
as leading personalities – what position they may have held before
did not matter to me, for God does not look upon a person's outer
standing – these men made no further demands of me. 7On the
contrary, they recognized that the Gospel for the uncircumcised
has been entrusted to me, just as that for the circumcised has been
to Peter – 8for he who has given Peter the power to work as an
apostle among the circumcised has given me the power to work
likewise among the heathen peoples – 9and when they recognized
the grace which has been granted me, James and Peter and John,
who were regarded as the pillars of the community, gave me and
Barnabas their hand in confirmation of our community with them;
we should go to the heathen, they themselves would go to the
Jews. 10Only, they reminded us that we should do something for
the poor, which I have also wholeheartedly tried to do.

11But then when Peter once came to Antioch, I had to confront
him to his face. There really was a reason for complaint against
him. 12For, before some of those who were of the circle around
James came there, he had sat at table with non-Jews; but when they
came, he withdrew and kept himself apart because he was afraid
of those strict upholders of the circumcision. 13The rest of the Jews
joined in his hypocrisy, so that ultimately Barnabas, too, was drawn
into it. 14When I saw that they were not behaving correctly, as we
owe it to the truth of the Gospel, I said to Peter in the presence of
everyone, 'If you as a Jew live as the heathen live and not like the
Jews, how is it that you want to compel the heathen to live like the
Jews?'

15We are Jews by birth; we are not of heathen descent and
therefore by definition regarded as sinners. 16But we have recog-

nized that Man does not attain to the true higher life by carrying
out the duties prescribed by the Law, but only through a heart-re-
lationship built on faith in Christ Jesus. We have come to the
faith in Christ Jesus, so that our share in the true higher existence
shall proceed from this faith in Christ, not from the works of the
Law. No human being incarnated on the earth can find the true
higher existence through the works of the Law.
17Now if we who are striving in Christ towards true being are
nevertheless found to be sinful, does that not make Christ a servant of sin? Not at all! 18For if I reinstate the Law which I have
declared invalid, then I myself become a lawbreaker.

Christ in me
19But through the Law my higher self died to the Law, in order
to live for the realm of God. 20I am crucified with Christ. So it is
not I who live, but Christ lives in me. The life which I have now
in my earthly incarnation I have through devotion and faith in the
Son of God who loves me and has given himself for me. 21I do not
reject the grace of God, for if the true higher life could be found
through the Law, then Christ died for no reason at all.

3 *Only faith, not the Law, leads to righteousness*
O you ignorant Galatians! Who has cast such a spell over you that
the truth no longer means anything to you? You, for whom Jesus
Christ was described as vividly as if it were in your midst that he
was crucified! 2Only one thing I want to know from you: did you
receive the Spirit through carrying out the deeds prescribed by the
Law or through listening with the open-heartedness of faith? 3How
can you be so foolish! Do you now want to complete by earthly,
physical means what you began in the Spirit? 4Have all the sufferings you endured been for nothing? Everything does really seem
to have been in vain. 5Does he who bestows the Spirit on you and
gives such evidence of higher power among you do it on the basis
of the works of the Law or through the open-heartedness of your
faith?

[6]It is as it once was with Abraham, who put his trust and faith
in God and to whom this was 'counted as righteousness.' [7]From
this you can understand: those who live out of the power of faith
are the true sons of Abraham. [8]The scriptures foretold that God
would open the realm of higher life to the heathen peoples through
faith; that is why it says in the promise made to Abraham:

> In you all peoples shall be blessed.

[9]So now all who tread the path of faith are blessed with Abraham
who was rich in faith.

[10]Those who remain upon the path of the works of the Law are
doomed. For scripture says:

> Cursed be he who does not keep all that is written
> in the book of the Law and does not act strictly in
> accordance with it.

[11]It is quite clear that no human being can be perfect before God
in the sense of the Law. The life of one who has a share in the
higher life flows out of faith. [12]The Law did not proceed out of the
faith. It is said:

> Whoever acts strictly according to the Law will
> receive his life from it.

[13]Christ has freed us from the curse which lies upon the Law, by
becoming a curse for us, for it says in scripture:

> Cursed is everyone who hangs on the gibbet.

[14]The blessing which Abraham received is to be passed on to all
peoples, including the heathen, through Jesus Christ: the promise
of the Spirit is to be fulfilled in us through faith.

[15]Dear brothers, I will speak in human terms: it is as with the
will and testament of a human being; once it has taken effect, no
one can set it aside and no one can add to it. [16]Now the promises
were, of course, made to Abraham and to his seed. It does not say
'seeds,' as though it were a question of many, but there is only
mention of one:

> And to your seed.

By this is meant: Christ. [17]Now what I want to say is this: the testament which God put into effect in advance cannot be set aside

by the Law given four hundred and thirty years later, so as to make
the promise invalid. 18For if the inheritance could be acquired
through the Law, then it would no longer be flowing from the
promise; but God gave it freely to Abraham through the promise.

The Law is our teacher towards Christ

19Then what really is the point of the Law? It was added because of
the strayings of human beings, until the seed should come to whom
the promise applied. It came into being with the help of the angels
and was placed in the hand of a mediator. 20There is no such thing
as a mediator who deals with one party only. But God is One.

21So is the Law something which contradicts the divine promises? Not in the least! For if a law had been given which was able
to bestow life, then in truth righteousness could have proceeded
from the Law. 22But scripture regarded the whole human race as
belonging in the realm of sin, and so it is clear that the promise which is linked to union in faith with Jesus Christ appears as
something quite new, namely for those in whom faith lives.

23Before faith came into the world we were guarded by the Law
and under restraint by the Law, waiting for the future which was
to draw back the curtain from before the mystery of faith. 24Thus
the Law became our educator towards Christ, so that we should be
able to find the realm of true being through faith. 25Ever since faith
has come into the world we are no longer subject to the educator.
26You all are sons of God through the faith in Christ Jesus. 27You
all, having been baptized into Christ, have put on Christ. 28Then
there are no longer Jews or Greeks, no longer slaves or freemen, no
longer male or female: you are all one in Christ Jesus. 29But if you
are one in Christ, then you are the real seed of Abraham, and the
inheritance is yours, in accordance with the promise.

4 *Free from the Law through the Son*

And furthermore I say: as long as the heir is a minor, he is not yet
different from a servant, although he is lord of everything; 2he is
subject to his tutors and the stewards of the estate until the time

determined by his father. 3So, too, it was with us: as long as we
were minors, we were subject to the elements of earthly nature, and
served them. 4But then, in the fullness of time, God sent HIS Son,
born of a woman and subject to the Law: 5he was to set free those
who were under this spell of the Law, so that we might receive
sonship. 6Now that you have become sons, God has sent the Spirit
of HIS Son into your hearts; it calls out: Abba! Father! 7So you
are no longer a servant, but a son; and if a son, then also an heir
through the will of God.

8In the days when you did not yet know God, you were in thrall
to powers who are not divine in their essential nature. 9Now you
know God – or rather, you are known by God; how can you then
turn back again to those poor, feeble elemental beings, why do you
want to serve them again? 10Anxiously you observe special days
and months, seasons and years. 11When I think about you, I fear
that my efforts on your behalf have been in vain.

12I beg of you, do go my way as I am going yours. Dear brothers, I come before you, entreating you. You have done me no
wrong. 13You know that I was frail, physically, when I came to
you the first time, proclaiming the Gospel. 14You did not succumb
to the temptation to respond to my bodily state with contempt and
rejection; rather, you received me as an angel sent from God, as
though I were the Christ Jesus himself. 15Where now is the sympathetic good feeling toward me which filled you then? I assure
you: had it been possible, you would have plucked out your eyes
and given them to me. 16Have I then become your enemy because
I now tell you the truth? 17There are those who are making a great
show of regard for you, but they do not mean well by you. They
want to break up your circle and make you join in their enthusiasm. 18It is good to be enthusiastic for a cause – provided always
that the cause is good; and that you are not reverent only when I
am with you! 19You are my dear children, for whom I suffer birth-
pangs again until Christ takes on form in you. 20I wish I could be
with you now and change my tone; for I am deeply concerned
about you all.

[21]Tell me, you who want to be subject to the Law, why do you then not listen to the Law? [22]For it is written that Abraham had two sons, one by the maid and one by the free woman. [23]The son of the maid was born because of an earthly creative impulse; but the son of the free woman was born because of the divine promise. [24]We can understand this as an allegory: we are here concerned with the two covenants. The one of Mount Sinai which bears children for servitude: that is Hagar. In Arabia, [25]the word Hagar means 'Mount Sinai'; it corresponds to the earthly, temporal Jerusalem; for she is in servitude, together with her children. [26]But the heavenly Jerusalem is free; she is the mother of us all. [27]For scripture says:

> Rejoice, you who are barren and have borne no children.
> Dance and sing, you who are not with child;
> for she who is bereft shall have many children,
> more than she who has a husband.

[28]Dear brothers, you – like Isaac – are children of a promise. [29]But, just as then he who was born according to the flesh persecuted him who was born according to the spirit, so it is also now. [30]But what does scripture say?

> Cast out the maid and her son, for the son of the maid shall not be heir together with the son of the free woman!

[31]Therefore, dear brothers, understand this: we are not children of the serving-maid but of the free woman.

5 *Call to freedom*

So stand firm in the freedom into which the Christ has freed us; do not let yourselves be harnessed again in the yoke of servitude. [2]Look, now I, Paul, say to you: if after all this you let yourselves be circumcised, Christ cannot bring you further. [3]I must say again with emphasis to everyone who lets himself be circumcised that then he is also obliged to observe the whole of the Law. [4]You have separated yourselves from Christ, you who think that you can attain to higher life through the Law, and you have fallen away from grace. [5]Our spiritual nature creates in us the faith to expect and the hope for life from on high. [6]In Christ Jesus neither circumcision nor uncircumcision is of any consequence, but only the faith which becomes an active power through love.

[7]You were doing so well. Who has put a hindrance in your way, so that now you no longer follow the truth? [8]What they are now trying to make you believe has nothing to do with him who called you. [9]A little leaven soon leavens the whole dough. [10]Out of my oneness with Christ I have confidence in you, that basically you do not really think otherwise. He who is confusing you will have to take the consequences, no matter who he may be. [11]I, dear brothers, if I still spoke in favour of circumcision, how is it then that I am persecuted? For then, that scandal about the cross would have been cleared away. [12]May the hardest blows of destiny strike those who unsettle you!

[13]You are called to freedom, dear brothers. Only this should not be thought of as that freedom which gives free rein to the bodily desires; but rather that which leads you to serve one another in love. [14]For the whole of the Law is fulfilled in the one saying:

> Love your neighbour as yourself.

[15]If you flare up against one another as though you could bite and devour one another: take care that you do not in all reality destroy one another.

Living out of the spirit

[16]I say to you: structure your lives out of the spirit, then you will not be driven by the desires of your earthly senses. [17]For the bodily desires are all directed against the spirit; and the spirit is opposed to the flesh. These two are in conflict with one another, and that is why you cannot do what you want to do in reality. [18]But if you let the spirit be the mainspring of your actions, then you are not subject to the Law. [19]It is plain to see what the merely earthly, bodily in us leads to:

> sexual gratification without commitment, and perverse practices,
> unclean and lascivious sensual cravings,

[20]idolizing the world of the senses, and frivolous, magical playing with the sensory world,
the desire to wound and to stir up discord,
resentment, anger,
the urge to make quarrels and the compulsion to deny everything,
the inclination to dissension,
[21]enmity against everything which has soul and against everything which has life,
enslavement to earthly matter, so that there is nothing left except gluttony and excess of eating and drinking,
and everything that is of like nature
and against which I have given you timely warning again and again:
those who let their actions be determined by these powers
cannot be heirs to the Kingdom of God.

[22]But the fruit which matures on the way of the spirit is:
Love, joy, peace,
patience of soul, gentleness of soul, goodness,
faith, [23]forgivingness, self-mastery.

The Law has nothing to say against these. [24]Those who belong
to Christ Jesus crucify their earthly-physical nature with all the
passions and cravings which arise from it. [25]If we owe our life to
the spirit, then let us also order our lives by the spirit. [26]Let us
beware of all vanity; let us avoid trying to outdo one another and
being envious of one another.

6 *Life in the congregation*

Dear brothers, if someone slips into error, you who have received the Spirit should try, out of the inner harmony which you have from the Spirit, to help him recover. And let everyone look to himself, that he does not fall into temptation also. [2]Bear one another's
burdens; so shall you fulfil the law of Christ. [3]If someone thinks
himself to be something and yet is not, he deceives himself in his

own mind. [4]Let each examine his own deeds; for then he will find out for himself what is good in them and does not need the praise of others. [5]For everyone has to learn to bear his own burden. [6]Let him who is taught the Word be at one in all that is good with him who teaches. [7]Do not fool yourselves: one cannot deceive God. What a human being sows, that he will also reap. [8]Whoever sows only on the field of his earthly nature will merely reap progressive decay from his physical nature; but he who sows into his spiritual nature will harvest from his spiritual nature a life that endures through all cycles of time.

[9]Let us not tire of doing good. At the right moment we shall reap, if we do not relax our efforts. [10]So therefore, during the time granted us, let us work and do good to all human beings, especially to those who are united with us through faith into one spiritual household.

Concluding words

[11]See with what great letters I am now writing to you, with my own hand! [12]Those who want to make an impression in external matters are also those who urge you to be circumcised. They do not wish to suffer persecution because of the cross of Christ. [13]Even they, who are circumcised, do not keep the Law. They want you to be circumcised in order that on your bodies they can proudly show external evidence of success.

[14]Far be it always from me to show pride unless it be in the cross of Jesus Christ, our Lord. Through him the world is crucified to me and I to the world. [15]So neither circumcision nor uncircumcision counts for anything; the only thing that matters is the new creation. [16]May peace and divine goodness descend upon all who will be guided by this rule: they are the Israel of God. [17]Henceforth let no one make unnecessary difficulties for me, for I bear the crucifixion marks of Jesus on my body.

[18]The grace of Jesus Christ our Lord be with your spirit, brothers. Amen.

The Letter of Paul to the Ephesians

Introduction

Paul, an apostle of Christ Jesus by the will of God which guides destinies, to all in Ephesus who unite themselves in faith with Christ Jesus:

[2]Grace be with you and peace from God our Father and from Jesus Christ, the Lord.

Song of praise

[3]The highest praise be to the Father of our Lord Jesus Christ. HE it is who bestows on us the great fullness of spiritual blessings which are prepared for us through Christ in the heavenly worlds. [4]In him HE chose us all even before the world was created, so that we can stand before HIS countenance, hallowed and without blemish, [5]in the stream of HIS love. HE formed us inwardly so that we can, according to HIS will and pleasure, be of HIS sonship in Jesus Christ [6]to the praise of HIS gracious revelation, bestowed on us in the One who is HIS Beloved.

[7]In HIM we receive the redemption through his blood, the lifting of the curse which hangs over us because of our strayings: all flows from the riches of HIS grace [8]which HE pours over us and so lavishes on us all wisdom and insight.

[9]HE has granted us insight into the mystery which lies hidden in HIS world-aims, into HIS healing intention which HE let appear in Christ, [10]to give purpose to the fulfilment of the cycles of time: all that is in the heavens and on the earth shall be renewed and united into one being in Christ. [11]In Christ indeed the lot has fallen to us to partake in the heritage which has been provided for us in accordance with the purposeful will of HIM who is the driving force

in all things. 12For it was HIS intention that we who have hoped
for Christ, have waited for Christ, should be the ones in whom his
light-glory is revealed. 13In him you also are sheltered, you who
have heard the word of truth, the Gospel of the salvation which is
intended for you. Through your faith in him you have been sealed
with the promised Holy Spirit, 14which is the certain promise of
our inheritance of the Spirit and of our salvation through which he
makes us his own that we enhance his glory.

Prayer of thanksgiving for the community
15For this reason, because I have heard of your faith in Jesus the
Lord and of your love for all who strive devotedly, 16I do not cease
to give thanks for you and to remember you in my prayers, 17that
the divine Father of Jesus Christ our Lord, the Father of the light
of revelation, may grant you the spirit of wisdom and revelation,
so that you can draw near to HIM as those who perceive; 18as those,
the eyes of whose hearts are enlightened.

So shall you know the aims of hope towards which your calling
leads you; what a wealth of revelation is determined in the destiny
of those who devote themselves to HIM, 19and how immeasurably
great is the power which HE would grant us. Through our faith
we gain access to the mighty working of the power of HIS sunlike strength 20which HE made active in Christ when HE raised him
from the dead and gave him the place on HIS right in the highest
heavenly spheres; 21above all Spirits of Might and all Creating
Spirits, above all World-Powers, even the World-Guides, above
every name that can be named, not only in the present age, but also
in the aeon to come. 22He has placed everything under his feet and
has made him the head of all things in the great community which
is his body, the divine fullness of him who fulfils all in all.

2 *New life as an endowment from God*
Death has penetrated you through your strayings and through sin
2which is active in you; for you have led your life according to
the laws of the present aeon to which everything in this world is

subject. You have followed the compelling will of him whose force rules the air and is now the spirit which is active in the self-willed rebels whom he dupes into following him. 3As such we also once lived our lives, given over to the desires of our earthly nature, working merely out of the instincts of our physical body and of our head-bound reasoning. We were by nature children ripe for punishment, just like everyone else.

4Nevertheless, God, rich in merciful goodness, has enveloped us in HIS great and profound love 5and has awakened us, who were dead through our sins, to a new life together with Christ. You have been saved through grace – 6HE has raised us from the dead with him and together with him designated us a place in the spheres of heaven. 7From there shall the overflowing wealth of HIS grace be visible and active in future ages of time, arising from the great goodness which HE shows to us in Jesus Christ.

8For it is by grace that you have been saved through faith, not out of your own strength, but as a gift from God – 9certainly not as a result of your own doing, so that you can hardly boast about it. 10We are a product of God's workmanship, created anew in Christ Jesus, and now we can do the good works for which God had laid the potential in us right at the very beginning, so that they can become the content of our lives.

The new community

11Remember, once you were heathens; that is, men who were orientated towards nature, and were designated, by those who took the path of circumcision, as the uncircumcised. 12Then you were separated from Christ, just as you also stood as strangers outside the bounds of the people of Israel and had no part in the testament of God's promise. You stood in the world without hope and without God. 13Now, however, you are in Christ Jesus; you, who were 'far,' are now 'near' through the blood of Christ. 14For he is our peace, he has made one out of two and has broken down the dividing fence. 15He has dissolved, through his physical body, that which stood there as rigid rules and which caused enmity, namely the Law

and its commandments. He wanted to transform the duality into the
unity of the New Man, in that he brought about peace; [16]he wanted
to transform back what had been divided, towards the divine in *one*
body, and that he did through the cross. On the cross he has killed
enmity. [17]Through his coming he brought the message of peace
for you who were 'far' and the same message for those who were
'near.' [18]So out of what was twofold we have access through him to
the Father, in the unity of the Spirit.

[19]Now you are no longer strangers and guests, you are fellow
citizens of those who strive for holiness, and members of the house
of God. [20]You belong to the house, the foundations of which are
built on the apostles and the prophets; the foundation-stone thereof
is Christ Jesus [21]in whom the harmoniously fashioned building
grows upwards into a holy temple. [22]That is so, because he is the
Lord in whose name you will also be formed into a dwelling-place
for God in the spirit.

3 *The share of the heathens in the Christ mystery*
I, Paul, receive my strength from the same source; I, who bear
the chains of Christ Jesus for you who have come from the heathen peoples. [2]For I expect you have sensed how I have received
the task to be there for you through the wise and merciful plan
of God's grace. [3]Through a real revelation I have received understanding and insight into the mystery, as I have already written
to you with few words; [4]and so you, when you read these words,
can gain a share of insight into my understanding of the Christ
Mystery, [5]which was not made known to mankind in bygone ages,
but which now has been revealed in the spirit to his holy apostles
and prophets. [6]The heathen nations are to become fellow heirs,
they shall be members and partakers of the promise in Christ Jesus
through the Gospel, [7]whose servant I have become by the merciful gift of God, and which has become his indwelling, active
power in me. [8]I, the very least among those who have a share in the
salvation, was favoured with grace to proclaim the inexhaustible
richness of the being of Christ to the heathen nations, [9]and to bring

them enlightenment about the purposeful unfolding of this mystery
which will take place from now on.

For aeons it has remained hidden in the divine worlds whence all
creation has gone forth, in order that it may now be opened to men's
consciousness. [10]Through the striving human community the Spirits
of Might and the Creating Spirits in the heavenly spheres shall be
made aware how many-coloured and many-sided is the wisdom of
God. [11]The divine purpose, alive through the aeons, now takes on
visible form in Christ Jesus, our Lord. [12]He gives us free courage and
a trusting approach through our faith in him. [13]Therefore I ask you:
do not become discouraged because of the trials which I have to go
through for your sake; they shall serve towards your enlightenment.

Prayer for the community

[14]So now I bow my knees before the Father [15]in whom all beings in
the heavens and on the earth have their birthplace and their home.
[16]May HE grant you, out of the wealth of HIS light-glory, that the
higher power may take hold of you which through HIS Spirit brings
to birth the Inner Man in you. [17]This happens when the Christ dwells
in your hearts through your faith, and when you are firmly rooted
and grounded in love. [18]Then you will also have the power, together
with all who have a share in the salvation, to grasp what the secret
is of length and of breadth, of height and of depth; [19]you will comprehend the love of Christ which is greater than all comprehension,
and you will be filled with all the fullness of the highest God.

[20]To HIM who can fulfil beyond all measure what we ask for or
what we simply carry in our minds, in that HE lets higher forces
become active in us: [21]to HIM belongs all the glory of revelation
which enlightens the community through Christ Jesus in all generations and in the ages of time to come. Amen.

4 *Exhortation to peaceful co-operation in the community*

I, who bear my chains in the service of the Lord, implore you to
fashion your lives in a way that is worthy of your calling: [2]in all
humility and inner harmony, in greatness of heart, bearing with one

another in love, 3eagerly endeavouring to care for the unity of spirit
in which peace is the bond which joins you all 4as one body and
one spirit, in the one hope that has ensouled you since your calling.
5One Lord, one faith, one baptism, 6one God, the Father of all, who
is above all, through all and in all.

7Each one of us receives grace according to the measure of
Christ's generously given love. 8For it is said:

> He has ascended to the heights, in order to put into
> captivity that power which holds you captive, and so
> can he give his gifts to men.

9That 'he has ascended,' is that not, in fact, the same as his having descended into the lowest regions of the earth? 10He who has
descended is the same as he who has ascended higher than all the
heavens; he wanted to fill all existence with his own being. 11He it
is who makes some into apostles, others into prophets or proclaim-
ers of the Gospel and others into pastors and teachers. 12They, who
have a part in the processes of healing, are equipped for actively
carrying out the service of building up the body of Christ 13until we
all together reach the goal of unity in faith and in the knowledge
of the divine Son out of whom the consecrated Man goes forth,
whose measure of maturity depends on how much the fullness of
Christ's Being is in him.

14We are no longer to be children, tossed to and fro and swayed
by every kind of teaching. Clever men, full of cunning, know well
how to make the most of this and use it in their crafty deceits.
15Let us breathe forth the air of truth, and grow in the love of the
Son. Let all our senses be turned to him, to Christ: he is the head;
16through him the whole body becomes harmonious, all members
and limbs working together, each according to its own strength,
helping each other towards proper growth of the body, that this
body be totally built up out of that love which is Christ.

A call to live out of the strength of renewal

17So I speak as follows and call you to wakefulness in the name
of the Lord, that you no longer follow the path of the heathen

peoples. [18]They have given themselves over to the illusions of
the senses, with an intellectual way of thinking that grows ever
darker, estranged from divine life by extinguishing the knowledge
of their souls through the hardening of their hearts. [19]So it cannot
be helped that they lose control of themselves and, following base
instincts, make the soul become ever more dull and subject to selfishness and egoism. [20]It was not on this path that you heard about
the Christ. [21]You have perceived him and have been taught in his
spirit; in the Being of Jesus you can read the truth: [22]so free yourselves from the old way of life and put off your old nature which
destroys itself in following beguiling desires. [23]Renew yourselves
through taking the Spirit into your thinking [24]and put on the New
Man who is created in God's image, and in righteousness and in
the holiness of truth.

[25]Therefore, strip off all that is untrue and false. Let truth hold
sway when conversing with one another, for we are all members
of one body. [26]You may be angered by one thing or another, but
do not be drawn into acting intemperately. Do not let the sun go
down upon your wrath, [27]and do not give any opportunity to the
Adversary. [28]May he, who has taken what is not his, desist from
now on; with increased effort and strength may he now bring about
the Good through the work of his hands and give to those who are
in need of it. [29]Let no foul word pass your lips: what you speak
should be good and edifying and relate to a need. Also it should
impart grace to those who hear it. [30]Do not injure the holy Spirit
of God with which you are sealed until the day of redemption.
[31]All bitterness and passion, every anger and wantonness, and all
irreverence for the Word be far from you, as well as the bad consequences which arise therefrom. [32]Be friendly to one another with
a sympathetic heart, forgive one another as God has shown HIS
grace to you in Christ's forgiving you.

5 *Life in the light*
Become real imitators of God as HIS beloved children. [2]Shape your
lives out of love, as also Christ loved us and gave himself for us as

a gift of offering whose fragrance ascends to God. [3]Let impure
sexuality, uncleanness and self-seeking no longer even be named
among you; thus it is fitting for those who have a share in the salvation. [4]Words without shame, without content and without earnestness are not fitting for you, rather practise all the more the word
of thanksgiving. [5]For you must realize that everyone who loses
himself in immorality, uncleanness and self-seeking is a servant of
false idols; there is no inheritance for him in the kingdom of Christ
nor of God.

[6]Do not be deceived by empty words. They call down the wrath
of God on those who turn away. [7]Have nothing to do with them.
[8]Once your being was darkness, now it is light in the Lord. Live
like the children of light – [9]the fruit of light ripens into every kind
of goodness, into higher levels of life, into truth itself.

[10]You must be able to judge what belongs to the Lord. [11]Take no
part in the unfruitful machinations of the darkness; rather unmask
them. [12]For what in reality lies hidden in them is revealed as dam-
aging and shameful when it is called by its right name. [13]Everything
comes to light when the light exposes the illusion. Everything that
appears openly belongs to the light. [14]And so it is said:

> Awake, you who are sleeping,
> Arise from the dead,
> The Christ shall be your light!

[15]Always strive to stand in life with care and wakeful attention,
not as unwise men, but as wise. [16]Make good use of time and the
right moments, for the powers of evil rule the hour. [17]Therefore
be not without serenity, but try to understand what the will of the
Lord is. [18]Do not let yourselves become intoxicated with wine, for
thereby everything loses its healthy order. Rather strive to carry
the fullness of the Spirit in you. [19]In your gatherings, strike up
psalms and hymns and spirit-filled songs; in your hearts singing
and accompanying, to the praise of the Lord. [20]At all times cherish
the act of thanksgiving for all that you have received in the name of
Jesus Christ, our Lord, before the countenance of the divine Father.

Order in the home
21Let each one of you be beholden to the other in the feeling of
the nearness of Christ. 22Let the feminine be related to its corresponding masculine in the same way as the soul itself relates to the
Lord. 23For the masculine is the head of the feminine as Christ is
the head of the community. In that he is the head, he is the healing
power for the whole body. 24So, as the community bows to serve
the Christ, let the feminine serve the masculine in all things. 25The
masculine shall love the feminine as Christ loved the community
and gave himself for it.
26He will hallow it by cleansing it, bathing it in the water of his
word-deed. 27He will make the community a light-filled revelation
of himself, so that there shall be neither a blemish nor a wrinkle
nor any other flaw in it; holy and pure shall it be. 28So also shall
the love be with which the masculine loves the feminine which has
been given to it. Let the masculine love the feminine as if it were
his own body. Thus it will, in reality, love itself in the feminine
which belongs to it. 29For no-one hates his own physical nature;
rather he feeds it and takes care of it. That is how Christ is with
the community, 30and we are members of his body.

> 31For this reason a man will leave his father and his
> mother and turn to his wife and be joined to her; the
> duality will become a unity, even into their physical
> natures.

32That is a great mystery. I say this with Christ and the congregation in view. 33So also you, each single one of you, shall love the
feminine which belongs to him as he loves himself; and let the
feminine look up to the masculine.
6 You, who are children, follow the word of those who are your
parents in the Lord. Thus you will be on the right path.

> 2Honour your father and your mother,

that is the first commandment, which is tied to the promise,

> 3then things will go well with you, and your life on
> earth will be full.

4And you, who are fathers, do not incite angry feelings in those

who are your children; guide and lead them as if Christ himself
were their educator and teacher.

5You, who are servants, follow the word of those who, here on
earth, are your masters, in all reverence and humility and simplicity of heart. Relate to them as you would relate to Christ. 6Let your
services not just be show with which to find favour in the eyes of
men. As servants of Christ, work out of your heart powers that
the will of God may be fulfilled. 7Serve with a good will as if you
were serving not men, but the Lord. 8You know that every good
that is done by a man shines out from the realm of the Lord back
to him, whether he be a slave or a free man.

9And you, who are masters, treat them as they should treat you.
Lay aside all harsh pride which causes rifts. You know that above
them and above you the same Lord holds sway in the spiritual
worlds, in whose sight all differences of person lose their meaning.

The armour of God

10What it comes to in the end is this: let the intense strength of his
might flow through those who want to serve the Lord. 11Put on the
full armour of God that you may resist the well-aimed attacks of
the Adversary. 12For our part is not to fight against powers of flesh
and blood, but

> against spirit-beings,
> mighty in the stream of time,
> against spirit-beings,
> powerful in the moulding of earth's substance,
> against the cosmic powers
> whose darkness rules the present time,
> against beings who, in the spiritual worlds,
> are themselves the powers of evil.

13Therefore courageously take up the armour of God, that you
can resist the evil on the day when it unfolds its greatest strength.
You should stand firm, following everything through to the very end.

> 14Stand fast, girded about the loins with truth.
> Put on the breastplate of the higher life

which fulfils our human destiny.
15Shoe your feet with preparedness
to spread the message of peace that comes from the
angels.
16In all your deeds continually hold
to your hearts' vision of Christ's presence,
with which you can quench all the flaming darts of the
evil one.
17Take into your thoughts the certainty of the coming
world-healing,
that it protect you as with a helmet,
and grasp the sword of the Spirit
which is the word of God which you utter.

18May this armour cover you in all your supplications and
prayers, may your inmost heart light up in spirit in your prayers.
To this end direct your spirit-strength in all your efforts of soul
and in your intercessions for all who would know Christ's healing power. 19Take me into your prayers, so that when I open my
mouth the strength of the Word may be given me. Then I can courageously and openly expound the mysteries of the Gospel, 20for
which I am a priestly messenger, in spite of the chains which I
bear. Out of the Gospel itself there streams to me the free strength
to speak with the courage I need.

Conclusion

21Tychicus, the beloved brother and faithful minister in the service
of the Lord, will tell you all that you should know about me and
my work. 22I have sent him to you so that you may know about us
and that your hearts may be strengthened through his news.

23Peace be with all brothers, and love united with faith. May
they be given to you from the divine Father and from Jesus Christ,
the Lord. 24Grace be with all whose love for Jesus Christ our Lord
lives on, incorruptible.

The Letter of Paul to the Philippians

1 *Introduction*
Paul and Timothy, fully committed to the service of the Christ
Jesus, to all those in Philippi, including the leaders of the congregation and those serving as priests, who strive for holiness through
the power of Christ Jesus:
[2]May grace be yours, and peace from God our Father and from
Jesus Christ, our Lord.

Prayer of thanks for the congregation
[3]My every thought of you rises up in me like a thanks-offering to
God. [4]Full of joy I always include you in my prayers. [5]The source
of this joy is the wholehearted way in which, from the first day
until now as a community, you have turned to the essence which
lives in the Gospel. [6]I am certain: HE who has initiated in you the
working of the Good will also lead you to the goal of the way – to
the dawning of the Day of Christ. [7]I have the right to think about
you all like this, for I bear you in my heart. In my fetters, but also
in all my work for the Gospel, whether I defend it or carry it further out into the world – you are involved, because the same grace
is at work in you as in me. [8]God HIMSELF can confirm how much I
long for you all in my innermost being where Christ dwells. [9]And
I pray for this, that your love will make even more progress in
knowledge and discernment, [10]so that you acquire the ability to
distinguish between spirits. Then, when the Day of Christ dawns,
you will prove yourselves full of sunlike clarity and without a
shadow. [11]Through the power of Christ the full fruit of the higher
being will ripen in you. You will be a revelation of God and a
song of praise to HIM.

News of the work in Rome
[12]Dear brothers, I want you to know that my destiny – whatever
form it has taken – has helped the Gospel forward. [13]The fetters
I bear have become a visible symbol of faith in Christ for the
whole praetorium, the court of the ruler, but also for all others.
[14]And many of our brothers with whom we are united in the Lord
have become trusting and confident because of my fetters: all
the more fearlessly they now dare to proclaim the word of God.
[15]Some, however, are not free from envy and quarrelsomeness;
but the others proclaim Christ with a good and pure will. [16]They
draw the strength for this from the love which encompasses us
all; they know that I have only come to my present state because I
represent the Gospel. [17]When the others proclaim Christ, they are
following personal and conflicting interests, their will is not pure.
Perhaps they want to add further distress to my fetters. [18]But what
of it? Just so long as Christ is proclaimed, whether as a pretence
or sincerely! And that is why I am filled with joy. [19]And my joy
will endure, for I know that this will serve as my salvation; your
prayers help me, and also my awareness of the spiritual guidance
of Jesus Christ.

[20]It is my deep longing and hope not to fail in any way, but
rather to make the greatness of Christ apparent as always, so also
now, right into my physical, bodily nature in powerful freedom,
whether it be through my life or through my death. [21]For Christ
is my life, and so dying is gain to me. [22]Even if my life in the
physical body allows me to continue bearing fruit through active
work, I still do not know which form of existence I should rather
wish for. [23]Both forms of existence matter to me; and yet I feel a
longing for dissolution and for total union with Christ. I think I
would prefer that to anything else.

[24]But for your sakes it is necessary for me still to remain in the
physical body. [25]And so I know with absolute certainty that I shall
remain. I will be near you all and help you to progress inwardly,
and be full of joy through your faith; [26]so that through me you will
find fulfilment of life in your oneness with Christ in ever greater

measure. This I wish when I think that I shall be coming to you again some time.

Call to order the life of the congregation worthily

27Only, order the life of your congregation in such a way that it
become worthy of the Christ-Gospel. Then, whether I come to you
and see you or am far from you, I shall be able to sense

that you are standing firm in unity of spirit,
that you are one heart and soul in your striving
for the faith in the Gospel,
28and that you are not to be shaken in any
way by the adversaries.

For them, every stirring and activity of the power of faith is
an omen of their defeat; but for you it is a sign of salvation. That
is God's will. 29You have been granted the grace to be allowed
to form your lives into a service of Christ; not only by uniting
yourselves with him through prayer, but also by suffering for
him. 30You have to face the same struggle in which you have also
seen me engaged, and which you now also hear that I have to go
through.

2 If the power of the spirit-word is in the Being of Christ; if
there is encouragement of the heart through the divine love; if we
experience how the Spirit makes us into a community; if there is
tenderness and warm-heartedness – 2then you can make my joy
complete by directing your thinking and your whole minds towards
the same aims:

cultivate the same loving will;
feel your souls to be intimately united;
strive for harmony of thought between you!

3Do not allow your community to be spoiled by strife and
ambition. With simple modesty let each one regard the other more
highly than himself. 4Overcome that in you which makes each one
see only himself. Let each one strive to be open to other human
beings.

Christ emptied himself and offered up his divine form
[5]Be imbued with the same state of mind which also filled Christ
Jesus himself. [6]For although he was of divine nature and form,
he chose not to lay claim for himself to be equal to God. [7]Rather,
he emptied himself in offering and took on the form of a servant.
In human form he took on body, [8]and he showed himself in the
form of a man throughout his whole life. Humbly and selflessly
he submitted to the laws of earth-existence, even to the experience
of death, the death on the cross. [9]Therefore God has also exalted
him to the highest heights and given him the name which is above
every other name. [10]In the name of Jesus the knees of all beings
should bow, in the heavens, on the earth and in the depths of existence. And so that the Father, the Ground of all existence shall
be revealed, [11]every tongue should declare the confession: JESUS
CHRIST, THE LORD!

[12]Therefore, beloved, just as you always did, listen to the voice
of the Spirit, not only when I am with you, but now all the more,
since I am far from you.

Work with anxious effort and trembling expectation, to the end
that the realm of healing power may open to you. [13]For it is God
who awakens the will in you and who brings about the fulfilment
so that everything can become good. [14]Do not let yourselves be
held back in that work by sluggishness of the will or by restless
thoughts which make you indecisive. [15]Only so can you live, without blemish and falseness, as pure children of God in the midst of
a dissipated and twisted humanity. You are to shine among human
beings like the bright stars in the sky, [16]by keeping to the Word of
Life. And when the Day of Christ dawns you will be my pride and
prove that my efforts have not been meaningless, nor my work in
vain. [17]And even if I were to be offered up as a sacrifice for my
priestly service to your faith: I would be filled with joy and be
closely united in joy with you all. [18]So therefore you also should
be filled with joy and be closely united in joy with me.

News of Timothy and Epaphroditus
[19]My life in Jesus the Lord makes me hope that I can soon send
Timothy to you, so that my soul may be cheered by hearing about
you. [20]I have no one with whom I am so at one and who would
more devotedly care for you. [21]There are so many who seek their
own interests instead of serving Christ Jesus in purity. [22]You know
Timothy's worth. As a child does his father, he has served the
Gospel with me. [23]Him I hope to send to you as soon as I can see
how things will turn out with me. [24]My life in the Lord makes me
hope that I can also soon come to you myself.

[25]I have thought it necessary to send Epaphroditus to you, my
brotherly fellow worker and fellow fighter; he comes to you as a
messenger and as the fulfiller of my obligation to you. [26]He longed
for you all and was worried because you had heard that he was ill.
[27]And, in fact, he has been so ill that he has been near to death.
But God had mercy on him, and not only on him but also on me,
so that I should not suffer grief upon grief. [28]Therefore I have sent
him to you as quickly as possible so that you should see him and
be glad again, and that I should be released from grief and care.
[29]So now receive him in the name of the Lord with all joy. Honour
such men; [30]for it was his work for Christ that brought him near to
death. He put his life into completing your service to me, in so far
as you yourselves were not able to fulfil it.

3 *Faith in Christ and the Law*
Yet it remains so, dear brothers: rejoice in the Lord! For me it is
not irksome to keep writing the same things to you. Let it give you
firmness.

[2]Beware of the dogs, do not let yourselves become drawn in by
those forces which are of merely natural origin.

Beware of all who are instruments of evil.

Beware of the bad consequences of circumcision.

[3]We are the bearers of the true circumcision because, serving
the Spirit of God and strengthened in our true selves by the Christ
Jesus, we no longer place all our trust in what is physical and

bodily; [4]although, of course, I could have good reason to trust in what I am by physical descent. If anyone thinks that he has grounds for confidence because of his bodily descent, I have even more. [5]I was circumcised on the eighth day as a true descendant of Israel, of the tribe of Benjamin. Descended from Hebrews I became a Hebrew, as a Pharisee I followed the direction of the Law. [6]Through an excess of zeal I became a persecutor of the congregation. In so far as perfection can be achieved by following the Law, I was blameless and did it full justice.

[7]But all the things which once I strove for and achieved, I had to recognize on the way of Christ as hindering and harmful. [8]Yes, even now I see them only as hindrances, since the spirit-knowledge of Jesus Christ, my Lord, has blossomed in fullness within me. For his sake have I had to travel these roundabout ways. Now all that has become unimportant to me. Important is only that I win Christ [9]and can be recognized as belonging to him. The righteousness which is found through the Law is not mine, but rather that which I attain through faith in Christ. That is the true higher being which I receive from God, grounded in the faith. [10]Knowledge of Christ flows from it, as well as the power which was made manifest by his resurrection. Through it I also understand the mystery of fellowship with his sufferings by which I am formed towards his kind of death, [11]so that perhaps I may also grow into his resurrection, his victory over death.

The apostle's example

[12]Not that I have already reached the aim or received the ultimate consecration. But I strive onwards on the path, so as to take hold of that for which Christ Jesus took hold of me. [13]Dear brothers, I do really not think that I have achieved it. But one thing I may say: what is behind me is forgotten; my whole being stretches out towards what lies before me. [14]My whole striving is for the prize that I see: the call from the heavenly heights to become one with Christ.

[15]Let those many of us who are minded to partake of the consecration think in this way. If you still have other things in mind,

God will also grant you revelation through them; [16]only, let us continue on the path by which we have come.

[17]Work hard to follow in my footsteps, dear brothers, and,
in following my example, pay close attention to those who are
on the same way. [18]For many also travel this road – I have often
told you, and now I say it again with tears – who in reality are
enemies of the cross of Christ. [19]They are heading for destruction. Their belly is their god, and their fame is their shame, since
their hearts and minds are set only on earthly things. [20]But the
true being and life of us all is in the heavens, from where we
expect the spiritual coming of the Saviour. That is Jesus Christ,
the Lord. [21]He will transform the lowliness of our earthly body
and make it of like form as his transfigured body. He can do this
through the mighty power by which he can subject all existence
to himself.

4 *Rejoice!*

Therefore, my brothers whom I love and long for, my joy and my
crown of glory, stand firm in the power of the Lord!

[2]I admonish both Euodia and Syntyche to strive to be of one
mind in the power of the Lord. [3]And I ask you, my faithful fellow
worker, to look after them. They have shared in my struggles on
behalf of the Gospel, together with Clement and my other helpers,
whose names are in the Book of Life.

[4]Rejoice in the Lord at all times! And I say it again: rejoice!
[5]Let your kindliness of soul be evident to all human beings. The
Lord is near! [6]Let no anxiety take root in your hearts, but let your
concerns in all things be known to God by sending your thankful
thoughts upwards in supplication and prayer. [7]And the peace of
God which transcends anything that the intellect can grasp will
keep safe your hearts and thoughts in the Being of Christ.

[8]And lastly, dear brothers, I say to you:

all that is true,
all that is worthy of reverence,
all that is good and holy,

all that is lovely to look at
and beautiful to hear,
all that has virtue
and all that deserves praise:

let these be the content of your thinking. [9]All that you have learned
from me and have had handed on to you, what you have heard
from me and seen in me – put all this into practice: then the God
of peace will be with you!

Thanks for the gift that was sent

[10]It is a great joy for me, living in the Lord, that you have begun
to be concerned about my needs again. Of course, you always
wanted to, but you had no opportunity. [11]I am not speaking about
this because I am in any kind of need. I have learned to be satisfied with whatever is available at any given time. [12]I know what
it is to be in need, but also what it is to have plenty.

In all and in everything I have walked my inner path,
well fed or hungry, in abundance or in want. [13]All this I can
do through him who lives as a power in me. [14]You did well to
let me feel the life of your community when I was in distress.
[15]You Philippians will recall that at that time, at the beginning
of my work for the Gospel when I moved on from Macedonia,
no congregation except yours supported me according to the
principle that one good gift deserves another. [16]Not just once,
but on two occasions did you send me what I needed while I
was in Thessalonica. [17]It is not that I am after gifts, but I am
looking out for the fruits which ripen due to my work; their
abundance is to your credit. [18]I lack everything, and yet I have
everything in abundance. My heart was full when Epaphroditus
brought me your gifts. Sweet fragrance rose from this
offering, an offering well-pleasing to God.

Concluding words

[19]May the God whom I serve grant you all your needs out of the
riches of HIS being. May HE give to you in the light of revelation

of Christ Jesus. [20]All revelation in all aeons is the due of God our
Father. Amen.

[21]Greet everyone who consecrates himself in Christ Jesus. The
brothers who are with me greet you; [22]so do all those here who
strive for holiness send greetings, especially those who are of
Caesar's household. [23]May the grace of Jesus Christ the Lord fill
your spirit.

The Letter of Paul to the Colossians

Introduction

Paul, an apostle of Christ Jesus through the divine guidance of
destiny, and Timothy our brother: 2to all the brothers in Colossae
who seek the salvation through Christ and are united with him
through faith:

Grace be with you and peace from God our Father.

Prayer of thanks

3At all times in our prayers we thank God, the Father of our Lord
Jesus Christ, for you; 4for we have heard of your *faith,* by which
you are united with the Being of Christ Jesus, of your *love* for
all who seek the salvation, 5inspired by the *hope* which has been
prepared for you in the heavenly spheres and which has been proclaimed to you in the word of truth, the Gospel 6which has come
to you. Just as it is growing and bearing fruit in the whole world,
so also among you, from the day you received the message, and
full understanding of the divine grace awoke in you. 7You were
taught it through Epaphras, our beloved companion in service,
who is a faithful servant of Christ for you. 8He has given us a clear
picture of your love in the Spirit.

Prayer for the congregation

9That is why we have not ceased praying and petitioning for you
since the day when we heard of you, that you may be filled with
insight into the divine will; may it live in you as wisdom and awareness of the spiritual relationships, 10so that you can shape your
lives to be worthy of Christ and pleasing to him, bearing fruit in
every good work, growing in awareness of God, 11empowered by

all the strength which flows in might from HIS light-glory. You are
to develop true patience and greatness of soul, thanking the Father
with joy [12]who makes you worthy to share the lot of the saints in
light. [13]HE has freed us from the might of darkness and translated
us into the realm of the Son who is the embodiment of HIS love,
[14]and through whom we attain redemption by becoming free of the
sickness of sin.

The cosmic dimension of Christ

[15]He is the visible image of the invisible God, the first-born of all
created beings; [16]for in him has come into existence everything
that is in the heavens and on the earth, the visible and the invisible world, the Thrones and the World Guides, the Archai and the
Creator Spirits. All things were created through him and for him.
[17]He was there before all else; everything coheres in him. [18]He
is the head of the body, and his body is the great community of
congregations. He is also the very beginning, the first-born among
those who rise from the dead; that he may be the One who goes
before in all things and everything. [19]For in him all the fullness of
God was pleased to dwell, [20]to transform and reconcile everything
to himself, and laying the foundations of peace through the blood
of his cross. Through him, all beings on the earth as well as in the
heavenly spheres are to attain their goal.

[21]You, too, were once alienated and hostile in your thinking,
caught up in deeds by which you served the powers of evil; [22]but
now he has penetrated you with the power of transformation, as
members of his body: through the death which he suffered in his
earthly body. You are to stand before his countenance, hallowed,
cleansed of impurity and guilt, [23]if only you do not let the power
of faith grow lame in you. Faith is the ground on which you stand;
it gives you inner certainty, so that you do not waver in your confidence in the future, through the Gospel which you have heard,
which is being proclaimed among all creatures under heaven, and
whose servant I, Paul, have become.

The mystery revealed: Christ in you
[24]In the midst of all suffering I rejoice because of you. Willingly
I take upon myself what still remains to be suffered to make up
the measure of the trials of Christ. In my body I will endure what
makes me into his body; for his body is the great congregation
[25]whose servant I have become. That is in accordance with God's
plan of salvation in which I am involved, so that I should bear the
essence of the divine Word into your midst, [26]the mystery which
has remained hidden for generations and aeons – now it is revealed
to his saints. [27]Now it is the will of God that they should become
aware what immeasurable fullness of revealing light for all peoples lies in this mystery: it is 'Christ in you,' the certain hope of
all future revelation. [28]He it is whom we proclaim; towards him
do we guide the heart and mind of each individual human being;
we teach the all-embracing wisdom to each individual, so that we
may lead him as a free human being to the stage where he becomes
consecrated in Christ. [29]All my efforts are for this purpose, it is
for this that I wrestle and fight, armed with his strength which is
powerfully at work in me.
2 I want you to know how great a battle I am fighting for you
and for the congregation in Laodicea, and also for all those who
do not yet know me by sight in earthly life. [2]Let their hearts
be comforted by this, that they become knit firmly together in
love, able to receive the overflowing riches of spiritual understanding and to have seeing awareness of the mystery of God,
that is: Christ. [3]In him are hidden all treasures of wisdom and
knowledge.

Warning against teachings which lead astray
[4]I say this, so that no one shall lead you astray with beguiling
words. [5]Though I am absent in body, yet I am in your midst in
spirit, seeing with joy the harmonious order of your community and
the powerful sphere of faith by which you are united with Christ.
[6]Since, then, Christ Jesus has become the guide of your souls, walk
your ways in his power, [7]be rooted in him, build up your being in

his Being, unshakable in the faith as you have been taught, richly
endowed through your life in the Eucharist.

[8]Take care that no one comes to ensnare you with philosoph-
ical cunning and empty deceits by invoking purely human traditions. That kind of thinking may reach as far as the elements of
external nature, but not to the world of Christ. [9]For in Christ the
whole fullness of the being of God lives and has taken on body.
[10]And now this fullness can also live in you through him who is
the head of all primal powers and creating spirits. [11]In him you
have received a circumcision which was not performed outwardly:
by being divested of the merely earthly bodily nature; that is the
circumcision of Christ. [12]With him you have also been laid in the
grave: through baptism. But with him you have also risen again:
through faith in the effective power of God who has raised him
from the dead. [13]He has awakened you, too, to life with him, in
that he in his mercy forgave you your strayings, dead though you
were as the result of your strayings, lost to the uncircumcision of
your earthly, physical body. [14]He has extinguished and suspended
the commandments and the violations which were written into the
book of the world and which were an accusation against us; they
no longer stand against us, barring us from the heavenly worlds.
He has nailed them to the cross. [15]By stripping the primal powers
and the creator-spirits of their might which had become darkened,
he made them emerge with power into the light and made them
subject to his triumphant revelation.

[16]Now no one shall sit in judgment on you any more, for instance
about eating and drinking or about the observance of a festival,
the new moon or the Sabbath. [17]For all these things are only the
shadow falling in advance of a future world, and their essential
substance is the body of Christ. [18]No one must cheat you of victory
by claiming to have converse with angels through self-denial and
ascetic practices, even if he can lay claim to having visions. That
is all mere empty boosting of soul powers which rise up out of the
physical body [19]and are not controlled by the head. Only through
the head is the whole body with its joints and limbs held together

like a choir by its choirmaster; through it alone can the growth
of its forces be divine growth. [20]If, with Christ, you have died
to the elements of the world, why do you still let yourselves be
compelled by commandments, like those whose life is bound up
with the world? Such rules as: [21]do not touch this; do not eat that;
avoid this! [22]only bind him who lives by them all the more to what
is transitory. It is here as with all merely human rules and pre-
cepts: [23]although claims are made that it is wisdom when arbitrary
spiritual paths are promoted, when penitential fervour is indulged
in and the body is maltreated, it is all without value in the end, and
only makes the importance of the physical body be overrated.

3 *The old and the new human being*
If, then, you have risen with Christ, direct your striving and your
longing upwards to where Christ wields at the right hand of God.
[2]Let the higher being fill your thoughts, not the earthly. [3]For you
have died, and your true life and being is united with Christ and hidden in the spiritual world. [4]But when Christ becomes apparent, who
bears our true being, then also your true being shall be revealed
with him in the light of the Spirit.

[5]Therefore let die that in the members of your being which is
earthly, such as

unchastity of body,
impurity of life,
uncontrolled feelings,
baseness of desires,
self-seeking in your personal lives.

[6]All this is service of demons which calls up divine wrath. [7]Once
your lives, too, were full of these failings and errors; they were a
way of life for you. [8]Now, however, you are to free yourselves
from all that:

from anger, through which you lose yourselves,
from passion which is not controlled from the centre of
your being,
from malice which falsifies your true being,

from misuse of the Word, which is the beginning of
demonic power,
from distortion of the world through the word of your
mouth.

[9]Let not lies hold sway among you. Lay aside the former human
being and his practices, [10]and put on the New Man who grows
with his renewed being into knowledge and insight according to
the image of the One who created him. [11]Here there are neither
Greeks nor Jews, neither circumcised nor uncircumcised, neither
barbarians nor Scythians, neither slaves nor free men: Christ is all,
and in all.

[12]As those who are chosen of God, consecrated and beloved,
clothe yourselves with the power

of heartfelt compassion,
with healing goodness,
with humility and selflessness,
with self-achieved harmony of soul,
with all-embracing greatness of heart.

Life in the congregations

[13]Bear with one another, and if one of you has a reproach to make
to another, let friendliness and reconciliation be your way. As the
Lord has forgiven you, so you, too, should forgive one another.
[14]And love is above everything, it is the bond of highest perfection
and consecration. [15]Let the peace of Christ be the prevailing power
in your hearts. It is the meaning and purpose of the divine calling
which makes you into members of one body. Cultivate a mood of
thankfulness as in the Eucharist. [16]The World-Word of Christ live
in you in its fullness. Educate and guide one another in all wisdom.
Learn to cultivate converse with God in your hearts with dignified
devoutness, by singing psalms, hymns and spiritual songs. [17]All that
you do, in word and in deed, do it in the sense and in the name of
Jesus the Lord, as if you were thereby bringing a thanks-offering
out of his power to the Father.

Ordering the house-community

18You women, follow the men, as is right in the community of the
Lord.

19You men, love the women and be not bitter towards them.

20You children, be obedient to your parents in all things, for this
is well-pleasing in the community of the Lord.

21You fathers, do not quarrel with your children so that they lose
heart.

22You servants, be obedient in all things to those who are your
earthly masters, not merely in appearance as do those who want
to please men, but out of a true heart and in reverence before the
highest Lord. 23Whatever you do, do it whole-heartedly, knowing
that thereby you serve the Lord and not men. 24You may be certain
that in return you will receive the inheritance of the Spirit from the
Lord. Serve Christ the Lord. 25Whoever does wrong will draw to
himself the wrong he has done. Before this law, all differences in
personal status become irrelevant.

You masters, give your servants what is their due in justice and
fairness. Be mindful that you also have a master, namely in heaven.

Call to prayer

2Cultivate your life of prayer with perseverance. Practise it in
wakefulness of spirit and in that mood of thankfulness which
grows out of the Eucharist; 3and pray also for us, that God may
open to us the door of the Word, that we may speak of the mystery
of Christ. This mystery is the reason for my chains: 4I am also to
make manifest in my life what I have to proclaim in words.

Attitude towards outsiders

5Let your attitude towards outsiders be governed by wisdom. Make
use of favourable times, always seizing the right moment. 6Let your
word be always gracious, seasoned with salt. Pay attention to the
ways in which you must answer each individual person.

News about Tychicus and Onesimus

7Tychicus will tell you all about my affairs; he is a beloved brother, a faithful worker and fellow servant in the power of the Lord. 8I have sent him to you for this reason, that you may have news of us and that he may comfort and encourage your hearts.
9I sent him with Onesimus, our faithful and beloved brother who comes from your congregation. They will give you all the news from here.

Greetings

10Greetings from Aristarchus, my fellow prisoner, and Mark, the nephew of Barnabas (about whom you have already received letters; when he comes to you, make him welcome), 11and Jesus, who is also called Justus, that is: Righteous. Among my fellow workers for the Kingdom of God, these are the only ones who are of the circumcision; they have strengthened my courage. 12Greetings also from Epaphras, the servant of Christ Jesus, who is of your congregation. At all times he wrestles in his prayers for you, that you may continue as consecrated souls, in all things moved by the will of God. 13I can testify for him that he takes many difficulties upon himself for your sakes and for the congregations in Laodicea and in Hierapolis. 14Greetings likewise from Luke the beloved physician, and from Demas.

15Greet the brothers in Laodicea, as well as Nympha and the congregation in her house. 16And when this letter has been read in your circle, see to it that it is also read in the congregation in Laodicea; and similarly you should read out among you the letter addressed to Laodicea. 17And say to Archippus: give heed to the office which you have to administer in the name of the Lord, that you fulfil it rightly!

18This is the greeting by my own hand, the hand of Paul. Remember my chains. Grace be with you!

The First Letter of Paul to the Thessalonians

Introduction and words of thanks

Paul, Silvanus and Timothy to the congregation of the Thessalonians, in the name of the Father and of Jesus Christ, the Lord:

Grace be with you and peace!

[2]Without ceasing we thank God for you all. We remember you
in our prayers. [3]Constantly, we bear in our consciousness

your faith, whose power is revealing itself,
your love, which strives untiringly,
your hope, which is proving itself in patience,

and by which you walk before God, filled with the power of Jesus Christ, the Lord.

The special position of the congregation in Thessalonica

[4]We know, you brothers beloved of God, that the will of God has
chosen you out of humanity, [5]for the Gospel which we proclaim
did not come to you only as a stream of words, but as a mighty
power, as an outpouring of Holy Spirit in overflowing fullness. You
know the events which overtook us in consequence of our working
among you and for you. [6]But you followed our example and that of
Christ himself. Although you were in great danger, you received
the Word with the enthusiastic joy which is the very nature of the
Holy Spirit. [7]And thus you, in turn, have become an example to
all the faithful in Macedonia and Achaia. [8]The sound and tone of
the Christ-Word has not only been transmitted from you throughout Macedonia and Achaia, but the fame of your faith, which keeps you in a living relationship to God, has spread everywhere;

nowhere do we need to say anything about it any more. 9People
of themselves tell us how readily we have been received by you,
and how you have turned away from the false gods towards the
true Godhead in order to serve the God of life and truth, 10aware
of HIS Son who came from the heavens and is coming. HE has
awakened the Son from the dead: Jesus, our saviour from the
coming storm of wrath.

2 *Remembering the apostle's work in Macedonia*
You yourselves know very well, dear brothers, what inner
acceptance we found among you straight away. What happened
there was not without higher power. 2After we had had to endure
much suffering and much arrogance in Philippi, as you know,
we were full of courageous confidence that we would be able to
proclaim the Gospel of God to you out of our enthusiasm for the
divine, in spite of all opposition. 3We have not been charged with
this out of some delusion or selfish striving by impure means.
4We have been entrusted with the proclamation of the Gospel
as men who have been tested by God, and we spread the Word
further, not for the sake of winning human approval but to strive
to please God who tests our hearts. 5We have not indulged in
flattering chatter, you know that. 6Nor have we tried to set ourselves up as something great; God vouches for that in us. We did
not look for praise from men, neither among you nor elsewhere.
For we could, of course, have invoked our authority as apostles
of Christ; 7but we were active among you in a quiet and inconspicuous way, like a nurse feeding her children. 8So, out of our
heart's joy in you, we want not only to bring you the Gospel as
God's gift but also our very selves; for you have become very
dear to us. 9Dear brothers, remember our toil and our weight of
work. Day and night we have worked so as not to be a burden
on any of you. Thus we have proclaimed the Gospel to you as
divine tidings. 10You are witnesses, and God HIMSELF can testify,
that we have behaved in a holy, just and pure way towards you
faithful. 11And we spoke as a father to his children – as you well

know – to encourage and strengthen each one of you. [12]By our
witnessing we have urged you to walk your ways so as to be worthy of God who calls you to HIS kingdom and to the revelation
of HIS light.

How the Gospel was received in the congregation
[13]And we also thank God without ceasing for this, that you did not
receive as human words the divine Word which it was granted us
to make heard, but as what it is in truth: the Word of God. Now it
works in you through the power of faith. [14]Dear brothers, by growing into the destiny of Christ Jesus you have become followers of
the congregations of God in Judea. For you have suffered from
your own kin what they have had to endure from the Jews [15]who
killed the Lord and the prophets; now they have persecuted us, too.
Their deeds are not pleasing to God, and indeed, they are enemies
of all human beings. [16]They are the ones who want to prevent us
from proclaiming the healing word to the peoples, and thus the
measure of their alienation from God grows ever greater. In the
end, the revealing storm of wrath comes upon them.

The apostle's visit thwarted
[17]But we, dear brothers, who have been orphaned from you for a
while (as regards seeing you face to face, not as regards the heart)
are all the more eager and full of longing to see you again, face
to face. We were getting ready to begin our journey. [18]I, Paul, was
preparing – not once, but twice – to come to you. Every time the
Adversary prevented it. [19]Where else would be our hope, our joy
and our crown of fame if it is not you – before the countenance of
Jesus our Lord, whose coming in the Spirit we await? [20]You are
the light of our glory and our joy.

3 *The sending out of Timothy*
Therefore, when we could not bear it any longer, we decided to
remain behind alone in Athens [2]and to send to you Timothy, the
servant of God in the proclamation of the tidings of Christ. He was

to give you strength and make firm the certainty of your heart
through the living word of the Spirit, [3]so that no one should begin
to waver because of the present afflictions. You yourselves know
that this is our task. [4]When we were with you, we foretold that
hard trials were before us; and so it has come to pass, as you know.
[5]That is the reason why I could not bear it any longer and sent
someone, so that I could make sure of your inner strength and that
the Tempter should not gain power over you by his wiles, thus
robbing our work of its fruits. [6]Now Timothy has returned to us
after being with you and has brought us good news of your faith
and of your love. He has reported that you bear us in your good
thoughts always, and that you long to see us again, just as we
long to see you. [7]And so, dear brothers, we are reassured in our
thoughts about you. The certainty of your faith raises us above all
our sufferings and afflictions. [8]We feel re-enlivened, knowing how
firmly you are rooted in the Being of Christ.

[9]Can we thank God enough for the joy and happiness which
has become ours through you, before the countenance of our
God? [10]Day and night we pray all the more earnestly that it may
be granted us to see you again, face to face, and by our work to
give you what is still lacking in your faith. [11]May God HIMSELF, our
Father, and Jesus, our Lord, guide our way to you.

[12]May the Lord fill your souls; may he make you rich to overflowing with love for one another and for all men, as we have love
for you, [13]so that your hearts may become strong, without flaw,
hallowed by the Spirit, before God our Father, in the light-glory
of the coming of Jesus our Lord in the midst of those who devote
themselves to him.

4 *Encouragement to strive on the right way*

Dear brothers, there is still this to say: we ask you and urge you in
the name of Jesus the Lord that you continue to strive onward on
the way, following the directions you have been given by us. Guide
your lives in such a way – and you are already doing this – that
you win ever greater inner wealth by pleasing God. [2]You know the

tasks which we have given you in our commission by the Lord
Jesus. [3]If you intend to strive for holiness as the divine will would
have it, then keep your souls free from all things indecent. [4]Each
one of you knows how he can work to form his body and soul into
a garment which is hallowed by the Spirit and shines with true
dignity. [5]Do not lose yourselves in wishes and passionate desires
like the heathen peoples who know nothing of God. [6]Nor should
anyone strive to outdo or cheat his brother in the external affairs
of life. In all these things, the Lord will cause justice to be done,
as we have always told you and shown you. [7]For God has not
called us to live as impure beings, but to be filled with Spirit and
holiness. [8]Whoever inwardly rejects this, does not reject a human
being but God HIMSELF who, out of HIS grace, has poured HIS Holy
Spirit into your being.

[9]Concerning brotherly love, you need no instruction from me.
God himself teaches you to love one another. [10]And you take this
further to all the brothers in the whole of Macedonia.

We cannot urge you enough, dear brothers, to strive for ever
greater inner wealth. [11]Learn to value it, and strive hard to become
inwardly still, and thus carry out your individual tasks, right into
the outer work you do with your hands, as we recommended to
you. [12]That will also give you the right bearing towards those who
do not belong to the congregation, and it makes you independent
of everyone.

Those who have died, and the coming of Christ

[13]Dear brothers, we will not leave you in ignorance about those
who have fallen asleep, so that you are not overshadowed by sadness like those for whom the future is not brightened by hope.
[14]As certainly as our hearts know through faith that Jesus broke
through death to resurrection, as certain may we be that the divine
Ground of the World will lead those who have fallen asleep, united
with Christ, towards the same goal through him. [15]We say this to
you with a word of the Lord himself: we who are living, being
saved for the new revelation of the coming of Christ, will have no

precedence over those who have fallen asleep. [16]For he himself, the
Lord, will descend from the sphere of the heavens when the signal
sounds forth in the thundering call of the archangel, in the sound
of the trumpet of God. Then, as the first, those who have died
united with Christ, will experience the resurrection; [17]after them,
we living ones who have been kept till now. Our souls, united
with the souls of the dead, will be lifted up as if on clouds to meet
Christ in an airy realm of soul. Thus we shall be inseparably united
with him, the Risen One. [18]Give one another courage and strength
with such words and thoughts.

5 Concerning time-spans and right moments, dear brothers, you
have no need for me to write to you. [2]You yourselves know well
that the Day of Christ comes like a thief in the night. [3]When people say, 'Now there is peace, and everything is safe and secure,'
then suddenly the catastrophe comes upon them like the birth-
pangs upon a woman with child, and there will be no escape
for them.

[4]But you, dear brothers, are not to remain in the darkness, so
that the breaking of the Day will not surprise you like a thief. [5]For
you all are sons of the light and sons of the day. Our being is not
filled with night and darkness. [6]Therefore, let us not sleep as the
others do, but cultivate an alert and sober state of mind. [7]Those
who sleep, sleep at night, and those who are drunk are also drunk at
night. [8]But, since we belong to the brightness of the day, let us be
sober, putting on the breastplate of faith and love, the head armed
with the helmet of hope of salvation. [9]For God has not destined
us to be victims of the great wrath. HE wills it that we make ourselves sharers in the salvation which has been achieved through
Jesus Christ, our Lord. [10]He died for us, so that we, whether we are
now awake or asleep, may find true life through union with him.
[11]Therefore speak words of comfort and strength to one another;
give one another upbuilding strength, from one person to another,
as indeed you are doing already.

Conduct within the congregation

12We ask you, dear brothers, to show understanding towards those
who work among you, those who are your leaders in the name
of Christ and who guide your hearts and minds. 13For the sake of
their work, let them experience your special loving regard. Within
yourselves, nourish peace. 14And we admonish you, dear brothers,
to guide the minds and hearts of those who are unable to bring
order into their inner being; strengthen the faint-hearted; support
those who are ill; embrace all human beings with your great-heartedness. 15Take care that no one repays evil with evil; rather,
always strive to do good to one another, both within your own
circle and towards all other people.

16Have joy within yourselves always.
17Do not neglect your practice of prayer.
18In all things, cultivate the sacramental mood of thanksgiving.
Then God's will shall work in your will through the
power of Christ.
19Let not the flame of the Spirit be quenched.
20Do not let the power of prophecy wither away for
lack of care and practice.
21Test everything, hold fast what is good.
22Keep clear of the evil, in whatever form it appears.

Words of blessing and greeting

23May God HIMSELF, the source of all peace, hallow your whole
being. May your complete and undivided being, your spirit, your
soul and your body remain, unpolluted and pure, at the coming in
the Spirit of Jesus Christ, our Lord. 24You can trust him who calls
you; he will also act.

25Pray for us, dear brothers. 26Greet all the brothers with the holy
kiss. 27I lay it upon your hearts in the name of the Lord, that this
letter be read to all the brothers.

28The grace of Jesus Christ, our Lord, be with you!

The Second Letter of Paul to the Thessalonians

1 *Introduction and words of thanks*

Paul, Silvanus and Timothy to the congregation of the Thessalonians, in the name of our divine Father and of Jesus Christ, the Lord:

[2]Grace and peace be with you from God the Father and from Jesus Christ, the Lord.

[3]We owe constant thanks to the divine world for you, dear brothers – that is both right and good – because your faith grows so wonderfully, and the love you bear for one another grows stronger all the time. [4]Because of you, we can stand, crowned with fame, in the congregations of God: because of your long-suffering patience and strong faith which enables you to stand firm in the persecutions and afflictions you have to endure. [5]You are living proof that the crisis which God has imposed leads to the Good. You are to become worthy of the Kingdom of God for which you are suffering now. [6]It is quite certainly in the spirit of the divine justice that those who now oppress you, in due course themselves will suffer oppression through the compensation of destiny; [7]you who are being oppressed, however, will experience re-enlivening.

The renewed coming of Christ

All this is fulfilled through the revealing appearing of Jesus, the Lord, out of the spheres of the heavens where he is seen in the midst of the angels of power. With flames of fire [8]he causes a stern judgment to come upon those who refuse to know anything about the divine and who shut off their soul-hearing from the Gospel of

Jesus, our Lord. 9When the countenance of the Lord appears in
very essence, and the light-revelation of his sun-power dawns,
then they will experience this as a decline and a punishment. 10In
those, however, who have devoted themselves to him, his coming
will engender the light of seeing, and those who unite with him in
faith will, full of wonder, perceive and recognize his Being. We
entrust this our testimony to you; when the great dawning of the
Day comes, it will be proved in you.

11That is the aim of our unceasing prayer for you: that the
Godhead, who reigns over us, will make you worthy of HIS enduring
call upon you, and that HE will fulfil all HIS will for good towards
you, as well as making your faith effective and blessed with power;
12so that the name and the Being of Jesus, our Lord, may shine in
your being, and that your being shine in him. Thus it is willed by
the grace of our divine Father and Jesus Christ, the Lord.

2 *The coming of Christ and the approach of the Adversary*
Bearing in mind the spiritual coming of our Lord Jesus Christ,
and the inner composure which we need for it, we ask you, dear
brothers: 2do not let yourselves be shaken so quickly in your conviction, nor let your souls be led astray, neither by a spirit-ap-
pearance nor by a word or a letter which purports to be from us:
as though the dawning of the Christ-Day were imminent. 3Let no
one deceive you, however he may try.

For first there must come the great breach of faith, the separation from the world of Spirit; the man of chaos must be revealed,
the son of perdition, 4the spirit of opposition who considers himself exalted over everything that is called divine and deserves
reverence, and who ultimately puts himself in place of God in the
temple of God and poses as a god. 5Do you not remember that
I told you this repeatedly when I was still with you? 6Then you
also know that a power still restrains him, until, when his time has
come, he will appear openly. 7The mysteries of chaos are already
working. If there were not a power which still restrains them, they
would even now break out from the centre. 8In time, the magical

destroyer will be revealed without disguise. But Jesus the Lord will sweep him aside with the breath of his mouth and destroy him by his coming in the Spirit; [9]him, the destroyer, whose appearing is instigated by the satanic powers with boundless violence and with deceiving signs and wonders. [10]Those who have given themselves over to the abyss will be exposed to every kind of temptation to evil, because they have not taken into themselves the love for the truth by which they could have found salvation. [11]God HIMSELF sends them the active power of error, so that, in the end, they even believe the lie. [12]Thus, all must be judged who do not give over their hearts to truth but allow themselves to be spellbound by the revelation of the evil.

[13]We, however, owe God continued thanks for you, dear brothers, who are beloved of the Lord. From the first beginnings God implanted the direction towards healing into your being by hallowing through the Spirit and by trust in the truth. [14]To this end HE has also called you through our proclamation. Now you can make the light-form of our Lord Jesus Christ your own. [15]Therefore, dear brothers, stand firm and remain faithful to the traditions which you have been taught, whether by word of mouth or by our letter. [16]And he himself, Jesus Christ, our Lord, and God, our Father who loves us and gives us comforting strength for all coming times by bringing hope for the Good to life in us by HIS grace: [17]may HE give comfort and strength to your hearts for every good deed and word.

3 *Request for the prayer of the congregation*
There is still this to say: pray for us, dear brothers, so that the word of the Lord may take its course and everywhere unfold the same power of light as it did among you. [2]Pray, too, that we may be delivered out of the hands of men who have no inner strength and therefore become instruments of the evil; for the faith is not something for just everyone! [3]The Lord is faithful; he will strengthen you and protect you from the evil. [4]With his power in our souls we have confidence in you that – now, and in the future – you will turn what we proclaim to you into deeds. [5]May the Lord

direct your hearts to the love of God and the supportive patience
of the Christ.

Keeping one's distance from dissolute people

[6]Dear brothers, we have to instruct you in the name of Jesus Christ,
the Lord, that you should distance yourselves from all those brothers who are without order in their lives and who do not live in
accordance with the traditions which you have received from us.
[7]You yourselves know that the right thing for you is to walk the
path which we also walk. When we were among you, we did not
stray from the spiritual order of things [8]and did not eat anyone's
bread for nothing; rather, we worked day and night under great
difficulties in order not to be a burden to any of you. [9]It is not as
if we did not have the freedom and right to it, but we wanted to
be an example to you which you can follow. [10]When we were with
you we said to you: whoever is not willing to work should also
not eat. [11]Now we hear that some of you live without order, do not
work and loaf about. [12]To them we have to say, and to give this
directive in the name of Jesus Christ, the Lord, that they should
work and eat their bread with inner calm and composure. [13]But
you, dear brothers, do not tire of serving the Good. [14]If anyone
closes his ears to the word we speak to you in this letter, take note
of him, but be reticent in his company so that you do not become
drawn in; for he has to come to insight. [15]Do not treat him as an
enemy, but correct him as a brother.

Words of blessing and greeting

[16]But may he, the Lord of peace, give you the peace for all of your
being and for everything in your life. The Lord be with you all.
[17]This is my greeting which I, Paul, write with my own hand. It is
the sign in every letter. Thus I write. [18]The grace of our Lord Jesus
Christ be with you all!

The First Letter of Paul to Timothy

1 *Introduction*
Paul, an apostle of Christ Jesus in accordance with the commis-
sion from God who gives us the salvation, and from Christ Jesus
who is our hope: 2to Timothy, a true child of the faith:
May grace, merciful goodness and the peace be with you from
God the Father and from Jesus Christ, our Lord.

Defending the teaching against distortions
3I have a task for you again, as I did when I was going to Macedonia
and asked you to remain in Ephesus. You must point out to certain
persons that they are about to distort our teachings. 4They occupy
themselves with mythological ideas and endless deductions from
genealogies which only lead to ever new problems, instead of
making clearer the divine plan and guidance of destiny which
works where the faith is alive. 5The aim of our proclamation is the
love which springs from a pure heart, a good conscience and from
genuine faith. 6Now some have strayed from this and have ended
up with empty words. 7They want to be teachers of the Law, but
they neither understand what they themselves are saying, nor the
things about which they make assertions.
8We do not underestimate the value of the Law, when it is rightly
applied. 9Only, one must also know that the Law does not exist for
those in whom the Good is alive. It was given for those in whose
souls there is no order and no will to order; it is for those who are
alienated from the divine and are under the spell of sin, who have
fallen from holy heights into unholy depths; those who profane
both the maternal and paternal principles in the world, who force
the masculine element into death and misuse the feminine, 10those

who pollute and falsify the nature of the youthful human being,
and of the human being altogether; who pervert the truth into a
lie and commit perjury. [11]To that belongs everything which is in
opposition to the soul-healing power of the teaching of the Gospel
which has been entrusted to me by the light-revelation of the divine
world which ensouls and blesses.

Words of thanks and the summons to fight in the spirit

[12]Full of thanks, my soul rises up to him who lives in me as a
power, to the Christ Jesus, our Lord. He has so much trust in me
that he has appointed me to his priestly service, [13]although I once
was a cursing and fanatical persecutor. In spite of everything, forgiving goodness has come towards me; for what I did before faith
lived in me, that I did out of ignorance. [14]But when I came to the
faith and experienced the love which proceeds from life in Christ
Jesus, then it was granted me to feel in superabundance the touch
of the grace of him who is our Lord.

[15]Now I speak a word to you which is sure and which everyone
should take into their innermost being: Christ Jesus came into the
world to heal those who suffer from the sickness of sin. I am first
and foremost of all in being enmeshed in sin. [16]But because of that,
the merciful love of God was shown me, so that the whole greatness of soul of Jesus Christ was revealed to me, as the first. This
was so that an example, an archetypal image, might be created for
all who unite with him in faith and thereby become sharers of the
eternal life. [17]To HIM, the king of the aeons, in whom there is no
death, who is exalted above all sense-perception, the One Being
of God: to HIM belong all dignity of soul and all light of Spirit
through all cycles of time to come. Amen.

[18]This message I lay upon your heart, you my child Timothy. It
is in accord with the prophetic indications which you have already
received. Out of the power of these words of the Spirit, be a true
fighter in the war of the Spirit. [19]Foster the faith and a good conscience within you. Some have scorned their conscience and have
suffered shipwreck in their faith; [20]among these are Hymenaeus

and Alexander, whom I had to abandon to the Adversary, so that they might profit from experience and learn not to scorn what is holy.

2 *Summons to earnest prayer*

The most important thing I have to urge you to practise is prayer: supplication, intercession and thanks-offerings; and these are for all human beings, [2]including kings and all who are in positions of authority. Only in this way can we fulfil our life's task with surety and harmony, sustained by devoutness and dignity. [3]And we can know ourselves to be accepted and confirmed before the countenance of that divine Being from whom we receive salvation, [4]and who desires to heal all human beings and lead them to full recognition of the truth. [5]For there is only one God for all men, and there is only one mediator between the divine world and the human world: the man Jesus Christ [6]who offers himself as a ransom for all human beings. Always, when the times need it, he is the proof of the Spirit. [7]I have been appointed as his herald and apostle – what I say is the truth and no deception – I am to be a teacher of the heathen peoples out of the power of faith, in the light of the truth.

Particular tasks for man and woman

[8]What I want to achieve is that everywhere the masculine element in human beings should learn to pray, lifting up holy hands, free from the blind tempest of the will and from unrest in thinking. [9]And the feminine, too, should strive towards its aim: let it clothe itself with a garment of inner beauty; let it be adorned with devout reticence and inner calm, not with costly braids and gold and rich dress. [10]As a promise for the future, the feminine being has been given a special aptitude for devotion, and therefore it is particularly fitting that she should do good deeds. [11]The feminine being should be a disciple of the Spirit with great inner stillness and openness. [12]That she should work as a teacher of the Spirit, I do not consider right. She should not claim authority as a leader over the masculine

being, but should be fulfilled in silence of soul. [13]For Adam was the first to receive his earthly form, and only afterwards Eve. [14]And it was not Adam who fell for the Tempter: the feminine being let itself be deceived and fell. [15]Through her ability to give birth, however, she can win her original being again, only she must have her foundation in the faith and in love, and must strive for holiness with a calm soul.

Congregation-leaders and congregation-helpers

Now another word about fundamentals: whoever aspires to the office of congregation-leader desires a noble task. [2]The leader of a congregation must give no cause for reproach. His soul must have reached complete unity between what is masculine and what is feminine. He must cultivate a sober consciousness with inner calm and dignity. He must always be open to other human beings and be ready to guide them on the path of the teachings. [3]Everything tempestuous, and all actions out of impulses of anger be far from him. With mildness and goodness let him avoid all quarrelling and let him not think about personal advantage. [4]In his own house let him prove his ability to create social order, let him guide his children to be good-natured and capable of reverence. [5]For if he is not able to lead his own household, how will he be able to lead with care and wisdom in the congregation of God? [6]He must not be a beginner on the inner paths, otherwise he may easily fall prey to arrogance and thus to the influence of the demonic powers. [7]Moreover, he must also be well thought of by outsiders; otherwise he will be beset by reproach and shame and be caught in the snare of the Adversary.

[8]The congregation-helpers, too, must be honourable people, not two-faced, free of tempestuous desires and evil avarice. [9]They must cultivate the mystery of the faith with purified consciousness. [10]They should be submitted to a test first; only when they have proved themselves reliable should they be allowed to do their service. [11]The women among them, too, must be venerable personalities, they must not be susceptible to demonic influence; they must

be of wakeful consciousness and dependable in all things. [12]As
regards the relationship between male and female, the congregation-helpers, too, must have reached harmony in their souls and
remain so. Let them be good educators of the children; above
all, they must prove themselves in their own house-community.
[13]Whoever has fulfilled his task as helper in the right way will also
rise to a higher stage in his personal life, namely to the freedom
and authority which he derives from his union in faith with Christ
Jesus.

The mystery of the way of God

[14]I write all this to you, hoping to be able to come to you soon. [15]If I
am delayed, however, you will know how you are to be at work in
the house of God. This house is the congregation of the life-bearing and life-giving Godhead, the corner-stone and foundation
of the truth.

[16]We confess to the great mystery of the way of God:
In the earthly body has he revealed himself
who is the bearer and bringer of true being through the
power of his Spirit.
The angels saw him in his full being,
but the peoples of the earth heard his message.
He found firm ground in the hearts of men,
he rose up in the light of revelation.

4 *The teachings of deceitful spirits*

There is a clear word, spoken by the Spirit himself. It says that
in the end-times there will be some who will refuse the power of
the faith and cling to deceitful spirits and heed the instructions of
demonic powers. [2]They fall for the deceits of liars with burnt-out
consciences: [3]they want to kill off sexuality and abstain from the
enjoyment of food. And yet, the Godhead has created all this, so
that it may be received with holy feelings of gratitude by human
beings who live in faith and in awareness of the truth. [4]Everything
created by God is good, and nothing can be reprehensible that is

received with gratitude and blessing. 5It is made holy by the divine Word which lives in it, and by the word of prayer that is spoken over it.

Hints for the work in the congregation

6If you lay this upon the hearts of the brothers, you will be a good servant of Christ Jesus. Let only the words of the faith and the good teachings which you follow be the nourishment of your soul. 7Do not hold on to obsolete and inane mythological images. Train yourself in the right kind of devoutness. 8The value you gain from training in bodily ability is slight, but training in devotion really does lead you to the aim, for it has been given the promise of true life, both present and future. 9Our soul can build on this word. Everyone ought to take it into his innermost being: 10all our struggle and striving is meaningful because of our certain hope in God, the life-giver, the bringer of healing to all human beings, above all to those in whom the faith is alive. 11This shall be your message and your teaching.

12No one should despise you because of your youth. Just see that you are always an example to those in whom the faith lives: in your working with the Word, in the conduct of your life, in love, in faith and in purity. 13Until I come, devote yourself to the reading of the Word, to spiritual instruction and to the proclamation of the teaching. 14Do not neglect the spiritual gift which has come alive in your soul through the words, pointing to the future, and the laying on of hands of those who lead as priests. 15Devote yourself to these things, live in them. The progress you make on this path is to be clear to everyone. 16Take heed to yourself and to the teaching. Inwardly, unite yourself completely with it. If you do that, you call in healing powers for yourself and for those who hear your word.

5 *Various groups in the congregation*

Do not speak to an older man in a reproachful manner, but speak to him as you would to a father. To the younger men speak as to brothers, [2]to older women as to mothers and to the younger as to sisters. Always speak out of a pure soul.

[3]Show respect to those who bear the dignity of widowhood with real justification. [4]If a widow has children or grandchildren with her, she should be concerned, above all, to make her own house a place where devotion is nurtured; for thereby she will also do justice to the parents of the children. Where things are like this, the eye of God can look with pleasure.

[5]A rightful bearer of the dignity of widowhood experiences the blessing of being alone when she lives in constant hopeful openness towards the divine world. Neither by night nor by day does she leave the realm of prayer and worship. [6]But she who gives herself up to a life of luxury is already dead, although she is still living. [7]If you tell them that, you protect them from straying. [8]If someone does not look after those who belong to him, especially if they are members of his house-community, then his faith has proved worthless. He is worth less than an unbeliever.

[9]The dignity of widowhood can be awarded to a woman when she is not less than sixty years of age. She must only have been the wife of one man [10]and must have proved herself in doing good. By this is meant that she has brought up children, has shown hospitality, has washed the feet of her fellow Christians, has given help to afflicted souls and altogether has worked on the path of all good works. [11]Do not admit younger widows. For if they let themselves go in the feelings they have towards Christ, they easily develop a desire for physical marriage also. [12]Then they have spoken the verdict about themselves, in that they have made invalid the faith that was beginning to grow in their heart. [13]To begin with, they become indolent in their inner striving, then they begin to gad about restlessly from house to house, and ultimately do nothing but gossip and pry and offend against all decent behaviour with what they say. [14]I consider it better that the younger women should marry, bear children and manage their household. Then they give the Adversary no occasion for slander. [15]Some have already strayed onto the ways of Satan. [16]Let the women who belong to the congre-

gation look after the widows in the vicinity, so that they are not a
burden on the congregation. The congregation must be responsible
for those who genuinely bear the dignity of widowhood.

17The elders who have proved themselves to be good leaders
should be considered worthy of double deference, especially those
who work through proclamation of the Word and the teachings.
18As the scripture says:

> You shall not muzzle the ox when it is treading out the
> grain,

and:

> Whoever works is worthy of his wages.

19If complaints are made against an elder, you should only accept
them in the presence of two or three witnesses. 20Make those who
really are at fault give account of themselves before everyone,
so that the others also get a feeling for the wrong that has been
done.

21Solemnly I ask you, before the countenance of God, before
the Christ Jesus and his angels, to follow these rules without prej-
udice, and not to let yourself be guided in your actions by your
personal inclinations. 22Do not be too hasty in dispensing the ordination to someone by the laying on of hands. Also, do not burden
yourself with other people's failings. Keep your being pure. 23Do
not always drink water only, rather take a little wine; it is good
for your stomach, and will help you to overcome the ailment that
troubles you frequently.

24Some people's transgressions lead to obvious consequences of
destiny, straight away; others are only affected later. 25In the same
way, the consequences of good deeds will become obvious, and
where they are not apparent, they can still not remain hidden in the
long run.

6 All who live under the yoke of slavery should show their masters due respect, so that no shadow may fall on the divine name
and the path of the teachings. 2Those whose masters are Christians
should not respect them less highly on the grounds that they are also
brothers, but rather they should serve them all the more willingly,

for they share in the faith and the community of love which sustains their actions. Let this be your teaching and advice.

The dangers of self-importance and greed for money
[3]Whoever follows another teaching and does not abide in the soul-healing words of Jesus Christ, our Lord, or in the teachings which are in accordance with true devoutness, [4]he is blinded by his own sense of superiority, and his heart and mind are closed. Such people have a morbid tendency to hair-splitting and arguing; nothing comes of it except envy and cantankerousness, hate and evil suspicions, [5]an ongoing quarrelling of people whose senses are confused and who have distorted the truth, thinking that devoutness is a means of commerce. [6]Certainly, devoutness gains us much, in so far as it is combined with self-sufficiency and modesty. [7]We have brought nothing into the earthly world, and neither can we take anything out of it. [8]If we have food and clothing, we can be satisfied with that.

[9]Those who yearn for riches fall into temptation, and the snare closes about them. They lose themselves in all kinds of senseless wishes which sneak in unnoticed. These throw men into destruction and ruin. [10]The root of all evils is greed for money. How many have already strayed from the path of the faith by succumbing to it, and thus have fallen into great unhappiness and suffering!

Final admonition to Timothy
[11]You, who are a man of God: avoid this danger. Strive onwards on the path that leads to righteousness, to devoutness, to faith, to love, to patience and the strength to bear suffering. [12]Be a true fighter in the good battle of the faith, take hold of the power of eternal life. To that you have been called, and to that you have confessed with a full heart before many witnesses. [13]Before the countenance of God who leads all beings into life, and before the countenance of Christ Jesus who put the seal on the good confession before Pontius Pilate by giving himself, [14]I urge you: cherish your spiritual task; let it not be darkened, and do not expose it to any reproach

until the gracious appearing of Jesus Christ, our Lord. [15]This
appearing will be opened for our seeing souls when the time for
it has come, through HIM who fills the universe, the one and only
Sovereign, the King of all kings, the Lord of all lords. [16]To HIM
who alone has deathless life, who dwells in a light to which no
path leads; whom no man has seen nor can see: to HIM all honour
is due, to HIM belongs all eternal might. Amen.

[17]To those who are rich in the sense of this present cycle of
time give this directive: they should not be proud of it, and should
not rely upon uncertain riches, but rather on God who gives us
everything we need in rich abundance. [18]They should be active in
a meaningful way, and should seek their wealth in doing good, in
giving generously and bringing about the wonder of community.
[19]Thus, they will lay up for themselves a treasure which will be
a firm foundation for them for all future time. On this path they
should strive after the true life.

Closing words

[20]Dear Timothy, guard the gift that has been entrusted to you. Turn
away from all inane and empty speech and from the objections
from the kind of knowledge which, in reality, is no knowledge
[21]and which is being propagated by some who have strayed from
the path of the faith.

The grace be with you!

The Second Letter of Paul to Timothy

1 *Introduction and words of thanks*
Paul, by divine guidance of destiny an apostle of Christ Jesus,
appointed to proclaim the promise of the higher life which is given
us through Christ Jesus: [2]to Timothy, his beloved child:
Grace, mercy and peace be with you from God the Father and
from Christ Jesus, our Lord. [3]Full of thanks my soul lifts itself to
God, whom I serve from my forefathers with clear consciousness,
when I can include you in my prayers night and day and constantly
bear you in mind. [4]I long to see you, remembering your tears.
How full of joy I should be [5]if I could renew my certainty of the
unfeigned faith which already then lived in your grandmother Lois
and your mother Eunice and, I am sure, also fills your heart.

Exhortation to persevere
[6]Therefore I would remind you to rekindle, ever and again, the
fire of awakened spiritual power which you received by my laying
on of hands. [7]For God has not given us a spirit of timidity, but a
spirit of power, of love and wise conduct of life. [8]You must not
be ashamed of the martyrdom of our Lord, nor of mine who serve
him in chains. You, too, take on yourself the suffering that the
service of the Gospel brings with it. By doing this, you will find
in yourself the moving power of God [9]who gives us the salvation
and calls us to a sacred destiny. This destiny is not the result of
our works; it proceeds from the creative purpose of God HIMSELF
and from HIS gracious will which HE turned towards us before all
times in Christ Jesus. [10]But now it has become manifest in the merciful appearing of Christ Jesus, the bringer of our healing. He has
destroyed the might of death and has lit the light of the true, death-

less life through the Gospel [11]whose herald, apostle and teacher I have been appointed to be. [12]For the sake of this task I take on myself all sufferings and am not ashamed of them. I know who it is with whom I unite myself in faith, and so I know also that he gives the strength to carry through what has been laid upon me until the breaking of the new Day. [13]Take what you have heard from me as an example for how you may work with the soul-healing Word, out of the power of faith and out of love for Christ Jesus. [14]Nurture and enliven the good treasure which has been given to you by the power of the Holy Spirit who dwells within our souls.

[15]You know that in Asia everyone turned away from me, and among them Phygelus and Hermogenes. [16]But may the Lord turn towards the household of Onesiphorus with mercy, for often he has refreshed my soul and was not ashamed of my chains. [17]When he came to Rome, he searched for me at once until he found me. [18]May the Lord grant that he will find the merciful love of the Lord at the breaking of the new Day. And how many services he rendered us in Ephesus, you yourself know better than anyone.

Summons to be prepared to suffer like Christ

You, who are my child, take strength from the spiritual grace which you have received through Christ Jesus. [2]What you have heard from me through many witnesses, pass it on to such people as we can trust and who are able to teach others. [3]As a good fighter for Christ Jesus, take on yourself the sufferings on the way of Christ. [4]No one who is engaged in fighting can concern himself with the small affairs of everyday life; he is concerned to fulfil the expectations of his leader. [5]And no one who is taking part in a contest can win the wreath if he does not fulfil the conditions of the contest. [6]However, the farmer who has done his work is the first to receive a share of the fruits of the field. [7]Take my words into your thoughts. The Lord will open the meaning of everything to you.

[8]Bear in your consciousness Jesus Christ, the Risen One, who descended from David, as you know him from the Gospel I have proclaimed. [9]Out of his power I take all sufferings upon myself,

including the chains I am wearing as though I were a criminal. But
the divine Word cannot be fettered. [10]And so I endure everything
with patience, that those who are ripening towards being chosen by
God may attain the healing which lives in Christ with eternal light
of revelation.

[11]Our soul can build on this word: if we die with his death, we
shall also live with his life. [12]And when our endurance is proved,
we shall also win a share in his spiritual kingdom; but if we close
ourselves to him, he will also close himself to us. [13]If we do not
find the faith, he still is and remains the source of all faith; for he
cannot be untrue to his own being.

Warnings against untruth, discussion and dispute

[14]Impress this indelibly on everyone's consciousness, and implore
them before the countenance of God not to engage in disputes about
words which lead to nothing but inner conflicts in the hearers.
[15]With all your enthusiasm strive to be able to stand before God as
one who has been proved; as one who need not be ashamed of his
work and who knows how to dispense rightly the spiritual word that
proclaims the truth. [16]Avoid all empty phraseology, all inane word
content. Those who use such language will only become ever more
alienated from God; [17]their word poisons the surroundings like a
cancer-growth. Among them are Hymenaeus and Philetus [18]who
have strayed from the path of truth. They say that the resurrection
is completed already, and so they bring some away from the faith.
[19]But God's foundation stands firm, and this is its seal:

> The Lord knows his own.

And:

> Whoever rightly names the name of the Lord, let
> him leave the false trails of the world of appearances
> behind him.

[20]In a great house there are not only vessels of gold and silver,
but also of wood and clay, some for noble and some for common
purposes. [21]Now, whoever purifies himself from every aberration,
he makes himself into a noble vessel, one that is consecrated and

can give useful service to the lord of the house, well made for every good work.

22Keep yourself free from the life of desires which stirs in Man as long as he is still immature. Strive ahead on the path to righteousness, to faith, to love and to peace, in company with all those who call on the Lord out of a pure heart. 23Avoid foolish and unskilled arguments; you know that they only lead to quarrels and strife. 24A servant of the Lord is not there to quarrel. He should be open to all human beings, be able to lead them spiritually, bear evil with goodness. 25By his own inner harmony he should lead those who resist, so that perhaps God yet may cause a change in their hearts and minds and they may come to know the truth, 26and awaken from their numbness in the snare of the Adversary in which they had been caught to do his will.

The strayings of human beings in coming times

Know this: there are bad times to come for the end-days of the present cycle of time. 2Men will be infatuated with themselves, greedy for belongings, arrogant in word, arrogant in attitude, ruthless in negation, disobedient to their parents, ungrateful, profaning everything, 3without love, implacable, possessed by demons, without self-control, unrestrained, without love for the Good, 4treacherous, wanton, darkened, more devoted to their base desires than to the divine. 5They know how to feign devotion, but they deny the inner strength of piety. Be on your guard against these dangers. 6Among these people there will also be some who desire to use their will to force themselves on other human beings and to coerce and spellbind their unconscious soul-life. 7Their victims, full of impure desires, begin to roam about without inner control, addicted to the most varied cravings. Although they have various experiences in that way, they actually become ever less able really to perceive the truth. 8Just as Jannes and Jambres opposed the will of Moses, so these people oppose the truth. They are men of corrupt mind, unable to develop the strength of faith. 9They

will not get far; for in the end their spiritual incompetence will
be apparent to everyone, as was that of those opponents of Moses.
[10]You have followed after me on the path of the teaching, in
the schooling of soul, in the inner aims, in the faith, in the striving
for greatness of heart, in love, in patience, [11]in all persecutions
and sufferings, in everything which I had to endure in Antioch, in
Iconium and in Lystra. What trials I had to withstand! Out of all
dangers the Lord saved me. [12]All who choose to form their lives
in Christ Jesus out of devotion will have to suffer persecution.
[13]The people who have given themselves over to the evil, and use
magical powers to that end, will become worse and worse. They
are, at one and the same time, deceivers and deceived.

Summons to persevere with the message

[14]But you – cultivate faithfully what you have learnt and what
has become certainty for you. You know who your teachers were.
[15]And since you have been familiar with the holy scriptures since
you were a child, they can continue to be sources of wisdom for
you and lead you to the salvation, you who are united in faith with
Christ Jesus. [16]Every scripture which is inspired by the Spirit of
God is productive for the teachings, for self-examination, for finding the inner direction, for the education of the soul to righteousness, [17]that the man of God may acquire his true dignity and be
equipped for every good work.

4 Before the countenance of God and before Christ Jesus I bear
witness to the One who is to come as the lord of destiny for the
living and the dead, and to his gracious appearing and the rising
of his kingdom: [2]be a herald of the divine Word, be committed to
it whether the times are favourable or not, lead souls to the test,
point out errors, give comfort of spirit. Do all this with greatness
of heart, as a good teacher. [3]A time will come when men will
have no sense for the power of the teaching to heal souls. They
will not be able to bear it and, driven by their personal cravings,
they will run from one teacher to another for ever new sensa-
tions. [4]Their hearts and minds will move further and further from

the truth; they will be drawn by all kinds of obsolete, traditional imagery.

[5]But you – cultivate a sober consciousness in all things, take difficulties upon yourself willingly, work as you must work as a proclaimer of the Gospel, fulfil your priestly service!

Personal report and request for Timothy to come soon

[6]I have already begun my path of sacrifice. For me, the time draws near when what is earthly will begin its dissolution. [7]I have fought the good fight to the end, I have completed my course, the power of the faith I have carried through. [8]It remains for me to win the wreath of righteousness. At the breaking of the new Day, the Lord will give it to me, he who is the just judge of destiny. And not only to me, but to all who have longed for his Epiphany, his gracious appearing, with loving hearts.

[9]Hurry, so that you may come to me soon. [10]Demas has left me; he is still bound up with the present state of the world. He has gone to Thessalonica. Crescens has gone to Galatia, Titus to Dalmatia. [11]Only Luke is still with me. Take Mark and bring him with you. I can well use him for the work. [12]I have sent Tychicus to Ephesus. [13]When you come, please bring the cloak which I left with Carpus at Troas, and also the books, and above all the parchments. [14]Alexander the coppersmith has done me much harm. The Lord will cause compensation to be made for his deeds. [15]Beware of him yourself, he has made many difficulties for our working with the Word. [16]At my first defence, no one stood by me. Everyone deserted me. May it not be laid to their charge. [17]But the Lord stood by me and gave me strength. For through me the proclamation is to be so fulfilled that all the peoples of the world will hear it. Therefore I was rescued from the lion's maw. [18]And in the time to come, the Lord will again rescue me from all deeds of the evil; he will let me find salvation in his kingdom which already is in the heavenly spheres. To him the light of revelation is due through all cycles of time. Amen.

Greeting and blessing
[19]Greet Prisca and Aquila and the household of Onesiphorus.
[20]Erastus remained in Corinth. Trophimus I left ill in Miletus.
[21]Hurry, so that you can come before the winter. Eubulus, Pudens
and Linus send greetings, as do Claudia and all the brothers.
[22]The Lord be with your spirit. Grace be with you all!

The Letter of Paul to Titus

1 *Introduction*
Paul, a servant of God, an apostle of Jesus Christ.
I am there for the faith of those whom God chooses so that
HE may dwell in them, and for the recognition of the truth which
opens up for the devout soul. [2]Thus the presentiment of eternal
life, borne up by hope, is enlivened – the life which was promised
before all cycles of time by God, in whom there is no deception.
[3]When the time for it was fulfilled, HE revealed HIS Word; and I
have been entrusted with its proclamation by the God who gives us
salvation. [4]I am writing to Titus who is my true child in the faith
which we share:

Grace be with you and peace from God the Father and from Christ Jesus, our Saviour.

About the appointing of elders
[5]I left you in Crete so that you might complete the work of bringing form and order which has been begun. In each town you were
to induct elders according to the rules which I gave you, [6]namely
such as give no occasion for reproach, and whose life of soul as
regards the relationship between the male and female is completely
mastered in inner unity. They must be fathers of children who are

believers and who do not have an air about them of an impure and
disorderly way of life. 7The leader of a congregation, above all,
must be above every reproach, since he is God's steward. He must
not be arrogant or ill-tempered, everything of an ecstatic character,
all quarrelsomeness and every base lust after gain be far from him.
8Rather, he should be a hospitable host, a lover of goodness, master
of himself, just, his nature filled with Spirit, self-controlled, 9faith-
ful to the Word which, when it is taught rightly, leads to faith. Then
he will be able to give spiritual courage through the soul-healing power of the teaching, and to convince those who resist it
of their error.

About false and misleading teachings

10For there are many who will not bow to the rulership of the Spirit.
Their speaking is without substance, and just because of that it is
misleading. Mostly they are of the circumcision. 11They must be
made to be silent, for by their false teaching they bring confusion
to whole communities; and, to crown it all, they do it out of base
greed for gain. 12Even one of their own prophets has said:

> All Cretans are liars, wild beasts; they are bone-idle
> and think only about gorging themselves.

13This judgment is true. Therefore call them to account, sternly,
so that they remain healthy in the faith. 14They should not give
heed to Jewish myths and rulings by people who have turned away
from the truth. 15To those who are purified and clean, everything
can serve for purification. But for those who are without purity
and without faith, there is nothing pure. 16They speak as though
they confess to God, but by their deeds they deny HIM. They are
possessed by dark powers, and so they do not follow the voice of
the Spirit, and prove incapable of doing the Good.

2 *The right conduct of groups in the congregation*

Always shape your work with the Word in such a way that it
corresponds to the soul-healing power of the teaching.

2Say to the elders that they should be of wakeful mind,

dignified, temperate, raying forth the healing which comes about
through faith, love and patience. 3To the older women say that they
also should strive for a bearing which is worthy of the holy service.
They must not make themselves into tools of demonic powers, and
should not give themselves over to immoderate drinking of wine.
They should be good teachers who show the younger ones the way
to inner harmony 4and teach them to find the right relationship to
the male nature and the nature of children. 5They should be of temperate, calm mind, of pure heart, caring mistresses of the house,
devoted to the Good, followers of the masculine spiritual power
within their own being. The divine Word must not be devalued
through them.

6I also urge the younger men to strive for inner collectedness.
7You, yourself, be an example of right behaviour in all things. In
teaching, develop an unbroken spiritual impulse and dignified
greatness. 8Let your word have power to heal souls and let it be so
unassailable that the opponents are put to shame and are unable to
say anything derogatory about us.

9Those who are servants should certainly be subject to those
who are their masters. They should not oppose them, but should
strive to please them. 10They should not be guilty of unreliability,
but should prove themselves trustworthy through and through. In
that way, by everything they do, they will adorn the teaching which
proclaims our divine Saviour.

11The grace of God has been revealed as a source of healing
for all human beings. 12It educates us, so that we may renounce
all alienation from God and the cravings of the earthly world, and
place into our present age an image of a collected and calm life,
dedicated to what is good and holy. 13We may live towards the
blessed hope and the sight of the light of revelation that proceeds
from the all-encompassing Godhead and from Christ Jesus 14who
gives us the salvation. He gave himself for us, to free us out of the
chaotic life of outer appearances, so that he might distil out for
himself a people who are of one being with him and ensouled with
enthusiasm for every good work.

[15]Let this be the content of your proclamation and your advice. Thus you are to lead souls to the test with the whole authority of your task and commission. No one should have a low opinion of you.

About order in the congregation

Bring to the consciousness of those who have tasks as leaders that they must conform to the order which reflects the working of the hierarchies of the Mights and Revealers. In this they must develop inner obedience and constant preparedness to be active for the Good. [2]They must not make wrong use of the power of the Word, they must be free from all quarrelsomeness, full of gentleness and inner acceptance of all human beings.

[3]We ourselves were once without any sense for the Spirit, without willingness to follow, without a sure goal, ruled by various cravings and desires; we led our lives without kindness and compassion, we were inhuman and full of mutual hate. [4]But then God's goodness and love for Man was made manifest. [5]He brings salvation to us, not as a result of our moral achievements, but the healing power flowed to us from *his* offering mercy through the bath of new birth and the renewal of being which is brought about by the Holy Spirit. [6]This Spirit was poured out upon us in fullness through Jesus Christ who gives us the salvation. [7]By his grace the true higher being was to enter into us; we were to become heirs of the longed-for eternal life.

[8]Our soul can build upon this word. It is my will to strengthen you ever more in this, so that everyone's heart will become set on proving this connection in faith with the heavenly world by exemplary conduct. That will be good and helpful to the people among whom you are living. [9]Do not join in useless speculations and deductions from genealogies, nor in quarrels and disputes about interpretations of the Law. That is all futile and also without sense. [10]If someone begins to follow heretical directions, then withdraw from him after you have tried once or twice to turn his heart and mind to the right path. [11]You must know that such a person has

come apart inwardly and himself will attract the necessary consequences of destiny by his error.

Personal tasks and greetings

12As soon as I send Artemas or Tychicus to you, hurry and come to
me at Nicopolis, for I intend to spend the winter there. 13As soon
as possible send Zenas, the expert on the Law, and Apollos ahead
of you, and see that they lack nothing. 14Those who belong to us
must prove themselves more and more by exemplary behaviour
wherever there is a need, so that their life shall not be without
fruit.

15All who are with me send greetings to you. Greet those who
love us and are united with us in the faith.

Grace be with you all!

The Letter of Paul to Philemon

Introduction

Paul, the chain-bearer of Christ Jesus, and Timothy our brother, to Philemon our beloved fellow worker [2]and to Apphia our sister and Archippus our fellow fighter, and to the whole congregation which gathers in your house:

[3]Grace be with you and peace from God our Father and from Jesus Christ, the Lord.

Faith and love of Philemon

[4]Always, when I think of you in my prayers, my thanks rise up to God [5]because I hear of the great power of your love and your faith which unite you with the Lord Jesus and also with all who strive for holiness in him. [6]May the community which develops for you through your faith work powerfully in you in your awareness of the good that lives in us and leads us to the Christ. [7]The love which streams from you gives me great joy and encouragement in spirit; through you, dear brother, the hearts of those who strive for holiness have been entirely refreshed.

On behalf of Onesimus

[8]I would certainly have the right to order you in the name of Christ to do what is right. [9]For the sake of our love, however, let me put a request to you instead. I do it as who I am, I speak as the old Paul and now also a chain-bearer of Christ Jesus. [10]The request concerns my child Onesimus whose father I have become in my chains.

[11]At one time he proved useless to you, but now he is of great value to you and to me. [12]I am sending him to you, take him as

though he were my own heart. 13I would have been glad to keep
him with me, so that he might be helpful to me rather than you in
the chains which I bear in the service of the Gospel; 14but I did not
want to do anything without knowing your views. The good deed
which you can do now should not come about through any kind of
compulsion but entirely out of your free will.

15Perhaps that is why he was parted from you for a while, in
order that you now may receive him back as yours for eternity:
16now no longer as a slave but as something higher, as a beloved
brother. He is that to me already; how much more he can be it to
you, both in the earthly community as well as in the community of
the Lord. 17If you feel me as close to you, then receive him as you
would receive me. 18If he has wronged you or owes you anything,
charge it to my account. 19I, Paul, write here with my own hand: I
will reimburse you. Actually, here I could say: reimburse me, for
you owe me even your own self. 20Yes, my dear brother, I would
wish some time to have some benefit from you in the service of
the Lord. Refresh my heart in the name of Christ.

21I have written to you with confidence in your ready willingness. I know that you will do even more than I ask of you. 22Please
be prepared to offer me hospitality, for I hope that I shall be given to
you all again through the power of your prayers.

Greetings

23Epaphras greets you, my companion in the chains I bear in the
service of Christ Jesus. 24Also Mark, Aristarchus, Demas and Luke,
my fellow workers.

25May the grace of Jesus Christ the Lord fill your spirit!

The Letter to the Hebrews

The Son of God: higher than the angels
When God had spoken in bygone times to our fathers through the
prophets on many occasions and in many ways, [2]HE finally spoke
to us in these last days through the Son. HE has appointed him
the all-embracing heir of all being, for it was through him that HE
created all cycles of being in the stream of time. [3]He is the visible
reflection of the divine Light Being; he is imprinted on existence
as the embodiment of the essential nature of the divine. He bears
all things through the creative power of his word. When he had
fulfilled the purification of our sins he took his seat at the right
hand of the exalted might in the heights. [4]He has become as much
exalted above all the realms of the angels as the name he has won
for his inheritance is greater than they. [5]For to which of all angels
would God ever have said:

> You are my Son, today I have begotten you

or,

> I will be Father to him, and he shall be a Son to me?

[6]And again, when HE brings the first-born into the world of earth
existence, HE says:

> Let all the angels of God kneel in worship of him.

[7]To the angels HE says:

> He makes the spirits of the air into his angelic messengers, and the flames of fire into his ministering servants.

[8]But to the Son HE says:

> Your throne, O divine Being, endures from aeon to aeon,

and,

> The sceptre of your kingdom is the sceptre of upright-
> ness; 9you have loved righteousness and hated
> injustice. Therefore, O God, the God above you has
> anointed you with the oil of rejoicing as the leader of
> all beings who belong to you.

10And further,

> You, O Lord, laid the foundations of the earth in the
> realm of primal beginnings; the heavenly spheres
> are the work of your hands. 11Yet when they perish,
> you will remain. They all become old like a garment.
> 12Like a mantle you will roll them up, they will be
> changed as a garment is changed. But you are and
> remain the same; your years will not pass away.

13To which of the angels would HE ever have said:

> Sit at my right hand, till I place your enemies as a
> stool under your feet?

14Are they not all ministering spirits, sent forth with the task of
serving those who in the future are to obtain healing?

2 Therefore we must hold on even more closely to what has
reached our ears, if our life is not to be dissipated in nothingness.
2For if the word once spoken through the angels already had such
firm validity that every transgression and every disobedience
received its deserved retribution, 3how then shall we escape our
destiny if we despise so great a salvation, whose origin is in the
active word of the Lord himself? It has been reliably passed on
to us by those who still heard him themselves. 4God HIMSELF has
borne witness to it through signs and wonders, through many kinds
of powerful deed and by dispensations of the Holy Spirit by which
HE revealed HIS will.

5For it was not to the angels that God subordinated the world
to come, of which we are speaking. 6That has been testified somewhere:

> What is Man that you are mindful of him, and what is
> the son of Man that you direct your gaze at him? 7For
> a little while you have given him a lower rank than the

> angels; but then you have crowned him with the light
> of the Spirit and with dignity of soul. 8You have put
> everything in subordination under his feet.

In subordinating everything to him, God left out nothing from
this subordination; only for us it is not yet apparent that HE has
subordinated everything to him. 9That God wished Man to be
lower than the angels for a short while we see in Jesus who went
through suffering and death, but then was crowned with glory and
dignity of soul. It was the will of the divine grace that he should be
permeated by the taste of death on behalf of all beings.

10It was fitting that HE, for whom and through whom everything
has been created, after HE had led many sons to enlightenment,
should also lead the pioneer and first-born of their salvation to
perfection through suffering. 11For he who gives healing and those
who receive it have all one and the same origin. That is why he is
not ashamed to call them brothers:

> 12I will proclaim your name to my brothers;
> in the midst of the congregation I will sing your praise.

13And again:

> I will put my trust in HIM,

and,

> See, it is I, and these are the children God has given me.

14Now since the children have had to unite with flesh and blood,
he, too, clothed himself in like manner and so became like them,
in order that, through his death, he might destroy the one who
wields the power of death: the diabolical Adversary. 15Thus those
were to be delivered who through fear of death were subject to
lifelong bondage. 16It is no longer the angels that he works for; his
helping will extends to the human race from the days of Abraham.

17Therefore he had to become like his brothers in every way,
so that he could be their merciful and faithful High Priest in their
relationship to God, and so that he could make expiation for the
sins of the people through the presence of God. 18Because he himself suffered temptations, he is able to help those who have to
endure the same trials.

3 *The Son of God: higher than Moses*
Therefore, you ordained brothers who are sharers in a heavenly
calling, turn your hearts and minds to Jesus, the messenger and
High Priest of our confession. [2]He serves his creator faithfully, as
did Moses and his whole house. [3]He has been counted worthy of
a greater form of glory than Moses, just as the builder of a house
deserves more honour than the house itself. [4]For every house is built
by someone, but God is the builder of everything. [5]Moses worked
faithfully in the midst of HIS house as a caring servant, witnessing
to the words which would only be spoken in the future. [6]But Christ
is a son of the house. And we are his house if we hold fast our courageous and proud confidence in the salvation until its fulfilment.
[7]Therefore, as the Holy Spirit says:

> Today, when you hear my voice, [8]do not harden your
> hearts as you did in the bitterness which came over you
> on the day of temptation in the desert. [9]In those days
> your fathers were put to a test of their souls, although
> they had lived in the sight of my works for forty years.
> [10]Therefore I was full of displeasure with that gener-
> ation and said: They always go astray in their hearts;
> they have not recognized my ways. [11]In my wrath I
> swore: They shall find no way into the calm of my
> Being.

[12]See to it, dear brothers, that there is no one among you who
has an evil, faithless heart which turns away from the living God.
[13]Every day stand by one another with words of spiritual comfort,
until the great 'today' comes, so that none among you will become
hardened in the errors of sin. [14]For we have become sharers in the
Being of Christ, if only we keep firmly to the original power which
goes out from him, until its fulfilment. [15]That is why it is said:

> Today, when you hear his voice, do not harden your
> hearts as in the bitterness.

[16]Who were they who became bitter when hearing the word?
Was it not all those who left Egypt under the leadership of Moses?
[17]And with whom was HE displeased for forty years? Was it not

with those who succumbed to sin and whose bones were left in
the desert? [18]And to whom did HE swear that they should not enter
the calm of HIS being? Was it not to those who closed their hearts?
[19]We can see that they could not enter into that calm because of
their unbelief.

4 It must be our anxious concern that none of you should come to
think that entrance into the divine calm will be denied him because
he has not received the words of encouragement which point to
the future. [2]The message of promise is for us just as it was for
them. The spirit of the word which they heard did not benefit them,
because they were unable to hear with an ear of unmixed faith.
[3]For we who have come to the faith enter into the sphere of divine
calm, remembering the word:

> In my wrath I swore: They shall not enter into the
> calm of my Being.

That also becomes clear from the sequence of creative deeds which
happened at the creation of the world. [4]Scripture says about the
seventh day:

> And God rested on the seventh day from all HIS crea-
> tive deeds.

[5]With that in mind we can understand the word:

> They shall not enter into the calm of my Being.

[6]Since it is possible for human beings to enter into that sphere,
although those who first received the promise did not find the way
in because of their closed minds, [7]then that must mean that God
has instituted a new day, the great 'today,' of which David says
that it will come after a certain time, according to the prophetic
word:

> Today, when you hear HIS voice, do not harden your
> hearts.

[8]If Joshua had already been able to lead the way into the world
of calm, there would be no need after those days to speak of a
new day. [9]Therefore, a Sabbath-sphere is still open to the people
of God. [10]He who enters into the calm of God also rests from his
labours as God did from HIS. [11]Let us therefore strive eagerly to

enter into the sphere of calm, so that no one fall because of his
closed heart after that warning example. 12Full of life is the divine
Word, powerfully active and sharper than any two-edged sword;
it penetrates to the extent that it separates soul and spirit; it goes
through joint and marrow; it judges the intentions and thoughts of
the heart. 13No created being can hide from him; everything lies
open, uncovered and in every detail, before his gaze. That is the
Word of whom we speak with our words.

Christ, the true High Priest

14Since then we have a great High Priest who has passed through
all the heavens, sphere by sphere, Jesus, the Son of God, let us hold
to our confession with all our strength. 15For we do not have a High
Priest who cannot suffer our weaknesses with us. He made himself
like us and endured the same temptations in everything, only he
remained free of sin. 16Let us then approach the throne of grace
with confident freedom, that we may experience compassionate
goodness and find a share in the grace which sends us help in
the right hour.

5 For every High Priest chosen from among men is appointed
for the dealings of men with God, to offer gifts and sacrifices for
the expiation of sins. 2That is why he is able to have understanding sympathy with those whose consciousness and will are weak,
because he himself is subject to weakness, 3and therefore he must
offer sacrifice not only for the sins of the people, but also for his
own.

4No one can give himself the dignity of priesthood. For that he
needs to be called by God, just as Aaron needed to be. 5Even Christ
did not give himself the light-form which made him a High Priest,
but rather he received it from HIM who spoke to him:

> You are my Son, today I have begotten you.

6And in another place it says:

> You are a priest for ever, after the order and rite of
> Melchizedek.

7In the days of his earthly incarnation he offered up prayers and

entreaties to HIM who had the power to save him out of the might
of death. With intense cries of pain and with tears he offered up his
soul, and he was heard because of his readiness to fulfil destiny.
[8]He conducted himself like that, although he was the Son. Through
his suffering he learned obedience, [9]and, because he won through
to ultimate perfection, he has become the source of eternal healing
for all who would follow him, [10]he who has been declared by God
HIMSELF the High Priest after the order of Melchizedek.

Dangers to the faith and inner certainty

[11]About him we have spirit-words in plenty which, however, can
scarcely be expressed in human words, because your inner hearing
has become dull. [12]Though by this time you should have become
teachers, you now need to be taught all over again about the first
principles and beginnings of the sayings of God. You have become
people who need milk, not solid food. [13]For anyone who still lives
on milk is inexperienced in the word of righteousness, for he is not
of age. [14]Solid food is only for those who are becoming mature,
because they have achieved the higher faculties which are practised
in distinguishing between good and evil.

6 Let us therefore leave the first principles of the Christ-teaching
behind us and strive with all our might towards the highest aim.
We do not have to lay the foundation again which consists of a
change of heart and mind and turning away from dead works,
of faith as a turn towards the divine world, [2]of instruction about
the baptisms, about the laying-on of hands, about the resurrection
of the dead and about the great decision which leads over to the
coming aeon.

[3]All this we will turn into reality, in so far as God enables us
to do it. [4]Those who have had a share of enlightenment and have
experienced the taste of the heavenly grace, who have felt the
indwelling of the Holy Spirit, [5]who have sensed the upbuilding
might of the deeds of the divine Word and the wonderful powers
of the coming aeon – [6]once they have experienced these things,
they cannot possibly simply begin again with the change of heart

and mind when they have fallen, because thereby they crucify and
expose the Son of God in their souls.

7The earth, which ever and again drinks the rain that falls on
it and brings forth the wonderful green for those who cultivate it,
partakes of the blessing of the heavenly world. 8But because it also
brings forth thorns and thistles it proves to be less than good and
comes close to the curse whose end is the burning fire. 9However, as
regards you, dear brothers, we are quite sure that you are close to the
salvation, even though our words may give a different impression.
10God is not unjust and does not blot out the memory of your deeds
and the love which you have shown to the divine name in your service among those who strive for the healing; you have done this and
will continue to do it. 11Our hope and wish is that each one of you
will also show the same eagerness in the future, so that you may
achieve the aim of being filled by the Spirit – the aim upon which
we base our hope. 12Do not become lame; rather, imitate those who
themselves have experienced the fulfilment of the promise through
their faith and patience.

13Abraham received such a promise from God. Since God had
no one greater by whom to swear, HE swore by HIMSELF 14and said:

> For certain, I will pour out my blessing upon you and
> multiply you exceedingly.

15And as Abraham received the promise with a patient heart, it was
fulfilled for him. 16Human beings usually swear by those powers
which are greater than they; for them, an oath is a confirmation
which excludes all contradiction. 17How much more did God intend
to prove HIS unalterable will to those who are heirs to HIS promise,
when HE made use of an oath! 18Through two unchangeable com-
mitments, in which it is impossible that God should prove false, we
were to receive a strong consolation, we, who have sought refuge
in seizing the hope which has been offered us. 19This hope we have
as a secure and firm anchor of our soul. By it, the innermost part of
the shrine behind the curtain has been opened to us; 20there Jesus
has gone before us, preparing the way. He has become a High Priest
for ever after the order of Melchizedek.

Christ, the High Priest after the order of Melchizedek

This Melchizedek of whom we are speaking is king of Salem, the priest of the highest God. He went out to meet Abraham who was returning from the war of the kings. He blessed Abraham, 2and Abraham gave him a tenth of all that he possessed. His name when translated means, firstly, king of righteousness, and then he is also called king of Salem, that means king of peace. 3He is without father, without mother and without ancestors, without beginning of days or end of life: he is of similar nature as the Son of God and he is a bearer of priesthood for ever. 4Imagine how great he must be that Abraham, our patriarch, sacrificed a tenth of all the spoils of war as an offering to him! 5As you know, those sons of Levi who have taken on the task of priesthood were given the instruction to receive tithes from the people according to the Law, that is, from their brothers who themselves are also descended from Abraham. 6But he, who is without ancestors, received the tithe from them by accepting it from Abraham, and he blessed him who was the bearer of the promise. 7It is beyond dispute that the inferior receives the blessing from the superior. 8Whereas it usually is mortal men who accept the tithes, here it is the one of whom we know that he is the bearer of life itself. 9One might say that when Abraham paid the tithe, Levi, who otherwise receives it, paid it with him; 10for he lay, as yet unborn, in the loins of the father when Melchizedek came to meet him.

11But if a true stream of consecration flowed through the Levitical priesthood – and the Law was given to the people on that basis – why was it necessary to institute another priest of the order of Melchizedek, of whom it is expressly said that he does not belong to the succession of Aaron? 12For if there has been a transformation of the priesthood, it necessarily follows that the role of the Law has changed, too. 13The one of whom this is said belongs to another tribe, from which no one has ever served at the altar. 14It is, of course, an evident fact that our Lord has come forth from the tribe of Judah, of which Moses said nothing about priesthood. 15And so it is all the more evident that he, in the same way as Melchizedek, stands before us as a priest of another kind. [16]He has his task, not because of the Law with its physical rules, but out of the power of imperishable life. [17]Of him the word gives testimony:

> You are a priest for ever, after the order of
> Melchizedek.

[18]That means an annulment of the earlier Law, which, in fact, has become without power and fruitfulness. [19]The old Law no longer has any power to consecrate. But in its place a new and greater hope has come into the world, by virtue of which we can draw near to God anew. [20]And this new thing is accompanied by God's oath. [21]In the past they became priests without such an oath by God, but *he* was ordained according to the oath of him who said to him:

> The Lord HIMSELF has sworn and will never break
> faith: you are a priest for ever.

[22]That is how Jesus has become the surety for us of a new and greater covenant with God.

[23]The former priests were many in number, because death prevented them from remaining in office. [24]But he, since he remains for ever, is the bearer of an imperishable priesthood. [25]Thereby he can give those who come to God through him a share of unlimited salvation; by virtue of his everlasting life he intercedes for them for ever. [26]We have need of such a High Priest: holy, free from evil, unblemished, separated from all sinfulness, exalted above all the heavens. [27]He has no need, like the former High Priests, always first to make daily offerings for his own sins, and only after that be able to make offerings for the people. He did this once for all when he offered up himself. [28]The Law appointed men as priests who themselves were weak. But the word of God's oath, which replaces the Law, appoints the Son who is consecrated for ever.

8 *The mediator of the New Covenant*
The most important thing of all that we have to say is this: we
have such a High Priest who has his seat in the spheres of the

heavens, on the right of the throne of the most exalted power. 2He is the priestly ruler in the sanctuary and the true tabernacle which has not been built by man, but by the Lord HIMSELF. 3Every High Priest is appointed to offer gifts and sacrifices; therefore this priest also depends on having something to offer. 4Now if he were an earthly being he could not be counted among the priests, for on earth there are already those who offer gifts in accordance with the Law. 5But priestly service on earth is nothing but a likeness and shadow of the archetypal images in the heavens. That is the meaning of the word of God which was spoken to Moses as he prepared to erect the tabernacle. He was told:

> Look up, and form everything like the spiritual image which was shown you on the mountain.

6But he, Christ, has become the bearer of a completely different and new kind of priestly service, the mediator of a new, higher covenant with God, whose Law consists of new, higher promises. 7If the first priestly service had still been blameless there would have been no need for a new one to come about. 8But scripture finds fault with them:

> The Lord says, 'See, the days will come when I establish a new covenant with the house of Israel and the house of Judah. 9It will not be like the covenant which I made with their fathers when I took them by the hand and led them out of Egypt. They did not remain faithful to my covenant, and therefore I could no longer care for them, says the Lord. 10This shall be the covenant which I will make with the house of Israel after those days: into their understanding and insight I will place my laws; on the tablets of their hearts I will write them. So will I be their God, and they shall be my people. 11Then they will no longer need to teach one another, each one his neighbour or brother: know the Lord. For then all will know me, from the least to the greatest of them. 12Then I will look mildly on their failings and no longer remember their sin.'

13When a new covenant is spoken of like this, it means that the
first is obsolete. And what has become obsolete and grown old is
near to extinction.

9 *Christ's unique sacrifice*
The Old Covenant, too, had its legitimate ritual and the sanctuary
which depicted the cosmos. 2The interior of the holy tabernacle
was arranged like this: a room contained the lamp stand and the
table with the shewbread; it was called 'the Holy Place.' 3Behind
the second curtain was the room which was called 'the Holy of
Holies.' 4In it stood the golden censer and the ark of the covenant,
completely covered with gold. It contained the golden urn holding the manna, the rod of Aaron which had blossomed, and the
stone tablets of the covenant. 5Above the ark were the Cherubim as
guardians of the revelation, overshadowing the place of the divine
presence. About this, it is not possible to speak more precisely
now. 6These things having been arranged thus, the priests who at
all times have to fulfil the holy rituals, enter the front part of the
Temple. 7But into the second, innermost room only the High Priest
enters, and that only once a year, alone and with the blood which
he has to offer for his own errors and those of the people. 8Through
these patterns the Holy Spirit enables us to see in picture that
the way to the inner sanctuary is not yet revealed, as long as the
first tabernacle is in existence. 9That building is a parable for the
present age, in which external gifts and sacrifices are still offered,
although they cannot lead the worshipper to enlightenment and
consecration of his consciousness.

10For the time being, the ritual still rests upon food and drink and
various rites of baptism, that is, on regulations for the body, until
the time for its renewal shall have come.

11But now Christ has appeared as the High Priest of future evo-
lution. He reigns in a higher and more perfect tabernacle which is
not built with hands and indeed does not belong to this creation.
He does not make use of the sacrificial blood of rams and calves;
12through the power of his own blood he has entered once and

for all into the innermost sanctuary and has achieved an eternal
redemption. [13]If even the sacrificial blood of rams and bulls and the
ashes of a calf had the power to sanctify those who were touched
by them, including purification of their bodily nature, [14]must not
then the blood of Christ, who gave himself through the power of
the eternal Spirit as an offering without blemish to God, be able
beyond that to purify our consciousness and lead us from dead
works to serving and sharing the life of the divine? [15]That is why
he is the mediator of a New Covenant. By passing through the
death which dissolved the transgressions of the Old Covenant,
he has enabled the appointed bearers of the promise to become
partakers of the eternal inheritance.

[16]Whenever a legacy is made, the death of the one making the
legacy is necessarily taken into consideration, [17]for the bequest
only takes effect on his death. As long as he is living, the legacy
has no force. [18]In a similar way, the Old Covenant could also only
be established through blood. [19]When Moses had proclaimed the
commandments contained in the Law to the whole people, he took
the blood of the bulls and rams, mixed it with water, dipped scarlet
wool and a hyssop-sponge in it and sprinkled the book and then the
whole people with it. [20]And he said:

> This is the blood of the covenant which God makes
> with you.

[21]In the same way he also sprinkled the tabernacle and all the uten-
sils for the ritual with the blood. [22]When the Law rules, almost
everything has to be purified with blood; without the shedding of
blood there is no taking away of sin.

[23]Now if it was necessary that the representations of the heavenly archetypal images should be given such purification, those
heavenly archetypes themselves require greater sacrifices than the
representations. [24]For Christ did not enter into a sanctuary built by
human hands, which could, after all, only be a counter-image of the
true archetypes; rather, he entered into heaven itself, there to appear
for our salvation before the countenance of God. [25]He does not need
to offer himself repeatedly as a sacrifice, as the High Priest, every

year anew, must enter into the sanctuary, offering blood which is
not his own. [26]Otherwise he would often have had to suffer since
the creation of the world. Now, as the aeons approach fulfilment, he
has revealed himself once for all, so that he might make sin powerless by the sacrifice of himself. [27]Just as it is ordained for human
beings that one day they must die and then enter into the sphere of
decision, [28]so also Christ sacrificed himself once to wipe out the
sins of many. Free from the spell of sin he will then reveal himself a
second time to those who wait for him, hoping for the salvation.

10 The Law merely casts a shadow in advance of the future treasures of the Spirit; it is not yet itself the true form of those facts of
salvation. That is why, for all the offerings brought year after year,
it can never lead those to consecration and fulfilment who take part
in the offerings. [2]Otherwise, of course, the offerings would have
ceased, because the devout would no longer be conscious of sin
if they had really been cleansed by them. [3]Therefore the offering
cannot be anything other than a reminder, renewed every year, of
the fact of sin. [4]The blood of bulls and rams cannot possibly wipe
out sin. [5]Therefore he said, as he was still about to enter into our
world:

> Sacrifices and offerings you have not desired, but
> you have prepared a body for me. [6]Burnt offerings
> and atonement offerings no longer give you pleasure.
> [7]Then I said, 'See, I come! The holy scriptures speak
> of me, that I fulfil your will, O God.'

[8]First he said:

> Sacrifices and offerings, burnt offerings and atonement
> offerings you do not want, they no longer give you
> pleasure,

even when they are brought exactly according to the Law. [9]And
after that he went on:

> See, I come to fulfil your will.

He abolishes the first in order to establish the second. [10]By being
within this streaming of will we have experienced holiness through
the unique deed of Jesus Christ who offered up his life.

11Every priest is appointed to serve at the altar daily, and repeatedly to offer the same sacrifices which can never remove sin. 12But
he brought the one sacrifice for the sins of men, and now sits at
the right hand of God for all time, 13looking to the future until the
powers which are hostile to him shall be forced entirely under his
feet. 14By that one sacrifice he has fulfilled and consecrated for all
time those who let themselves be penetrated by the power of his
spirit. 15The Holy Spirit also bears witness to us about this. First he
says:

> 16This is the covenant which I will make with them
> after those days, says the Lord.

Then he says:

> I will lay my laws upon their hearts, and write them
> on their thinking consciousness; 17I will eradicate the
> memory of their sins and failings.

18But if this redemption has begun to work, there is no longer any
need for offerings for sin.

Free access to the Holy of Holies

19Therefore, dear brothers, as those who strive towards the salvation we have free access to the Holy of Holies through the power
of the blood of Jesus. 20He has opened for us an open and living
way through the curtain; that means, through his earthly, bodily
nature. 21That is to say, we have a High Priest over the house of
God; 22let us draw near to him with true hearts, with the fulfilling
power of the faith, with hearts cleansed, by sprinkling, of darkened
consciousness, washed in our whole body with the water of purity.
23Let us unshakably hold fast the confession of our hope; for he
who made us the promise is faithful. 24Let us spur one another on
to love and to work in the service of the Good, 25not neglecting our
shared community-life, as has become the habit of some. Rather,
let us help one another up, ever and again, and all the more so
since you see the great Day drawing near.

26If we wilfully cling to sin, after we have once found our way
through to an awareness of the truth, then we also throw away the

possibility of offering sacrifice for our sin. 27Nothing remains for
us but a fearful prospect of the hour of decision and of the fire of
wrath which consumes those who oppose. 28If someone violates the
Law of Moses, he is condemned to death without mercy on the
testimony of two or three witnesses. 29Do you not think that a much
worse punishment will fall on anyone who tramples the Son of God
underfoot, who regards as nothing the blood of the New Covenant
by which he has been sanctified and who mocks the power of the
Spirit of grace? 30We know HIM who said:

> Vengeance is mine; I will repay.

And:

> The Lord is the judge of HIS people.

31It is terrible to fall into the hands of the living God.

32Remember the days recently past, when you had become
enlightened and then at once had to endure great struggles and much
suffering. 33Subjected to oppression and humiliation, you became a
spectacle for the world, but thereby you also became closely united
with those who had to endure similar treatment. 34You felt the sufferings of those who were imprisoned, and you allowed the plunder
of your belongings with a cheerful heart, conscious of having a
better possession within you, and, what is more, a lasting one. 35Let
your courageous trust never waver; from it flows unending blessing.
36What you need above all is patience, so that you may completely
fulfil the will of God which works in destiny, and may obtain the
promised treasure. 37For:

> Only a little, quite short while, and *he* will come who
> is to come; and he will not tarry. Whoever would do
> justice to me must learn to live out of trust and faith.
> 38But my power of soul cannot be revealed in anyone
> who, cowardly, shrinks back.

39Let us not be among those who draw back and fall victim to
the decline. We stride forwards on the path of faith, so that we can
make that soul-power completely our own.

1 *The path of faith in the Old Covenant*
Faith is the intrinsic working-in-advance of that which we hope
for, an inner proof of that which still rests, unseen, in the lap of the
future. 2By it, those who have gone before us become witnesses
to the Spirit. 3Through faith our spirit perceives that the cycles of
creation have been structured by the power of God's word, so that
the sense-perceptible came into being out of the supersensible.
4Through faith, Abel was superior to Cain when offering sacrifice to God. Through it, he was testified to as a bearer of righteousness, in that God HIMSELF bore witness to his offerings. Through
it, he could still speak when he was already dead. 5Through faith,
Enoch was taken up so that he should not see death; he was found
on earth no longer because God HIMSELF had taken him up. It is
testified of him that his ways were pleasing to God even before
he was taken up; 6but without faith it is impossible to become
well-pleasing to God, for whoever would draw near to HIM must, of
course, first believe that HE exists and that HE will give those who
seek HIM their reward for their striving.
7Through faith, Noah received the divine directive about that
which had not yet become visible to earthly eyes, and with a devout
heart he built the ark for the saving of his family. Thereby he caused
a division in mankind to come about, and himself became an heir to
the righteousness which is the fruit of faith.
8Through faith, Abraham obediently followed his call and set
out for the place which, in time, he was to receive as the promised
inheritance. He set out without knowing his destination. 9Through
faith, he settled in the promised land, although it still was foreign
to him, and he lived there in tents with Isaac and Jacob, the fellow
heirs to the same promise. 10Full of expectation he looked forward
to the firmly grounded city, whose builder and creator is God HIM-
SELF.
11And lastly, through faith Sarah received the power to conceive and so to lay the foundation for the continuation of her tribe,
in spite of her advanced age. For she faithfully trusted HIM who had
given the promise. 12Thus it could come about that from *one* womb

– and, what is more, one that had already died – all those were born who were like the stars of heaven in the fullness of their number and uncountable like the sand by the seashore.

[13]These all died in the power of the faith, without themselves having experienced the fulfilment of the promises. They only saw and greeted it from afar, acknowledging that they were only strangers and guests on the earth. [14]Those who speak thus make it clear that they are searching for the true homeland. [15]If they had had the earthly home in mind, they would, of course, have had the opportunity to go back there. [16]What they long for is a greater home which belongs to the spheres of the heavens. Therefore God does not consider it beneath HIS dignity to be called their God, for HE has prepared a city for them.

[17]Through faith, Abraham was willing, when he had to withstand the test, to offer up Isaac. His only son he offered, [18]he who had received the promise:

> With Isaac your lineage begins which shall be called your seed.

[19]He thought that God surely also would be able to awaken the dead, and so his son was given him anew in that allegorical event.

[20]Through faith, and full of trust in the future, Isaac blessed Jacob and Esau. [21]Through faith, the dying Jacob, in his turn, blessed the two sons of Joseph and prayed over the point of his staff. [22]Through faith, the dying Joseph turned his inner gaze upon the exodus of the sons of Israel, and gave directions as to what was to happen to his remains.

[23]Through faith it came about that Moses was kept hidden by his parents for three months after his birth, because they saw the beauty of the child. They did not fear the stern decree of Pharaoh. [24]Through faith, Moses, when he was grown up, declined any longer to be regarded as the son of Pharaoh's daughter. [25]He would rather share the sufferings of the people of God than have an advantage for a while through sin. [26]He held the humiliation to be endured when serving the Christ to be a greater treasure than all the wealth of Egypt; he saw how this humiliation would, in

time, receive its reward. 27Through faith he achieved the exodus
from Egypt and was not afraid of Pharaoh's anger. He held to the
invisible Being as though he saw HIM with eyes. 28Through faith
he instituted the Passover and the sprinkling of the doorposts with
sacrificial blood, so that the Destroyer should not touch the first-
born of his people. 29Through faith they walked through the Red
Sea as though it were dry land. And when the Egyptians tried to do
the same, they were engulfed by the waves.

30Through faith the walls of Jericho were brought tumbling
down after they had been encircled for seven days. 31Through faith,
Rahab the harlot did not perish with the unbelievers, since she had
received the scouts with a peaceful heart.

32What more shall I still say? There would not be time enough
to tell of Gideon, Barak, Samson, Jephthah, David and Samuel and
the prophets – 33who, through faith, conquered kingdoms, wrought
works of divine righteousness, received promises, rent the maws of
lions, 34quenched the might of fire, escaped the edge of the sword,
won strength out of sicknesses, proved themselves heroes in war
and put enemies to flight. 35Women received back their dead as resurrected ones. Others let themselves be tortured and did not accept
the release they were offered, so that they might share in a greater
resurrection. 36Still others took mocking and scourging and even
chains and imprisonment upon themselves; 37they endured stoning, torment, beating to death; they died by the murderous sword.
They walked about in skins of sheep and goats, suffering want,
hard-pressed and ill-treated – 38the world was not worthy of such
sufferings. In deserts they wandered, in mountains and ravines they
dwelt. 39And they all became witnesses to the Spirit through faith,
although they did not themselves experience the fulfilment of the
promise. 40But God has planned a better lot for us, so that they
now also can reach the goal of their ways through us.

12 *The path of faith in the New Covenant*
Since, then, so great a cloud of witnesses surrounds us, let us cast
aside everything which pulls us down, and free ourselves from

the enticing spell of sin. Let us continue with endurance in the
fight which has been laid upon us. [2]Let us look to him who is the
founder and fulfiller of our faith: Jesus. Instead of the joy that was
his due, he willingly took the cross upon himself and did not heed
the shame. Now his place is at the right hand of the throne of God.

[3]Consider what it means that he so willingly endured the enmity
of sinful humanity; then your courage will not fail nor the power
of your soul grow weak. [4]In your fight against sin you have not
yet resisted to the point of shedding blood; [5]you have forgotten the
word of the Spirit which is spoken to you as sons:

> My Son, do not regard the education by the Lord
> lightly. Do not weaken when HE puts you to the test.
> [6]For the Lord disciplines him whom HE loves. With HIS
> blows HE strikes just him whom HE receives as a son.

[7]Endure this education. You are being treated as sons by God.
Can someone be a son if his father does not discipline him? [8]As
long as you are without this education, which is intended for
everyone, you are illegitimate children and not sons. [9]After all, we
acknowledge our earthly fathers and show them respect. Should
we then not all the more obey the Father of spirits who gives us
true life? [10]For *they* brought us up for a short time as they considered best; but *he* is concerned about our progress for ever, so that
HE may give us a share in the holiness of HIS being. [11]At the time,
all discipline seems to us to lead to sorrow rather than joy; but later
it yields the peaceful fruit of righteousness to those who have been
educated by it.

[12]Therefore lift your tired hands and straighten your bowed
knees once more; [13]take purposeful strides with your feet, so that
you do not become lame and go astray, but instead attain to new
healing power. [14]Let peace with all men be your aim, and the
holiness without which no one can behold the Lord.

[15]See to it that no one remains without the touch of the divine
Spirit; otherwise it can happen that a root of bitterness springs up
which blocks the path and takes away the purity of their being from
many. [16]Take care that no one strays onto the path of unspiritual

and external ways of being, like Esau who gave away his right as
the firstborn for a single meal. 17You know that afterwards he was
found unworthy when he wanted to inherit the blessing; he could
not change his heart and mind, although he strove for it with tears.

18The spiritual place you have come to is not the peak touched
by God in burning fire, in gloomy clouds where darkness dwells
and the tempest is let loose; 19where the trumpet blares and mighty
voices sound. There, those who heard it begged that the word
should not apply to them, 20for they could not bear the directive:

> Even an animal that comes near this mountain shall be
> stoned.

21Since the sight was so terrifying, even Moses said:

> I am filled with fear and trembling!

22The place you have come to, rather, is Mount Zion and the city
of the living God, the heavenly Jerusalem with a myriad angels, a
festive choir 23and the congregation of the first-born whose names
are inscribed in the heavens. There God rules as judge of all destinies among the spirits of those who have won through to the
perfection of righteousness. 24There also Jesus reigns, the mediator
of the New Covenant with God, and the power of that sprinkled
blood is felt which speaks a higher language than the blood of
Abel. 25See that you do not reject him who speaks to you. If those
who closed themselves against the divine voice sounding on earth
could not escape their fate, much less shall we be able to, if we
turn away from HIM who speaks to us out of the heavens. 26At one
time HIS voice caused the earth to tremble; but now HE has spoken
the promise for the future:

> Once more I will shake not only the earth but also
> heaven.

27This 'once more' indicates the transformation that shall come
upon everything created because of the tremor. Then only that will
remain which no longer can be shaken. 28Since we have been given
a kingdom which cannot be shaken, let us be thankful; for thereby
we serve God as it pleases HIM, with reverence and awe. 29For our
God is a consuming fire.

13 *Advice on various matters*
Let brotherly love endure. 2Do not neglect to show hospitality to
strangers; thereby some have had angels as guests without knowing it. 3Remember those who are in chains, as though you were
bearing chains yourselves. Care for those who have difficult things
to endure, since you also live in the body.
4Marriage is to be honoured in every respect, and the relationship
between the sexes is to be kept pure. He who gives himself up to
sexual abuses and whoever breaks marriage will be made account-
able to God.
5Let your conduct be free of greed; be content with what you
have, for God has said:

I will not fail you or forsake you.

6And so we may confidently say:

The Lord is with me as a helper; I need have no fear.
What harm can a human being do to me?

7Bear in your good thoughts those who guided you and proclaimed the word of God to you. Look at the outcome of their
ways of life and let their faith be an example to you. 8Jesus Christ
is the same yesterday and today and in all coming cycles of time.
9Do not let yourselves be pulled this way and that by many kinds
of other teachings. It is good to ground the heart firmly on the
power of the touch of the Spirit, not on external rules of nutrition
which bring no real benefit to those who follow them.
10We have an altar of sacrifice from which those who serve
the old tabernacle may not eat. 11The bodies of the animals whose
blood is brought as an offering for sin by the High Priest in the
inner sanctuary are burned outside, beyond the precincts of the
Temple. 12Therefore Jesus also suffered death outside the gates of
the city in order to sanctify mankind through his blood. 13Let us
go to him, outside those confines, and take his humiliation upon
ourselves. 14For here we have no lasting city. The city we seek
rests in the lap of the future. 15Through his power let us continually
offer up a sacrifice of praise to God; that is the fruit of lips that
confess HIS name. 16Do not neglect to do good to one another and

to nurture the community; that is the service of offering which is
pleasing to God. [17]Follow your leaders and submit to them, for
they watch over your souls and will one day have to give account
for them. Take care that they can do it with joy and not with sighs.
That would also be harmful for you.

[18]Pray for us. We may be certain that we are on a right path with
our conscience. Our striving is to use the whole of our lives in the
service of the Good. [19]All the more fervently I ask that you also
should do this, so that I may be in a position to come to you again
very soon.

Words of blessing, greetings

[20]May the God of peace who raised up the great shepherd of the
flock, Jesus our Lord, from the realm of the dead through the blood
of the eternal covenant, [21]equip you with all good forces, so that
you can fulfil HIS will. Thus HE HIMSELF brings about in us what
is pleasing to HIM: through the power of Jesus Christ, to whom
belongs the revelation through all cycles of time. Amen.

[22]I urge you, brothers: keep to the word of fulfilment by the
Spirit. I have sent it to you, couched in brief terms. [23]You should
know that our brother Timothy has been set free again. If he comes
soon, he and I will see you together. [24]Greet all those who guide
you, and all those in the congregations who strive for holiness. The
friends from Italy greet you.

[25]The grace be with you all!

The Letter of James

1 *Introduction*

James, a servant of God and of Jesus Christ the Lord; to the twelve
tribes who are scattered throughout the world. Greeting.

Standing firm in temptation

[2]When you have to endure many kinds of trial, my brothers, then
you can only be glad of it, [3]for you know that inner strength of
patience grows in you through the testing of your faith. [4]But this
patience must lead to fulfilment so that you become complete and
whole human beings, not held back in any respect.

[5]If anyone lacks the gift of wisdom, let him ask it of God who
gives to all human beings without reservation and without making
reproaches, and what he asks for will be given him. [6]Only he must
ask out of a believing heart, not with a doubting soul. A doubter
is like a wave on the sea which is moved and thrown hither and
thither by the wind. [7]Such a man should not think that he is able
to receive anything from the Lord. [8]His soul is divided and he is
unsteady on all his ways. [9]A brother who considers himself among
the lowly may pride himself on his greatness; [10]whoever is rich
may be proud of his lowliness, for he will perish like a flower in
the grass. [11]When the sun rises with its scorching heat it makes the
green grass wither and the flower drop off. The beauty in which
it appeared to us perishes. So also all human wealth will fade
away along Man's paths. [12]Blessed is the man who withstands the
temptation. If he proves himself, he will receive the wreath of life
which HE has promised to those who love HIM.

The origin of temptation
[13]No one who is tempted should say, ‘I am being led into
temptation by God’; for God is not tempted by evil and HE does
not lead anyone into temptation. [14]Every temptation which a
human being experiences arises out of his own cravings and
desires which lure and entice him. [15]When human desire once
has conceived, then it gives birth to sin. And sin is complete
when it brings forth death. [16]Do not be deceived, my beloved
brothers. [17]Every gift which is truly good and every perfect
present descends to us out of the higher world from the Father
of lights in whom there is no alternation and no phases of light
and darkness. [18]Out of HIS cosmic will, HE called us into life
through the truth-bearing Word. We were to be the first fruits
among HIS creatures.

Right hearing and right doing
[19]You know, my beloved brothers: every human being should
quickly be prepared to listen, slow to speak, and above all slow
to anger. [20]Out of angry impulses a human being can do nothing
which brings him close to the divine righteousness. [21]Therefore
make yourselves free of everything that pollutes your being and
from the mastery of the lower powers in you. In striving for harmony of soul, make yourselves into good soil for the seed of the
Word which can heal your souls. [22]Become fulfillers of the word;
not only hearers, imagining that you thereby already have it. [23]If
someone is a hearer of the word without being a fulfiller of it,
he is like a man who looks in a mirror at the face he was born
with, [24]and when he has observed himself like this, goes away
and at once forgets again what he looks like. [25]Whoever attains
to insight into the perfect laws of freedom and keeps to that, not
as a forgetful hearer, but as an active doer: blessed shall he be
through what he fulfils! [26]If someone thinks that he is cultivating
devotion genuinely, but has no mastery of his tongue and even
deceives himself about this in his heart, his devoutness is without
content. [27]This is true, pure and undefiled devoutness before God

the Father: taking care of the orphans and the widows in their need, and keeping oneself free from the dulling influence of the sense world.

2 *Before God all human beings are equal*
My brothers, do not allow personal considerations to become
mixed up in your faith in Jesus Christ, our Lord, and in his
light-revelation. 2Imagine: while you are gathered together, a man
wearing gold rings and splendid garments comes in, and then
there comes a poor man in shabby clothes. 3If you then turn to the
well-dressed man and say, 'Sit here in this good seat,' while you
say to the poor man, 'You can stand there' or 'sit down there by
my footstool,' 4have you then not already pronounced judgment
on yourselves as judges who make their judgments out of a base
attitude of mind?
5Listen, my beloved brothers! Has not God chosen those who
are regarded as poor in the world to be rich through the faith, as
heirs of the kingdom which he has promised to those who love him?
6But you have despised the poor man. Is it not the rich who do
violence to you and drag you before the courts? 7Do they not scorn
the good name by which you are called? 8But if you fulfil the royal
law which is stated in the scripture:

Love your neighbour as yourself,

then you do well. 9If, however, you let yourselves be guided by
personal considerations, then you are acting out of sin, and the
Law unmasks you as breakers of the Law. 10For whoever keeps the
whole Law but fails in only one point, he is guilty on all points.
11He who said:

Do not commit adultery,

has also said:

You shall not kill.

So even if you are not an adulterer but a murderer, you break the
whole of the Law. 12Therefore form your speaking and doing as
men who can be measured by the law of freedom. 13When the final
verdict comes, no compassion will be shown to one who himself

has been without compassion. Yet true compassion triumphs in
every judgment.

Faith without works is fruitless
14What use is it, dear brothers, if someone says he has faith but
does not act in accordance with the faith? Can faith by itself help
him? 15If a brother or sister is without clothing and lacks the daily
bread, 16what use is it if one of you says to them, 'Go in peace,
keep warm and eat until you are satisfied,' without giving them
what they need for daily life? 17So it is with the faith: if it is not
proved by works, by itself it is dead. 18Now someone could say,
'You have the faith, I do the works.' Well, show me your faith
without the works that spring from it, then, by my works, I will
show you my faith. 19You believe that there is a God who is One?
You are right in that. But even the demons believe that – and
shudder. 20Will you not realize, you man without inner content,
that faith without the fruit of works is meaningless? 21Was not our
father Abraham justified by his deeds when he laid his son Isaac
on the sacrificial altar? 22You see how his faith was active in his
works and that the faith was only made complete by the fruit of
the works. 23Thus the scripture was fulfilled:

> Abraham united himself with God in faith;
> it was reckoned to him as righteousness,
> and he was called a friend of God.

24You see, therefore, that a human being is justified by his deeds
and not by faith alone. 25In the same way, was not also Rahab the
harlot justified by her deeds when she received the messengers
and sent them out another way? 26As the body without the spirit is
dead, so also the faith is dead without the fruit of works.

3 *The power of the tongue*
Let not too many of you feel called to the task of teaching, my
brothers. You know that then we are judged by even stricter
standards. 2We all make many mistakes. If anyone makes
no mistakes in his work with the word, then he is a perfect

human being and will also be able to hold the reins of all bodily
urges.
[3]When we put bits into the mouths of horses to make them
obedient to our will, we thereby take control of their whole bodies. [4]Think of the ships: however great they are, driven by strong
winds, they can still be guided by the inconspicuous rudder in the
direction that the helmsman wants. [5]So also the tongue is a small
member and yet can call up great effects. See, how small a fire,
and how great a forest is set ablaze by it! [6]And the tongue is a fire:
a whole world of harm can slumber in it.

Among the members of our body the tongue holds an important
position. It can pollute the whole body; it sets the wheel of becoming on fire and can itself be set on fire by the flames of hell. [7]Every
species of animal, including the birds, reptiles and sea-creatures,
are mastered by Man; for they are tamed within human nature.
[8]But no human being is able so to master the tongue. A restless
evil lives in it, it is full of deadly poison. [9]With it we send words
of blessing and praise to the Lord and Father; but with it we also
hurl curses at human beings who are created in the image of God.
[10]From the same mouth sounds forth blessing and cursing. But,
dear brothers, it does not have to be like that. [11]Does a spring give
out both fresh and bitter water from the same opening? [12]Can a
fig tree, my brothers, yield olives, or a vine figs? No more can
a salty spring yield fresh water.

Wisdom from above

[13]Who among you has wisdom and understanding? Let him prove
it by conducting his life well and by deeds which come from a
soul which is harmonious through wisdom. [14]If bitter jealousy and
quarrelling is the tenor of your heart, you cannot speak with proud
words about yourselves without offending against the truth. [15]That
would not be a wisdom which comes down from above; at best, it
would be earthly, arising merely in the soul, flowing from demonic
sources. [16]For where jealousy and quarrelsomeness rule, there are
disorder and bad deeds of every kind. [17]The wisdom that comes

from above is, firstly, of holy purity; but it is also peaceable, gentle, agreeable, full of cordial helpfulness and rich in good fruits,
impartial and without false appearances. [18]But the fruit of righteousness springs from the seed of peace in the souls of those who
themselves beget peace.

4 *The origin of conflicts*

How does it come about that there is fighting and arguing among
you? Does not the reason for it lie in the cravings which are at war
with each other in your members? [2]Desires you have, but you do
not achieve true fulfilment. You are full of hatred and jealousy, but
what do you gain by it? That is why there is fighting and quarrelling among you. The reason why you cannot find satisfaction is
that you do not pray. [3]And when you do pray, it does not help you
because you pray wrongly. You only want to have the enjoyment
of what you wish for.

[4]You adulterous souls: do you not know that friendship with the
world of the senses means enmity with the divine world? Whoever
wishes to be friends with the sense-world easily makes himself
an enemy of God. [5]Or do you think that the word of scripture is
meaningless:

> It is precisely the spirit HE has caused to dwell in us
> which craves jealousy. [6]In contrast, the grace which HE
> gives appears all the greater.

That is why it is said:

> God resists those who think themselves important, but
> to the humble HE gives grace.

[7]Place yourselves under the guidance of God, and resist the
Tempter, then he will depart from you. [8]Seek the nearness of God,
and HE will be near to you. Cleanse your hands, you who are sinful; make your hearts holy, you who are divided in soul. [9]Become
aware of your degradation, mourn and weep because of it. Let your
laughter be turned to sorrow and your superficial joy to a feeling of
dejection. [10]Humble yourselves before the Lord and HE will exalt
you.

Warning against disparaging judgments and self-praise
[11]Do not speak disparagingly about each other, dear brothers. He
who speaks disparagingly about one of the brothers or pronounces
judgment on him, he debases the Law and pronounces judgment
on the Law. But when you make judgments about the Law you
cease to follow it in your deeds and make yourself a judge of it.
[12]But there is only one true lawgiver and judge. HE can bring about
healing or decline. Who are you, that you make yourself a judge
of your fellow men? [13]Now as for you who say, 'Today or tomorrow we will go to such and such a town and stay there a year, do
business and earn money.' [14]You do not even know what tomorrow
will bring. What is your life? You are a cloud of smoke which is
visible for a short time and soon vanishes again. [15]You ought rather
to say, 'If it is the will of the Lord and we are still living, then we
will do this or that.' [16]As things are now, your self-confidence is
based on empty boasting. Such self-praise is always evil. [17]Anyone
who knows the right and good thing to do, but does not do it,
becomes enmeshed in sin.

5 *The judgment upon the rich*
O, you rich, weep and lament because of the sufferings that will
come upon you! [2]Your riches have rotted, your garments are moth-
eaten, [3]your gold and your silver have rusted, and the rust will be
evidence against you and in the end will consume your existence
like fire. You have laid up treasure in the last days. [4]See, the wages
of the labourers who harvested your fields, which you embezzled,
cry out, and the cries of the reapers have reached the ears of the
Lord of the heavenly hosts. [5]While you have lived on earth you have
given yourselves up to pleasure and feasting; you have indulged
the sensuality of your hearts as if at a butcher's feast. [6]You have
condemned the righteous man, you have killed him and he has not
defended himself against you.

Reminder to be patient
7Therefore, brothers, in view of the spiritual coming of the Lord
be patient and long-suffering. Consider the farmer: he waits for
the precious fruit of the earth; he looks forward to it with patient
expectation until it has received both early and late rain. 8You, too,
be patient and strengthen your hearts: the spiritual coming of the
Lord is near! 9Do not complain about one another, dear brothers,
so that you will not be judged. See, the judge is already at the
door! 10In order to endure suffering and strengthen your patience,
dear brothers, let the prophets be an example to you, who spoke in
the name of the Lord. 11See, we call those blessed who bore their
destiny with patience. You have heard of the patience of Job; you
know how the Lord enabled him to reach his goal. The Lord has
great goodness and compassion.

12My brothers, be especially careful to avoid using the magic
powers of oaths. Swear neither by the Beings of the heavens nor
by those of the earth. Shun any kind of swearing altogether. Let
your yes be a yes and your no a no, if you do not want to fall into
severe crises.

Anointing the sick and the healing power of prayer
13If anyone among you has hard things to bear, let him cultivate his
life of prayer. If anyone is cheerful, let him sing songs of praise.
14If someone is ill, let him call on the help of the elders in his
congregation, and they will pray for him and anoint him with oil
in the name of the Lord. 15Then the prayer out of strong faith will
give strength to the one who is weak and the Lord will raise him
up again. If he has burdened himself with sin, it will be forgiven
him. 16Confess your transgressions to one another and pray for
one another, that you may find healing! The prayer of a righteous
human being is powerful in its effect. 17Elijah was a human being
of the same nature as ourselves, and yet: when he had completed
his prayer that no rain should fall, for three years and six months
no rain fell on the earth. 18Then he prayed again, and the heavens
gave rain and the earth brought forth its fruit.

Responsibility for those who have strayed
[19]My brothers, if anyone can bring about a change of heart in someone who has strayed from the path of truth, then he can know: [20]whoever helps another to turn back from a path of sinful aberration will free the soul of that human being from the power of death and will obliterate a great amount of sinfulness.

The First Letter of Peter

1 *Introduction*
Peter, an apostle of Jesus Christ, to the chosen homeless souls who are scattered over the lands of Pontus, Galatia, Cappadocia, Asia and Bithynia, [2]who owe their being to the providence of the Father God, whose striving is for hallowing by the Spirit and who are devoutly committed to the purifying power of the blood of Jesus Christ:

May grace and peace be yours in fullness!

Words of thanks for hope fulfilled
[3]God be praised with words of blessing, the Father of Jesus Christ, our Lord! Out of HIS great goodness HE has led us to a new birth, and thereby to the living hope which is founded on the resurrection of Jesus Christ from the dead. [4]The prospect has been opened for us of an imperishable, undefiled and unfading inheritance which is preserved for you in the heavenly spheres. [5]Through your faith you are protected by the sheltering care of the divine might; for you is intended the healing which will reveal itself when this cycle of time comes to an end. [6]About this you can rejoice, even if you still have to bear some sorrow and have to endure various trials. [7]If

your faith proves itself, then it is a treasure greater than gold which
perishes, although it also has had to be proved by fire. Through
being proved you will find the praise of God, the light of the Spirit
and the true worth of the soul when the revelation of the Being of
Christ begins. 8Your love is for him whom you have not seen with
eyes; your faith streams towards him whose presence you do not
perceive. You will rejoice with inexpressible and spirit-radiating
joy 9when you make the goal of the faith, the healing of souls, your
own.

10The prophets sought and enquired after this salvation; they
foretold the grace that was intended for you. 11They wanted to
discover what time or time-character was indicated by the Spirit
of Christ who spoke within them when he foretold the sufferings which the Christ would have to endure, as well as the light-
filled revelations of his Being which would arise out of them. 12It
was revealed to the prophets that with their proclamations they
were to serve not themselves, but you. Now this proclamation
is made to you anew through those who bring you the message
of the Gospel. They are working among you out of the power
of the Holy Spirit which has been sent down from the heavens.
Even the angels desire to learn that which is now proclaimed
to you.

Summons to a holy life

13Therefore gird up the loins of your mind in sober wakefulness,
hoping for nothing save the grace which streams to you from the
revelation of the Being of Jesus Christ. 14Be as children, of willing
mind, do not let yourselves be shaped by the stirrings of desires
as previously, when you did not yet live with insight. 15In view of
the holy nature of him who has called you, you also should hallow
everything that you do; 16as it says in the scripture:

> You shall be holy as I am holy.

17Since you call HIM Father who sternly judges the deeds of
each one without regard for persons, then you must also live
in awareness of the sternness of HIS Being as long as you are

living on earth. 18You know that you were not redeemed from the
life of appearances – transmitted to you from your fathers – by
perishable things, by silver or gold, 19but by the precious blood
of Christ which is like that of a lamb without blemish or flaw.
20Already before the creation of the world the creating thought of
God contained him, but only now, as the cycles of earthly time
are approaching their end, has he appeared for your sakes who are
united in faith with God through him. 21For God has awakened
him from the dead and given him a shining spiritual form, so that
your faith is also a hope in God. 22Purify your souls, unconditionally committed to the truth, to unfeigned brotherly love. Love one
another from the heart with all devotion 23as souls reborn who have
your lives not from perishable but from imperishable seed: from
the life-giving Word of the Godhead who bears all present and
future life in HIMSELF.

> 24For all physical existence is like grass; and all its
> glory is like the flower in the grass. The grass with-
> ers and the flower drops off, 25but the word which the
> Lord speaks outlasts the cycle of time.

That is the word which comes to you in the proclamation of the
Gospel.

2 *The living edifice of those born anew*

Therefore shed all malice, guile, insincerity and mutual slander.
2Rather be like newborn babes, hungry for the pure milk which is
offered you in the spirit-word and which makes you grow up to
receive the salvation; 3for you have tasted the mild goodness of the
Lord. 4Your way led to him, the living stone which is regarded as
worthless by men, but which is particularly highly prized by God.
5Like living building stones let yourselves also be built into the
spiritual edifice in which the holy priestly service is performed.
This is done by bringing spiritual offerings on which the eye of
God can look with pleasure, because they are brought through the
power of Jesus Christ. 6Scripture speaks of it like this:

> See, I am laying in Zion a chosen foundation stone; I

raise up a precious corner stone. Whoever is founded
on it will not be put to shame.

7 To you, who are founded on it through faith, it is valuable. But
to those without faith it has become – as the stone which builders
have called useless – the main corner stone, 8 that is to say the
stumbling-block and the rock which causes them to fall. They
stumble over it because they close their inner hearing against the
Word, as they were destined to do. 9 You, however, are the chosen
tribe, a royal priesthood, a holy people, a people belonging to God,
and you are to proclaim the marvellous deeds of him who called
you out of the darkness to his wonderful light. 10 Once you were not
a people, but now you are a people of God; once no one had pity
on you, but now you are shown mercy.

The good example

11 Beloved, I urge you, you who are strangers in your house and
homeless souls in this world, to free yourselves from the cravings
that arise out of the physical body and oppose the soul. 12 By your
way of life be a good example to the non-Christians among whom
you live, so that those who denigrate you as evildoers may awaken
to the goodness that shines from you and will come to praise God
when the day of the Visitation dawns.

13 Out of love for the true Lord be subject to every institution
which exists to guide human beings, be it the king as the leader,
14 be it those who have authority from him to punish evildoers and
to praise those who do good. 15 For that is the will of God, that you
should silence the stupidity of foolish men by giving a good example. 16 As truly free human beings you can act like that, but do not
use your freedom as a cover for wrongdoing. As free human beings
be servants of God. 17 Honour every human being, love the brotherhood, feel the greatness of God, meet the king with respect.

Admonition to slaves

18 Those of you who are slaves, with all modesty be subject to your
masters – not only to those who are gentle and kind, but also to

those who are unpredictable and irascible. 19For a human being
is raised above himself when he is able to endure suffering in the
awareness of being in the sight of God, and especially so when
he suffers without having deserved it. 20For what is special about
enduring the blows which you have earned by your failings? But
when you have done the Good and then patiently accept what you
have to suffer: that raises you above yourselves before the countenance of God. 21For to this you have been called, for did not
Christ also suffer for you? Thus he has given you his example and
the way you can follow in his steps. 22His deeds were without sin,
no false word came from his mouth. 23When he was reviled, he
did not revile in return. His suffering forced no word of bitterness
from him. He offered it all up to HIM who compensates justly. 24He
raised our sin up on to the wood of the cross in his own body so
that we, freed from sin, might find the power of true life. By his
wounds you are healed. 25You were like straying sheep, but now
you have returned to the shepherd who cares for your souls.

3 *Admonitions to women and men*

I have to speak to you women in the same way. You should entrust
yourselves to masculine guidance. It should be so that people who
do not open themselves to the Word may be won by the life and
bearing of the women, 2because they see your reverent and pure
way of being. 3Let your adornment not be external, let it not consist of artful braiding of the hair, of dangling gold ornaments and
of beautiful clothes. 4Rather, let the hidden person of the heart be
your adornment, with indestructible harmony of soul and with the
strength to be spiritually contained within yourselves. That is a precious jewel before the countenance of God. 5The holy women who
trusted in masculine guidance have always adorned themselves
like that, devoted and full of hope in God. 6That is how Sarah
trusted the guidance of Abraham, calling him 'Lord.' If you want
to be her children, devote yourselves to doing good and do not be
afraid of any intimidation.

7For you men this means: your relationship with the women

should be guided by the insight that the female body is weaker.
You should honour and respect the feminine being, since it is
intended to be the bearer of powers of life which come from
higher worlds. In this way you will also avoid disturbances in
your life of prayer.

Admonitions to the congregation

[8]Let the aim for all of you be unity of mind, common ground of
feeling, brotherliness, mutual compassion, modesty. [9]Do not repay
evil with evil and insult with insult, but rather bless; for you have
been called in order that you may pass on the power of blessing.

> [10]He who would love life
> and see good days,
> let him keep his tongue from evil
> and his lips from speaking untruth.
> [11]Let him turn away from the evil and do good.
> Let him seek peace and walk the path of peace.
> [12]For the eyes of the Lord are upon the righteous,
> and HIS ears are open to their prayer
> but the sternness of HIS countenance is against those who
> do evil!

[13]And who can do evil to you if you serve the Good with all
your heart? [14]And if you have to suffer for the sake of the Good,
then may you be called blessed. You need not fear what people
in general fear; let nothing shake you. [15]Give Christ the Lord a
holy dwelling-place in your hearts. Be always prepared to stand
up for your expectation of the future when you are required to give
account of yourselves. Give this account with a harmonious and
devout soul [16]and a good conscience, so that those who decry you
and slander the good conduct of your lives which you lead with the
power of Christ, may one day be ashamed and admit that they were
wrong. [17]It is better to suffer in the service of the Good than to be
a servant of evil.

[18]Christ suffered death once for all for the healing of the sickness
of sin, he, the bearer of the higher being, for those who have lost

the higher being. Access to the divine world was to be opened to
you. In the realm of earthly matter he suffered death; in the realm
of the Spirit he won through to new life. [19]And in the Spirit he also
went and brought the proclamation to the spirits in prison, [20]who
once closed themselves off from the will of God in the days when
the divine magnanimity still allowed a period of waiting. That was
in the days of Noah when the ark was built and only a few, namely
eight souls, were saved from the flood. [21]You now have an image
of this in the baptism which imparts healing power to you. It does
not mean being freed from earthly impurity, it is rather an appeal
to God for a conscience in which the Good lives. Baptism has its
power from the resurrection of Jesus Christ [22]and his ascent to the
right hand of God. He has risen up to the heavens, and all Angels,
Revealers and World Powers are subject to him.

4 *About the meaning of suffering*
In his earthly body Christ took suffering upon himself. Let this
same attitude of mind be your armour. Whoever takes on himself
the suffering which is the consequence of being in an earthly body,
he is at rest as far as sin is concerned; [2]for the remaining time that
he still has to live in the earthly body it is no longer human desires
but the divine will which gives impetus and direction to his life.

[3]In the past you have lived long enough in the manner of the
heathen peoples. You have lived out of unconscious depths of
the will, and you have let yourselves go in ecstatic indulgence,
in unleashing of your base desires, in Dionysian intoxication, in
greedy enjoyment of food and drink and in orgiastic rituals. [4]Now
people draw back from you, because you no longer take part in
such excesses of passion, and they turn their abuse against you.
[5]They will have to give account of themselves for this to him who
is preparing, as Lord of destiny, to judge the living and the dead.
[6]That is why the Gospel has also been proclaimed to the dead, in
order that – though they, too, have to bear the consequences of
having been physical human beings – they still can win a share
in the life of the divine Spirit.

[7]The goal of all things has come near; therefore practise calmness of will and wakefulness of consciousness as regards your life of prayer. [8]Above all, let the love which unites you become inward and deep. Love enfolds and covers all the might of sin. [9]Be hospitable to one another, without grudging. [10]Let each one use his particular ability in such a way that you serve one another, for you are to be good stewards of the many forms of the divine grace: [11]if someone has the gift of speaking, then let him make the divine word audible through the human word; if someone has the office of helper, then let him work out of the power given by God. The light of the revelation of God should shine forth in everything through the power of Jesus Christ. To him belong spiritual light and power of soul through all cycles of time. Amen.

[12]Beloved brothers, do not lose your composure in the fiery ordeal which is coming upon you to test you; for, of course, it does not descend upon you as something totally alien. [13]On the contrary – rejoice: the more you experience community with the suffering of Christ, the greater will be your joyful, rejoicing share in his light-form when it reveals itself. [14]Blessed are you when you are reviled because of the name of Christ, for the Spirit of revelation, the Spirit of God, rests upon you. [15]None of you should be affected by the test of suffering as a murderer or a thief is, one who does evil or who presumptuously assumes power over other people. [16]Whoever endures the test as a Christian need not be ashamed of it; but just at such a time let him glorify God in this name! [17]The time has come; in the house-community of God will the final decisions begin. And if it begins with us, what will become of those who do not open themselves to the divine Gospel? [18]If it is difficult even for a devout person to find salvation, how will it be for him who is without reverence, ensnared in sin?

[19]Therefore let those who have suffering laid upon them by the will of God, entrust their souls to the faithful safe keeping of the Creator and steadfastly serve the Good.

5 *Admonition to the elders and to the young*
And now I turn to the elders among you. I do this as a fellow elder,
as a witness of the suffering of Christ and as one who has a share
in the ongoing revelation of his light-form. [2]Be good shepherds
of the flock of God that has been entrusted to you. Do not do
this out of any compulsion, but fulfil the task given you by God
out of your free will. Do not act out of selfish motives but out of
enthusiastic devotion; [3]not as rulers, as though you were the own-
ers, but as men who wish to be examples to the members of their
congregation. [4]Then, when the shepherd of shepherds becomes
visible to our seeing, you will receive the unfading wreath of the
shining light of the Spirit. [5]Likewise, you that are younger: be
subject to the elders, indeed all of you should practise humility
towards one another. God works against those who are arrogant,
but to the humble HE gives grace. [6]Bow down in humility under
the mighty hand of God, so that, when the time has come, HE can
raise you up. [7]Leave all your anxieties to HIM, for HE cares for you.
[8]Be sober and be of wakeful mind. Your Adversary, the demonic
power, prowls about like a roaring lion, greedy for prey. [9]Resist
him, firm in the faith. You know that your brotherhood, which
is spread throughout the world, has to endure the same tests of
suffering. The divine source of all grace has called you in Christ to
be bearers of HIS eternal spiritual light. [10]Your sufferings are slight
compared to the strength that HE gives you: HE will establish and
strengthen you and make you the foundation of the new world.
[11]To HIM belongs all power through all cycles of time. Amen.

Conclusion: greetings and words of blessing
[12]By Silvanus I have written you these few words. In him I see
a faithful brother. Take my words as a call of the Spirit and as
a proof that it is the true grace of God on which you are based.
[13]The congregation in Babylon, which is chosen like you, sends you
greetings, as does Mark, my son. [14]Greet one another with the kiss
of love.

The peace be with you all – you, who are in Christ.

The Second Letter of Peter

1 *Introduction*
Simon Peter, a servant and apostle of Jesus Christ, to all those who
have the same treasure of faith as we, partakers of the righteousness
which is given to us by God and by Jesus Christ, the bringer of
healing:
[2]Grace and peace be yours in abundance in the knowledge and
awareness of God and of Jesus Christ, our Lord.

The importance of the Promise
[3]Because we have been granted his divine power we have all that
we need for our forces of life and for the devoutness of our soul.
We have it through knowledge of him who has called to us and has
opened to us the source of his own revealing light and his ordering
power. [4]Thereby we have been granted the most precious and significant promises; through them you will win an ever greater share
in the nature of the divine Being; you are meant to escape from
the declining, craving-filled life of the world of the senses. [5]Now
use all your enthusiasm and devotion so that true morality may
grow out of the power of your faith; and with morality spiritual
insight, [6]and with spiritual insight purity of soul, and with purity
of soul the strength to bear your destiny, and with the strength to
bear your destiny piety, [7]and with piety brotherliness, and with
brotherliness love. [8]If all this lives and grows among you, then
you will not remain without deeds and unfruitful on the path of
recognition of Jesus Christ, our Lord. [9]But anyone, for whom all
this is not present, is blind, he is short-sighted and has allowed the
purification of his past sins to be forgotten.
[10]Therefore, dear brothers, strive all the more zealously to make

firm and sure what has come alive in you since you were called and chosen. If you succeed in this you will no longer stumble on your way; [11]the entrance to the eternal spirit-kingdom of Jesus Christ who is our Lord and bringer of healing will be opened, wide and glorious, to you.

[12]I intend to bring this to your consciousness anew ever and again, although you know it and have already won a substantial share in the truth which streams towards you. [13]As long as I am living in this earthly dwelling I believe I have the right to call and awaken your consciousness; [14]for I know that I soon will have to lay aside this dwelling of mine. Thus it has also been made known to me by Jesus Christ, our Lord. [15]But I will strive to ensure that also after my departure from earthly life you will always be able to call these things to mind anew.

The Transfiguration: the fundamental experience

[16]We did not follow thought-out ideas when we brought you knowledge of the power of being and the spiritual coming of Jesus Christ, our Lord. We spoke to you as those to whom it has been granted to perceive the majestic revelation of his being. [17]From the Father God he received dignity of soul and spiritual light when the voice spoke to him out of the exalted revelation:

> This is my beloved Son, in him I have revealed
> myself.

[18]This voice we heard sound forth out of the heavenly heights when we were with him on the holy mountain.

[19]For us, therefore, the spiritual word which points to the future is even more securely founded, and you do well to pay heed to it as to a light which illumines a dark place until the day dawns brightly, and the light-bearer, the morning star, rises in your hearts. [20]But, from the beginning, be clear about this, that no prophetic word in the scriptures may be understood merely personally. [21]No prophecy ever flowed from human willing; rather, human beings, carried by the Holy Spirit, spoke as the mouth of God.

2 *Judgment upon false teachers*
There have always been false prophets among the people, and there
will also be false teachers among you. They will cause harmful ten-
dencies to schism to arise, since they deny the Master who bought
them their freedom. Thus they will bring about their own rapid
decline. [2]Many will follow their unbridled desires, whereby the
path of truth is profaned. [3]Driven by self-seeking, they will try to
win you with brilliance in speaking. The ancient judgment of them
is in force; the powers of decline and destruction, towards whom
they are drifting, do not sleep.

[4]Neither did God spare the angel-beings who strayed; HE cast
them bound into the dark depths of Tartarus where they await the
great decision. [5]Nor did HE spare the old earth-cosmos; besides
seven others, HE only saved Noah, a herald of righteousness, when
HE caused the flood to rise over mankind which had fallen away
from God. [6]The cities of Sodom and Gomorrah HE also caused
to be extinguished, by burning them to ashes as a warning and
example to all who would turn away from God in the future. [7]He
saved only the righteous Lot, who suffered great anguish because
of the wanton lives of the sinners; [8]for since he, being devoted to
the Good, lived among them, they tortured his devout soul day
after day with deeds of chaos which were done within his sight and
hearing.

[9]The Lord's intention is to rescue from every trial the souls
who are devoted to the Spirit. But the enemies of the Good HE
keeps for the Day of Decision which delivers them into torment.
[10]This will be so, especially for those who lose themselves completely to earthly matter in impure desire, and who despise all
spiritual guidance. Insolent in their overestimation of themselves,
they have no inhibitions about ridiculing all revelations; [11]and yet
the angels, though they are so high above them in strength and
might of being, do not pronounce judgment before the Lord about
their blasphemy. [12]Like irrational animals, whose natural instincts
lead them to hunt for prey and to cause destruction, they revile
things about which they know nothing. [13]By their destructive

attitude they ruin themselves; they are cheated of the reward of
their fraud. They consider luxurious feasting in broad daylight a
great joy. They are stained and polluted in their being, and even
when they live in your community they still do not tear themselves
free from the fascination of their deceptive pleasures. 14Their eyes
are full of unchastity and insatiable, sinful greed. They entice
unsteady souls; their heart has become accustomed only to seek
for selfish aims; like immature beings they are under a curse.
15They have departed from the true path and therefore they wan-
der aimlessly. They have entered upon the path of Balaam, the son
of Beor. When he chased after unjust gain 16he experienced how
his magic rebounded upon him. A beast of burden, without the
gift of language, spoke in human words and restrained the mad
undertaking of the prophet.

17These people are springs without water, clouds of mist driven
by the storm; the abyss of darkness yawns before them. 18They
speak pompous words which in reality are without content; and,
by playing on uncontrolled sensual desires, they entice others who
are just about to free themselves from a false path. 19They promise
them freedom, although they themselves are slaves of corruption;
for everyone is a slave to the power to which he is subject. 20Those
who have freed themselves from the obscuring might of the world
of the senses and have come to recognize Jesus Christ, the Lord and
bringer of healing, but then once more fall prey to those entangle-
ments – for them the last state is worse than the first. 21It would be
better for them if they had not come to know the path of goodness
at all, than that they now, when they know it, fall away and become
unfaithful to the holy task which they have been given. 22To them
applies the true proverb:

> The dog craves for its own filth,

and

> The sow goes to the watering place only to wallow
> once more in the mud.

The apparent delay in the reappearing of Christ

Now this, beloved, is the second letter that I write to you; and once
again may my words be an awakening call to sun-clear consciousness in you. 2Cultivate remembrance of the words once spoken by
the holy prophets and the directions of the apostles of the Lord and
Saviour who worked among you. 3Above all, be aware of this: in
the last days will come people with utterly mocking minds, who
let themselves be guided entirely by their personal wishes and
desires. 4They will say, 'What about the promise of his coming,
then? The patriarchs died ages ago, and still everything is exactly
the same as it always has been since the beginning of creation.'
5Those who speak like that will not admit the fact that originally
the heavenly spheres and the earth together consisted of water, and
that all existence was condensed out of the water by the power of
the creating Word of God. 6That is also why the old earth-condi-
tion was swallowed up by water and perished. 7But by the same
Creator-Word the heavens and the earth in their present form are
being gathered and kept for the element of fire; they are being preserved until the Day of the last decision and decline comes upon
humanity which is alienated from God.

8This one thing, beloved, should not remain hidden from you:
with the Lord one day is as a thousand years, and a thousand years
are as one day. 9The Lord is not delaying his promise, as some
think who regard him as slow to act. Rather, he is patient with
us, not wishing that anyone should perish, but that all should find
the way to a change of heart and mind. 10The Day of the Lord
will come like a thief. With an enormous uproar the spheres of
the heavens will enter into a new form of existence. The realm of
the elements will be dissolved in fire. Then the face of the earth
is fully revealed, and all deeds that have been done on earth are
written upon its face.

11Since the dissolution of all being takes place in this way, how
powerful must be your striving to prepare a place for what is holy
by the whole of your lives and all your devotion! 12You must wait
for the dawning of the Day of God with never-resting longing,

when the spheres of the heavens will dissolve in fire and the realm
of the elements will melt in it. [13]Within us we bear the expectation
of new heavens and a new earth, according to the divine promise
in which righteousness dwells.

Concluding admonition and reference to Paul

[14]Therefore, dcar brothers, for the sake of this expectation of the
future strive with devoutness to stand before him as bearers of
peace, without spot or blemish. [15]Look upon the patience of the
Lord as a saving grace. Paul, our beloved brother, has also written
to you about this out of the wisdom given him. [16]In all his letters
he speaks in a similar way about these things, although there are
also some things in them which are hard to understand, so that
those who are of unteachable and superficial mind twist them, as
they also do the other scriptures, to their own destruction.

[17]But you, my beloved, who know in advance what is to come,
take care that you do not let yourselves be robbed of inner certainty and be led astray by the error of those lawless people. [18]Let
the power of spiritual fulfilment and the clarity of knowledge of
our Lord and Saviour Jesus Christ grow ever stronger in you.
To him belongs the light of spiritual revelation, now and at the
dawning of the day of the coming cycle of time.

The First Letter of John

1 *The message concerning the divine Word*
It was from the Beginning. We have heard it, we have seen it
with our eyes, we have beheld it and touched it with our hands:
the divine Word which bears all life within itself. 2The very life
revealed itself and we saw it, and so we bear witness to it and
proclaim it to you as the life which is through all cycles of time.
It was with the Father; now it has revealed itself to us. 3We have
seen it and heard it, and we proclaim it to you, so that you also can
live in spiritual community with us; that is, our community with
the Father and with Jesus Christ, HIS Son. 4We are writing this so
that your joy may be full.

Life in the Light
5And this is the message we have received from him and which
we proclaim to you; God is Light and there is not any kind of
darkness in HIM. 6If we say that we have community with HIM, yet
conduct our lives in darkness, then what we say is a lie and what
we do is without reality. 7Only when our life is fully permeated by
light, as HE is in the light, are we truly united in community, and
the blood of Jesus, HIS Son, cleanses us of all sin. 8If we say that
we are without sin, we deceive ourselves and the truth is not in us.
9But if we are conscious of our sinfulness and confess to it, then
HE proves faithful and just; HE takes the sins from us and cleanses
us of all unrighteousness. 10If we say that we have never fallen
into sin, we make HIM a liar, and the divine Word which goes forth
from HIM is not in us.

2 I write this, my little children, so that you may not fall into sin.
Should anyone still fall into sin, we have an advocate, a Paraclete,

with the Father: Jesus Christ, the righteous one. 2He is the atonement for our sins, and not only for ours but also for the sins of the whole world.

3That is how we know whether we are filled by knowledge of him, if we faithfully bear the aims of his will in us. 4Whoever says that he knows him, yet does not follow the aims of his will, is a liar, and the truth is not in him. 5But whoever faithfully bears his word within his own will, in him the love of God has, in truth, reached its fulfilment. This is how we can know whether our being is within his Being: 6whoever says that his own being is enveloped by his Being must walk the same paths that he walked.

Brotherly love

7My beloved, I am writing you no new commandment. It is the old commandment which has been given you from the beginning: the old commandment is the divine Word which you have perceived, 8and yet it is a new commandment that I write to you. In him it became reality, and also in you. For the time of the darkness is past – already the true light is shining. 9Whoever says that he is in the light, and yet hates his brother, he is still in darkness. 10But whoever loves his brother, he lives in the light. Nothing which separates him from the Spirit is present in him. 11Whoever hates his brother is in the darkness and walks the path of darkness; he does not know where he is going, because the darkness has blinded his eyes.

12I am writing to you, little children, because the sins have been taken from you through the power of his name. 13I am writing to you, fathers, because you have recognized him who is from the Beginning. I am writing to you, young men, because you have won the victory over the might of the evil. 14I have written to you children, because you have recognized the Father. I have written to you fathers, because you have recognized him who is from the Beginning. I have written to you young men, because you are strong, and because the divine Word lives in you, and because you have won the victory over the might of the evil.

15 In your love, do not lose yourselves to the world and to that
which is in the world. If anyone loses himself in love to the world,
then the love of the Father is not in him. 16 For all that belongs
to the world: the life of desires which rises up out of our bodily
nature, the cravings which are aroused through the eyes, the arrogant self-will which enslaves our forces of life – all this does not
originate from the Father, but comes from the external side of the
world. 17 The outer world is transitory, as are the desires which it
awakens. But whoever fulfils the will of God endures through the
cycles of time.

The signs of Antichrist

18 Children, it is the last hour. As you have heard, the Antichrist
is coming. He is already at work in many forms; that is how we
recognize that a last hour has begun. 19 Those, through whom the
Antichrist works, have come forth out of our midst, but they did
not belong to us. If they had belonged to us they would have
remained with us; but it had to become apparent that they do
not all belong to us. 20 You all have received the anointing from
him who is holy. You all are men who know. 21 I do not write to
you as to men who do not know the truth, but as to men who
know it and who know that no lie can come forth out of truth. 22 Is
not he the actual liar who denies that Jesus is the Christ? In him
lives the spirit of the Antichrist; he denies the Father and the Son.
23 Whoever denies the Son has no part of the Father, either. Whoever
confesses the Son has the Father also. 24 Let what you have heard
from the beginning live lastingly in you. If what you have heard
from the beginning lives as enduring power in you, then you will
remain in the Son and in the Father. 25 That is the promise which he
himself has proclaimed to us: the life which endures through all
cycles of time.

26 I have written all this to you because of those who would
lead you astray. 27 And as regards you, may the anointing, which
you have received from him, live in you. Then you have no need
for anyone to teach you, but rather you learn every kind of thing

through the anointing which you have received from him, and what
you learn is true and no deception. Be founded in him, in accordance with the teaching which he gives you in this way.
[28]Therefore remain in him, little children, so that we may look
towards his appearing with confidence and not fail shamefully at
his coming in the Spirit. [29]When you know that he is just, then you
also know that every one who makes righteousness come alive is
born of him.

3 *Distinguishing features of the children of God*
See how great is the love that the Father has shown us, that we can
be called children of God and also really *be* that. The reason why
the world cannot know us is that it did not know HIM. [2]Beloved,
we are children of God now, and what we shall be in the future is
not yet manifest. We know that when he reveals himself we shall
be like him, for we shall see him as he is. [3]And so everyone who
looks toward him with this hope purifies himself according to the
example of his holy being. [4]Everyone who acts out of sin brings
about chaos; sin is chaos. [5]But you know that he has revealed
himself in order to break the power of sin. His being is free from
sin. [6]Everyone who is founded in him ceases to be a tool of sin.
Whoever acts out of sin has neither seen him nor recognized him.
[7]Little children, do not be led astray by anyone! Whoever practises
righteousness is just, as he is just. [8]Whoever acts out of sin has
his being from the realm of the Adversary; for it is the Adversary
who has been the cause of sin from the very beginning. For that
reason the Son of God appeared and revealed himself to dissolve
the works of the Adversary. [9]Whoever is born of God does not act
out of sin, for the divine seed works in him as enduring power.
He cannot act out of sin, because he is born of God. [10]Thus the
children of God and the children of the Adversary are revealed.
Whoever does not practise righteousness is not of God; neither is
he who does not love his brother.
[11]That is the message which you have perceived from the very
Beginning: that we should love one another. [12]We should not

be like Cain who made himself a tool of the evil and slew his
brother. And why did he slay him? Because evil was active in his
deeds, whereas the Good worked in his brother's. [13]Do not wonder, dear brothers, when the world hates you. [14]We know that we
have passed out of the realm of death into that of life, for we love
the brothers. Whoever does not love remains within the power of
death. [15]Everyone who hates his brother kills what is human in
him, and you know that the eternal life cannot be in a murderer.

[16]By this we have recognized the Being of love, that he gave his
life for us; and so it is also for us to give our lives for our brothers.
[17]Someone may have all the life in the world: if he sees his brother
in need and yet closes his heart against him, how can God's love
dwell in him? [18]Little children, let us not only love one another
in thoughts and words but with deeds and in truth. [19]By that we
shall know whether we are of the truth. And before the countenance of God we may be certain: [20]even if our heart accuses us,
God is greater than our heart and understands everything. [21]Then,
beloved, when our heart no longer accuses us, we can come before
God with confidence, [22]and what we ask for we will receive from
HIM. For we have taken the aims of HIS will into ourselves and do
what is pleasing before HIM. [23]This is the aim that he sets before
us, that we trust in the name of HIS Son Jesus Christ, and that we
love one another as he laid it upon us to do. [24]All who take his
aims into their will remain in him, and he in them. By this we
can recognize that he remains in us: out of the Spirit which he has
given us.

4 *The Spirit of God and the spirit of Antichrist*

Beloved, do not trust every spirit, but test the spirits to see whether
they are of God. For many false prophets have begun to work
among men. [2]By this you can recognize the Spirit of God: every
spirit who acknowledges that in Jesus the Christ entered as man
into earthly incarnation is of God; [3]and every spirit who does not
acknowledge Jesus is not of God. Rather, it is the spirit of Antichrist,
of whom you have heard that he is coming. He is already at

work among men. 4Little children, you are of God and have conquered the hostile powers; for he who works in you is greater than he who is at work in the world. 5They are of the world, and that is why what they say is also of the world, and the world listens to them. 6But we are of God. Whoever knows God listens to us; whoever is not of God does not listen to us. That is how we can distinguish between the spirit of truth and the spirit of error.

The love of God and brotherly love

7Beloved, let us love one another, for love is of God, and everyone who loves is born of God and knows God. 8Anyone who does not love has not recognized God, for God is love. 9The love of God appeared visibly among us through this, that God sent HIS only begotten Son into the world, so that we might have true life through him. 10That is the nature of this love, not that we loved God, but that HE loved us and sent HIS Son as atonement and healing for our sins. 11Beloved, if God so loved us, then it is incumbent upon us to love one another. 12No one has ever seen God; but if we love one another, God abides in us and HIS love reaches fulfilment in us. 13By this we know that we remain in HIM and HE in us; HE has given us of HIS own Spirit. 14We have seen it for ourselves and can testify to it that the Father has sent the Son to bring healing to the world. 15Whoever confesses that the Son of God has appeared among us in Jesus, in him God dwells, and he dwells in God. 16We have perceived the love with which God dwells in us, and have founded our faith on it.

God is love, and he who remains in love remains in God, and God remains in him. 17And this is the most perfect fruit of love among us, that we can be full of joyful confidence on the day of the great decision. Let us, too, stand in this world in the same way as he did. 18There is no fear in love, but perfect love drives out all fear. Fear bears its own punishment within it; he who is fearful remains imperfect in love. 19Let us love, because HE first loved us. 20Whoever says that he loves God, and yet hates his brother, he is a liar. For if someone does not love the brother whom he can see,

he will be unable to love God whom he cannot see. [21]This commandment we have received from him, that everyone who loves
God should love his brother also.

5 *The power of faith*

Every one who believes that Jesus is the Christ is born of God.
And every one who loves the one who brings to birth, also loves
the one who is born. [2]By this we recognize that we love the children of God, when we love God and act according to HIS spirit-aims. [3]That is how our love to God reveals itself, that we take
HIS spirit-aims into our will. And the aims HE lays upon us are not
heavy burdens, [4]for everything that is born of God overcomes the
world. And the victory with which we conquer the world is the
faith in our hearts.

The threefold testimony to Christ

[5]Who else can be a victor over the world but he who believes that
Jesus is the Son of God?

[6]He it is who comes close to us in the elements water and blood:
Jesus Christ. He does not come close to us in water only, but in
water and in blood. And in the element air, [7]the Spirit makes us
aware of his nearness, for the Spirit is the truth. [8]Thus we have a
threefold witness to his presence: through the Spirit, through the
water and through the blood; and these three are one.

[9]If we can have confidence in the testimony of human beings,
the testimony of God is very much greater: this is HIS testimony, that
HE has confirmed the sending of HIS Son. [10]Whoever unites himself
in faith with the Son of God finds the testimony of God in his own
inner being. Whoever does not open himself in faith to God makes
HIM a liar, for he does not believe the testimony with which God
has confirmed the sending of HIS Son. [11]This testimony is that God
gives us eternal life, and that is life in HIS Son. [12]Whoever has the
Son has life. Whoever does not have the Son of God does not have
life either.

Certainty that prayer is heard

13I have written all this to you, so that you may know that you
have eternal life, you who bear the faith in the name of the Son
of God as a power within you. 14Out of our life with him grows
the joyful confidence that we are heard by him in everything we
ask of him in accordance with his will. 15And since we know that
he hears our prayers, we can also be sure that we will receive the
fulfilment of the pleas we send to him.

16If anyone sees that his brother is caught up in sin, and it is not
a sin which leads to death of the soul, then he should pray for him,
and life will be granted to him. However, this is only so for sin
which does not have death of the soul as its consequence. For there
is a sin which causes soul-death. That is not the sin I mean when I
say that one should pray. 17Every injustice is already sin, but it is
not a sin that leads to death of the soul.

Shelter in Christ

18We know that anyone who is born of God does not fall prey
to sin. He who was born of God takes HIM into his will, and the
power of the evil cannot touch him. 19We know that we are of God,
although the whole world is in the power of the evil; 20but we also
know that the Son of God has come and has given us the perception by which we recognize him whose very being is truth. We are
within this true Being, the Son of God, Jesus Christ. He is the true
God and eternal life.

21Little children, guard against the spirits of mere appearances!

The Second Letter of John

Greeting

The elder to the elect soul of the congregation and to her children,
whom I love in truth, and not I alone but with me all who have
recognized the truth. [2]This love flows from the truth which dwells
in us and will be with us for ever. [3]Grace, goodness and peace
will work among us from God the Father and from the Son of the
Father, Jesus Christ, in truth and love.

Love for the brothers

[4]My joy was great, because among your children I found such as
walk the path of truth, in accordance with the aim which we have
been given by the Father. [5]And now I ask you, you guiding soul,
not in order to give you a new commandment but to renew that
aim within you which we have all been given from the beginning:
let us love one another! [6]And this is the nature of love, that we
lead our lives in accordance with the divine spiritual aims. This is
the commandment which you have heard from the beginning: that
you should walk the path of love.

Warning against being led astray

[7]Many deceiving spirits have begun to work among men. They will
not admit the truth that in Jesus the Christ was incarnated in an
earthly body. That is the spirit of error and enmity towards Christ.
[8]Look out, that you do not lose the fruits of our work; you are to
reap the full yield. [9]Someone may make ever such great progress,
but if he does not remain faithful to the Christ-teachings he will
lose all his share of the divine world. But whoever remains filled
by this teaching has a share in the Being of both the Father and

the Son. [10]If anyone comes to you who does not bring this teaching with him, do not include him in your community and do not offer him your greeting. [11]Whoever offers him this greeting makes himself an accomplice to his deeds with which he is ultimately serving the evil.

Concluding words and greeting

[12]There is still much I could have written to you, but I did not want to use paper and ink; rather, I hope to come to you. Then we can speak face to face, and our joy will be complete.

[13]The children of your elect sister greet you.

The Third Letter of John

Greetings and words of blessing

The elder to Gaius, the beloved whom I love in truth. [2]Beloved,
above all my wish and my prayer are that you may find the right
path and the healthy way, and I know that your soul is on the right
course. [3]I was overjoyed when the brothers came and testified to
me that you are founded in the truth and lead your life in the truth.
[4]No greater joy can I have than this: to hear that my children walk
the way of truth.

Conduct towards foreign brothers

[5]Beloved, you prove your faithfulness by what you do for the
brothers and, in addition, for strangers. [6]They have testified to your
love before the congregation: how well you did to care for their
further journey, as befits the service of God. [7]They have set out
in order to serve the divine name, and they have accepted no gifts

from the non-Christians. [8]Therefore it is our duty to receive them, so that we show ourselves to be their fellow workers in the service of the truth.

Diotrephes and Demetrius

[9]I have written to the congregation; but Diotrephes, who would like to be foremost in the congregation, does not accept anything from us. [10]Therefore, when I come, I will have to bring to his awareness what he is actually doing. He disparages us with hostile words, and, not content with that, he does not welcome the brothers and prevents those who are prepared to receive them from doing so, and drives them away from the congregation.

[11]Beloved, do not take the evil but the good as your example. He who does the good is of God. He who does evil has not seen God. [12]Everyone has stood up for Demetrius, and the truth itself has borne witness to him. We also stand by him, and you know that our testimony is truthful.

Concluding words and greeting

[13]There is still much I could write to you, but I will not write it to you with pen and ink. [14]I hope to see you soon, and we will speak together, face to face.

[15]The peace be with you. The friends greet you. Greet the friends, each one by name.

The Letter of Judas (Jude)

Greeting and words of blessing
Judas, a servant of Jesus Christ and brother of James, to all who
have been called and live in the love of the Father God and the
protecting guidance of Jesus Christ:
2May goodness, peace and love be yours in fullness!

Fight for the faith
3Beloved, always I have wanted to write to you about the salvation in which we all share. Now it has become necessary for me
to write to you to urge you to fight for the substance of the faith,
which has been handed on in the same way to all who strive for
salvation. 4For some persons have sneaked in, whose ominous
attitude of soul has been noticeable for a long time: they are without reverence; the power of grace which God has given to us
they pervert into means for their licentiousness, and they deny the
only Master, Jesus Christ, our Lord.
5I want to call to your mind all that you know, once for all:
when the Lord had saved the people out of Egypt, HE caused those
who became unfaithful to perish. 6So also the angels who did not
keep the connection with their very beginning, and even deserted
from the spheres of activity which had been allotted to them, have
been kept in eternal chains by HIM until the decision at the great
dawning of the Day. 7So also Sodom and Gomorrah and the surrounding towns became a warning and an example: because they
gave themselves up to sexual perversions and set their minds on
illicit bodily mutations, they drew upon themselves, as just compensation, the fire that, in time, will destroy the aeon.
8The ones we are speaking about here err in a similar way.

They fall into somnambulistic trances, and defile the physical body
through misuse; they despise spiritual guidance and pour scorn
upon revelations. [9]When the Archangel Michael fought with the
Adversary in the Spirit for the life-body of Moses, he still did not
dare to make the final decision about those blasphemous words,
but rather he said, 'May the Lord be your judge!' [10]These people
talk blasphemously of something about which they know nothing,
because, like the irrational animals, they only know of it through
the appearance to the senses. They bring ruin upon themselves.

The error of Balaam and Korah's rebellion

[11]Woe to them: they walk in the way of Cain; by their greed they
have abandoned themselves to the error of Balaam, and they perish in the spirit of contradiction of Korah. [12]These are the people
who desecrate your sacramental life by taking part in it without
reverence. They want to be their own shepherds, but they are waterless clouds, driven along by the winds, barren trees in late autumn,
twice dead and uprooted; [13]wild waves of the sea who spray abroad
their own insubstantiality, wandering stars for whom the abyss of
darkness waits until the end of the aeon.

[14]About them, Enoch, the seventh after Adam, prophesied:

> Behold, the Lord will come in the midst of his holy
> myriads [15]to lead all beings to the final decision. The
> true nature must be revealed of all those who are with-
> out reverence, the consequences of their irreverence
> must show themselves and all the hardheartedness and
> rigidity of the words which they have uttered against
> him in their sinful irreverence.

[16]With embittered souls they form their disparaging judgments
about everything; they let themselves be guided only by their
desires, their mouths speak arrogant words. When they speak with
approval of anything, they only do it to gain an advantage by it.

[17]But you, my beloved, cultivate the remembrance of the words
once spoken by the apostles of our Lord Jesus Christ. [18]For they did
tell you that at the end of the age there will be people with mock-

ing minds who are guided solely by the desires of their irreverent
nature. 19They are only out to cause divisions. They are human
beings who only live out of their soul-natures; they have no share
of the Spirit.

Stand firm in love

20But you, my beloved, with inner work make use of the upbuilding forces which are given to you by your faith which is most
sacred to you. Be filled with the Holy Spirit through the practice of
prayer. 21Remain in the love of God and stand firm in it, open yourselves in longing to the goodness of our Lord Jesus Christ unto
eternal life. 22Let the wavering souls experience your helping love,
23snatch them out of the consuming fire and lead them to healing;
but also give compassionate help to those for whom you must
already fear, even when you feel revulsion for their garment, soiled
as it is by earthly matter.

Words of praise

24To HIM who has the power to keep you from stumbling and who
so fills you that you can stand before HIS shining revelation with
purified hearts and minds and full of joy; 25to HIM, the one God
who gives us healing through Jesus Christ, our Lord, to HIM belong

light of revelation
greatness of being
strength of being
and creating power

before all aeons and now and in all cycles of time to come. Amen.

The Revelation to John

The origin of the revelation

This is the revelation of the Being of Jesus Christ which God has
given him to show those who would serve HIM what is to come
in the future and is approaching speedily. HE formed this revelation in picture language and sent it to HIS servant John through HIS
angel; 2and so John speaks as a witness to the divine Word, and to
the life of Jesus Christ which served as a testimony and which he
himself saw. 3Blessed is he who knows how to read the prophetic
words, and blessed are those who know how to hear them, and all
who take into their souls what is written in this book; for the time
is pressing!

Greetings to the seven congregations

4John to the seven congregations in Asia:
May grace and peace be yours
From HIM who is and who was and who is coming
And from the seven creating spirits before HIS throne
5And from Jesus Christ.
By his witnessing he is the archetype of faith,
He is the firstborn from the realm of death,
He is the spirit that leads the Kings on earth.
He has turned to us in love, and by the power of his blood
he has released us from the spell of sin which lay upon us.
6He has established us as true Kings and made us into priests
before the divine Ground of the World, his Father.

To him belongs all light of the spirit and all power of
soul from aeon to aeon. Amen.

7See, he comes in the realm of clouds. All eyes shall see him,
also the eyes of those who pierced him. And men down the ages
will lament about him. Yes, Amen.

8I am the Alpha and the Omega,
thus speaks the Lord, our God,
who is and who was and who is coming,
the divine ruler of the world.

9I, John, your brother and your companion in all trials and also
in the inner kingdom and in the power of endurance which we
possess through our one-ness with Jesus: I was on the island of
Patmos. There it was to be granted me to receive a share of the
divine word and to bear witness to the sufferings of Jesus.

10On the Lord's day I was lifted up to the world of spirit, and
I heard behind me a mighty voice like the sound of a trumpet.
11It said: write what you see in a book and send it to the seven
congregations, to Ephesus and to Smyrna and to Pergamum and
to Thyatira and to Sardis and to Philadelphia and Laodicea. 12And
I turned to see him whose voice was speaking to me. And as I
turned I saw seven golden lampstands, 13and in the midst of the
lampstands a figure like that of the Son of Man:

clothed with a long, flowing garment,
a golden girdle round his breast,
14his head white, with hair shining white
like white wool and like snow,
his eyes as if they were a flame of fire,
15his feet as of bronze refined by fire,
his voice like the rushing of many streams of water.
16In his right hand he held seven stars,
from his mouth issued as it were a sharp two-edged
sword,
and his face shone like the sun in its full power.

17And when I saw him I fell at his feet and was as if dead.
But he laid his right hand upon me and said: do not be afraid. I

am the first and the last 18and the living one. I was dead, and yet
I bear the life of the world through all aeons. Mine is the key to
the realm of death and of the shades. 19Write down what you see,
what is now and what is to come.

20The secret of the seven stars which you see in my right hand,
and of the seven golden lampstands is this:

The seven stars are the angels of the seven congregations, and
the seven lampstands are the seven congregations themselves.

2 *To Ephesus*

To the angel of the congregation in Ephesus write: speaking to
you is the one who holds the seven stars in his right hand, and
who walks among the seven golden lampstands. 2I see through
your deeds and I see your striving and your power of endurance.
But I also see that you are not able to carry those who lack the
strength to resist evil. You have put to the test those calling themselves apostles, and you have discovered that they are not and
that they are frauds. 3You have power of endurance. For the sake
of my name you have borne heavy burdens and have not become
weary. 4But I have the reproach to make against you that you have
deviated from your first love. 5Cultivate the remembrance of the
heights from which you have fallen back. Change your heart and
mind and once more act in the same spirit as you did at first. If
not, I will come and take away your lampstand, that is if you do
not transform your heart and mind. 6But this can be said for you,
that you loathe the deeds of the Nicolaitans which I also abhor.

7He who has ears, let him hear what the spirit says to the
congregations! To him who overcomes I will give to eat from the
tree of life which stands in the paradise of God.

To Smyrna

8And to the angel of the congregation in Smyrna write: speaking to
you is the First and the Last, who was dead and who won through
to life again. 9I know and see the difficulties of your destiny and
how poor you have become; yet you are rich. And I also see

through the mocking of the spirit of those who call themselves
Jews but who in reality are an assembly of Satan.
10Do not be afraid of the sufferings that are before you. See, the
Adversary is making ready to bind some of you with chains. That
is so that you may be tested. You have ten days of grievous destiny
before you. Have faith unto death, then I will give you the crown
of life.
11He who has ears, let him hear what the spirit says to the
congregations! He who overcomes will suffer no harm from the
second death.

To Pergamum

12And to the angel of the congregation in Pergamum write: speaking to you is the one who has the sharp two-edged sword. 13I
know and see your dwelling place. You dwell where the throne
of Satan is. You hold fast to the power of my name, and you have
not denied your faith in me, not even in the days of Antipas, my
faithful witness, who was killed in your midst at the place of the
satanic power. 14And yet I must reproach you. Some of you adhere
to the teaching of Balaam, who taught Balak to set a trap for the
sons of Israel by enticing them to eat of meat offered in pagan sacrifices, and to practise licentiousness. 15And there are also some
among you who in a similar way adhere to the teaching of the
Nicolaitans. 16Strive to change your heart and mind. If not I will
come upon you unexpectedly and will fight against them with the
sword of my mouth.
17He who has ears, let him hear what the spirit says to the
congregations! To him who overcomes I will give of the hidden
manna and a white stone on which a new name is written which no
one knows except he who receives it.

To Thyatira

18And to the angel of the congregation of Thyatira write: speaking to
you is the divine Son whose eyes are like flames of fire and whose
feet are like glowing bronze. 19I know your deeds, your love and

your faith and your willingness to help and your power of endurance. Your latter deeds exceed your former.

[20]But I must reproach you that you tolerate the woman Jezebel. She calls herself a prophetess and teaches and entices those who serve me to spiritual adultery and to eat meat offered in pagan sacrifice. [21]I gave her time to change her consciousness, but she refuses to change her heart and mind and to desist from spiritual adultery. [22]See, I throw her on a sickbed, together with all those who have sinned against the spirit with her.

There, they will be struck by grievous destiny unless they still achieve a change of heart and mind and distance themselves from her former deeds. [23]Her children shall be exposed to the power of death.

All congregations shall know that I Am and that I know how to test them, heart and sinew, and that I give to each one of you the destiny that corresponds to his deeds. [24]But now I am also speaking to those among you in Thyatira who have not accepted that teaching and who have not entered into the depths of the Satan's being, as one says. I will lay no new burden on you. [25]I only urge you: hold fast to what you have achieved, and so prepare for my coming! [26]To him who overcomes and who faithfully strives to work out of my power until the aim has been reached, I will give the authority of the true self which is above all merely national characteristics, [27]and he will be a shepherd of the peoples, with the iron staff. He will be able to break them like earthenware pots. He will have the same authority of the true self as I have received from my Father. [28]And I will give him the morning star. [29]He who has ears, let him hear what the spirit says to the congregations!

3 *To Sardis*

And to the angel of the congregation in Sardis write: he it is who speaks to you who has power over the seven divine creating spirits and the seven stars: I see through your deeds. You have the name of a living being, yet you are dead. [2]Strive to awaken in your

consciousness, and strengthen what is still living in your soul so
that it die not. I cannot say that your deeds are of real worth before
the countenance of God. 3Therefore revive in your memory all that
you have received and heard from the spiritual worlds. Care for
it in your soul, and change your heart and mind. If you do not
awaken to higher consciousness, I will come like a thief; you will
not know at what hour I will come upon you. 4Yet you do still have
a few names in Sardis who have not soiled their garments. They
shall walk in my ways, clothed in white, for they are worthy of it.

5He who overcomes shall also be clothed in white, and I will
not blot out his name from the Book of Life. I will confess his
name before the countenance of my Father and before HIS angels.
6He who has ears, let him hear what the spirit says to the congregations!

To Philadelphia

7And to the angel of the congregation in Philadelphia write: speaking to you is the one who is holy, who is true, who has the key
of David. When he opens, no one shuts, and when he shuts, no
one opens. 8I see through your deeds. See, I have caused the door
before you to be open so that no one can close it. Your strength is
yet small, but you have kept my word in your soul and have not
denied my name. 9See, I will cause some of those of the assembly of
the satanic spirit, who wrongfully and untruthfully call themselves
Jews, to come to you and throw themselves at your feet. They shall
know that I love you. 10You have kept my word of patient endurance in your heart, and so I will keep you in the hour of the great
trial which is breaking in upon the whole of mankind. All inhabitants of the earth must withstand this trial. 11I come unexpectedly
quickly. Hold fast to what you have achieved inwardly, so that no
one may rob you of your crown.

12Him who overcomes I will make a pillar in the temple of
my divine Father. He will no longer leave this temple. And I will
inscribe the name of my divine Father upon him, and the name
of the city of God, the New Jerusalem, which descends from my

divine Father out of heaven; and my own name, which is new. [13]He
who has ears, let him hear what the spirit says to the congregations!

To Laodicea
[14]And to the angel of the congregation in Laodicea write: thus speaks
the Amen, the divine-creative principle of the world who makes
faith and insight true by the testimony of his own Being: [15]I see
through your deeds; you are neither cold nor warm. If only you were
at least cold or warm! [16]But since you are lukewarm, and neither
cold nor warm, I spew you out from my mouth. [17]You say: I am rich
and have everything and lack for nothing. You do not know how
pitiful, pathetic and poverty-stricken you are, how blind and how
naked. [18]Therefore I counsel you to obtain gold from me which is
refined by fire, so that you may be rich again; also white garments so
that you may be clothed, and the disgrace of your nakedness be not
made apparent; and lastly also the salve to anoint your eyes so that
you may become seeing.
[19]Those whom I love, I educate through blows of destiny; so,
do all that you can to change your heart and mind. [20]See, I stand
before the door and knock. Whoever hears my voice and opens
the door to me, to him will I come in and share the holy meal with
him and he with me. [21]He who overcomes, I will grant him to sit
on the throne with me, as I, too, have won the victory of the spirit
and sit on the throne with my Father. [22]Whoever has ears, let him
hear what the spirit says to the congregations!

4 *The throne in the heavens*
After this, I looked – and see! An open door in heaven. And the
first voice which I had heard like the sound of a trumpet, said,
'Come up here! I will show you what is to happen in the future,
after all that has gone before.' [2]And at once I was raised to the
realm of the spirit. See, a throne stood in heaven and there was one
seated on it. [3]In his radiance he was like jasper and carnelian, and
round the throne was a bow of colour which shone like an emerald.
[4]Standing in a circle about the throne were twenty-four thrones, and

seated on them were twenty-four elders clad in white garments
and with golden crowns on their heads. [5]From the throne, lightning
flashed, voices sounded, thunders rolled, and seven flaming torches
burned before the throne. They are the seven creator-spirits of God.
[6]And before the throne something like a sea of glass, crystalline,
as it were.

In the midst and surrounding the throne, four living Beings full
of eyes in front and behind. [7]The first living Being like a lion, the
second like a bull-calf, the third with a face like a human being
and the fourth like a flying eagle. [8]The four living Beings, each
with six wings, are bedecked with eyes all around and within. And
without ceasing they call out by day and by night:

> Holy, holy, holy the Lord, the divine Ruler of the World,
> who was and who is and who comes.

[9]And whenever the living Beings bring light of the spirit, dignity of soul and thanks-offerings to HIM who sits on the throne and
bears all life through the ages, [10]the twenty-four elders bow down
in worship of HIM who sits on the throne and bears the life of the
world from aeon to aeon, and they lay down their crowns before
the throne and say:

> [11]Worthy are you, our Lord and God, to receive radiant
> light of the spirit,
> dignity of the soul and active, creative power,
> for you have created the universe.
> By your will, all things exist and have their form.

5 *The book with seven seals*

And I saw in the right hand of HIM who was seated on the throne
a book with outer and inner writing and sealed with seven seals.
[2]And I saw an angel of great strength who proclaimed with a great
voice: who is worthy to open the book and undo its seals? [3]But no
Being in heaven nor on the earth nor under the earth was able to
open the book and read in it. [4]And I wept much because no one
proved worthy to open the book and read in it. [5]Then one of the
elders said to me: do not weep! See, the Lion of the tribe of Judah,

the Root of David, has won the victory. He can open the book and
its seven seals.
6And I saw: in the midst of the throne and the four living
Beings and in the midst of the elders stood a Lamb as though it
had already been slain. It had seven horns and seven eyes. They
are the seven divine creator-spirits who have been given the whole
earthly realm as their place of working. 7The Lamb came and
took the book from the right hand of HIM who was seated on the
throne. 8And when he took the book, the four living Beings and
the twenty-four elders fell down before the Lamb. Each of them
had a harp and golden censers with incense: they are the prayers
of those who are devoted to the spirit. 9And they sing a new
song:
You are worthy to receive the book and to open its seals, for you
were slain, and by your blood you have ransomed for God human
beings from all tribes and languages and peoples and races. 10You
have made them kings and priests for our God. They will be kings
in the realm of earth.
11And as I saw, I heard the voice of many angels in a circle
around the throne and the living Beings and the elders; they numbered ten thousand times ten thousand and a thousand times a
thousand. 12They said with a great voice:
'The Lamb, the sacrificial One, is worthy to be given power
and wealth and wisdom and strength of self and dignity of soul and
light of the spirit and strength of blessing.'
13And I heard all created Beings in heaven and on the earth and
under the earth and on the sea, and all Beings who work in them.
They said:
'To HIM who sits upon the throne and to the Lamb belong all
strength of blessing, dignity of soul, light of the spirit and creating
power in all cycles of time to come.'
14And the four living Beings said: 'Amen!' And the elders fell
down and worshipped.

6 *Opening the first six seals*
And I saw: the Lamb opened one of the seven seals, and I
heard one of the four living Beings say with a voice of thunder:
'Come!' 2And I saw: see, a white horse, and its rider held a bow
in his hand and a crown was placed on his head; like a conqueror
he went forth to further victories.

3And when he opened the second seal I heard the second living
Being say: 'Come!' 4And a second horse came forth, fiery red. And
to its rider was given the power to take peace from the earth so
that a general massacre began. He was given a great sword.

5And when he opened the third seal I heard the third living
Being say: 'Come!' And I saw: see, a black horse, and its rider held
a pair of scales in his hand. 6And I heard a voice in the midst of
the four living Beings saying: a measure of wheat for a denarius,
three measures of barley for a denarius. But do not harm the oil
and the wine!

7And when he opened the fourth seal, I heard the voice of the
fourth living Being say: 'Come!' 8And I saw: see, a pale horse,
and the name of its rider is Death, and the spirits of death are his
retinue. They were given authority over a quarter of the earth, that
they might kill with the sword, with hunger and death, and through
the wild beasts of the earth.

9And when he opened the fifth seal, I saw under the altar the
souls of those who had suffered death as a sacrifice for the sake
of the divine Word and because of their witnessing. 10And they
cried out with a loud voice: holy and true Lord of the World, how
long will you delay your judgment upon those who live on the
earth, to atone for our blood? 11And each one of them was given
a white garment and they were told that they should remain yet a
short time in the realm of repose until the destinies of their fellow
servants and their brothers should also be fulfilled, who, like they,
would also suffer death.

12And I saw, as he opened the sixth seal: a great earthquake
occurred. And the sun became black as a mourning garment made
of hair, and the full moon became red as blood, 13and the stars of

the sky fell to the earth as when a fig tree shakes off its unripe fruits
in a strong gale. [14]And the sky drew back like a scroll being rolled
up. All mountains and islands moved from their place. [15]And the
kings of the earth, the leaders and the generals of armies, the rich
and the strong and all slaves and all free men hid in the caves and
among the rocks of the mountains, [16]and said to the mountains and
to the rocks: fall on us and hide us from the countenance of HIM
who sits on the throne and from the surging will of the Lamb! [17]The
great Day of the divine wrath has come; who can stand up to it?

7 *The one hundred and forty-four thousand sealed*

After this I saw four angels standing at the four corners of the
realm of earth. By their power they held back the four winds of
the earth, that no wind should blow on the earth or on the sea or
on any tree. [2]And I saw another angel ascend at the place where
the sun rises. He had the seal of the living, creative forces of God,
and he called out with a loud voice to the four angels into whose
capricious will the earth and the sea had been given: [3]do not harm
the earth or the sea or the trees, until we have set our seal on the
foreheads of those who serve our God. [4]And I heard the number of
those who had been sealed: a hundred and forty-four thousand from
every tribe of the sons of Israel shall receive the seal, [5]of the tribe
of Judah twelve thousand were sealed,

of the tribe of Reuben twelve thousand,
of the tribe of Gad twelve thousand,
[6]of the tribe of Asher twelve thousand,
of the tribe of Naphtali twelve thousand,
of the tribe of Manasseh twelve thousand,
[7]of the tribe of Simeon twelve thousand,
of the tribe of Levi twelve thousand
of the tribe of Issachar twelve thousand
[8]of the tribe of Zebulun twelve thousand
of the tribe of Joseph twelve thousand
of the tribe of Benjamin twelve thousand bearers of the seal.

The great assembly in white garments

9After this I saw: see, a great assembly which no one could count, from all peoples and tribes and races and languages. They stood before the throne and the Lamb, clad in white garments, with palm branches in their hands. 10And they called out with a great voice: healing is of our God who sits upon the throne, and of the Lamb! 11And all angels stood in a circle about the throne and the elders and the four living Beings, and they fell on their faces before the throne and worshipped the divine Ground of the World 12and said, 'Amen – the word which blesses, the revelation, the wisdom, the thanks-offering, the dignity of soul, the strength of worlds and the power of the spirit belong to our God in all aeons. Amen!'

13And one of the elders answered and said to me, 'These who are clothed in white garments, who are they and from where do they come?' 14And I said, 'My Lord, you know.' And he said to me, 'These are they who come out of the great suffering. They have washed their garments and made them white with the blood of the Lamb. 15Therefore they can stand before the throne of God and serve HIM day and night in HIS temple. And HE who sits upon the throne will shelter them. 16They will hunger no more, neither thirst any more; they can no longer be overwhelmed by the heat of the sun nor by any other scorching fire. 17For the Lamb in the midst of the throne will be their shepherd and will lead them to the springs from which flows the water of life. And God will wipe away every tear from their eyes.'

8 *The seventh seal and the seven angels*

And when the Lamb opened the seventh seal, there was profound silence in the spiritual world, lasting for half a cycle of time. 2And I saw the seven angels who stand before God, and they were given seven trumpets.

3And another angel came and stood at the altar with a golden censer; and he was given much incense to offer with the prayers of all those who are devoted to the Spirit, on the golden altar in the sight of the throne. 4And the smoke of the incense rose up with the

prayers of those who are devoted to the Spirit, from the hand of
the angel before the countenance of God. 5Then the angel took the
censer, filled it with the fire of the altar and scattered it over the
earth. Then thunder pealed, voices sounded, lightning flashed and
the earth shook.

Sounding the first four trumpets

6And the seven angels who had the seven trumpets made ready to
trumpet.

7And the first trumpeted: then there came hail and fire, mixed
with blood, and it rained down on the earth. A third of the earth
was burnt up, a third of the trees were burnt up and all green grass
was burnt up.

8And the second angel trumpeted: then something like a great
mountain, burning with fire, was thrown into the sea. 9And a third
of the sea was turned into blood, a third of all the ensouled, living creatures in the sea perished and a third of all ships were
destroyed.

10And the third angel trumpeted: then a great star fell from
heaven, blazing like a torch. And in falling it struck a third of
all streams and all springs of water. 11The name of the star is
Wormwood. A third of all waters was turned into wormwood,
and many human beings died of the water which had become so
bitter.

12And the fourth angel trumpeted: Then a blow struck a third
of the sun and a third of the moon and a third of the stars, so that a
third of them was darkened and the day lost a third of its light and
the night likewise.

The three woes

13And as I saw, I heard an eagle flying through the zenith of
heaven and calling out with a great voice: 'Woe, woe, woe to all
who dwell on earth because of the blasts of the remaining trumpets which the last three angels are about to sound!'

9 *Sounding the fifth and sixth trumpets*
And the fifth angel trumpeted: then I saw a star which had fallen
from heaven to earth. To it was given the key to the shaft of the
abyss. 2And it opened the shaft of the abyss. Then smoke rose up
from the shaft, as if it were smoke from a great furnace, so that
the sun was darkened, as well as the whole atmosphere, by the
smoke from the shaft. 3And out of the smoke there came swarms
of locusts over the earth. They were given power similar to that
which the scorpions have on earth. 4But a voice told them not to
harm the grass of the earth nor any greenery nor any tree. They
were only to turn on those who did not have the seal of God on
their foreheads. 5Yet they were not to kill them, but only to torment
them for five months. The anguish that they caused was like the
agony caused by a scorpion when it stings a man. 6In those days
men will long for death but will be unable to find it. They will wish
to die, but death will flee from them. 7In appearance the locusts
are like horses armed for battle. They appear to be wearing gold
crowns on their heads, and their faces are like human faces. 8They
have hair like women's hair, and their teeth are like those of lions.
9They have armour like breastplates of iron, and the sound of their
wings is like the clatter of chariots of war drawn by many gallop-
ing horses. 10They have tails and stings like scorpions, and their
power to bring disaster upon mankind for five months lies in their
tails. 11As their king they have the angel of the abyss leading them,
whose name is Abaddon in Hebrew, Apollyon in Greek.

12The first woe is over. See, two woes are still to come.

13And the sixth angel trumpeted: and I heard a single voice; it
sounded from the four horns of the golden altar before the countenance of God. 14It said to the sixth angel who had the trumpet,
'Release the four angels who are bound at the great river Euphrates.'
15And the four angels were freed of their bonds; they were ready
in this hour, on this day, in this month and year to kill a third of
mankind. 16And the number of the troops of cavalry was twenty
thousand times ten thousand. I heard their number. 17And to my
seeing consciousness the horses and the riders appeared in fiery

red, hyacinth-coloured and sulphur-yellow breastplates. The heads
of the horses were like lions' heads, and fire and smoke and sulphur
fumes belched from their maws. [18]By these three destructive forces
a third of all human beings were killed: by the fire, the smoke and
the sulphur fumes which belched from the maws of the horses.
[19]The great power that the horses possess is in their maws and
in their tails; for their tails are like serpents with stinging heads,
and by means of them they do harm. [20]The rest of mankind, who
were not killed by these plagues, still did not change their heart
and mind and did not desist from what they were doing. They did
not give up serving the demons and the idols of gold, silver, iron,
stone and wood, although these images can neither see nor hear
nor move. [21]They did not change their heart and mind and did not
give up their way of life, tainted though it was by death-forces,
that is by poison and immorality and greed.

10 *The strong angel*
And I saw another angel of great strength; he descended from
heaven, clothed in a cloud. About his head the rainbow shone, his
face was like the sun and his feet were like pillars of fire. [2]In his
hand he held a small open book. He placed his right foot on the
sea, the left on firm ground. [3]And he called out with a great voice
which was like the roar of a lion. The seven thunders answered
his call with their voices. [4]And when the seven thunders spoke
I wanted to write down their words. Then I heard a voice from
heaven which said, 'Seal up what the seven thunders said, do not
write it down!'

[5]And the angel, whom I saw as he stood both on the sea and on
the firm ground, raised his right hand to heaven [6]and swore in the
name of HIM who bears the life of the world through all aeons, who
created the heavens and all Beings in it, as well as the earth and all
Beings on it, and the sea, and all Beings within it: time will be no
more, [7]but rather, in the days when the seventh angel lifts up his
voice and sounds his trumpet, the mystery of the Godhead shall
be fulfilled as HE proclaimed it to HIS servants the prophets.

Eating the book

8And the voice which I had heard from heaven spoke to me anew:
'Go and take the open book from the hand of the angel who is
standing on the sea and on the earth!' 9And I went to the angel
and spoke to him that he might give me the little book. And he
said to me, 'Take and eat it, it will be bitter in your stomach, even
though it is sweet as honey in your mouth.' 10And I took the little
book from the hand of the angel and ate it. And in my mouth it
tasted sweet as honey; but when I had eaten it, it filled me inwardly
with a bitter taste. 11Then it was said to me, 'You must again be
a prophet before the races and peoples and languages, and before
many kings.'

11 *The two witnesses*

I was given a reed like a staff and I heard these words: 'Arise and
take the measure of the temple of God and of the altar within it
and of those who worship there. 2But omit the forecourt outside the
temple, and from now on count it wholly as belonging to the outer
world. You do not need to measure it, for it will be given over to
the heathen peoples, and they will trample over the holy city for
forty-two months.

3'And I will call upon my two witnesses. For one thousand two
hundred and sixty days they shall proclaim the word of the Spirit,
clothed in mourning garments.' 4They are the two olive trees and
the two lampstands which stand before the Lord of the earth. 5If
anyone wants to harm them, flames of fire will leap from their
mouth and consume their enemies. Whoever wants to hurt them
must die. 6It is they who have the authority to lock the sky so that
no rain shall fall in the days of their working as prophets. And they
also have the authority to turn the water into blood and to strike
the earth with every kind of plague whenever they wish.

7And when the time of their witnessing is fulfilled, the beast
which rises from the abyss will fight them and defeat them and kill
them. 8Their corpses will lie in the streets of the great city which
spiritually is called: Sodom and Egypt. That is also where their

Lord was crucified. [9]Human beings from all races and tribes and
languages and peoples will see their dead bodies for three and a
half days, and they will not permit their bodies to be laid in the
tomb.

[10]And the inhabitants of the earth will rejoice over their death
and celebrate and shower one another with presents, for these two
prophets had been a provocation to the inhabitants of the earth.
[11]And after three and a half days the life-spirit from the heavenly
world entered them again, and they were able to stand on their
feet. Great fear fell on all who saw them. [12]And they heard a great
voice speaking to them from heaven: 'Come up here!' And they
ascended into the sphere of the heavens in a cloud of surging
forces of life. That, too, their enemies had to look upon. [13]In that
hour there came a great earthquake, and a tenth of the city fell in
ruins and seven thousand human souls met their deaths through the
earthquake. Those remaining were overcome with fear and bowed
down before the radiant revelation of God in the spheres of heaven.

[14]The second woe is over, a third is approaching fast.

The seventh trumpet: the twenty-four elders

[15]And the seventh angel trumpeted: then great voices were heard in
heaven which said:

The cosmos has been appointed to be the kingdom of our Lord and HIS Christ. He shall reign over this realm through all aeons.

[16]And the twenty-four elders who sat on their thrones before the
countenance of God fell on their faces in worship [17]and said:

Our thanks-offering is for you,
O Lord, divine Ruler of all,
who is and who was.
You have seized your mighty power, you are king of the kingdom.

[18]The peoples of the world are filled with anger, but your cosmic wrath has stirred also.

The time has come when the destiny of the dead will be decided.

Each one will receive the fruits of his life, your servants, the

prophets, and all those who are devoted to the Spirit, and also those
who revere your name; both small and great. Destruction will be the
reward of those who destroy the earth.
[19]And the temple of God in the heavens was opened, and the
altar of HIS covenant could be seen in the sanctuary. And lightning
flashed, voices sounded, thunders rolled, the earth trembled and
there was a great fall of hail.

12 *The woman with child*

And an exalted sign was unveiled in the world of spirit: a woman
clothed with the sun, the moon under her feet, her head adorned
with the crown of the twelve stars. [2]And she was with child and
cried out in the labour and pain of giving birth.
[3]And a second image was revealed in the heavens: see, a great
fiery-red dragon with seven heads and ten horns. On his heads he
had seven diadems, [4]and with his tail he drew down a third of all
the stars in heaven and threw them on the earth. And the dragon
stood before the woman who was about to give birth, so that he
could devour her child when it was born. [5]And the woman gave
birth to a child: a son. He shall shepherd all peoples with an iron
staff. And the woman's child was caught up to God and to HIS
throne. [6]And the woman fled into the desert. It was in the divine
world-plan that she must go there. There she is to eke out her
existence for twelve hundred and sixty days.

Michael's fight with the dragon

[7]And a war flared up in the heavenly world. Michael and his angels
fought against the dragon. And the dragon fought in the midst of
his angels. [8]But his strength failed, and so there was no longer a
place for them in the heavens. [9]The great dragon was overthrown,
the primeval serpent who is of both diabolic and satanic nature, the
Tempter of all mankind. Onto the earth he was thrown, and all his
angels with him. [10]And I heard a great voice in heaven:

Now has been founded the salvation and the power and the
kingdom of our God, and the creative might of HIS Christ.

Overthrown is the accuser of our brothers. Now he can no longer
accuse them day and night before the countenance of God. 11They
have overcome him by the blood of the Lamb and by the divine
Word to which they bore witness. They did not love their own lives
too dearly, and they did not fear death. 12Therefore rejoice, you
heavens and you Beings in the heavens!

But woe to the earth and the sea: the Adversary has come down
to you, and he seethes with raging fury, for he knows that his time
is only short.

13And when the dragon saw that he had been cast onto the earth,
he began to persecute the woman who had borne the son. 14Then
the woman was given the two wings of the great eagle, so that she
could fly into the desert to her appointed place, where she is to
eke out her existence for a cycle of time, for cycles of time, and
for half a cycle of time, far from the face of the serpent. 15And the
serpent poured a stream of water after the woman out of his mouth,
in order to destroy her. 16But then the earth came to the woman's
assistance; it opened its mouth and swallowed the stream of water
which the dragon spewed from his mouth. 17And the dragon raged
in fury against the woman. He stormed away to fight against those
who remained of the woman's offspring. That is those who keep
to the divine world-aims and who are united with the destiny and
witnessing of Jesus.

13 *The beast from the sea and the beast from the earth*
As I saw that, I was standing on the sand at the sea. And I saw a
beast rise up out of the sea. It had ten horns and seven heads, and
on the horns, ten diadems, and on its heads were names of enmity
against the spirit. 2The beast which I saw was like a leopard, but
it had feet like a bear,and its maw was like that of a lion. And
the dragon handed on to it his power, and his throne, and great
authority. 3One of its heads seemed to be mortally wounded, but its
deadly wound was healed. The whole earthly world followed the
beast, full of admiration. 4Everyone worshipped the dragon because
he gave the beast such authority. And they worshipped the beast

and said: who is like the beast, and who would dare to fight against
it? 5 And it was given a mouth with which it could utter haughty
words and words of enmity against the spirit; and it was also
allowed to exercise authority for forty-two months. 6 And it opened
its mouth to hurl its curses against the divine world, against the
divine name, and against the sphere of the divine dwelling, and
against all Beings who dwell in the spheres of heaven.

7 And it was given the power to unleash a war against those
human beings who were devoted to the spirit, and to defeat them.
All-embracing power was given to it over all tribes and peoples
and languages and races. 8 All inhabitants of the earth will worship
the beast, although its name has not at any time been written in the
Book of Life which belongs to the Lamb, who has been sacrificing
himself since the foundation of the world.

9 He who has ears, let him hear! 10 If anyone takes away freedom,
he himself shall become unfree; he who wields a murderous sword
shall himself become a victim of the murderous sword. Here only
the power of endurance and the faith of those who are devoted to
the Spirit will stand the test.

11 And I saw a second beast. It rose out of the earth, and it had
two horns so that it looked like a lamb. But its speech was like that
of a dragon. 12 It works magically, in league with everything which
is within the authority of the first beast. It causes the earth and all
its inhabitants to worship the first beast, whose mortal wound was
healed. 13 And it performs great magic deeds. It even calls down
fire from heaven, and makes it flash down onto the earth before
the eyes of men. 14 It leads the inhabitants of the earth astray by the
wonders which it is able to do in the presence of the first beast. By
its words it makes the inhabitants of the earth set up an image to
the beast which was wounded by the sword and yet remained alive.
15 It is also permitted to send a spirit into the image of the beast so
that it can speak. It does this, because it desires the death of all
those who do not worship the image of the beast. 16 Furthermore it
causes everyone, small and great, rich and poor, free or unfree, to
become imprinted with a mark on the right hand or the forehead.

17No one is to buy or sell who does not bear the name of the beast or the number of his name as a mark and an imprint.

18Here wisdom itself speaks. Whoever has the ability to think it, let him seek the meaning of the number of the beast. It is the number of Man. And its number is six hundred and sixty-six.

14 *The Lamb and the hundred and forty-four thousand*
And I saw: see, the Lamb stood on Mount Zion, and gathered about him were the one hundred and forty-four thousand who had his name and the name of his Father written on their foreheads.

2And I heard a voice out of the heavens like the rushing of great streams of water and like the sound of mighty thunder. But the voice that I heard was also like the sound of harpers playing on their harps 3and singing the new song before the throne and before the four living Beings and the circle of the elders. No one could learn that song except the hundred and forty-four thousand who had been freed from slavery of the earth. 4These are they who have not defiled their spiritual nature with base soul cravings – they are virginal in their hearts. They follow the Lamb, wherever his way leads. They have been brought out of mankind to become the foundation of a new humanity which belongs to God and to the Lamb. 5No false word was heard from their mouths. They are of perfect purity.

The eternal Gospel and the harvest of the earth
6And I saw another angel flying through the zenith of heaven. He bore the eternal Gospel, to proclaim it to those who dwell on earth, to all peoples and tribes and languages and races. 7He said with a great voice, 'Have reverence for the divine world, the source of all revelation. The hour of the divine decision has come. Worship the creator of the heavens and the earth and the sea and all springs of water!'

8And another angel, a second, followed and said, 'Fallen, fallen is the great city of Babylon, who poured out the seething wine of her lewdness to all peoples of the world.'

9And another angel, a third, followed the first two and said
with a great voice, 'Whoever worships the beast and its image,
and whoever receives its mark on his forehead or on his hand,
10he shall drink of the wine of the seething divine wrath which is
poured unmixed into the chalice of HIS anger; before the countenance of the holy angels and before the Lamb he will be in torment
as if by fire and sulphur. 11The smoke of their torment will rise up
through all cycles of time, they will have no rest, day or night.
This applies to all who worship the beast and its image and who
have accepted the mark of its name.'

12Here the only thing that stands the test is the power of endurance of those who are devoted to the Spirit, who hold to the divine
aims and keep the faith in Jesus.

13And I heard a voice from heaven which said, 'Write this:
Blessed are the dead who from now on die in the power of Christ.'
'Yes,' the Spirit says, 'They shall find rest after their hardships.
The fruits of their lives shall not be lost on their further ways of
soul.'

14And I saw: see, a white cloud. And on the cloud one like
a son of man. On his head he had a golden crown, and in his
hand he held a sharp sickle. 15And another angel came out of
the temple and called out with a great voice to him who was
coming on the cloud: 'Wield your sickle and reap, for the time of
harvest has come. The harvest field, the earth, is ripe.' 16And he
on the cloud swung his sickle over the earth, and the earth was
harvested.

17And yet another angel came out of the temple in the heavens,
and he, too, had a sharp sickle. 18And again another angel came
out from the altar; it was he who had authority over fire. He called
loudly to the angel who had the sharp sickle: 'Strike with your
sharp sickle and reap the grapes of the vineyard, the earth, for
the fruits of the vine are ripe.' 19And the angel swung his sickle
over the earth and harvested the vineyard of the earth and cast the
grapes into the great wine press of the divine will of destiny. 20And
the wine press was trodden outside the town. And blood flowed

from the wine press, as high as a horse's bridle, for one thousand
six hundred stadia.

15 *The song of Moses and the song of the Lamb*
And a new great and amazing sign was revealed in heaven to my
sight: seven angels with the seven last trials which are the fulfilment of God's mighty will.
[2]And I saw, and it was like a sea of crystal mixed with fire. And
those who had overcome the beast and the allure of its image and
the number of its name I saw standing by the crystal sea with the
harps of God. [3]And they sang the song of Moses, the servant of
God, and the song of the Lamb:

Great and wonderful are your works,
O Lord, divine Ruler of all.
Your ways lead to the good and to the true,
you king of all peoples.
[4]Who does not hold you in awe, O Lord?
Who does not praise your Being
as the source of all revelation?
You alone are holy.
All peoples shall come to worship before your countenance,
for now your divine ordinances have been clearly revealed.

[5]After this I saw that the temple in heaven was opened, the tabernacle of God's testimony to HIMSELF. [6]And the seven angels came
out of the temple with the seven trials. They were clothed in pure
shining linen, about the waist they had golden girdles. [7]And one of
the four living Beings gave the seven angels seven golden bowls
filled with the quickening will of God, who bears the life of the
world through all aeons. [8]And the temple was filled with the smoke
which went forth from the spiritual light and the strength of soul of
the divine Being. And no one could enter the temple until the seven
afflictions by the seven angels had been fulfilled.

16 *Pouring out the seven bowls*

And I heard a great voice. It spoke out of the temple to the seven angels: 'Go forth and pour out over the earth the seven bowls of the divine will!'

[2]The first went and poured out his bowl over the earth. Then those human beings who had the mark of the beast and who worshipped the image of the beast were afflicted with foul and malignant sores.

[3]And the second poured out his bowl into the sea, and it was turned into blood as from a corpse, and all living and ensouled beings in the sea perished.

[4]And the third poured out his bowl into all rivers and springs of water, and all water was turned into blood. [5]And I heard the angel of the waters call: 'You bear the very truth within yourself, you who are and who were, you holy One. This is why you are imposing this judgment: [6]they have spilt the blood of the saints and the prophets, and now you give them blood to drink. This fate they have brought upon themselves.' [7]And from the altar I heard: 'Yes, Lord, divine Ruler of all, your judgment leads to Truth and to the Good.'

[8]And the fourth poured out his bowl over the sun. It was given to him to scorch mankind with fire. [9]And so men were seared by fierce heat and cursed the name of the divine Being who had the power to impose such trials on mankind. They did not find the way to a change of heart and mind; they remained closed to the divine revelation.

[10]And the fifth poured out his bowl over the throne of the beast. Then its realm was darkened, and men bit their tongues in anguish [11]and cursed the divine power of heaven because of their pain and their suppurating wounds. They did not find the way to a change of heart and mind; they did not desist from what they were doing.

[12]And the sixth poured out his bowl into the great river Euphrates. Then all its waters dried up, so that a way was prepared for the kings from the lands of the rising of the sun. [13]And I saw issuing from the jaws of the dragon and from the maw of the beast

and from the mouth of the false prophet three unclean spirits in the form of frogs. 14They are demonic beings who can perform deeds of magic. They set about the kings of the whole world so as to assemble them for the war which will break out when the great Day of the divine Ruler of all dawns.

15See, I am coming like a thief. Blessed is he who knows how to remain alert and who takes care of his garments so that he may not go naked and his unsightliness be exposed.

16And he assembled his throngs in the place which is called Armageddon in Hebrew.

17And the seventh poured out his bowl into the atmosphere. Then a mighty voice was heard from the temple, coming from the throne: 'It is done!' 18And lightning flashed, the voices sounded, the thunders rolled and there was the roar of a great earthquake such as there had never been since men have lived on the earth, so tremendous was that earthquake. 19And the great city was split into three parts, and the towns of all the peoples fell in ruins. And Babylon the great appeared before the thought of the Godhead: she was to be given the cup with the wine of the divine will as the cup of wrath. 20And all islands disappeared, and no mountains were to be found. 21And great hailstones which seemed heavy as a hundredweight fell from heaven on men. And humanity cursed the divine world because of their suffering from the hail; their suffering was exceedingly great.

17 *Great Babylon and her fall*

Then one of the seven angels who had the seven bowls came and said to me, 'Come! I will show you the judgment upon the great whore who sits on many streams of water, 2with whom the kings of the earth have united themselves unchastely; and the inhabitants of the earth are drunk with her impure wine.' 3And he led me up on a spiritual plane into a desert. There I saw a woman sitting on a scarlet beast. The beast was bedecked all over with names cursing the spirit, and it had seven heads and ten horns. 4The woman was clad in purple and scarlet garments, and she was

brilliantly adorned with gold and precious stones and pearls. In
her hand she held a golden cup full of hideous and impure Beings,
the offspring of her unchastity.
[5]And on her forehead a name was written, a mystery:

GREAT BABYLON, THE MOTHER OF ALL WHORING
AND OF ALL MONSTROUS FORMS ON EARTH.

[6]And I saw the woman drunk with the blood of those who are
devoted to the Spirit, and with the blood of the martyrs of Jesus.
When I saw the woman, I was greatly astonished.
[7]Then the angel said to me, 'What are you astonished about?
I will tell you the secret of the woman, and of the beast which
carries her and has seven heads and ten horns. [8]The beast that you
see was there once; now it is not; but it will arise anew out of the
abyss, and then it will meet its destruction. The dwellers on earth
whose names were never written in the Book of Life since the
foundation of the world, will be greatly astonished at the sight
of the beast which was in the past, now is not, but will be in the
future. [9]Here speaks a mind with the power of thought as well as
wisdom.
[10]'The seven heads are seven mountains on which the woman
is seated. They are also seven kings. Five of them have fallen, one
is there, and one is not yet there. When he comes, he must remain
for a short time. [11]And the beast which was there and is not there
is itself the eighth king and yet it also belongs to the seven; it will
meet its destruction. [12]The ten horns which you see are ten kings
who have not yet begun to reign, but with the beast they will rule
as kings for one cycle of time. [13]They are all of one mind. They
put their strength and authority at the service of the beast. [14]And so
they will make war against the Lamb, but the Lamb will conquer
them, for he is the Lord of all lords and the King of all kings. And
all those who have been called and chosen, all who have faith, are
on his side.'
[15]And he said to me, 'The streams of water that you see where
the whore sits are the races and the multitudes, the peoples and the
languages. [16]And the ten horns that you see and the beast: they will

come to hate the great whore. They will cause her to stand there
lonely and naked in the end. They will devour her flesh and let her
perish in flames. [17]For God has implanted into their hearts a will
so that they will ultimately act according to HIS purposes after all.
And so they also serve HIS purpose by placing their realm at the
service of the beast until the aims of the words of God shall be
fulfilled. [18]The woman that you see is the great city which rules
over all kings of the earth.'

18 After this, I saw another angel coming down out of heaven. He
had mighty authority and the whole earth was enlightened by the
spiritual light that shone from him. [2]He called out with a resound-
ing voice:

'Fallen, fallen is great Babylon, she has become a dwelling place
of demons and a prison of all kinds of impure spirits, and of eerie
and hateful birds. [3]All peoples have drunk the wine of her drunk-
enness and her unchastity, the kings of the earth have shared in her
licentiousness, and the merchants of the earth have become rich
through the craving of the senses which she has aroused in them.'

[4]And I heard another voice speaking from heaven: 'Leave the
city, my people! Do not be drawn into her community of aberrations, so that you will also not share the blows of her destiny.
[5]Her aberrations reach from earth to heaven; God was aware of
her injustices. [6]Give back to her what she has given you; repay her
double for all that she has done to you. Give her twice the draught
of the cup which she gave you to drink. [7]Give her anguish and
mourning by the measure of her self-glorification and craving of
the senses. For she says in her heart: I reign as queen and am not a
widow; I wish to see nothing that makes me sad. [8]For this reason
all the blows of her destiny will strike her in one single day; death,
mourning and hunger, and she will be consumed by fire. For God,
the Lord who judges her, is severe in HIS might.' [9]The kings of the
earth who have let themselves be drawn into her unchastity and
senses' craving will weep and wail over her when they see the
smoke of the fire in which she burns. [10]But they will only look on
from a distance, because they are afraid of her torment. They will

say, ‘Woe, woe, you great city, Babylon, you mighty city; in one single hour your destiny has been fulfilled.’ [11]And the merchants of the earth weep and mourn for her, for now no one buys their wares any more: [12]gold, silver, precious stones and pearls, fine linen and the purple, silk and scarlet, sweet-scented woods and vessels of ivory, costly wood, iron and marble; [13]also cinnamon, pepper, incense, myrrh and frankincensc, wine and oil, flour and corn, cattle, sheep, horses and chariots, and also the bodies and souls of human beings.

[14]The sweet fruit of life for which your soul has been craving has been lost to you; all wealth and all splendour has perished for you, and never will you be able to win back any of it. [15]The merchants who traded with these things and became rich through them will stand far off; for they fear her torment. They will weep and lament and say, [16]‘Woe, woe, you great city who were clothed with fine linen, purple and scarlet and brilliantly adorned with gold, precious stones and pearls; [17]in one hour such great wealth has been laid waste!’ And all helmsmen and seafaring men, all sailors and all others who have anything to do with the sea, they stood far off, [18]and when they saw the smoke of the fire in which she burned they said, ‘Who could compare with you, you great city!’ [19]They threw dust on their heads, and with tears and laments they cried: ‘Woe, woe, you great city! All those who sail the seas have become rich through your wealth. In one hour you have been turned into a desert.’ [20]So now rejoice over her, you heavens and all saints, apostles and prophets! God HIMSELF has given judgment for you against her.

[21]Then the one mighty angel lifted up a huge stone which looked like a millstone and threw it into the sea and said, ‘So shall Babylon, the great city, be cast down with one throw. Never will she rise again. [22]Never will there sound again in you the voice of harpists, singers, flautists and trumpeters. No work of whatever kind will be done in you any more. The sound of the mill will not be heard in you any more, [23]and the light of the lamp will not shine in you any more. Never again will the voice of the bridegroom and the

bride be heard in you. Your merchants were the great men of the
earth; you led all peoples astray with your draught of magic. [24]In
you flowed the blood of the prophets and the saints, the blood of all
those who met their sacrificial death on earth.'

19 *The coming marriage of the Lamb*
After this I heard a mighty voice as from a great multitude in the
heavens:

> Hallelujah! The healing and the revelation and the
> world-power belongs to the God whom we serve. [2]HIS
> decisions lead to the Truth and to the Good. HE has
> passed judgment upon the great whore who corrupted
> all earthly existence with her impure way of being. HE
> has avenged the blood of HIS servants which was shed
> by her hand.

[3]And once more the voices said:

> Hallelujah! The smoke of her burning will not cease
> rising from aeon to aeon.

[4]Then the twenty-four elders and the four living Beings fell down
and worshipped the exalted divine Being who sat on the throne and
said, 'Amen, Hallelujah!'

[5]And a voice spoke from the throne:

> Give praise to the God whom we serve, all you, small
> and great, who are devoted to HIM and who bow down
> before HIM with reverence!

[6]And I heard a voice as from a great multitude and like the
rushing of many streams of water and like the roar of mighty
thunder:

> Hallelujah! The Lord our God, the divine Ruler of
> all, has become King. [7]Let us rejoice and jubilate and
> praise HIS revelation: the marriage of the Lamb begins;
> his bride has prepared herself. [8]It was given to her to
> be clothed with a garment of pure shining linen. The
> white garment is woven out of the just consequences
> of the deeds of those who are devoted to the Spirit.

9And he said to me, 'Write! Blessed are those who are called to
the marriage feast of the Lamb.' And he went on: 'These are true
words of God.' 10And I fell at his feet to worship him. And he said
to me, 'Do not do that. I am a fellow servant with you and your
brothers who hold to the destiny and witnessing of Jesus. Offer
your worship to God.' The life and testimony of Jesus is the spirit
of prophecy.

The rider on the white horse and his battle

11And I saw that heaven had been opened. See, a white horse!
And the rider who sat upon it is he who makes faith and knowledge true. Morality arises through his decisions and his battles.
12His eyes are like flames of fire, and many crowns shine on his
head. He has a name inscribed which no one understands but he
himself. 13He is clad in a blood-sprinkled robe, whose name is:
The Word of God. 14And the armies of heaven, clad in pure white
linen, follow him on white horses. 15A sharp sword issues from his
mouth, with which he strikes the peoples of the world. He is the
shepherd of the peoples, and he carries the iron staff. He treads the
winepress from which flows the wine of God's will as the anger
of the Lord Almighty.

16On his robe and on his thigh the name is written:

KING OF ALL KINGS, LORD OF ALL LORDS.

17And I saw an angel standing in the sun. He called with a great
voice to all the birds flying through the zenith of heaven: 'Come,
gather for the great heavenly meal of God! 18Let your food be the
bodies of the kings and the bodies of the generals, the bodies of
great men and the bodies of the horses and their riders, the bodies
of all who are free and unfree, of small and of great.'

19And I saw the beast and the kings of the earth and their armies
gathered for war against the rider and his army. 20And the beast was
captured and with it the false prophet who by his wonders had led
mankind astray in its presence, namely those who bore the mark of
the beast and who worshipped its image. These two were thrown
alive into the fiery swamp, alight with sulphur flames. 21The rest

met their death by the sword that issued from the mouth of the rider.
And all the birds gorged themselves upon their corpses.

20 *Sealing up the dragon for a thousand years*
And I saw an angel coming down from heaven. In his hand he
had the key of the abyss, and a massive chain. [2]And he seized the
dragon, the serpent power from the very beginning, whose power
is of both diabolic and satanic nature; and fettered him for a thousand years, [3]and hurled him into the abyss which he then closed
over him and sealed so that he should not lead human beings on
earth astray any more until the thousand years are fulfilled. After
that he shall become free of his fetters for a short time.
[4]And I saw thrones and those who sat upon them. It was given
to their charge to make the decisions of destiny. I saw also the
souls of those who had been slain because of their testimony to
Jesus, and for the sake of the divine Word. They had worshipped
neither the beast nor its image nor, therefore, received its mark on
their forehead and hand. They lived and reigned with Christ for a
thousand years. [5]The remaining dead could only come to life again
when the thousand years were fulfilled. This is the first resurrection: thus it was revealed. [6]Blessed and holy are those who share
in the first resurrection. Over them the second death has no power;
they shall be priests of God and of Christ and shall be kings with
Christ for a thousand years.
[7]And when the thousand years are fulfilled, the satanic power
will be loosed from his prison [8]and he will appear as the deceiver
of all peoples at all four corners of the earth. He will herd mankind together in Gog and Magog and altogether entangle them in
wars; their number will be like the sand on the sea shore. [9]And they
marched up over the whole realm of the earth and surrounded and
laid siege to the stronghold of the saints and the beloved city. But
then fire flashed down from heaven and consumed them. [10]And the
diabolic power who led them astray was thrown into the swamp
of fire and sulphur like the beast and the false prophet before him,
suffering torment day and night through all aeons.

The judgment upon the old world
11And I saw a great white throne and before the countenance of
HIM who sat upon it the earth and the sky withdrew and were not
to be found any more in the world of space. 12And I saw the dead,
great and small, who stood before the throne, and books were
opened. And yet another book was opened: the Book of Life. And
the destinies of the dead were determined by what was written
in the books, according to their deeds. 13And the sea gave up its
dead, and the realm of death and of the shades also gave up its
dead. And the destiny of each one was determined according to his
deeds. 14And the realm of death and of the shades was also hurled
into the smouldering swampy abyss; that is the second death, the
fiery swamp. 15And every one whose name was not found in the
Book of Life was also thrown into the fiery swamp.

21 *The appearance of the new world*
And I saw a new heaven and a new earth. The former heaven and
the former earth had passed away, and the sea was no more. 2And
I also saw the holy city, the New Jerusalem. It descended from
the heavenly world, out of the realm of the Godhead. In its beauty
of form it was like a bride adorned for marriage. 3And from the
throne I heard a great voice: 'See, the dwelling of God among
men! He will dwell in their midst, and they shall be HIS people.
God HIMSELF will be with them 4and will wipe away every tear
from their eyes. There shall be no more death, no pain and no
sorrowing, no heavy burdens; for the old world has passed away.'
5And HE who sat upon the throne said, 'See, I make all things
new!' And HE said, 'Write this! These are words of faith and
knowledge.'

6And HE said to me, 'It is done. I am the Alpha and the Omega,
both the very beginning and the ultimate purpose of the world.
To the thirsty I will give unconditionally from the fountain of the
water of life. 7He who overcomes shall have all this. I will be his
God and he shall be my son.

8'But as for the fearful souls, those who have no faith, who pervert the image of Man, those who spread death about them, who tread impure paths of the soul, make use of dark magic forces and serve the demonic powers, as well as all frauds – the fiery swamp of the abyss opens for them, and flames of sulphur blaze. That is the second death.'

The new Jerusalem

9 Then came one of the seven angels who had the seven bowls with the seven last trials and he said to me, 'Come! I will show you the bride, the wife of the Lamb.' 10 And he led me up in the realm of the spirit to a great and lofty mountain and showed me the holy city Jerusalem descending out of heaven out of the realm of the Godhead. 11 It shone in the light of the revelation of God. Its radiance was like that of a most valuable precious stone, it was like that of a crystal clear jasper.

12 The city had a great and high wall and twelve gates. And on the gates twelve angels, and names were written on them: the names of the twelve tribes of the sons of Israel. 13 Three gates faced east, three gates faced north, three gates faced south and three gates faced west. 14 And the wall of the city rested on twelve foundations, and on them were the twelve names of the twelve apostles of the Lamb.

15 He who spoke to me had a golden measuring rod, to measure the city and its gates and its walls. 16 The city lies like a square; its length the same as its width. And he measured the city with the rod and found that its length was twelve thousand stadia. Its length and its width and its height are equal. 17 And he measured the wall: one hundred and forty-four cubits. That is the measure of Man, and equally that of an angel.

18 The wall was built of jasper, the city itself of pure gold which was like a transparent crystal. 19 The foundations of the city wall were adorned with precious stones of every kind:

The first foundation with jasper,
the second with sapphire,
the third with chalcedony,

the fourth with emerald,
[20]the fifth with onyx,
the sixth with carnelian,
the seventh with chrysolite,
the eighth with beryl,
the ninth with topaz,
the tenth with chrysoprase,
the eleventh with hyacinth,
the twelfth with amethyst.

[21]And the twelve gates were twelve pearls; each one of the gates
was formed out of one single pearl. And the street of the city was
of pure gold which was like a transparent crystal.

[22]A temple I did not see in the city. The Lord, the divine Ruler
of all, is HIMSELF its temple together with the Lamb. [23]And the city
does not need the sun or the moon to light it. The light of the revelation of God enlightens it, and its lamp is the Lamb. [24]And the
peoples shall walk in its light, and the kings of the earth shall bring
their splendour into it. [25]The gates of the city are never shut by
day; there is no night there. [26]All spiritual treasures of the peoples
and all achievements of soul shall be brought into this city. [27]But
nothing unconsecrated shall enter it, nothing which perverts the
image of Man blasphemously and falsifies Truth by fraud. Only he
can gain entrance whose name is written in the Book of Life which
belongs to the Lamb.

22 And he showed me a river: the water of life, bright as a crystal.
Its source was the throne of God and of the Lamb. [2]In the middle
of the streets of the city and on this side of the river and on that,
the tree of life bearing fruit twelvefold, so that it yielded of its fruit
each month. And the leaves of the tree were healing medicine for
the peoples; [3]thereby every curse loses its power. And the throne
of God and of the Lamb will stand in the city, and his faithful will
serve him. [4]They will see his countenance, and his name will shine
on their foreheads. [5]Night shall be no more, they need no light of
lamp nor of the sun; for the Lord God HIMSELF will shine out over
them. And they will be kings through all aeons.

The high worth of the revelation

6And he said to me, 'These are words of faith and of insight. The
Lord, from whose divine being the revelation is given to all prophetic spirits, has sent forth HIS angel to show HIS faithful what
is approaching speedily.

7'See, I come in a moment of time.' Blessed is he who takes
into his heart the words of this book which are the spirit of prophecy.

8I, John, am he who heard and saw this. And when I heard it
and saw it I fell at the feet of the angel to worship him who showed
me all this. 9And he said to me, 'Do not do that. I am a fellow
servant with you and your brothers, those who herald the future
and those who take the words of this book into their hearts. Offer
your worship towards God only.' 10And he said to me, 'Do not seal
up the words of prophecy of this book; for the time is pressing!
11Whoever is far from the Good now will also be far from the
Good in the future. Whoever is full of impurity now will be so
in the future also. But whoever has a share in the higher life now
will also be able to shape his existence out of the higher life in the
future. And whoever is devoted to the Spirit will also be filled with
the Spirit in the future.

12'See, I come quickly. And I will be Lord of destiny; I will
give to everyone the compensation of destiny that corresponds to
his deeds. 13I am the Alpha and the Omega, the first and the last,
the very beginning and also the ultimate purpose of the world.'
14Blessed are those who cleanse their festive garments. They have
authority over the tree of life and they may enter the city through
the gates. 15Outside must remain the cynics and those who make
use of magic, those who follow unclean ways of soul, those who
spread death about them, those who serve demonic powers and also
every one who by his attitude and deeds serves falsehood.

16'I, Jesus, have sent my angel to you. He shall confirm these
words to you in the congregations. I am the root and the stem of
David. I am the radiant morning star.'

17And the Spirit and the bride say, 'Come!' And he who hears

this call let him also say, 'Come!' Let him who is thirsty come.
Let him who desires freely drink of the water of life! [18]I myself
declare to everyone who hears the prophetic words of this book:
whoever adds anything extra to these words, to him God will also
add the trials which are described in this book. [19]And if anyone
takes anything away from the prophetic words of this book, from
him God will take away his share in the tree of life and in the holy
city which are described in this book.

[20]He who lends power to these words says, 'Yes, I am coming
quickly.' Amen, come, Jesus our Lord. [21]The grace of Jesus our
Lord be upon all.

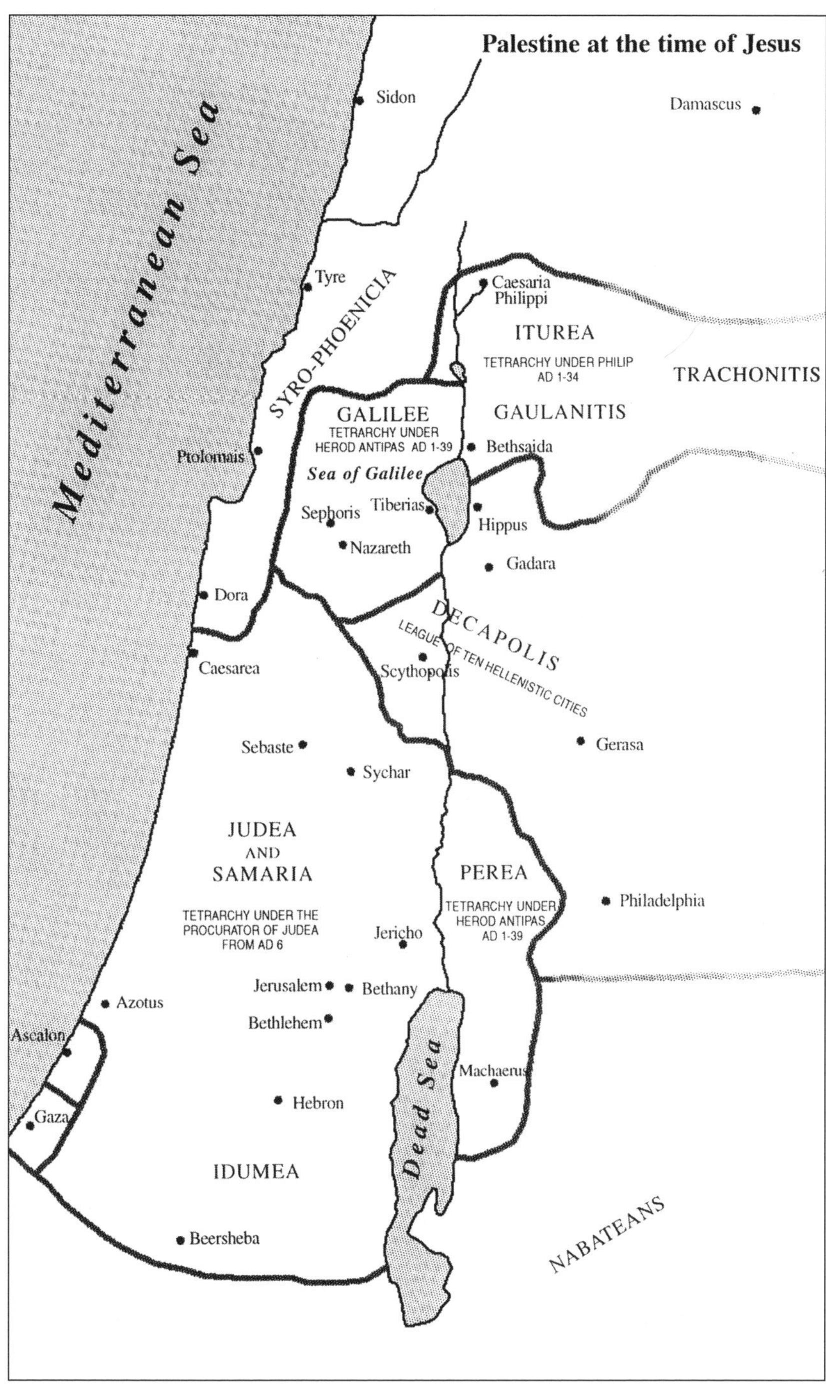
Palestine at the time of Jesus
Mediterranean Sea
Sidon
Damascus
Tyre
SYRO-PHOENICIA
Caesaria
Philippi
ITUREA
TETRARCHY UNDER PHILIP
AD 1-34
TRACHONITIS
GALILEE
TETRARCHY UNDER
HEROD ANTIPAS AD 1-39
GAULANITIS
Bethsaida
Ptolomais
Sea of Galilee
Sephoris
Tiberias
Hippus
Nazareth
Gadara
Dora
DECAPOLIS
LEAGUE OF TEN HELLENISTIC CITIES
Caesarea
Scythopolis
Sebaste
Gerasa
Sychar
JUDEA
AND
SAMARIA
TETRARCHY UNDER THE
PROCURATOR OF JUDEA
FROM AD 6
PEREA
TETRARCHY UNDER
HEROD ANTIPAS
AD 1-39
Philadelphia
Jericho
Jerusalem
Bethany
Azotus
Bethlehem
Ascalon
Dead Sea
Machaerus
Hebron
Gaza
IDUMEA
Beersheba
NABATEANS

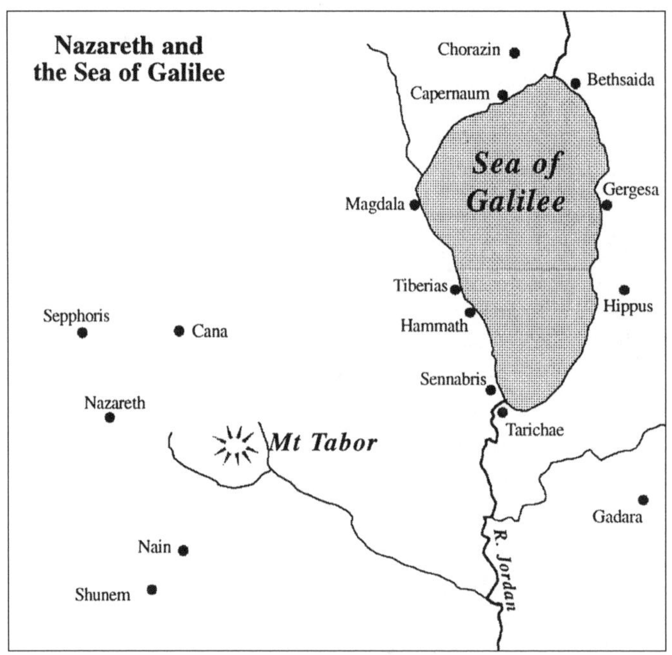
Nazareth and the Sea of Galilee
Chorazin
Bethsaida
Capernaum
Sea of Galilee
Magdala
Gergesa
Tiberias
Hippus
Hammath
Sepphoris
Cana
Sennabris
Nazareth
Tarichae
Mt Tabor
Gadara
R. Jordan
Nain
Shunem

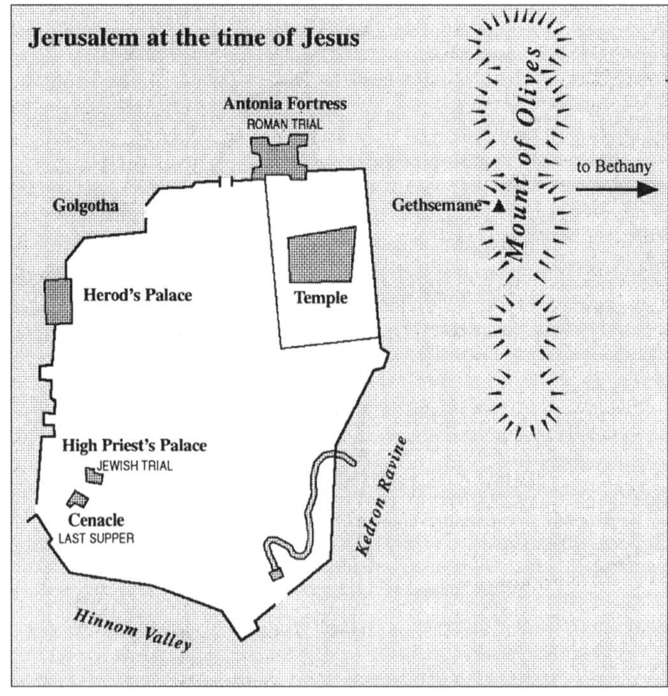
Jerusalem at the time of Jesus
Mount of Olives
Antonia Fortress
ROMAN TRIAL
to Bethany
Golgotha
Gethsemane
Herod's Palace
Temple
High Priest's Palace
JEWISH TRIAL
Kedron Ravine
Cenacle
LAST SUPPER
Hinnom Valley

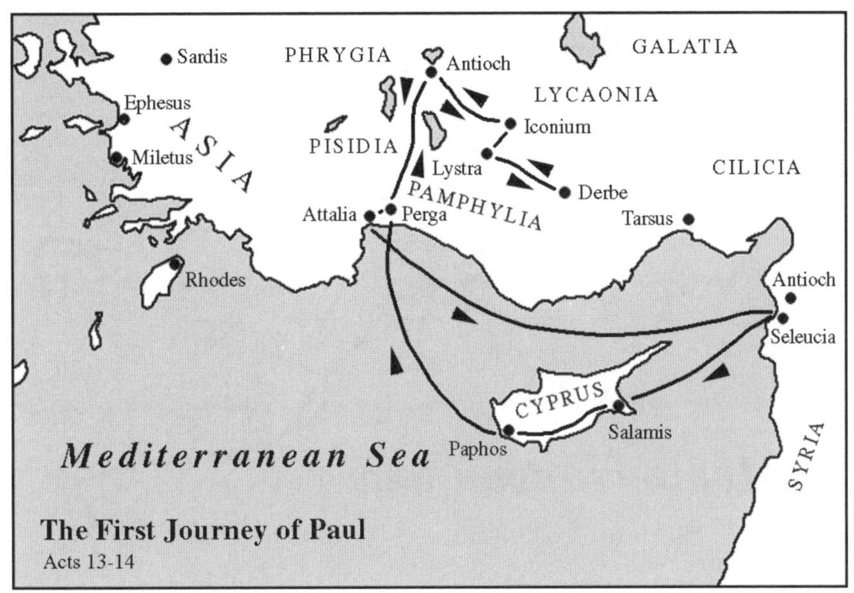

The First Journey of Paul
Acts 13-14

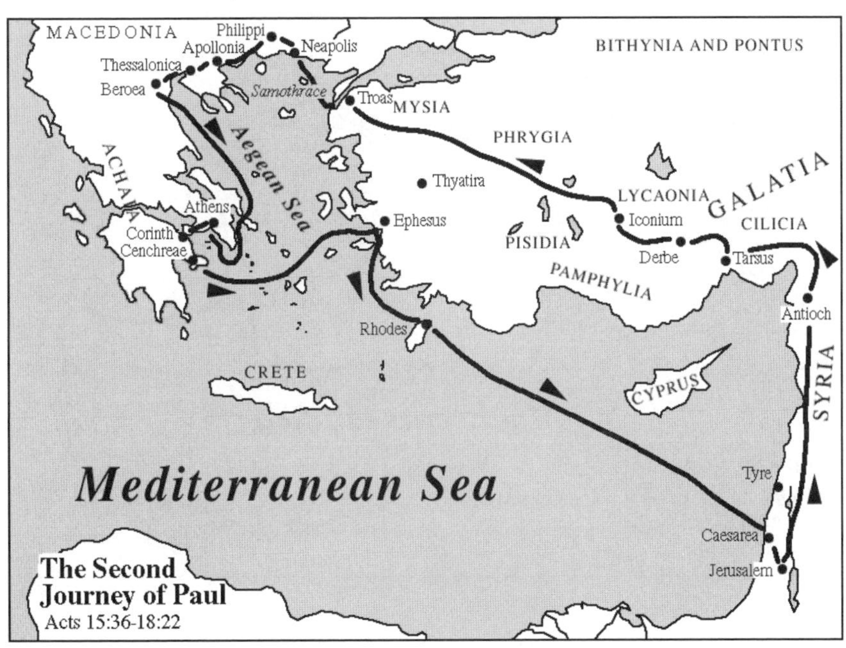

The Second Journey of Paul
Acts 15:36-18:22

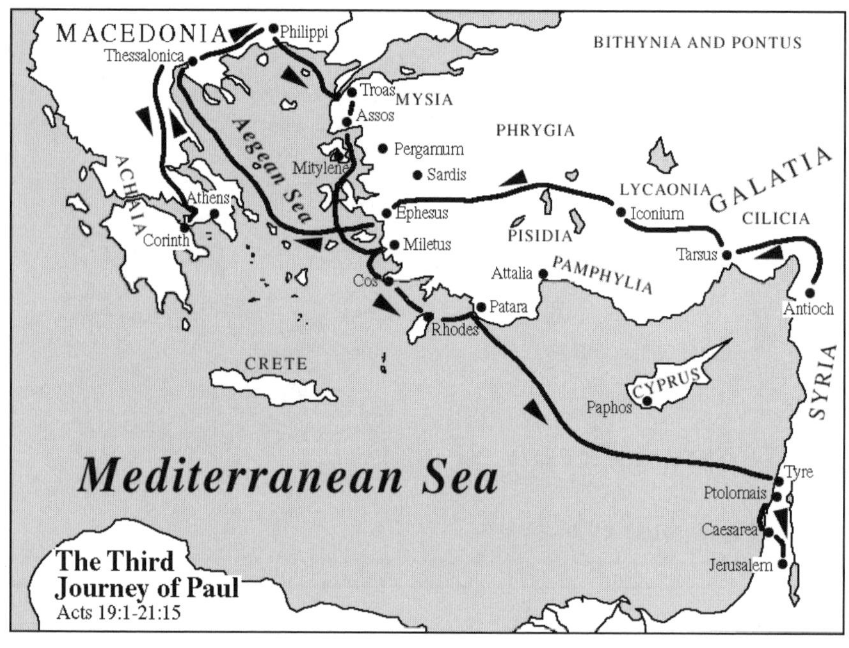

The Third Journey of Paul
Acts 19:1-21:15

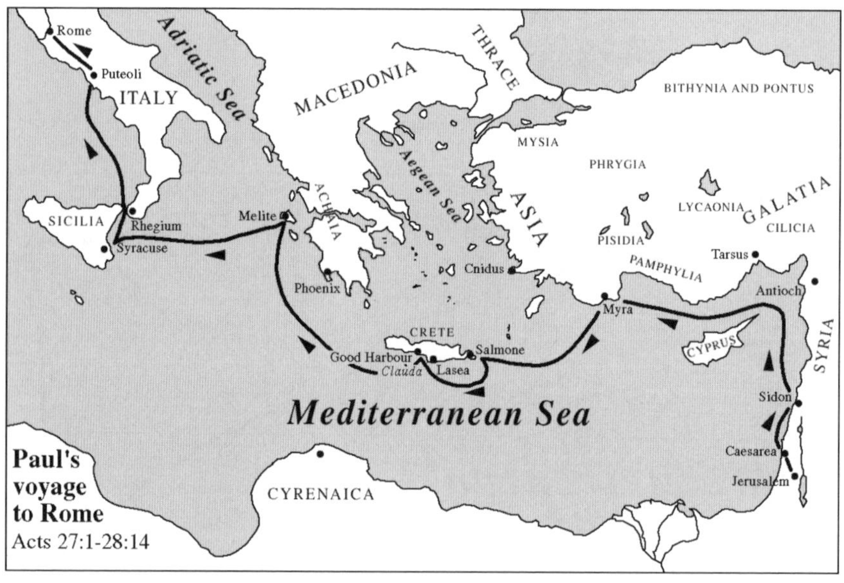

Paul's voyage to Rome
Acts 27:1-28:14

References to the Old Testament and Notes

Matthew

1:2 Gen.21:2f, 25:26, 29:32-30:24
1:3 Gen.38:29f
1:3-6 Ruth 4:18-22; 1Chr.2:1-15
1:6 2Sam.12:24
1:7-12 1Chr.3:10-19
1:23 Isa.7:14
2:2 Num.24:17; Jer.23:5
2:6 Mica 5:2; 2Sam.5:2
2:15 Hos.11:1; Exod.4:22
2:18 Jer.31:15
2:23 Judg.13:5; Isa.11:1 *(Nazer,* a branch)
3:3 Isa.40:3
3:4 2Kings 1:8; Lev.11:22; Zech.13:4
3:17 Ps.2:7; Isa.42:1
4:2 Exod.34:28; 1Kings 19:8
4:4 Deut.8:3
4:6 Ps.91:11f
4:7 Deut.6:16
4:10 Deut.5:9, 6:13
4:15 Isa.9:1f
5:3 Isa.61:1
5:4 Isa.61:2
5:5 Ps.37:11
5:8 Ps.24:3f
5:21 Exod.20:13; Deut.5:17; 16:18
5:27 Exod.20:14; Deut.5:18
5:31 Deut.24:1
5:33 Lev.19:12; Num.30:2; Deut.23:21
5:34f Isa.66:1
5:35 Ps.48:2
5:38 Exod.21:24
5:39 Prov.20:22, 24:29
5:43 Lev.19:18
5:48 Lev.19:2
6:6 2Kings 4:33
6:29 1Kings 10:5
7:23 Ps.6:8
8:4 Lev.13:49, 14:2-32
8:17 Isa.53:4
9:13 Hos.6:6
9:36 Num.27:17; 1Kings 22:17; Ezek.34:5
10:15 Gen.19:24f
10:35 Mic.7:6
11:5 Isa.26:19, 29:18, 35:5f, 61:1
11:10 Exod.23:20; Mal.3:1
11:21 Joel 3:4
11:22 Esther 4:1
11:23 Isa.14:13-15
11:25 Isa.29:14
11:28 Jer.31:25
11:29 Jer.6:16; Isa.28:12
12:1 Deut.23:25
12:3 1Sam.21:1-6; Lev.24:9
12:5 Num.28:9f
12:7 Hos.6:6
12:18 Isa.42:1-4
12:29 Isa.49:24
12:40 Jonah 1:17
12:41 Jonah 3:5
12:42 1Kings 10:1-10; 2Chr.9:1-12
13:14 Isa.6:9f
13:25 Regarding weeds, the Greek *zizania* is a rye-grass with poisonous seeds. In its early stages of growth it is virtually indistinguishable from wheat.
13:32 Dan.4:10f; Ezek.17:23
13:35 Ps.78:2
13:43 Dan.12:3
14:4 Lev.18:16, 20:21
14:19 2Kings 4:43f
15:4 Exod.20:12, 21:17; Lev.20:9; Deut.5:16
15:8 Isa.29:13
16:27 Ps.28:4
17:5 Ps.2:7; Isa.42:1; Deut.18:15
17:11 Mal.4:5
17:21 *Later texts add:* This kind [of demon] can only be overcome by the power which is won through prayer and through fasting. *(Compare Mark 9:29).*
17:24 Exod.30:13, 38:26

18:11 *Other texts add:* For the Son of Man came to save that which is lost. *(Compare Luke 19:10).*
18:15 Lev.19:17; Deut.19:15
18:22 Gen.4:24
19:5 Gen.1:27, 2:24
19:7 Deut.24:1-4
19:18 Exod.20:12-16; Deut.5:16-20
19:19 Lev.19:18
19:26 Gen.18:14; Job 42:2
20:8 Lev.19:13; Deut.24:15
20:28 Isa.53:12
21:5 Isa.62:11; Zech.9:9
21:9 Ps.118:25f
21:13 Exod.30:13; Lev.1:14; Isa.56:7; Jer.7:11
21:16 Ps.8:2
21:33 Isa.5:1f
21:42 Ps.118:22f
22:24 Deut.25:5; Gen 38:8
22:32 Exod.3:6
22:37 Deut.6:5
22:39 Lev.19:18
24:7 Isa.19:2
24:15 Dan.9:27, 11:31, 12:11
24:21 Dan.12:1; Joel 2:2
24:29 Isa.13:10; Ezek.32:7; Joel 2:10f; Zeph.1:15
24:30 Dan.7:13
24:37 Gen.6:5-8, 7:6-24
25:32 Ezek.34:17
25:46 Dan.12:2
26:11 Deut.15:11
26:15 Exod.21:32; Zech.11:12
26:17 Exod.12:14f
26:24 Ps.41:9
26:28 Exod.24:6f; Jer.31:31
26:31 Zech.13:7
26:63 Isa.53:7
26:64 Dan.7:13; Ps.110:1
26:65 Num.14:6; Lev.24:16
26:67 Isa.50:6
27:6 Deut.23:18
27:9 Zech.11:12f; Jer.32:6-15, 18:2f
27:30 Isa.50:6
27:34 Ps.69:21
27:35 Ps.22:18
27:38 Isa.53:12
27:39 Ps.22:7f, 109:25
27:43 Ps.22:8
27:46 Ps.22:1
27:48 Ps.69:21
27:51 Exod.26:31f
27:58 Deut.21:22

Mark
1:2 Exod.23:20; Mal.3:1
1:3 Isa.40:3
1:11 Gen.22:22; Ps.2:7; Isa.42:1
1:44 Lev.13:49; 14:2-32
2:23 Deut.23:25
2:26 1Sam.21:1-6; 2Sam.8:17
2:27 Exod.23:12; Lev.24:5f; Deut.5:14
3:27 Isa.49:24f
4:12 Isa.6:9f
4:29 Joel 3:13
4:32 Dan.4:8f,18; Ezek.17:23
6:18 Lev.18:16; 20:21
6:23 Esther 5:3,6; 7:2
6:34 Num.27:17; 1Kings 22:17; Ezek.34:5
6:37 2Kings 4:42-44
7:6f Isa.29:13
7:10 Exod.20:12; 21:17; Lev.20:9; Deut.5:16
7:37 Isa.35:5
8:17 Isa.6:9f; Jer.5:21
9:7 Deut.18:15; Ps.2:7; Isa.42:1
9:12 Ps.22:2-20; Isa.52:13-15; Mal.4:5
9:38f Num.11:27-29
9:46 *Later texts add:* Where their worm does not die and the fire is not quenched. *(See 9:48).*
9:48 Isa.66:24
10:4 Deut.24:1-4
10:6 Gen.1:27; 5:2
10:7f Gen.2:24
10:19 Exod.20:12-16; Deut.5:16-20; 6:4
10:27 Gen.18:14; Job 42:2
10:45 Isa.53:10f
11:9 Ps.118:25f
11:17 Isa.56:7; Jer.7:11

11:26 *Later texts read:* But if you do not forgive, then your Father in heaven will also not forgive your transgressions. *(Matt.6:15).*
12:1 Isa.5:1-7
12:10 Ps.118:22f
12:19 Gen.38:8; Deut.25:5f
12:26 Exod.3:6
12:29 Deut.6:4f
12:31 Lev.19:18
12:32 Deut.4:35; 6:4f
12:33 1Sam.15:22; Hos.6:6; Mic.6:6-8
12:36 Ps.110:1
13:7 Dan.2:28
13:8 Isa.19:2
13:12 Mic.7:6
13:14 Dan.9:27; 11:31; 12:11
13:19 Dan.12:1; Joel 2:2
13:24 Isa.13:10; 34:4; Joel 2:10
13:25 Hag.2:6,21
13:26 Dan.7:13
13:27 Zech.2:10
14:7 Deut.15:11
14:12 Exod.12:14f
14:18 Ps.41:9f
14:24 Exod.24:8; Isa.53:11f; Jer.31:31
14:27 Zech.13:7; 24:7
14:34 Ps.42:6,12; 43:5
14:62 Ps.110:1; Dan.7:13
14:64 Lev.24:16
15:23 Ps.69:22
15:24 Ps.22:18f
15:28 *Later texts insert:* Thus the scripture was fulfilled: He was reckoned as one of the criminals. *(Compare Luke 22:37).*
15:29,31 Ps.22:7f
15:34 Ps.22:1
15:36 Ps.69:21
15:42 Deut.21:22f
16:19 2Kings 2:3,11; Ps.110:1
An alternative ending to the Gospel of Mark: With brief words I have told of all that it was laid upon Peter and his companions to do. After all this, Jesus himself spread, through their mouth, from East to West, the holy and undying message of the salvation which endures through all cycles of time.

Luke
1:5 1Chr.24:10; 2Chr.31:2
1:9 Exod.30:7
1:13 Exod.17:9
1:15 Num.6:3; Judg.13:4
1:17 Mal.4:5
1:19 Dan.8:16; 9:21
1:25 Gen.30:23; Isa.4:1
1:31 Gen.17:19; Isa.7:14
1:32 2Sam.7:13
1:33 Isa.9:6; Dan.2:44
1:37 Gen.18:14; Job 42:2
1:46ff 1Sam.2:1-10
1:47 Hab.3:18
1:48 1Sam.1:11; Gen.30:13
1:49 Deut.10:21; Ps.111:9
1:50 Ps.103:13f
1:51 Ps.89:11
1:52 Ps.147:6; Job 5:11; Ezek.21:31
1:53 Ps.107:9; 34:11
1:54 Ps.98:3; Isa.41:8f
1:55 Gen.17:7; 18:18; 22:17; 2Sam.22:51; Mic.7:20
1:59 Gen.17:12; Lev.12:3
1:68 Ps.41:14; 72:18; 106:48; 111:9
1:69 1Sam.2:10; Ps.18:3; 132:17
1:71 Ps.106:10
1:72 Exod.2:24; Lev.26:42; Ps.105:8; 106:45
1:73 Gen.22:16f; Jer.11:5; Mic.7:20
1:76 Exod.23:20; Mal.4:5
1:78 Isa.60:1f; Zech.6:12; Mal.4:2
1:79 Ps.107:10; Isa.9:2; 42:7; 59:8
2:12 1Sam.2:34; 2Kings 19:29; Isa.7:14
2:14 Isa.57:19
2:22f Lev.12:2-8; Num.18:15f
2:23 Exod.13:2,12
2:24 Lev.12:8
2:30 Isa.40:5; 52:10
2:32 Isa.42:6; 46:13; 49:6
2:34 Isa.8:14

2:40 Judg.13:24; 1Sam.2:26
2:41 Exod.23:15; Deut.16:1-8
2:43 Exod.12:15,18
2:52 1Sam.2:26
3:4ff Isa.40:3-5
3:22 Gen.22:2; Ps.2:7; Isa.42:1
3:23-38 1Chron.1:1-4,24-28; 2:1-15; Ruth 4:18-22; Gen.5:3-32; 11:10-26
4:2 Deut.9:9; 1Kings 19:8
4:4 Deut.8:3
4:8 Deut.5:9; 6:13
4:10f Ps.91:11f
4:12 Deut.6:16
4:18 Isa.61:1f; 29:18; 58:6
4:25f 1Kings 17:1,8-16; 18:1
4:27 2Kings 5:1-14
5:14 Lev.13:49; 14:2-32
6:1 Deut.23:25
6:2 Exod.20:10; 23:12; Deut.5:14
6:3 1Sam.21:1-6
6:4 Lev.24:9
7:11ff 1Kings 17:17-24; 2Kings 4:32-37
7:22 Isa.26:19; 29:18; 35:5f; 61:1
7:27 Exod.23:20; Mal.3:1
8:10 Isa.6:9f; Jer.5:21; Ezek.12:2
9:13 2Kings 4:42-44
9:35 Deut.18:15; Ps.2:7; Isa.42:1
9:54 2Kings 1:9-16
9:61 1Kings 19:20
10:5 1Sam.25:6
10:7 Deut.24:15
10:15 Isa.14:13f
10:19 Ps.91:13
10:20 Exod.32:32; Ps.69:28; Dan.12:1
10:21 Isa.29:14
10:27 Deut.6:5; Lev.19:18
10:28 Lev.18:5
10:29 Lev.19:16f
11:20 Exod.8:15; Ps.8:4
11:21 Isa.49:24
11:29,32 Jonah 3:4f
11:31 1Kings 10:1-10; 2Chron.9:1-12
11:42 Lev.27:30; Mic.6:8
11:51 Gen.4:8f; 2Chron.24:20f; Zech.1:1
12:14 Exod.2:14
12:20 Jer.17:11; Job 27:8; Ps.39:6
12:27 1Kings 10:1-10
12:47f Deut.25:2f; Num.15:29f
12:53 Mic.7:6
13:14 Exod.20:9f
13:19 Dan.4:8f.18; Ezek.17:23
13:27 Ps.6:9
13:35 Jer.12:7; 22:5; Ps.118:26
14:8 Prov.25:6f
14:20 Deut.24:5
15:12 Deut.21:15-17
15:22 Gen.41:42; Zech.3:4
16:15 1Sam.16:7; Prov.21:2
17:3 Lev.19:17
17:12 Lev.13:45f
17:14 Lev.13:49: 14:2-32
17:26f Gen.6:5-8; 7:6-24
17:27 Gen.7:7
17:28f Gen.18:20-33; 19:15,23f
17:32 Gen.19:26
17:36 *Later texts add:* When two men are in the field, one will be taken and the other left behind.
18:13 Ps.51:3
18:19 Deut.6:4
18:20 Exod.20:12-16; Deut.5:16-20
18:27 Gen.18:14; Job 42:2; Jer.32:17
19:8 Exod.22:1; Lev.6:5; Num.5:6f
19:36 2Kings 9:13
19:38 Ps.118:26
19:40 Hab.2:11
19:43 Isa.29:3; Jer.6:6; Ezek.4:2
19:44 Ps.137:9
19:46 Isa.56:7; Jer.7:11
20:9 Isa.5:1-7
20:17 Ps.118:22f
20:18 Isa.8:14f
20:28 Gen.38:8; Deut.25:5f
20:37 Exod.3:6
20:42 Ps.110:1
21:9 Dan.2:28
21:10 2Chron.15:6; Isa.19:2
21:18 1Sam.14:45
21:22 Deut.32:35
21:24 Isa.63:18; Dan.8:13; Zech.12:3
21:25 Isa.13:10; 34:4; Joel 2:10; Zeph.1:15

21:26 Hag.2:6,21
21:27 Dan.7:13f
22:7 Exod.12:18-20; Deut.16:5-8
22:20 Exod.24:8; Jer.31:31
22:31 Job 1:6-12; Amos 9:9
22:37 Isa.53:12
22:69 Ps.110; Dan.7:13
23:17 *Some texts add:* But at the festival he was obliged to release a prisoner to them.
23:30 Hos.10:8
23:34 Ps.22:18
22:35 Ps.22:8
22:36 Ps.69:21
23:45 Exod.26:31-35
23:46 Ps.31:5
23:49 Ps.38:12
23:54 Deut.21:23
23:56 Exod.12:16; 20:10
24:12 *Some texts add:* But Peter stood up and ran to the tomb. He bent forward, but he saw only the linen bandages. Then he went home, full of wonder at what had happened.
24:36 *In some texts this verse continues:* and he said to them: Peace be with you!
24:40 *Some texts add:* so saying, he showed them his hands and his feet.
24:46 Hos.6:2
24:51 *Some texts add:* and was borne up into the heavens.

John
1:1 Gen.1:1
1:18 Exod.33:18-20
1:21 Deut.18:15, 18
1:23 Isa.40:3
1:29 Isa.53:7
1:41 Dan.9:25
1:47 Ps.32:2
1:49 Ps.2:7
1:51 Gen.28:12
2:13 Deut.16:1-6
2:17 Ps.69:9
3:5 Ezek.11:19; 36:25-27
3:6 Gen.6:3; Job 34:14f
3:8 Ezek.37:9
3:14 Num.21:8f
4:5 Gen.33:18f; 48:22; Josh.24:32
4:9 Ezra 4:3-6
4:14 Ps.36:9; Isa.58:11
4:18 2Kings 17:24; Hos.2:7
4:20 Deut.11:29; Josh.8:33
4:21 Mal.1:11
4:22 2Kings 17:28-41; Isa.2:3
4:25 Deut.18:18
4:36 Ps.126:5f; Isa.9:3
4:37 Job 31:8; Mic.6:15
4:48 Dan.4:2
4:50 1Kings 17:23
5:2 Neh.3:1; 12:39
5:10 Neh.13:19; Jer.17:21
5:17 Gen.2:3
5:21 1Sam.2:6; 2Kings 5:7
5:27 Dan.7:13f
5:29 Dan.12:2
6:9 2Kings 4:42f
6:14 Deut.18:15f
6:27 Isa.55:2
6:31 Exod.16:4, 15; Num.11:8; Neh.9:15; Ps.78:24; 105:40
6:44 Jer.31:3; Hos.11:4
6:45 Isa.54:13
7:2 Lev.23:34; Deut.16:16
7:22 Gen.17:10; 21:4; Lev.12:3
7:24 Isa.11:3; Zech.7:9
7:37 Lev.23:36
7:38 Isa.44:3; 55:1; 58:11
7:41 Deut.18:15
7:42 2Sam.7:12f; Mic.5:2
7:51 Exod.23:1; Deut.17:6
7:52 2Kings 14:25
8:5 Deut.22:22f
8:6 Jer.17:13
8:7 Deut.17:7
8:17 Deut.17:6; 19:15
8:24 Isa.43:11
8:35 Gen.21:10
8:41 Deut.32:6; Isa.63:16; 64:8
8:44 Gen.3:4
8:56 Gen.17:17

9:2 Exod.20:5; Ezek.18:20
9:7 2Kings 5:10; Isa.8:6
9:24 Josh.7:19; 2Chron.30:8; Ps.65:2; Isa.42:12
9:34 Ps.51:7
10:7 Ps.118:20
10:8 Jer.23:1; Ezek.34:2
10:9 Isa.49:9f; Ezek.34:12f
10:11 Isa.40:11; Ezek.34:11-16
10:16 Isa.56:8
10:21 Exod.4:11
10:33 Lev.24:16
10:34 Ps.82:6
11:19 Job 2:11
11:24 Dan.12:2
11:50 Jonah 1:8f
11:55 Num.9:6ff; 2Chron.30:15f
12:8 Deut.15:11
12:13 Ps.118:26
12:15 Isa.40:9; Zech.9:9
12:34 Ps.89:36; 110:4; Isa.9:7; Ezek.37:25; Dan.7:14
12:38 Isa.53:1
12:40 Isa.6:10
12:41 Isa.6:1f
12:50 Deut.32:47
13:8 Deut.12:12
13:18 Ps.41:9
13:34 Lev.19:18
15:1 Isa.5:1-7; Ps.80:9f; Ezek.19:10
15:6 Ezek.15:2f
15:25 Ps.35:19; 69:4
16:2 Isa.66:5
16:21 Isa.13:8; Hos.13:13; Mic.4:9
16:32 Zech.13:7
17:12 Ps.41:9
18:1 2Sam.15:23
19:7 Lev.24:16
19:24 Exod.28:32; Ps.22:19
19:28 Ps.22:16
19:29 Ps.69:21
19:31 Exod.12:16; Deut.21:23
19:36 Exod.12:46; Num.9:12; Ps.34:20
19:37 Zech.12:10
20:8 Ps.16:8f

Acts

1:20 Ps.69:25; 109:8
1:26 1Sam.14:41f; Prov.16:33
2:17 Joel 2:28-32
2:25-28 Ps.16:8-11
2:30 Ps.132:11; 2Sam.7:12f
2:31 Ps.16:10
2:34f Ps.110:1
2:39 Isa.57:19; Joel 2:32
2:40 Deut.32:5; Ps.78:8
3:13 Exod.3:6-15; Isa.52:13
3:22 Deut.18:15f
3:23 Lev.23:29; Deut.18:19
3:25 Gen.12:3; 18:18; 22:18; 28:4
4:11 Ps.118:22
4:24 Exod.20:11; Ps.146:6
4:25-27 Ps.2:1f
5:30 Deut.21:22f
7:2 Gen.11:31; 15:7; Ps.29:3
7:3 Gen.12:1
7:4 Gen.11:31; 12:5; 15:7
7:5 Gen.12:7; 17:8 Deut.2:5;
7:6f Gen.15:13f
7:7 Exod.3:12
7:8 Gen.17:10-14; 21:2-4; 25:26; 29:31-35; 30:1-24; 35:16-18,23-6
7:9 Gen.37:11,28; 39:2; 45:4
7:10 Gen.39:21; 41:37ff; Ps.105:21
7:11 Gen.41:54f; 42:5
7:12 Gen.42:2-5
7:13 Gen.45:1-4,16
7:14 Gen.45:9f; 46:27; Exod.1:5; Deut.10:22
7:15 Gen.46:1; 49:33
7:16 Gen.23:16f; 33:19; 50:13; Josh.24:32
7:17f Exod.1:7f,22
7:19 Exod.1:10f,15-22
7:20 Exod.2:2
7:21 Exod.2:3-10
7:23 Exod.2:5-6,10 2:11
7:23-29 Exod.2:11-15
7:26 Exod.2:13
7:27 Exod.2:14
7:29 Exod.2:22; 18:3f
7:30-34 Exod.3:1-10

7:32 Exod.3:6
7:35 Exod.2:14
7:36 Exod.7:3; 14:21; Num.14:33
7:37 Deut.18:15,18
7:38 Exod.19:3; 31:18
7:39 Num.14:3f
7:40 Exod.32:1,23
7:41 Exod.32:4,6
7:42 Amos 5:25f; Jer.19:13
7:44 Exod.25:9,40
7:45 Deut.32:49; Josh.3:14-17; 18:1
7:46 2Sam.7:2-16; Ps.132:1-5
7:47 1Kings 6:1
7:49 Isa.66:1f
7:51 Exod.33:3-5; Jer.9:26; 6:10; Num.27:14; Isa.63:10
7:52 2Chron.36:16
7:53 Exod.20:18f; Deut.5:2f
8:21 Ps.78:37
8:23 Isa.58:6
8:32f Isa.53:7f
8:37 *Some texts add:* Then Philip said to him, 'If you believe with all your heart, it is possible.' He answered, 'I believe that Jesus Christ is the Son of God.'
8:39 1Kings 18:12
10:14 Lev.11; Ezek.4:14
10:34 Deut.10:17
10:36 Isa.52:7
10:38 Isa.61:1
10:39 Deut.21:22
10:43 Isa.53:5f; Jer.31:34; Dan.9:24
13:10 Hos.14:9
13:17 Exod.6:1,6
13:18 Exod.16:35; Num.14:34; Deut.1:31
13:19 Deut.7:1; Josh.14:1
13:22 Ps.89:20; 1Sam.13:14; Isa.44:28
13:23 2Sam.7:12; Isa.11:1
13:26 Ps.107:20
13:33 Ps.2:7
13:34 Isa.55:3
13:35 Ps.16:10
13:41 Hab.1:5
13:47 Isa.42:6; 49:6
14:15 Exod.20:11; Ps.146:6; Isa.37:16; Jer.32:17
15:15 Amos 9:11f; Jer.12:15
15:18 Isa.45:21
15:20 Lev.18:6ff
17:24f Isa.42:5;
17:25 Ps.50:10f
17:26 Deut.32:8; Job 12:23
17:27 Isa.55:6; Jer.29:12f; Ps.145:18
17:28 Epimenides; Aratus, *Phaenomena* 5
17:31 Ps.9:8; 96:13; 98:9
18:9f Isa.43:5; Jer.1:8
20:10 1Kings 17:21
20:33 1Sam.12:3
21:26 Num.6:1-21
23:3 Lev.19:15
23:5 Exod.22:28
24:15 Dan.12:2
26:16f Ezek.2:1,3
26:18 Isa.35:5; 42:7,16; 61:1
27:12 Phoenix: *See note to 28:1.*
27:14 Euraquilo: an east-north-easterly wind
28:1 Melite: *Heinz Warnecke in* Die tatsächliche Romfahrt des Apostels Paulus *(Stuttgart 1987) demonstrates convincingly that "Melite" cannot be Malta, but rather the present-day Cephalonia, off the west coast of Greece. He also shows that Acts 27:12 is best rendered "Phoenix, a harbour serving Crete," Phoenix being located on the southern tip of Messinia, part of the Peloponnese peninsula.*
28:26f Isa.6:9f
28:28 Ps.67:2; 98:3
28:29 *Some texts add:* When he said this, the Jews went out, discussing and arguing among themselves.

Romans

1:17 Hab.2:4
1:18 Isa.66:15
1:20 Ps.19:1-4

1:23 Ps.106:20; Deut.4:15f
1:27 Lev.18:22
2:6 Ps.62:13
2:11 Deut.10:17; 2Chron.19:7
2:16 Eccles.12:14
2:17 Isa.48:1f
2:24 Isa.52:5; Ezek.36:20
2:25 Jer.9:25
2:29 Deut.30:6
3:2 Ps.147:19
3:4 Ps.51:4; 116:11
3:10-12 Ps.14:1-3; 53:1-3
3:13 Ps.5:9; 140:3
3:14 Ps.10:7
3:15-17 Isa.59:7f; Prov.1:16
3:18 Ps.36:1
3:20 Ps.143:2
3:25 Lev.16:12f
3:30 Deut.6:4
4:3 Gen.15:6
4:7 Ps.32:1f
4:9 Gen.15:6
4:11 Gen.17:10f
4:13 Gen.17:4-6; 22:17f
4:17 Gen.17:5
4:18 Gen.15:5
4:19 Gen.17:17; 18:11
4:21 Gen.18:14
4:22 Gen.15:6
4:25 Isa.53:4f,12
5:5 Ps.22:6; 119:116
5:12 Gen.2:17
6:12 Gen.4:7
7:7 Exod.20:17; Deut.5:21
7:10 Lev.18:5
7:14 Ps.51:7
7:18 Gen.6:5; 8:21
7:22 Ps.1:2
8:20 Gen.3:17f; Eccles.1:2
8:22 Jer.12:4,11
8:27 Ps.139:1f
8:31 Ps.118:6
8:33 Isa.50:8f
8:36 Ps.44:22
9:3 Exod.32:32
9:4 Exod.4:22; 40:34f
9:7 Gen.21:12
9:9 Gen.18:10
9:10 Gen.25:21
9:12 Gen.25:23
9:13 Mal.1:2f
9:14 2Chron.19:7
9:15 Exod.33:19
9:17 Exod.9:16
9:18 Exod.7:3
9:20 Isa.29:16; 45:9
9:21 Jer.18:6
9:22 Prov.16:4
9:25 Hos.2:25
9:26 Hos.1:10
9:27 Gen.22:17; 2Kings 19:4; Isa.10:22f; 11:11; Hos.1:10
9:29 Isa.1:9
9:31 Isa.15:1
9:33 Isa.8:14; 28:16
10:5 Lev.18:5; Neh.9:29; Ezek.20:11,13,21; Deut.9:4
10:6 Deut.30:12f; Ps.107:26
10:8 Deut.30:14
10:11 Isa.28:16
10:13 Joel 2:32
10:15 Isa.52:7
10:16 Isa.53:1
10:18 Ps.19:4
10:19 Deut.32:21
10:20 Isa.65:1
10:21 Isa.65:2
11:1 1Sam.12:22; Jer.31:37; 33:24-26
11:2 Ps.94:14; 1Kings 19:10f
11:4 1Kings 19:18
11:5 2Kings 19:4; Isa.11:11
11:8 Isa.29:10; Deut.29:4
11:9 Ps.69:22f
11:26 Isa.59:20f
11:27 Isa.27:9; Jer.31:33
11:29 Num.23:19
11:33 Job 11:7f; Ps.139:17
11:34 Isa.40:13f
11:35 Job 35:7; 41:11
12:16 Prov.3:7; 26:12
12:17 Prov.20:22
12:19 Lev.19:18; Deut.32:35f
12:20 Prov.25:21f
13:1 Prov.8:15

13:9 Exod.20:13f; Deut.5:17f; Lev.19:18
14:11 Isa.45:23
15:3 Ps.69:9
15:9 Ps.18:49; 2Sam.22:50
15:10 Deut.32:43
15:11 Ps.117:1
15:12 Isa.11:10
15:21 Isa.52:15
16:20 Gen.3:15
16:24 *Later texts add:* The grace of Jesus Christ, our Lord, be with you all! Amen.

1 Corinthians
1:19 Ps.33:10; Isa.29:14
1:20 Isa.19:12; 33:18; 44:25
1:31 Jer.9:24
2:9 Isa.64:4; 65:17
2:10 Dan.2:22
2:16 Isa.40:13
3:9 Isa.61:3
3:15 Job 23:10
3:18 Isa.5:21
3:19 Job 5:13
3:20 Ps.94:11
5:1 Deut.22:30; 27:20
5:6 Exod.12:15
5:7 Exod.12:19
5:8 Exod.13:7; Deut.16:3
5:13 Deut.17:7; 19:19
6:2 Dan.7:22
6:16 Gen.2:24
7:5 Exod.19:15
7:18 1Macc.1:15
8:4 Deut.6:4
8:6 Mal.2:10
9:9 Deut.25:4
9:12 Num.18:8,21; 18:1f
9:13 Deut.18:1
10:1 Exod.13:21; 14:22,29; Ps.78:13f
10:3 Exod.16:4,35; Ps.78:24
10:4 Exod.17:6; Num.20:11; Ps.78:15f
10:5 Num.14:29f
10:6 Num.11:4,34
10:7 Exod.32:4,6
10:8 Num.25:1-8
10:9 Num.21:5f
10:10 Exod.16:2f; Num.14:2; 16:41f,49
10:18 Lev.7:6; Deut.18:1f
10:20 Deut.32:17
10:21 Mal.1:7,12
10:22 Deut.32:21; Eccles.6:10; Isa.45:9
10:26 Ps.24:1; 50:12
11:3 Gen.3:16
11:7 Gen.1:27
11:8 Gen.2:21-23
11:9 Gen.2:18
11:10 Gen.6:2
11:25 Jer.31:31
13:1 Ps.150:5
14:5 Num.11:29
14:16 1Chron.16:36; Ps.106:48; Neh.8:6
14:21 Isa.28:11f
14:25 Isa.45:14; Zech.8:23
14:34 *Some authorities consider this verse to be a later insertion.*
15:3 Isa.53:5-12
15:4 Ps.16:8; Hos.6:2
15:21 Gen.3:17f
15:25 Ps.110:1
15:27 Ps.8:6
15:30 2Esdras 7:89
15:32 Isa.22:13
15:33 *Menander,* Thais
15:38 Gen.1:11
15:42 Dan.12:3
15:45 Gen.2:7
15:49 Gen.5:3
15:54 Isa.25:8
15:55 Hos.13:14
16:13 Ps.31:24; Josh.1:7

2 Corinthians
3:3 Exod.24:12; 31:18; 32:15f; Jer.31:33; Ezek.11:19
3:6 Jer.31:31
3:7 Exod.34:29-35
3:14 Isa.6:10
3:16 Exod.34:34
3:17 Isa.61:1f
3:18 Exod.16:7,10; 24:17

4:6 Gen.1:3
4:13 Ps.116:10
6:2 Isa.49:8
6:9 Ps.118:17f
6:11 Ezek.33:22; Isa.60:5
6:14 Deut.22:10
6:16 Exod.25:8; 29:45; Lev.26:12; Ezek.37:27; Jer.31:1
6:17 Isa.52:11; Jer.51:45; Zeph.3:20
6:18 2Sam.7:14; Jer.31:9; Isa.43:6; Hos.1:10
8:4 in the hallowed circle. *This refers to the congregation in Jerusalem.*
8:12 Prov.3:27f
8:15 Exod.16:18
8:21 Prov.3:4 (Septuagint)
9:1 *See note to 8:4*
9:6 Prov.11:24
9:7 Prov.22:8 (Septuagint)
9:9 Ps.112:9
9:10 Isa.55:10; Hos.10:12
10:5 Isa.2:11f
10:17 Jer.9:24
11:2 Hos.2:19f
11:3 Gen.3:4,13
11:24 Deut.25:3
12:7 Num.33:55; Job 2:6; Ezek.28:24
12:9 Isa.40:29
13:1 Deut.19:15

Galatians

1:15 Isa.49:1; Jer.1:5
2:6 Deut.10:17
2:16 Ps.143:2
3:6 Gen.15:6
3:8 Gen.12:3; 18:18
3:10 Deut.27:26
3:11 Hab.2:4
3:12 Lev.18:5
3:13 Deut.21:23
3:14 Joel 3:1f
3:16 Gen.12:7
3:17 Exod.12:40
3:20 Deut.6:4
4:22 Gen.16:15; 21:2,9
4:23 Gen.17:16
4:24 Exod.19:20; Gen.16:1
4:27 Isa.54:1
4:29 Gen.21:9
4:30 Gen 21:10-12
5:14 Lev.19:18
6:16 Ps.125:4f

Ephesians

1:18 Deut.33:3
1:20 Ps.110:1
1:22 Ps.8:6
2:12 Isa.57:19
2:17 Isa.57:19
4:8 Ps.68:18
4:24 Gen.1:26
4:25 Zech.8:16
4:26 Ps.4:5
5:2 Exod.29:18; Ezek.20:41
5:14 Isa.60:1f. *Clement of Alexandria* (Protr. *IX.84) has a continuation of the verse, from which it can be seen that this is an early Christian hymn. The full text is:*
Awake, you who are sleeping,
Arise from the dead!
The Christ shall be your light,
the Kyrios, the sun of resurrection, begotten before the Morning Star, giving life, full of grace, in his own rays.
5:18 Prov.23:31
5:19 Ps.33:2f
5:31 Gen.2:24
6:2 Exod.20:12
6:3 Deut.5:16
6:14 Isa.11:5; 59:17
6:15 Isa.52:7
6:17 Isa.49:2

Philippians

1:19 Job 13:16
2:10 Isa.45:23
2:16 Isa.65:23; 49:4
4:3 Ps.69:29

Colossians

1:17 Prov.8:22-31

2:3 Isa.45:3; Prov.2:2f
2:22 Isa.29:13
3:1 Ps.110:1
3:10 Gen.1:26f
4:1 Lev.25:43,53

1 Thessalonians
2:4 Jer.11:20
2:16 Gen.15:16; Dan.8:23
4:5 Jer.10:25; Ps.79:6
4:6 Ps.94:1
4:8 Ezek.36:27; 37:14
5:8 Isa.59:17
5:14 Isa.35:4
5:15 Prov.20:22
5:22 Job 1:1,8; 2:3

2 Thessalonians
1:8 Isa.66:4,15; Jer.10:25; Ps.79:6
1:9 Isa.2:10,19,21
1:10 Isa.2:11,17; Ps.89:8
1:12 Isa.24:15; 66:5; Mal.1:11
2:3 Dan.7:25; 8:25
2:4 Dan.11:36; Ezek.28:2
2:8 Isa.11:4; Job 4:9
2:13 Deut.33:12
3:16 Ruth 2:4

1 Timothy
2:13 Gen.2:7,21f
2:14 Gen.3:1-6,13
4:4 Gen.1:31
5:18 Deut.25:4
5:19 Deut.19:15
6:7 Job 1:21
6:16 Ps.104:2; Exod.33:20

2 Timothy
2:19 Num.16:5; Isa.26:13
3:8 Exod.7:11
4:14 Ps.62:13; 28:4
4:17 Ps.22:22; Dan.6:21,28

Titus
1:12 Epimenides
2:14 Exod.19:5; Deut.14:2; Ps.130:8; Ezek.37:23

Philemon
1:11 *The name Onesimus means useful or (1:20) beneficial.*

Hebrews
1:3 Ps.110:1
1:5 Ps.2:7; 2Sam.7:14
1:6 Deut.32:43 *(Septuagint);* Ps.97:7
1:7 Ps.104:4
1:8f Ps.45:6f
1:10-12 Ps.102:25-27
1:13 Ps.110:1
2:6-9 Ps.8:4-6
2:12 Ps.22:22
2:13 Isa.8:17f; 2Sam.22:3
2:16 Isa.41:8f
2:17 Ps.22:23
3:2 Num.12:7
3:5 Num.12:7
3:7-11 Ps.95:7-11
3:15 Ps.95:7f
3:16-19 Num.14:1-35
4:3 Ps.95:11
4:4 Gen.2:2
4:5 Ps.95:11
4:7 Ps.95:7f
4:10 Gen.2:2
4:11 Ps.95:11
5:3 Lev.9:7
5:5 Ps.2:7
5:6 Ps.110:4
5:9 Isa.45:17
5:10 Ps.110:4
6:7 Gen.1:11f
6:8 Gen.3:17f
6:13f Gen.22:16f
6:19 Lev.16:2,12
6:20 Ps.110:4
7:1-10 Gen.14:17-20
7:3 Ps.110:4
7:5 Num.18:21
7:11,15 Ps.110:4
7:17 Ps.110:4
7:21 Ps.110:4
7:24 Ps.110:4
7:27 Lev.16:6,15

7:28 Ps.2:7; 110:4
8:1 Ps.110:1
8:2 Num.24:6 *(Septuagint)*
8:5 Exod.25:40
8:8-12 Jer.31:31-34
9:1-10 Exod.25:10-40
9:2 Lev.24:5
9:3 Exod.26:31-33
9:4 Exod.16:32f; 30:1-5; Num.17:8-10
9:7 Exod.30:10; Lev.16
9:13 Lev.16:6,16; Num.19:9,17f
9:19f Lev.14:4; Num.19:6; Exod.24:3f; 24:6-8
9:22 Lev.17:11
9:28 Isa.53:12
10:5-9 Ps.40:6-8
10:12f Ps.110:1
10:16f Jer.31:33f
10:20 Zech.6:11f
10:27 Isa.26:11
10:28 Deut.17:2-6
10:29 Exod.24:8
10:30 Deut.32:35f
10:37 Isa.26:20 *(Septuagint)*
10:37f Hab.2:3f
11:4 Gen.4:3-10
11:5 Gen.5:21-24
11:7 Gen.6:13-22; 7:1
11:8f Gen.12:1-8
11:9 Gen.26:3
11:11 Gen.17:19; 18:11-14; 21:2
11:12 Gen.15:5f; 22:17; 32:12
11:13 Gen.23:4; Ps.39:13; 119:19
11:16 Exod.3:6,15; 4:5
11:17 Gen.22:1-10
11:18 Gen.21:12
11:20 Gen.27:27-29,39f
11:21 Gen.48; 47:31 *(Septuagint)*
11:22 Gen.50:24f; Exod.13:19
11:23 Exod.1:22; 2:2
11:24 Exod.2:10f,11-15
11:26 Ps.69:10; 89:51f
11:27 Exod.2:15
11:28 Exod.12:21-28,29f
11:29 Exod.14:21f
11:30 Josh.6:1-21
11:31 Josh.2:1-24; 6:17,22-25
11:32 Judg.6-8; 4-5; 13-16; 11-12; 1Sam.16-30; 2Sam.1-24; 1Kings 1-2:11; 1Sam.1-12; 15; 16:1-13;
11:33 Dan.6:23
11:34 Dan.3:23f
11:35 1Kings 17:17-24; 2Kings 4:25-37
11:37 2Chron.24:21
11:38 1Sam.13:6
12:2 Ps.110:1
12:5-8 Prov.3:11f
12:7 Ps.73:14f
12:8 Num.16:22; 27:16f
12:12 Isa.35:3; Job 4:3f
12:13 Prov.4:26 *(Septuagint)*
12:14 Ps.34:15
12:15 Deut.29:18 *(Septuagint)*
12:16 Gen.25:29-34
12:17 Gen.27:30-40
12:18f Exod.19:12-22; 20:18-21; Deut.4:11; 5:22-27
12:19 Exod.20:19
12:20 Exod.19:12f
12:21 Deut.9:19
12:24 Gen.4:10
12:25 Exod.20:19
12:26 Hag.2:6
12:29 Deut.4:24; Isa.33:14
13:2 Gen.18:1-8; 19:1-3
13:5 Deut.31:6,8; Josh.1:5
13:6 Ps.118:6
13:11 Lev.16:27
13:15 Lev.7:12; Isa.57:19; Hos.14:2; Ps.50:14
13:20 Isa.63:11; Zech.9:11; Isa.55:3; Ezek.37:26

James
1:10f Isa.40:6f
1:25 Ps.19:7f
2:8 Lev.19:18
2:11 Exod.20:13f; Deut.5:17f
2:19 Deut.6:4
2:21 Gen.22:1-14
2:23 Gen.15:6; Isa.41:8; 2Chron.20:7
2:25 Josh.2:1-21
3:9 Gen.1:26f

4:6 Prov.3:34
5:5 Jer.12:3
5:11 Job 1:21f; 2:10; Ps.103:8; 111:4
5:17 1Kings 17:1; 18:1
5:18 1Kings 18:42
5:20 Prov.10:12

1 Peter
1:11 Dan.12:6ff; Ps.22; Isa.53; Hab.2:3
1:16 Lev.11:44f; 19:2
1:18 Isa.52:3
1:24f Isa.40:6-9
2:3 Ps.34:8
2:4 Ps.118:22; Isa.28:16
2:6 Isa.28:16
2:7 Ps.118:22
2:8 Isa.8:14f
2:9 Exod.19:5f; 23:22; Isa.43:20f
2:10 Hos.1:6,9; 2:23
2:11 Ps.39:13; 119:19
2:17 Prov.24:21
2:22 Isa.53:9
2:24 Isa.53:12 *(Septuagint)*
2:24f Isa.53:5
3:6 Gen.18:12; Prov.3:25
3:10-16 Ps.34:12-16
3:14f Isa.8:12f
3:20 Gen.6-8
4:8 Prov.10:12
4:14 Isa.11:2
4:18 Prov.11:31 *(Septuagint)*
5:5 Prov.3:34
5:7 Ps.55:22
5:8 Ps.22:14

2 Peter
2:5 Gen.8:18; 6:6-8
2:6 Gen.19:24
2:7 Gen.19:16,29
2:15 Num.22:5,7
2:16 Num.22:21,23,28,30f
2:22 Prov.26:11
3:5f Gen.1:6-8; 7:11
3:8 Ps.90:4
3:12 Isa.34:4
3:13 Isa.65:17; 66:22

1 John
1:5 Dan.2:22
1:9 Exod.34:6f; Deut.32:4; Prov.28:13
2:16 Prov.27:20
3:8 Gen.3:14
3:12 Gen.4:8

2 & 3 John
-

Jude
6 Gen.6.1-4
7 Gen.19:4-25
9 Zech.3:2
11 Gen.4:3-8; Num.22-24; 16.
14f Enoch 1:9
23 Amos 4:11; Zech.3:3f

Revelation
1:1 Dan.2:28f
1:4 Exod.3:14
1:5 Ps.89:27; 130:8
1:6 Exod.19:6; Isa.61:6
1:7 Dan.7:13; Zech.12:10
1:8 Exod.3:14
1:13 Dan.7:13; 10:5
1:14 Dan.7:9; 10:6
1:15 Ezek.1:24; 43:2
1:16 Judg.5:31; Exod.34:29
1:17 Isa.44:2,6
1:18 Hos.13:14
1:19 Dan.2:29
2:7 Gen.2:9; Ezek.31:8 (Septuagint)
2:8 Isa.44:6
2:10 Dan.1:12
2:14 Num.31:16; 25:1f
2:17 Ps.78:24; Isa.62:2
2:18 Dan.10:6
2:20 Num.25:1; 1Kings 16:31; 2Kings 9:22
2:23 Ps.7:10; 62:12; Jer.17:10
2:26 Ps.2:8f
3:5 Exod.32:32; Ps.69:28; Dan.12:1
3:7 Isa.22:22

3:9 Isa.60:14; 49:23; 43:4
3:12 Isa.62:2; Ezek.48:35
3:14 Ps.89:28; Prov.8:22
3:17 Hos.12:8
3:19 Prov.3:12
4:1 Exod.19:16,24; Dan.2:29
4:2 Isa.6:1; Ezek.1:26-28
4:3 *Jasper. In earlier times this name was also used for other precious stones, most frequently for the diamond.*
4:5 Exod.19:16; Zech.4:2; Ezek.1:13
4:6 Ezek.1:5,18
4:7 Ezek.1:10
4:8 Isa.6:2f; Ezek.1:18; Exod.3:14
4:9 Ps.47:8; Isa.6:1; Dan.6:27; 12:7
5:1 Ezek.2:9; Isa.6:1; 29:11
5:5 Gen.49:9; Isa.11:10
5:6 Isa.53:7; Zech.4:10
5:7 Isa.6:1
5:8 Ps.141:2
5:9 Ps.33:3
5:10 Exod.19:6; Isa.61:6
5:11 Dan.7:10
5:12 Isa.53:7
5:13 Isa.6:1
6:2 Zech.1:8; 6:1-3
6:4 Zech.1:8
6:6 2Kings 6:25
6:8 Hos.13:14; Ezek.5:12; Jer.14:12; 15:3
6:10 Zech.1:12; Ps.79:5; Gen.4:10; Deut.32:43; 2Kings 9:7
6:12 Joel 2:31; Isa.13:10
6:13 Isa.34:4
6:15 Ps.2:2; Isa.2:10; 24:21
6:16 Hos.10:8; Isa.6:1
6:17 Joel 2:11; Mal.3:2
7:1 Zech.6:5; Ezek.7:2; 37:9
7:3 Ezek.9:4
7:10 Isa.6:1
7:14 Dan.12:1; Gen.49:11
7:15 Isa.6:1
7:16 Isa.49:10; Ps.121:6
7:17 Ezek.34:23; Ps.23:2; Jer.2:13; Isa.25:8
8:3 Ps.141:2; Amos 9:1
8:5 Lev.16:12; Ezek.10:2
8:7 Exod.9:23-25; Joel 3:3
8:8 Jer.51:25; Exod.7:20f
8:10 Isa.14:12
9:2 Gen.19:28; Exod.19:18; Joel 2:10
9:3 Exod.10:12-15;
9:4 Ezek.9:4
9:6 Job 3:21
9:7 Joel 2:4
9:8 Joel 1:6
9:9 Joel 2:5
9:11 Apollyon: 'the Destroyer'
9:13 Exod.30:1-3
9:14 Gen.15:18
9:17 Dan.8:1f
9:20 Isa.17:8; Ps.115:4-7; 135:15-17; Dan.5:4,23
10:3 Amos 3:8
10:4 Dan.12:4,9
10:5 Deut.32:40; Exod.14:22; Neh.9:6; Dan.12:7
10:9 Ezek.2:8; 3:1-3
10:11 Jer.1:10; Dan.3:4; 7:14
11:1 Ezek.40:3
11:2 Zech.12:3; Isa.63:18
11:4 Zech.4:3,11-14
11:5 2Kings 1:10; 2Sam.22:9; Jer.5:14
11:6 1Kings 17:1; Exod.7:17,19; 1Sam.4:8
11:7 Dan.7:3; 7:21
11:8 Isa.1:9
11:11 Ezek.37:5,10; Gen.15:12
11:12 2Kings 2:11
11:13 Ezek.38:19f
11:15 Ps.22:28; Dan.7:14,27; Zech.14:9
11:17 Exod.3:14; Ps.99:1
11:18 Ps.2:1,5; 115:13
11:19 1Kings 8:1-6; Exod.19:16; 2Macc.2:4-8
12:2 Isa.66:7; Mic.4:10
12:3 Dan.7:7
12:4 Dan.8:10
12:5 Isa.66:7; Ps.2:9; Mic.5:2f
12:7 Dan.10:13,21
12:8 Dan.2:35

12:9 Gen.3:1,14f; Zech.3-1
12:10 Job 1:9-11
12:12 Isa.44:23; 49:13
12:14 Dan.7:25; 12:7
13:1 Dan.7:1-6
13:2 Dan.7:4-6
13:5 Dan.7:8
13:7 Dan.7:21
13:8 Dan.12:1; Ps.69:29; Isa.53:7
13:10 Jer.15:2; 43:11
13:14 Deut.13:1-5
13:15 Dan.3:5f
14:1 Ezek.9:4
14:2 Ezek.1:24; 43:2
14:3 Ps.33:3; Isa.42:10
14:5 Isa.53:9; Zeph.3:13
14:7 Exod.20:11
14:8 Isa.21:9; Dan.4:27; Jer.51:7f
14:10 Isa.51:17,22; Ps.75:9; Jer.25:15; Gen.19:24
14:11 Isa.34:10
14:14 Dan.7:13
14:15 Joel 3:13
14:20 Joel 3:13; Isa.63:3
15:1 Lev.26:21
15:3 Exod.15:1; Ps.145:17; 92:5; 139:14
15:4 Jer.10:7; Ps.86:9f
15:5 Exod.40:34
15:6 Lev.26:21; Dan.10:5; Ezek.9:2,11
15:8 1Kings 8:10; Isa.6:4; Ezek.44:4; Exod.40:34f; Lev.26:21
16:1 Isa.66:6; Ps.69:24; Zeph.3:8
16:2 Exod.9:10f; Deut.28:35
16:3f Exod.7:17-21
16:5 Ps.119:137; Exod.3:14
16:6 Ps.79:3; Isa.49:26
16:7 Ps.19:10; 119:137
16:10 Exod.10:21f
16:12 Isa.11:15f; Gen.15:18; Jer.50:38
16:13 1Kings 22:21-23; Exod.8:3
16:16 2Kings 9:27
16:16 Armageddon: the hill Megiddo
16:17 Isa.66:6
16:18 Exod.19:16; Dan.12:1
16:19 Dan.4:27; Isa.51:17,22; Jer.25:15
16:21 Exod.9:23
17:1 Jer.51:13
17:2 Isa.23:17; Jer.25:15f
17:3 Dan.7:7
17:4 Jer.51:7
17:5 Dan.4:27
17:8 Dan.7:3; Ps.69:29
17:12 Dan.7:20-24
17:14 Deut.10:17; Dan.2:47
17:15 Jer.51:13
17:18 Ps.2:2
18:1 Ezek.43:2
18:2 Isa.21:9; Jer.50:39; Dan.4:27
18:3 Jer.25:15,27; Ezek.27:33
18:4 Isa.48:20; Jer.50:8
18:5 Jer.51:9
18:6 Ps.137:8; Jer.50:15,29
18:7 Isa.47:8f
18:8 Isa.47:9; Jer.50:34
18:9 Ezek.26:16f; Isa.23:17
18:10 Dan.4:27; Ezek.26:17
18:11 Ezek.27:36
18:12 Ezek.27:12f,22
18:13 Ezek.27:13
18:15 Ezek.27:36
18:17 Isa.23:14; Ezek.27:26-30
18:19 Ezek.27:30-34
18:20 Deut.32:43; Isa.44:23; Jer.51:48
18:21 Jer.51:63; Ezek.26:21; Dan.4:27
18:22 Isa.24:8; Ezek.26:13
18:23 Jer.25:10; Isa.23:8; 47:9
18:24 Jer.51:49
19:2 Deut.32:43; 2Kings 9:7; Ps.19:10
19:3 Isa.34:10
19:4 Isa.6:1
19:5 Ps.134:1; 115:13
19:6 Ezek.1:24; 43:2; Ps.93:1; Dan.7:14
19:7 Ps.118:24
19:8 Ps.45:14f
19:11 Ezek.1:1; Ps.96:13
19:12 Dan.10:6
19:13 Isa.63:1f
19:15 Ps.2:9; Isa.11:4; 49:2; 63:2f
19:16 Deut.10:17; Dan.2:47
19:17 Ezek.39:4,17-20
19:19 Ps.2:2

19:20 Isa.30:33; Dan.7:11
19:21 Ezek.39:17f
20:2 Gen.3:1; Zech.3:1; Job 1:6
20:4 Dan.7:9,22,27
20:6 Isa.61:6
20:8 Isa.11:12; Ezek.7:2; 38:2,9,15
20:9 Hab.1:6; Ps.87:2; 2Kings 1:10-12; Ezek.39:6
20:10 Ezek.38:22
20:11 Isa.6:1; Ps.114:3,7; Dan.2:35
20:11f Dan.7:9f
20:12 Ps.69:29; 28:4
20:13 Hos.13:14; Ps.28:4
20:14 Isa.25:8
20:15 Exod.32:32f; Dan.12:1; Ps.69:29
21:1 Isa.66:22; 65:17. *See also Note to 4:3.*
21:2 Isa.52:1; 61:10
21:3 Lev.26:11; Ezek.37:27; Zech.2:10
21:4 Isa.25:8; 35:10
21:5 Isa.6:1; 43:19
21:6 Isa.55:1; Zech.14:8
21:7 2Sam.7:14; Ps.89:27f
21:8 Isa.30:33; Ezek.38:22
21:9 Lev.26:21. *See also Note to 4:3.*
21:10 Ezek.40:2; Isa.52:1
21:11 Isa.60:1f
21:12 Exod.28:21; Ezek.48:30-35
21:13 Ezek.48:31-34
21:15 Ezek.40:5
21:16 Ezek.43:16; 48:35
21:17 Ezek.40:5
21:18f Isa.54:11f; Ezek.28:13. *See also Note to 4:3.*
21:20 *Hyacinth was also known as jacinth.*
21:23 Isa.24:23; 60:1,19.
21:24 Isa.60:3,11; Ps.72:10f
21:25 Isa.60:11; Zech.14:7
21:27 Isa.4:3; 52:1; Dan.12:1; Ps.69:29
22:1 Gen.2:10; Zech.14:8
22:2 Ezek.47:12; Gen.2:9
22:3 Zech.14:11
22:4 Ps.17:15
22:5 Isa.60:19; Dan.7:18,27
22:6 Dan.2:28
22:10 Dan.12:4
22:11 Dan.12:10
22:12 Isa.40:10; Ps.28:4; Jer.17:10
22:13 Isa.44:6; 48:12
22:14 Gen.2:9; 3:22
22:16 Isa.11:1,10; Num.24:17
22:17 Isa.55:1; Zech.14:8
22:18 Deut.4:2; 13:1; 29:20
22:19 Deut.4:2; Gen.2:9; 3:22